Serving the Stigmatized

Serving the Stigmatized

Working Within the Incarcerated Environment

Edited by

Wesley T. Church II

and

David W. Springer

OXFORD
UNIVERSITY PRESS

OXFORD
UNIVERSITY PRESS

Oxford University Press is a department of the University of Oxford. It furthers
the University's objective of excellence in research, scholarship, and education
by publishing worldwide. Oxford is a registered trade mark of Oxford University
Press in the UK and certain other countries.

Published in the United States of America by Oxford University Press
198 Madison Avenue, New York, NY 10016, United States of America.

© Oxford University Press 2018

Library of Congress Cataloging-in-Publication Data
Names: Church, Wesley T., editor. | Springer, David W., editor.
Title: Serving the stigmatized : working within the incarcerated environment /
[edited by] Wesley T. Church II, David W. Springer.
Description: New York, NY : Oxford University Press, [2018] |
Includes bibliographical references and index.
Identifiers: LCCN 2018002216 (print) | LCCN 2018004447 (ebook) |
ISBN 9780190678760 (updf) | ISBN 9780190678777 (epub) |
ISBN 9780190678753 (preprinted case cover : alk. paper)
Subjects: LCSH: Social work with criminals—United States. |
Prisoners—Services for—United States. |
Criminals—Rehabilitation—United States. | Corrections—United States.
Classification: LCC HV7428 (ebook) | LCC HV7428 .S445 2018 (print) |
DDC 365/.660973—dc23
LC record available at https://lccn.loc.gov/2018002216

9 8 7 6 5 4 3 2 1

Printed by Sheridan Books, Inc., United States of America

CONTENTS

FOREWORD

Most people probably encounter a social worker during their lifetime. It may be a brief, fleeting event that occurs during our normal routines, and we may not even recognize that person as a social worker. For many other people, however, it is a much more intense experience. This is especially true for populations that are both stigmatized and institutionalized, such as the residents of a closed mental health facility or the inmates in a prison.

Social work with incarcerated populations has been going on through the efforts of settlement houses since the late 19th century, although there have been times when the profession's core values such as self-determination were viewed by some as excluding work with prisoners. In modern times, however, forensic social work has become a well-established field of practice, with the Council on Social Work Education formally sanctioning a curriculum for education in correctional social work in 1959.

The United States has the largest incarcerated population in the world. About 2.3 million people currently reside in prisons and jails, or about 1 of every 110 adults, according to the US Bureau of Justice Statistics. Only recently have we come to realize that many, if not most, of these prisoners have other serious health, mental health, and relationship problems, as well as skill and resource deficits that require the attention of social workers and other helping professions. We are just beginning to address these problems. Many prisons still do not have adequate financial and personnel resources to provide adequate services to inmates. The proportion of professionally trained social workers who are employed full time to work with incarcerated inmates is pitifully small. According to an NASW survey, only 2% of members identified their field of practice as the "justice system," and that includes everything from public defenders' offices to halfway houses. The number of social works in prison settings is a tiny fraction of that 2%.

Perhaps one of the reasons for the dearth of social work professionals in this field is the lack of information about prison inmates and their problems. Until recently, comparatively few social work researchers showed much interest in them, and not many social work education programs provided more than a cursory survey of this field.

The trend began to change in the late 20th century due to efforts of pioneers such as the late Albert Roberts, the author of dozens of research studies in this neglected area. His contributions led to a number of encyclopedic works such as *Social Work in Juvenile and Criminal Justice Settings* (1997). He recruited and collaborated with other researchers like David Springer, who recently coauthored the fourth edition of that book. Springer worked with Dr. Roberts on other similar projects, and he recruited still other researchers into this field. Additionally, and building on Dr. Robert's work, Dr. Church and Dr. Springer collaborated in updating Dr. Robert's *Juvenile Justice Sourcebook* (2014). Dr. Springer soon became one of the leading scholars in correctional social work, and Dr. Church has become a leading scholar in juvenile justice.

Professors Springer and Church have brought together an impressive team of experts to address the issues of special stigmatized populations in prison. Their team covers the most stigmatized of these inmate groups—from the mentally ill to HIV and terminally ill inmates, from immigrants to veterans and LGBT inmates. Unfortunately, record keeping in prisons and jails has generally been woefully inadequate, but this volume provides much useful data on these inmate populations, where available. They also examine and evaluate treatment approaches. Readers, especially those involved in these special areas of practice, will find the book's provision of case examples and resources extremely helpful.

This book should be a valuable addition to the curricula of educational programs for all the helping professions, especially those focused on correctional settings, as well as a useful guide to prison administrators and their staff. It will assist both in the understanding of the problems experienced by these underserved and stigmatized populations, and in the application of this knowledge to practice.

C. Aaron McNeece, PhD
Dean and Walter W. Hudson Professor (Emeritus)
College of Social Work
Florida State University

PREFACE

My frustration with the criminal justice system began in earnest in 1995. It was at this time that I had just graduated from the University of Utah with a degree in history and was looking for something to do with my life. Like most looking for employment at that time, I responded to an advertisement in the local newspaper for Correctional Officers at the Utah State Prison. I must say, with all candor, that I knew nothing of the correctional system and really had no interest in it, short of getting a paycheck to make ends meet. However, after my 16 weeks of training, I was thrown into a world only seen by a select few individuals. Since that time I have been fascinated by, frustrated with, challenged by, and concerned about the criminal justice system. After working as a correctional officer for 1.5 years, I was given the opportunity to become a rehabilitative specialist, which is essentially a case worker. It was at this time that I decided I wanted to go into social work and saw this as my first step of "fixing a broken system."

My time at the Utah State Prison was short—only 5 years—but in that time I was able to witness a system that was breaking down in terms of providing services to offenders, and my example of "Sam" is of but one who taught me about the "revolving door" and a system that is not about "correction" but about warehousing. Sam was a career petty criminal who had been in and out of prison and jail for most of his life. Like most criminals, Sam entered the system as a juvenile and when he became of age he graduated into the adult system; unfortunately, for his graduation he did not get to walk across a stage and receive his diploma.

Sam was one of the many on my caseload, and he is especially memorable because he was one of the first inmates I prepared to leave prison. I had worked with him to set up his release plan and we were both excited when the day came for him to walk out the front gate. He left; I went about my business saving the next soul. However, 2 weeks later I was walking down the main hall, here comes Sam walking toward me. My heart sank and my idealistic visions vanished. I asked him what happened, and he told me something that has always stayed with me: He said, "This is all I know. I do not belong out there and have no idea how to function out in the real world." I was devastated and I wanted to know why we have a system that sets people up to fail rather than helping them succeed.

Thus, as a society, we must ask ourselves, "What can we do?" Do we continue the same trend (which fiscally is not possible), or do we create ways to better serve inmates who need services that will allow them to be productive members of society?

The current trend of locking up just to punish has done nothing but increase the prison population and drain the coffers of many of our states' budgets. Over the past 30 years the United States has become home to more prisoners than any other country in the world. During these 30 years, the prison population in the Unites States has grown from about 400,000 in 1985 to roughly 2.2 million in 2015. In addition, 68% to 70% reoffend within 3 years of release. Although during this time incarceration rates have risen, the reason behind it is not clear because crime rates have followed no clear path. Violent crime has risen, then fallen off, only to rise again. To me, it is clear, as I examine the past 30 years, that the best explanation I can devise for the rise in incarceration is not rising crime rates (or increase in the number of criminals for that matter), but the policy choices made by legislators to greatly increase the use of imprisonment as a response to *any* activity seen as a crime and not focus on the reduction of crime through nonpunitive means. In my mind, what we are currently doing is not working.

—Wesley T. Church II, PhD

I began my professional career as a clinical social worker across various settings—inpatient, community-based, nonprofits, schools—working with adolescents and their families. Many of these youth had involvement in the juvenile justice system, which often brought with it additional challenges for them and their families. When I left the field to return to Florida State University for my doctoral studies, I was fortunate to have Dr. Aaron McNeece as a faculty mentor. McNeece was a former probation officer, and he introduced me to the world of juvenile and criminal justice research. For 20 years, my work has focused on the reform of juvenile justice systems and the delivery of effective community-based services with juvenile and criminal offenders. There is much work left to do.

The evidence about what works is very clear. Study after study indicates that prevention and treatment programs are more effective than incarceration, and that it is cheaper and more effective to keep less serious juvenile offenders in the community, where they can access needed services and avoid or limit disruption in their home lives. The evidence also shows that it is ineffective to lump delinquent kids together in large state institutions far from home. An investment in school- and community-based prevention and diversion programs will save money over time and increase accountability because more youths will stay in the community.

It is in our best interest to ensure that youth receive a well-rounded education. Research has found that the single greatest predictor of future involvement in the juvenile justice system is a history of disciplinary referrals at school. Indeed, a good education is a critical component of stopping the juvenile-to-adult-criminal pipeline. Preventing adolescents from continuing a criminal lifestyle will save taxpayers millions of dollars. Each teen prevented from becoming an adult offender could save between $1.7 and $2.3 million *per* youth. The ultimate goal is to enhance public safety and prevent victimization by stopping this cycle of offending.

If we want our neighborhoods and communities to be safer, we must be more than tough on crime. We must be smart on crime.

—David W. Springer, PhD

The impetus for this book grew out of our 40+ years of combined experience in being involved with the juvenile and criminal justice system. The decision to edit this book was based on our belief that an up-to-date text that addressed trends, critical issues, policies, programs, and research was needed by upper-division undergraduate and graduate students who were considering a career in the criminal justice system. This volume should also prove useful to those already working within the criminal justice system—practitioners, administrators, and court officials—as a desk reference and as a resource for updating their knowledge about the most effective interventions and practices for the diverse populations with the criminal justice system.

This book has six distinct features:

1. It provides a comprehensive discussion of the critical issues, public policies, and intervention strategies and programs that are effective in serving distinct criminal justice populations.
2. It features current case studies to illustrate and profile mentally-ill offenders, sex offenders, suicidality, HIV/AIDS, geriatric, youth offenders, substance abuse, LGBTQ and transgender, minority confinement, veterans, and death row inmates.
3. It presents the latest data indicating that treatment/training and education, as well as alternative sentencing, is more beneficial than punitive sanctions for inmates.
4. It discusses the benefits of alternative sentencing to society from a cost perspective as well as a human compassion perspective.
5. It discusses in detail the heterogeneity of the prison population and distinguishes between "cookie-cutter" services and individualized treatment options.
6. It provides an extensive discussion of the strengths and limitations of institutions, alternative sentencing options, probation, and specialized interventions.

The criminal justice system is too complex in its systems for any one person to be an expert in all facets of it. Therefore, we have invited 29 prominent scholars, each with extensive knowledge and expertise in a specific area of the criminal justice system, to write or coauthor original chapters for this book. These chapters thoroughly summarize and document the most up-to-date developments and emerging trends in the care, treatment, and rehabilitation of the populations presented in each respective chapter. *Serving the Stigmatized* is the first comprehensive volume devoted exclusively to examining the scope of the problems, risks, and evidence-based institutional and community-based interventions of these populations within the criminal justice system. The overriding objective of this volume is to focus on the current trends of rehabilitation and explore the possibility of resolving the issues of incarceration in the United States from a rehabilitative perspective rather than punitive.

Wesley T. Church II, PhD
David W. Springer, PhD

CONTRIBUTORS

David L. Albright, PhD, MSW
Hill Crest Foundation Endowed Chair
  in Mental Health
School of Social Work
The University of Alabama
Tuscaloosa, Alabama

Eprise R. Armstrong
PhD Student
Indiana University School of
  Social Work
Indianapolis, Indiana

Katie Ropes Berry, MSW
College of Social Work
Florida State University
Tallahassee, Florida

Wesley T. Church II, PhD, LMSW
Director and J. Franklin Bayhi
  Endowed Professor
Louisiana State University
School of Social Work
Baton Rouge, Louisiana

David Patrick Connor, PhD
College of Arts and Sciences
Criminal Justice Department
Seattle University
Seattle, Washington

Susan De Luca, PhD
Assistant Professor
The University of Texas at Austin
Steve Hicks School of Social Work
Austin, Texas

Daley DiCorcia
Master's of Social Work Candidate
School of Social Welfare
Stony Brook University
Stony Brook, New York

J. Mark Eddy, PhD
Senior Research Scientist
Director of Community-Based
  Research Family Translational
  Research Group
NYU Health
New York University
New York, New York

Matthew Gilmour, MSW
College of Social Work
Florida State University
Tallahassee, Florida

Matthew Hiller, PhD
Associate Professor
Department of Criminal Justice
Temple University
Philadelphia, Pennsylvania

Jeremiah W. Jaggers, PhD
Assistant Professor
School of Social Work
Indiana University
Indianapolis, Indiana

Stephanie C. Kennedy, PhD
Assistant Professor
School of Social Work
University of Connecticut
Hartford, Connecticut

Khadija Khaja, PhD
Associate Professor
School of Social Work
Indiana University
Indianapolis, Indiana

George Leibowitz, PhD, LICSW
Professor
School of Social Welfare
Stony Brook University
Stony Brook, New York

Tina Maschi, PhD
Associate Professor
Fordham University Graduate School
of Social Service
Founder and Director of the Justia
Agenda Initiative at Fordham
University GSS
Bronx, New York

Ellen P. McCann, PhD
Adjunct Professor
Department of Criminology, Law,
and Society
George Mason University
Fairfax, Virginia

Susan McCarter, PhD, MS, MSW
Associate Professor
School of Social Work
University of North
Carolina—Charlotte
Charlotte, North Carolina

Stephen W. Phillippi Jr, PhD,
LCSW, CCFC
School of Public Health
Program Chair, Behavioral &
Community Health Sciences
Director, Institute for Public Health &
Justice
LSU Health–New Orleans
New Orleans, Louisianna

Elizabeth C. Pomeroy, PhD, LCSW
Distinguished Teaching Professor
Bert Kruger Smith Professor of Mental
Health and Aging
Steve Hicks School of Social Work
The University of Texas at Austin
Austin, Texas

Stephanie Grace Prost, PhD
Assistant Professor
Louisville University
Kent School of Social Work
Louisville, Kentucky

James Roffee, PhD
Associate Professor of Law
Swinburne University of Technology
Melbourne, Australia

Christine Saum, PhD
Associate Professor
Law and Justice Studies
Rowan University
Glassboro, New Jersey

Jean E. Schumer, PhD, LCSW
College of Public Health and Human
Sciences
Oregon State University
Corvallis, Oregon

Evan R. Seamone, LLM, JD, MPP
Clinic Attorney
Veterans Legal Clinic at the Legal
Services Center
Harvard Law School
Cambridge, Massachusetts

David W. Springer, PhD
Director of the RGK Center for
   Philanthropy and Community
   Service
University Distinguished Teaching
   Professor
The University of Texas at Austin
Lyndon B. Johnson School of Public
   Affairs
Austin, Texas

Kate H. Thomas, PhD, MCHES
Assistant Professor
College of Health Sciences
Charleston Southern University
Charleston, South Carolina

Stephen J. Tripodi, PhD
Doctoral Program Director
Associate Professor
Florida State University
College of Social Work
Tallahassee, Florida

Andrea Waling, PhD
Australian Research Centre in Sex,
   Health & Society
La Trobe University
Melbourne, Victoria

Drew E. Winters
PhD Student and Research Assistant
Indiana University School of
   Social Work
Indianapolis, Indiana

Serving the Stigmatized

Mental Health in Prison Populations

Policy, Practice, and Challenges

EPRISE R. ARMSTRONG, DREW E. WINTERS,
AND JEREMIAH W. JAGGERS

Mental health diagnoses and issues within the criminal justice system have been the focus of practitioners and researchers. Incarcerated individuals face specific needs when it comes to reentry into society after incarceration and meeting and maintaining their mental health needs.

SCOPE OF THE PROBLEM

Prevalence of Mental Health Issues in Prisons

It is generally understood that people with mental illnesses are overrepresented in the US criminal justice system (Prins, 2014; Skeem, Winter, Kennealy, Louden, & Tatar, 2014). However, the prevalence rates among the academic literature and national samples vary. The most recent meta-analysis of the academic literature found a range between 10% and 31% of sampled prisoners suffered from mental illness (Prins, 2014). On the other hand, the most recent Bureau of Justice Statistics (BJS) reports, among state prisoners, 61% of offenders had mental health issues, and 76% had substance use issues (James & Glaze, 2006). Standardization of sampling methods and methods for determining mental health issue prevalence is needed. The most robust samples likely use validated instruments and clinical interviews as opposed to correctional health records (Prins, 2014). Despite the inconsistency of findings, current and lifetime prevalence of mental illness is higher among incarcerated population in comparison to the general population.

The most reported diagnoses among prisoners are attention-deficit/hyperactivity disorder (ADHD), bipolar disorder, generalized anxiety disorder, major depressive disorder, and posttraumatic stress disorder (PTSD; Prins, 2014).

Schizophrenia appears to be the least prevalent disorder, ranging between 2% and 10%, although psychotic symptoms have been reported in up to 15% of prisoners (James & Glaze, 2006; Prins, 2014). The most prevalent diagnosis is PTSD, which has been estimated to affect between 2% and 48% of prisoners (Prins, 2014). However, several studies have found that untreated childhood trauma exposure, with symptoms considered subclinical under the current standards in the *Diagnostic and Statistical Manual of Mental Disorders* (American Psychiatric Association, 2013), is prevalent in over 90% of prisoners (Dierkhising et al., 2013; Wolff & Shi, 2012). Many have linked childhood trauma exposure with involvement in the criminal justice system (Dierkhising et al., 2013; Marsiglio, Chronister, Gibson, & Leve, 2014; Wolff & Shi, 2012).

The prevalence of these disorders varies among subsets of the population. Females are more likely to report symptoms and are twice as likely to have symptoms related to PTSD (James & Glaze, 2006; Lynch et al., 2014; Prins, 2014). Although antisocial personality disorder (43%) and co-occurring substance use and mental illness subsumes a larger portion of male offenders (Ogloff, Talevski, Lemphers, Wood, & Simmons, 2015), other mental health conditions are more likely to be reported among females (Sarteschi, 2013). One reason for this disparity may be that women are more likely to report traumatic experiences, such as sexual abuse, than males (James & Glaze, 2006; Lynch et al., 2014; Sarteschi, 2013). There could be a number of reasons for this phenomenon other than males having fewer issues, such as male reticence, decreased awareness, increased stigma, and professional attitudes toward gender.

There are similar disparities in mental health in relation to race. Those identifying as non-Latino and White are most likely to have an *identified* mental health issue (James & Glaze, 2006; Ricks & Eno Louden, 2016; Sarteschi, 2013). Similar to gender disparities, stigma and attitudes toward mental illness may play a role in these differences. Ricks and Eno Louden (2016) assert that minority's mental health issues are similar to European Americans and that minorities, specifically Latino minorities, are not getting the care they need. Cultural and language issues may play a significant barrier to receiving care (Ricks & Eno Louden, 2016). Although national samples indicate that those with European descent are more likely to have an identified mental health issue, percentages based on population demonstrate a comparable proportion across race (James & Glaze, 2006). Further disparities may arise, not as a result of who is identified as having mental health issues, but as a result of access to treatment.

MENTAL ILLNESS AND CRIMINAL BEHAVIOR

Existing literature makes a strong connection between mental illness and criminal behavior; the prevalence of particular diagnoses tends to be higher in prisons than in community settings (Prins, 2014). Marcotte and Markowitz (2011) report that incarcerated adults and adolescents have higher rates of mental illness than individuals in the general population. Half of all incarcerated individuals have been diagnosed with a mental illness, when compared to 11% of the people in the general population (Hoke, 2015). Several factors influence criminal behaviors among those suffering from mental illness, including the type of mental illness, crime type, recidivism, race, and attitudes of professionals toward those suffering from mental illness. Though high levels of comorbid psychiatric disorders have been found among prisoners in a variety of countries over four decades, rates (apart from increasing instances of depression) appear to be remaining steady (Fazel & Seewald, 2012).

In prison settings, major depressive disorder is the most common severe mental illness; in one study, nearly a quarter of state prisoners met criteria for major depressive disorder (James & Glaze, 2006). Using the Beck Depression Inventory, Boothby and Durham (1999) found feelings of mild depression to be common among North Carolina prisoners (n = 1,494). This rate is nearly triple the national 12-month prevalence. Depression has been found to predict delinquent or criminal behavior (Broidy & Agnew, 1997). Individuals suffering from depression are more likely to commit crimes of a violent nature (Fazel et al., 2015; Hawkes, 2015). Fazel et al. (2015) conducted two studies to determine the association between violent crime and depressive behaviors in Sweden. The study found that when accounting for family, demographic, and individual factors, instances of violent crime increased in individuals suffering from depression. Substance abuse, gender, and other mental health issues each contribute to the relationship between depression and crime. Douzenis, Ferentinos, and Lykouras (2005) analyzed data from three studies and found that individuals who suffered from depression were less likely to be involved in criminal activities than those with other mental illnesses, but when they did commit crimes, they were more likely to commit violent crimes. Generally, depression is believed to have a negative correlation with criminal behaviors, but comorbid personality and conduct disorders, and alcohol and substance abuse do serve to increase the risk of criminality in persons suffering from depression (Douzenis, Ferentinos, & Lykouras, 2005).

Many prisoners do not receive adequate treatment for mental health conditions while in prison. This has an impact on recidivism. In an analysis of data from the Survey of Inmates in State and Federal Correction Facilities, Reingle Gonzalez and Connell (2014) found that inmates with less overt types of diagnoses (e.g., depression) were less likely to receive pharmacotherapy in prison than inmates with more overt diagnoses (e.g., schizophrenia). By contrast, Matejkowski, Lee, and Han (2014) propose that the criminal justice system serves as a significant referrer for mental health services, or, as supported by extensive literature, that a large number of people who have a serious mental illness have justice involvement.

Anderson, Cesur, and Tekin (2015) used data from the National Longitudinal Study of Adolescent Health (ADD Health) to examine the relationship between adolescents and depression. The analysis controlled for individual, family, and neighborhood factors. Findings from this study suggest that depression in adolescence results in increased probability of engagement in criminal behavior directed at property. Adolescent depression was not found in this study to increase the likelihood of engagement in violent or drug-selling-related crime (Anderson, Cesur, & Tekin, 2015).

Those with severe mental illness diagnoses are at increased risk for victimization themselves. Khalifeh et al. (2015) examined the prevalence and impact of crimes committed against people with severe mental illnesses (SMI). They interviewed 361 psychiatric patients using a national crime survey questionnaire. The responses were compared to control responses from a concurrent national crime survey completed by 3,138 participants from the general population. Kalifeh et al. (2015) found that people with severe mental illness were at much greater risk for experiencing crime in the last year (40% SMI versus 3% control) and violent assaults (19% SMI versus 3% control). Additionally, victimization, especially during childhood, is correlated with higher rates of depression, anxiety, and stress than those in the general population (Unver, Yuce, Bayram, & Bilgel, 2013).

Mental illness prevalence varies by the type of crime committed. Individuals labeled as firesetters were found to be more likely to have engaged with psychiatric services than other offenders and community controls (37% versus 29.3% versus 8.7%) (Ducat, Ogloff, & McEwan, 2013). Firesetters were also more likely to use various public mental health services. Additionally, they were also more likely to have diagnoses of affective and personality disorders, and substance abuse. There is emerging evidence that suggests that high-risk sexual offenders have an increased likelihood of suffering from complex trauma; complex PTSD has been found to be related to serious mental health difficulties (Abracen & Looman, 2015).

Co-occurring Disorders

Literature suggests that inmates with both mental illness diagnoses and substance abuse disorders are more likely to commit more serious and frequent crimes than people in the general population (Ogloff, Talevski, Lemphers, Wood, & Simmons, 2015). More than 60% of inmates with mental illness who were incarcerated at a state prison used drugs in the months before they were arrested (Fischer et al., 2014).

Rates of mental illness have been reported to be higher among female inmates (73%) than male inmates (55%) (James & Glaze, 2006). High incidence of substance abuse exists among female prisoners (Mir et al., 2015). Anxiety, personality, and affective disorders accompany substance abuse disorders in female prisoners. Lynch et al. (2014) conducted a multisite study ($n = 491$) in rural and urban jails to determine the prevalence and level of impairment of serious mental illnesses for women in jail and the proportion of women who present with substance abuse disorders or PTSDs. Findings revealed that nearly half (43%) met the criteria for a serious mental illness and for PTSD individually; about one third (29%) met the criteria for both PTSD and a severe mental illness, 38% had a serious mental illness and a substance abuse disorder, and about a quarter (26%) experienced all three in their lifetime.

James and Glaze report that a majority (80%) of women who are involved with the criminal justice system have a history of substance abuse and various co-occurring mental illness disorders. Scott, Dennis, and Lurigio (2015) explored psychiatric disorder comorbidity and prevalence in 253 women detained in a single county jail participating in drug treatment programs. In addition to substance abuse, more than 75% of those involved in the study also had a psychiatric diagnosis. These comorbid diagnoses were related to low self-esteem, increased substance use severity, and higher levels of criminal thought. Using these findings, Scott, Dennis, and Lurigio (2015) suggest that recidivism interventions for those involved with the criminal justice system address both psychiatric and substance abuse issues. Modestin, Hug, and Ammann (1997) found higher rates of criminality in male inpatients diagnosed with affective disorders, when compared with those with depressive disorders.

Wallace et al. (1998) discovered that increases in criminal offences committed by persons diagnosed with schizophrenia and affective disorders is small, and they can possibly be mediated by the existence of a comorbid personality disorder or substance abuse issue. In reviewing studies examining prevalence of mental health disorders in prisoners, Fazel and Seewald (2012) discovered high rates of mental illness, notably, depression, personality disorders, and psychosis.

Mental Illness, Criminal Behavior, and Recidivism

The disproportionate representation of the mentally ill in the prison system and the movement to increase care for these conditions bring along the assumption that mental illness is directly associated with criminal behavior. As such, efforts to address mental illness in those who are incarcerated implicitly assume that reducing mental illness will decrease crime (Peterson, Skeem, Kennealy, Bray, & Zvonkovic, 2014; Skeem et al., 2014). However, there is strong empirical support that mental illness is not directly associated but rather indirectly related or independent of criminal behavior. For example, Peterson et al. (2014) found that crimes were rarely motivated by symptoms with only 4% related to psychosis, 3% to depression, and 10% to bipolar disorder. Similarly, Skeem et al. (2014) found that offenders with mental illnesses had more risk factors for recidivism and that this predicted recidivism, but, because of this relationship, mental illness was indirectly related to criminal behavior, and that criminological needs were present independently. Finally, Walters and Crawford (2014) found major mental illness did not achieve significance related to future antisocial behavior; rather, a history of violence was a consistent predictor of recidivism.

Others have demonstrated a correlation between mental health issues and reincarceration. Wilson, Draine, Barrenger, Hadley, and Evans Jr. (2014) found that the risk of recidivism was not different for those with serious mental illness than those in the general population. Fisher et al. (2014) found the presence of a juvenile record and history of previous incarcerations to be significant risk factors, whereas substance abuse and other clinical risk factors were not indicators of recidivism. Wilson et al. (2014) also found that people with a serious mental illness remained in the community after incarceration longer than any others included in the study. Baillargeon, Binswanger, Penn, Williams, and Murray (2009) call this the revolving door of the prison system, indicating that those with mental illnesses are two to three times more likely to be reincarcerated in comparison to controls. On the other hand, Ogloff et al. (2015) found those with co-occurring mental health and substance use issues were responsible for more serious offenses than mental illness alone. Although not common, hallucinations precede up to 10% of violent offenses (Skeem et al., 2014). Certainly, there is some association with imprisonment and mental illness; however, addressing mental illness alone is not sufficient to meet the needs of this population (Peterson et al., 2014; Sarteschi, 2013; Skeem et al., 2014; Walters & Crawford, 2014).

Alternative models have been created to capture the complexity of mental illness and criminal behavior. For individual factors, Andrews, Bonta, and Wormith (2006) propose that the strongest factors for recidivism are (1) an established criminal history pattern, (2) antisocial traits, (3) antisocial cognition, and (4) antisocial peers. Four additional moderate risk factors are substance use, employment instability, family problems, and a lack of prosocial activity engagement. These factors have been found to be involved with those who suffer from mental illness, but not specific to those who have a mental illness. Cognitive errors, attitudes, and values supportive of crime (antisocial cognition) have been found equally as common among those with mental illness as those without mental illness (Morgan, Fisher, Duan, Mandracchia, & Murray, 2010; Wolff, Morgan, Shi, Huening, & Fisher, 2011). The cognitive capacity for proactive antisocial cognition appears to be more salient than reactive antisocial cognition, which may render many with mental illness unable (Walters & DeLisi, 2015).

The aforementioned risk factors for recidivism are independent of mental illness and provide a framework for understanding how mental health may play a part in criminal behavior. Others have identified that mental illness, even though it is prevalent in prisoners, more likely is an indirect cause of criminal behavior by promoting general risk factors for crime or often happens independently of criminal behavior (Skeem et al., 2014). Findings in the literature support that the relationship between recidivism and mental illness is largely indirect. If the goal is to reduce recidivism for mentally ill offenders, then antisocial features must be explicitly assessed, acknowledged, and targeted in correctional treatment efforts.

In the context of these findings, competent mental health treatment is an important factor to reducing recidivism by reducing indirect factors associated with criminal behavior. Greater success may be possible by treating mental illness while also treating criminology factors. Reducing criminal behavior is not the only reason for addressing mental health in those who are imprisoned. Other factors such as stress on society, the cost of care outside of prison, quality of life, and the potential for successful reintegration are of significant importance.

Access to Mental Health Treatment for Prisoners

According to national samples, prison mental health services are deficient (Abramsky, Fellner, & Watch, 2003). James and Glaze (2006) in the BJS report indicates only a third of state prisoners with mental health issues receive care with federal and state facilities as low as 17.5%. Medication is the most frequent form of mental health care received, but national samples only indicate around 18% of those in need are receiving medication (Reingle Gonzalez & Connell, 2014). Of those who do receive services, only 7% of prisoners with mental health issues have received any professional counseling or therapy while incarcerated (James & Glaze, 2006). Reingle Gonzalez and Connell (2014) found that in a national sample of state and federal prisoners, over 50% who were prescribed medication prior to incarceration were not receiving these medications as an inmate. These disparities in the need for care and access to these services are not commensurate to access equivalence outside of prisons.

International bodies have issued position statements calling for the equivalence of care, including mental health care, to prisoners as what is available outside of prison (United Nations General Assembly, 1990; World Health Organisation, 2008). The position asserts that prisoners should not be denied full access to health care as a result of incarceration (Forrester, MacLennan, Slade, Brown, & Exworthy, 2014). However, treatment equivalence may be more challenging due to differences between general population and prison populations. Niveau (2007) states that the environment of prison is inherently detrimental to mental health because it does not have supportive factors, such as family support, work, and liberty. Similarly, it may be impossible for prison psychiatrists to offer patient-centered and compassionate care due to the ethical dilemma of loyalties to both patient and institution (Dlugacz, Low, Wimmer, & Knox, 2013). Furthermore, prisoners often present with a complex mixture of mental health problems that typical primary care models from the general community may not address (Forrester et al., 2014). Addressing the needs for services that are commensurate with outside levels of care may have different measures for meeting this standard.

Increasing accessibility may not be a matter of meeting minimal equivalent standards to what is found in the general population. Rather, a commitment to a rights-based provision that seeks a right to health that takes no account of one's legal status may be more appropriate to find measures to realize a commensurate level of care (Forrester et al., 2014). Examining whether relevant health care services are available, accessible, and of good quality would ignore a false comparison between care for the general population and care for those who are imprisoned (Exworthy, Samele, Urquía, & Forrester, 2012). Attitudes toward prisoners may be a significant barrier to care access and treatment.

The correctional system has a difficult task of delivering correctional punishment while trying to provide care when needed; these two functions historically have been confused with a compromise on the latter for the former. Among staff and correctional workers in the state prison system, prisoners with severe mental illness are generally considered to be malingering (Abramsky et al., 2003). Toch (2007) reports that the limited number of services are only distributed to those who prove to be the most worthy. The reported attitudes of the correctional workers and staff are a concern due to the consistency of numbers indicating the overrepresentation of those with mental health issues in prison. Deinstitutionalization has led to transinstitutionalization as the prison system has subsumed the majority of this population (Sisti, Segal, & Emanuel,

2015). It is clear that greater efforts for accessibility to mental health care are needed for prison populations, but mental health care is not necessarily the only need these populations need.

EVIDENCE-BASED PRACTICES RELATED TO THE CRIMINAL JUSTICE SYSTEM

The increased risks for recidivism among mentally ill offenders remains an increasingly troubling phenomenon for researchers and practitioners alike. As a result, there are several evidence-based interventions attempting to improve outcomes and reduce recidivism for offenders suffering from serious mental health issues. Unfortunately, the bulk of these interventions does not fully address issues of recidivism; however, despite this, several programs do result in positive outcomes. We outline four of these approaches next.

Mental Health Courts and Modified Therapeutic Community

Mental health courts are a cost-effective and successful treatment course to reduce recidivism (Aos & Drake, 2013). However, mental health courts (MHCs) are used to keep offenders from jail or prison time; these programs are not meant to treat offenders while in prison (Duwe, 2014). In response, the nodified therapeutic community (MTC) program was developed. The MTC program was found to significantly reduce incarceration rates of offenders with comorbid substance abuse and mental illness diagnoses (Sacks, Sacks, McKendrick, Banks, & Stommel, 2004). Individuals involved with the MTC program used Personal Reflections, which was a residential treatment program modified to change an individual's attitude and lifestyle as it related to substance abuse, criminal thinking and behavior, and mental illness and health. The model uses psychoeducational classes with cognitive-behavioral elements and therapeutic interventions such as group therapy with peers and medication administration and management. The program is designed to last approximately 12 months, but it can vary depending on the individual's progress and needs. The program requires that while incarcerated, the inmates participate in formal program activities; the average participant will attend activities for 4 to 5 hours per day, up to 5 days a week. Once released from jail or prison, the participant can enroll in the postprison MTC program. The aftercare program requires the individual to live on location and continues the work begun during incarceration (Sacks et al., 2004).

Individual Community-Based Treatment

The ACT service delivery model was designed to provide individualized mental health services; needs are assessed by a multidisciplinary group of providers, and services include treatment, support services, and rehabilitation (Morrissey,

Meyer, & Cuddeback, 2007). The multidisciplinary team works to determine the needs of the individual and provide comprehensive treatment without a time limit. Aimed at improving symptoms and reducing hospitalizations, ACT can include treatment within a hospital (with as-needed 24/7 crisis support), intensive pharmacology treatment, and community living skills. ACT interventions, while successful at reducing psychiatric hospitalization rates and improving stability with housing, were not shown to be effective at reducing arrest or incarceration rates. To reduce costs in comparison to the ACT models, forensic intensive case management (FICM) models were developed. FICM models are considered extensions of the assertive community treatment (AFT) model, but they do not provide psychiatric services (Abracen, Gallo, Looman, & Goodwill, 2016). Rather than directly providing services, in the FICM model, providers assist participants in obtaining appropriate services. However, outcomes from the updated model were inconsistent, and there was not a strong evidence base to support the provision of services at a reduced cost.

The Risk-Need-Responsivity Model

The Risk-Need-Responsivity (RNR) model is one that promotes assessment and treatment of those clinically involved with the criminal justice system (Skeem, Steadman, & Machak, 2015). The RNR model goes beyond the historical focus of assessment and treatment and attempts to ascertain an individual's risk of recidivism.

Abracen et al. (2015) developed a model to treat individuals involved with the criminal justice system who were suffering from severe mental illness. This model, the Integrated Risk-Need-Responsivity (RNR-I) model, is developed with the assumption that factors related to criminal activity and severe mental illness should be incorporated into treatment and management of moderate- and high-risk offenders. Additionally, for treatment to be comprehensive, complex trauma and associated issues should be included in treatment. This model incorporates group- and individual-based treatments similar to the RNR model, but it is argued to be more integrated. The RNR-I model was designed for treatment with sexual offenders, but it is possible that the model could be useful with other types of offenders (Abracen et al., 2015).

Release Planning

Release planning was designed to help with serious and persistently ill offenders. The program is implemented while participants are still incarcerated. To participate, program participants must meet one of six criteria: be hospitalized and/or treated by a crisis team at least twice within 24 months for mental health issues; have been hospitalized at least 6 months in the last year; have a diagnosis considered one of the "big four": major depression, borderline personality disorder, schizophrenia, or bipolar disorder; the court has committed the individual as mentally ill; or a mental health professional has written a letter finding the individual to have future episodes or attacks if not treated. Release planning services address issues with housing, transportation vocation, substance use and abuse, disability, and mental and health care needs (Duwe, 2014). This model includes case planning, life skills training, and other skills.

CRIMINAL JUSTICE POLICY ISSUES AND IMPLICATIONS

A number of social and economic issues related to policy influence the prevalence and experience of prisoners suffering from mental illness. Policies related to gun violence, homelessness, and substance abuse and misuse all have an impact on crime. Those involved with the criminal justice system who also have experience with mental illness might have experiences with unemployment and homelessness as well. The perspective that homelessness is a mental health problem has been prevalent since the 1980s (Bassuk, Rubin, & Lauriat, 1984). When first studied, it was found that nearly 90% of the homeless population had a mental health issue of some type (Bassuk, Rubin, & Lauriat, 1984). Homelessness may influence criminal behavior; additionally, previous incarceration may have influenced homelessness. The economic impact of incarcerated individuals struggling with mental illness is also of concern. While incarcerated, individuals lose income, which impacts their community's tax base. Additionally, the loss of income may result in the loss of housing, removal of social support, and the absence of health care to treat any mental health concerns.

Another issue concerns the increasingly high number of individuals with one or more mental illnesses incarcerated; some have labeled American prisons as the "new asylums" (Torrey et al., 2014). Individuals with mental illness who might previously have been treated in psychiatric facilities are now being housed, and sometimes treated, in jails and prisons. Many individuals, receiving inadequate mental health care services, and possibly facing additional victimization while incarcerated, leave sicker than when they entered (Torrey et al., 2014). Policy should focus on providing adequate mental health services to incarcerated individuals and ensuring that care can continue after individuals leave the jail or prison.

Public versus privately funded prisons are another policy issue. Some argue that increasing numbers of private prisons incentivize the incarceration of increasing numbers of individuals, even those who might be better treated in alternative institutions. Also, for-profit institutions are focused primarily on profit, rather than the rehabilitation of citizens.

TRENDS AND FUTURE DIRECTIONS

One of the greatest impacts on future directions in the population of currently or formally incarcerated individuals with one or more mental illness diagnoses is that public knowledge relies on movies and media. As a result of this, any stigma faced by mentally ill and/or incarcerated individuals is bolstered by negative portrayals. The future direction of policy or practice is often driven by public perception.

SAMPLE CASE

Thomas is a 34-year-old African American man who was recently convicted of domestic violence and illegal possession of a controlled substance. Police responded to a motel room where Thomas was living. He appeared disheveled and had blood on one hand. After investigation, officers determined that Thomas had repeatedly hit his live-in girlfriend on the face. They also found small amounts of marijuana and crack cocaine. Subsequent to their investigation, Thomas was arrested. He pled guilty to a reduced sentence and was remanded to a state prison.

This is one of many convictions for Thomas, including four previous convictions for violent behavior. After his first arrest at the age of 19, Thomas was diagnosed with bipolar disorder. At that time, Thomas reported being awake for approximately 36 hours and was arrested after assaulting a homeless man whom he described as a "government agent." Subsequently, he enrolled in a court-directed mental health treatment program. Larry, a social worker who assisted the court, was assigned to Thomas's case. Larry arranged and paid for transportation for Thomas, helped advocate for him with court officials, and helped Thomas to develop a plan for his transition out of court supervision. Thomas participated in weekly group sessions that taught him about bipolar disorder and how to manage it. He also met weekly with Leah, a therapist, to address his underlying mental health issues. After completing his treatment, the court placed him on probation for 1 year. During that time, he continued meeting with Leah and began taking lithium to help manage symptoms.

After 1 year, Thomas was released from probation and his charges were dropped. Larry referred him to the community mental health center and to a psychiatrist who could continue the medical management of his illness. Thomas began working with a local construction company and rented his first apartment. After working for some time, Thomas was hurt while at work. His physician prescribed a narcotic to treat his pain. During the ensuing months, Thomas ceased taking lithium and began relying on prescription pain medications, even after his treatment for the injury stopped. A drug test by his employer revealed the presence of opioids in his blood, so Thomas was fired. Consequently, Thomas began engaging in criminal activity, burglarizing homes, selling drugs, and committing assault. Whereas the first treatment program seemed to have worked, subsequent efforts did not. In every instance, Thomas refused to participate in treatment or violated the conditions of his probation.

At 25, Thomas was convicted for assaulting a police officer and pled guilty and received a 5-year prison sentence. This was his first time in prison. While there, he received monthly visits from the prison psychiatrist. Each visit lasted no more than 15 minutes and each time the psychiatrist continued his prescription for lithium, a medication that he was forced to take in front of the prison medical staff. Besides his visits from the psychiatrist, he received an annual evaluation by a psychologist to assess for declining mental health, manifestation of other mental illnesses, and to provide recommendations for further treatment. He received no other treatment.

After completing 4 years of his sentence, he was placed on parole. A condition of his release was that he continue his treatment for bipolar disorder. However, the court did not provide resources (such as a case manager, referral, or a prescription for lithium) for him to utilize. Without a job or place to live, Thomas was unable to continue his treatment. The years following his release Thomas again began to engage in criminal activity. His mental health also began to decline. His life became punctuated by two events: long periods of mania and psychosis followed by serious depression.

Thomas lost touch with his family and friends. His repeated stays in jail/prison had left them unwilling to assist Thomas with his illness or with his basic needs such as a place to stay. In addition to his longtime recurring difficulties with bipolar disorder, he has also become dependent upon crack cocaine. With his criminal history and no stable residence, Thomas is unable to acquire a job. Despite his early success with the treatment of his illness, Thomas has limited resources and no desire to engage in treatment. Most recently, he was found living under a bridge.

WEB-BASED RESOURCES

There are a number of resources available to practitioners, policy makers, and clients. Following are a few of those resources:

- Justice Center, Resource Package on Offenders with Mental and/or Substance Use Disorders: https://csgjusticecenter.org/nrrc/publications/resource-package-on-offenders-with-mental-illnesses-andor-substance-use-disorders/
- Justice and Mental Health Collaboration Program: https://www.bja.gov/ProgramDetails.aspx?Program_ID=66
- Mental Health America, Criminal Justice: http://www.mentalhealthamerica.net/issues/criminal-justice
- National Institute of Justice: https://www.nij.gov/Pages/welcome.aspx

Unique Challenges of the Prisoner Population

Prisoners with mental health issues face unique challenges that need to be addressed to facilitate rehabilitation. One important consideration is the difficulty with obtaining and maintaining insurance for medical and mental health care, including any necessary medication (Freudenberg, Daniels, Crum, Perkins, & Richie, 2005). The inability to start or maintain care for mental health issues creates significant barriers for functioning once released. Issues with mental health create significant barriers to functioning in the domains of physical, mental, and social health (including employment and meeting demands of daily life) that are not required while incarcerated (Haney, 2003). Job availability after incarceration relegates those who re-enter society to low-skill and low-paying jobs, which do not support a basic cost of living (Visher, Debus-Sherrill, & Yahner, 2011). Public assistance such as food stamps is often denied to prisoners re-entering society (Western, Braga, Davis, & Sirois, 2015), thus placing an additional burden by creating barriers to receiving assistance that these individuals would have otherwise qualified for. Many prisoners reintegrating into society are reliant on alternative sources such as family for financial support, if they have family support (Visher, Debus-Sherrill, & Yahner, 2011). Similarly, obtaining and maintaining housing has been a consistent difficulty for this population (Visher, Debus-Sherrill, & Yahner, 2011), which is likely an extension of difficulties obtaining employment. The difficulties of gaining employment and housing after incarceration compounded with barriers associated with mental illness and the difficulties with continuing treatment or medication place an unjustifiably excessive burden on these individuals (Barrenger, Draine, Angell, & Herman, 2017). These barriers must be addressed to facilitate rehabilitation and reintegration into society in a sustainable way.

REFERENCES

Abracen, J., Gallo, A., Looman, J., & Goodwill, A. (2016). Individual community-based treatment of offenders with mental illness: Relationship to recidivism. *Journal of Interpersonal Violence, 31*(10), 1842–1858.

Abracen, J., & Looman, J. (2015). *Treatment of high-risk sexual offenders: An integrated approach.* Hoboken, NJ: John Wiley & Sons.

Abramsky, S., Fellner, J., & Watch, H. R. (2003). *Ill-equipped: U.S. prisons and offenders with mental illness.* Washington, DC: Human Rights Watch.

American Psychiatric Association. (2013). *Diagnostic and Statistical Manual of Mental Disorders* (5th ed.). Arlington, VA: Author.

Anderson, D. M., Cesur, R., & Tekin, E. (2015). Youth depression and future criminal behavior. *Economic Inquiry, 53*(1), 294–317.

Andrews, D. A., Bonta, J., & Wormith, J. S. (2006). The recent past and near future of risk and/or need assessment. *Crime & Delinquency, 52*(1), 7–27.

Aos, S., & Drake, E. (2013). *Prison, police and programs: Evidence-based options that reduce crime and save money.* Olympia, WA: Washington State Institute for Public Policy.

Baillargeon, J., Binswanger, I. A., Penn, J. V., Williams, B. A., & Murray, O. J. (2009). Psychiatric disorders and repeat incarcerations: The revolving prison door. *American Journal of Psychiatry, 166*(1), 103–109.

Barrenger, S. L., Draine, J., Angell, B., & Herman, D. (2017). Reincarceration risk among men with mental illnesses leaving prison: A risk environment analysis. *Community Mental Health Journal, 53*(8), 1–10.

Bassuk, E. L., Rubin, L., & Lauriat, A. (1984). Is homelessness a mental health problem. *American Journal of Psychiatry, 141*(12), 1546–1550.

Boothby, J. L., & Durham, T. W. (1999). Screening for depression in prisoners using the Beck Depression Inventory. *Criminal Justice and Behavior, 26*(1), 107–124.

Broidy, L., & Agnew, R. (1997). Gender and crime: A general strain theory perspective. *Journal of Research in Crime and Delinquency, 34*(3), 275–306.

Dierkhising, C. B., Ko, S. J., Woods-Jaeger, B., Briggs, E. C., Lee, R., & Pynoos, R. S. (2013). Trauma histories among justice-involved youth: Findings from the National Child Traumatic Stress Network. *European Journal of Psychotraumatology, 4*, 1–12. doi:10.3402/ejpt.v4i0.20274

Dlugacz, H. A., Low, J. Y., Wimmer, C., & Knox, L. (2013). Ethical issues in correctional psychiatry in the United States. In N. Konrad, B. Völlm, & D. N. Weisstub (Eds.), *Ethical issues in prison psychiatry* (pp. 49–75). New York, NY: Springer.

Douzenis, A., Ferentinos, P., & Lykouras, E. (2005). Depression and criminality. *Archives of Hellenic Medicine, 22*(6), 535–543.

Ducat, L., McEwan, T., & Ogloff, J. R. (2013). Comparing the characteristics of firesetting and non-firesetting offenders: Are firesetters a special case? *The Journal of Forensic Psychiatry & Psychology, 24*(5), 549–569.

Duwe, G. (2014). The development, validity, and reliability of the Minnesota screening tool assessing recidivism risk (MnSTARR). *Criminal Justice Policy Review, 25*(5), 579–613.

Exworthy, T., Samele, C., Urquía, N., & Forrester, A. (2012). Asserting prisoners' right to health: Progressing beyond equivalence. *Psychiatric Services, 63*(3), 270–275.

Fazel, S., & Seewald, K. (2012). Severe mental illness in 33 588 prisoners worldwide: Systematic review and meta-regression analysis. *The British Journal of Psychiatry, 200*(5), 364–373.

Fazel, S., Wolf, A., Chang, Z., Larsson, H., Goodwin, G. M., & Lichtenstein, P. (2015). Depression and violence: A Swedish population study. *The Lancet Psychiatry, 2*(3), 224–232.

Fischer, W. H., Hartwell, S. W., Deng, X., Pinals, D. A., Fulwiler, C., & Roy-Bujnowski, K. (2014). Recidivism among released state prison inmates who received mental health treatment while incarcerated. *Crime & Delinquency, 60*, 811–832.

Forrester, A., MacLennan, F., Slade, K., Brown, P., & Exworthy, T. (2014). Improving access to psychological therapies in prisons. *Criminal Behavior and Mental Health, 24*(3), 163–168. doi:10.1002/cbm.1898

Freudenberg, N., Daniels, J., Crum, M., Perkins, T., & Richie, B. E. (2005). Coming home from jail: The social and health consequences of community reentry for women, male adolescents, and their families and communities. *American Journal of Public Health, 95*(10), 1725–1736.

Haney, C. (2003). The psychological impact of incarceration: Implications for post-prison adjustment. In J. Travis & M. Waul (Eds.), *Prisoners once removed: The impact of incarceration and reentry on children, families, and communities* (pp. 33–66). Washington, DC: The Urban Institute.

Hawkes, N. (2015). People with depression are more likely to commit violent crime, study concludes. *British Medical Journal, 350*, h1083.

Hoke, S. (2015). Mental illness and prisoners: Concerns for communities and healthcare providers. *Online Journal of Issues in Nursing, 20*(1), Manuscript 3.

James, D. J., & Glaze, L. E. (2006). *Highlights mental health problems of prison and jail inmates*. Washington, DC: U.S. Department of Justice, Bureau of Justice Statistics.

Khalifeh, H., Johnson, S., Howard, L. M., Borschmann, R., Osborn, D., Dean, K., . . . & Moran, P. (2015). Violent and non-violent crime against adults with severe mental illness. *The British Journal of Psychiatry, 206*(4), 275–282.

Lynch, S. M., DeHart, D. D., Belknap, J. E., Green, B. L., Dass-Brailsford, P., Johnson, K. A., & Whalley, E. (2014). A multisite study of the prevalence of serious mental illness, PTSD, and substance use disorders of women in jail. *Psychiatric Services, 65*(5), 670–674.

Marcotte, D. E., & Markowitz, S. (2011). A cure for crime? Psycho-pharmaceuticals and crime trends. *Journal of Policy Analysis and Management, 30*(1), 29–56.

Marsiglio, M. C., Chronister, K. M., Gibson, B., & Leve, L. D. (2014). Examining the link between traumatic events and delinquency among juvenile delinquent girls: A longitudinal study. *Journal of Child & Adolescent Trauma, 7*(4), 217–225. doi:10.1007/s40653-014-0029-5

Matejkowski, J., Lee, S., & Han, W. (2014). The association between criminal history and mental health service use among people with serious mental illness. *Psychiatric Quarterly, 85*(1), 9.

Mir, J., Kastner, S., Priebe, S., Konrad, N., Ströhle, A., & Mundt, A. P. (2015). Treating substance abuse is not enough: Comorbidities in consecutively admitted female prisoners. *Addictive Behaviors, 46*, 25–30.

Modestin, J., Hug, A., & Ammann, R. (1997). Criminal behavior in males with affective disorders. *Journal of Affective Disorders, 42*(1), 29–38.

Morgan, R. D., Fisher, W. H., Duan, N., Mandracchia, J. T., & Murray, D. (2010). Prevalence of criminal thinking among state prison inmates with serious mental illness. *Law and Human Behavior, 34*(4), 324–336.

Morrissey J., Meyer P. C., Cuddeback G. (2007). Extending assertive community treatment to criminal justice settings: Origins, current evidence, and future directions. *Community Mental Health Journal, 43*, 527–544.

Niveau, G. (2007). Relevance and limits of the principle of "equivalence of care" in prison medicine. *Journal of Medical Ethics, 33*(10), 610–613. doi:10.1136/jme.2006.018077

Ogloff, J. R., Talevski, D., Lemphers, A., Wood, M., & Simmons, M. (2015). Co-occurring mental illness, substance use disorders, and antisocial personality disorder among clients of forensic mental health services. *Psychiatric Rehabilitation Journal, 38*(1), 16–23. doi:10.1037/prj0000088

Peterson, J. K., Skeem, J., Kennealy, P., Bray, B., & Zvonkovic, A. (2014). How often and how consistently do symptoms directly precede criminal behavior among offenders with mental illness? *Law and Human Behavior, 38*(5), 439–449. doi:10.1037/lhb0000075

Prins, S. J. (2014). Prevalence of mental illnesses in US state prisons: A systematic review. *Psychiatric Services, 65*(7), 862–872. doi:10.1176/appi.ps.201300166

Reingle Gonzalez, J. M., & Connell, N. M. (2014). Mental health of prisoners: Identifying barriers to mental health treatment and medication continuity. *American Journal of Public Health, 104*(12), 2328–2333. doi:10.2105/AJPH.2014.302043

Ricks, E. P., & Eno Louden, J. (2016). Slipping through the cracks. *Criminal Justice and Behavior, 43*(4), 525–538. doi:10.1177/0093854815605525

Sacks, S., Sacks, J., McKendrick, K., Banks, S., & Stommel, J.(2004). Modified therapeutic community for MICA offenders: Crime outcomes. *Behavioral Sciences and the Law, 22*, 477–501.

Sarteschi, C. M. (2013). Mentally ill offenders involved with the U.S. criminal justice system. *SAGE Open, 3*(3), 215824401349702. doi:10.1177/2158244013497029

Scott, C. K., Dennis, M. L., & Lurigio, A. J. (2015). Comorbidity among female detainees in drug treatment: An exploration of internalizing and externalizing disorders. *Psychiatric Rehabilitation Journal, 38*(1), 35.

Sisti, D. A., Segal, A. G., & Emanuel, E. J. (2015). Improving long-term psychiatric care: Bring back the asylum. *Journal of the American Medical Association, 313*(3), 243–244. doi:10.1001/jama.2014.16088

Skeem, J. L., Steadman, H. J., & Manchak, S. M. (2015). Applicability of the Risk-Need-Responsivity model to persons with mental illness involved in the criminal justice system. *Psychiatric Services, 66*(9), 916–922.

Skeem, J. L., Winter, E., Kennealy, P. J., Louden, J. E., & Tatar, J. R., 2nd. (2014). Offenders with mental illness have criminogenic needs, too: Toward recidivism reduction. *Law and Human Behavior, 38*(3), 212–224. doi:10.1037/lhb0000054

Toch, H. (2007). Prevalence estimates: The numbers game. *Correctional Mental Health Report, 8*(5), 67–68.

Torrey, E. F., Zdanowicz, M. T., Kennard, A. D., Lamb, H. R., Eslinger, D. F., Biasotti, M. C., & Fuller, D. A. (2014, April). The treatment of persons with mental illness in prisons and jails: A state survey. *Treatment Advocacy Center.* Arlington, VA.

United Nations General Assembly. (1990). Basic principles for the treatment of prisoners: Resolution 45/111. United Nations General Assembly 45th Session (14 December 1990). Retrieved June 17, 2017 from http://www.un.org

Unver, Y., Yuce, M., Bayram, N., & Bilgel, N. (2013). Prevalence of depression, anxiety, stress, and anger in Turkish prisoners. *Journal of Forensic Sciences, 58*(5), 1210–1218.

Visher, C. A., Debus-Sherrill, S. A., & Yahner, J. (2011). Employment after prison: A longitudinal study of former prisoners. *Justice Quarterly, 28*(5), 698–718.

Wallace, C., Mullen, P., Burgess, P., Palmer, S., Ruschena, D., & Browne, C. (1998). Serious criminal offending and mental disorder. Case linkage study. *The British Journal of Psychiatry, 172*(6), 477–484.

Walters, G. D., & Crawford, G. (2014). Major mental illness and violence history as predictors of institutional misconduct and recidivism: Main and interaction effects. *Law and Human Behavior, 38*(3), 238–247. doi:10.1037/lhb0000058

Walters, G. D., & DeLisi, M. (2015). Psychopathy and violence: Does antisocial cognition mediate the relationship between the PCL: YV factor scores and violent offending? *Law and Human Behavior, 39*(4), 350–359. doi:10.1037/lhb0000123

Western, B., Braga, A. A., Davis, J., & Sirois, C. (2015). Stress and hardship after prison. *American Journal of Sociology, 120*(5), 1512–1547.

Wilson, A., Draine, J., Barrenger, S., Hadley, T., & Evans, A. (2014). The role of substance abuse in explaining time to re-incarceration among people with serious mental illness. *Administration and Policy in Mental Health and Mental Health Services Research, 41*(3), 293–301.

Wolff, N., Morgan, R. D., Shi, J., Huening, J., & Fisher, W. H. (2011). Thinking styles and emotional states of male and female prison inmates by mental disorder status. *Psychiatric Services, 62*(12), 1485–1493.

Wolff, N., & Shi, J. (2012). Childhood and adult trauma experiences of incarcerated persons and their relationship to adult behavioral health problems and treatment. *International Journal of Environmental Research and Public Health, 9*(5), 1908–1926. doi:10.3390/ijerph9051908

World Health Organisation. (2008). Trencin statement on prisons and mental health. Retrieved June 17, 2017 from http://www.euro.who.int/prisons

2

Suicide Risk Among Adolescents Involved in the Justice System

Risk and Suggestions for Prevention

SUSAN DE LUCA AND DALEY DICORCIA

Suicide has been the third leading cause of death among 10- to 24-year-olds for the past 35 years (CDC, 2015). For every death by suicide, roughly 25 people attempt suicide, (American Foundation for Suicide Prevention, 2014), reflecting that su-icide affects far more than just the individual who attempts or dies. Since 1991, rates of adolescent (ages 12–18 years; National Library of Medicine, 2015) sui-cidal thoughts and behaviors remain relatively unchanged (CDC, 2013) and have increased among certain marginalized groups (Bridge et al., 2015). The Centers for Disease Control (CDC) conducts biennial surveys on a variety of health outcomes, including suicidal thoughts and behaviors, to middle and high school students, consistently reports gender and racial/ethnic disparities, and recently started collecting data on sexual minorities (2014).

The CDC found that sexual minority youth are at an increased risk of suicide; a nationally representative study of adolescents in grades 7–12 found that lesbian, gay, and bisexual youth were more than twice as likely to have attempted suicide as their heterosexual peers (CDC, 2014a; Russell & Joyner, 2001) and transgender youth (25%) attempted suicide (CDC, 2014a; Grossman & D'Augelli, 2007). Bridge and colleagues' 2015 study found females (23%) reported more suicidal ideations than males (12%). Examining the intersection of race/ethnicity and gender, Latinas (26%) reported higher rates of ideation compared to non-Hispanic White (23%) and Black females (19%). Regarding attempts, females (12%) reported double the proportion of attempts than males (6%). Among females, Latinas (15%) reported higher rates of attempts compared to non-Hispanic Whites (10%). Latino males (8%) reported twice the proportion of attempts than non-Hispanic White males (4%). Injuries sustained from attempts were higher for females (4%) than males (2%), and higher among underserved groups (e.g., Latinas (5%) and

Latino males (3%)) compared to non-Hispanic White males (0.9%; Kann et al., 2016). Even more pressing is that Latinas (Latinos will comprise over 25% of the US youth population by 2020; Childstats, 2014) have reported higher rates of suicidal thoughts and behaviors than non-Hispanic Whites and Blacks for 25+ years (CDC, 2014b). By 2060, Latinos 18 and younger will comprise more than one third of the US population, and overall, racial/ethnic minorities will constitute more than two thirds of the population.

RISK FACTORS

Behavioral Health

Mental illness and substance use are most strongly associated with an increased risk for suicide, suicidal thoughts, and suicidal behaviors (Chapman & Ford, 2008; Chavira et al., 2010; Gould et al., 2004). Often related to mental and behavioral health are traumatic experiences (Chapman & Ford, 2008; Chavira et al., 2010; Esposito & Clum, 2002; Morris et al., 1995), including sexual abuse history (Chavira et al., 2010; Esposito & Clum, 2002; Morris et al., 1995), and these risk factors are only amplified in the juvenile justice system. Roughly 70% of those involved in the juvenile justice system have a diagnosed mental illness (Skowyra & Cocozza, 2007), and most have comorbid mental health and substance use disorders (National Council on Disability, 2002). For example, more than two thirds of youth in custody have a mental illness and/or a substance use disorder (Teplin et al., 2002; Wasserman et al., 2002). Females (75%) are more likely than males (66%) to have reported abuse (King et al., 2011). And whereas mental health is a key risk factor for suicide, suicidal thoughts, and suicidal behaviors, feelings of hopelessness are a driving factor in risk for harm. When detainees were asked if they had felt hopeless, more than 33% of males and almost 50% of the females reported that their feelings of hopelessness led to ideating suicide (Abram et al., 2004). Furthermore, the experience of separation from family (Pogrebin, 1985), sharing tight (Parent et al., 1994) and locked housing quarters (Gallagher & Dobrin, 2006), or even placement in solitary confinement (Marcus & Alcabes, 1993; Parent et al., 1994), not surprisingly, increases the likelihood of suicide and suicidal behaviors.

Connections to Others and Help Seeking

Connectedness (Whitlock, 2006) is the level of attachment one has in his or her dyadic relationships. More than just the number of people one associates with, connectedness also involves the feeling of belonging and reciprocal positive regard. Connectedness is often a key factor in determining one's level of risk for suicide within social systems (Wyman et al., 2010). Family often functions as the main repository for a child's reported level of connectedness. Numerous authors have found that increased perceived connectedness to family decreases risk of suicidal behaviors (Borowsky et al., 1999; De Luca, Wyman, & Warren, 2012; Guiao & Esparza, 1995; Kerr, Preuss, & King, 2006).

Social-ecological factors are also strongly associated to suicide and suicidal behaviors, including family conflict (O'Donnell, O'Donnell, Wardlaw, & Stueve, 2004; Zayas, 2011), degree of access to trusted adults to turn to during times of distress (Whitlock, 2006), and having a suicidal peer in your social network (De Luca & Wyman, 2012). Creating a culture that encourages seeking formal support (i.e., mental health services) during times of increased distress is essential in any system for suicide prevention, including educational and juvenile systems (Husky et al., 2011). Individuals, regardless of age, tend to associate with peers who have similar behaviors as their own. This also means that adolescents at heightened risk for suicide seek help only from their peers (Raviv, Raviv, Vago-Gefen, & Fink, 2009) who are often also dealing with suicidal thoughts and behaviors themselves (De Luca, Wyman, & Warren, 2012) and are less likely to get support from trusted adults (Pagura, Fotti, Katz, & Sareen, 2009). Therefore, understanding mechanisms that may affect not only adolescents' individual help-seeking thoughts and behaviors are crucial among higher risk groups.

Research is still emerging on specific subgroups' risk for maladaptive coping norms and lower help seeking related to suicidal behaviors, especially among racial and ethnic minority adolescents (Freedenthal, 2007) but nonexistent for children in the juvenile justice system (Burke, Mulvey, & Schubert, 2015). Among the general population, research indicates that racial/ethnic minority youth are less likely to endorse seeking mental health services when in distress compared to non-Hispanic White adolescents (De Luca & Wyman, 2012; Freedenthal, 2007). Some of these disparities might be related to cultural differences to seeking help outside of the family unit (Cabassa, Zayas, & Hansen, 2006). Latino families traditionally believe that personal issues are private, family matters. Minority families, especially among Latino households, are often portrayed as collective and interdependent, and place a strong emphasis on respecting elders (i.e., *respeto*) (Marin & Marin, 1991). Therefore, a child who discloses any problems to a mental health professional could be seen as disrespecting long-held family norms.

Gender Differences

There are noted gender differences in help-seeking behavior among adolescent samples (De Luca, Schmeelk-Cone, & Wyman, 2012; De Luca & Wyman, 2012; Rickwood & Braithwaite, 1994). Societal norms posit that it is more acceptable for females to seek help (Vaux et al., 1986), especially from family (Feiring & Coates, 1987), and they often present deeper emotional connections with individuals compared to males (Youniss & Smollar, 1987). As a result, this may suggest the notable gender differences related to seeking help (Blyth & Foster-Clark, 1987), and these differences have also been observed in ethnic minority samples (De Luca & Wyman, 2012; Ocampo, Shelley, & Jaycox, 2007). For example, the Latino cultural norm of machismo stresses that males should encompass a number of characteristics simultaneously, including virility, independence, and emotional restraint (Torres, Solberg, & Carlstrom, 2002). Therefore, disclosing any type of emotional distress would be contradictory to this norm. Latinas have their own gendered norms, which include marianismo. This norm stresses that females are responsible for the level of harmony in the household and defer to others' instead of their own opinions and needs (Gil & Vazquez, 1996). Marianismo could influence Latinas' lower endorsement of help seeking to decrease family discord (Rew, 1997) by seeking help during times of distress for the betterment of the family (Gulbas et al., 2015).

Family conflict is common in adolescents' homes (Borowsky et al., 1999; Zayas, 2011). But this strain might present differently with Latinos due to the cultural norms addressed previously (Marin & Marin, 1991). As conflict increases, the number of trusted adults a child can turn to decreases. Whereas nonsuicidal adolescents often disclose more positive help-seeking attitudes, including talking to trusted adults outside of the family (Landale, Oropesa, & Bradatan, 2006), some racial and ethnic minorities might not share these more positive coping strategies. Individuals endorsing recent ideation also are likely to have increased feelings of hopelessness, isolation, and burdensomeness, especially resulting from the strained relationships with their parents (Winterrowd, Canetto, & Chavez, 2010). Therefore, racial and ethnic minorities are at increased risk to employ maladaptive beliefs and behaviors, including thoughts that no one, including trusted adults, can help them during periods of distress.

Ideation and Attitudes Toward Help Seeking

Lower levels of connectedness have been associated with suicidal risk (Durkheim, 1912) and linked to lower help-seeking norms and connections to adults (e.g., Asarnow, Carlson, & Guthrie, 1987). Youth engaging in suicidal behaviors often have discord with family or other adults in their life or are in environments where attachments to adults are strained (O'Donnell et al., 2004). Adolescents who utilize adults as a coping resource report feeling more hopeful about their situation. A recent study examined gender differences among Latino males' and Latinas' self-reported level of school engagement and seeking help after recent suicidal ideation (De Luca & Wyman, 2012). Stronger ties to school were positively associated with Latino males reporting positive engagement with adults or trying to get help, whereas no such associations were found among Latinas. These findings are not surprising, given the wealth of literature positing that mental and physical health outcomes are related to an individual's perception of the quality of the connections in his or her social network.

Race, ethnicity, and gender can also impact processes associated with suicidal risk in several settings by influencing self-reported stress and access to coping resources (Goebert et al., 2012). Congruent with systems theory, access to fewer social connections, especially with peers, have also been linked to suicidal risk, most notably among female adolescents (Bearman & Moody, 2004; Roberts & Chen, 1995). Gender disparities related to suicidal risk could be linked to the socialization processes, including with fellow adolescents. For example, females might have higher expectations of their friendships, resulting in a higher vulnerability to relationship losses (Allgood-Merten, Lewinsohn, & Hops, 1990). Additionally, having a friend who has attempted suicide in the past year increases one's own risk for an attempt more than two-fold (De Luca, Wyman, & Warren, 2012), and risk of dying by suicide increases 2–4 times if someone in a teen's network dies by suicide (Gould, Wallenstein, & Kleinman, 1990).

School Engagement and Help Seeking

School connectedness is related to numerous health-promoting outcomes (Whitlock, 2006), including decreased sexual activity compared to those not reporting strong associations with their school (Markham et al., 2010), decreased substance use, and decreased mental illness but also higher grades in school (Bond et al., 2007) and increased openness to seek out adults to report bullying and other forms of violence while in school (Eliot et al., 2010). Increasing school engagement, even in the juvenile justice system, is appropriate for a variety of prevention services as roughly 70%–80% of mental health services adolescents obtain are in their school system (Burns et al., 1995).

Schools also offer the opportunity to interact with a number of trusted adults each day (i.e., teachers, administration, and staff). Adults in schools can engage with students in formal but also informal encounters that might be less intimidating to children in terms of seeking out help. These more informal interactions can create stronger bonds to adults where they can become confidants to students and act as extended family to the child. This could be very beneficial to children who live in homes with higher levels of conflict where support might not be offered in the household. Students who are hesitant to discuss concerns or have few connections to adults at school have several obstacles for seeking help (Cigularov et al., 2008; Whitlock, 2006). Students who shared higher levels of reluctance to seek help from adults received services less and presented more avoidant coping responses than those who did seek help from an adult, even if they believe they needed help (Evans et al., 2004).

Some of the disparities related to suicidal thoughts and behaviors could be attributed to how adolescents respond while in distress. Distraught non-Hispanic White adolescents are more likely than peers to access services (Angold et al., 2002; Freedenthal, 2007; Snowden & Thomas, 2000; Wu et al., 2001; Yeh, McCabe, Hough, Dupuis, & Hazen, 2003), and Hispanics are the least likely to obtain care (Hough et al., 2002; Katatoka, Zhang, & Wells, 2002) among diverse groups and are more quickly discharged from care (Chakravarthy, 2014). Of adolescents hospitalized for a suicide attempt, roughly 37% to 52% sought care 30 days before their attempt (Barnes, Ikeda, & Kresnow, 2001; Suominen, Isometsä, Marttunen, Ostamo, & Lönnqvist, 2004). Suicidal youth often do not disclose suicidal thoughts and behaviors to trusted adults even after recent thoughts and behaviors (Pisani et al., 2012), especially racial/ethnic minorities (De Luca & Wyman, 2012), and even after participating in a suicide prevention program (Freedenthal, 2010). Fewer than half of detainees with recent thoughts of suicide had told anyone about their suicidal thoughts (Abram et al., 2014).

JUVENILE JUSTICE

Each year, more than 2 million juveniles are arrested (Puzzanchera & Adams, 2011) and roughly 71,000 are housed in detention centers (Office of Juvenile Justice and Delinquency Prevention, 2011). Roughly 70% of justice system involved youth met criteria for at least one mental health disorder (Lane, Goldstein, Heilbrun, Cruise, & Pennacchia, 2012; Teplin et al., 2002). Given the sheer number of minors involved in the juvenile justice system and the high proportion that needs mental health services, a deeper understanding of risk and protective factors for the development of evidenced-based interventions and patient-centered approaches for care are warranted. This starts with the rigorous assessment for treatment modalities that many federal, state, and local agencies reportedly support (Elliot & Mihalic, 2004; Mihalic et al., 2004). Yet few researchers have published such findings due to numerous obstacles, including selecting and accessing facilities, receiving institutional review board (IRB) approval in addition to informed consent/assent (often difficult to do in residential settings), mandated reporting concerns, and addressing staff attrition and buy-in (Lane et al., 2012). As a result, there is little recent information on suicidal behaviors and its mechanisms related to risk but also to care, specifically focusing on those in detention. Although some of the obstacles can be overcome by educating administrators on the positive outcomes related to empirical research on such a high-risk population to decrease their workload and increase the health of those in their care, many of the barriers are static in nature. Researchers must learn how to address these obstacles and anticipate them in order to gain entrée to such a closed system. Therefore, the information presented is limited, yet thorough, with the empirical information that is available to date.

Deaths by suicide is higher in the juvenile justice system than the general population (Gray et al., 2002; Hayes, 2009), roughly 3 times higher (Gallagher & Dobrin, 2006). Prevalence rates of suicidal ideation in juvenile justice–involved youth are also significantly higher than the general population, ranging from 3% to 52% (Abram et al., 2008; Archer et al., 2004; Cauffman, 2004; Esposito & Clum, 2002; Goldstein et al., 2003; Nolen et al., 2008; Rohde, Mace, & Seeley, 1997; Vincent et al., 2008; Wasserman & McReynolds, 2006). Differing assessment tools, as well as demographic differences within samples, may contribute to the varying prevalence rates. There is limited research on the rates of lifetime suicidal behaviors among youth in custody. Two known studies (Archer et al., 2004; Rohde, Mace, & Seeley 1997) reported lifetime suicidal ideation rates of detained youth ranging from 14% to 35%.

Attempts

Again, in terms of suicide attempts, there are a range of reported suicidal behaviors in the juvenile justice system ranging from 1.4% to 9% (Abram et al., 2008; Nolen et al., 2008; Wasserman & McReynolds, 2006; Wasserman et al., 2010) and are most often disproportionally reported by non-Hispanic White youths (Esposito

& Clum, 2002). Studies are limited to the demographics of the population (race, ethnicity, gender, and/or geography and the site's facility). For example, a seminal study found that roughly 16% of youth attempted suicide in the past 12 months (Morris et al., 1995), but this could be attributed to the agency's demographics or that the study included both short and longer term placements. One point that is agreed upon is that the longer a child is in the criminal justice system, the more at risk the individual is for suicidal thoughts and behaviors (Wasserman et al., 2010). The experience of residing in a juvenile justice facility may have long-ranging effects on the child well into adulthood. For example, the lifetime reported rates of attempts by juvenile justice–involved youth range from 10% to 37% (Abram et al., 2008; Archer et al., 2004; Chavira et al., 2010; Esposito & Clum, 2002; Kempton & Forehand, 1992; Mallett et al., 2012; Nolen et al., 2008; Rohde, Mace, & Seeley, 1997; Wasserman & McReynolds, 2006; Wasserman et al., 2010).

Gender and Racial/Ethnic Disparities

Similar to the general population, there are racial, ethnic, and gender disparities related to suicidal thoughts and behaviors. A study by Freedenthal and colleagues (2007) found that more than 58% of incarcerated youth reported a lifetime history of suicidal thoughts and behaviors. At least 31% of confined, incarcerated youth in a study by Robertson and Husain (2001) had self-reported a suicide attempt. Comparable to non–juvenile justice populations, females in detention reported higher rates of suicidal thoughts and behaviors (recent and lifetime). Furthermore, females are at even greater risk for suicidal thoughts and behaviors if their offense was running away from home or due to behavioral concerns as these girls often leave due to abuse by a family member (Chesney-Lind, 2001). In addition, there might be racial bias with practitioners, guards, and allied professionals among male and female youth because non-Hispanic Whites are more likely to receive rehabilitation compared to racial/ethnic minorities (Chesney-Lind, 2001). Racial/ethnic minorities also disproportionately represent the juvenile justice system's population, thus potentially reinforcing the negative stereotypes of minority youth.

Again, suicidal behaviors in the juvenile justice system mirror trends in the overall population yet indicate higher risk. For example, Black females had the lowest reports of lifetime suicidal thoughts among all adolescents while non-Hispanic White males disclosed more suicidal thoughts and behavior histories than their Black and Hispanic male peers and Latinas reported higher rates of suicidal thoughts and behaviors than their peers (Abram et al., 2008; Cauffman, 2004; Vincent et al., 2008). Nolen and colleagues (2008) also reported that non-Hispanic Whites and Latinos disclosed higher lifetime rates of attempts compared to Blacks.

Suicide Prevention in the Juvenile Justice System

Suicide prevention in the juvenile justice system begins at the moment of arrest (National Action Alliance for Suicide Prevention [NAASP], 2013). As offered by the NAASP, this initial interaction is filled with anxiety, stress, and quick transitions—all of which can make an already vulnerable child at an even higher risk for harm. The time of arrest is not only when officers and practitioners can learn much about the child to assess suicidal risk but also when communication between professionals is imperative to relay salient information pertaining to the child. With that said, assessment is an ongoing practice and not a solitary event. Assessment can occur during individual and/or group meetings with the child, informal observations but also during shift reports noting any changes in a child's observed behavior (i.e., increased aggressiveness, decreased affect, impulsivity), and during more formal discussions such as clinical team meetings. Furthermore, the child's family and friends should be part of the intake process or assessment meeting, if possible, to triangulate information to agency staff. When warranted, the child should be provided pharmacotherapy and placed under suicide observation in a safe room. The child should be taken to an environment which is free from any materials that could aid in a suicide attempt or staff must transport the child to an inpatient facility on their own grounds or at a local medical center.

Screening

A recent study by Aalsma, Schwartz, and Perkins (2014) found that a higher percentage of non-Hispanic White (25%) and female (33%) juvenile justice–involved youth screened positive for mental health concerns, including suicidal behaviors, as compared to Blacks (18%), Hispanics (16%), and males (18%). Female youth were more likely to receive mental health services, but no more likely to receive referrals, than males. The percentage of both males and females who received services during detention or referrals for services postdetention declined with their age. Receiving a positive mental health screen was associated with receiving services within 24 hours of detention but also receiving a mental health referral upon discharge. The impact of a positive mental health screen on receiving services may be dependent upon time, as the relationship between a positive screen and services during detention was more significant than that between a positive screen and referral upon discharge.

Due to the high risk of suicide and suicidal behaviors in juvenile justice facilities, universal screening should be implemented in all facilities at intake but also during multiple points while in detention. Individuals can become increasingly at risk for suicide while in the care of the juvenile justice system. While in detention, these periods are often found to be the most distressing to youth, and the following periods are considered times of high risk (National Commission on Correctional Health Care, 2015): (1) admission; (2) returning to the facility from court after adjudication; (3) receiving bad news, experiencing rejection or feelings of humiliation; (4) confinement, isolation, or segregation; and (5) following a prolonged stay in the facility. Therefore, these are crucial times that screening and assessment are needed for adjudicated youth.

There are over 50 suicidal screening and assessment tools specifically designed for adolescents (Goldston, 2000). Unfortunately, most these instruments are not validated with juvenile justice populations. Therefore, finding a tool to quickly but accurately assess a child's risk for suicide can become overwhelming to an already taxed staff. Screening, often in the form of a questionnaire that quickly addresses higher risk behaviors, can be completed by most staff with minimal effort. A recent study found that more than three fourths of agencies (76%) do not use a validated screener, and they ask only one question about suicidality in their health screener. Also, roughly 64% of agencies questioned used a screening tool that their facility or their state/county created on their own (Hockenberry, Wachter, & Sladky, 2016) and did not evaluate the efficacy of their tool. Although screeners do not necessarily require training or a specialized degree, they should be used with caution. For example, the screener might provide a score (if using a scale) that is considered high in and of itself, and the staff member may make the mistake to assume that the child is suicidal. The screening tool is just a starting point and requires a more thorough conversation (i.e., a mental health assessment) to determine one's risk for suicide.

Empirically based assessment and evaluations often require more time and specialized training. Additionally, many assessors (less than half in some reports; Hockenberry, Wachter, & Sladky, 2016) do not have any mental health training or have earned a master's degree in social work or another allied field. Some facilities require trained mental health professionals for screening instruments, but the majority do not (Hayes, 2009). In many states, those without the relevant credentials (i.e., probation and correctional officers) are not able to provide clinical judgements or even referrals. And with these restrictions, suicide assessment is either not done or is an afterthought.

Many of these factors place facilities at a disadvantage to care for at-risk youth, and sometimes agencies might not believe they have the capacity to assess or screen for suicide risk effectively or ethically. So, while upward of 90% of facilities reported providing some type of suicide screening, roughly 3% reported they assessed some youth and approximately 7% did not evaluate any youth in their public (97%) or private (82%) facilities (Hockenberry, Wachter, & Sladky, 2016). Among those agencies that reported screening for suicide, there was a substantial increase in positive screening from 94% in 2014 compared to 81% in 2002 (Hockenberry, Wachter, & Sladky, 2016). As a result, there is overwhelming agreement that using evidence-based instruments can provide the most benefit to agencies and their clients (American Psychological Association, 2008), given such resources have been tested and designed to assess suicide risk in youth, which is an issue that has clearly increased over time. To aid in this movement to utilize evidenced-based tools in agencies, Table 2.1 details the most common suicidal risk screening tools for adolescents and young adults.

Safety While in Custody

One of the most important yet daunting tasks for facilities is to provide an environment that is not only safe to the distressed child but also to their employees and other clients. Once an assessment has been made to determine the level of

Table 2.1. Empirically Tested Screening Instruments for Suicidal Ideation and Attempts

Questionnaire	Population	No. of Items on Scale	Scope of Items
Suicidal Ideation Questionnaire (SIQ) (Reynolds, 1987a)	15- to 18-year-olds	30	History and frequency of suicidal ideation
Suicidal Ideation Questionnaire-Junior (SIQ-JR) (Reynolds, 1987b)	12- to 14-year-olds	15	History and frequency of suicidal ideation
Suicidal Behaviors Questionnaire-Revised (SBQ-R) (Osman et al., 2001)	Adolescents and adults	4	History of suicidal ideation, attempt, and disclosure to others
Massachusetts Youth Screening Instrument-Second Version (MAYSI-2) (Grisso & Barhum, 2000)	Juvenile justice–involved youth	52 in total Suicide Ideation subscale = 5	Suicide Ideation subscale assesses history and frequency of suicidal ideation
Global Appraisal of Individual Needs–Short Screener (GAIN-SS) (Dennis, Chan, & Funk, 2006)	Adolescents and adults	15	Suicidal ideation; depressed mood and internalizing symptoms

risk, providing a physical place for the child is the first point of care. Often, staff decide upon two options: seclusion or physical restraints. Although well intentioned, these options place youth at an even higher risk for harm because quarantine decreases connectedness to others, which is essential to mental health (Parent et al., 1994). For instance, Hayes (2009) found that roughly half of juveniles who died by suicide were under room confinement at the time of their deaths, and the majority of those died during waking hours. Therefore, potentially counter to the intuition to separate the distressed youth from others for safety, every effort should be used to keep the youth in their current environment. Because again, transitions can often trigger individuals, resulting in increased anxiety, depression, and hopelessness. This also makes the youth accessible to clinicians in case of emergency. Some facilities also believe they should quickly confiscate children's clothing and provide them differently colored clothing to easily identify them from other youth. But this should be done only in the most acute cases, and they should be under constant supervision regardless. Other agencies take away any clothing that could be used during an attempt (shoelaces, belts, earrings) while allowing them to blend in with their peers to decrease stigma and maintain confidentiality. The key is to not dehumanize or depersonalize individuals during the time that they acutely need the support of others.

If a seclusion room is warranted, due to the extremely high risk of injury to themselves or to others, the environment should be free of any devices or materials that could aid in an attempt. The room should also be constantly observed by a staff member or provide an unobstructed view. A child should not be "imprisoned," meaning that there should be some comforts, if possible, including a soft place to sit albeit free of hooks, wires, or other protrusions (i.e., anything that could be fashioned to cut or used to aid in asphyxiation). It should be noted that a child does not have to verbally endorse suicidal thoughts or behaviors to warrant suicidal watch. Therefore, youth who present behavior that indicates any self-injury should be taken seriously. Although staggered observations are also utilized in facilities, and often the order is to never stagger for longer than 5 minutes, caution should be taken with this approach because it does not take long (often 3–4 minutes) to die of asphyxiation. Therefore, every effort should be made to continuously observe the client. In addition, interpersonal contact should be made with the youth throughout the day to compare current and past behavior for even potentially slight changes in behavior. Unfortunately, even doctoral-level clinicians are not fully trained on how to assess and treat suicidal patients (Almeida, O'Brien, Gross, & Gironda, in press); therefore, yearly trainings should be mandated for all staff.

FUTURE DIRECTIONS

Training

Regardless if an agency is screening all clients with empirically tested instruments, assessing all youth that are deemed at-risk, and providing safe guards in the facility, ongoing training is the key to effective suicide prevention. The most important factor to any prevention initiative is properly trained staff, but this can be easily averted. Although agencies often think to offer trainings exclusively to mental health professionals, suicide prevention training should include all staff on all shifts and work responsibilities. Disclosure of suicidal thoughts and behaviors can occur at any time, including times when staff might be on a lighter schedule, including weekends and holidays (Cocozza & Skowyra, 2000).

In addition to structured trainings, unplanned simulations where staff must respond to an emergency are effective tools to ascertain the application of protocols. These simulations should also include an assessment of CPR training in addition to other medical procedures. This is essential if a youth has attempted suicide and medical interventions are needed before emergency medical technicians, nurses, or physicians can provide care. After such trainings, quality control and assessment of current policies should be reviewed and changes made accordingly based on best practices and potential barriers to care.

Initial Points of Contact With Child

Although we often train support care staff to create an environment that is empathetic and supportive for clients, there needs to be a cultural shift in the juvenile justice system from sanction to rehabilitation. Staff who are welcoming and engaging to the youth they serve can also build trust and rapport that is beneficial in numerous ways. First, when youth have trusted adults in their social network, they are more open to share important information that could be imperative to their care and treatment (Wyman et al., 2010) and ultimately could prevent a suicide attempt (Roush, 1996).

One example of how law enforcement have been trained in mental health crisis intervention is the "Memphis Model" (University of Memphis, n.d.). This nationally recognized program focuses on the prearrest experience when mental health outcomes can become maladaptive. The idea is that if mental illness is addressed before children are potentially sent to juvenile justice facilities or engage in the criminal justice system longer term (i.e., probation), the potential for serious mental health outcomes, including suicide, could be prevented. The model stresses that all law enforcement should be trained in the intervention from judges, lawyers, and other allied court professionals. This upstream prevention training includes education on the risk factors for suicide and how to respond to suicidal youth during stressful transitions, including sentences and detention.

EMPIRICALLY TESTED SUICIDE PREVENTION PROGRAMS

The Suicide Prevention Resource Center and the American Foundation for Suicide Prevention (SPRC) created the Best Practices Registry for Suicide Prevention (http://www.sprc.org/bpr/section-iii-adherence-standards) that lists carefully reviewed and rigorously evaluated interventions. Recently, the Registry included an intervention specifically focusing on the juvenile justice settings. Shield of Care utilizes a systems approach to prevention by increasing levels of connectedness in a youth's network but also seeks to understand the impact of policy and potential barriers in the micro and macro systems of care. This approach not only empowers the facility itself but all members, including youth, in improving services.

There are a variety of interventions focused on adolescent populations that also have the potential to work with detained youth (Table 2.2). A recent study found that roughly 21% of juvenile justice–involved youth screened positive for mental illness with scores resulting in the "caution" or "warning" range on a suicide ideation screening measure. Additionally, these children were more likely to score higher on additional measures strongly associated with suicidal behaviors, including depression, anxiety, substance use, traumatic experiences, anger, irritability, somatic complaints, and thought disturbances (SPRC, 2014). What is needed are empirically based interventions for detained youth in juvenile justice settings to ascertain feasibility, effectiveness, and potential adaptations for this population.

As stated earlier, the detention environment itself can exacerbate mental health outcomes and increase suicidal risk. The risk factors strongly associated with suicide include feelings of hopelessness and isolation. These feelings can increase due to living away from family in addition to the punitive culture in many facilities. Therefore, detention centers should be used as a last resort for children, especially

Table 2.2. Empirically Tested Interventions for Suicide Prevention

Intervention	Population	Scope
Question, Persuade, Refer (QPR) https://www.qprinstitute.com/about-qpr	Community members and professionals (aka gatekeepers)	Gatekeepers recognize early suicide warning signs Question their meaning to determine suicide intent or desire Persuade the person to accept or seek help Refer the person to appropriate resources
Applied Suicide Intervention Skills Training (ASIST) https://www.livingworks.net/programs/asist/	All ages	Preparing, Connecting, Understanding (focuses on providing participants with skills to recognize risk and develop safeplans to reduce the risk of suicide), Assisting, and Networking (generates information about resources in the local community)
safeTALK https://www.livingworks.net/programs/safetalk/	Ages 15+	Identify those who are at risk, confidently ask them about the topic of suicide, and connect them with resources that can help them stay safe
Shield of Care http://www.tn.gov/behavioral-health/article/shield-of-care-curriculum	Juvenile justice staff	Emphasizes connectedness to youth, and communication between staff are essential system-level elements of suicide prevention; Specific steps: Seeing, Protecting, Listening, Assessing, Networking Reflection of policies, barriers, and how to take action in their specific facility's context
Functional Family Therapy (FFT) for Juvenile Offenders https://www.ncjrs.gov/pdffiles1/ojjdp/184743.pdf	Trained clinicians work with families	Focuses on the treatment system, family and individual functioning, and the therapist as major components Three specific, interdependent, intervention phases: engagement and motivation, behavior change, and generalization Develops family members' inner strengths and sense of ability to improve their situations
Multi-Systemic Therapy (MST) for Juvenile Offenders http://mstservices.com/what-is-mst/what-is-mst	Trained clinicians work with families in community-based settings	The therapist works with parents and caregivers to keep adolescents focused on education and gaining job skills in addition to decreased rearrests and substance use and management of mental health conditions.

since there are likely long-lasting negative effects on mental health for children who have lived in juvenile justice facilities. Therefore, suicide prevention should include decreasing the use of detention centers and focusing more on evidence-based treatments that focus on family systems, including such interventions like multisystemic therapy (MST) for juvenile offenders, which have been shown to decrease future involvement in the criminal justice system and suicidal behaviors (Trupin, 2007).

CONCLUSION

With few studies in the literature fully detailing the incidence and risk factors associated with suicidal risk among juvenile justice youth (Gallagher & Dobrin, 2006; Memory, 1989), it is crucial to understand this higher risk population. Adding to the call to action is that there is such variance in the reported outcomes for suicide in the juvenile justice system. For example, two widely cited studies (i.e., Gallagher & Dobrin, 2006; Memory, 1989) varied significantly (21.9 per 100,000 versus 57 per 100,000) in reports of suicidal deaths. Obtaining relevant data is wrought with bureaucracy because children are already a vulnerable group and then adding their juvenile justice status just increases the risk for coercion and harm. Therefore, institutions are often reluctant to approve studies focusing on suicide in the juvenile justice system. As a result, some researchers decide to study "easier" groups, whereas others become increasingly frustrated with the bureaucracy in these systems and others are ultimately shut out of these closed systems for fear of bad publicity.

With that said, we must learn more about those in detention to provide ethical and effective care. First, we need to know the current rate of suicide and suicidal behaviors occurring in the juvenile justice system. Second, researchers must incorporate variables on suicidal ideation and attempts and their history of suicidal behaviors in their studies. Although we know this is often difficult to do when researching underrepresented or vulnerable groups, educating institutional review and executive boards is crucial to allow these studies to continue.

Additionally, few studies have focused on the development and evaluation of preventive interventions for juvenile justice–involved youth. A greater understanding of the specific risk and protective factors of suicide and suicidal behaviors among juvenile justice–involved youth, including their family's history of suicide and detention history, can inform the development of effective intervention strategies. Juvenile justice agencies should ensure that at-risk youth receive evidence-based services in the least restrictive settings as possible. Agencies should provide mental health services that respect the gender, ethnicity, and sexual orientation status, and their intersections, of youth at risk of suicide.

Intensive follow-up and support should be provided to youth who are re-entering the community from detention, especially those who have a history of suicidal thoughts and behaviors. Finally, youth who are at risk for suicide should receive appropriate mental health resources and care, rather than punitive detention sentencing, if juvenile detention is considered only based on attaining some form of mental health services for the youth. Evidence-based mental health care that is sensitive to cultural, trauma, and identity should always be provided to youth at risk for juvenile detention and/or suicide.

CASE STUDY

Maria last attempted suicide at age 15 by harboring her asthma medications over a prolonged time and then ingesting them. Her mother raised her from the time she was an infant and has had no contact with her biological father. Her mother was diagnosed with depression shortly after Maria was born by her primary care physician. Although she was treated for postpartum depression, her mother does not believe in taking selective serotonin reuptake inhibitor (SSRI) medication and refuses to try narrative therapy. Because depression is strongly linked to problems with childrearing, and the additional stressors of living in a single-parent family with limited economic means, Maria reports that her relationship with her mother is strained.

Her family was referred into the child welfare system when she was 10 years old when they both became homeless. Child Protective Services (CPS) workers were diligent in meeting with the family and identified various outcomes to improve: (1) ensuring that her mother would maintain remission of her depression diagnosis; (2) introducing family therapy; (3) and addressing Maria's emerging depressive symptoms and feelings of hopelessness. Maria reported to her social worker that she believes that "ever since I was born, my mom was depressed. I'm the reason why she's depressed and now homeless. If I wasn't around, her life would be better. She'd be happier." Shortly afterward, Maria attempted suicide twice over an extended holiday weekend. Her mother was aware of the first attempt (she decided to cut her legs with a household knife), but Maria reported that she told her mother as she walked into her bedroom that she was "just fooling around." Maria stated that she "didn't want her mother to see her dead and just played it off." Over the course of the day, Maria grew increasingly guilty for making her mother upset (furthering her idea that she was a burden to her mother). She decided to take a handful of Tylenol at night and decided to rest in her bedroom. Her mother called her to breakfast and she did not answer, so she entered to find an initially nonresponsive Maria in her bed. Her mother thought she was 'faking it as teenagers do" and "didn't have time to deal with her," so she decided to have breakfast without her. When Maria woke up in the mid-afternoon, she complained of a stomach ache and went back to bed. She then missed lunch and by the time dinner was ready, Maria was vomiting and complained of severe stomach aches. Her mother took her to the hospital because she was in increasing pain. A social worker did conduct a suicide assessment, and Maria eventually admitted that her goal was to die with both attempts. The social worker referred her to the inpatient unit for observation overnight, and Maria repeatedly stated that she was not going to kill herself and her assessments indicated that she was a low risk for ideation. After Maria's discharge, her mother was referred to an outpatient social worker but failed to initiate treatment. Maria's teacher also encouraged treatment to the school social worker whom Maria's mother felt more comfortable with in terms of care because she had met with Maria previously, and it was a positive experience.

Maria did not want to increase her mother's distress and decided to go to the school social worker. Their former CPS worker also connected with them again, and despite ongoing efforts to supervise and support Maria's family, was unable to make contact with her family. Over the past few years, Maria was hospitalized roughly once per year and was referred for intensive outpatient services. Unfortunately, her mother could not aid in the intensive care, and her own depressive symptoms increased due to feeling overwhelmed with working, maintaining a home, and also working with Maria's practitioners. Maria started to self-cope with drugs and alcohol and was arrested for underage drinking and possession of controlled substances.

Maria was sent to juvenile detention for her charges and also to monitor her treatment. When Maria arrived, she tested positive for marijuana and barbiturates. When Maria was discharged from the detention, she was kicked out of her home the following week after getting into a fight with her mother about a boy she was dating. Her probation officer secured housing with Maria's aunt as a temporary solution because Maria was adamant about staying with someone she knew. Ten days later, Maria died of an overdose of heroin.

Because family relationships are often strained in children's lives who are also dealing with behavioral health issues, especially when cultural norms toward professional help seeking are often negative, suicidal behaviors can increase. Although it is difficult to surmise if Maria's family had been more supportive or intervened sooner she would not have died by suicide, family appraisals of her care and also deciding to get treatment might have contributed to her care. With that in mind, care is related to a variety of systems, including the schools, mental health centers and hospitals, and also juvenile and welfare systems. So, collaborative approaches—that is, systems working together—are essential.

REFERENCES

Aalsma, M. C., Schwartz, K., & Perkins, A. J. (2014). A statewide collaboration to initiate mental health screening and assess services for detained youths in Indiana. *The American Journal of Public Health, 104*(10), e82–e88.

Abram, K. M., Choe, J. Y., Washburn, J. J., Teplin, L. A., King, D. C., & Dulcan, M. K. (2008). Suicidal ideation and behaviors among youths in juvenile detention. *Journal of the American Academy of Child & Adolescent Psychiatry, 47*(3), 291–300. doi:10.1097/CHI.0b013e318160b3ce

Abram, K. M., Teplin, L. A., Charles, D. R., Longworth, S. L., McClelland, G. M., & Dulcan, M. K. (2004). Post-traumatic stress disorder and trauma in youth in juvenile detention. *Archives of General Psychiatry, 61*(4), 403–410.

Allgood-Merten, B., Lewinsohn, P. A., & Hops, H. (1990). Sex differences and adolescent depression. *Journal of Abnormal Psychology, 99,* 55–63.

Almeida, J., O'Brien, K., Gross, E., & Gironda, C. (in press). Development, implementation, and evaluation of a comprehensive course on suicide in a Masters of Social Work program. *Journal of Social Work Education.*

American Foundation for Suicide Prevention. (2014). Suicide statistics. Retrieved from https://www.afsp.org/understanding-suicide/facts-and-figures

American Psychological Association Task Force on Evidence-Based Practice for Children and Adolescents. (2008). *Disseminating evidence-based practice for children and adolescents: A systems approach to enhancing care.* Washington, DC: American Psychological Association.

Angold, A., Erkanli, A., Farmer, E. M. Z., Fairbank, J. A., Burns, B. J., Keeler, G., & Costello, E. J. (2002). Psychiatric disorder, impairment, and service use in rural african american and white youth. *Archives of General Psychiatry, 59*(10), 893–901. doi:10.1001/archpsyc.59.10.893.

Archer, R. P., Stredny, R., Mason, J. A., & Arnau, R. C. (2004). An examination and replication of the psychometric properties of the Massachusetts Youth Screening Instrument-Second Edition (MAYSI-2) among adolescents in detention settings. *Assessment, 11*(4), 290–302. doi:10.1177/1073191104269863

Asarnow, J. R., Carlson, G. A., & Guthrie, D. (1987). Coping strategies, self-perceptions, hopelessness, and perceived family environments in depressed and suicidal children. *Journal of Consulting and Clinical Psychology, 55*(3), 361.

Barnes, L. S., Ikeda, R. M., & Kresnow, M. (2001). Help-seeking behavior prior to nearly lethal suicide attempts. *Suicide and Life-Threatening Behavior, 32*(Suppl.), 68–75.

Bearman, P. S., & Moody, J. (2004). Suicide and friendships among American adolescents. *American Journal of Public Health, 94*(1), 89–95.

Blythe, D. A., & Foster-Clark, F. S. (1987). Gender differences in perceived intimacy with different members of adolescents' social networks. *Sex Roles, 17,* 689–718.

Bond, L., Butler, H., Thomas, L., Carlin, J., Glover, S., Bowes, G., & Patton, G. (2007). Social and school connectedness in early secondary school as predictors of late teenage substance use, mental health, and academic outcomes. *Journal of Adolescent Health, 40*(4), 357–e359.

Borowsky, I. W., Resnick, M. D., Ireland, M., & Blum, R. W. (1999). Suicide attempts among American Indian and Alaska Native youth: Risk and protective factors. *Archives of Pediatrics & Adolescent Medicine, 153*(6), 573–580.

Bridge, J. A., Asti, L., Horowitz, L. M., Greenhouse, J. B., Fontanella, C. A., Sheftall, A. H., Kelleher, K. J., & Campo, J. V. (2015). Suicide trends among elementary school-aged children in the United States from 1993 to 2012. *Journal of the American Medical Association, 169*(7), 673–677.

Burke, J. D., Mulvey, E. P., & Schubert, C. A. (2015). Prevalence of mental health problems and service use among first-time juvenile offenders. *Journal of Child and Family Studies, 24*(12), 3774–3781.

Burns, B. J., Costello, E. J., Angold, A., Tweed, D., Stangl, D., Farmer, E. M., & Erkanli, A. (1995). Children's mental health service use across service sectors. *Health Affairs, 14*(3), 147–159.

Cabassa, L. J., Zayas, L. H., & Hansen, M. C. (2006). Latino adults' access to mental health care: A review of epidemiological studies. *Administration and Policy in Mental Health and Mental Health Services Research, 33*(3), 316–330.

Cauffman, E. (2004). A statewide screening of mental health symptoms among juvenile offenders in detention. *Journal of the American Academy of Child & Adolescent Psychiatry, 43*(4), 430–439. doi:10.1097/00004583-200404000-00009

Center for Disease Control. (2013). Trends in the prevalence of suicide-related behavior National YRBS: 1991–2013. Retrieved from http://www.cdc.gov/healthyyouth/data/yrbs/pdf/trends/us_suicide_trend_yrbs.pdf

Center for Disease Control. (2014a). LGBT youth. Retrieved from https://www.cdc.gov/lgbthealth/youth.htm

Center for Disease Control. (2014b). Morbidity and mortality weekly report, youth risk behavior surveillance—United States, 2013. Retrieved from http://www.cdc.gov/mmwr/preview/mmwrhtml/ss6304a1.htm

Center for Disease Control. (2015). Suicide: Facts at a glance. Retrieved from http://www.cdc.gov/ViolencePrevention/pdf/Suicide-DataSheet-a.pdf

Chakravarthy, B., Hoonpongsimanont, W., Anderson, C. L., Habicht, M., Bruckner, T., & Lotfipour, S. (2014). Depression, suicidal ideation, and suicidal attempt presenting to the emergency department: Differences between these cohorts. *The Western Journal of Emergency Medicine, 15*(2), 211–216.

Chapman, J. F., & Ford, J. D. (2008). Relationships between suicide risk, traumatic experiences, and substance use among juvenile detainees. *Archives of Suicide Research, 12*(1), 50–61. doi:10.1080/13811110701800830

Chavira, D. A., Accurso, E. C., Garland, A. F., & Hough, R. (2010). Suicidal behavior among youth in five public sectors of care. *Child and Adolescent Mental Health, 15*(1), 44–51. doi:10.1111/j.1475-3588.2009.00532.x

Chesney-Lind, M. (2001). Out of sight, out of mind: Girls in the juvenile justice system. In Claire Renzetti and Lynne Goodstein (eds.), *Women, crime, and criminal justice: Original feminist readings* (pp. 27–43). Los Angeles, CA: Roxbury Pub. Co.

Childstats. (2014). Pop3 race and Hispanic origin composition: Percentage of U.S. children ages 0–17 by race and Hispanic origin, 1980–2014 and projected 2015–2050. Retrieved from http://www.childstats.gov/americaschildren/tables/pop3.asp.

Cigularov, K., Chen, P. Y., Thurber, B. W., & Stallones, L. (2008). What prevents adolescents from seeking help after a suicide education program? *Suicide and Life-Threatening Behavior, 38*(1), 74–86.

Cocozza, J. J., & Skowyra, K. R. (2000). Youth with mental health disorders: Issues and emerging responses. *Juvenile Justice, 7*(1), 3–13.

De Luca, S., Schmeelk-Cone, K., & Wyman, P. (2015). Latino and Latina adolescents' help-seeking behaviors and attitudes regarding suicide compared to peers with recent suicidal ideation. *Suicide and Life-Threatening Behavior, 45*(5), 577–587.

De Luca, S. M., & Wyman, P. A. (2012). Association between school engagement and disclosure of suicidal ideation to adults among Latino adolescents. *The Journal of Primary Prevention, 33*(2–3), 99–110.

De Luca, S. M., Wyman, P., & Warren, K. (2012). Latina adolescent suicide ideations and attempts: Associations with connectedness to parents, peers, and teachers. *Suicide and Life-Threatening Behavior, 42*(6), 672–683.

Dennis, M. L., Chan, Y. F., & Funk, R. R. (2006). Development and validation of the GAIN Short Screener (GAIN-SS) for psychopathology and crime/violence among adolescents and adults. *The American Journal on Addictions, 15*(Supplement 1), 80–91.

Durkheim, E. (1912). *Le suicide: Étude de sociologie* (2nd ed.). Paris, France: Félix Alcan.

Eliot, M., Cornell, D., Gregory, A., & Fan, X. (2010). Supportive school climate and student willingness to seek help for bullying and threats of violence. *Journal of School Psychology, 48*(6), 533–553.

Elliot, D. S., & Mihalic, S. (2004). Issues in disseminating and replicating effective prevention programs. *Prevention Science, 5*(1), 47–53.

Esposito, C. L., & Clum, G. A. (2002). Social support and problem-solving as moderators of the relationship between childhood abuse and suicidality: Applications to a delinquent population. *Journal of Traumatic Stress, 15*(2), 137–146. doi:10.1023/A:1014860024980

Feiring, C., & Coates, D. (1987). Social networks and gender differences in the life space of opportunity: Introduction. *Sex Roles, 17*(11), 611–620.

Freedenthal, S. (2007). Racial disparities in mental health service use by adolescents who thought about or attempted suicide. *Suicide and Life-Threatening Behavior, 37*, 22–34.

Freedenthal, S., Vaughn, M. G., Jenson, J. M., & Howard, M. O. (2007). Inhalant use and suicidality among incarcerated youth. *Drug and Alcohol Dependence, 90*(1), 81–88. doi:10.1016/j.drugalcdep.2007.02.021

Freedenthal, S. (2010). Adolescent help-seeking and the yellow ribbon suicide prevention program: An evaluation. *Suicide and Life-Threatening Behavior, 40*(6), 628–639.

Gallagher, C. A., & Dobrin, A. (2006). *Deaths in juvenile justice residential facilities. Journal of Adolescent Health, 38*(6), 662–668. doi:10.1016/j.jadohealth.2005.01.002

Gil, R. M., & Vazquez, C. I. (1996). *The Maria paradox: How Latinas can merge old world traditions with new world self esteem.* New York, NY: G. P. Putnam's Sons.

Goldstein, N. E., Arnold, D. H., Weil, J., Mesiarik, C. M., Peuschold, D., Grisso, T., & Osman, D. (2003). Comorbid symptom patterns in female juvenile offenders. *International Journal of Law and Psychiatry, 26*(5), 565–582. doi:10.1016/S0160-2527(03)00087-6

Goldston, D. B. (2000). *Assessment of suicidal behaviors and risk among children and adolescents.* Washington, DC: National Institute of Mental Health.

Gould, M. S., Velting, D., Kleinman, M., Lucas, C., Thomas, J. G., & Chung, M. (2004). Teenagers' attitudes about coping strategies and help-seeking behavior for suicidality. *Journal of the American Academy of Child & Adolescent Psychiatry, 43*(9), 1124–1133.

Gould, M. S., Wallenstein, S., & Kleinman, M. (1990). Time-space clustering of teenage suicide. *American Journal of Epidemiology, 131*(1), 71–78.

Gray, D., Achilles, J., Keller, T., Tate, D., Haggard, L., Rolfs, R., & McMahon, W. M. (2002). Utah Youth Suicide Study, phase I: Government agency contact before death. *Journal of the American Academy of Child & Adolescent Psychiatry, 41*(4), 427–434. doi:10.1097/00004583-200204000-00015

Grisso, T., & Barhum, R. (2000). *Massachusetts Youth Screening Instrumentt-2 (MAYSI-2).* Worchester, MA: University of Massachusetts Medical School.

Grossman, A. H., & D'Augelli, A. R. (2007). Transgender youth and life-threatening behaviors. *Suicide and Life-Threatening Behavior, 37*(5), 527–537.

Guiao, I. Z., & Esparza, D. (1995). Suicidality correlates in Mexican American teens. *Issues in Mental Health Nursing, 16*(5), 461–479.

Gulbas, L., Hausman-Stabile, C., De Luca, S., Tyler, T., & Zayas, L.H. (2015). An exploratory study of nonsuicidal self-injury and suicidal behaviors in adolescent Latinas. *American Journal of Orthopsychiatry, 85*(4), 302–314.

Hayes, L. M. (2004). *Juvenile suicide in confinement: A national survey.* Mansfield, MA: National Center on Institutions and Alternatives.

Hayes, L. M. (2009). Juvenile suicide in confinement—Findings from the First National Survey. *Suicide and Life-Threatening Behavior, 39*, 353–363. doi:10.1521/suli.2009.39.4.353

Hockenberry, S., Wachter, A., & Sladky, A. (2016, September). Juvenile residential facility census, 2014: Selected findings. *Juvenile Justice Statistics National Report Series Bulletin*, 1–19. NCJ 250123.

Hough, R. L., Hazen, A. L., Soriano, F. I., Wood, P., McCabe, K., & Yeh, M. (2002). Mental health services for Latino adolescents with psychiatric disorders. *Psychiatric Services, 53*, 1556–1562.

Husky, M. M., Kaplan, A., McGuire, L., Flynn, L., Chrostowski, C., & Olfson, M. (2011). Identifying adolescents at risk through voluntary school-based mental health screening. *Journal of Adolescence, 34*(3), 505–511.

Kann, L. and colleagues (2016). *Youth risk surveillance – United States, 2015.* Atlanta, GA: Centers for Disease Control and Prevention.

Kataoka, S. H., Zhang, L., & Wells, K. B. (2002). Unmet need for mental health care among U.S. children: Variation by ethnicity and insurance status. *American Journal of Psychiatry, 159*, 1548–1555.

Kempton, T., & Forehand, R. L. (1992). Suicide attempts among juvenile delinquents: The contribution of mental health factors. *Behaviour Research and Therapy, 30*(5), 537–541. doi:10.1016/0005-7967(92)90038-I

Kerr, D. C., Preuss, L. J., & King, C. A. (2006). Suicidal adolescents' social support from family and peers: Gender-specific associations with psychopathology. *Journal of Abnormal Child Psychology, 34*(1), 99–110.

King, D. C., Abram, K. M., Romero, E. G., Washburn, J. J., Welty, L. J., & Teplin, L. A. (2011). Childhood maltreatment and psychiatric disorders in detained youth. *Psychiatric Services, 12*, 1430–1438.

Lane, C., Goldstein, N. E., Heilbrun, K., Cruise, K. R., & Pennacchia, D. (2012). Obstacles to research in residential juvenile justice facilities: Recommendations for researchers. *Behavioral Sciences & the Law, 30*(1), 49–68.

LivingWorks Education. (n.d.). Applied Suicide Intervention Skills Training (ASIST). Retrieved from https://www.livingworks.net/programs/asist/

LivingWorks Education. (n.d.). SafeTALK. Retrieved from https://www.livingworks.net/programs/safetalk/

Mallett, C., DeRigne, L. A., Quinn, L., & Stoddard-Dare, P. (2012). Discerning reported suicide attempts within a youthful offender population. *Suicide and Life-Threatening Behavior, 42*(1), 67–77. doi:10.1111/j.1943-278X.2011.00071.x

Marcus, P., & Alcabes, P. 1993. Characteristics of suicides by inmates in an urban jail. *Hospital and Community Psychiatry, 44*(3), 256–261.

Marin, G., & Marin, B. V. (1991). *Research with Hispanic populations.* Thousand Oaks, CA: Sage

Markham, C. M., Lormand, D., Gloppen, K. M., Peskin, M. F., Flores, B., Low, B., & House, L. D. (2010). Connectedness as a predictor of sexual and reproductive health outcomes for youth. *Journal of Adolescent Health, 46*(3), S23–S41.

Memory, J. M. (1989). Juvenile suicides in secure detention facilities: Correction of published rates. *Death Studies, 13*(5), 455–463. doi:10.1080/07481188908252324

Mihalic, S., Irwin, K., Fagan, A., Ballard, D., & Elliot, D. (2004). *Successful program implementations: Lessons learned from blueprints.* Washington, DC: Office of Juvenile Justice and Delinquency Prevention. Retrieved from http://www.ncjrs.gov/pdffiles1/ojjdp/204273.pdf.

Morris, R. E., Harrison, E. A., Knox, G. W., & Tromanhauser, E. (1995). Health risk behavioral survey from 39 juvenile correctional facilities in the United States. *Journal of Adolescent Health, 17*(6), 334–344. doi:10.1016/1054-139X(95)00098-D

National Action Alliance for Suicide Prevention. (2013). *Guide to developing and revising suicide prevention protocols for youth in contact with the juvenile justice system.* Washington, DC: Author.

National Commission on Correctional Health Care. (2015). Correctional Mental Health Care: Standards and Guidelines for Delivering Services. Retrieved from https://www.ncchc.org/juvenile-standards-2015-what's-new.

National Council on Disability. (2002). The well-being of our nation: An intergenerational vision of effective mental health services and supports. Washington, DC: Author. Retrieved from http://www.ncd.gov/publications/2002/Sept162002

National Library of Medicine. (2015). Adolescent development. Retrieved from https://www.nlm.nih.gov/medlineplus/ency/article/002003.htm

Nolen, S., McReynolds, L. S., DeComo, R. E., John, R., Keating, J. M., & Wasserman, G. A. (2008). Lifetime suicide attempts in juvenile assessment center youth. *Archives of Suicide Research, 12*(2), 111–123. doi:10.1080/13811110701857087

Ocampo, B., Shelley, G., & Jaycox, L. (2007). Latino teens talk about help seeking and help giving in relation to dating violence. *Violence Against Women, 13*(2), 172–189.

O'Donnell, L., O'Donnell, C., Wardlaw, D. M., & Stueve, A. (2004). Risk and resiliency factors influencing suicidality among urban African American and Latino youth. *American Journal of Community Psychology, 33*(1-2), 37–49.

Office of Juvenile Justice and Delinquency Prevention. (2011). *Census of juveniles in residential placement 1997, 1999, 2001, 2003, 2006, 2007, and 2010* [machine-readable data files]. Washington, DC: Office of Juvenile Justice and Delinquency Prevention.

Osman, A., Bagge, C. L., Gutierrez, P. M., Konick, L. C., Kopper, B. A., & Barrios, F. X. (2001). The Suicidal Behaviors Questionnaire-Revised (SBQ-R): Validation with clinical and nonclinical samples. *Assessment, 8*(4), 443–454.

Pagura, J., Fotti, S., Katz, L. Y., & Sareen, J. (2009). Help seeking and perceived need for mental health care among individuals in Canada with suicidal behaviors. *Psychiatric Services, 60*(7), 943–949.

Parent, D. G., Leiter, V., Kennedy, S., Livens, L., Wentworth, D., & Wilcox, S. (1994). *Conditions of confinement: Juvenile detention and corrections facilities.* Washington, DC: U.S. Department of Justice, Office of Justice Programs, Office of Juvenile Justice and Delinquency Prevention.

Pisani, A. R., Schmeelk-Cone, K., Gunzler, D., Petrova, M., Goldston, D. B., Tu, X., & Wyman, P. A. (2012). Associations between suicidal high school students' help-seeking and their attitudes and perceptions of social environment. *Journal of Youth and Adolescence, 41*(10), 1312–1324.

Pogrebin, M. (1985). Jail and the mentally disordered: The need for mental health services. *Journal of Prison and Jail Health, 5*(1), 13–19.

Puzzanchera, C., & Adams, B. (2011). Juvenile arrests 2009. Juvenile Offenders and Victims: National Report Series Bulletin (NCJ 236477). Washington, DC: Office of Juvenile Justice and Delinquency Prevention.

Raviv, A., Raviv, A., Vago-Gefen, I., & Fink, A. S. (2009). The personal service gap: Factors affecting adolescents' willingness to seek help. *Journal of Adolescence, 32*(3), 483–499.

Rew, L. (1997). Health-related, help-seeking behaviors in female Mexican-American adolescents. *Journal for Specialists in Pediatric Nursing, 2*(4), 156–161.

Reynolds, W. M. (1987a). *Suicidal Ideation Questionnaire (SIQ)*. Odessa, FL: Psychological Assessment Resources.

Reynolds, W. M. (1987b). *Suicidal Ideation Questionnaire-Junior*. Odessa, FL: Psychological Assessment Resources.

Rickwood, D. J., & Braithwaite, V. A. (1994). Social-psychological factors affecting help-seeking for emotional problems. *Social Science & Medicine, 39*(4), 563–572.

Roberts, R. E., & Chen, Y. W. (1995). Depressive symptoms and suicidal ideation among Mexican-origin and Anglo adolescents. *Journal of the American Academy of Child & Adolescent Psychiatry, 34*(1), 81–90.

Robertson, A., & Husain, J. (2001). *Prevalence of mental illness and substance abuse disorders among incarcerated juvenile offenders*. Jackson, MS: Mississippi Department of Public Safety and Mississippi Department of Mental Health.

Rohde, P., Mace, D. E., & Seeley, J. R. (1997). The association of psychiatric disorders with suicide attempts in a juvenile delinquent sample. *Criminal Behaviour and Mental Health, 7*(3), 187–200. doi:10.1002/cbm.172

Roush, D. W. (1996). *Desktop guide to good juvenile detention practice: Research report*. Washington, D.C.: U.S. Dept. of Justice, Office of Justice Programs, Office of Juvenile Justice and Delinquency Prevention.

Russell, S. T., & Joyner, K. (2001). Adolescent sexual orientation and suicide risk: Evidence from a national study. *American Journal of Public Health, 91*(8), 1276–1281.

Skowyra, K. R., & Cocozza, J. J. (2007). *Blueprint for change: A comprehensive model for the identification and treatment of youth with mental health needs in contact with the juvenile justice system*. Policy Research Associates, Inc. Delmar: New York.

Snowden, L. R., & Thomas, K. (2000). Medicaid and African American outpatient mental health treatment. *Mental Health Services Research, 2*, 115–120.

Suicide Prevention Resource Center (SPRC). (2014, December 5). Youth in juvenile detention centers. Retrieved from http://www.sprc.org/news/youth-juvenile-detention-centers

Suicide Prevention Resource Center (SPRC). (2016). Resources and programs. Retrieved from http://www.sprc.org/resources-programs

Suominen, K., Isometsä, E., Marttunen, M., Ostamo, A., & Lönnqvist, J. (2004). Health care contacts before and after attempted suicide among adolescent and young adult versus older suicide attempters. *Psychological Medicine, 34*, 313–321.

Tennessee Department of Mental Health and Substance Abuse Services (TDMHSAS). (n.d.). Shield of care. Retrieved from http://www.tn.gov/behavioral-health/article/shield-of-care-curriculum

Teplin, L. A., Abram, K. M., McClelland, G. M., Dulcan, M. K., & Mericle, A. A. (2002). Psychiatric disorders in youth in juvenile detention. *Archives of General Psychiatry, 59*(12), 1133–1143. doi:10.1001/archpsyc.59.12.1133

Torres, J. B., Solberg, V. S. H., & Carlstrom, A. H. (2002). The myth of sameness among Latino men and their machismo. *American Journal of Orthopsychiatry, 72*(2), 163.

Trupin, E. (2007). Evidence-based treatment for justice-involved youth. In *The mental health needs of young offenders: Forging paths toward reintegration and rehabilitation* (pp. 340–367). Cambridge: Cambridge University Press.

The University of Memphis. (n.d.). Memphis model: Crisis intervention training (CIT). Retrieved from http://www.cit.memphis.edu/aboutCIT.php

Vaux, A., Phillips, J., Holly, L., Thomson, B., Williams, D., & Stewart, D. (1986). The social support appraisals (SS-A) scale: Studies of reliability and validity. *American Journal of Community Psychology, 14*, 195–218.

Vincent, G. M., Grisso, T., Terry, A., & Banks, S. (2008). Sex and race differences in mental health symptoms in juvenile justice: The MAYSI-2 National meta-analysis. *Journal of the American Academy of Child & Adolescent Psychiatry, 47*(3), 282–290. doi:10.1097/CHI.0b013e318160d516

Wasserman, G. A., Jensen, P. S., Ko, S. J., Cocozza, J., Trupin, E., Angold, A., . . . & Grisso, T. (2003). Mental health assessments in juvenile justice: Report on the consensus conference. *Journal of the American Academy of Child & Adolescent Psychiatry, 42*(7), 752–761.

Wasserman, G. A., & McReynolds, L. S. (2006). Suicide risk at juvenile justice intake. *Suicide and Life-Threatening Behavior, 36*(2), 239–249. doi:10.1521/suli.2006.36.2.239

Wasserman, G. A., McReynolds, L. S., Lucas, C. P., Fisher, P., & Santos, L. (2002). The voice DISC-IV with incarcerated male youths: Prevalence of disorder. *Journal of the American Academy of Child & Adolescent Psychiatry, 41*(3), 314–321. doi:10.1097/00004583-200203000-00011

Wasserman, G. A., McReynolds, L. S., Schwalbe, C. S., Keating, J. M., & Jones, S. A. (2010). Psychiatric disorder, comorbidity, and suicidal behavior in juvenile justice youth. *Criminal Justice and Behavior, 37*(12), 1361–1376. doi:10.1177/0093854810382751

Whitlock, J. L. (2006). Youth perceptions of life at school: Contextual correlates of school connectedness in adolescence. *Applied Developmental Science, 10*(1), 13–29.

Winterrowd, E., Canetto, S. S., & Chavez, E. L. (2010). Friendships and suicidality among Mexican American adolescent girls and boys. *Death Studies, 34*(7), 641–660.

Wu, P., Hoven, C. W., Cohen, P., Liu, X., Moore, R. E., Tiet, Q., Okeezie, N., Wicks, J., & Bird, H. (2001). Factors associated with use of mental health services for depression by children and adolescents. *Psychiatric Services, 52*, 189–195.

Wyman, P. A., Brown, C. H., LoMurray, M., Schmeelk-Cone, K., Petrova, M., Yu, Q., . . . & Wang, W. (2010). An outcome evaluation of the sources of strength suicide prevention program delivered by adolescent peer leaders in high schools. *American Journal of Public Health, 100*(9), 1653–1661.

Yeh, M., McCabe, K., Hough, R. L., Dupuis, D., & Hazen, A. (2003). Racial/ethnic differences in parental endorsement of barriers to mental health services for youth. *Mental Health Services Research, 5,* 65–77.

Youniss, J., & Smollar, J. (1987). *Adolescent relations with mothers, fathers and friends.* Chicago, IL: University of Chicago Press.

Zayas, L. H. (2011). *Latinas attemping suicide: When cultures, families, and daughters collide.* New York, NY: Oxford University Press.

3

Sex Offenders as Prison Inmates

DAVID PATRICK CONNOR

There are a lot of misconceptions about people who have sexually offended. The most common myths that the media perpetuate, which the public tend to accept as conventional wisdom, include sex offenders are unfamiliar to victims (Berliner, Schram, Miller, & Milloy, 1995; Craun & Theriot, 2009; Fortney, Levenson, Brannon, & Baker, 2007; Fuselier, Durham, & Wurtele, 2002; Levenson, Brannon, Fortney, & Baker, 2007), highly recidivistic (Fortney et al., 2007; Katz-Schiavone et al., 2008; Levenson et al., 2007; Levenson & D'Amora, 2007; Quinn, Forsyth, & Mullen-Quinn, 2004), specialists (Magers, Jennings, Tewksbury, & Miller, 2009; Miethe, Olson, & Mitchell, 2006), and unable to be rehabilitated (Katz-Schiavone et al., 2008; Levenson et al., 2007). In addition to acknowledging these misunderstandings, it is important for correctional and treatment professionals who are working with sex offenders to recognize that such individuals are not homogenous (Sample & Bray, 2006). Sex offenders are quite different with respect to personal characteristics, offense patterns, sexual preferences, treatment amenability, and risk levels. If professionals who work with sex offenders fail to take into consideration their differences, assessment efforts, correctional and treatment interventions, and other efforts to help them may be undermined.

CHARACTERISTICS OF SEX OFFENDERS

Despite the fact that they are a heterogeneous population, it may be possible to describe some common characteristics of many individuals who participate in illegal sexual activities. Keep in mind that not all of these attributes are present in all sex offenders, some people who commit sex offenses have none of these qualities, and some individuals may possess these characteristics without necessarily being sexual lawbreakers. In essence, the following descriptions are merely attributes that have been found in samples of sex offenders, but they may provide general insight into potential characteristics of the sex offender population behind bars.

Sex offenders may engage in sexual behaviors and have sexual interests that are considered by mainstream society to be unhealthy or inappropriate (Laws & O'Donohue, 2008). Examples may include participating in sexual contact with children or adults who cannot or do not consent, intentionally humiliating or causing pain to others, exposing genitals in public settings, and secretly observing others who are undressing or taking part in sexual activities. It is also widely believed that sex offenders utilize cognitive distortions or attitudes that support sex offending so they do not feel as badly about themselves for participating in illegal sexual behaviors (Bumby, 1996). The idea is that most sex offenders understand that their offenses are illegal and harmful to others, but they decide to do it anyway and reduce feelings of accountability through a variety of so-called thinking errors. Sex offenders may attempt to minimize their transgressions by convincing themselves and others that their behaviors are not harmful or not very serious. They may also believe that their victims enjoyed or initiated what happened. In addition, sex offenders may justify their actions by feeling that their victims deserved to be assaulted.

At the same time, poor communication and interpersonal skills, problems with intimacy, and isolation are said to commonly characterize the social experiences of sex offenders (Bumby, 2000). Further, many sex offenders tend to have ineffective coping skills that prohibit them from controlling their emotions and allow them to act impulsively. In addition, physical and sexual abuse histories are not uncommon among sex offenders (Dhawan & Marshall, 1996).

PREVALENCE OF SEX OFFENDING

It is difficult to describe the prevalence of sexual offending and victimization in the United States. What is known about sexual perpetration is largely derived from individuals who are arrested, charged, or convicted of illegal sexual activities. Between 10,000 and 20,000 sex offenders are released annually from US correctional institutions (Center for Sex Offender Management, 2007; Harrison & Beck, 2006; Hughes & Wilson, 2003). At the same time, more than 700,000 individuals in the United States are registered sex offenders (National Center for Missing and Exploited Children, 2014). These people, however, likely constitute a very small segment of the sex offender population. Many perpetrators of sex offenses are neither detected nor successfully prosecuted, and some may avoid the sex offender label through plea agreements. At the same time, individuals who are sexually victimized often do not report their experiences to law enforcement. Hart and Rennison (2003) found that only about 3 in 10 rapes and sexual assaults were reported to the police between 1992 and 2000.

Nonetheless, the actions of people who participate in illegal sexual activities often negatively impact a significant proportion of US society and represent a serious social problem. Nearly one quarter of all children are sexually assaulted at some point in their first 17 years of life (Spinazzola et al., 2005). In addition, between 17% and 22% of women and between 2% and 8% of men have been sexually victimized (Levenson & D'Amora, 2007). As a result of their victimization, many survivors of sex offenses report a variety of long-term consequences, including depression, substance abuse, and posttraumatic stress disorder (Chapman, Dube, & Anda, 2007).

The remainder of this chapter will initially describe evidence-based practices surrounding risk assessment and treatment for incarcerated sex offenders. Next, several criminal justice policy issues and corresponding implications germane to sex offenders and their prison and reentry experiences will be discussed. A case example featuring a convicted sex offender's incarceration and return to society will be presented. Finally, a web-based resources is provided.

EVIDENCE-BASED PRACTICES

Sex offenders who are confined to correctional institutions are commonly evaluated for recidivism risks and other characteristics of interest to prison officials. Based on these assessments, incarcerated sex offenders are frequently referred to sex offender treatment and other correctional programs. This section highlights the most commonly utilized risk assessment models. It also describes the most popular forms of sex offender treatment that are available inside correctional institutions today.

Risk Assessment Models

While inside correctional institutions, many sex offenders are evaluated by prison officials for the purposes of establishing their likelihood of recidivism, identifying their individual needs, and recommending appropriate types of institutional programming. Such assessments traditionally involved unstructured professional judgment. It is now quite common, however, for correctional and treatment professionals to use actuarial decision making and structured professional judgment to help them make decisions about sex offender risk and treatment.

Decisions about sex offenders that rely on unstructured professional judgment are based on discretion. In this model, no guidelines or restrictions exist for correctional and treatment professionals. Determinations of risk and treatment assignments are supported by the credentials and work experience of the evaluator. One advantage to using this approach is that it provides analysis of risk on an individual basis. In this way, risk management strategies and treatment recommendations may be afforded to sex offenders that consider the context behind their unlawful behaviors. However, evaluators who utilize unstructured professional judgment may overlook important factors that could otherwise be addressed. At the same time, without any direction or instruction for assessment, evaluators have no accountability and their conclusions tend to lack reliability and validity (Litwack & Schlesinger, 1999; Quinsey, Harris, Rice, & Cormier, 1998).

Another approach to sex offender assessment utilizes actuarial risk instruments. These tools quantitatively measure the risks and needs of incarcerated sex offenders. Specifically, actuarial assessments require correctional and treatment professionals to obtain total risk scores and probabilistic estimates of reoffending by adding together weighted risk factor items. Risk factor items represent a variety of dynamic and static characteristics. Dynamic risk factors may be changed through correctional intervention or treatment (i.e., antisocial lifestyle, cognitive distortions, and deviant sexual interest), whereas static risk factors are stable over time or cannot be changed through correctional intervention or treatment (i.e., age, family history, previous sex offenses, and stranger victims). With actuarial assessments, the focus is on prediction of sexual recidivism.

One advantage of using the actuarial approach is that it is generally more reliable and valid compared to unstructured professional judgment. However, actuarial methods may present challenges for prison officials. Some correctional and treatment professionals may not view prediction of sexual recidivism as a part of their responsibilities and may be reluctant to adopt tools that eliminate their discretion (Douglas & Kropp, 2002; Heilbrun, 1997). At the same time, evaluators who utilize actuarial assessment instruments are instructed to only consider a fixed set of factors. As a result, distinct or unusual characteristics that are relevant to individual sex offenders that may provide important context about their risks and needs cannot be considered (Hart, 1998).

The Static-99 (Hanson & Thornton, 2000) is the most common actuarial risk assessment instrument administered to incarcerated sex offenders. It consists of five items that measure sexual deviance factors and five items that measure nonsexual criminal history factors. The sexual deviance factors include presence of male victims (no = 0, yes = 1), noncontact sex offenses (no = 0, yes = 1), unrelated victims (no = 0, yes = 1), and stranger victims (no = 0, yes = 1). At the same time, prior sex offenses in terms of charges (none = 0; 1–2 = 1; 3–5 = 2; 6+ = 3) and convictions (none = 0; 1 = 1; 2–3 = 2; 4+ = 3) are considered. The nonsexual criminal history factors include whether or not the offender ever lived with a significant other for at least 2 years (no = 0, yes = 1), is 24 years of age or younger (no = 0, yes = 1), has current nonsexual violence (no = 0, yes = 1), has prior nonsexual violence (no = 0, yes = 1), and has four or more prior sentencing dates (no = 0, yes = 1). The 10 scores are summed to generate a single score that represents one of four risk groups, including low (0–1), moderate–low (2–3), moderate–high (4–5), and high (6+). Other examples of actuarial risk assessment tools are the Minnesota Sex Offender Screen Tool-Revised (MnSOST-R) (Epperson, Kaul, Huot, Goldman, & Alexander, 2003), Rapid Risk Assessment for Sex Offense Recidivism (RRASOR) (Hanson, 1997), and the Sex Offender Risk Appraisal Guide (SORAG) (Quinsey et al., 1998).

Structured professional judgment constitutes a third model of sex offender assessment. These instruments provide correctional and treatment professionals with a list of empirically validated risk factors that must be considered in the evaluation of sex offenders. However, this simply represents a starting point for assessment, and evaluators may often include additional risk factors, assign weights to risk factors, and combine risk factors at their discretion. In this way, structured professional judgment may be thought of as middle ground between unstructured professional judgment and actuarial decision making. Advocates of structured professional judgment commonly assert that the approach maintains professional responsibility and the flexibility of discretion while improving consistency and visibility of decision making. Examples of structured professional judgment tools are the Risk for Sexual Violence Protocol (RSVP) (Hart et al., 2003) and the Sexual Violence Risk-20 (SVR-20) (Boer, Hart, Kropp, & Webster, 1997).

Beyond conducting evaluations for risk level, prison staff members who are assessing sex offenders for treatment may attempt to gauge additional characteristics. It is not unusual for correctional and treatment professionals to appraise the personalities and cognitive abilities of sex offenders before recommending individualized treatment plans. When evaluators are interested in understanding personalities of sex offenders, the Minnesota Multiphasic Personality Inventory-2 (MMPI-2) (Butcher et al., 2001) is a common assessment tool. If evaluators want to know something about the cognitive operations of sex offenders, they often turn to the Wechsler Adult Intelligence Scale (WAIS-IV) (Wechsler, 2008).

At the same time, many correctional and treatment professionals are concerned about deviant sexual preferences in the sex offender population, and they may attempt to gauge whether or not certain sex offenders have deviant sexual interests through physiological testing. Specifically, penile plethysmography (PPG) determines whether or not sex offenders experience deviant sexual arousal by measuring blood flow to their penises. Sexualized audio and images of adults, children, and objects are presented to sex offenders, and devices attached to their genitals measure and record their penile circumferences that exist in response to the stimuli. The Abel Assessment for Sexual Interest (AASI) (Abel, Huffman, Warberg, & Holland, 1998) is often used in conjunction with PPG, as it also attempts to determine whether or not individuals have deviant sexual interest in various areas. The Abel Assessment shows images of adults and children of various ages and measures viewing times across the images. When sex offenders have longer viewing times associated with specific images than normative viewing times, they are said to have deviant sexual interests in such areas.

Treatment Models

Contemporary sex offender treatment programs inside correctional institutions are most commonly informed by a cognitive-behavioral therapeutic approach to addressing sex offending. Under cognitive-behavioral treatment (CBT) modalities, illegal sexual activities are considered to be behavioral in nature and indicative of thinking patterns that are established and preserved through observational learning and reinforcement of attitudes, beliefs, and experiences (Yates, 2013). Sex offenders who are exposed to CBT are likely to encounter one (or a combination) of three distinct models.

One treatment model that is commonly aimed at incarcerated sex offenders is relapse prevention (RP). Although it was initially used to thwart substance abuse, RP was modified in the 1980s to address deviant and unlawful sexual behaviors (Pithers, Marques, Gibat, & Marlatt, 1983). The idea behind RP is to increase self-awareness among individuals who have sexually offended. Specifically, by helping such people to recognize factors—behaviors, environments, feelings, habits, and situations—that facilitated their past sex offenses, it is thought that these individuals may subsequently learn how to avoid putting themselves at risk for committing future sex offenses. According to RP advocates, people who understand what made it possible for them to sexually offend are equipped to refrain from participating in additional sex crimes.

In the RP model, a sex offense chain or cycle is often described that provides a sequential narrative about how a person ultimately engaged in illegal sexual activities. This recollection almost always must be entirely free of justification, minimization, and other thinking errors that supposedly reduce the seriousness of the transgressions and mitigate blameworthiness. Through this process, treatment participants and providers identify factors that are allegedly responsible for sexual lawbreaking. What is more, people inside prisons who are participating in treatment curriculums that feature RP are usually obligated to define and provide examples of dangerous behaviors, tempting environments, negative feelings, bad habits, and high-risk situations that are unique to themselves and their former crimes. It is believed that persons who previously committed sex offenses may be able to monitor themselves and their future decision-making processes once they are aware of their offense chains or cycles from the past. RP posits that individuals who know what caused them to sexually offend may proactively exit identified offense cycles or never enter such chains at all.

Under the RP model, sex offender treatment participants are told that lapses (fantasies or initial instances of sexually deviant behaviors) are possible, but these are not necessarily indicative of relapses (fantasies that turn into realities or complete returns to sexually deviant behaviors) (Yates, 2013). Instead, participants are informed that relapses usually happen after several seemingly irrelevant decisions (SIDs). A single SID represents a relatively harmless and insignificant choice; however, multiple SIDs, it is said, may lead to reoffending. Thus, participants are offered coping strategies and guidance on what to do around particular people and in specific situations to inhibit the accumulation of SIDs. For incarcerated sex offenders, responding to hypothetical scenarios of a risky nature that may be encountered in the free world is not an uncommon component of RP treatment. Treatment providers often want to know exactly what inmates say they will do when faced with situations in outside society that may cause them to enter again into a sex offending cycle. The successful participant will recognize the scenarios as high-risk situations and subsequently provide approved coping strategies that they will use to deal with their circumstances. Inmates who acknowledge factors and SIDs that may trigger their sex offending and articulate alternative resolutions that will convincingly prevent continued participation in illegal sexual activities are commonly viewed as open and responsive to treatment and less of a public safety risk.

Risk-need-responsivity (RNR) is another form of treatment that sex offenders inside correctional institutions may experience. This modality is based on three distinct propositions that allegedly characterize effective treatment and other correctional interventions for sex offenders (Andrews & Bonta, 2010). The first proposition focuses on the level of risk associated with people who have committed sex offenses. Specifically, under the RNR model, the degree of sex offender treatment received by individuals should correspond to their assessed degree of risk. This means that sex offenders who are believed to be more likely to reoffend should be exposed to more intense treatment and other correctional interventions (for longer periods of time, more frequent applications, and greater number of contact hours) compared to sex offenders who are believed to be less likely to reoffend. Relatedly, if sex offenders deemed low risk receive too much treatment, it is thought that their likelihood of recidivism increases.

The second proposition centers on the needs of incarcerated sex offenders. That is, sex offender treatment should address the criminogenic needs or factors that led to the illegal sexual activities. This means that treatment and other correctional interventions for sex offenders who reported feeling isolated and alone prior to their past offenses should feature family reunification or other forms of social support to reduce the likelihood of recidivism.

The third proposition focuses on responsivity or the degree to which sex offender treatment responds to the attributes of its participants. In other words, programs that follow the RNR approach to sex offender treatment are adapted to the qualities of participants. This means that sex offender treatment curriculums should be adjusted to take the cognitive abilities, culture, interpersonal communication skills, language, learning styles, motivation levels, and personalities of its participants into consideration. When treatment programs are delivered in a way that is responsive to the abilities, characteristics, and styles of individuals who are participating, RNR advocates believe that they are more likely to resonate with participants and subsequently help them avoid unlawful behaviors.

In addition, the Good Lives Model (GLM) represents a popular and relatively new approach toward sex offender treatment. The GLM asserts that sex offenders are like other people in that they seek to meet basic human needs, maintain intimate relationships, and achieve other life goals (Ward & Stewart, 2003). However, under the GLM, it is purported that sex offenders often meet basic human necessities, maintain intimate associations, and achieve personal ambitions through antisocial and unlawful behaviors. Interestingly, treatment that follows the GLM approach to sex offender treatment aims to help participants find more prosocial and lawful ways to meet their needs, maintain relationships, and achieve other goals. Rather than focusing entirely on avoidance and prevention, the GLM assists participants to realize their desires without harming others in the process.

CRIMINAL JUSTICE POLICY ISSUES AND IMPLICATIONS

There are many criminal justice policy issues and corresponding implications that concern convicted sex offenders. Many of these topics reflect the fact that people who have committed sex offenses are highly stigmatized inside and outside of correctional institutions. This section first describes the challenges that sex offenders may face during their incarcerations. It then discusses the subsequent obstacles that convicted sex offenders encounter once they are released from confinement and return to the free world.

Prison Problems

One reality that is difficult to ignore is that sex offenders are more likely than other inmates to have daunting incarceration experiences. Sex offenders are often at the bottom of the prison inmate power/status hierarchy (Clemmer, 1940; Colvin, 1982; Irwin, 1980; Schwaebe, 2005; Waldram, 2012). Throughout their incarceration, they are commonly rejected and excluded from full participation in prison life. Other criminal offenders (Akerstrom, 1986) and prison staff members (Connor, 2012; Connor & Tewksbury, 2013; Sapp & Vaughn, 1990) view sex offenders as representing the lowest status in the prison community. As a direct result of their inferior standing, sex offenders are seemingly more prone to neglect, exploitation, and victimization. This is supported by Connor and Tewksbury (2013), who surveyed 68 prison wardens and found that nearly 60% of them felt that sex offenders were not as safe inside prisons as inmates convicted of other crimes.

There is evidence that sex offenders who are stigmatized and likely mistreated inside prisons may be actively engaged in avoidance behaviors in order to escape perceived or actual violence. Tewksbury, Connor, and Denney (2014) examined predictors of receiving institutional disciplinary infractions among 585 adult male inmates. They found that, in spite of the fact that sex offenders were significantly more likely than other inmates to receive any type of disciplinary infraction, sex offenders were also significantly less likely than other inmates to receive a serious disciplinary infraction. Thus, rather than becoming involved in serious transgressions while incarcerated, sex offenders behind bars largely participated in more trivial and less serious forms of prison misconduct. This suggests that sex offenders may, for example, intentionally avoid their prison job assignment or programming, or simply avoid settings where large numbers of inmates congregate.

When incidents cannot be successfully avoided and violence ensues, sex offenders may still receive a less serious disciplinary infraction (Tewksbury et al., 2014). In the case of actual physical violence directed toward sex offenders, for instance, where they are neither an aggressor nor blameworthy, it is still likely that sex offenders would receive a disciplinary infraction for fighting. Unable to readily differentiate between perpetrators and victims, many prison staff members will issue a disciplinary infraction to each inmate involved.

Both a strong cultural loathing of sex offenders that often permeates the prison environment and sex offenders' common proclivity toward becoming a target may also lead prison staff members to intentionally or unintentionally ignore these inmates and their requests for assistance. In turn, this may cause incarcerated sex offenders to act out to receive attention. Such overt expressions and attention-seeking behavior that arises from deprivation may lead to receipt of a less severe disciplinary infraction, such as disobeying a direct order (Tewksbury et al., 2014). Correctional and treatment professionals who are working with sex offenders inside prisons should remain cognizant of the fact that people convicted of illegal sexual activities are often the most marginalized and subsequently deprived inmates and may experience unique difficulties inside prisons because of their offenses.

Although some jurisdictions house sex offenders in separate institutions or housing units designed specifically for such inmates, only a minority (20%) of wardens see this as a valuable approach (Connor & Tewksbury, 2013). Therefore, other proactive measures from institutional leadership to facilitate the well-being of inmates with sex offense convictions may be necessary. Prison wardens, for instance, should make it a point to closely monitor the safety of their inmates with sex offense convictions through consultation with their correctional and treatment officers (Tewksbury et al., 2014).

Apart from safety concerns, incarcerated sex offenders may receive less social support from the outside world than other inmates. Connor and Tewksbury (2015) obtained a sample of 615 inmates from one Midwestern jurisdiction and analyzed how inmate characteristics influenced the visits they received from specific types of visitors. Incarcerated sex offenders were less likely to receive visits from children and friends than inmates who were not serving time for sex offense convictions. This makes sense with respect to children as visitors, as many convicted sex offenders are legally prohibited from interacting with individuals below the age of majority. At the same time, sex offenders inside prisons may have victimized their own children, and such victims are not likely to visit their perpetrators. Qualitative interviews with incarcerated sex offenders support this notion, revealing that such inmates often expect at least some family members, especially children, to reject them outright (Tewksbury & Connor, 2012a). It is also not surprising that sex offenders may have fewer or no friends from whom to receive visits, as convicted sex offenders are generally regarded as social outcasts while incarcerated (Connor & Tewksbury, 2013; Schwaebe, 2005; Tewksbury et al., 2014; Waldram, 2012) and on the outside (Robbers, 2009; Tewksbury, 2012; Tewksbury & Lees, 2006, 2007). Correctional management that features positive social interaction, such as a direct supervision approach, may prove beneficial for sex offenders. At the same time, because visitation may be particularly challenging for incarcerated sex offenders, prison chaplains and religious volunteers may prove useful in affording social support and connections to the outside world.

In addition to worrying about their safety and dealing with limited social support, sex offenders behind bars must confront the prospect of participating in treatment to address their unlawful behaviors. As discussed earlier, individuals who are serving prison time for sex offense convictions often engage in some form of sex offender treatment while incarcerated. Although participation in sex offender treatment programming is almost always voluntary, many incarcerated sex offenders are essentially compelled to take part in such curriculums. More often than not, their opportunities for early release from confinement are directly tied to involvement in sex offender treatment. In some jurisdictions, state statutes specify that inmates convicted of sex offenses are not eligible for parole and other types of early release until they have satisfactorily completed a sex offender treatment program. In other jurisdictions, it is merely a norm for individuals who enter prisons on sex offense convictions to complete sex offender treatment programs.

Connor (2016) found that parole board members expected inmates to participate in and subsequently complete a variety of prison programs before they would agree to release them on parole supervision. What is more, his qualitative analysis revealed that these parole gatekeepers believed that program involvement by inmates should be related to the criminal offenses that led to their imprisonment. In addition, for each additional program completed, Tewksbury and Connor (2012b) found that inmates were 1.3 times more likely to be recommended for parole. Thus, correctional and treatment professionals should encourage people who are incarcerated for illegal sexual activities to participate in institutional sex offender treatment programs, as well as other available programming, especially when assessments indicate that such curriculums are warranted and helpful in addressing risk factors.

Sex Offender Registration and Notification

Once sex offenders exit correctional institutions and reenter society, they commonly face considerable setbacks in communities. A primary reason for these challenges is that people who are convicted of sex offenses must comply with sex offender registration and notification (SORN) laws upon leaving prisons. For many such individuals, this means being publicly identified as sexual lawbreakers in their neighborhoods.

SORN policies obligate most individuals convicted of sex offenses to register as convicted sex offenders. In other words, sex offenders are typically required to provide local law enforcement and correctional authorities with their names, photographs, addresses, birth dates, Social Security numbers, fingerprints, offense histories, dates of convictions, and locations of convictions. At the same time, they must verify the accuracy of this information, especially their home addresses, on a routine basis for the duration of their registration, which may range from 10 years to life (Tewksbury & Connor, 2014). Sex offender registries are utilized in every jurisdiction in the United States, and these repositories of information provide online access to a wide array of facts about convicted sex offenders and their sex offenses (Mustaine & Tewksbury, 2013; Tewksbury & Higgins, 2005).

Some jurisdictions went beyond the creation of sex offender registries by enacting notification laws designed to warn community members when sex offenders live nearby (Farkas & Stichman, 2002). Notification laws assume that community members will not only use this information to protect themselves and their children, but that they will also report risky behaviors displayed by convicted sex offenders to their local police department. Many states that use community notification have a three-tiered system based on the purported dangerousness of sex offenders that determines the degree of notification that will take place (Finn, 1997; Goodman, 1996). When sex offenders are categorized as the lowest risk to public safety, notification is typically reserved for law enforcement officials only. Schools, daycares, and other neighborhood organizations are notified of the presence of sex offenders posing a medium risk to public safety. Those sex offenders considered the most dangerous, designated at high risk, will generate the most widespread notification, as the general public is notified. However, some jurisdictions subject all convicted sex offenders to community notification.

Like community notification mandates, restrictions on where one may establish a residence may be an accompanying reality that registered sex offenders must face. Well over one half of all states and numerous municipalities have sex offender residency restriction laws. In some cases, these policies determine where sex offenders are allowed to work, travel, and be in public (Meloy, Miller, & Curtis, 2008). Today, the most common residency restriction laws feature nebulous language to restrict registered sex offenders from living near locations described as "child congregation" areas (Tewksbury & Connor, 2014). Such places are typically defined to include schools, parks, playgrounds, daycare centers, bus stops, and recreational facilities. Fluctuating between 500 feet and 2,500 feet, residency restriction laws assert that specific distances must be preserved between a sex offender's residence and various landmarks in the community. Registered sex offenders in Kentucky, for instance, who were convicted in July 2006 or after, cannot live within 1,000 feet of a school, park, or playground.

People convicted of sex offenses have reported significant obstacles resulting from SORN laws that have prevented them from easily reintegrating into society. The social damage caused by SORN policies is often insurmountable, as the social stigmatization (Robbers, 2009; Tewksbury, 2005, 2012; Tewksbury & Lees, 2006) experienced by registered sex offenders leads to their ostracism by community members (Zevitz & Farkas, 2000), in the forms of harassment (Levenson & Cotter, 2005a; Tewksbury, 2004, 2005; Tewksbury & Lees, 2006; Zevitz & Farkas, 2000), threats (Zevitz & Farkas, 2000), and vigilante attacks (Tewksbury & Lees, 2006; Zevitz & Farkas, 2000). These active demonstrations of contempt aimed at registered sex offenders cause them to have persistent feelings of vulnerability (Tewksbury & Lees, 2006), undergo heightened levels of stress (Robbers, 2009), and witness emotional harm to their family members (Zevitz & Farkas, 2000). Individuals who are publicly identified as sex offenders through SORN struggle with maintaining relationships and developing new associations (Tewksbury & Lees, 2006), even with family members (Tewksbury & Connor, 2012a). Once individuals are subjected to SORN, most of their friendships are lost altogether and the quality of the few relationships that persist is greatly diminished (Tewksbury, 2004, 2005). As a result of their social exclusion, registered sex offenders tend to internalize their spoiled identity (Tewksbury, 2012) and intentionally withdraw from community involvement, which further reduces their social support (Robbers, 2009).

Beyond social impacts, people frequently lose their jobs (Tewksbury, 2004, 2005; Zevitz & Farkas, 2000) when coworkers and employers discover their status through SORN. Unemployed registered sex offenders appear to have particularly onerous and unsuccessful experiences with finding work (Levenson & Cotter, 2005a; Tewksbury, 2004, 2005; Tewksbury & Lees, 2006). The loss of housing (Tewksbury, 2004, 2005; Zevitz & Farkas, 2000) and need to locate to a new residence (Levenson & Cotter, 2005a) are more common experiences for sex offenders subjected to SORN.

In many cases, the challenges associated with housing are connected to SORN's accompanying residency restriction laws (Levenson & Cotter, 2005b). However, residency restriction laws for sex offenders certainly exacerbate the limited choices for home placement already facing many ex-offenders (Tewksbury & Connor, 2012c). Policies that limit where registered sex offenders live may restrict their possible housing options to as little as 2% of all housing stock (Zandbergen & Hart, 2006, 2009). As a result of residency restrictions, registered sex offenders are also likely to be concentrated in very dense, socially disorganized communities or in rural locations with limited employment, treatment, and transportation opportunities (Minnesota Department of Corrections, 2003; Tewksbury & Mustaine, 2006, 2008; Zandbergen & Hart, 2006, 2009).

Ultimately, SORN legislation should be reconsidered. It is not simply that individuals who are obligated to register and cooperate with public notification procedures under SORN laws endure numerous negative ramifications that make it more difficult for them to reintegrate into society and live law-abiding lives. It is also not simply that the family members of publicly identified sex offenders who have participated in no wrongdoing tend to experience harmful consequences (Farkas & Miller, 2007; Levenson & Tewksbury, 2009; Tewksbury & Levenson, 2009). It is that, in addition to producing human suffering, SORN policies do not increase public safety. Advocates of SORN policies set out to increase awareness about the locations of sex offenders so that nearby communities could protect themselves; however, a large majority of the public does not actively utilize available information that is disseminated through SORN mandates (Anderson & Sample, 2008; Burchfield, 2012; Craun, 2010; Kernsmith, Comartin, Craun, & Kernsmith, 2009). This reduces the ability of SORN laws to protect community members from sex offenders in their neighborhoods. Alternatively, when the public utilizes information that is provided to them through SORN policies, this strategy often leads to excessive precautionary behavior and fear of crime that may be unnecessary (Beck & Travis, 2004; Caputo & Brodsky, 2004). What is more, proponents of SORN mandates believe that such laws deter convicted sex offenders from committing additional sex offenses. And yet data from Arkansas (Maddan, 2008), Iowa (Adkins, Huff, & Stageberg, 2000; Tewksbury & Jennings, 2010), Massachusetts (Petrosino & Petrosino, 1999), New Jersey (Tewksbury, Jennings, & Zgoba, 2012; Zgoba, Witt, Dalessandro, & Veysey, 2008), New York (Sandler, Freeman, & Socia, 2008), and Washington (Schram & Milloy, 1995) show that there are no significant differences in sexual recidivism rates between sex offenders who were subjected to SORN and sex offenders who were not subjected to SORN. Despite these empirical realities, SORN policies persist across the United States as popular mechanisms of sex offender management.

CASE EXAMPLE

Mike, a 21-year-old White man, was arrested on suspicion of third-degree rape. After a jury trial, he was found guilty on one count of third-degree rape and was subsequently remanded into custody. He was sentenced to 5 years in prison 2 weeks later at his sentencing hearing. Upon arriving at the state penitentiary, Mike was assigned a case manager, Jenny, who introduced him to the prison and informed him of the rules and regulations.

The following week he was evaluated by Jenny to establish his risk of recidivism. Mike was told that his assessment would be used to identify correctional and treatment interventions that would best suit his needs. One of the assessments that Jenny utilized in evaluating Mike was the Static-99. Based on her interview with him, as well as court and institutional records, Jenny assigned various scores to the items on the instrument. She ultimately gave Mike a score of 2, which meant that his risk level was moderate–low for reoffending. Mike reported that his victim was his underage girlfriend and acknowledged that they had sexual intercourse, so Jenny assigned the scores of 0 to the risk factor items of male victims, noncontact sex offenses, unrelated victims, and stranger victims. Mike's court and institutional records showed that he had never been charged with or convicted of any earlier criminal offenses. His criminal history only included the third-degree rape arrest and conviction. As a result, Jenny assigned the scores of 0 to the risk factor items of prior sex offenses, current nonsexual violence, prior nonsexual violence, and four or more sentencing dates. However, because Mike was 21 years of age, did not live with his girlfriend, and had never had another significant other, Jenny assigned the scores of 1 to the risk factor items of age and cohabitation.

Because Mike did not pose a substantial risk of repeating his sex offense, Jenny did not believe intense treatment was necessary and that it could unnecessarily cause harm. As a result, rather than a daily curriculum, she recommended that Mike participate in a weekly sex offender treatment group with other relatively low-risk inmates. Jenny told Mike that completing sex offender treatment may help his chances of receiving parole.

Mike enrolled in the sex offender treatment program. He reported that his experiences in treatment helped him to learn that he should seek out his parents and siblings when he begins feeling lonely. Based on interactions with the treatment provider and other participants, Mike realized that long periods of social isolation may trigger him to sexually offend. He devised a safety plan whereby he intends to call his family members any time he feels shut off from others. With the approval of the treatment provider, Mike decided that he would become involved in the local church to meet new people and form healthy adult relationships once he was released.

Although Mike looked forward to his treatment sessions, his time behind bars was arduous. He constantly worried about his safety, because he feared what other inmates would do if they knew he was a sex offender. Mike thought about telling other inmates that he was doing time for a drug offense, but he never had the chance. By the fourth week of his prison sentence, Mike was verbally harassed and threatened on multiple occasions. At one point, he refused to leave his cell out of fear of being assaulted, which led to a write-up for failure to follow a direct order by a correctional officer. At the same time, Mike did not receive any visits. A majority of his friends ceased contact with him after learning of his sex offense with a minor. His closest contact on the outside was his sister, but she could not visit, as she had to take care of two young children.

After 3 years, Mike completed sex offender treatment. He was soon eligible for a hearing before the parole board. Along the way, he had also completed several different educational and vocational training programs while incarcerated. The parole board recommended that Mike be released on parole, and he completed the remainder of his sentence on the outside.

Upon leaving the state penitentiary, Mike had only a few days to formally register as a sex offender at the county sheriff's office. He arrived at the sheriff's office the following day, where he submitted his name, address, birth date, Social Security number, fingerprints, offense history, date of conviction, and location of conviction. At the same time, Mike's photograph was taken by a police officer. Mike verifies the accuracy of the SORN information that he submitted shortly after getting out of prison every 90 days, and he must continue to do so for the next 25 years as a publicly identified sex offender. This is particularly challenging for him, as Mike believes that his status as a registered sex offender prevents him from achieving lasting friendships and fully engaging in community activities. He went on a few dates, but when women discovered that he was labeled as a convicted sex offender online, they no longer returned his phone calls or text messages. Mike's neighbors no longer wave to him when they drive by his house. However, he is still happy to be able to live in his hometown in the same house as his parents. The land surveyor his father hired determined that their house was roughly 3,000 feet away from the nearest park, playground, or school.

WEB-BASED RESOURCES

Abel Assessment for Sexual Interest: http://www.abelscreening.com

Association for the Treatment of Sexual Abusers: http://www.atsa.com

Center for Sex Offender Management: http://www.csom.org

Office of Sex Offender Sentencing, Monitoring, Apprehending, Registering, and Tracking: http://www.smart.gov

Static-99: http://www.static99.org

REFERENCES

Abel, G. G., Huffman, J., Warberg, B., & Holland, C. L. (1998). Visual reaction time and plethysmography as measures of sexual interest in child molesters. *Sexual Abuse, 10*(2), 81–95.

Adkins, G., Huff, D., & Stageberg, P. (2000). *The Iowa Sex Offender Registry and recidivism*. Des Moines: Iowa Department of Human Rights.

Akerstrom, M. (1986). Outcasts in prison: The cases of informers and sex offenders. *Deviant Behavior, 7*(1), 1–12.

Anderson, A. L., & Sample, L. L. (2008). Public awareness and action resulting from sex offender community notification laws. *Criminal Justice Policy Review, 19*(4), 371–396.

Andrews, D. A., & Bonta, J. (2010). *The psychology of criminal conduct*. Cincinnati, OH: Anderson.

Beck, V. S., & Travis, L. F. (2004). Sex offender notification and protective behavior. *Violence and Victims, 19*(3), 289–302.

Berliner, L., Schram, D., Miller, L., & Milloy, C. D. (1995). A sentencing alternative for sex offenders: A study of decision making and recidivism. *Journal of Interpersonal Violence, 10*(4), 487–502.

Boer, D. P., Hart, S. D., Kropp, P. R., & Webster, C. D. (1997). *Manual for the Sexual Violence Risk-20: Professional guidelines for assessing risk of sexual violence*. Vancouver, BC: British Columbia Institute Against Family Violence.

Bumby, K. M. (1996). Assessing the cognitive distortions of child molesters and rapists: Development and validation of the MOLEST and RAPE scales. *Sexual Abuse, 8*(1), 37–54.

Bumby, K. M. (2000). Empathy inhibition, intimacy deficits, and attachment difficulties in sex offenders. In D. R. Laws, S. M. Hudson, & T. Ward (Eds.), *Remaking relapse prevention with sex offenders: A sourcebook* (pp. 143–166). Thousand Oaks, CA: Sage.

Burchfield, K. B. (2012). Assessing community residents' perceptions of local registered sex offenders: Results from a pilot survey. *Deviant Behavior, 33*(4), 241–259.

Butcher, J. N., Graham, J. R., Ben-Porath, Y. S., Tellegen, A., Dahlstrom, W. G., & Kaemmer, B. (2001). *MMPI-2: Minnesota Multiphasic Personality Inventory-2: Manual for administration, scoring, and interpretation*. Minneapolis: University of Minnesota Press.

Caputo, A. A., & Brodsky, S. L. (2004). Citizen coping with community notification of released sex offenders. *Behavioral Sciences and the Law, 22*(2), 239–252.

Center for Sex Offender Management. (2007). *Managing the challenges of sex offender reentry*. Washington, DC: US Department of Justice.

Chapman, D. P., Dube, S. R., & Anda, R. F. (2007). Adverse childhood events as risk factors for negative mental health outcomes. *Psychiatric Annals, 37*(5), 359–364.

Clemmer, D. (1940). *The prison community*. New York, NY: Rinehart.

Colvin, M. (1982). The 1980 New Mexico prison riot. *Social Problems, 29*(5), 449–463.

Connor, D. P. (2012). *Prison wardens' perceptions of sex offenders, sex offender registration, community notification, and residency restrictions* (Master's thesis). University of Louisville, Louisville, KY.

Connor, D. P. (2016). How to get out of prison: Views from parole board members. *Corrections: Policy, Practice, and Research, 1*(2), 107–126.

Connor, D. P., & Tewksbury, R. (2013). Examining prison wardens' perceptions of inmates incarcerated for sex offenses. *Corrections Today, 75*(3), 60–61, 68.

Connor, D. P., & Tewksbury, R. (2015). Prison inmates and their visitors: An examination of inmate characteristics and visitor types. *The Prison Journal, 95*(2), 159–177.

Craun, S. W. (2010). Evaluating awareness of registered sex offenders in the neighborhood. *Crime and Delinquency, 56*(3), 414–435.

Craun, S. W., & Theriot, M. T. (2009). Misperceptions of sex offender perpetration: Considering the impact of sex offender registration. *Journal of Interpersonal Violence, 24*(12), 2057–2072.

Dhawan, S., & Marshall, W. L. (1996). Sexual abuse histories of sexual offenders. *Sexual Abuse, 8*(1), 7–15.

Douglas, K., & Kropp, P. R. (2002). A prevention-based paradigm for violence risk assessment: Clinical and research applications. *Criminal Justice and Behavior, 29*(5), 617–658.

Epperson, D. L., Kaul, J. D., Huot, S., Goldman, R., & Alexander, W. (2003). *Minnesota Sex Offender Screening Tool-Revised (MnSOST-R) technical paper: Development, validation, and recommended risk level cut scores.* Arnes, IA: Authors.

Farkas, M. A., & Miller, G. (2007). Reentry and reintegration: Challenges faced by families of convicted sex offenders. *Federal Sentencing Reporter, 20*(2), 88–92.

Farkas, M. A., & Stichman, A. (2002). Sex offender laws: Can treatment, punishment, incapacitation, and public safety be reconciled? *Criminal Justice Review, 27*(2), 256–283.

Finn, P. (1997). *Sex offender community notification.* Washington, DC: National Institute of Justice.

Fortney, T., Levenson, J. S., Brannon, Y., & Baker, J. (2007). Myths and facts about sex offenders: Implications for practice and public policy. *Sex Offender Treatment, 2*(1), 1–17.

Fuselier, D. A., Durham, R. L., & Wurtele, S. K. (2002). The child sexual abuser: Perceptions of college students and professionals. *Sexual Abuse, 14*(3), 267–276.

Goodman, E. A. (1996). Megan's Law: The New Jersey Supreme Court navigates uncharted waters. *Seton Hall Law Review, 26,* 764–802.

Hanson, R. K. (2007). *The development of a brief actuarial risk scale for sexual offense recidivism.* Ottawa, Ontario: Department of the Solicitor General of Canada.

Hanson, R. K., & Thornton, D. (2000). Improving risk assessment for sex offenders: A comparison of three actuarial scales. *Law and Human* Behavior, *24*(1), 119–136.

Harrison, P. M., & Beck, A. J. (2006). *Prison and jail inmates at midyear 2005.* Washington, DC: US Department of Justice.

Hart, S. D. (1998). The role of psychopathy in assessing risk for violence: Conceptual and methodological issues. *Legal and Criminological Psychology, 3*(1), 121–137.

Hart, S. D., Kropp, P. R., Laws, D. R., Klaver, J., Logan, C., & Watt, K. A. (2003). *The Risk for Sexual Violence Protocol (RSVP).* Burnaby, British Columbia: Mental Health Law and Policy Institute.

Hart, T. C., & Rennison, C. (2003). *Reporting crime to the police, 1992–2000.* Washington, DC: US Department of Justice.

Heilbrun, K. (1997). Prediction versus management models relevant to risk assessment: The importance of legal decision-making context. *Law and Human Behavior, 21*(4), 347–359.

Hughes, T. A., & Wilson, D. J. (2003). *Reentry trends in the United States.* Washington, DC: US Department of Justice.

Irwin, J. (1980). *Prisons in turmoil.* Boston, MA: Little, Brown & Company.

Katz-Schiavone, S., Levenson, J. S., & Ackerman, A. R. (2008). Myths and facts about sexual violence: Public perceptions and implications for prevention. *Journal of Criminal Justice and Popular Culture, 15*(3), 291–311.

Kernsmith, P. D., Comartin, E., Craun, S. W., & Kernsmith, R. M. (2009). The relationship between sex offender registry utilization and awareness. *Sexual Abuse: A Journal of Research and Treatment, 21*(2), 181–193.

Laws, D. R., & O'Donohue, W. T. (2008). *Sexual deviance: Theory, assessment, and treatment.* New York, NY: Guilford.

Levenson, J. S., Brannon, Y. N., Fortney, T., & Baker, J. N. (2007). Public perceptions about sex offenders and community protection policies. *Analyses of Social Issues and Public Policy, 7*(1), 137–161.

Levenson, J. S., & Cotter, L. P. (2005a). The effect of Megan's Law on sex offender reintegration. *Journal of Contemporary Criminal Justice, 21*(1), 49–66.

Levenson, J. S., & Cotter, L. P. (2005b). The impact of sex offender residence restrictions: 1,000 feet from danger or one step from absurd? *International Journal of Offender Therapy and Comparative Criminology, 49*(2), 168–178.

Levenson, J. S., & D'Amora, D. A. (2007). Social policies designed to prevent sexual violence: The Emperor's new clothes? *Criminal Justice Policy Review, 18*(2), 168–199.

Levenson, J. S., & Tewksbury, R. (2009). Collateral damage: Family members of registered sex offenders. *American Journal of Criminal Justice, 34*(1–2), 54–68.

Litwack, T. R., & Schlesinger, L. B. (1999). Dangerousness risk assessments: Research, legal, and clinical considerations. In A. K. Hess & I. B. Weiner (Eds.), *Handbook of forensic psychology* (pp. 171–217). New York, NY: Wiley.

Maddan, S. (2008). *The labeling of sex offenders.* Lanham, MD: University Press of America.

Magers, M., Jennings, W. G., Tewksbury, R., & Miller, J. M. (2009). An exploration of the sex offender specialization and violence nexus. *Southwest Journal of Criminal Justice, 6*(2), 133–144.

Meloy, M. L., Miller, S. L., & Curtis, K. M. (2008). Making sense out of nonsense: The deconstruction of state-level sex offender residence restrictions. *American Journal of Criminal Justice, 33*(2), 209–222.

Miethe, T. D., Olson, J., & Mitchell, O. (2006). Specialization and persistence in the arrest histories of sex offenders: A comparative analysis of alternative measures and offense types. *Journal of Research in Crime and Delinquency, 43*(3), 204–229.

Minnesota Department of Corrections. (2003). *Level three sex offenders' residential placement issues.* St. Paul, MN: Author.

Mustaine, E. E., & Tewksbury, R. (2013). What can be learned from an online sex offender registry site? An 8 year follow-up. *Journal of Community Corrections, 23*(1), 5–10.

National Center for Missing and Exploited Children. (2014). *Map of registered sex offenders in the United States.* Washington, DC: Author.

Petrosino, A. J., & Petrosino, C. (1999). The public safety potential of Megan's Law in Massachusetts: An assessment from a sample of criminal sexual psychopaths. *Crime and Delinquency, 45*(1), 140–158.

Pithers, W. D., Marques, J. K., Gibat, C. C., & Marlatt, G. A. (1983). Relapse prevention with sexual aggressives: A self-control model of treatment and maintenance change. In J. G. Greer & I. R. Stuart (Eds.), *The sexual aggressor: Current perspectives on treatment* (pp. 214–239). New York, NY: Van Nostrand Reinhold.

Quinn, J., Forsyth, C., & Mullen-Quinn, C. (2004). Societal reaction to sex offenders: A review of the origins and results of the myths surrounding their crimes and treatment amenability. *Deviant Behavior, 25*(3), 215–233.

Quinsey, V. L., Harris, G. T., Rice, M. E., & Cormier, C. A. (1998). *Violent offenders: Appraising and managing risk.* Washington, DC: American Psychological Association.

Robbers, M. L. P. (2009). Lifers on the outside: Sex offenders and disintegrative shaming. *International Journal of Offender Therapy and Comparative Criminology, 53*(1), 5–28.

Sample, L. L., & Bray, T. M. (2006). Are sex offenders different? An examination of rear-rest patterns. *Criminal Justice Policy Review, 17*(1), 83–102.

Sandler, J. C., Freeman, N. J., & Socia, K. M. (2008). Does a watched pot boil? A time-series analysis of New York State's sex offender registration and notification law. *Psychology, Public Policy, and Law, 14*(4), 284–302.

Sapp, A. D., & Vaughn, M. S. (1990). The social status of adult and juvenile sex offenders in prison: An analysis of the importation model. *Journal of Police and Criminal Psychology, 6*(2), 2–7.

Schram, D. D., & Milloy, C. D. (1995). *Community notification: A study of offender characteristics and recidivism.* Olympia, WA: Washington Institute for Public Policy.

Schwaebe, C. (2005). Learning to pass: Sex offenders' strategies for establishing a viable identity in the prison general population. *International Journal of Offender Therapy and Comparative Criminology, 49*(6), 614–625.

Spinazzola, J., Ford, J.D., Zucker, M., van der Kolk, B.A., Silva, S., Smith, S.F., & Blaustein, M. (2005). Survey evaluates: Complex trauma exposure, outcome, and intervention among children and adolescents. *Psychiatric Annals, 35*(5), 433–439.

Tewksbury, R. (2004). Experiences and attitudes of registered female sex offenders. *Federal Probation, 68*(3), 30–33.

Tewksbury, R. (2005). Collateral consequences of sex offender registration. *Journal of Contemporary Criminal Justice, 21*(1), 67–81.

Tewksbury, R. (2012). Stigmatization of sex offenders. *Deviant Behavior, 33*(8), 606–623

Tewksbury, R., & Connor, D. P. (2012a). Incarcerated sex offenders' perceptions of family relationships: Previous experiences and future expectations. *Western Criminology Review, 13*(2), 25–35.

Tewksbury, R., & Connor, D. P. (2012b). Predicting the outcome of parole hearings. *Corrections Today, 74*(3), 54–56.

Tewksbury, R., & Connor, D. P. (2012c). Inmate reentry. In D. McDonald & A. Miller (Eds.), *Race, gender, and criminal justice: Equality and justice for all?* (pp. 141–157). San Diego, CA: Cognella Academic Publishing.

Tewksbury, R., & Connor, D. P. (2014). Sex offenders and criminal policy. In G. Bruinsma & D. Weisburd (Eds.), *Encyclopedia of criminology and criminal justice* (pp. 4782–4791). New York, NY: Springer.

Tewksbury, R., Connor, D. P., & Denney, A. S. (2014). Disciplinary infractions behind bars: An exploration of importation and deprivation theories. *Criminal Justice Review, 39*(2), 201–218.

Tewksbury, R., & Higgins, G. E. (2005). What can be learned from an online sex offender registry site? *Journal of Community Corrections, 14*(3), 9–11, 15–16.

Tewksbury, R., & Jennings, W. G. (2010). Assessing the impact of sex offender registra-tion and community notification on sex offending trajectories. *Criminal Justice and Behavior, 37*(5), 570–582.

Tewksbury, R., Jennings, W. G., & Zgoba, K. M. (2012). A longitudinal examination of sex offender recidivism prior to and following the implementation of SORN. *Behavioral Sciences and the Law, 30*, 308–328.

Tewksbury, R., & Lees, M. B. (2006). Perceptions of sex offender registration: Collateral consequences and community experiences. *Sociological Spectrum, 26*(3), 309–334.

Tewksbury, R., & Lees, M. B. (2007). Perceptions of punishment: How registered sex offenders view registries. *Crime and Delinquency, 53*(3), 380–407.

Tewksbury, R., & Levenson, J. S. (2009). Stress experiences of family members of registered sex offenders. *Behavioral Sciences and the Law, 27*(4), 611–626.

Tewksbury, R., & Mustaine, E. E. (2006). Where to find sex offenders: An examination of residential locations and neighborhood conditions. *Criminal Justice Studies, 19*, 61–75.

Tewksbury, R., & Mustaine, E. E. (2008). Where registered sex offenders live: Community characteristics and proximity to possible victims. *Victims and Offenders, 3*(1), 86–98.

Waldram, J. B. (2012). *Hound pound narrative: Sexual offender habilitation and the anthropology of therapeutic intervention.* Berkeley: University of California Press.

Ward, T., & Stewart, C. (2003). Criminogenic needs and human needs: A theoretical model. *Psychology, Crime, and the Law, 9*(2), 125–153.

Wechsler, D. (2008). *Wechsler Adult Intelligence Scale: Fourth edition.* San Antonio, TX: The Psychological Corporation and Harcourt Brace.

Yates, P. M. (2013). Treatment of sexual offenders: Research, best practices, and emerging models. *International Journal of Behavioral Consultation and Therapy, 8*(3–4), 89–95.

Zandbergen, P. A., & Hart, T. C. (2006). Reducing housing options for convicted sex offenders: Investigating the impact of residency restrictions laws using GIS. *Justice Research and Policy, 8*(2), 1–24.

Zandbergen, P. A., & Hart, T. C. (2009). *Availability and spatial distribution of affordable housing in Miami—Dade County and implications of residency restriction zones for registered sex offenders.* Miami: American Civil Liberties Union of Florida.

Zevitz, R. G., & Farkas, M. A. (2000). Sex offender community notification: Managing high risk criminals or exacting further vengeance? *Behavioral Sciences and the Law, 18*(2–3), 375–391.

Zgoba, K. M, Witt, P., Dalessandro, M., & Veysey, B. (2008). *Megan's Law: Assessing the practical and monetary efficacy.* Washington, DC: National Institute of Justice.

4

HIV/AIDS and the Incarcerated Population

ELIZABETH C. POMEROY

Human immunodeficiency virus (HIV) infection has transformed from an acute, life-threatening disease to a potentially controllable chronic illness in a span of approximately 30 years as a result of improvements in pharmaceuticals available to treat this life-altering condition. Although for some the normalization of this chronic disease has occurred, for many it still manages to be a challenging illness, especially among underserved populations (Moyer & Hardon, 2014). Despite these advances in treatment therapies, individuals can further impair their health, risk transmission, and diminish their longevity by ignoring their status or not maintaining care of their disease.

The epidemiology of the HIV epidemic in the United States is changing from its inception to include greater incidence among minority racial/ethnic/sexual groups and women. Although it is most prevalent among young adults, the incidence among older persons is continuing to increase (Moore, 2011). The most recent data from the Centers for Disease Control and Prevention (CDC) estimates that more than 1.2 million persons over the age of 13 years in the United States had an HIV diagnoses (at year end 2013), including an estimated 161,200 (13%) living with the disease without a diagnosis (CDC, 2016a). Furthermore, the growing number of individuals incarcerated in correctional systems throughout the United States are at high risk for contracting HIV/ AIDS and vulnerable to suboptimal care (CDC, 2015; Westergaard, Spaulding, & Flanigan, 2013; Wohl, 2016). Globally, over 36 million people are estimated to be living with HIV, and a staggering 78 million have been diagnosed since the start of the epidemic (at year end 2015). Regrettably, an estimated 35 million people have died as a result of an AIDS-related disease since the start of the epidemic for the same time period (UNAIDS, 2016). Consequently, prevention and treatment programs and retention in health care services are essential to improved quality of life for individuals living with HIV/AIDS and their communities.

PSYCHOSOCIAL ISSUES

Psychosocial factors and challenges to coping for HIV-positive MSM need to be include in the outreach messaging and intervention strategies rather than just messaging about sexual risk. Effective interventions need to address psychosocial factors, including anxiety about health decline and death due to HIV; struggles with medication side effects; information on coping strategies for depression and substance abuse; dealing with financial stress; lack of social supports; and difficulty forming supportive relationships (Vanable et al., 2012).

Although the number of women diagnosed with AIDS is doubling every 1–2 years, little is known about the psychological and behavioral factors influencing the transmission of HIV in women, the majority of whom are impoverished and socially disadvantaged (Ickovics & Rodin, 1992). Across all ethnic and racial groups, HIV-positive women are challenged by issues of poverty, lack of educational opportunities, racism, stigma, and unemployment. Many of these women have experienced physical and sexual abuse. In addition, inequality and discrimination in terms of gender roles leads many women to remain silent about their physical and psychological needs, which in turn leads to depression. Many women with HIV who are incarcerated have histories of prostitution, drug abuse, and/or partners who are intravenous drug users. Often women incarcerated with HIV/AIDS contracted the illness from their drug-abusing partners. Most often, they are incarcerated for nonviolent crimes (such as prostitution and drug use) or have plead guilty to crimes in order to prevent their partners from being incarcerated with long sentences (particularly in "three strikes and you're out states").

These are problematic issues in terms of accessing necessary services and treatment in the face of a chronic illness such as HIV/AIDS. Research suggests that resilience can be a positive coping skill that can lead to adaptive outcomes. Resilience can be considered a set of qualities such as being committed and optimistic; possessing a sense of humor and self-efficacy; developing self-esteem and a practical sense of control; having a goal orientation to problem solving; perceiving stress as a challenge; and being able to adapt to change (Connor & Davidson 2003; Dale et al., 2014; Werner, 2004). Most important, studies indicate that resilience is a coping mechanism that can be acquired through education (Steinhardt & Doblier, 2008). Employment is determined to be a key factor in empowering women and decreasing the risk factors associated with HIV/AIDS (Dale et al., 2014).

Another relevant minority population at risk for HIV/AIDS is the incarcerated population. HIV-positive male inmates are often in jail or prison for short periods of time but also have had multiple incarcerations. In addition, when released from jail or prison, they return to their needle-sharing partners who are not infected. Released with a 30-day supply of HIV medication, they do not seek health care services for months after their release. Medication adherence is a key factor in controlling viral load, and this is a challenge for postrelease inmates. One study (Baillargeon et al., 2009) indicated that 70% of HIV-positive male inmates had not accessed medical services for 2 months or more following release from prison. Psychosocial factors associated with poor medication adherence include financial problems, unemployment, lack of family and social support, and psychological distress. Depression, psychoticism, anxiety, obsessive-compulsive behaviors, hostility, interpersonal distress, somatic symptoms, and phobias were evident in HIV-positive inmates during incarceration (Feaster et al., 2013). In addition, a meta-analysis of 34 articles addressing HIV disease progression and psychosocial factors, researchers found that personality types (i.e., antisocial personality disorders, borderline and narcissistic personality disorders) and poor coping styles and psychological distress may determine disease progression more often than other types of stress (i.e., socioeconomic). Some of these personality types and coping styles are prevalent among persons who are incarcerated. Again, educating HIV-positive clients about positive coping skills may be beneficial in slowing the progression of HIV/AIDS (Chedha & Vedhara, 2009).

HIV INFECTION RATES AMONG MARGINALIZED POPULATIONS

The demography of HIV has changes since its inception. Trends in research show that new HIV diagnoses are higher in marginalized populations, including economically disadvantaged persons, communities of color, sexual minorities, and women (Moore, 2011; Pellowski, Kalichman, Matthews, & Adler, 2013; Prejean et al., 2011). The disparity of HIV prevalence among individuals in correctional facilities exposes the underlying socioeconomic and racial inequalities that characterize both mass incarceration of non-White individuals and the current state of HIV/AIDS in the United States (Westergaard, Spaulding, & Flanigan, 2013).

HIV Infection Rates in Racial/Ethnic Minority Groups

Racial and ethnic minorities are disproportionately affected by HIV/AIDS and underrepresented in HIV clinical research trials, and this is complicated by poor retention in HIV care maintenance (Castillo-Mancilla et al., 2014; Steele, Meléndez-Morales, Campoluci, DeLuca, & Dean, 2007). In 2010, the percentage of HIV-positive persons diagnosed with a suppressed viral load was lowest for Black Americans (34.9%) followed closely by Hispanics (37.2%). Black Americans account for more new HIV infections, persons living with HIV (PLWH), and HIV-related mortalities than any other racial/ethnic group in the United States. Although death from HIV/AIDS in the United States has been going down in recent years, for Black men it still represents the fifth leading cause of death and the seventh for Black women (ages 25–44, in 2010), which is higher than any other racial/ethnic group (The Henry J. Kaiser Family Foundation, 2014). Also, the national lifetime risk (6.25%) of receiving an HIV/AIDS diagnosis is highest for Black males (Lanier & Sutton, 2013).

State and federal correctional facilities in the United States have an overrepresentation of people with HIV/AIDS, at 3–5 times the rate of the general population

(CDC, 2015; Dumont, Brockmann, Dickman, Alexander, & Rich, 2012). Given this factor, the overrepresentation of African Americans and people of color in the correctional system means that a greater share of this HIV burden falls on minority populations (Beckwith, Zaller, Fu, Montague, & Rich, 2010; National Minority AIDS Council, 2013). The CDC (2015) indicates that African American men in US correctional facilities are 5 times more likely than White men, and twice as likely as Hispanic/Latino men, to be diagnosed with HIV. This overrepresentation holds for incarcerated African American women, who have a more than twofold chance of having an HIV diagnosis, compared to White or Hispanic/ Latino women in prison (CDC, 2015).

Prisons are an established high-risk environment for HIV transmission due to drug use, high-risk sexual behaviors, and the incarceration of drug users and sex workers (UNAIDS, 2014). The war on drugs has resulted in the mass incarceration of African Americans, which for many represents a system of racial and social control, and has had negative public health implications for communities of color, especially since drug use is an established risk factor for HIV (Alexander, 2012; Fullilove, 2011; Rich et al., 2013). Additionally, the spread of HIV in disadvantaged communities may inadvertently be linked back to the revolving door of the correctional system since most prisoners are released back into their communities (Frazier, Sung, Gideon, & Alfaro, 2015; Rich et al., 2013). For example, one research study from 2006 showed that 20% of Black Americans infected with HIV pass through the correctional system each year (Beckwith, Zaller, Fu, Montague, & Rich, 2010).

HIV RATES AMONG INCARCERATED INDIVIDUALS

Worldwide, over 10 million people were incarcerated in 2011. It is estimated that more than 1% of all adults in the United States are incarcerated, and this disproportionally affects African American men (Wohl, 2016). The CDC (2015) reported that in 2010, more than 20,000 inmates with HIV/AIDS were incarcerated in federal and/or state prisons, with the majority being males (91%).

There are twice as many LGBTQ persons in correctional facilities in the United States (7.1% to 7.9%) in comparison to the Americans who self-identify as LGBT (3.8%) according to Gallup in 2015 (Center for American Progress & Movement Advancement Project, 2016). Additionally, the National Transgender Discrimination Survey (Grant et al., 2011) found that 16% of 6,450 transgender and gender-nonconforming study respondents indicated that they had been sent to jail or prison for "any reason," highest for transgender women (21%). This rate was much higher than lifetime imprisonment rates reported by the general US population (for prisons not including jails) in 2003 by the US Department of Justice.

Incarcerated individuals represent the largest population affected by HIV/ AIDS in the United States (Beckwith, Zaller, Fu, Montague, & Rich, 2010). Also, individuals who are incarcerated have an unequal and higher risk of

HIV infection, substance abuse, mental illness, and poor access to care, all risk factors for underutilization of antiretroviral therapy (Westergaad, Spaulding, & Flanigan, 2013).

Although incarcerated individuals make up less than 1% of the US population, they represent almost 20% to 26% of people living with HIV (McLemore, 2008). The Centers for Disease Control and Prevention (CDC, 2009) reported the rate of confirmed AIDS cases among the US prison population for the years 1999 until 2006 was between 2.7 to 4.8 times higher than in the general population.

Moreover, HIV is overrepresented in the correctional system due to the higher prevalence of people who inject drugs [PWID] (Dolan et al., 2015). Thirty million people are being detained and released in US correctional facilities each year, and a large proportion of this population is either injecting drugs and/or sharing needles (Dolan et al., 2015). Nationally, half of prison inmates have a substance use disorder in comparison to only 9% of the general population (Peters, Wexler, & Lurigio, 2015). Furthermore, few inmates (under 20%) who meet the *Diagnostic and Statistical Manual for Mental Disorders* (DSM) criteria for a substance use disorder receive treatment (Chandler, Fletcher, & Volkow, 2009). Some studies report that male inmates at the state and federal levels had a HIV-positive rate at 8 to 10 times that of the general population. Inmates, parolees, and those persons charged with crimes being held in prisons and jails are less likely to receive medical care for their HIV or to have their disease under control (Dolan et al., 2015). The Department of Justice defines the entire correctional population as all persons under the authority of the correctional systems, including those persons on parole and individuals being held in federal or state prisons and jails (Bureau of Justice Statistics, 2017).

Furthermore, a disproportionate number of minorities are represented in US correctional facilities for both men and women (Beckwith, Zaller, Fu, Montague, & Rich, 2010). African American and Black American offenders are imprisoned at a high rate compared to White and Hispanic offenders, most often due to racial biases when applying the laws regarding illegal drugs (Rowell-Cunsolo, El-Bassel, & Hart, 2016). Among jail populations, African American men are 5 times as likely as White men, and twice as likely as Hispanic/Latino men, to be diagnosed with HIV. Among jail populations, African American women are more than twice as likely to be diagnosed with HIV as White or Hispanic/Latino women (CDC, 2015). Nationally, broken down by race/ethnicity, HIV infection rates for the incarcerated population were highest for African American inmates (2.0%) followed closely by Hispanic/Latino inmates (1.8%) and lowest (1.0%) for White inmates (Feaster et al., 2013; Maruschak, 2007).

The CDC reported that in 2010, more than 20,000 inmates with HIV/AIDS were incarcerated in federal and/or state prisons, with the majority being males (91%). Furthermore, African American men were more likely to have an HIV diagnosis in comparison to their White and Hispanic/Latino counterparts, 5 times and 2 times greater risk, respectively (CDC, 2015).

- In 2010, there were 20,093 inmates with HIV/AIDS in state and federal prisons with 91% being men.

- Rates of AIDS-related deaths among state and federal prisoners declined an average of 16% per year between 2001 and 2010, from 24 deaths/100,000 in 2001 to 5/100,000 in 2010.
- Among jail populations, African American men are 5 times as likely as White men, and twice as likely as Hispanic/Latino men, to be diagnosed with HIV.
- Among jail populations, African American women are more than twice as likely to be diagnosed with HIV as White or Hispanic/Latino women (CDC, 2015). Incarcerated women in US correctional facilities are disproportionately affected by the HIV epidemic. Incarcerated women make up a little over 7% of the US prison population, but they are twice as likely as incarcerated men to be diagnosed with HIV and 15 times more likely than nonincarcerated women to be HIV positive (Kramer & Comfort, 2011).

Risk Factors

While the prison environment is a high risk one for HIV transmissions (Krebs, 2006), it is important to note that much of the HIV infection happens prior to in-carceration (Harawa & Adimora, 2008). Further, as research bears out, when HIV-positive inmates are released back into the community, HIV often spreads from the ex-inmate to others in the general population either through shared injecting drug use or unprotected sex (Dolan, Kite, Black, Aceijas, & Stimson, 2007). Moreover, drug use is a major risk factor and pathway for contracting HIV in the United States.

For 2010, state and federal prison authorities reported HIV infection rates that were 3 to 5 times higher than the general US population (National Minority AIDS Council, 2013). Some studies report that male inmates at the state and federal levels had a HIV-positive rate at 8 to 10 times that of the general population. Nationally, broken down by race/ethnicity, HIV infection rates for the incarcerated population were highest for African American inmates (2.0%) followed closely by Hispanic/Latino inmates (1.8%) and lowest (1.0%) for White inmates (Feaster et al., 2013; Maruschak, 2007). Prevalence of AIDS cases among incarcerated individuals is 2.5 times that of nonincarcerated populations in the United States (Beckwith et al., 2010). Sadly, incarcerated women in US correctional facilities are disproportionately affected by the HIV epidemic. Incarcerated women make up a little over 7% of the US prison population, but they are twice as likely as incarcerated men to be diagnosed with HIV and 15 times more likely than nonincarcerated women to be HIV positive (Kramer & Comfort, 2011).

RISK FACTORS AND BARRIERS TO OUTREACH, CARE, AND PREVENTION

Barriers for Inmates

The complex dynamics of the social networks of inmates and parolees within their communities also need to be understood when developing HIV prevention interventions.

HIV stigma, HIV-based discrimination, and HIV-specific criminal laws in addition to recent history of incarceration and lack of housing are identified risk factors for poor HIV health outcomes and ongoing HIV transmission (National Minority Aids Council, 2013).

Stigmatization, lack of confidentiality, and misunderstandings about HIV transmission are acknowledged barriers to HIV-related services for inmates and their female partners (Beckwith et al., 2010; Mahoney, Bien, & Comfort, 2013). The costs associated with highly active antiretroviral therapy, which must be also be paid for out of overburdened state and federal correctional budgets, are also barriers (Beckwith et al., 2010).

Another recognized barrier for HIV-positive inmates and their families is the lack of linkage to community HIV services post release (Beckwith et al., 2010). An estimated 25% of the entire HIV-positive population in the United States is believed to pass through the prison system yearly. Adapting evidence-based interventions aimed at reducing HIV risk (condom and needle distribution programs, antiretroviral treatments) and improving treatment adherence among inmates as they transition back into their community has been associated with improved outcomes (Copenhaver, Chowdhury, & Altice, 2009).

Incarceration of male partners has been found to increase HIV risks for their female partners as evidenced by their low rates of HIV testing, but higher rates of substance use and unprotected sex (Beckwith et al., 2010). This disproportionately affects racial/ethnic minority women and women affected by intimate partner violence (Meyer et al., 2013; Oliver & Hairston, 2008). Research shows that by structuring culturally and gender-appropriate HIV prevention services (i.e., HIV testing service, education on HIV-risk behaviors for both partners, substance abuse and violence treatment) into a conveniently located community/social service organization might mitigate some associated structural barriers (i.e., lack of housing and lack of employment) and negative health consequences (i.e., lack of health care utilization and medication noncompliance), especially given the inverse relationship between violence and HIV status (Mahoney, Bien, & Comfort, 2013). The HIV risk factors for incarcerated women could be greatly reduced by the provision of substance use treatment, job training, mental health services, and linkage to health care; as well as programs to support and maintain family and community connections (Forbes et al., 2014; Kramer & Comfort, 2011).

In 2000, one Texas study of over 2,300 parolees showed that medical noncompliance was routine. Among parolees, only 5% had obtained their antiretroviral medications in order to remain compliant with treatment. Furthermore, only 30% had filled prescriptions within 60 days of release. These results have serious ramifications for the transmission of HIV and for the seropositive status of the general population (Beckwith, Zaller, Fu, Montague, & Rich, 2010).

According to recent research on racial and ethnic minority populations (Texas DSHS, 2014; Forbes et al., 2014; Keesee, Natale, & Curiel, 2012; Moore, 2011; Pulerwitz et al., 2010), there are numerous barriers that impact HIV/AIDS prevention and treatment services:

- Insufficient service delivery systems for African American and Latino men who have sex with men (MSM) due to the lack of evidence-based interventions for nonidentifying African American and Latino MSM, especially in rural areas
- Insufficient research of HIV among sex workers
- Lower levels of linkage to care are especially critical for young Black MSM
- Distrust of the health care system and its ability to protect confidentiality of individuals infected with HIV or sexually transmitted infections (STIs)
- Inadequate community-level programming to address the stigma associated with HIV and STI disease

Structural inequalities within our social and economic systems, also known as social determinants of health, are deemed critical factors for racial/ethnic/sexual disparities seen among the HIV/AIDS epidemic within the United States. Although researchers recognize that differences in individual risk behaviors (i.e., frequency of unprotected sex, coexisting STI infections, numbers of sexual partners) may play a role in some of these differences; they do not account for all of the observed disparities (Sullivan & Wolitski, 2007; Sullivan et al., 2014). Research has shown that

> Historical psychosocial determinants in the rural geography of the south also play a central part in the disproportionate impact of HIV such as the prevailing social stigma, HIV denial, misconceptions about the disease, and distrust of the health-care system. The concatenation of these pervasive social inequities disempowers people and deprives them from having some degree of control over their lives. In this context, HIV/AIDS need to be considered as a neglected infection of poverty in the region by further reducing lifetime opportunities of social and economic mobility among affected communities. (Chastain, Ezigbo, & Callins, 2017, p. e101)

Stigma, homophobia, discrimination, racism, and poverty as well as behavioral risk factors all contribute to prevalence disparities in HIV/AIDS. In addition, unequal access to health care, racially skewed incarceration, and fewer jobs/educational opportunities in minority communities characterize the structural and socioeconomic factors that contribute to the higher minority community burden of HIV/AIDS. Furthermore, these social determinants of health, which include the complex social and sexual networks that all people belong to, are understood by many to be better predictors of HIV outcomes than behavioral risk factors alone (Lanier & Sutton, 2013; Millet, Flores, Peterson, & Bakeman, 2007; Sullivan et al., 2014).

A socio-ecological model of HIV prevention (see Figure 4.1) developed by Poundstone, Strathdee, and Celentano identifies many components that need to be incorporated into HIV/AIDS prevention interventions (Schield & Beets,

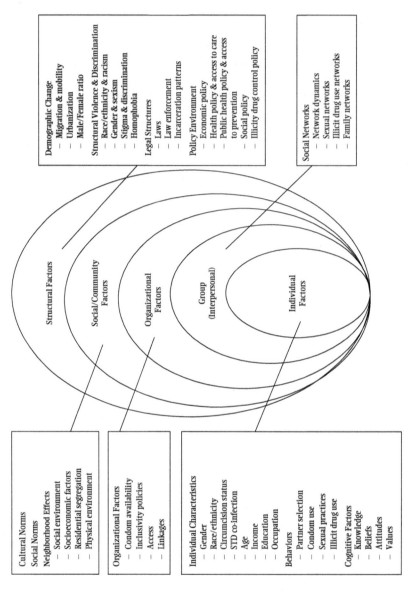

Figure 4.1 A socioecological model of HIV prevention.

Adapted from Poundstone, K. E., Stratdee, S. A., & Celentano, D. D. (2004). The social epidemiology of human immunodeficiency virus/acquired immunodeficiency syndrome. *Epidemiologic Reviews, 26*(1), 22–35.

2011). Structural interventions addressing many of these social determinants of HIV vulnerability in the United States have been identified and include comprehensive sexual education, universal access and availability of condoms, universal access to syringes for drug users, universal health care coverage, and access to housing (Adimora & Auerbach, 2010). However, progress on this front is slow.

Network dynamics have been used to explain the greater burden of HIV and AIDS among African Americans compared with other racial groups in the United States (Kottiri, Friedman, Neaigus, Curtis, & Des, 2002; Latkin et al., 2011; Rothenberg, 2009).

To address the HIV/AIDS epidemic, prevention efforts must incorporate sexual network differences that allow for higher transmission of HIV/STIs (Adimora & Schoenbach, 2005). Poverty and lower socioeconomic status are associated with high-risk social networks and greater exposure to sexual risk factors in regard to sexually transmitted diseases (Adler & Newman, 2002). Indeed, there is evidence that network structural characteristics, such as network density (the extent to which social network members know one another) and partner concurrency (having a sexual relationship with more than one person at a time), may lead to high rates of sexually transmitted infectious diseases, but more research is needed (Rothenberg, 2009).

Barriers to Care—Stigma

Goffman (1963) has defined "stigma" as "a dynamic process of devaluation that 'significantly discredits' an individual in the eyes of others" (p. 3). Few studies have been done on interventions aimed at reducing the stigma associated with HIV/AIDS (Sengupta, Banks, Jonas, Miles, & Smith, 2011). Research indicates that the following factors contribute to the stigma of HIV/AIDS:

- Lack of knowledge or understanding about the illness
- Misconceptions about how HIV/AIDS is transmitted
- Media reporting
- Lack of a cure
- Discrimination toward marginalized populations

Stigma is a major barrier to HIV/AIDS prevention and intervention. Part of the stigma surrounding HIV stems from the historical context of its identification in the 1980s among marginalized groups, including homosexual men and intravenous drug users (Ramirez-Valles, Fergus, Reisen, Poppen, & Zea, 2005). Ethnic/racial minority homosexuals may experience greater incidences of stigma both within their cultural communities as well as externally from the larger population. In particular, Latinos may have to contend with questions of immigration. To further complicate the matter, Latino men may not identify as homosexual or gay despite engaging in sex with other men (Zellner et al., 2009). This lack of identity with the MSM community may stymie efforts to engage these individuals in prevention and treatment efforts.

In addition to the stigma of homosexual behavior, HIV-positive Latino MSM must also contend with the stigma of HIV and rejection from their families and communities resulting from disclosing their serostatus. Mistaken cultural beliefs that HIV infection is only associated with Blacks or Anglos and that it remains an acute, mortal illness rather than a treatable chronic condition abound. Exposure to the public health system for assistance also contributed to fears of deportation that did not dissipate over time in the given study. Thus, undocumented HIV-positive Latinos may deal with the added burden of immigration status along with the intersectionalities of ethnicity and sexual orientation (Dang, Giordano, & Kim, 2012).

To further evaluate the role that discrimination has on health care outcomes in stigmatized (e.g., sexual orientation, and HIV-serostatus) and ethno-racially marginalized groups, one study of HIV-positive Black and Latino MSM sought to investigate which types of discrimination were more hostile in terms of their impact on health. Although both marginalized groups reported similar discrimination in terms of sexual orientation and HIV serostatus, for Black MSM racism alone was found to relate to negative health outcomes (e.g., antiretroviral treatment/ART nonadherence and sexual dysfunction). In comparison, for Latino MSM, the combined effect (versus one specific type of discrimination) was seen as responsible for hindering positive health care outcomes (e.g., producing more severe symptoms/side effects, and poorer illness experiences). Data suggest that discrimination functions differently by race/ethnicity, producing worse health implications for stigma-reducing interventions for coping across all types of discrimination (Bogart, Landrine, Galvan, Wagner, & Klein, 2013).

RISK FACTORS: NOT TESTING, LACK OF HIV STATUS DISCLOSURE, INJECTING DRUG USE, AND RISKY SEX PRACTICES AMONG INCARCERATED PERSONS

The CDC estimates that most new HIV infections in the United States are the result of HIV-positive individuals who are unaware of their infection status (Millet, Flores, Peterson, & Bakeman, 2007). This is especially valid for persons who have been incarcerated. Often testing in correctional facilities is only conducted at the time of an inmate's release. In both the cases of HIV and Hepatitis C, persons who are incarcerated may have contracted these illnesses long before they entered the correctional facility (Adams et al., 2013; CDC, 2015; Dolan et al., 2015). Globally, studies indicate that 10%–48% of males and 30%–60% of females have a history of drug use prior to incarceration (Fazel, Bains, & Doll, 2006). Adams et al. (2013) identified high levels of unprotected sex and risky injection drug use both pre and post incarceration as high risk factors for HIV in inmate populations. Research has shown that there is an overrepresentation of persons who inject drugs and share needles in prisons (Dolan et al., 2015). More than 200,000 heroin users pass through the revolving doors of the prison system in the United States (Boutwell, Nijhawan, Zaller, & Rich, 2007). One unintended consequence of the war on drugs in the United States has been the astounding rise in the imprisonment of drug offenders. Both federal and state prisons have had a dramatic increase in persons held for drug offense with nearly a two-thirds increase at the federal level and over 50% increase at the state level (Alexander, 2012). Given these statistics, the risk that drug users will contract HIV while in correctional facilities is evident. Furthermore, inmates who formerly injected drugs and who enter the prison system with HIV are more likely to continue with their addiction and share needles with other inmates as opposed to HIV negative inmates (Dolan et al., 2015).

Given that more than half of PLWH in the United States are MSM, knowledge of their HIV risk behaviors and use of HIV testing and prevention services is vital to reducing prevalence in this high-risk population. The National HIV Behavioral Surveillance (NHBS) System gathered data from 8,175 MSM on their use of prevention services and HIV behavioral interventions. This survey screened out men who were HIV positive or had no male sexual partner in the previous year. Nearly half of the men who were HIV newly diagnosed during this survey were unaware of their infection status. Of note, nondisclosure of HIV status by both partners was very common in the casual partnerships of the MSM surveyed. Most survey participants reported having been tested for HIV during their lifetime (90%), and many reported being tested in the previous year (62%). For those who reported no HIV testing during the prior year (38%), the top reason sited was a perception of low personal risk (62%) followed by fear of having a positive test (42%). Testing increased with education level of participant and being under 40 years old (Finlayson et al., 2011).

Research attests to the fact that stigma and discrimination are common for people living with HIV, and having a history of incarceration is a compounding factor (Collins et al., 2008; Whetten, Reif, Whetten, & Murphy-McMillan, 2008). In addition, HIV prevention interventions are rare in facilities housing incarcerated persons. Since many inmates enter the prison system with a history of injection drug use, the spread of HIV, without any intervention, can occur rapidly in some facilities (Dolan et al., 2015).

HIV/AIDS INTERVENTIONS FOR INCARCERATED MALES AND FEMALES

Interventions for HIV-positive male and female inmates are limited. There are several reasons for the lack of interventions inside the prison system, including the stigma related to HIV/AIDS, lack of disclosure, the voluntary testing within the prison system, and lack of availability of counselors to provide interventions. In general, most correctional facilities only have a few mental health counselors who spend much of their time dealing with mental health emergencies; inmates in mental health units; and in the case of social workers, assisting with postrelease issues such as family, housing, finances, and job opportunities. Although the majority of inmates who are HIV positive enter correctional facilities with the disease, they will not disclose their status while incarcerated due to fears of ostracism, harassment, and potential assault by others.

Given these facts, the next section encompasses prevention and educational interventions that would be beneficial before a person commits a crime and enters the prison system, interventions that have been studied for inmates while they are in jails and prisons, and postrelease interventions that provide assistance to inmates leaving the prison system.

HIV PREVENTION PROGRAMS BEFORE
AND AFTER INCARCERATION

Successful HIV prevention programs for at-risk populations (i.e., MSM) are known to include the following: community-based outreach; distribution of commodities (e.g., condoms); HIV testing and counseling; linkage to health care and antiretroviral treatment (ART); targeted information, education, and communication (IEC); and STI prevention, screening, and treatment. Furthermore, the use of peer-led or facilitated outreach and intervention programs has been shown to successfully engage difficult-to-reach populations, such as MSM, and engage and retain them in HIV prevention services (US PEPFAR, 2011).

Vanable et al. (2012) developed a formative research study designed to optimize the development of prevention interventions for HIV-positive MSM. In total, 52 HIV-positive MSM participants were engaged through individual interviews and recruited to participate in focus groups for evaluation research. Participants completed a questionnaire prior to focus group participation. Results indicated that stress-reduction techniques, developing a positive attitude, and abstaining from heavy substance use were important factors to reducing risky sexual behavior. Such topics should be an important part of preventions interventions with this population. Medication adherence was also considered an important aspect of maintaining a healthy lifestyle. In addition, participants recommended a support group intervention that focused on coping with life stressors beyond sexual risk reduction. Furthermore, having the ability to meet other HIV-positive MSM through discussion groups in an informal setting was paramount to the success of this intervention.

CULTURALLY BASED HEALTH PREVENTION INTERVENTIONS
TARGETING RACIAL/ETHNIC MINORITIES

Capitman, Gonzalez, Ramirez, and Pacheco (2009) developed a culturally based intervention designed to measure the effectiveness of utilizing "Promotora" community health educators in improving medically underserved participants' access to health care services, public health insurance enrollment, receipt of preventative health care screenings, and self-efficacy. The "Promotora" model utilizes peer-led, trained advocates who are fluent in the languages/cultural nuances of the community they support in order to reach underserved populations, minority populations, and medically underserved communities. The "Promotora" acts as a bridge between underserved members of their community and key community health and social service organizations/resources. For this intervention, eligibility criteria included ethnicity (e.g., Latinos/as), age (e.g., 18 years or older), low-income level (e.g., below 250% of federal poverty level), and residency (e.g., living in Fresno County). Also, to draw from this medically underserved population, participants could be undocumented, permanent legal residents or US citizens.

This intervention identified the following system barriers to accessing services for this underserved population, including (1) eligibility barriers (i.e., understanding the health insurance requirements as well as the application process itself); (2) language barriers (i.e., experiencing limited to poor quality translation services offered at healthc are systems); and (3) poor-quality customer service. Two personal attitude barriers were identified, and they were linked to the participants' experience of any system barriers; they included (1) participants' lack of trust and (2) participants' reluctance to follow up or seek services. The intervention demonstrated that Promotoras are an important community resource that can be utilized to overcome system barriers and participant attitudes that are known to result in underutilization of community health care services. These advocates identified the following crucial components for why Promotoras can be a successful intervention, including (1) shared identification with participants due to shared language, culture, and economic levels; (2) availability made the participants feel supported when seeking health care services; and (3) time (they could provide as much time as necessary to achieve a successful intervention).

SOCIAL SUPPORT INTERVENTIONS

To discover sources of social support to engage HIV-positive Latinos/as and African Americans, Project MUSE recruited 24 participants of color. These 24 adults of color included HIV-positive MSM and heterosexual women. Qualitative interviews were conducted and participants received a monetary incentive ($50). The following factors were identified by the participants as contributing to engagement and retention in HIV care:

Sources of Emotional Support
- support groups
- encouragement for medical adherence
- keeping appointments

Instrumental Support
- transportation vouchers
- translation services
- mental health services
- primary care and referrals to specialist

Informational Support
- education about HIV nutrition
- medications
- treatment options through conferences workshops and word of mouth
- information about other resources (i.e., Legal Aid, Food Bank)

Of note, the importance of the church as a source of support was paramount for African Americans but not for Latinos. In fact, Latinos stated that the church could be a source of stigma. In conclusion, the authors found that formal social support networks such as health care organizations appear to be crucial for engagement in medical and allied HIV treatment and case management. However, family and peer supports are more influential in other psychosocial needs (Erausquin et al., 2009). Further, strong linkages between medical and other AIDS organizations are critical to address the needs of these underserved populations (George et al., 2009).

INTERVENTIONS TARGETING RACIAL/ETHNIC MINORITY MEN WHO HAVE SEX WITH MEN

There is growing consensus that HIV/AIDS prevention strategies must incorporate knowledge about how social determinants impact social networks and community supports in order to eliminate racial, ethnic, and sexual disparities in HIV/AIDS (Millet et al., 2007). Recognizing the interrelated components of HIV risk is crucial to determining the most effective HIV prevention response (CHIPTS & SYPP, 2012). Millet et al. (2007) reported less identification as gay and less disclosure of same-sex behavior in Black MSM compared to White MSM. Furthermore, he identified the need to decrease stigma, homophobia, and discrimination in order to increase the disclosure of same-sex behavior among Black MSM. Sadly, Jones et al. (2008) report almost a 25-year absence of research on Black MSM. Few interventions have been developed for Black MSM, and still fewer have been adapted for Black MSM who do not identify as gay.

One of the first HIV prevention interventions developed for Black MSM showed that interventions developed on other MSM (White and Latino) and women could be adapted for Black MSM with good success. Jones et al. (2008) showed that by adapting these interventions for Black MSM, there was a decrease in unprotected anal intercourse (UAI) (35.2% for insertive UAI, 44.1% for receptive UAI, and 31.8% for any UAI) and increase in condom use.

Another evidence-based HIV prevention intervention targeting at-risk Black MSM focused on a more holistic strategy, one that included addressing the social determinants of health (i.e., stigma, racial/sexual discrimination) in order to build health-promoting behaviors in preference to promoting prevention alone through condom use. This intervention could be delivered as a weekly group session for 7 weeks or as a 3-day weekend workshop. This prevention strategy encouraged the development of risk reduction behaviors among participants. It also encouraged the formation of supportive relationships that reinforced positive health behaviors on an individual level as well as among social and sexual networks (Herbst, Painter, Tomlinson, & Alvarez, 2014).

In a very large study, data from the National HIV Behavioral Surveillance System (NHBS-2008), which included 21 cities in the United States, was used to measure engagement in HIV care among HIV-positive MSM (Paz-Bailey et al., 2014). This study involving 8,153 MSM (self-reported HIV-positive status) found that 33% were not receiving care; and 30% were not receiving care who had at least one prior HIV health care visit following their initial diagnosis. Delayed linkage to HIV care was associated with testing positive at first testing, denial about HIV-positive status, and lower income level. Also, having public insurance in comparison to no insurance and or/private insurance was associated with being in care. Top reasons cited for not being in care were adequate viral load (31%) and feeling good (21%). Critically, 12% reported that a doctor advised them to delay treatment. Additionally, youth (ages 18–29 years) in comparison to older adults (aged 50 years or more) was associated with not currently being in care as was drug use and being from a southern city. Also, Black MSM (17%) were less likely to be in care versus White MSM (11%), which is consistent with the research.

HOUSING AND PREVENTION IN REDUCING INCARCERATION

There is increased recognition of the importance that housing plays in successful approaches to HIV prevention and care (Velsey, 2014). One study showed that the cost of housing as an HIV intervention would be cost-effective if it prevented one transmission of HIV to a seronegative partner for every 64 clients served (Holtgrave et al., 2007). The Department of Housing and Urban Development (HUD) in their February 2011 report to The White House stated that approximately half of all individuals diagnosed with HIV will face homelessness or unstable housing over the course of their illness. Homeless persons who are HIV positive have a heightened risk for poor access and adherence to HIV care (Wolitski et al., 2010) as well as being at risk for incarceration.

Buchanan, Kee, Sadowki, and Garcia (2009) designed a randomized, controlled trial study (2003 to 2006) to assess the impact of a housing and case management program known as "the Chicago Housing for Health Partnership," on the health service utilization of homeless, HIV-positive individuals. This study built on earlier research showing that housing could reduce hospital stays and supportive case management could improve medication adherence in homeless persons (Buchanan et al., 2006; Kessell et al., 2006).

Psychoeducational groups, support groups, and individual counseling are types of mental health interventions available to reduce emotional stress related to HIV and to increase the levels of coping. Not all cultural and ethnic populations are comfortable with these types of interventions. Women raised in different cultures may need other models of support, such as incorporation of family and community networks. This is supported by quantitative and qualitative research (Runnels, 2012) that reveals that members of minority cultures tend to reach out for help from their families and kinship networks (which may be defined differently than mainstream society traditionally defines it) before utilizing service agencies.

Studies show that minority women tend to utilize alternative coping strategies when faced with dual mental and physical health challenges. The rich historical and spiritual traditions commonly found within African American communities provide the frameworks that incorporate spiritually based interventions into mental health services. Among African American women, spirituality has been found to have a direct relationship with cognitive and social functioning and inversely related to HIV symptoms (Runnels, 2012). Through spiritual networks, social networks are formed and a sense of personal identity and autonomy is supported. Personal autonomy leads to a sense of control over one's own health and well-being as well as the necessary decision-making capacities to maintain health-related behaviors (medication adherence, diet, exercise, etc.). Insofar as HIV/AIDS may impact a woman's social and spiritual networks, it is important for practitioners to assess these connections and provide psychosocial support for developing and maintaining these networks.

Stress reduction programs that reduce the stress response system and improve well-being have proven to be beneficial to HIV/AIDS clients. Mindfulness meditation programs have been shown to increase immune functioning and facilitate positive coping of stressors. HIV/AIDS clients are confronted with a myriad of stressors (physical, psychological, cognitive, economic, and social) that appear to respond well to mindfulness techniques. One researcher suggests that mindfulness meditation is "effective in reducing pain, physical complaints, addictive behavior/substance abuse, anxiety, and depression, all of which are common occurrences within the HIV/AIDS population" (Logsdon-Conradsen, 2002, p. 69). In a controlled study of 41 HIV-positive, ethnically diverse participants, an 8-week, mindfulness-based intervention indicated that participants who received and completed the intervention had a reduction in CD-4 + T lymphocyte counts. Mindfulness interventions have been shown to reduce stress levels and viral loads (Creswell, Myers, Cole, & Irwin, 2009).

To help identify effective HIV prevention intervention strategies for Black MSM, a comprehensive literature review was performed enlisting three (Pubmed, Scopus, and Google Scholar) databases by Maulsby et al. (2013). This review included published peer review research articles of studies conducted in the United States. It excluded dissertations, editorials, letters, and commentaries. From the original 127 records, 16 published articles were identified (12 intervention studies and 4 formative research studies) in addition to 7 ongoing research studies.

Of the 12 intervention studies, 8 sought to reduce HIV sexual risk behaviors, including unprotected anal intercourse (7 studies) and consistent condom use (1 study). Five of the 8 behavioral risk reduction interventions resulted in a statistically significant reduction in HIV risk behaviors. The 8 study designs ranged from the accepted benchmark, the randomized comparison group (5 studies), to the pre-post test (2 studies) and repeated cross-sectional (1 study) studies. The health education and skills building were provided through group sessions (5 studies), individual (1 study) counseling, and partner/couples (1 study) counseling. Multisession interventions (7 studies) addressed a range of topics, including condom usage, relationship dynamics, and skills building around partner communication and risk reduction. The one study that was not multisession was a community popular opinion leader method, which trained community leaders to engage friends in discussions about safe sex practices.

These results suggest that behavioral risk interventions are more successful at reducing risky sexual behaviors when involving more (i.e., triple over single) sessions. All of the interventions focusing on behavioral risk reductions also addressed the social context of HIV risk reduction for Black MSM, including discussion of known barriers such as stigma, racism, and homophobia.

The four peer-reviewed articles on evaluated health services interventions among Black MSM found that men who were provided with motivational interviewing and enhanced linkage to care were more likely to receive HIV counseling and testing and were more likely to return for their test results than men who received standard care. Also, enhanced linkage-to-care services increased the likelihood of making HIV medical appointments. Feeling respected by staff was also associated with retention in care. Additionally, more intensive case management was associated with retaining previously intermittent care participants in care. A significant dose–response trend was found between number of hours in the intervention and retention in HIV care. Furthermore, when a social marketing campaign was combined with outreach and availability of a medical social support network, minority YMSM were 2.58 times more likely to attend clinic visits.

Four formative research articles were identified on intervention development. One focused on the development of an online HIV/STI prevention intervention for young Black MSM. Another sought to reduce HIV risk behavior and increase racial and cultural pride. Still another intervention was an adaptation of a methamphetamine-involved heterosexual couples' intervention for methamphetamine-involved African American MSM couples.

The research is promising in the expanding number of studies and intervention services being targeted to Black MSM—a traditionally underserved, high-risk population. In addition, the growing inclusion of subgroups (MSM, drug users, and youth) in these studies is warranted. The high occurrence of diagnosed HIV-seropositive Black MSM can be partially explained by the lack of or a delay in HIV testing, high rates of coexisting STIs, low rates of antiretroviral therapy (ART), and low HIV medical adherence. There is some hope for improvement, as the research indicates a small number of study interventions aimed at increasing HIV testing and treatment services among Black MSM. However, the research demonstrates that a reliance on behavioral interventions to reduce sexual risk behaviors and substance use will not address all the causes for this higher rate of HIV infections. These finding indicate that social and environmental factors coincide to result in these negative health outcomes for Black MSM. Study authors propose that the insight gained from this literature review be used to direct further interventions.

INTERVENTIONS FOR INCARCERATED INMATES

The Centers for Disease Control and Prevention (CDC, 2009) suggests best practices include "opt-out" HIV testing for inmates upon intake into correctional facilities. Research shows that inmates are more likely to obtain voluntary HIV testing when correctional facilities offer all prisoners "opt-out" HIV testing (i.e., everyone is tested unless they ask not to be) in comparison to "opt-in" HIV testing (i.e., inmates have to request to be tested). Also, the CDC reports that opt-in testing has the ability to aid identification of more HIV-infected inmates who may not be aware of their serostatus (CDC, 2009). Other studies show that utilizing an "opt-out" option for STIs and HIV testing during incarceration can facilitate greater continuity of care for prisoners while serving their sentences as well as upon reenter into the community (John Howard Association, 2012). Finally, a study by Jurgens, Nowack, and Day (2011) indicated that inmates used condoms when a condom distribution program was implemented in correctional facilities, thereby reducing the risk of contracting HIV while incarcerated.

A group of public health researchers in Texas implemented a peer education prevention in 36 prison units in the state titled Project Wall Talk. Peer educator inmates ($n = 590$) received a 40-hour intensive training workshop on HIV/AIDS prevention from professionals in community-based HIV/AIDS organizations. The intervention was delivered to 2,506 inmates over an 8-month period of time. Results indicated an increase in HIV testing among both peer educators and students who received the prevention education program and that the knowledge was disseminated to as many as 150,000 or more inmates in a 12-month follow-up questionnaire. Other peer education prevention interventions in prisons have yielded positive results, suggesting that peer education prevention strategies may be beneficial in increasing the knowledge and reducing the fear and stigma associated with HIV testing among prison inmates (Martin, O'Connell, Inciardi, Surratt, & Maiden, 2008).

Finally, one study evaluated the effectiveness of three different types of brief intervention for inmates who were being released from prison back into the community. The interventions included a DVD peer-led intervention, a NIDA Standard HIV intervention delivered by health staff, and a standard HIV and hepatitis test with education only. Three hundred forty-three inmates were tested for HIV and hepatitis C prior to release. Follow-up research at 30 and 90 days indicated that the DVD video involving peers significantly reduced risky behaviors, while the other two interventions showed no significant changes (Martin, O'Connell, Inciardi, Surratt, & Maiden, 2008).

Four DVD videos were made based on gender and ethnicity, including a White ex-offender, African American ex-offender, White female ex-offender, and African American female ex-offender. Given the fact that the research was conducted in Kentucky and Delaware, there were a very low number of Hispanics in the inmate population and therefore a Spanish version of the DVD was not created. The ex-offender talked directly to the inmate in a nonscripted format about safe sex practices, needle cleaning, role-playing condom negotiation or confrontation of someone selling drugs, and testimonials from the ex-offenders. The results indicated that the videos reduced risky behaviors and may be one of the first successful brief interventions for offenders following release from prison (Martin, O'Connell, Inciardi, Surratt, & Maiden, 2008).

CONCLUSION

This chapter covered the most current literature and data on HIV/AIDS research related to the incarcerated population in the United States and cultural factors, barriers to care, retention and engagement of HIV-positive and out-of-care individuals, and evidence-based prevention and intervention practices. The incarcerated population is both a difficult underserved minority in which to study the effectiveness of interventions. Many persons incarcerated enter the prison system already HIV positive. Others leave prison with an HIV-positive diagnosis. Providing assistance for these individuals has also been challenging due to the very limited funding given for postrelease programs.

Major findings suggest that a holistic, multifactorial approach to HIV prevention is needed. There are clearly many reasons why it is difficult to engage and retain individuals at risk for HIV and who are HIV positive in care, as delineated in this review. Stigma, racism, discrimination, homophobia, substance abuse, mental health issues, incarceration, homelessness, financial instability, and lack of social support are major barriers to HIV/AIDS prevention and care. Psychological barriers (e.g., low perceived risk for HIV infection) can further complicate access to care. Facilitators to improve access and retention in care include linguistic and cultural competency in service providers, greater diversity in health care service providers, availability of services for special populations (e.g., transgender), service access for immigrants, health insurance coverage, partnerships with community organizations to address barriers (i.e., racism, HIV stigma), coordination and service linkages to address socioeconomic/psychosocial problems (i.e., community food banks, homeless shelters), and engaging social networks in HIV prevention services. Hard-to-reach populations will require HIV/AIDS professionals to critically examine existing prevention efforts. The person-in-environment model has shown that HIV/AIDS prevention outreach must meet the client where he or she is and provide demonstrable benefits, which often means addressing the client's socioeconomic and psychosocial problems in order to engage him or her in care. Social marketing campaigns will need to incorporate new technologies to communicate and connect with this ever-changing and diverse audience. This review provides a starting point from which to develop and implement new and creative strategies for HIV/AIDS prevention and intervention for incarcerated persons.

Interventions for incarcerated inmates need to be implemented throughout the US correctional facilities. From the few evidence-based studies that have been published, it is clear that interventions to reduce the risk of inmates contracting or spreading the illness when released are needed. Medication that covers at least 90 days after release for those who are HIV positive is a necessity. Clearly, the ability to obtain and use condoms while incarcerated reduces the risk of contracting HIV while in prison. Further research is needed to best address the issues confronting this population.

CASE EXAMPLE

Ronald, a 38-year-old African American male, is currently at the end of a 15-year prison sentence for possession of a considerable quantity of cocaine and heroin with intent to sell. He had previously served two shorter prison terms (2 years and 4 years, respectively) for drug possession, but due to living in a "three strikes and your out state" he received a lengthy sentence for his last offense. Ronald is currently working with the social worker, Carver, at the prison to plan for his impending release from the facility. Carver notes that Ronald's only job experience was working at a fast food restaurant as a teenager since he has spent most of his adult life involved with drugs or in the prison system. Ronald obtained a GED and a Community College degree while in prison and wants to finish a 4-year degree once he is released. He has obtained some job skills, including computer data entry and systems analyst training. He also belonged to the prison's AA group and completed a drug rehabilitation program in the past 5 years. He tells Carver that he has no intentions of going back to drugs. "I'm clean now and I'm going to stay clean," Ronald declares.

Ronald has another problem, however, that has created problems for Ronald since he entered the correctional facility 15 years ago. Ronald entered the facility and discovered 2 years into his sentence that he was HIV positive. He wasn't aware of his HIV status until he became ill and underwent voluntary HIV testing while in the infirmary. He believes he must have contracted the virus using dirty needles prior to entering the prison system. He did admit to Carver that he had a couple of sexual encounters with other male inmates but has not had any sex since finding out his HIV status. Ronald states that he is heterosexual and had a live-in girlfriend when he was "outside." She abandoned him when he went to prison.

Carver lets Ronald know that it's going to be an uphill battle when he gets released from prison. He will be on probation and must meet weekly with the probation officer or risk being sent back to prison. He must find housing and a job as soon as possible, which will be very difficult given his record. In addition, he must be under medical supervision and comply with a medication regime that he has only taken sporadically while in prison. Ronald states that they just make it "so damn hard" to get medication. "You have to be in line at the medication counter at 4 a.m. and then everyone knows what you're doing there. The officers hassle you, the inmates abuse you, and there's no peace if they find out you're positive. I'd rather take my chances and hope I don't get sick."

Carver contacted Ronald's brother who lives in the same city as Ronald and let him know that Ronald was being released from prison soon. His brother has agreed to let Ronald stay at his place until he can find another place to live. Carver also contacted two AIDS organizations that have food pantries and medical care at no cost. Finally, Carver referred Ronald to the Prison Post Release Agency, a nonprofit, that helps ex-inmates with jobs, housing, and other forms of assistance in an effort to reduce the revolving door of correctional facilities today.

REFERENCES

Adams, L. M., Kendall, S., Smith, A., Quigley, E., Stuewig, J. B., & Tangney, J. P. (2013). HIV risk behaviors of male and female jail inmates prior to incarceration and one year post-release. *AIDS and Behavior, 17*(8), 2685–2694. doi:10.1007/s10461-011-9990-2

Adler, N. E., & Newman, K. (2002). Socioeconomic disparities in health: Pathways and policies. *Health Affairs, 21*(2), 60–76.

Adimora, A. A., & Auerbach, J. D. (2010). Structural interventions for HIV prevention in the United States. *JAIDS Journal of Acquired Immune Deficiency Syndromes, 55*, S132–S135.

Adimora, A. A., & Schoenbach, V. J. (2005). Social context, sexual networks, and racial disparities in rates of sexually transmitted infections. *Journal of Infectious Diseases, 191*(Supplement 1), S115–S122.

Alexander, M. (2012) *The new Jim Crow: Mass incarceration in the age of colorblindness.* New York, NY: The New Press.

Baillargeon, J., Giordano, T. P., Rich, J. D., Wu, z. H., Wells, K., Pollack, B. H., & Paar, D. P. (2009). Accessing antiretroviral therapy following release from prison. Journal of the American Medical Association, 301, 848–857.

Beckwith, C. G., Zaller, N. D., Fu, J. J., Montague, B. T., & Rich, J. D. (2010). Opportunities to diagnose, treat and prevent HIV in the criminal justice system. *Journal of Acquired Immune Deficiency Syndromes, 55*(1), S49–S55.

Bogart, L. M., Landrine, H., Galvan, F. H., Wagner, G. J., & Klein, D. J. (2013). Perceived discrimination and physical health among HIV-positive black and Latino men who have sex with men. *AIDS and Behavior, 17*(4), 1431–1441.

Boutwell, A. E., Nijhawan, A., Zaller, N., & Rich, J. D. (2007). Arrested on heroin: A national opportunity. *Journal of Opioid Management, 3*(6), 328.

Buchanan, D., Doblin, B., Sai, T., & Garcia, P. (2006). The effects of respite care for homeless patients: A cohort study. *American Journal of Public Health, 96*(7), 1278–1281.

Buchanan, D., Kee, R., Sadowski, L. S., & Garcia, D. (2009). The health impact of supportive housing for HIV-positive homeless patients: A randomized controlled trial. *American Journal of Public Health, 99*(Suppl 3), S675–S680.

Bureau of Justice Statistics. (2017). *Total correction population.* Retrieved from https://www.bjs.gov/index.cfm?ty=tp&tid=11

Capitman, J. A., Pacheco, T. L., Ramirez, M., & Gonzalez, A. (2009). *Promotoras: Lessons learned on improving healthcare access to Latinos.* Fresno, CA; Central Valley Health Policy Institute.

Castillo-Mancilla, J. R., Cohn, S. E., Krishnan, S., Cespedes, M., Floris-Moore, M., Schulte, G., . . . & Smith, K. Y. (2014). Minorities remain underrepresented in HIV/AIDS research despite access to clinical trials. *HIV Clinical Trials, 15*(1), 14–26. doi:10.1310/hct1501-14

Center for American Progress & Movement Advancement Project. (2016). *Unjust: How the broken criminal justice system fails LGBT people.* Washington, DC: Center for American Progress.

Centers for Disease Control and Prevention [CDC]. (2009). HIV testing implementation guidance for correctional settings. Retrieved from http://www.cdc.gov/hiv/topics/testing/resources/guidelines/correctional-settings.

Centers for Disease Control and Prevention. (CDC). (2013). *National HIV Prevention Progress Report.* Retrieved from http://www.cdc.gov/hiv/pdf/policies_NationalProgressReport.pdf

Centers for Disease Control and Prevention. (2015, July). HIV among incarcerated populations. Retrieved from https://www.cdc.gov/hiv/group/correctional.html

Centers for Disease Control and Prevention. (2016a, November). HIV in the United States: At a Glance [fact sheet]. Retrieved from https://www.cdc.gov/hiv/statistics/overview/ataglance.html

Centers for Disease Control and Prevention. (2016b, December). Terms, definitions, and calculations used in CDC HIV surveillance publications. Retrieved from https://www.cdc.gov/hiv/pdf/statistics/systems/nhbs/cdc-hiv-terms-surveillance-publications-2014.pdf

Center for HIV Identification, Prevention and Treatment Services (CHIPTS) and Center for Strengthening Youth Prevention Paradigms (SYPP). (2012). *HIV prevention at the structural level: the role of social determinants of health and HIV.* Los Angeles, CA: Author.

Chandler, R. K., Fletcher, B. W., & Volkow, N. D. (2009). Treating drug abuse and addiction in the criminal justice system: Improving public health and safety. *JAMA, 301*(2), 183–190. doi:10.1001/jama.2008.976

Chastain, D. B., Ezigbo, C., Callins, K. R. (2017). Reducing transmission of HIV in southeastern USA. *The Lancet, 4*(3), e101. Retrieved from http://www.thelancet.com/hiv.

Chedha, Y., & Vedhara, K. (2009). Adverse psychosocial factors predict poorer prognosis in HIV disease: A meta-analytic review of prospective investigations. *Brain, Behavior, and Immunity, 23*, 434–445.

Collins, P. Y., Elkington, K. S., von Unger, H., Sweetland, A., Wright, E. R., & Zaybert, P. A. (2008). Relationship of stigma to HIV risk among women with mental illness. *American Journal of Orthopsychiatry, 10*(78), 498–506.

Connor, K. M., & Davidson, J. R. T. (2003). Development of a new resilience scale: The Connor-Davidson Resilience Scale (CDRISC). *Depression and Anxiety, 18*, 76–82.

Copenhaver, M., Chowdhury, S., & Altice, F. L. (2009). Adaptation of an evidence-based intervention targeting HIV-infected prisoners transitioning to the community: The process and outcome of formative research for the Positive Living Using Safety (PLUS) intervention. *AIDS Patient Care & STDs, 23*(4), 277–287.

Creswell, J. D., Myers, H. F., Cole, S. W., & Irwin, M. R. (2009). Mindfulness meditation training effects on CD4+ T lymphocytes in HIV-1 infected adults: A small randomized controlled trial. *Brain, Behavior, and Immunity, 23*(2), 184–188.

Dale, S. K., Cohen, M. H., Kelso, G. A., Cruise, R. C., Weber, K. M., Watson, C., . . . & Brody, L. R. (2014). Resilience among Women with HIV: Impact of silencing the self and socioeconomic factors. *Sex Roles, 70*(5–6), 221–231.

Dang, B. N., Giordano, T. P., & Kim, J. H. (2012). Sociocultural and structural barriers to care among undocumented Latino immigrants with HIV infection. *Journal of Immigrant and Minority Health, 14*(1), 124–131.

Dolan, K., Kite, B., Black, E., Aceijas, C., & Stimson, G. V. (2007). HIV in prison in low-income and middle-income countries. *The Lancet Infectious Diseases, 7*(1), 32–41.

Dolan, K., Moazen, B., Noori, A., Rahimzadeh, S., Farzadfar, F., & Hariga, F. (2015). People who inject drugs in prison: HIV prevalence, transmission and prevention. *International Journal of Drug Policy, 26*, S12–S15.

Dumont, D. M., Brockmann, B., Dickman, S., Alexander, N., & Rich, J. D. (2012). Public health and the epidemic of incarceration. *Annual Review of Public Health, 33*(1), 325–339. doi:10.1146/annurev-publhealth-031811-124614

Erausquin, J. T., Duan, N., Grusky, O., Swanson, A. N., Kerrone, D., & Rudy, E. T. (2009). Increasing the reach of HIV testing to young Latino MSM: Results of a pilot study integrating outreach and services. *Journal of Health Care for the Poor and Underserved, 20*(3), 756–765.

Fazel, S., Bains, P., & Doll, H. (2006). REVIEW: Substance abuse and dependence in prisoners: A systematic review. *Addiction, 101*(2), 181. doi:10.1111/j.1360-0443.2006.01316.x.

Feaster, D. J., Reznick, O. G., Zack, B., McCartney, K., & Gregorich, S. E., & Brincks, A. M. (2013). Health status, sexual and drug risk and psychosocial factors relevant to postrelease planning for HIV+ prisoners. *Journal of Correctional Health Care, 19*(4), 278–292.

Finlayson, T., Le, B., Smith, A., Bowles, K., Cribbin, M., Miles, I., . . . & Dinenno, E. (2011). *HIV risk, prevention, and testing behaviors among men who have sex with men—National HIV Behavioral Surveillance System, 21 U.S. cities, United States, 2008.* Washington, DC: US Department of Health and Human Services, Centers for Disease Control and Prevention.

Forbes, A. L., Khanna, N., Rastogi, S., Cardell, B., Griffith, K., & Shabazz-El, W. (2014). Understanding the promise: Considering the experiences of women living with HIV to maximize effectiveness of HIV prevention technologies. *Women's Health Issues, 24*(2), e165–e170.

Fullilove, R. E. (2011). Mass incarceration in the United States and HIV/AIDS: Cause and effect. *Ohio State Journal of Criminal Law, 9*, 353.

Frazier, B. D., Sung, H., Gideon, L., & Alfaro, K. S. (2015). The impact of prison deinstitutionalization on community treatment services. *Health & Justice, 3*(1), 1–12. doi:10.1186/s40352-015-0021-7

George, S., Garth, B., Wohl, A. R., Galvan, F. H., Garland, W., & Myers, H. F. (2009). Sources and types of social support that influence engagement in HIV care among Latinos and African Americans. *Journal of Health Care for the Poor and Underserved, 20*(4), 1012.

Goffman, E. (1963). *Stigma: Notes on the management of spoiled identity.* Englewood Cliffs, NJ: Prentice-Hall.

Grant, J. M., Mottet, L. A., Tanis, J., Harrison, J., Herman, J. L., & Keisling, M. (2011). *Injustice at every turn: A report of the national transgender discrimination survey.* Retrieved from http://www.transequality.org/issues/resources/national-transgender-discrimination-survey-full-report

Grant, J. M., Mottet, L. A., Tanis, J., Harrison, J., Herman, J. L., & Keisling, M. (2011). *Injustice at every turn: a report of the National Transgender Discrimination Survey.* Washington, DC: National Center for Transgender Equality and National Gay and Lesbian Task Force.

Harawa, N., & Adimora, A. (2008). Incarceration, African Americans and HIV: Advancing a research agenda. *Journal of the National Medical Association, 100*, 57–62.

The Henry J. Kaiser Family Foundation. (2014a). Black Americans and HIV/AIDS. Retrieved from http://kff.org/hivaids/fact-sheet/black-americans-and-hiv-aids/

Herbst, J. H., Painter, T. M., Tomlinson, H. L., & Alvarez, M. E. (2014). Evidence-based HIV/STD prevention intervention for black men who have sex with men. *Morbidity and Mortality Weekly Report Supplement, 63*(1), 21–27. Retrieved from https://www.ncbi.nlm.nih.gov/pmc/articles/PMC4680977/

Holtgrave, D. R., Briddell, K., Little, E., Bendixen, A. V., Hooper, M., Kidder, D. P., . . . & Aidala, A. (2007). Cost and threshold analysis of housing as an HIV prevention intervention. *AIDS and Behavior, 11*(2), 162–166.

Ickovics, J., & Rodin, J. (1992). Women and AIDS in the United States: Epidemiology, natural history, and mediating mechanisms. *Health Psychology, 11,* 1–16.

John Howard Association. (2012). Unasked questions, unintended consequences: Fifteen findings and recommendations on Illinois' prison healthcare system. Retrieved from http://thejha.org/sites/default/files/Unasked%20Questions-Unintended%20Consequences.pdf.

Jones, K. T., Gray, P., Whiteside, Y. O., Wang, T., Bost, D., Dunbar, E., . . . & Johnson, W. D. (2008). Evaluation of an HIV prevention intervention adapted for Black men who have sex with men. *American Journal of Public Health, 98*(6), 1043–1050.

Jürgens, R., Nowack, M., & Day, M. (2011). HIV and incarceration: Prisons and detention. *Journal of the International AIDS Society, 14,* (26). doi:10.1186/1758-2652-14-26 Retrieved from https://www.ncbi.nlm.nih.gov/pmc/articles/PMC3123257/

Keesee, M. S., Natale, A. P., & Curiel, H. F. (2012). HIV positive Hispanic/Latinos who delay HIV care: Analysis of multilevel care engagement barriers. *Social Work in Health Care, 51*(5), 457–478.

Kessell, E. R., Bhatia, R., Bamberger J. D., & Kushel, M. B. (2006). Public health care utilization in a cohort of homeless adult applicants to a supportive housing program. *Journal of Urban Health, 83*(5), 860–873.

Kottiri, B. J., Friedman, S. R., Neaigus, A., Curtis, R., & Des, J. (2002). Risk networks and racial/ethnic differences in the prevalence of HIV infection among injection drug users. *Journal of Acquired Immune Deficiency Syndromes, 30*(1), 95–104. http://www.ncbi.nlm.nih.gov/pmc/articles/PMC2884281/

Kramer, K., & Comfort, M. (2011). Considerations in HIV prevention for women affected by the criminal justice system. *Women's Health Issues, 21,* S272–S277.

Krebs, C. P. (2006). Inmate factors associated with hiv transmission in prison. *Criminology & Public Policy, 5*(1), 113–135. doi:10.1111/j.1745-9133.2006.00101.x

Lanier, Y., & Sutton, M. Y. (2013). Reframing the context of preventive health care services and prevention of HIV and other sexually transmitted infections for young men: New opportunities to reduce racial/ethnic sexual health disparities. *American Journal of Public Health, 103*(2), 262–269.

Latkin, C., Yang, C., Tobin, K., Penniman, T., Patterson, J., & Spikes, P. (2011). Differences in the social networks of African American men who have sex with men only and those who have sex with men and women. *American Journal of Public Health, 101*(10), e18–e23. Retrieved from http://www.ncbi.nlm.nih.gov/pmc/articles/PMC3222365/#!po=86.1111

Logsdon-Conradsen, S. (2002). Using mindfulness meditation to promote holistic health in individuals with HIV/AIDS. *Cognitive and Behavioral Practice, 9*(1), 67–72.

Mahoney, M., Bien, M., & Comfort, M. (2013). Adaptation of an evidence-based HIV prevention intervention for women with incarcerated partners: Expanding to community settings. *AIDS Education and Prevention, 25*(1), 1–13.

Martin, S. S., O'Connell, D. J., Inciardi, J. A., Surratt, H. L., & Maiden, K. M. (2008) Integrating an HIV/HCV brief intervention in prisoner reentry: Results of a multisite prospective study, *Journal of Psychoactive Drugs, 40*(4), 427–436. doi:10.1080/02791072.2008.10400649

Maruschak, L. M. (2007). *HIV in prisons, 2005* (NCJ 218915). Washington, DC: Bureau of Justice Statistics. Retrieved from http://www.bjs.gov/content/pub/pdf/hivp05.pdf

Maulsby, C., Millett, G., Lindsey, K., Kelley, R., Johnson, K., Montoya, D., & Holtgrave, D. (2013). A systematic review of HIV interventions for black men who have sex with men (MSM). *BMC Public Health, 13*(1), 625. Retrieved from http://www.ncbi.nlm.nih.gov/pmc/articles/PMC3710496/

McLemore, M. (2008). Access to condoms in US prisons. *HIV/AIDS Policy & Law Review, 13*(1), 20–24.

Meyer, J. P., Wickersham, J. A., Fu, J. J., Brown, S., Sullivan, T. P., Springer, S. A., & Altice, F. L. (2013). Partner violence and health among HIV-infected jail detainees. *International Journal of Prisoner Health, 9*(3), 124–141.

Millet, G. A., Flores, S. A., Peterson, J. L., & Bakeman, R. (2007). Explaining disparities in HIV infection among Black and White men who have sex with men: A meta-analysis of HIV Risk Factors. *AIDS, 21*(15), 2083–2091.

Moore, R. D. (2011). Epidemiology of HIV infection in the United States: Implications for linkage to care. *Clinical Infectious Diseases, 52*(2), S208–S213.

Moyer, E., & Hardon, A. (2014). Introduction: A disease unlike any other? Why HIV remains exceptional in the age of treatment. *Medical Anthropology, 33*(4), 263–269.

National Minority AIDS Council. (January 2013). *Mass incarceration, housing instability and HIV/AIDS: Research findings and policy recommendations.* Retrieved from nmac.org/wp-content/uploads/2013/02/Incarceration-Report-FINAL_2-6-13.pdf   (June 18, 2017).

Oliver, W., & Hairston, C. F. (2008). Intimate partner violence during the transition from prison to the community—Perspectives of incarcerated African American men. *Journal of Aggression, Maltreatment and Trauma, 16*(3), 258–276.

Paz-Bailey, G., Pham, H., Oster, A. M., Lansky, A., Bingham, T., Wiegand, R. E., . . . & Heffelfinger, J. D. (2014). Engagement in HIV care among HIV-positive men who have sex with men from 21 cities in the United States. *AIDS and Behavior, 18*(3), 348–358.

Pellowski, J. A., Kalichman, S. C., Matthews, K. A., & Adler, N. (2013). A pandemic of the poor: Social disadvantage and the US HIV epidemic. *American Psychologist, 68*(4), 197. doi:10.1037/a0032694

Peters, R. H., Wexler, H. K., & Lurigio, A. J. (2015). Co-occurring substance use and mental disorders in the criminal justice system: A new frontier of clinical practice and research. *Psychiatric Rehabilitation Journal, 38*(1), 1–6. doi:10.1037/prj0000135.

Prejean, J., Song, R., Hernandez, A., Ziebell, R., Green, T., Walker, F., . . . & Hall, H. I. (2011). Estimated HIV incidence in the United States, 2006–2009. *PloS One, 6*(8), e17502.

Pulerwitz, J., Michaelis, A., Weiss, E., Brown, L., & Mahendra, V. (2010). Reducing HIV-related stigma: Lessons learned from Horizons research and programs. *Public Health Reports, 125*(2), 272.

Ramirez-Valles, J., Fergus, S., Reisen, C. A., Poppen, P. J., & Zea, M. C. (2005). Confronting stigma: Community involvement and psychological well-being among HIV-positive Latino gay men. *Hispanic Journal of Behavioral Sciences, 27*(1), 101–119.

Rich, J. D., DiClemente, R., Levy, J., Lyda, K., Ruiz, M., Rosen, D. L., & Dumont, D. (2013). Correctional facilities as partners in reducing HIV disparities. *Journal of Acquired Immune Deficiency Syndromes (1999), 63*(1), S49.

Rothenberg, R., (2009). HIV transmission networks. *Current Opinion in HIV and AIDS, 4*(4), 260–265.

Rowell-Cunsolo, T. L., El-Bassel, N., & Hart, C. L. (2016). Black Americans and incarceration: A neglected public health opportunity for HIV risk reduction. *Journal of Health Care for the Poor and Underserved, 27*(1), 114.

Runnels, R. C. (2012). *Constructing spirit-level interventions for African American women living with HIV* (Dissertation thesis). University of Texas at Austin. Retrieved from http://hdl.handle.net/2152/22111

Sengupta, S., Banks, B., Jonas, D., Miles, M. S., & Smith, G. C. (2011). HIV interventions to reduce HIV/AIDS stigma: A systematic review. *AIDS and Behavior, 15*, 1075–1087.

Schield, J., & Beets, G. (2011). *Texas HIV/STD Prevention Plan 2011: The Texas HIV/ STD Prevention Community Planning Group* (TxCPG), p. 24, Austin, TX.

Steele, C. B., Meléndez-Morales, L., Campoluci, R., DeLuca, N., & Dean, H. D. (2007). *Health disparities in HIV/AIDS, viral hepatitis, sexually transmitted diseases, and tuberculosis: Issues, burden, and response, a retrospective review, 2000–2004*. Retrieved from http://www.cdc.gov/nchhstp/healthdisparities/

Steinhardt, M., & Dolbier, C. (2008). Evaluation of a resilience intervention to enhance coping strategies and protective factors and decrease symptomatology. *Journal of American College Health, 56*(4), 445–453.

Sullivan, P. S., Peterson, J., Rosenberg, E. S., Kelley, C. F., & Cooper, H. (2014). Understanding racial HIV/STI disparities in black and white men who have sex with men: A multilevel approach. *PLoS ONE, 9*(3), e90514.

Sullivan, P. S., Wolitski, R. J. (2007). HIV infection among gay and bisexual men. In R. J. Wolitski, R. Stall, & R. O.Valdiserri (eds.), *Unequal opportunity: Health disparities affecting gay and bisexual men in the United States* (pp. 220–247). New York, NY: Oxford University Press.

UNAIDS. (2014). *The gap report*. Retrieved from http://www.unaids.org/en/resources/ campaigns/2014/2014gapreport/gapreport

UNAIDS. (2016). *Fact sheet November 2016*. Retrieved from http://www.unaids.org/en/ resources/fact-sheet

US President's Emergency Plan for AIDS Relief (USPEPFAR). (2011). *Technical guidance on combination HIV prevention: As part of PEPFAR's overall prevention strategy, this guidance document addresses prevention programs for Men Who Have Sex with Men*. Washington, DC: Office of the US Global AIDS Coordinator.

Vanable, P. A., Carey, M. P., Brown, J. L., Littlewood, R. A., Bostwick, R., & Blair, D. (2012). What HIV-positive MSM want from sexual risk reduction interventions: Findings from a qualitative study. *AIDS and Behavior, 16*(3), 554–563.

Velsay, K. (2014). Affordable housing or lack thereof: With new mayor and different governor at the helm, increased HIV/AIDS housing subsidy to become a reality. *New York Observer*. Retrieved from http://observer.com/2014/02/with-a-new-mayor-and-different-governor-at-the-helm-hivaids-housing-subsidy-to-become-a-reality/

Werner, E. E. (2004). Journeys from childhood to midlife: Risk, resilience, and recovery. *Pediatrics, 114*, 492.

Westergaard, R. P., Spaulding, A. C., & Flanigan, T. P. (2013). HIV among persons incarcerated in the US: A review of evolving concepts in testing, treatment and linkage to community care. *Current Opinion in Infectious Diseases, 26*(1), 10–16. doi:10.1097/ QCO.0b013e32835c1dd0.

Whetten, K., Reif, S., Whetten, R., & Murphy-McMillan, L. K. (2008). Trauma, mental health, distrust, and stigma among HIV-positive persons: Implications for effective care. *Psychosomatic Medicine, 70*(5), 531–538. doi:10.1097/PSY.0b013e31817749dc

Wohl, D. A. (2016). HIV and mass incarceration where infectious diseases and social justice meet. *North Carolina Medical Journal, 77*(5), 359–364. doi:10.18043/ ncm.77.5.359

Wolitski, R. J., Kidder, D. P., Pals, S. L, Royal, S., Aidala, A., Stall, R., . . . & Courtnenay-Quirk, C. (2010). Randomized trial of the effects of housing assistance on the health and risk behaviors of homeless and unstably housed people living with HIV. *AIDS and Behavior, 14*(3), 493–503.

Zellner, J. A., Martínez-Donate, A. P., Sañudo, F., Fernández-Cerdeño, A., Sipan, C. L., Hovell, M. F., & Carrillo, H. (2009). The interaction of sexual identity with sexual behavior and its influence on HIV risk among Latino men: Results of a community survey in northern San Diego County, California. *American Journal of Public Health, 99*(1), 125.

5

Aging, Stigma, and Criminal Justice

Toward Human Rights–Based Assessment and Intervention

TINA MASCHI AND GEORGE LEIBOWITZ

The stigmatization and mass incarceration of the elderly is international in scope but is particularly problematic in the United States, which has the largest incarceration rate per capita. This chapter reviews the intersectional issues of age, health, mental health, legal, economic, and social care–related needs and rights of justice-involved older adults. We provide an overview and scope of the problem, promising and best practices, and policy and population trend issues that perpetuate or reduce ageism and other forms of stigmatization, neglect, and mistreatment of this population, and trends and future issues. It concludes with select case examples to illustrate the diversity among the aging prison population. We assert that the biggest challenges for professionals and prisons to best serve this population is to develop competencies to work effectively at the practice intersection of aging, health/mental health, and the criminal justice system to prevent or effectively intervene with the justice-involved aging population at the programming and policy level.

INTRODUCTION AND SCOPE OF THE PROBLEM

Background and Profile of Population

The steady rise of the mass incarceration of the elderly is international in scope but is particularly problematic in the United States, which has the largest incarceration rate per capita (American Civil Liberties Union, 2012). As of 2009, prisoner population rates per 100,000 were 760 in the United States, 624 for the Russian Federation, 153 in the United Kingdom, 119 in China, and 116 in Canada (OECD, 2010). Of the 2.3 million persons in custody in the United States, 16% ($n = 200,000$) are aged 50 and older (Guerino et al., 2011). In global corrections, the number of incarcerated adults aged 50 and older varies and has been steadily increasing over the past two decades (Aday, 2003; Carstairs & Keon, 2009). Prisoners aged 50 and older represent about 20% (2,800) of Canada's total inmate population of 14,000 (Hale & Swiggum, 2011; Sapers, 2008). In Australia, of a total general population of 19,082 prisoners, 7.4% (1,412) are aged 50 and older (Grant, 1999); in England and Wales, older prisoners aged 50 plus represent almost 11% (6,417) of the total prison population (Ministry of Justice, 2010).

The United States is particularly problematic in warehousing older people in prison, including to their death. Of the 2.6 million people in US prisons as of 2010, about 220,000 (16%) were aged 50 and older (ACLU, 2012). The Bureau of Justice Statistics (BJA) reports that in the past two decades the state prison population aged 55 and older has increased from 3% (1993) to 10% (Guerino et al., 2011. This increase has largely been attributed to the growing segment of incarcerated people who are aged 55+ serving long-term prison sentences, of which a large number have serious violent and sex offenses (Carson & Sabol, 2016).

In addition to ageism and stigma based on age, the disproportionality of stigmatized subgroups also is reflected in other characteristics of the US older population. In 2010, 8% of inmates were aged 55 and above, male (93%), and disproportionately racial and ethnic minorities (46%), had chronic health or mental health problems (36%), and came from lower socioeconomic backgrounds (Guerino et al., 2011; HRW, 2012; Maschi, Viola, & Sun, 2013). Health status also varied; some individuals have functional capacity, whereas others suffer from serious and terminal illnesses such as HIV/AIDs, cancer, and dementia or mental health and substance use problems (36%; James & Glaze, 2006). In addition to criminal offense histories, many have histories of victimization in the community and in prison, which include childhood physical and sexual assault, and witnessing violence (see Maschi et al., 2013).

Victimization that has occurred prior to prison often has gone undetected and/or untreated and results in varying levels of adaptive coping responses and access to justice, social support, and service networks (Aday, 2005; Maschi, Viola, & Morgen, 2013). There is a growing body of prison research on health and justice disparities in which minority groups have less access to quality care and justice and tend to experience more health and justice disparities than Whites (Adler & Rehkopf, 2008; Groman & Ginsburg, 2004). For example, Black men have a lifetime likelihood of imprisonment of 1 in 3, compared to 1 in 17 for White men (Sentencing Project, 2013). Evidence suggests that aging people in prison vary in their coping capacities or resources and this influences the degree interpersonal and social structural trauma, stigma, and oppression influences their health and well-being and criminal behavior (Maschi, Leibowitz, & Morgen, in press; Maschi, Viola, Morgen, & Koskinen, 2015).

Older people vary in their life course pathways to prison, which has implications for prevention and intervention efforts with this population. Maschi and colleagues' (2013) typology describes four distinct types of older adults in prison based on time served, which has implications for research, practice, and advocacy. These four groups are as follows: incarcerated persons with long-term sentences (a person with 20 or more years served), the lifer (life sentence), persons with histories of acute and chronic recidivism (two or more incarcerations), and persons who first were convicted as older adults (first convicted in old age). Thus, the differing pathways that result in prison for older adults may vary in one or more cumulative disparities or stigmatized social identities related to race, education, socioeconomic status, gender, disability, and legal or immigration status, which can influence their access to health and social services, economic resources, and justice throughout their life course. As the international human rights movement is gaining momentum in its efforts to advocate for the rights of stigmatized and vulnerable groups, such as justice-involved aging people, racial ethnic minorities, and persons with mental health and mental health issues, social work and allied professionals are challenged to address stigma and oppression at the structural and cultural levels as well as develop and refine evidence-based practices with this population (UN High Commissioner, 2012).

Moving From Stigma to Human Rights

The recent Report of the United Nations High Commissioner for Human Rights (2012) urges that special consideration be given to older adults involved in the justice system due to the accumulated or aggravated disadvantages and stigmatization inherent in their status and grave human rights conditions that they have endured, including in prison. An antithesis to stigma-fueled mistreatment, human rights values purport dignity and respect for all persons and the indivisible and interlocking holistic relationship of all human rights in civil, political, economic, social, and cultural domains (UN, 1948). In the working group documents leading to a Convention on the Rights of Older Persons, rights are framed by conceptions of equality, respect, autonomy, and dignity (UN, 2012). Areas of protections of older persons that are underscored for those in prison include age discrimination; legal capacity and equal recognition before the law; conditions of institutional and home-based long-term care; violence and abuse; access to productive resources, work, food, and housing; social protection and the right to Social Security; right to health and palliative and end-of-life care; disabilities in old age; access to justice; and legal rights. The United Nations classifies "older prisoners" as a special needs population along with racial/ethnic minorities, persons with disabilities or terminal illnesses, homosexuals (GBLT), and death row inmates with specific nonbinding guidelines for their treatment that include care transitions (United Nations Office on Drugs and Crime, 2009).

Incarcerated elders with violent records, including violent sex offense histories, experience a significant challenge based on the stigma of their criminal convictions in being granted parole or obtaining access to services post prison release (Maschi & Koskinen, 2015). Research suggests that incarcerated elders report on average three traumatic and stressful life experiences before, during, and after prison, and these cumulative traumatic events can place them at risk of later life physical and mental health decline (Maschi, Viola, & Morgen, 2013). Based on their complex health, mental health, social, legal, and economic concerns, many of the interventions that have been developed have taken a holistic approach to address these multiple rights and needs.

The High Costs of Incarcerating Older People

Health and social care costs associated with incarceration are growing in large part due to the aging inmate population. High medical expenditures for institutional care are common, especially those associated with serious illness, disabilities, or terminal illnesses (UNODC, 2009). In the United States, these costs represent approximately 10% of the total direct prison costs of care for those incarcerated. Average cost of care for the average prisoner is approximately $5,500, for prisoners aged 55 to 59; the costs double ($11,000) and are 8 times higher for prisoners aged 80 and older ($40,000; HRW, 2012). The adult correctional system is struggling with managing a diverse older prison population in need of specialized health, mental health, social service, and legal services (HRW, 2012). What is particularly concerning is long-term prison sentences for an older population that is estimated to have a low recidivism rate compared to a younger population and the high financial costs associated with it (Maschi & Koskinen, 2015; Maschi, Leibowitz, Rees, & Pappacena, 2016). There are many social workers and advocacy organizations that question the costs of warehousing older people in prison when their risk of recidivism based on their health conditions or age-related desistance from crime is much lower compared to their younger counterparts (ACLU, 2012; HRW, 2012).

If we fail to reform our current punitive practices and policies, the economic and human costs of sustaining strict criminal justice policies, which are already astounding, will likely become even more dramatic. In the United States, federal and state governments spend a combined $77 billion annually to operate correctional facilities (ACLU, 2012). About 20% or $16 billion is spent on older adults in prison for health care (HRW, 2012). People aged 50 and older cost approximately three times more ($68,000) per year to incarcerate compared with younger persons ($34,000) (Kinsella, 2004).

The human and moral costs also are high with regard to stigmatizing and marginalizing the aging population, including those that are dying in prison. More than three decades of local and global media coverage have often shown haunting images of seriously ill and frail and elderly people in prison, including those chained to beds within hours of their death. These images compel us to reevaluate our decision-making practices concerning crime and punishment (Finlay, 1998; Ridgeway, 2012). The media have also shared the stories and images of peer specialists or "inmate" volunteers who provide compassionate end-of- life care (e.g., Barens, 2014). Their altruistic behavior stands in stark contrast to many community service providers, who deny services to this vulnerable population, often based on their criminal conviction histories. The economic and human costs challenge communities to revisit a universal commitment to basic human rights for older persons, prisoners, and disenfranchised populations (Maschi, Viola, et al., 2012). These individuals, who include those with mental and physical disabilities, represent a large percentage of the aging prison population (BJS, 2006; HRW, 2012; Maschi, Sutfin, & O'Connell, 2012). Determining ethically appropriate sentencing policies and intervention practices that foster compassion and care, as opposed to punishment and incapacitation, are important areas for public debate and deliberation (Anno et al., 2004; Maschi, Marmo, & Han, 2014). A formerly incarcerated 50-year-old African American man describes his personal reaction to witnessing a fellow inmate near the end of his life:

> When I had my last surgery in prison, um, there was a 93-year-old man, White guy, he was a nice guy. He was in there, I believe, for, um, assault. He's been in there for like 17 years or 18 years, but this guy is in a hospital. He cannot even hold his bowels, so I'm like what is a guy like this going to do? What is he going to do? He cannot, he can barely walk. He's been in a hospital, in a hospital or infirmary, for a year. What is he going to do? You'll see guys in there that just sit there staring into space.

This incarcerated elder brings up an interesting moral and legal question, and the reader is encouraged to explore this issue. Should we release a person of this age and health condition even if he or she has committed a serious offense, such as murder?

PROMISING AND EVIDENCE-BASED PRACTICE PRISON AND REINTEGRATION PRACTICES

Many of the program or advocacy interventions on the older population are currently in their early stages of development. At best, we might refer to these interventions as "promising practices" as opposed to evidence-based practices that have demonstrated consistent outcomes on improving health and reducing criminal behavior. Older adults' health and well-being can be affected during prison placement and community reintegration efforts by the lack of programming or with the use of promising practices, such as those that target multiple domains of well-being related to physical, mental, social/cultural, economic/housing, educational, and legal/political well-being. Although there has been a time lag in which the needs of specific programming based on age for this population, in the past 5–10 years, there has been a wellspring of international programs that have emerged.

Prisons

Older adults' health and well-being are generally compromised while serving prison sentences. Currently, older adults across the globe lack specific programming promoting their health and well-being while incarcerated. Older adults in prison often do not benefit from prison programming targeting younger prisoners' needs, such as reducing offending behavior through education, vocational, and employment programs (Davies, 2011; Mesurier, 2011). According to the 2000 US Bureau of Justice Statistics Survey of Correctional Facilities, only 4% ($n = 38$) of state correctional institutions provided any type of geriatric-specific health care services. One percent of state institutions offered services in geriatric care facilities, 2% had segregated geriatric units, and 1% had mixed (younger-older) unit models (Thivierge-Rikard & Thompson, 2007). Palliative care and information and counseling about end-of-life options are needed in prison, especially since many older adult prisoners are chronically ill and over 3,000 prisoners may die each year while in prison in the United States (Williams & Abradles, 2007).

Older adults have a more difficult psychological adjustment than younger persons to prison life and community reintegration. The reality of declining health often places older adults in a state of high alert to victimization and/or a fear of dying in prison. Social well-being is an important concern for older adults, who are also more than likely to have elderly spouses and other family members that make the prison experience (and reentry process) more problematic (Maschi, Viola, Morgen, & Koskinen, 2015). Some scholars document the trauma of incarceration of older adults or the "institutional thoughtlessness" of staff in the treatment of older prisoners (Crawley & Sparks, 2005; Maschi, Viola, & Koskinen, 2015). In prisons, older adults often are less of a problem for staff, which may lead to them being neglected or forgotten. Staff may not provide older adults with needs supports such as wheelchairs or assistance climbing stairs. Sometimes they assign volunteer prisoners responsibilities without providing them with the proper training, which does not meet proper standards of care (Mesurier, 2011).

Community Reintegration

Upon community reentry, the health and well-being of older ex-prisoners are compromised. Older adults are often more difficult to resettle in the community, especially when they have longer sentences that result in institutionalization or the inability to survive outside of prison (Davies, 2011). Resettlement success for older adults may be hindered by limited financial resources, health and/or mental health problems, lack of family and peer support, ongoing substance use, lack of available health care and substance abuse services, and a paucity of suitable housing options, shelter services, and transportation (Maschi & Koskinen, 2015). Some older adults are in need of Medicare and/or Medicaid, or in need of retirement assistance. Even assistance with everyday practical issues, such as getting or replacing eyeglasses or hearing aids, taking care of personal hygiene and clothing, is warranted. This process takes time, and if not started early enough in prison, older adults may enter the community without the proper services in place (Mesurier, 2011). For able-bodied older adults, employment is another factor to consider in order to foster successful community reintegration. In contrast, for older adults who have physical and/or mental disabilities, access to community-based or institutional long-term care is essential (Maschi et al., 2014).

An important consideration in the current global economic climate is the relationship between economic policy and social welfare policy. With scant resources and stagnant economic growth, economic opportunities are limited. Therefore, older adults exiting prison will have an increasingly more difficult time obtaining needed economic and employment opportunities. They are also at an increased risk of homelessness (Williams et al., 2010). Ageism or age-related stigma that intersects with other forms of stigma, such as the stigma of incarceration or being diagnosed with a mental illness, contributes to this challenge, especially when community service providers deny them access to services based on their personal characteristics or history.

Very few institutions offer essential geriatric-specific services. Some innovative programs focus on care issues such as dementia that foster older adults' health and well-being. Characteristics of these programs include one or more of the following characteristics: age and cognitive capacity, sensitive environmental modifications, interdisciplinary staff and volunteers, and services such as hospice care designed specifically for older adults. These promising practices are outlined next.

THE TRUE GRIT PROGRAM
Nevada's True Grit Program (Harrison, 2006) is a structured-living program that attempts to deal with the special needs and well-being of geriatric inmates. Started in 2004, the program is designed to empower elderly inmates to live as healthfully as possible. By means of activities designed to enhance both cognitive and physical life skills, True Grit attempts to ensure that geriatric inmates contribute to their own well-being while at the same time enhancing the overall sociocultural environment of the institution. Together with Nevada's Division of Aging Services, the program was designed to enhance physical health (by means of various recreational and physical therapy activities); mental health (using group and individual therapy and self-help modalities); and spiritual health (coordinated with the prison chaplain and volunteers).

THE UNIT FOR THE COGNITIVELY IMPAIRED
The Unit for the Cognitively Impaired (UCI) program in New York is known for its innovative design such as adequate lighting, including windows, access to an outdoor patio, and the use of animal-assisted therapy to help relax and manage mood among inmates with dementia (Maschi, Viola, & Sun, 2013).

ENHANCING THE HEALING ENVIRONMENT
Enhancing the Healing Environment (EHE) is a British- based program that is a collaborative professional–patient model. Nurse-led teams work collaboratively with patients to improve the environment in which they deliver care to foster well-being among older prisoners (Kings Fund, 2011).

HOSPICE/MENTAL HEALTH–PRISON COMPANION PROGRAMS
In the United States, upward of 20 prison-based hospice programs are being developed to help foster dignity and respect among dying prisoners. The Robert Wood Johnson's Grace Project (Guiding Responsible Action for Corrections

at the End-Of-Life) collaborates with corrections to enable individuals close to the end of their lives to die with dignity and respect. Social workers are key players in palliative and end-of -life care. The development of core competencies is supported by social work advocacy groups such as the Social Work Hospice and Palliative Care Network and the Collaborative for Palliative Care. Professions such as social work have an established knowledge base and skill competencies in palliative and end-of-life care that enable qualified and trained social workers to provide the types of end-of-life care skills appropriate for correctional and noncorrectional settings. Developing and improving access to hospice and palliative care after prison release and in the process of community reintegration are priorities. Other programs use prisoner "companions" to assist inmates with dementia.

California Men's Colony
The California Men's Colony in San Luis Obispo, California, a medium-security care facility, has a peer-support dementia unit (Davidson & Rowe, 2010) that consists of six volunteer inmates or social aides. These social aides need a record of 10 years of exemplary behavior and receive training in dementia caregiving. They often do 12 hour shifts, 7 days a week, and earn $50 a month. These program aides are able to make requests matched for specific care recipients or for respite. Their role is to act as "buddies" to fellow prisoners with dementia. The responsibilities of program aides include making sure prisoners receive medical care, providing social support, and protecting them, because prison is often a dangerous environment in which older adults with cognitive disorders are vulnerable to victimization.

Angola Prison Hospice
The Angola Prison Hospice in Louisiana is a state prison hospice program that has served over 200 prisoners since it started in 1997. It is one of a growing number of hospice programs for dying inmates. Prisoners volunteer for the program and are taught basic hospice practices and how to counsel and provide assistance with activities of daily living.

EVERGREEN 50+ ADVOCACY GROUP
The Evergreen 50+ group advocates for the improved conditions for older people in British prisons. It helps older adults rebuild family relationships in an attempt to reduce loneliness (Prison Reform Trust, 2008).

AGE CONCERN OLDER OFFENDERS PROJECT
The Age Concern Older Offenders Project (ACOOP), another English program, is a day program that addresses the social service and reentry needs of older adults. It has a two-pronged strategy to reduce recidivism and improve community support by using such strategies of advocacy, social support (befriending), and social and community support (ACOOP, 2010; Prison Reform Trust, 2008).

PROJECT FOR OLDER PRISONERS

The Project for Older Prisoners (POPS) is a prison-to-community advocacy program that began at Tulane Law School in Louisiana in 1987 and has since expanded to other states. The POPS program uses laws students to assist low-risk prisoners over the age of 55 obtain paroles, pardons, or alternative forms of incarceration. In a typical case, a student will prepare an extensive background report on a prisoner to determine the likelihood of recidivism. If the risk is low, the student will then locate housing and support for the prisoner and help prepare the case for a parole hearing. POPS also addresses the needs of victim families because offenders cannot be considered for release unless they agree to it. The program boasts no known cases of recidivism among those released under its auspices (Turley, 2007).

SENIOR EX-OFFENDER PROGRAM

The Senior Ex-Offender Program (SEOP) also addresses the health and well-being of older adults exiting prison. Based in San Francisco, the program is based in a senior center for adults aged 50 and older who are incarcerated or about to be released. It provides medical, financial, social, mental health, and employment services. SEOP addresses the problems many older adults face when they are released from prison, such as homelessness, drug addiction, alcoholism, AIDS, untreated diabetes, hypertension and cardiovascular disease, depression, and unemployment. Comprehensive wrap-around services target basic needs (clothing, hygiene products), pre- and postrelease counseling (mental health, substance abuse), case management, gender-based transitional support groups, and health literacy and counseling (Maschi et al., 2012).

HOCKING CORRECTIONAL FACILITY

Hocking Correctional Facility (HCF) is the largest of six Ohio correctional institutions specifically for older prisoners and has a population of 450 prisoners. HCF offers a one-stop shop of services for prisoners preparing for community reintegration, including information on Social Security access, job-seeking skills, housing placement services, employment training, property maintenance, general education and literature courses, and self-care and psychoeducational classes that address age-related issues, such as the physical, psychological, and social processes of aging. The facility also provides staff training with knowledge and skills to deal effectively with geriatric populations, including chronic illnesses and death and dying issues. Community reintegration is an active component of services so that older prisoners have the necessary resources, including an approved placement in nursing homes if older adults' functional capacities necessitate such placement (Ohio Department of Corrections, 2011).

RESETTLEMENT AND CARE FOR OLDER EX-OFFENDERS

Resettlement and Care for Older Ex-offenders (Recoop) promotes older adults' health and well-being through the provision of support services, advocacy, financial advice, employment assistance, and housing advice that will enable them to take control of their lives, remain free from offending, and prevent them from becoming socially excluded (Prison Reform Trust, 2008).

RESTORE 50 PLUS

The Restore 50 Plus, another English program, uses older ex-prisoners to provide peer mentoring and social support to older adults returning to the community from prison in coordination with corrections staff (i.e., offender managers). It is a community-focused, holistic program, as contrasted with an "offender responsibility" model, which is better for older adults reentering the community who are more in need of age-related community supports (Prison Reform Trust, 2008).

REINTEGRATION EFFORT FOR LONG-TERM INFIRM AND ELDERLY FEDERAL OFFENDERS' PROGRAM

The Reintegration Effort for Long-Term Infirm and Elderly Federal Offenders' (RELIEF) program was established in Canada in 1999 to facilitate the transition of elderly and infirm prisoners into the community. Former prisoners in the program are screened and provided hospice care training. The program uses former prisoners and caregivers in an attempt to provide compassionate peer support to fellow ex-prisoners who are dying (Maschi et al., 2012).

CRIMINAL JUSTICE POLICY ISSUES AND POPULATION TRENDS

The Aftermath of Strict Sentencing Policies

Four major reasons have contributed to the global rise in aging prison populations: increases in the aging population coupled with the long-term aftermath of stricter sentencing policies from the 1980s (Gaydon & Miller, 2007). In the United States, for example, the number of aging prisoners is expected to continue to increase to 20% between 2010 and 2030. In addition, conservative criminal justice policies that began in the 1980s resulted in stricter public and legislative policies, such as restrictive drug and habitual offenders' laws (Aday, 2003, 2005). These laws included Truth in Sentencing Laws, Habitual Offender and Three Strikes You're Out Laws, and stricter drugs laws, such as the Rockefeller Drug Laws of New York. Overall, this conservative shift resulted in adjudicated offenders receiving longer mandatory minimum prison sentences, including an increase in the number of life sentences without parole. Additionally, official statistics also find that there is a growing group of older people who are incarcerated aged 50 and older that contribute to the rise in the aging prison population (Carson & Sabol, 2016). Currently, the global prison system is not prepared to address the growing numbers of the incarcerated aging in prison, especially those aged 65 and older, which increases the likelihood that costs for specialized long-term care or palliative and end-of-life care will continue to strain budgets and resources (Maschi, Marmo, & Han, 2014).

Parolee Reform: Compassionate and Geriatric
Release and Clemency

At the state and local levels, parole reform for aging people has become increasingly an issue of public concern. Two areas that have gained considerable attention are clemency and compassionate and geriatric release laws (DOJ, 2015). Clemency is a policy issue that has gained increased attention during the Obama Administration and often affected legal protections of older adults in prison (Shear, 2016). Clemency generally refers to an act of mercy in which a public official has the power, such as a governor or president, to reduce the harshness of punishment or sentencing of prisoners (Shear, 2017). For example, a *New York Times* article documents Obama's "merciful" record at the federal level, in which he granted 78 pardons and 153 commutations to incarcerated people who largely received long-term sentences for drug convictions during the 1980s "tough on crime" era.

Compassionate and geriatric release laws also have gained increased attention by scholars, policymakers, and the general public. For example, a study by Maschi, Leibowitz, Rees, and Pappacena (2016) analyzed the compassionate and geriatric release laws in the United States using content analysis methods. In a search of the LexisNexis legal database using the keyword search terms "compassionate release," "medical parole," "geriatric prison release," "elderly (or seriously ill)," and "prison," 47 identified federal and state laws using inductive and deductive analysis strategies. Of the possible 52 federal and state corrections systems (50 states, Washington D.C, and Federal Corrections), 47 laws for incarcerated people, or their families, to petition for early release based on advanced age or health were found. Six major categories of these laws were identified: (1) physical/mental health, (2) age, (3) pathway to release decision, (4) postrelease support, (5) nature of the crime (personal and criminal justice history), and (6) stage of review. The federal government also has called for the reform of compassionate and geriatric release laws, given that many incarcerated people have not been released based on their current provisions (Maschi et al., 2016).

Most relevant for this chapter, a human rights approach was applied to assess the laws, policies, and practices to the extent that provisions of existing compassionate and geriatric release laws meet basis human rights principles (Maschi et al., 2016). The principles of the human rights framework are as follows: dignity and worth of the person, the five domains of human rights (i.e., political, civil, social, economic, and cultural), participation, nondiscrimination, and transparency and accountability (UN, 1948).

The Compassionate and Geriatric Release Checklist (CGR-C; Maschi et al. 2015) was created for social workers and allied professionals, policymakers, advocates, and other key stakeholders to use as an assessment tool to develop or amend existing compassionate or geriatric release laws (see Table 5.1). This tool also can be used by social workers to prepare expert testimony for local, state, or federal hearings or as an educational or professional training exercise. Applying a human rights framework, the checklist consists of seven assessment

Table 5.1. Compassionate and Geriatric Release Checklist: Human Rights Principles Assessment for Compassionate and Geriatric Release Laws Regarding Physical and Mental Health, Age, Pathway to Release Decision, Postrelease Plan, Personal and Criminal History, and Style of Review

Assessor/s' Name: **Date:**

Federal/State/Institutional Law/Policy:

Yes	No	Does the law address any of the following minimum standards of existing laws? (Check yes or no)	Notes (Developing or improving practice/policy response)
		Dignity and Respect of the Person	
		Humane treatment of prisoners, esp. for advanced aged and infirmity	
		Postrelease plan vetted for safety and appropriateness	
		Placement are available in prison special medical units (e.g., hospice) prior to release	
		Holistic care models—prison and post release	
		Interprofessional pre- and postrelease care plans	
		Interprofessional pre- and postrelease service linkages set in place	
		Vetting postcare placement for safety and appropriate health care services	
		Promote Political, Civil, Economic, Social, and Cultural Rights	
		Legal language that refers to "cruel or inhumane" if release denied	
		No life limit for release based on health status (expected life expectancy)	
		Benefits (Medicaid/SSI/public assistance) available prior to release	
		Family and community involvement in pre- and postrelease process	
		Assigned surrogate/advocate when no family are identified that can provide care	
		Request made by incarcerated person or someone (e.g., family, lawyer) on their behalf	

(continued)

Table 5.1. CONTINUED

		Emotional and reintegration support for released person and caregiver/s
		If a person cannot represent oneself, a surrogate (e.g., lawyer) can take their place
		Home care supervision plans provided
		If released and recover, does not have to return to prison
		Nondiscrimination
		No constraint on sentence length to request release
		Released if determined there is a low public safety risk
		Age classified as aged 50 or above
		Does not discriminate based on chronological age (without infirmity)
		Does not discriminate based on sex offense history
		Does not discriminate based on murder, first- or second-degree history
		Does not discriminate based on felony (class A, B, C) history
		Does not discriminate based on length of time served (e.g., minimum sentence served)
		Participation
		Age (older people—aged 50 and above)
		Persons with disabilities (physical and/or mental)
		Persons with terminal illness (e.g., cancer, dementia)
		Correctional leaders (e.g., warden, commissioner, or medical director)
		Parole board or the courts
		Family members or surrogates
		Legal advocates/petitioners (including family and legal counsel)
		Crime survivors (victim involvement)

		Criteria
		Physician involvement
		Other professionals' involvement: psychiatrist, psychologist, social worker, lawyer
		Transparency
		Decisions based on evidence (e.g., assessment of risk, health status, other)
		Laws with clear definition of key terms (e.g., level of risk)
		Clear pathways for release determination
		Laws with specific, measurable, specific, and time-limited procedures for release
		% of parole/judicial petitions responded to in a timely fashion
		% of parole/judicial requests honored
		Accountability
		Time limits for each stage of review process
		Discharge planning evaluation
		Staff filing of release paperwork and follow-up
		Care coordination plan in place
		Community service providers that deny placement are held accountable
		Special Populations Reached
		Older persons (elderly)
		Persons with disabilities (physical and/or mental health status, developmental disabilities)
		Persons with terminal illnesses
		Persons with long-term or life sentences
		Other:

categories for compassionate and geriatric release laws: dignity and respect of the person; promotes political, civil, economic, social, and cultural rights; nondiscrimination; participation; transparency; accountability; and special populations served.

In the CGR checklist, assessment category 1 consists of items that address the principle of dignity and respect of the person. It includes such items as the legal references to the humane treatment of vulnerable populations in prison. Assessment category 2 addresses the promotion of political, civil, economic, social, and cultural rights. It includes such items as the use of legal language that refers to cruel or inhumane if, when released from prison, access to benefits post release is denied. Assessment category 3 refers to nondiscrimination. It includes items such as a law does not discriminate based on age, criminal justice history, or other background factors. Assessment category 4, participation, includes such items as the involvement of the incarcerated individual and family members, victims and/or their family members, and professionals. Assessment category 5, transparency, includes such items as that parole or judicial decisions are based on sound evidence, including reliable risk assessment. Assessment category 6 refers to accountability and includes items such that the law specifies time limits for each stage of the review. Assessment category 7 addresses special populations issues and includes United Nations special needs categories (UNODC, 2009) such as older persons, persons with disabilities, persons with terminal illnesses, and persons with serious and/or long-term prison sentences.

A human rights–based analysis using this checklist suggests that most of the provisions of each US compassionate and geriatric release often fall short of meeting the basic human rights principles that speak to the dignity and worth of the incarcerated person, family and victim rights and supports, and accountability and transparency on the part of the judicial and correctional systems to grant release. Additionally, the majority of the US compassionate and geriatric release laws fell short of inconclusive nondiscrimination provisions. This is especially true when assessing the level of risk of incarcerated people with histories of sex or violent offenses. Based on available research, this type of provision is overly restrictive. For example, in a study investigating whether risk factors for recidivism remained stable across age groups (N = 1,303), the findings showed that rates decreased in older age groups (ages 55 and older; Fazel, Sjostedt, Langstrom, & Grann, 2006). These findings are consistent with recidivism rates in studies with international samples of older sexual offenders, including research conducted in the United Kingdom, the United States, and Canada. Given these findings about older age and the reduced risk for recidivism, it is important to underscore that incarcerated individuals with violent offense histories (despite their failing health status) who are elderly in US federal and state prisons are often nevertheless excluded from compassionate or geriatric release provisions (HRW, 2012).

TRENDS AND FUTURE DIRECTIONS

Perhaps the most salient future trends and directions for the aging prison population are to further the evidence-based response to this population in regard to prison and reintegration programming, especially for the most vulnerable elders who are sick and dying in prisons. Another important and overlooked area is prevention efforts that seek to reduce the link between trauma and oppression and later life health and well-being and recidivism. A third trend and future direction is the development and evaluation of community-level, age-sensitive restorative justice practices that address the victim offender overlap, including specialized risk assessment and intervention with sex offenders. We highlight these future trends and directions next.

Intervention: Improving Prison and Community Reintegration Services

Over the past decade, there has been a growing movement to recognize and address the needs and rights of an aging prison population, including the US federal government. Many of the research, practice, and policy recommendations noted in the US Department of Justice, Office of the Inspector General's report (2015) can guide future trends and direction in responding to this crisis. Social workers can play a leading role in assisting in their implementation. These recommendations are as follows:

1. Consider the *feasibility* of placing *additional social workers* in more institutions, particularly those with larger populations of aging inmates.
2. *Provide all staff with training* to identify signs of aging and assist in communicating with aging inmates.
3. *Reexamine the accessibility and the physical infrastructure* of all institutions to accommodate the large number of aging inmates with mobility needs.
4. Study the *feasibility of creating units, institutions, or other structures* specifically for aging inmates in those institutions with high concentrations of aging inmates.
5. *Systematically* identify *programming needs* of aging inmates and develop programs and activities to meet those needs.
6. *Develop* sections in release *preparation courses* that address the postincarceration medical care and retirement needs of aging inmates.
7. Consider *revising the compassionate release policy* to facilitate the release of appropriate aging inmates, including lowering the age requirement and eliminating the minimum 10 years served requirement. (Office of Inspector General, United States Department of Justice, 2015, pp. 3–4)

These recommendations, if implemented and monitored for their effectiveness, certainly should improve conditions for the aging and seriously ill prison population.

Prevention: Interrupting the Cycle Between Trauma, Oppression, and Recidivism

In our most recent study (Maschi, Leibowitz, & Morgen, in press), we explored the role of cumulative trauma, stress, and minority oppression on recidivism among 344 older adults. It used a cross-sectional correlational design with 334 adult males aged 50 and older in a Northeastern correctional system. Logistic regression analyses were used to explore the relationship between cumulative trauma, minority status, coping, and offense histories. The analyses revealed that cumulative trauma, minority status, and drug and violent offense histories increased the likelihood for participants to report a history of recidivism. In contrast, physical coping also was found to decrease the likelihood of self-reported recidivism.

These findings build upon the sparse previous literature that examined trauma and racial/ethnic minority status and recidivism regardless of the type of prior offense. It also examined trauma history and race/ethnicity through the lens of cumulative inequality theory. As evidenced in bias in official statistics, racial ethnic minorities are disproportionately sentenced to the criminal justice system and this pattern may continue with a higher risk of receiving more harsh sentences, such as serious or violent offenses or being violated on parole regardless of their age (Sentencing Project, 2013). Those individuals regardless of race who reported higher levels of coping capacities, in particular physical coping resources, were less likely to report a history of recidivism. Consistent with cumulative inequality theory, individuals who reported higher levels of adaptive coping were less likely to report more than one imprisonment (Maschi, Viola, Morgen, & Koskinen, 2015). These findings suggest that when experiences of stigma and oppression are unavoidable, we can assist aging people with coping with these experiences.

As for the link between trauma, discrimination, and recidivism, prior research has shown that age is an important factor influencing who will return to prison and who will not. That is, adults aged 55 and older are less likely to recidivate than their younger counterparts (0%–2% and 43%, respectively). Official statistics consistently show that the public safety risk for crimes committed by released inmates is much lower for those 55 and older compared to their younger counterparts (Jhi & Joo, 2009; Lansing, 2012). In accord with the positive association between age and desistance from crime, adults aged 55 and older pose a low risk to public safety.

Our current findings suggest that undetected and untreated trauma and discrimination experiences based on race and ethnicity may be a potential driver as to why a low-risk older group may engage in behaviors that put them at risk of recidivating (Leach, Burgess, & Holmwood, 2009). For example, Leach and colleagues (2009) put forth an explanatory model as to how trauma, especially traumatic grief, may be linked to recidivism. Earlier life trauma and unresolved loss place individuals at a heightened risk of criminal activity and incarceration. Incarceration itself is often perceived as a type of trauma or stressor for incarcerated people, including older adults who served a long-term prison sentence. Incarcerated people may experience trauma, such as being a victim of physical or sexual assault and disenfranchised grief because they were separated from a loved one when they passed away or because of the loss of freedom or their health while incarcerated. It is highly likely that traditional offender rehabilitation, which most often focuses on accountability of one's crime, is ineffective in addressing their histories of both victimization and offending behaviors. If they are released from prison and the supports are not in place or they suffer from postincarceration PTSD-like symptoms commonly described by older adults released from prison, this puts them at a heightened risk for recidivism (Gorsky, 2006; Maschi et al., 2015). Additionally, as noted earlier, a minority elder released from prison may continue to experience the aggravated disadvantages and racial discrimination while in prison and post release (Maschi & Aday, 2014).

These findings also have important implications for understanding the possible underlying root causes of recidivism, such as structural and historical trauma, stress, and oppression (Maschi et al., 2013). Given that older adults are known for having low recidivism rates, these findings may have unearthed important risk factors among those older people that influenced recidivism prior to their most recent incarceration.

Community Level: Age Sensitive Restorative Justice Practices

Future prevention and intervention efforts might be most helpful if they addressed both the "victim and offender overlap," such as the use of trauma-informed care and restorative justice practices. The criminal justice system would benefit from adopting practice innovations that infuse trauma and oppression-informed care and restorative justice principles and practices that acknowledge the influence of trauma on offending behavior. Both trauma and restorative informed practices enable the telling of one's personal story as victim and/or as an offender. Addressing trauma, including historical trauma, has the potential to reduced recidivism and increase the quality of life for this stigmatized group.

Zehr and Gohar (2003) conceptualized restorative justice as a compass that invites community dialogue regarding a continuum of offenses, including the most severe, and he emphasizes that the Western legal system may exacerbate conflicts rather than fostering healing or peace. At the heart of restorative justice frameworks, also known as transformational justice, are three principles advanced: restoration, accountability, and engagement. The practice of restorative conferencing between victim, offender,and community is an alternative to offender-centered sanctions and punishment by attempting to balance the needs of all the stakeholders (victim, offender, community), which leads to restorative agreements, while encouraging accountability for offending behavior and promoting victim healing from traumatic stress. Types of restorations include damaged relationships, physical and mental health, and international peacemaking. To respond effectively to crime, victims, offenders, families, and community stakeholders are engaged to identify and repair the harm (Maschi, Leibowitz, & Mizus, 2014).

In our prior research, many elders experienced prior harm or wrongdoing by others that more than likely went unaddressed and untreated, and therefore was left unhealed (e.g., Maschi et al., 2015). Restorative justice practice also supports elders in being accountable, making apologies and restitution, and making amends to their families and communities. Restorative justice practices address both victim and offender issues in the context of family and community and can occur before, during, or after prison. Restorative justice practices that have relevance to older adults with histories of drug or violent offense histories may occur in prison and/or in the community before or after an individual's incarceration. Examples of specific restorative justice practices include the talking piece, circles of support, and community reparative boards. A structured method of equal dialogue among stakeholders uses a talking piece (e.g., a rock or feather) to facilitate speaking time; this is designed to illicit the victim's story and foster self-governance and community safety. Examples of Circles include Circles of Support and Accountability (COSA), enacted in many communities in the United States and Canada in high-risk violent sex offender cases, as a community reintegration model in line with the UN Standards for the Treatment of Prisoners. It involves offender accountability and community safety protocols, with the acknowledgment that traditional public safety measures and notification policies have been inadequate, and that accountability combined with support with community integration can prevent recidivism.

Reentry and transition planning circles for incarcerated individuals are a type of circle model designed to provide a space for offenders to express remorse and understand the impact of their crime, using solution-focused interventions (Maschi et al., 2014). Community reparative boards in states, such as Vermont, were shaped by restorative justice principles. They include community capacity-building and decision-making processes that involve recruiting and training board members who make recommendations regarding offender compliance with the probation, parole, or diversion contract, incorporating victim input (violations can result in renegotiation or a return to court). The goals include repairing the harm to victim and offender reintegration in the community, and boards can refer to victim–offender mediation. Other core practices and models include written or verbal apologies to victims; victim–offender dialogues; United Nations Truth Commissions (on human rights violations); financial restitution to victims; and community justice boards (Maschi et al., 2014).

Violence and Sex Offender Assessment and Intervention

Research suggests that the risk of recidivism is lower among older people compared to younger people, including those with sex and violent offense histories (e.g., Levenson & Shields, 2012). In 2014 in Vermont, about 63% of the male population and 40% of the female population are serving time for violent offenses (VT DOC, 2015).

Individuals aged 50 and older who committed a sexual offense (12%) are 50% less likely to recidivate than individuals who are younger (26%) and committed other types of offenses at release (35%; Levenson & Shields, 2012). Individuals who committed a violent offense generally commit one crime and do not repeat a pattern of violence. Moreover, after 5 years in the community offense-free, risk declines by half, and after 10 years by half again. Increased age is a protective factor against future offending, regardless of age at which the offense occurred, age at sentencing, or age at release from incarceration (Maschi, Viola, & Sun, 2013). Additionally, data from older offenders (N = 3,425) showed lower Static-99 scores than younger offenders, and the implications of this research is that evaluators using Static-99 (a commonly used risk sex offense risk assessment instrument) should consider advanced age in their overall estimate of risk (Hanson, Morton, & Harris, 2006). In a recent study assessing differences in trauma and coping among sex offenders, nonrecidivists were significantly older and had a greater capacity for social and physical coping, underscoring the importance of understanding the intersection of trauma, mental health, and increased risk for recidivism among older sex offenders (Leibowitz and Maschi, in press).

Circles of Support and Accountability (COSA) is an example of a tested and research-based community reintegration program designed for high-risk sex offenders based on principles of restorative justice aimed at increasing public safety and decreasing recidivism, while involving victims, offenders, and the community (e.g., Wilson, McWhinnie, & Wilson, 2008). Policy and legislative responses to sex offenders in reentry have historically involved strict registration, residency restrictions, and community notification laws, which can have iatrogenic consequences (Levenson, Grady, & Leibowitz, 2016), and along with intense media coverage can make successful reentry very challenging.

CASE EXAMPLES

As illustrated in the case vignettes (Box 5.1), older adults in prison are a diverse group. However, what they do have in common is that many of them experienced life challenges before, during, and after prison, and they have shared experiences involving stigma. We encourage the reader to evaluate and compare the life experiences illustrated in the vignettes.

SUMMARY AND CONCLUSION

This chapter reviewed the intersectional issues of health, mental health, legal, economic and social care needs, and rights of justice-involved older adults. We provide an overview and scope of the problem, promising and best practices, and policy and population trend issues that perpetuate or reduce stigmatization, neglect, and mistreatment of this population, and trends and future issues. The biggest challenges for professionals and prisons to best serve this population is to develop competencies to work effectively at the intersection of aging, health/ mental health, and the criminal justice system. Effectively addressing stigma and

BOX 5.1

Case Vignettes

Jesus: Jesus is a 56-year-old Puerto Rican male and the youngest of nine children. He has a history of the unexpected death of his father at age 5, sexual victimization, poverty, prostitution, drug dealing, substance abuse (heroin addiction), and recidivism (incarcerated two times). At age 17, he reported committing armed robbery to support his heroin addiction and was sentenced to 20 years in prison. During his prison term, he continued to use drugs. He violated parole within 15 months of release and, as a result, is now serving his second and current 45-year sentence. In prison, he has spent 8 of the past 15 years in solitary confinement. He perceives prison as "an overcrowded monster" designed to hold, degrade, and punish people. He views the staff as disinterested and disengaged and is despondent over the limited access to counseling and education rehabilitative services. Jorge developed a chronic lung condition while in prison and is projected to receive parole in 14 years when he is in his late seventies. He has not had any family visits in over 5 years.

Jane: Jane is a 54-year-old, Caucasian, Catholic woman who is incarcerated in a women's facility in a Northeastern state correctional facility. As a child, she experienced the divorce of her parents, abandonment by her mother, and physical and verbal abuse by her father, whom she described as having serious mental health problems. At age 25, Jane married a man 10 years younger, had two children, and divorced. This is her first criminal conviction, and she is serving a 10-year prison sentence (85% minimum) for conspiracy and the attempted murder of her husband. Jane describes this sentence as unfair and unjust based on mitigating circumstances. She has a medical history of hypertension and vision impairment. At age 54, Jane's extensive dental problems have resulted in a premature need for dentures. She describes her current prison experience as "degrading, especially the way correctional officers treat inmates." Jane copes with her prison experience by "finding meaning" in it through spirituality. Her projected parole date is in 5 years, when she will be 59 years old. Due to the long distance, she corresponds monthly by mail with her two children and every 3 months by phone but has not had any in-person visits since her incarceration.

Earl: Earl is a 57-year-old, bisexual, African American male with a history of homelessness and mental illness (schizoid-affective disorder). He describes his situation as unique since he committed a crime to get into prison. In 2007, he reports having had a nervous breakdown because he "lost everything," including his job and apartment. In 2009, in a drunken rage, he "broke the law" and spent 1 year in a county jail. After his release, he reports being unable to obtain basic needs, such as food, water, clothing, housing, and health care. He was reluctant to seek assistance from family and friends, social services, or church due to shame and embarrassment. He subsequently committed a crime (grand larceny) for the purpose of returning to prison, where his basic needs would be met. Earl reports improved coping capacity due to access to psychotropic medication and mental health treatment; however, in the past year he was diagnosed with diabetes. Earl is expecting to be released from prison in 2026 when he will be 70 years old. He has not been in communication with his family.

Ryan: Ryan is a 60-year-old Caucasian male of Irish and Polish descent; his family has an intergenerational history of alcoholism. Ryan is a Vietnam War veteran. As a child, he experienced "extreme" corporal punishment from his parents that left him generally fearful of communicating with them. Ryan was sexually molested for years by his Little League manager. At age 13, he made a conscious decision to "get tough" to protect himself; at 18 he joined the Marine Corp. After his release, Ryan witnessed a man in a bar offering cocaine to several young girls whom he believed would be sexually molested. In a blinding rage, he took the man outside the bar with another peer and murdered the man. In prison, Ryan spent time in solitary confinement. During these periods of isolation he describes engaging in self-reflection. Ryan is serving a life sentence in prison. He has not been in communication with his family while in prison.

---

oppression based on social identities, such as age, race, trauma and incarceration histories, and offense type is an integral aspect to prevent or effectively intervene with this population at the programming and policy level.

WEB-BASED RESOURCES

American Civil Liberties Union, Mass Incarceration of the Elderly Report: https://www.aclu.org/files/assets/elderlyprisonreport_20120613_1.pdf

Bureau of Justice Statistics, Aging of the Prison Population: https://www.bjs.gov/index.cfm?ty=pbdetail&iid=5602

Department of Justice Report on Federal Aging Prison Population: https://oig.justice.gov/reports/2015/e1505.pdf

Human Rights Watch, Old Behind Bars: https://www.hrw.org/sites/default/files/reports/usprisons0112webwcover_0.pdf

Penal Reform International, Global Prison Trends: https://www.penalreform.org/wp-content/uploads/2015/04/PRI-Prisons-global-trends-report-LR.pdf

REFERENCES

Aday, R. H. (2003). *Aging prisoners: Crisis in American corrections.* Westport, CT: Praeger.
Aday, R. H. (2005). Aging prisoners' concerns toward dying in prison. *OMEGA-Journal of Death and Dying, 52*(3), 199–216.
Adler, N. E., & Rehkopf, D. H. (2008). U.S. disparities in health: Descriptions, causes, and mechanisms. *Annual Review of Public Health, 29,* 235–252. doi: 10.1146/annurev.publhealth.29.020907.090852
Age Concern Older Offenders Project (ACOOP). (2010). Age Concern Older Offenders Project (ACOOP). Retrieved from http://www.acoop.org.uk/pages/home/index.php

American Civil Liberties Union. (2012). The mass incarceration of the elderly. Retrieved from http://www.American Civil Liberties Union.org/files/assets/elderlyprisonreport_20120613_1.pdf

Anno, B., Graham, C., Lawrence, J. E., Shansky, R., Bisbee, J., & Blackmore, J. (2004). Correctional health care: Addressing the needs of elderly, chronically ill, and terminally ill inmates. Retrieved from http://nicic.gov/library/018735

Barens, E. (2014). Prison terminal: The last days of Private Jack Hall. Retrieved from http://www.prisonterminal.com/index.html

Bureau of Justice Statistics (BJS). (2014). Probation and parole in the United States, 2013. Retrieved from http://www.bjs.gov/index.cfm?ty_pbdetail&iid_5135

Carson, E. A., & Sabol, W. J. (2016). *Aging of the state prison populations, 1993-2013.* NCJ 248766. Washington, DC: Bureau of Justice Statistics.

Carstairs, B., & Keon, D. (2009), *Canada's aging population: Seizing the opportunity report.* Ontario: Canada: Special Senate Committee on Aging. Retrieved from http://www.parl.gc.ca/Content/SEN/Committee/402/agei/rep/AgingFinalReport-e.pdf

Davidson, L., & Rowe, M. (2010). Peer support within criminal justice settings: The role of forensic peer specialists. Retrieved from http://gainscenter.samhsa.gov/pdfs/integrating/Davidson_Rowe_Peersupport.pdf

Davies, M. (2011). The integration of elderly prisoners: An exploration of services provided in England and Wales. *International Journal of Criminology.* Retrieved from http://www.internetjournalofcriminology.com/Davies_The_Reintegration_of_Elderly_Prisoners.pdf

Department of Justice Office of the Inspector General, United States Department of Justice. (2015). *The impact of an aging inmate population on the Federal Bureau of Prisons.* Washington, DC: Author.

Fazel, S., Sjostedt, G., Langstrom, N., & Grann, M. (2006). Risk factors for criminal recidivism in older sexual offenders. *Sexual Abuse: A Journal of Research and Treatment, 18*(2), 159-67.

Finlay, I. G. (1998). Managing terminally ill prisoners: Reflection and action. *Palliative Medicine, 12,* 457-461. http://dx.doi.org/10.1191/026921698674823377

Gaydon, L., & Miller, M. (2007). Elders in the justice system: How the system treats elders in trials, during imprisonment, and on death row. *Behavioral Sciences & the Law, 25,* 677-699. doi: 10.1002/bsl.781

Gorsky, T. (2006). Post incarceration syndrome and relapse. Retrieved from http://www.tgorski.com/criminal_justice/cjs_pics_&_relapse.htm

Grant, A. (1999). *Elderly inmates: Issues for Australia.* Canberra ACT 2601, Australia. Retrieved from http://www.aic.gov.au/documents/7/0/B/%7B70B4E5D4-3F91-416B-8670-0E3E4A1FF2AC%7Dti115.pdf

Groman, R., & Ginsburg J. (2004). Racial and ethnic disparities in health care: A position paper of the American College of Physicians. *Annals of Internal Medicine, 141*(3), 226-232.

Guerino, P., Harrison, P., & Sabol, W. (2011). *Prisoners in 2010.* Washington, DC: US Department of Justice, Bureau of Justice Statistics. Retrieved from http://bjs.ojp.usdoj.gov/content/pub/pdf/p10.pdf

Hale, L., & Swiggum, C. (2011, March). Older prisoners pose new challenges for Canada's prisons. *UBC Journalism News Service.* Retrieved from http://thethunderbird.ca/2011/03/31/older-prisoners-pose-new-challenges-for-canadas-correctional-service/

Hanson, K., Morton, K. E., & Harris, A. J. R. (2006). Sexual offender recidivism risk. *Annals of the New York Academy of Sciences, 989*, 154–166. doi:10.1111/j.1749-6632.2003.tb07303.x

Harrison, M. T. (2006). True Grit: An innovative program for elderly inmates. *Corrections Today, 1*, 46–49. Retrieved from http://www.aca.org/fileupload/177/prasannak/Stewart_dec06.pdf

Human Rights Watch. (2012). Old behind bars: The aging prison population in the United States. Retrieved from http://www.Human Rights Watch.org/reports/2012/01/27/old-behind-bars

James, D. J.,& Glaze, L. E. (2006). *Mental health problems of prison and jail inmates.* NCJ Publication No. 213600. Rockville, MD: US Department of Justice.

Jhi, K. Y., & Joo, H. J. (2009). Predictors of recidivism among major age groups of parolees in Texas. *Justice Policy Journal, 6*, 1–28.

Kings Fund. (2011). Improving the patient experience: Environment for care at end of life. Retrieved from http://www.kingsfund.org.uk/document.rm?id=9252

Kinsella, C. (2004). Correctional health care costs. Retrieved from http://www.csg.org/knowledgecenter/docs/TA0401CorrHealth.pdf.

Lansing, S. (2012). *New York State COMPAS-probation risk and need assessment study: Examining the recidivism scale's effectiveness and predictive accuracy.* Retrieved from http://www.criminaljustice.ny.gov/crimnet/ojsa/opca/compas_probation_report_2012.pdf http://www.criminaljustice.ny.gov/crimnet/ojsa/opca/compas_probation_report_2012.pdf

Leach, R.M., Burgess, T., & Holmwood, C. (2009). Could recidivism in prisoners be linked to traumatic grief? A review of the evidence. *International Journal of Prisoner Health, 4*, 104–119.

Leibowitz, G. S., & Maschi, T. M. (in press). Cumulative trauma, resilience, and the risk for recidivism among sex offenders in prison.

Levenson, J., Grady, M., & Leibowitz, G. S. (2016). Grand challenges: Social justice and the need for evidence-based sex offender registry reform. *Journal of Sociology and Social Welfare, 43*(2), 3–38.

Levenson,J.S.,&Shields,R.T.(2012).SexoffenderriskandrecidivisminFlorida.Retrieved from http://www.floridaatsa.com/Levenson&Shields_FloridaRiskRecidivism2012.pdf

Maschi, T., & Aday, R. (2014). The social determinants of health and justice and the aging in prison crisis: A call to action. *International Journal of Social Work, 1*(1), 1–15.

Maschi, T., & Koskinen, L. (2015). Co-constructing community: A conceptual map for reuniting aging people in prison with their families and communities. *Traumatology*, doi:10.1037/trm0000026.

Maschi, T., Leibowitz, G. S., & Mizus, L. (2014). Restorative justice. In L. Cousins (Ed.). *Encyclopedia of human services & diversity*, Vol. 3 (pp. 1142–1144). Thousand Oaks, CA: Sage.

Maschi, T., Leibowitz, G., & Morgen, K. (2018). Exploring the link between trauma and recidivism among incarcerated elders: Does race and offense history matter? Presentation at the Society for Social Work Research Conference, Washington, DC.

Maschi, T., Marmo, S., & Han, J. (2014). Palliative and end-of-life care in prisons: A content analysis of the literature. *International Journal of Prisoner Health, 10*, 172–197. http://dx.doi.org/10.1108/IJPH-05-2013-0024.

Maschi, T., Morgen, K., Westcott, K., Viola, D., & Koskinen, L. (2014). Aging, incarceration, and employment prospects: Recommendations for practice and policy reform. *Journal of Applied Rehabilitation Counseling, 45*(4), 44–55.

Maschi, T., Sutfin, S., & O'Connell, B. (2012). Aging, mental health, and the criminal justice system: A content analysis of the literature. *Journal of Forensic Social Work, 2,* 162–185. http://dx.doi.org/10.1080/1936928X.2012.750254

Maschi, T., Viola, D., Harrison, M., Harrison, W., Koskinen, L., & Bellusa, S. (2014). Bridging community and prison for older adults and their families: Invoking human rights and intergenerational family justice. *International Journal of Prisoner Health, 19,* 1–19.

Maschi, T., Viola, D., & Koskinen, L. (2015). Trauma, stress, and coping among older adults in prison: Towards a human rights and intergenerational family justice action agenda. *Traumatology.* http://dx.doi.org/10.1037/trm0000021

Maschi, T., Viola, D., & Morgen, K. (2013). Trauma and coping among older adults in prison: Linking empirical evidence to practice. *Gerontologist.* doi:10.1093/geront/gnt069.

Maschi, T., Viola, D., Morgen, K., & Koskinen, L. (2015). Trauma, stress, grief, loss, and separation among older adults in prison: The protective role of coping resources on physical and mental well-being. *Journal of Crime and Justice, 38*(1), 113–136.

Maschi, T., Viola, D., & Sun, F. (2013). The high cost of the international aging prisoner crisis: Well-being as the common denominator for action. *The Gerontologist, 53*(4), 543–554.

Mesurier, R. (2011). Supporting older people in prison: Ideas for practice. United Kingdom: X. London: Age UK. Retrieved from http://www.ageuk.org.uk/documents/en-gb/for-professionals/government-and-society/older%20prisoners%20guide_pro.pdf?dtrk=true

Ministry of Justice. (2010). *Offender management caseload statistics 2009.* London, UK: Author. Retrieved from http://www.justice.gov.uk/publications/statistics-and-data/prisons-and-probation/omcs-annual.htm

Office of the Inspector General, United States Department of Justice. (2015). *The impact of an aging inmate population on the Federal Bureau of Prisons.* Washington, DC: Author.

Ohio Department of Corrections. (2011). Hocking Correctional Facility. Retrieved from http://www.drc.ohio.gov/Public/hcf.htm

Organization for Economic Co-operation and Development (OECD). (2010). *Factbook.* Retrieved from http://www.oecdlibrary.org/economics/oecd-factbook-2010_factbook-2010-en

Prison Reform Trust. (2008). *Doing time: The experiences and needs of older people in prison.* London, UK: Prison Reform Trust.

Ridgeway, J. (2012). The other death sentence. *Mother Jones.* Retrieved from www.motherjones.com.

Sapers, H. (2008, February 4). Speaking notes for Mr. Howard Sapers, Correctional Investigator of Canada from the Office of the Correctional Investigator. Retrieved from http://www.oci-bec.gc.ca/comm/sp-all/sp-all20080204-eng.aspx

Sentencing Project. (2013). Racial disparity. Retrieved from http://www.sentencingproject.org/template/page.cfm?id=122.

Shear, M. (2016, December 19). Obama's 78 pardons and 153 commutations extend record of mercy. Retrieved from http://www.nytimes.com/2016/12/19/us/politics/obama-commutations-pardons-clemency.html?_r=0

Thivierge, R.V., & Thompson, M. S. (2007). The association between aging inmate housing management models and non-geriatric health services in state correctional institutions. *Journal of Aging and Social Policy, 19*(4), 39–56.

Turley, J. (2007). Testimony on prisoner reform and older prisoners before the House Judiciary Committee. Retrieved from http://jonathanturley.org/2007/12/06/testimony-on-prisoner-reform-and-older-prisoners-before-the-house-judiciary-committee

United Nations. (1948). The universal declaration of human rights. Retrieved from http://www.un.org/en/documents/udhr/

United Nations. (2012). *Report of the United Nations High Commissioner for Human Right*, Substantive session, July 23–27, Geneva, Switzerland.

United Nations Office on Drugs and Crime (UNODC). (2009). *Handbook for prisoners with special needs.* Retrieved from http://www.unhcr.org/refworld/docid/4a0969d42.html

Vermont Department of Corrections (2015). Annual Reprt. Retrieved May 1, 2016 from http://www.doc.state.vt.us

Williams, B., & Abraldes, R. (2007). Growing older: Challenges of prison and re-entry for the elderly. In R. Greifinger (Ed.), *Public health behind bars: From prisons to communities* (pp. 56–72). New York, NY: Springer, 2007.

Williams, B. A., McGuire, J., Lindsay, R. G., Baillargeon, J., Cenzer, I. S., Lee, S. J., & Kushel, M. (2010). Coming home: Health status and homelessness risk of older pre-release prisoners. *Journal of Gerontological Internal Medicine, 25*, 1038–1044.

Wilson, R. J., McWhinnie, A. J., & Wilson, C. (2008). Circles of support and accountability: An international partnership in reducing sexual offender recidivism. *The Prison Journal, 178*, 26–36.

Wronka, J. (2007). *Human rights and social justice: Social action and service for the helping and health professions.* Thousand Oaks, CA: Sage.

Zehr, H., & Gohar, Ali. (2003). *The little book of restorative justice.* Intercourse, PA: Good Books.

6

Parents in Prison

Promoting Success During Reentry to the Community

J. MARK EDDY AND JEAN E. SCHUMER

In the United States, more than half of men and women incarcerated in state prisons, and nearly two thirds incarcerated in federal prisons, or 809,800 people, are parents to a total of 1.7 million children under the age of 18 years (Glaze & Maruschak, 2010). Many more children, estimated in the multiple millions, have a parent currently incarcerated in city or county jails, or recently have had a parent released from jail or prison (e.g., Kemper & Rivara, 1993; Western & Wildeman, 2009). These children and their caregivers are often referred to as part of the "collateral damage" of incarceration due to the wide variety of negative impacts they experience (Comfort, 2007; Day, Acock, Bahr, & Arditti, 2005; Jensen, Gerber, & Mosher, 2004). For example, children and other family members present during the arrest of a parent may witness and be traumatized by aggressive apprehension and investigation tactics, including doors being broken down and the ransacking of one's home (Braman, 2004; Comfort, 2007). During parental incarceration, many families experience subsequent financial hardship, not only from losing a primary income earner (Glaze & Maruschak, 2010) but also from incurring new expenses that are a direct result of the incarceration.

Problems such as these often lead to new problems. They increase the risk of caregivers, who most often are single mothers or grandparents, for a variety of negative personal outcomes, including declines in physical and mental health (e.g., Arditti, Lambert-Shute, & Joest, 2003; Comfort, 2007; Dallaire & Wilson, 2010). A cascading array of problems can lead to decreases in parenting quality and may negatively impact the relationship between caregiver and child. With increasing difficulties in caregiver functioning, the vulnerability of the children of incarcerated parents to problems is increased in a number of areas, most notably, in the display of antisocial and delinquent behaviors. Unfortunately, it is these types of behaviors that most likely contributed to the incarceration of their parent, and which may lead to a child's own involvement in the juvenile justice system and, ultimately, the criminal justice system (Murray & Farrington, 2005; Murray, Bijleveld, Farrington, & Loeber, 2014).

Despite the fact that many incarcerated men and women are parents, this aspect of their lives is often ignored. In the United States, incarcerated individuals tend to be ostracized and marginalized, to be seen as fundamentally different from people who are not in prison or jail. Being a parent is viewed as incongruent with being in prison, and thus prisoners must not be parents. In part, this belief may be due to the fact that two thirds of the incarcerated parent population are minorities and tend to be from the lower socioeconomic classes. Their lives are outside of, and largely hidden from, the personal experiences of most current US policymakers and powerbrokers, who tend to be White males from the middle and upper classes (Porter, 2009). It is not just prison where differences in experience by race and ethnicity are found. Across the United States, members of most racial and ethnic minority groups are more likely than Whites to be arrested; once arrested, they are more likely to be convicted; once convicted, they are more likely to face stiffer sentences compared to their White counterparts (The Sentencing Project, 2013).

Not surprisingly, this chain of disparities results in vastly different experiences for children related to parental incarceration. At a given point in time, African American children are 7.5 times more likely and Latino children more than 2.5 times more likely than White children to have a parent in prison (Glaze & Maruschak, 2010). When lifetime exposure and key factors such as parent education are considered, differences by race and ethnicity are magnified even further. For example, by the age of 14 years, the cumulative risk for a child experiencing the incarceration of his or her father is estimated at 50.5% for African American children versus 7.2% for White children if the father had dropped out of high school, and 13.4% for African American children versus only 1.7% for White children if the father had some college (Wildeman, 2010).

Prevailing views on the incarcerated as not being parents may also be related to the fact that while women comprise less than 10% of the overall incarcerated population in the United States, women are more likely than men not only to be viewed as parents but also to be viewed as more connected to their children and family (Fearn & Parker, 2004; Harrison & Beck, 2004). For many, incarcerated men are viewed as estranged from their families. Since most people in prison are men, parenthood is an irrelevant and inconvenient detail. Regardless of such thinking, not only are a significant number of both men and women who are in prison and jail in the United States parents, but most of these fathers and mothers will maintain connections to their children and families during incarceration (Eddy & Poehlmann, 2010). Further, most will return to their communities and serve in some ongoing parental role with their existing children, and many will become new parents to additional biological and/or stepchildren. These parents and their families are an important part of the fabric of American society, and finding ways to ensure the successful return of parents from prison to their families is increasingly recognized as an imperative at the local, state, and federal levels alike (e.g., Gadsden, 2003; Gunnison & Helfgott, 2013). In this chapter, we provide a brief overview of the numerous challenges facing incarcerated fathers and mothers, highlight promising practices and programs that target some of these challenges in the hope of improving the likelihood of success after release, discuss implications for criminal justice practices and policies, and highlight trends and future directions related to this population.

Incarcerated Fathers and Mothers

Like other inmates, incarcerated parents typically have low levels of formal education (Dallaire, 2007; Glaze & Maruschak, 2010; Harlow, 2003). About 41% of inmates in prisons and jails did not complete high school, compared to 18% of the general population of adults (Harlow, 2003). Given the relation between education and income level, it is thus not surprising that these men and women also tend to have had low incomes prior to prison. Based on both national survey data from the Bureau of Justice Statistics and the US Census Bureau from 2004, 57% of incarcerated men age 27 to 42 years earned less than $22,500 prior to incarceration compared to only 23% of nonincarcerated men (Rabuy & Kopf, 2015). There was a similar gap for women, but women tended to be poorer than men, with 72% of incarcerated women age 27 to 42 years earning less than $22,500 prior to incarceration compared to 48% of nonincarcerated women.

Beyond socioeconomic status, incarcerated mothers and fathers tend to have histories, both during their childhoods and as adults, of personal and family difficulties in a variety of areas, from experiencing their own parent(s) being incarcerated, to being a victim of child abuse and neglect and/or intimate partner violence, and to struggling with substance abuse and/or mental health problems (Borja, Nurius, & Eddy, 2015; Dallaire, 2007; Kjellstand, Cearley, Eddy, Foney, & Martinez, 2012; Kjellstrand, Eddy, Schumer, Bridges Whaley, & Wheeler, 2017). For example, in the most recent available results from a national survey of prisoners, 40% reported living as a child in a home that received public assistance; 14% reported living for some amount of time in a foster home, agency, or institution; and 50% had a family member who had been incarcerated, including 19% who had an incarcerated father (Glaze & Maruschak, 2010). In the same survey, 20% reported ever experiencing physical or sexual abuse, 41% having a medical problem, 57% having a mental health problem, and 67% suffering from substance dependence or abuse.

Across a variety of studies, incarcerated mothers appear to have higher rates of problems than incarcerated fathers in three key areas, namely substance abuse, mental health problems, and trauma from domestic violence (Bloom, Owen, & Covington, 2003; Dallaire, 2007; Grella & Joshi, 1999; Kjellstrand et al., 2017). Probably most notable is the difference in the areas of physical or sexual abuse, where 60% of women who lived with their children prior to prison and 72% of women who had not lived with their children reported a history of these types of abuse versus only 16% of men (Glaze & Maruschak, 2010). In some studies, up to 90% of criminal justice–involved women report having experienced sexual or interpersonal violence (Women In Prison

Project, 2006). In contrast, the most commonly reported trauma by men is witnessing someone being killed or seriously injured (Sarchiapone, Carli, Cuomo, Marchetti, & Roy, 2009), followed by physical assault (Johnson et al., 2006). Notably, however, the next most common trauma for men is childhood sexual abuse (Weeks & Widom, 1998). Incarcerated fathers tend to have longer histories of justice system involvement, including more frequent and longer bouts of time in prison and jail and the potential for trauma exposure in lock-up (Kjellstrand et al., 2017; Liebling & Maruna, 2005).

As noted earlier, the number of incarcerated parents who are people of color is greater than the number of non-Hispanic White parents. Unfortunately, there have been very few examinations comparing incarcerated fathers and comparing incarcerated mothers of different races and ethnicities in terms of background characteristics such as those discussed here, but preliminary findings suggest more similarities than differences (e.g., Miller, Eddy, Borja, & Lazzari, 2017). Given the currently available information, what appears to be most important is that both incarcerated fathers and mothers face a variety of challenges that can have major implications not only for their lives as parents, partners, and family members but also for the lives of their children.

PROMISING PRACTICES AND PROGRAMS

Fortunately, there are a variety of practices and programs that have been developed to address many of the challenges facing incarcerated parents. Interest in these for parents in prison and their families has grown in recent years, particularly in relation to the period of "reentry" (Gunnison & Helfgott, 2013), during which an additional set of challenges commonly arise. Although the definition of the reentry period has varied across the decades, it most often is used to refer to experiences in the community after incarceration. A broader definition subsumes the time just both before and just after release, and within some jurisdictions, is now thought of as everything that takes place from the day a person is arrested and put in jail until the day the person completes community supervision. With an expansive time frame in mind, practices and programs relevant to parents are overviewed and presented by when they are typically delivered, namely before, during, and after incarceration. Outcomes related to some of these practices and programs have been examined, mostly through quasi-experimental studies, and mostly for incarcerated men and/or women rather than parents per se. Examples of promising findings are provided next.

Before Incarceration

TREATMENT COURTS
Keeping fathers and mothers who have committed certain lower level crimes both out of prison and positively engaged with their families and communities addresses multiple challenges simultaneously. Over the past several decades, a

variety of "problem solving" or "treatment" courts have been developed to meet these goals for offenders who have committed crimes and who have related co-occurring problems that are in need of intervention, such as drug abuse. While involved with a treatment court, an offender is on probation and must meet all the requirements of such. However, he or she also meets regularly with a judge, who monitors his or her progress in terms of staying substance-free, participating in programming, and gaining and maintaining employment. To provide the neces-sary support for an offender to be successful, a treatment court involves close col-laboration between and among all parties involved in a case, including the judge, the prosecution and defense, law enforcement and corrections officers, service providers, and the offender. Studies of outcomes due to treatment courts have consistently found positive effects (e.g., Marlowe, Hardin, & Fox, 2016; Mitchell, Wilson, Eggers, & McKenzie, 2012). Although most studies have not focused on parents per se, a few have examined courts that focus on child maltreatment cases (Gifford, Eldred, Vernerey, & Sloan, 2014). Preliminary evidence suggests that the children of adults who participate in family treatment courts spend less time in foster care and experience higher rates of reunification with parents than chil-dren of similar adults who do not (e.g., Bruns, Pullmann, Weathers, Wirschem, & Murphy, 2012; Worcel, Furer, Green, Burrus, & Finigan, 2008).

PARENTING ALTERNATIVE SENTENCING PROGRAMS

Other versions of probation have been tried as alternatives to incarceration, and some have been directed specifically at parents. In Washington State, for example, judges have the option to sentence eligible offenders who are convicted of certain crimes and who are parents with physical custody of their children to 1 year of close community supervision rather than incarceration. Similarly, the Washington Department of Corrections can release eligible inmates 1 year early to finish their sentence under electronic monitoring in the home of an approved sponsor. In both versions of the program, mothers or fathers must fulfill a variety of conditions to remain in good standing, such as checking in on a regular schedule with a community corrections officer and participating in certain programming (http://www.doc.wa.gov/corrections/justice/sentencing/parenting-alternative.htm). In a preliminary evaluation of the Department of Corrections version of the program, significant reductions were found in recidivism for program participants relative to a matched group of eligible parents who were in prison just before the pro-gram was launched (Agular & Leavell, 2017). The findings appeared promising enough to legislators in the nearby state of Oregon that a parenting alternative sentencing program is being piloted there in several counties (http://okb.oregon.gov/portfolio-item/fsap/).

During Incarceration

FAMILY VISITATION

Contact between incarcerated men and women and their families has long been thought to improve outcomes after release (e.g., Holt & Miller, 1972; see

Poehlmann, Dallaire, Loper, & Shear, 2010). Historically, contact takes place during face-to-face visits, phone calls, or letters. More recently, video visits and limited forms of email communication have been added as options in some institutions. In numerous recent studies, contact with family has been found to be related to a variety of positive outcomes for inmates during prison (e.g., Casey-Acevdeo, Bakken, & Karle, 2004; La Vigne, Naser, Brooks, & Castro, 2005; Loper, Carlson, Levitt, & Scheffel, 2009; McClure et al., 2014; Poehlmann, 2005; Visher, La Vigne, & Travis, 2004). Further, in-person visitation in particular has been found to be correlated with positive outcomes after release (e.g., Bales & Mears, 2008), including lower levels of recidivism for both men and women (Mitchell, Spooner, Jia, & Zhang, 2016).

PRISON NURSERIES

Approximately 4%–10% of incarcerated women are pregnant upon intake into a correctional facility. Most babies are separated from their mothers to live with kin caretakers or foster parents between 24 to 72 hours after birth. However, in a few US state prisons, eligible mothers are allowed to keep their infant with them within a special unit, typically for up to 12 to 18 months (Villanueva, From, & Lerner, 2009). These units, called "prison nurseries," are thought to promote the rehabilitation of incarcerated mothers, while also providing the physical closeness and supportive environment considered necessary for the development of a "secure attachment" (Ainsworth, Blehar, Waters, & Wall, 1978) between mothers and their infants (Byrne, Goshin, & Blanchard-Lewis, 2012). In the first longitudinal study of children who resided in a prison nursery, infants who participated in the program for at least 1 year were found to have attachment scores similar to low-risk infants living in the community (Byrne, Goshin, & Joestl, 2010). One year after release, mothers were found to have low recidivism rates (e.g., 0% new court convictions; 10% parole violations; Byrne, 2010).

MENTAL HEALTH PROBLEM TREATMENT

The mental health problems that many men and women bring with them when they enter prison can be exacerbated during their sentence, which in turn can add new challenges after release. In prison, both inpatient and outpatient types of interventions are employed to address mental health problems. Recognizing the centrality that trauma plays in the lives of both incarcerated women and men, a trauma-informed perspective is considered a best-practices approach for either type (Miller & Najavits, 2012). Trauma-informed treatment for women often emphasizes emotion regulation, empowerment, and safety, whereas for men it tends to emphasize relationships, feelings, and empathy. An example of a recent study of trauma-informed treatment compared outcomes for men who received the *Seeking Safety* or the *Male Trauma Recovery Empowerment Model* interventions versus men in a wait-list control group (Wolff, Juening, Shi, & Frueh, 2015). Both interventions use cognitive-behavioral skill-building approaches within a group setting, and *Seeking Safety* was developed specifically to address co-occurring posttraumatic stress disorder (PTSD) and substance abuse (Najavits, Weiss, Shaw, & Muenz, 1998). Significant improvements were found for men in the treatment groups in terms of PTSD symptom severity, self-esteem, proactive coping, and self-efficacy (Wolff et al., 2015).

Substance Abuse Treatment

Substance abuse is a problem for many prisoners and often had some relation to the crime that led to imprisonment (National Center on Addiction and Substance Abuse, 2010). Both inpatient and outpatient types of interventions also are utilized in prisons to address substance abuse. In some institutions, it is common for certain inmates with substance abuse problems who are nearing release to enter a specialized residential treatment unit where they participate in a variety of group- and individual-based interventions. Some units employ programs that are tailored to be responsive to the needs of a particular clients. For example, the *Women's Integrated Treatment Model* is a gender-responsive program that integrates trauma and substance abuse treatment, combining cognitive-behavioral interventions, expressive arts activities, and relational therapy to help women deal with the expression and containment of feelings (Covington, Burke, Keaton, & Norcott, 2008). In one study, women who successfully completed this program reported less depression and fewer trauma symptoms, including decreased anxiety, sleep disturbances, and dissociation, compared to baseline, before the program began (Covington et al., 2008).

Education Programs

As noted earlier, prisoners tend to have completed less formal education than the general population. Incarcerated men and women also tend to have lower literacy levels (Greenberg, Dunleavy, & Kutner, 2007). Both of these issues decrease employment options and income earning potential after release. To increase the chances of prosocial success in the community, a variety of educational experiences are available in prisons. Offerings typically range from basic skills instruction, to high school equivalency certification (i.e., GED), to vocational or career education, and may extend further to college coursework leading up to a degree (Davis et al., 2014). Several meta-analyses have found a positive relation between participating in educational programs in prison and a decreased likelihood of recidivating (Aos, Miller, & Drake, 2006; MacKenzie, 2006; Wilson, Gallagher, & MacKenzie, 2000). Further, education participation is also related to an increased likelihood of obtaining employment after release (Davis et al., 2014).

Employment Programs

In addition to obtaining housing, parents returning from prison often confront challenges on several other economic fronts, including minimal financial resources, accumulated debt, and a background that makes gaining employment difficult, including their criminal history and a weak employment history (Fontaine & Kurs, 2017; Visher, Debus, & Yahner, 2008; Visher, Yahner, & LaVigne, 2010). These and other barriers challenge the ability of those who seek employment to secure economic stability and maintain safe and stable housing (Holzer, 2007; Holzer, Raphael, & Stoll, 2003; Pager, 2003). A variety of prison-based programs have been created to assist with employment. For example, the *Fatherhood Reentry Initiative* included six programs intended to help stabilize fathers and their families by helping fathers move toward economic self-sufficiency (Fontaine & Kurs, 2017). The programs were offered to fathers (and family members) before and after release. Each program offered a wide array of services, including case management, vocational training, and certification services spanning industries such as construction, welding, home health care, and food handling, healthy relationship curricula, and parenting programs. Although outcomes related to these programs are not yet available, recommendations for future programs based on the analysis of performance measurement data from this initiative are available, and these are similar to those made in earlier reports of similar efforts (e.g., Drake & LaFrance, 2007; Petersilia, 2004; Seiter & Kadela, 2003). The first recommendation is casting a wide net to find partners (e.g., vocational schools, employers, and nonprofits) that can aid mothers and fathers in becoming more employable. The second is tailoring services to the specific needs of participants. The third is for program staff to advocate with potential employers in order to alter misconceptions about the reliability, trustworthiness, value, and benefits of formerly incarcerated persons as employees (Fontaine & Kurs, 2017).

Healthy Intimate Partner Relationship Skills Training

Maintaining a partnership while in prison is difficult. The lack of day-to-day interaction and opportunity for intimacy, the distance and travel times to visit partners in correctional facilities, the high costs of phone calls (at least historically), and other barriers to contact can add to feelings of estrangement and isolation. Nonincarcerated partners report feelings of stigma, shame, and loneliness (Arditti, Lambert-Shute, & Joest, 2003; Braman, 2004; Lowenstein, 1986), which may in turn affect their willingness to be supportive. Incarcerated men and women are often exposed to harsh environments and threats to their personal safety. Some may develop coping mechanisms, such as distrust and hypervigilance, which in prison may be functional behaviors but that take a toll on intimate partner relationships (McKay et al., 2010; Oliver & Hairston, 2008). These issues add to the stressors that many couples faced prior to prison, including low and unreliable incomes and bouts of joblessness. Relationship-strengthening programs have been used in prisons to try to assist men and women in prison with coping with problems as a couple. Usually these programs are offered in a group format, either in a series of sessions spanning multiple weeks or during weekend workshops. Sometimes complimentary programs are offered to partners in the community. In a recently conducted linked series of four matched comparison group studies of relationship skills training, positive impacts were found for the intervention group in only one (Lindquist, McKay, Steffey, & Bir, 2016). The incarcerated men and women in this study were living in faith-based housing units and attended a weekend relationship seminar. Three years following the seminar, program participants were more likely than control participants to have stayed in an exclusive relationship with their partner over time, to live with the partner after release, to support their children, and to engage in family-oriented activities.

PARENTING SKILLS TRAINING
Parenting programs have had lasting appeal within corrections for two important reasons. Over the short run, by developing and strengthening the communication skills of inmates, parenting programs are thought to increase the likelihood of positive contact between inmates and their families, which in turn may increase family support after release, and increase the probability of prosocial success in the community. Over the long run, by developing and strengthening an array of other parenting skills of inmates relevant to their lives back in the community, parenting programs are thought to decrease the likelihood of transmission of antisocial behavior from parent to child, and thus decrease the risk of the next generation becoming incarcerated (Eddy et al., 2008; Eddy, Kjellstrand, Martinez, & Newton, 2010). Parent education and skills training programs in prisons are usually group based. Common topics include child development, communication, and discipline techniques. Some programs also focus on specific skills helpful for parents when they are in prison, such as how to write a letter, have a phone call, or have a prison visit with a child at different stages of development (e.g., early childhood, middle childhood, adolescence). Only a few rigorous studies have been conducted of prison-based parenting programs. One of the largest was a randomized, controlled trial of *Parenting Inside Out* (PIO; Eddy & Clark, 2010), an evidence-informed cognitive-behavioral parent management training program developed for criminal justice–involved parents. Compared to parents in a services-as-usual control group, parents assigned to PIO reported less parental stress, less depression, and more positive parent–child intervention following intervention (Eddy, Martinez, & Burraston, 2013). Differences were found between the groups after release in both self-reports of criminal behavior and police arrest (Eddy, Martinez, Burraston, & Newton, 2017).

After Incarceration

TRANSITIONAL AND PERMANENT HOUSING
Formerly incarcerated persons face multiple barriers to successfully reintegrating into their families and communities. Many individuals return to impoverished communities in high-crime, unsafe areas with a shortage of affordable housing (Clear, 2007; Kirk, 2012; Kubrin & Stewart, 2006; Stewart, Schreck, & Simons, 2006). In addition, federal and state policies often prohibit felons, especially those convicted of drug or sex offenses, from accessing public housing, and most released offenders are unable to afford standard move-in expenses (e.g., first and last months' rent plus security deposit) and are thus excluded from securing housing in the private sector (Geller & Curtis, 2011; Malone, 2009; Mele & Miller,

2005; Roman & Travis, 2006). When rental units are available, many landlords are reluctant to rent to ex-felons (Helfgott, 1997; Roman & Travis, 2006). Living with family members can also be difficult due to limited financial resources or because of strained relationships owing to the offender's past behavior (Fontaine & Biess, 2012; Martinez & Christian, 2008). Thus, many released fathers and mothers are confronted with homelessness, and they bounce from living in temporary shelters, to living with friends or acquaintances for short periods of time, to living in low-cost hotels located in high-risk communities (Fontaine & Biess, 2012; Geller & Curtis, 2011; Gowan, 2002; Kushel, Hahn, Evans, Bangsberg, & Moss, 2005). In short, the need for safe, secure, and affordable housing is one of the most basic needs among released parents. A quasi-experimental evaluation was conducted that compared outcomes for released offenders who received housing and wrap-around services with similar offenders released to traditional community supervision. Participants in the housing condition had lower rates of recidivism on some indices compared to participants in community supervision only (Lutze, Rosky, & Hamilton, 2014).

CASE MANAGEMENT
After release, case managers develop and maintain working relationships with fathers and mothers, link them to needed resources (e.g., housing, employment training, or counseling), track progress in obtaining what they need, and monitor success in meeting goals. Often, the connection between a case manager and a father or mother may begin prior to release. In the end, whether or not case management is helpful depends on a number of factors, including the types of social services available in the local community, the individual's family and community networks, the intensity of supervision provided or required by parole or releasing agencies, and the status of the local economy and the availability of jobs (Seiter & Kadela, 2003). Case management was a part of several of the promising programs noted earlier. Across the plethora of studies that have included a case management component, there are a number of "best practice" case management elements that appear to be important if a program is going to be successful in reducing recidivism (e.g., Cullen & Gendreau, 2000; Domurad & Carey, 2010; Petersilia, 2004; Seiter & Kadela, 2003). These include having a well-trained and supervised staff; focusing on individuals who are assessed at medium or high risk to reoffend; beginning before release and continuing through a sufficiently long transition period (3–12 months); and engaging mothers and fathers in activities that occupy a significant amount of their time (e.g., 40%–70%) and that employ cognitive-behavioral skills training processes such as modeling, role playing, and reinforcement and content designed to target criminogenic thinking and behavior (Bourgon & Armstrong, 2005; Clark, 2010; Cullen & Gendreau, 2000; Lowenkamp, Latessa, & Holsinger, 2006; Morgan et al., 2012; Petersilia, 2004). The ability of case managers to develop interpersonally sensitive, quality relationships with mothers and fathers is thought to be key to success, and the first element, training and supervision,

is considered vital in terms of staff being successful in this area (Andrews, 1980, 2007; Dowden & Andrews, 2004).

MENTORING PROGRAMS

Mentors can act as prosocial role models and provide emotional support and practical advice to help an offender navigate everyday frustrations and barriers, both in prison and beyond, by reinforcing efforts in other program areas and by modeling problem-solving skills. Mentoring programs may be freestanding or be part of a larger, coordinated set of programs. An example of a program of the latter type is the *Ready4Work Reentry Initiative* (Bauldry, Korom-Djakovic, McClanahan, McMaken, & Kotloff, 2009), which included job training and placement services, intensive case management for other social service needs, and mentoring to strengthen social networks and support systems for formerly incarcerated adults. The Initiative operated in 11 sites, most of which started the program prior to release from prison, with services continuing for up to 1 year following release. Participants who met with a mentor at least once were twice as likely to obtain a job compared to participants who did not meet with a mentor. In all, 56% of participants became employed while in the program, and two thirds of these remained employed for at least three consecutive months.

CRIMINAL JUSTICE POLICY ISSUES AND IMPLICATIONS

There are a variety of practices and programs that appear to be promising in terms of assisting incarcerated fathers and mothers in their journey forward. This chapter provides just a sampling of this promise. In a just-released analysis of programs such as these, Bitney, Drake, Grice, Hirsch, and Lee (2017) examined the impacts of 59 programs and identified 43 that had been studied in a rigorous enough fashion to compute their impact on recidivism. Of these, 53% were found to significantly reduce recidivism. Further, they identified 45 of the 59 programs that had sufficient data on costs and benefits of the programs and found that about 80% demonstrated benefits that outweighed their costs. All and all, they found 29 programs that have at least a 75% chance of generating a benefit equal to their cost.

Unfortunately, despite this promise, the evidence base on most programs is quite slim, at least in terms of their application to incarcerated parents per se (e.g., Eddy & Burraston, in press). This is a common problem for any subpopulation within corrections. Further, on any given topic, not only are the number of outcome studies often few, but most that do exist suffer from a lack of scientific rigor both in terms of research design (e.g., quasi-experimental designs) but also in terms of attention to the quality of program implementation. A major weakness in terms of knowledge about most programs is a lack of information on how a program will perform, over time, under "conditions as usual" in the field. Given the number of parents who are incarcerated in this country, and the large number of children they have the potential to influence, there is a great need for the conduct of ongoing, quality research studies that can help guide the year-to-year decisions of policymakers and practitioners about what practices and programs to use with parents who are involved with the criminal justice system, and, if warranted by research findings, specific subpopulations of parents. A key question is how to achieve this goal.

The status quo in the fields of research and evaluation clearly has not been sufficient. The hallmark of this approach has been the support of "one-time" evaluations, often through funding from federal or private foundation sources, that, at best, demonstrate promise but nothing more. This tradition does not tend to support a focused, systematic approach to learning what programs or practices, including existing ones, work best for incarcerated parents, given the context of a particular jurisdiction or related set of jurisdictions on a day-to-day basis. Instead, it focuses on novel programs in various locations around the country with contexts that may, or may not, be relevant to a given jurisdiction. An alternative is for local and state governments to commit to developing and maintaining a culture of rigorous research of practices and programs both *within* and *across* criminal justice agencies, and to use the information generated to guide and shape ongoing policymaking regarding the criminal justice system at large, as well as regarding subpopulations within the system such as parents.

An example of such effort is currently in progress in the state of Oregon (cf. http://www.oregon.gov/cjc/justicereinvestment/Pages/default.aspx). In 2003, the Oregon legislature passed a bill, SB267, that required that 75% of correctional programs in Oregon be evidence based and cost-effective. Unfortunately, the statute was unclear on the definitions of these standards, and thus what types of evaluation were required to determine if a program qualified. Over the next decade, the number of incarcerated adults in Oregon increased at a rate of 4 times the national average to more than 14,000 inmates, and the biennial corrections budget exceed $1.4 billion for a state with only one major city and a total population of 3.8 million people. The consensus of policymakers in the state was that something needed to change.

In 2012, the Governor's Commission on Public Safety published a report that proposed a variety of policy recommendations, including several relevant to improving the situation regarding evidence-based programs and practices and the evaluation of such (Commission on Public Safety, 2012). The same year, Oregon joined the US Department of Justice Bureau of Justice Assistance's Justice Reinvestment Initiative. This initiative, now active in 27 states, is intended to assist states in better managing their criminal justice populations, including finding ways to spend their dollars in a more cost-effective way. The cost savings generated by such efforts are then to be reinvested in the use of evidence-based strategies that increase public safety, prevent crime, and ultimately decrease prison populations. Part of participation in the Initiative is receiving targeted technical assistance. Oregon began receiving such the following year from the Vera Institute of Justice.

That same year, the Oregon legislature passed HB3194, the Justice Reinvestment Act, which made several modest changes in sentencing and created the Justice Reinvestment Grant Program. The program provides financial support to Oregon counties to develop, implement, or expand practices and programs intended to reduce the prison population, increase public safety, and hold offenders accountable. It specifies a Governor-appointed commission, the Oregon Criminal Justice Commission, as the body to oversee the grant program, and sets aside 3% of total available grant funds to help fund rigorous evaluations of program outcomes and specifies randomized, controlled trials as a desirable research design. Further, it notes the importance of the following factors when choosing a program to be evaluated: "(a) The proposed program is promising and has the capability of being reproduced in other counties; (b) The proposed program is capable of being evaluated through randomized controlled trials when taking into account sample size and other practical requirements; (c) The proposed randomized controlled trial will meet the requirements of the institutional review board process; (d) Studying the program will benefit the State and more broadly the field of criminal justice by adding to the body of knowledge currently available." To date, the grant program has distributed over $53 million to Oregon counties. The prison forecast in 2017 was 839 beds below the 2013 forecast, and the estimated cost savings due to the Justice Reinvestment Act by 2019 is estimated to be over $250 million.

In short, the most significant issue facing criminal justice policymakers related to incarcerated parents is a lack of continually refreshed, reliable, and valid evidence on what truly "works" in reducing recidivism for the fathers and mothers in their custody. The major implication of this problem is that new strategies are needed to generate such evidence so that policymakers have the up-to-date information they need to make sound decisions about which practices and programs to implement to optimize outcomes for the incarcerated parents in their custody. Multiple targets are in need of focus, including the minimization of recidivism and the maximization of prosocial life outcomes, not only for incarcerated parents but also for their children and families. Making progress in this area will take collaboration across funders, sectors, and agencies as is taking place within the justice reinvestment movement, and it will require sustained and active leadership at multiple levels to be successful over the long run.

TRENDS AND FUTURE DIRECTIONS

Across the United States today, a variety of efforts focused on incarcerated parents are underway. Of keen interest is the reentry period, and what practices and programs are most useful to help parents get out and stay out of prison. Certainly, the justice reinvestment movement discussed earlier is an important trend that is very likely to continue and expand across the country. Examples of other work in progress at the local, state, and national levels and that reflect other trends are provided next. Each example includes a combination of program development, implementation, and evaluation, with a particular focus on programs that include multiple components (Eddy et al., 2010; Kjellstrand, 2017).

At the local level, over the past 40 years, Sponsors, Inc. of Eugene, Oregon, has worked with a wide variety of public and private partners, including local, state, and federal funders, to build a comprehensive reentry program for men and women thought to be at medium to high risk for returning to prison. The program begins with reach-ins by staff and volunteer mentors while men and women are still in prison; continues after release with the provision of basic needs, including short-term, transitional housing, food, and clothing, as well as job search support and appropriate psychosocial programming; and recently has been extended to include long-term, affordable, and permanent housing units. Programming includes parent education and other family relationship skills-building opportunities for both fathers and mothers. Transitional housing is available for mothers and their children. The administrative and Board leadership of Sponsors is committed not only to developing and maintaining the quality of each of the program components but also determining program outcomes through the conduct of scientifically rigorous studies such as randomized, controlled trials, and then making decisions for future programming based on results. One such randomized trial is currently underway through funding from the US Department of Justice and is focused on the impact of volunteer mentoring delivered within the context of transitional housing. Another randomized trial, focused on the multiple potential impacts of permanent housing on difficult-to-place men and women after release from prison or jail, is under development and will be funded through social impact bonds.

At the state level, the Washington State Department of Corrections has been building a new *Strength in Families* program through their Reentry Division. The program is funded through a Healthy Marriage and Responsible Fatherhood grant from the Administration for Children and Families (ACF) of the US Department of Health and Human Services (Becker-Green et al., 2015). ACF funds a wide variety of programs focused on the promotion of healthy relationships and positive parenting in various populations, including several that work specifically with criminal justice–involved parents. Washington State's program combines several evidence-based and promising practices to create a multimodal, multilevel, tailored approach to support reentering parents and their families around issues related to healthy intimate partner relationships, responsible parenting, and economic stability. The program begins with participation in evidence-informed prosocial skills training interventions, taught by trained and supervised Instructors, which focus on intimate partner relationships (i.e., *Walking the Line*; Erlacher, Stanley, & Markman, 2010) and parent–child relationships (i.e., *Parenting Inside Out*; Eddy et al., 2008). Instructors work with fathers, a trained and supervised Case Manager, and a trained and supervised Education and Employment Navigator to develop a tailored action plan based on the particular strengths, needs, and priorities of each reentering parent and his or her family. This plan then guides the day-to-day work of all involved in the program throughout the reentry process. The program continues in the home communities of each participant for a year following release. Work on the project includes the development and refinement of quality assurance processes. Discussions regarding the future of the program include the desire to conduct a randomized, controlled trial of *Strength in Families* through another funding mechanism.

At the national level, the Urban Institute and Community Works West has partnered with the US Department of Justice (and specifically the National Institute of Corrections and the Bureau of Justice Assistance) and the US Department of Health and Human Services to develop, implement, and evaluate the impact of model practices to facilitate communication and family strengthening for incarcerated parents while simultaneously maintaining safe and secure correctional institutions. The implementation of this effort, called *The Family Strengthening Project*, will take place in five sites around the United States. Participating sites will receive site-specific implementation strategies, training, and ongoing support. Outcomes will be tracked and used to guide other organizations and agencies interested in launching similar practices within their jurisdictions.

CASE EXAMPLES

A Mother

Callie is a 29-year-old, never married, White mother of three children, ages 10, 8, and 4 years. Callie's parents were alcoholics, and her father also abused prescription pain pills. She recalls things "falling apart" after her father lost his construction job. She and her siblings were exposed to violence from their father, not only directly toward them but also toward their mother. When Callie was in the fifth grade, she and a younger sibling were placed in foster care.

Callie reports moving to several homes while in foster care and having only one "nice" foster mother who didn't "treat me like a second-class citizen." Callie started drinking alcohol and using methamphetamine in middle school to "take my mind off things." She was eventually placed in residential treatment while in foster care for "cutting." Her mother regained custody of the children when Callie was in the eighth grade. By this time, her mother had remarried and her father had moved to another state.

Callie continued to have difficulties once she returned home. She eventually dropped out of high school and moved in with an older boyfriend, who was abusive to her. Despite involvement in a variety of antisocial behaviors, she had only fleeting contact with the juvenile justice system. Finally, at the age of 18 years, she spent time in jail several times for disorderly conduct and theft. Her first child was born the next year. She continued to spend brief periods of time in jail periodically and had another child. A few years later, she had a third child. A few months after this birth, she was arrested, tried, and convicted of several crimes, and subsequently sentenced to 26 months in prison. During her incarceration, her children were cared for by her mother and sister, who was a single mother with two children of her own. The prison was located a few hours away from their home.

While in prison, Callie attended a 12-step recovery group and took cognitive skills training and parenting classes. She spoke with her family weekly, wrote letters to them regularly, and saw them every few months. It was "hell" being away from the children, but, short of prison, she doesn't know what would have turned her life around. After spending 1 year in prison, she was released under an alternate sentencing arrangement that allows eligible parents to return to the community. Callie was placed at her mother's home with electronic monitoring surveillance. She was required to take parenting and other life skills training classes, attend drug and alcohol recovery groups, and submit to weekly urinalyses. Callie successfully completed her sentence and is now pursing an associate degree in business administration at a community college. She continues to live with her mother and has remained substance-free. She is currently single and hopes to have a "good" relationship someday, rather than an abusive one, so her kids can avoid "the system."

A Father

David is a 31-year-old Latino male in a maximum security prison. He has served 10 years of a 25-year sentence. He has twin 11-year-old boys who live with their mother, his common-law wife who works as a teacher's aide in a local public school. They live in a town about 4 hours away from the prison. They are in a committed relationship. She brings the children to visit when she can. The family keeps in contact with phone calls and letters between visits. His parents and one sibling also visit regularly. The other sibling is deceased from a gunshot wound.

David was sentenced to prison under a measure that limits judicial discretion in setting sentence lengths in favor of prescribed mandatory minimum sentences with no reductions for good time served or early parole. He doesn't know how he would handle "doing his time" if not for his family. Knowing he has people "out there" who love him gives him hope. David grew up in a neighborhood where violence was common—"Where I grew up was rough—fighting, being tough—that was the only way to get respect." He was a smart kid but did poorly in school. Through his deceased brother, he got involved with a gang. He went on to do "a lot of bad stuff" that he would take back if he could.

Prison stopped his behavior and likely stopped him from getting killed as well, he said. His gang is present in the prison, but he tries to stay out of things. So far, he has managed to do this and has no discipline reports. He wishes he could get out now, get away from the gang, and start over. He says he has learned to be a better parent and a softer guy, "even though prison is tough, very tough." He obtained a GED, attends 12-step recovery groups, and goes to parenting classes and other enrichment activities. He works in the prison's laundry operations and is considering getting a laundry certification for when he is released so that he can support his family. He loves to draw, is pretty good at it, and also wonders if perhaps he could be an artist.

Prison has been hard on his family, and David has many regrets. He has missed a lot of his boys' growing up but tries to look forward and maintain a "PMA" (positive mental attitude). The most important thing to him is that his boys do not end up "like me—stuck in here." He "tells them he loves them" often. He sees changes in them every time they visit. He does what he can to know what is going on with each of his family members and to support them in every way that he can think of given his situation. He is thankful for his family and looks forward to returning home to them some day.

WEB-BASED RESOURCES

Center for the Study of Social Policy: Ideas into Action:

http://www.cssp.org/reform/strengtheningfamilies/about/protective-factors-framework

This resource provides information on factors that protect against risks for problematic child and family outcomes, as well as a sampling of strengthening family programs around the United States.

Child Welfare Information Gateway: Supporting Children and Families of Prisoners:

https://www.childwelfare.gov/topics/supporting/support-services/prisoners/

This resource provides information on family-centered services for incarcerated parents and their children and families. Links are provided to reports and articles about relevant national initiatives, as well as to example programs delivered at the local and state levels.

Children of Inmates Family Strengthening Project: https://nicic.gov/coip

This resource has information on research relevant to the children of incarcerated parents, including articles and video content, as well as links to other Internet-based resources.

The National Resource Center on Children and Families of the Incarcerated:

https://nrccfi.camden.rutgers.edu/

This resource provides a compendium of information on the children of incarcerated parents and their families, including directories of state- and national-level support organizations. Fact sheets on various topics are provided, as well as information on some programs that have been evaluated for effectiveness.

The Urban Institute Justice Policy Center:

http://www.urban.org/policy-centers/justice-policy-center

The resource provides information on research and evaluations conducted to improve justice policy and practice at the national, state, and local levels. Typing "children of incarcerated parents" in the search bar yields links to research reports and tool kits covering a vast array of topics on the effects of incarceration, treatment approaches, and best practices.

REFERENCES

Agular, C. M., & Leavell, S. (2017). A statewide parenting alternative sentencing program: Description and preliminary outcomes. *Smith College Studies in Social Work,* *87*(1), 1–16.

Ainsworth, M., Blehar, M. C., Waters, E., & Wall, S. (1978). *Patterns of attachment. A psychological study of the strange situation.* Hillsdale, NY: Erlbaum.

Andrews, D. A. (1980). Some experimental investigations of the principles of differential association through deliberate manipulations of the structure of service systems. *American Sociological Review, 45,* 440–462.

Andrews, D. A. (2007). Principles of effective correctional programs. In L. L. Motiuk & R. C. Serin (Eds.), *Compendium 2000 on Effective Correctional Programming* (pp. 9–17). Ottawa, Canada: Correctional Service of Canada.

Aos, S., Miller, M., & Drake, E. (2006). *Evidence-based adult corrections programs: What works and what does not.* Olympia, WA: Washington State Institute for Public Policy.

Arditti, J. A., Lambert-Shute, J., & Joest, K. (2003). Saturday morning at the jail: Implications of incarceration for families and children. *Family Relations, 52*(3), 195–204.

Bales, W. D., & Mears, D. P. (2008). Inmate social ties and the transition to society: Does visitation reduce recidivism? *Journal of Research in Crime & Delinquency, 45,* 287–321.

Bauldry, S., Korom-Djakovic, D., McClanahan, W. S., McMaken, J., & Kotloff, L. J. (2009). *Mentoring formerly incarcerated adults: Insights from the Ready4Work Reentry Initiative.* Philadelphia, PA: Public/Private Ventures.

Becker-Green, J., House-Higgins, C., Eddy, J. M., Kjellstrand, J. M., Harris, M., Harding, M., & Meiko, J. (2015). *A pre- and post-release multimodal intervention for incarcerated fathers targeting parenting, economic stability, and healthy relationships.* Olympia, WA: Washington State Department of Corrections.

Bitney, K., Drake, E., Grice, J., Hirsch, M. & Lee, S. (2017). *The effectiveness of reentry programs for incarcerated persons: Findings for the Washington Statewide Reentry Council.* Olympia, WA: Washington State Institute for Public Policy.

Bloom, B., Owen, B., & Covington, S. (2003). *Gender responsive strategies: Research, practice, and guiding principles for women offenders.* Washington, DC: US Department of Justice, National Institute of Corrections.

Borja, S., Nurius, P., & Eddy, J. M. (2015). Adversity across the life course of incarcerated parents: Gender differences. *Journal of Forensic Social Work, 5,* 167–185.

Bourgon, G., & Armstrong, B. (2005). Transferring the principles of effective treatment into a "real world" prison setting. *Criminal Justice and Behavior, 32*(1), 3–25.

Braman, D. (2004). *Doing time on the outside: Incarceration and family life in urban America.* Ann Arbor: University of Michigan Press.

Bruns, E. J., Pullmann, M. D., Weathers, E. S., Wirschem, M. L., & Murphy, J. K. (2012). Effects of a multidisciplinary family treatment drug court on child and family outcomes: Results of a quasi-experimental study. *Child Maltreatment, 17*(3), 218–230.

Byrne, M. W. (2010). Interventions within prison nurseries. In J. M. Eddy & J. Poehlmann (Eds.), *Children of incarcerated parents: A handbook for researchers and practitioners* (pp. 161–188). Washington, DC: Urban Institute Press.

Byrne, M. W., Goshin, L., & Blanchard-Lewis, B. (2012). Maternal separations during the reentry years for 100 infants raised in a prison nursery. *Family Court Review, 50*(1), 77–90.

Byrne, M. W., Goshin, L. S., & Joestl, S. S. (2010). Intergenerational transmission of attachment for infants raised in a prison nursery. *Attachment & Human Development, 12*(4), 375–393.

Casey-Acevedo, K., Bakken, T., & Karle, A. (2004). Children visiting mothers in prison: The effects on mothers' behaviour and disciplinary adjustment. *Australian & New Zealand Journal of Criminology, 37*(3), 418–430.

Clark, P. (2010). Preventing future crime with cognitive behavioral therapy. *National Institute of Justice Journal, 265,* 22–25.

Clear, T. (2007). *Imprisoning communities: How mass incarceration makes disadvantaged neighborhoods worse.* New York, NY: Oxford University Press.

Comfort, M. (2007). Punishment beyond the legal offender. *Annual Review of Law and Social Science, 3*, 271–296.

Commission on Public Safety. (2012). *Report to the governor.* Salem, OR: State of Oregon.

Covington, S., Burke, C., Keaton, S., & Norcott, C. (2008). Evaluation of a trauma-informed and gender-responsive intervention for women in drug treatment. *Journal of Psychoactive Drugs, SARC Supplement, 5*, 1–12.

Cullen, F. T., & Gendreau, P. (2000). Assessing correctional rehabilitation: Policy, practice, and prospects. *Criminal Justice, 3*(1), 299–370.

Dallaire, D. (2007). Incarcerated mothers and fathers: A comparison of risks for children and families. *Family Relations, 56*, 440–453.

Dallaire, D., & Wilson, L. C. (2010). The relation of exposure to parental criminal activity, arrest, and sentencing to children's maladjustment. *Journal of Child and Family Studies, 19*, 404–418.

Davis, L. M., Steele, J. L., Bozick, R., Williams, M. V., Turner, S., Miles, J. N., . . . & Steinberg, P. S. (2014). *How effective is correctional education and where do we go from here?* Santa Monica, CA: RAND Corporation.

Day, R., Acock, A. C., Bahr, S. J., & Arditti, J. A. (2005). Incarcerated fathers returning home to children and families: Introduction to the special issue and a primer on doing research with men in prison. *Fathering, 3*, 183–200.

Domurad, F., & Carey, M. (2010). *Implementing evidence based practices.* Viera, FL: The Carey Group.

Dowden, C., & Andrews, D. A. (2004). The importance of staff practices in delivering effective correctional treatment: A meta-analysis of core correctional practice. *International Journal of Offender Therapy and Comparative Criminology, 48*, 201–214.

Drake, E., & LaFrance, S. (2007). *Findings on best practices of community re-entry programs for previously incarcerated persons.* San Francisco, CA: LaFrance Associates.

Erlacher, J., Stanley, S., & Markman, H. (2010). *Walking the line: PREP's curriculum for incarcerated men.* Greenwood Village, CO: PREP.

Eddy, J. M., & Burraston, B. (in press). Promoting the successful reentry of fathers coming home from jail or prison. In C. Wildeman, A. R. Haskins, & J. Poehlmann-Tynan (Eds.). *When parents are incarcerated: Interdisciplinary research and interventions to support children.* Washington, DC: American Psychological Association.

Eddy, J. M., & Clark, M. S. (Dec, 2010). Preparing for reentry with parent management training. *Corrections Today*, 44–48.

Eddy, J. M., Kjellstrand, J., Martinez, C. R., Jr., & Newton, R. (2010). Theory-based multimodal parenting intervention for incarcerated parents and their families. In J. M. Eddy & J. Poehlmann (Eds.), *Children of incarcerated parents: A handbook for researchers and practitioners* (pp. 237–264). Washington, DC: Urban Institute Press.

Eddy, J. M., Martinez, C. R., Jr., & Burraston, B. (2013). A randomized controlled trial of a parent management training program for incarcerated parents: Proximal impacts. In J. Poehlmann & J. M. Eddy (Eds.), *Relationship processes and resilience in children with incarcerated parents. Monographs of the Society for Research in Child Development, 78*(3), 75–93.

Eddy, J. M., Martinez, C. R., Burraston, B., & Newton, R. (2017). *A randomized controlled trial of a parent management training program for incarcerated parents: Distal impacts.* Manuscript submitted for publication.

Eddy, J. M., Martinez, C. R., Jr., Schiffmann, T., Newton, R., Olin, L., Leve, L., Foney, D. M., & Shortt, J. W. (2008). Development of a multisystemic parent management training intervention for incarcerated parents, their children and families. *Clinical Psychologist, 12*(3), 86–98.

Eddy, J. M., & Poehlmann, J. (Eds.) (2010). *Children of incarcerated parents: A handbook for researchers and practitioners.* Washington, DC: Urban Institute Press.

Fearn, N. E., & Parker, K. (2004). Washington state's residential parenting program: An integrated public health, education, and social service resource for pregnant inmates and prison mothers. *Californian Journal of Health Promotion, 2*(4), 34–48.

Fontaine, J., & Biess, J. (2012). *Housing as a platform for formerly incarcerated persons.* Washington, DC: Urban Institute.

Fontaine, J., & Kurs, E. (2017). *Promoting the economic stability of fathers with histories of incarceration: Activities and lessons from six Responsible Fatherhood programs.* Washington, DC: US Department of Health and Human Services, Administration for Children and Families.

Gadsden, V. L. (Ed.) (2003). *Heading home: Offender reintegration into the family.* Lanham, MD: American Correctional Association.

Geller, A., & Curtis, M. A. (2011). A sort of homecoming: Incarceration and the housing security of urban men. *Social Science Research, 40*(4), 1196–1213.

Gifford, E. J., Eldred, L. M., Vernerey, A., & Sloan, F. A. (2014). How does family drug treatment court participation affect child welfare outcomes? *Child Abuse & Neglect, 38*(10), 1659–1670.

Glaze, L. E., & Maruschak, L. (2010). *Parents in prison and their minor children.* Washington, DC: US Department of Justice, Bureau of Justice Statistics.

Gowan, T. (2002). The nexus: Homelessness and incarceration in two American cities. *Ethnography, 3*(4), 500–534.

Greenberg, E., Dunleavy, E., & Kutner, M. (2007). *Literacy behind bars: Results from the 2003 National Assessment of Adult Literacy Prison Survey.* Washington, DC: US Department of Education, National Center for Education Statistics.

Grella, C. E., & Joshi, V. (1999). Gender differences in drug treatment careers among clients in the national Drug Abuse Treatment Outcome Study. *The American Journal of Drug and Alcohol Abuse, 25*(3), 385–406.

Gunnison, E., & Helfgott, J. B. (2013). *Offender reentry: Beyond crime and punishment.* Boulder, CO: Lynne Rienner.

Harlow, C. W. (2003). *Education and correctional populations.* Washington, DC: US Department of Justice, Bureau of Justice Statistics.

Harrison, P. M., & Beck, A. J. (2004). *Prisoners in 2003.* Washington, DC: US Department of Justice, Bureau of Justice Statistics.

Helfgott, J. (1997). Ex-offender needs versus community opportunity in Seattle, Washington. *Federal Probation, 61*, 12.

Holt, N., & Miller, D. (1972). *Explorations in inmate-family relationships.* Sacramento, CA: California Department of Corrections.

Holzer, H. J. (2007). *Collateral costs: The effects of incarceration on the employment and earnings of young workers.* Bonn, Germany: IZA Institute of Labor Economics.

Holzer, H. J., Raphael, S., & Stoll, M. A. (2003). *Employment barriers facing ex-offenders.* Washington, DC: Urban Institute.

Jensen, E. L., Gerber, J., & Mosher, C. (2004). Social consequences of the War on Drugs: The legacy of failed policy. *Criminal Justice Policy Review, 15*(1), 100–121.

Johnson, R. J., Ross, M. W., Taylor W. C., Williams, M. L., Carvajal, R. I., & Peters, R. J. (2006). Prevalence of childhood sexual abuse among incarcerated males in county jail. *Child Abuse and Neglect, 30,* 75–86.

Kemper, K. J., & Rivara, F. P. (1993). Parents in jail. *Pediatrics, 92*(2), 261–264.

Kirk, D. S. (2012). Residential change as a turning point in the life course of crime: Desistance or temporary cessation? *Criminology, 50*(2), 329–358.

Kjellstrand, J. (2017). Building a tailored, multilevel prevention strategy to support children and families affected by parental incarceration. *Smith College Studies in Social Work, 87*(1), 112 129.

Kjellstrand, J., Cearley, J., Eddy, J. M., Foney, D., & Martinez, Jr., C. R. (2012). Characteristics of incarcerated fathers and mothers: Implications for preventive interventions targeting children and families. *Child and Youth Services Review, 34*(12), 2409–2415.

Kjellstrand, J. M., Eddy, J. M., Schumer, J., Bridges Whaley, R., & Wheeler, A. (2017). *Gender differences and implications for programming during the reentry of incarcerated men and women back into their communities.* Manuscript submitted for publication.

Kubrin, C. E., & Stewart, E. (2006). Predicting who reoffends: The neglected role of neighborhood context in recidivism studies. *Criminology, 44*(1), 165–197.

Kushel, M. B., Hahn, J. A., Evans, J. L., Bangsberg, D. R., & Moss, A. R. (2005). Revolving doors: imprisonment among the homeless and marginally housed population. *American Journal of Public Health, 95*(10), 1747–1752.

La Vigne, N.G., Naser, R. L., Brooks, L. E., & Castro, J. L. (2005). Examining the effect of incarceration and in-prison family contact on prisoners' family relationships. *Journal of Contemporary Criminal Justice, 21*(4), 314–335.

Leibling, A., & Maruna, S. (Eds.) (2005). *The effects of imprisonment.* Portland, OR: Willan.

Lindquist, C., McKay, T., Steffey, D., & Bir, A. (2016). *Impact of couples-based family strengthening services for incarcerated and reentering fathers and their partners.* Washington, DC: US Department of Health and Human Services, Office of the Assistant Secretary for Planning and Evaluation.

Loper, A. B., Carlson, L. W., Levitt, L., & Scheffel, K. (2009). Parenting stress, alliance, child contact, and adjustment of imprisoned mothers and fathers. *Journal of Offender Rehabilitation, 48*(6), 483–503.

Lowenkamp, C. T., Latessa, E. J., & Holsinger, A. M. (2006). The risk principle in action: What have we learned from 13,676 offenders and 97 correctional programs? *Crime & Delinquency, 52*(1), 77–93.

Lowenstein, A. (1986). Temporary single parenthood: The case of prisoners' families. *Family Relations, 35,* 79–85.

Lutze, F. E., Rosky, J. W., & Hamilton, Z. K. (2014). Homelessness and reentry a multisite outcome evaluation of Washington State's reentry housing program for high risk offenders. *Criminal Justice & Behavior, 41*(4), 471–491.

MacKenzie, D. (2006). *What works in corrections: Reducing the criminal activities of offenders and delinquents.* New York, NY: Cambridge University Press.

Malone, D. K. (2009). Assessing criminal history as a predictor of future housing success for homeless adults with behavioral health disorders. *Psychiatric Services, 60*(2), 224–230.

Marlowe, D. B., Hardin, C. D., & Fox, C. L. (2016). *Painting the current picture: A national report on drug courts and other problem-solving courts*. Alexandria, VA: National Drug Court Institute.

Martinez, D. J., & Christian, J. (2008). The familial relationships of former prisoners: Examining the link between residence and informal support mechanisms. *Journal of Contemporary Ethnography, 38*(2), 201–224.

McClure, H. H., Shortt, J. W., Eddy, J. M., Holmes, A., Van Uum, S., Russell, E., . . . & Snodgrass, J. J. (2014). Associations among mother–child contact, parenting stress, and mother and child adjustment related to incarceration and children's contact with incarcerated parents. In J. Poehlmann-Tynan (Ed.), *Children's contact with incarcerated parents: Implications for policy and intervention. Advances in child and family policy and practice* (pp. 59–82). New York, NY: Springer.

McKay, T., Corwin, E., Herman-Stahl, M., Bir, A., Lindquist, C., Smiley-McDonald, H., & Siegel, S. (2010). *Parenting from prison: Innovative programs to support incarcerated and reentering fathers*. Washington, DC: US Department of Health and Human Services, Administration for Children and Families.

Mele, C., & Miller, T. (2005). *Civil penalties, social consequences*. New York, NY: Routledge.

Miller, K. M., Eddy, J. M., Borja, S., & Lazzari, S. R. (2017). Variations in the life histories of incarcerated parents by race and ethnicity: Implications for service provision. *Smith College Studies in Social Work, 87*(1), 1–20.

Miller, N., & Najavits, L. M. (2012). Creating trauma-informed correctional care: A balance of goals and environment. *European Journal of Psychotraumatology, 3*, 1–8.

Mitchell, M. M., Spooner, K., Jia, D., & Zhang, Y. (2016). The effect of prison visitation on reentry success: A meta-analysis. *Journal of Criminal Justice, 47*, 74–83.

Mitchell, O., Wilson, D. B., Eggers, A., & MacKenzie, D. L. (2012). Assessing the effectiveness of drug courts on recidivism: A meta-analytic review of traditional and non-traditional drug courts. *Journal of Criminal Justice, 40*(1), 60–71.

Morgan, R. D., Flora, D. B., Kroner, D. G., Mills, J. F., Varghese, F., & Steffan, J. S. (2012). Treating offenders with mental illness: A research synthesis. *Law and Human Behavior, 36*(1), 37–50.

Murray, J., Bijleveld, C. C., Farrington, D. P., & Loeber, R. (2014). *Effects of parental incarceration on children: Cross-national comparative studies*. Washington, DC: American Psychological Association.

Murray, J., & Farrington, D. P. (2005). Parental Imprisonment: effect on boys' antisocial behaviour and delinquency through the life-course. *Journal of Child Psychology and Psychiatry, 46*(12), 1269–1278.

Najavits, L. M., Weiss, R. D., Shaw, S. R., & Muenz, L. R. (1998). "Seeking Safety": Outcome of a new cognitive-behavioral psychotherapy for women with posttraumatic stress disorder and substance dependence. *Journal of Traumatic Stress, 11*(3), 437–456.

The National Center on Addiction and Substance Abuse (CASA) at Columbia University. (2010). *Behind bars II: Substance abuse and America's prison population*. New York, NY: CASA.

Oliver, W., & Hairston, C. F. (2008). Intimate partner violence during the transition from prison to the community: Perspectives of incarcerated African American men. *Journal of Aggression, Maltreatment & Trauma, 16*(3), 258–276.

Pager, D. (2003). The mark of a criminal record. *American Journal of Sociology, 108*(5), 937–975.

Petersilia, J. (2004). What works in prisoner reentry: Reviewing and questioning the evidence. *Federal Probation, 68,* 4.

Poehlmann, J. (2005). Incarcerated mother's contact with children, perceived family relationships, and depressive symptoms. *Journal of Family Psychology, 19,* 350–357.

Poehlmann, J., Dallaire, D., Loper, A. B., & Shear, L. D. (2010). Children's contact with their incarcerated parents: Research findings and recommendations. *American Psychologist, 65*(6), 575.

Porter, N. (2009). *The state of sentencing 2009: Developments in policy and practice.* Washington, DC: The Sentencing Project.

Roman, C. G., & Travis, J. (2006). Where will I sleep tomorrow? Housing, homelessness, and the returning prisoner. *Housing Policy Debate, 17*(2), 389–418.

Rubay, B., & Kopf, D. (2015). *Prisons of poverty: Uncovering the pre-incarceration incomes of the imprisoned.* Northampton, MA: Prison Policy Initiative.

Sarchiapone, M., Carli, V., Cuomo, C., Marchetti, M., & Roy, A. (2009). Association between childhood trauma and aggression in male prisoners. *Psychiatry Research, 165*(1–2), 187–192.

Schiffmann, T., Eddy, J. M., Martinez, C. R., Leve, L., & Newton, R. (2006). *Parenting Inside Out: Parent management training for incarcerated parents in prison.* Portland, OR: Children's Justice Alliance.

Seiter, R. P., & Kadela, K. R. (2003). Prisoner reentry: What works, what does not, and what is promising. *NCCD News, 49*(3), 360–388.

The Sentencing Project (2013). *Report to the United Nations Human Rights Committee regarding racial disparities in the United States criminal justice system.* Washington, DC: The Sentencing Project.

Stewart, E. A., Schreck, C. J., & Simons, R. L. (2006). "I ain't gonna let no one disrespect me": Does the code of the street reduce or increase violent victimization among African American adolescents? *Journal of Research in Crime and Delinquency, 43*(4), 427–458.

Villanueva, C. K., From, S. B., & Lerner, G. (2009). *Mothers, infants, and imprisonment: A national look at prison nurseries and community-based alternatives.* New York, NY: Women's Prison Association.

Visher, C.A., Debus, S., & Yahner, J. (2008). *Employment after prison: A longitudinal study of releases in three states.* Washington, DC: Urban Institute, Justice Policy Center.

Visher, C., LaVigne, N., & Travis, J. (2004). *Returning home: Understanding the challenges of prisoner reentry in the Maryland Pilot Study: Findings from Baltimore.* Washington, DC: Urban Institute Justice Policy Center.

Visher, C., Yahner, J., & LaVigne, N. (2010). *Life after prison: Tracking the experiences of male prisoners returning to Chicago, Cleveland, and Houston.* Washington, DC: Urban Institute Justice Policy Center.

Weeks, R., & Widom, C. S. (1998). Self-reports of early childhood victimization among incarcerated adult male felons. *Journal of Interpersonal Violence, 13*(3), 346–361.

Western, B., & Wildeman, C. J. (2009). The black family and mass incarceration. *The Annals of the American Academy of Political and Social Science, 621*(1), 221–242.

Wildeman, C. (2010). Mass parental imprisonment, social policy, and the future of American inequality. In J. M. Eddy & J. Poehlmann (Eds.), *Children of incarcerated parents: A handbook for researchers and practitioners* (pp. 303–318). Washington, DC: Urban Institute Press.

Wilson, D. B., Gallagher, C. A., & Mackenzie, D. L. (2000). A meta-analysis of corrections-based education, vocation, and work programs for adult offenders. *Journal of Research in Crime and Delinquency, 37*(4), 347–368.

Wolff, N., Huening, J., Shi, J., Frueh, B. B., Hoover, D. R., & McHugo, G. (2015). Implementation and effectiveness of integrated trauma and addiction treatment for incarcerated men. *Journal of Anxiety Disorders, 30*, 66–80.

Women in Prison Project. (2006). *Why focus on incarcerated women?* New York, NY: Correctional Association of New York.

Worcel, S. D., Furrer, C. J., Green, B. L., Burrus, S. W., & Finigan, M. W. (2008). Effects of family treatment drug courts on substance abuse and child welfare outcomes. *Child Abuse Review, 17*(6), 427–443.

7

Youth Certified as Adults and Serving Adult Sentences

STEPHEN W. PHILLIPPI JR. AND ELLEN P. MCCANN

Transferring youth to adult courts and adult system processes to serve adult sentences is not new to the United States. Despite laws that distinguish between youth and adults in relation to issues such as voting, military service, serving on juries, entering into lawful contracts, marrying without parental consent, and others, the US criminal justice system currently eradicates these lines of age distinction between adults and youths in many cases, beginning at the point of arrest. Police arrest practices (driven by state age of criminal responsibility mandates), prosecutorial discretion, statutory exclusions, and judicial waivers all play a role in moving youths, still in the throes of junior high and high school adolescence, to be certified as adults, held as adults, and, when found guilty, serve adult sentences.

Laws vary considerably from state to state, as does the information available on the youth impacted by these practices. Currently 13 states in the United States report the total number youth transfers to adult courts (Griffin, Addie, & Adams, 2011). Even fewer report details such as demographics, offenses, and sentencing according to this same report. Best estimates for 21 of the 50 states suggest at least 14,000 youth are transferred annually in the states where some data are available (Griffin et al., 2011). This estimate, as of 2016, does not account for the tens of thousands more that are automatically processed in adult courts at the age of 17 years old in seven states and both 16 and 17 years old in two states. In a report from one state that studied its 17-year-olds being automatically treated as adult criminals, they found that almost 6,000 of these youth were being arrested annually and estimated over 650 were being jailed (Phillippi et al., 2016). Of those, none of the top-10 reported charges at jail booking included a violent crime as defined as defined by the Bureau of Justice Statistics Violent Crime Index (Phillippi et al., 2016). In other words, in this state example, these youth were being arrested as adults, jailed as adults, and now living with a permanent adult record, for minor offenses that might even be considered undesirable, but predictable, adolescent behaviors.

Of course, many of the crimes committed by young offenders are violent and generate public attention as they make their way through the courts, including the US Supreme Court. For over a decade now, including several heinous cases of violence (e.g., first-degree murder), the US Supreme Court has consistently ruled that youth (i.e., persons below the age of 18) are fundamentally different from adults and must be treated differently under the law. These rulings are filtering down in various translations to state policies and practices, but still today youth are held culpable to adult standards and serve adult sentences for their crimes. The common solution to keeping these youth "safe" as they await trial or serve their sentences is to separate them from adults through an overreliance on isolation. The iatrogenic effect of this practice alone places youth at a 36 times greater likelihood of committing suicide in an adult facility as compared to a juvenile detention—a practice that in 2016 was finally banned in the federal prison system by an executive order of President Obama.

The impact of these decisions, the long-term outcome of youth incarcerated as adults, is one of many current debates as the nation remains at a crossroads between getting tough on crime, reducing its dependence on mass incarceration, being smart on crime, and looking at the outcomes associated with each. To consider the issues, this chapter will examine how youth are transferred to the adult system, certified as adults, and serve adult sentences. The chapter will then consider how these policies and practices impact public safety and the trajectories for youth offenders. Finally, current best or emerging practices, policy implications, and a case example will be presented.

BACKGROUND: BRIEF HISTORY AND CURRENT LANDSCAPE OF YOUTH IN ADULT CRIMINAL JUSTICE SETTINGS

Federal guidelines have largely shaped the landscape for youth in the adult criminal justice system. That landscape is further determined by local policies and practices, particularly regarding youth being transferred into the adult system. These transfer practices vary but, in general, include judicial waivers, prosecutorial discretion, and statutory exclusions.

On the federal level, the Juvenile Justice and Delinquency Prevention Act of 1974 (JJDPA)[1] established sight and sound separation for juvenile offenders in adult facilities, but the definition of juvenile was set by local policy. This means that in a state where a 16-year-old is under the jurisdiction of the adult justice system, that same 16-year-old may be allowed in the same housing block as an adult. The second major change came with the Prison Rape Elimination Act (PREA) passed in 2003.[2] PREA recognized the increased risk faced by juveniles housed, and exposed to adults, in adult facilities. It established a set of youth

---

1. Information about the history of JJDPA can be found here: http://www.juvjustice.org/federal-policy/juvenile-justice-and-delinquency-prevention-act

2. Information about the history of PREA can be found here: https://www.prearesourcecenter.org/about

offender standards that were to apply equally to anyone under the age of 18. PREA recognized the dangers, including assault, sexual victimization, mental illness, and increased criminality, when young people are housed with adults and set standards to reduce and eliminate such harmful effects (Daugherty, 2015).

At the local level, judicial waivers allow juvenile courts to waive jurisdiction on a case-by-case basis. If waived, this allows for prosecution in adult criminal court. Prosecutorial discretion affords prosecutors the ability to decide whether a case is sent to a juvenile or a criminal court. There is not a hearing to determine which court is appropriate, and the decision rests solely with the prosecutor. Finally, statutory exclusions are state laws that direct certain classes of cases involving youth offenders to criminal court. Most often these exclusions are intended for the most heinous offenses such as murder, armed robbery, and other violent acts. Currently, all 50 states have at least one of these types of transfer laws (Griffin et al., 2011).

What varies state by state, and often jurisdictionally within states, is where these youth are held pretrial and posttrial. Some youth are immediately housed in adult jails awaiting trial if the prosecution charges them as adults. Typically, the standards for holding a youth in such facilities are considerably lower than juvenile detention facilities. In the latter, education and mental health programming are usually mandated and stays awaiting hearings tend to be significantly shorter. In some jurisdictions, youth, even when waived to adult courts, are held in juvenile detention centers awaiting trial. This allows youth to remain in juvenile settings until they are found guilty or released if found innocent. Finally, in a small, but growing number of states, youth, if waived to adult court and found guilty, serve the beginning of their adult sentences in juvenile secure facilities. They are transferred as they get older, typically between the ages of 18 to 21, to adult facilities to serve the remainder of their adult sentences.

DATA—YOUTH IMPACT ON STATE CRIMINAL JUSTICE SYSTEMS

At the end of 2014, according to the US Bureau of Justice Statistics census, there were 1,035 people under the age of 18 held in a state prison or in a jail (see Figure 7.1 [adapted from Carson, 2015] showing inmates 17 and younger incarcerated in the US). This is likely a low count, as some states did not respond to the census count (e.g., Alaska). Other states simply had no one under 18 in a facility for the year-end count, such as Idaho or Hawaii. Regardless, these numbers are a starkly lower number than those seen in past decades, largely a result of changes in federal guidelines, as noted earlier.

PUBLIC SAFETY IMPLICATIONS

A growing body of research supports keeping adolescents in the juvenile justice system (i.e., not transferring them to adult courts and adult jails or prisons); this enhances long-term community safety and better ensures the well-being of youth while in the justice system. It should be noted that, consistent with research, this is a long term view of public safety. Research on the "desistance" of crime shows

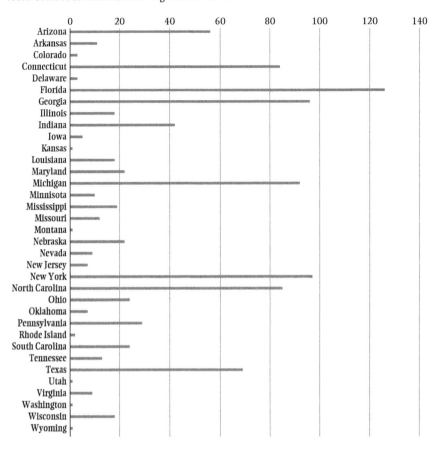

Figure 7.1 Inmates 17 years and younger in state prisons and jails (as of end of 2014); N = 1,035.
SOURCE: Carson, 2015.

similar criminal trajectories for most adolescents as they merge into adulthood and suggests that similar intervention approaches (i.e., all adolescents being served by the juvenile justice system) can yield similar results (Mulvey, 2011). In contrast, outcomes associated with youth transferred to adult courts indicate higher recidivism rates than similar youth handled by juvenile court processes (Butts, 2012; USDHHS-CDC, 2007). In other words, transferring youth to the adult system can increase risks to public safety and may fail to deter crime in the long term. Research shows an approximately 34% lower rate of recidivism for youth being processed through the juvenile justice system (USDHHS-CDC, 2007). Beyond recidivism, there is a significant body of research that shows youth are also safer in juvenile facilities in comparison to adult facilities (Redding, 2010).

Offender Desistance

Justice policymakers often rely on a false assumption. The false assumption is that the vast majority of offenders at the more serious end of the justice system are

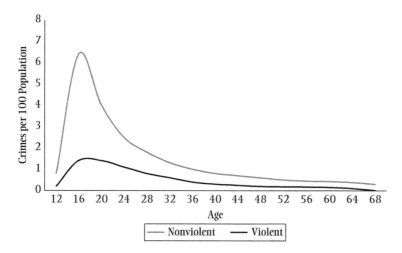

Figure 7.2 This shows that most adolescents desist from criminal activity as they mature psychosocially.
SOURCE: Adapted from the Pathways to Desistance Study; Stein, Cauffman, & Monahan, 2015.

uniformly treading down the path of continued, high-rate offending. The research on serious adolescent offenders shows otherwise (Borum, 2003; Lowencamp & Latessa, 2004; Mulvey et al., 2010).[3,4] The findings of the Pathways to Desistance study, which followed over 1,300 serious juvenile offenders for 7 years postconviction, show the link between psychosocial maturity and desistance from crime as youth transition from 14 to 25 years of age. The study found that "the vast majority (over 91%) of juvenile offenders, even those who commit serious crimes, grow out of antisocial activity as they transition to adulthood. (And) Most juvenile offending is, in fact, limited to adolescence" (see Figure 7.2, from Stein, Cauffman & Monahan, 2015). According to this research, the process of maturing out of much of adolescent criminal behavior (specifically felony-convicted offenses) is associated directly with the process of psychosocial maturity. Controlling one's impulses, considering the implications of one's actions on others, delaying gratification for longer term goals, and resisting peer influences are all part of this maturation process that is not fully achieved by teenagers. According to the researchers, "the most important conclusion of the study is that even adolescents

3. However, high-risk juvenile offenders gain a great deal more from services compared to low-risk juvenile offenders. See, generally, Karen Hennigan et al., *Final report, Five-year outcomes in a randomized trial of a community-based multi-agency intensive supervision juvenile probation program*, US Department of Justice, Grant No. 2007-JF-FX-0066 (Dec. 2010).

4. *Probation and parole FAQs*, American Probation & Parole Association. According to the Executive Director of the American Probation and Parole Association, "low risk offenders are more likely to recidivate with too much correctional intervention than no intervention." Carl Wicklund. See http://www.appanet.org/eweb/DynamicPage.aspx?WebCode=VB_FAQ#9.

who have committed serious offenses are not necessarily on track for adult criminal careers" (Mulvey, 2011; p. 3). In other words, most youthful felons are appropriate candidates for rehabilitation through the juvenile justice system as they are likely to desist in their patterns of future criminal behavior.

Criminal Justice Versus Juvenile Justice Recidivism

Due to the existence of states that allow youth to be transferred to the adult criminal justice system, researchers have the opportunity to match and compare outcomes of youth with similar characteristics who have committed similar crimes but experience two different system interventions—adult versus juvenile. Studies show that recidivism rates for youth transferred to the adult system are far higher than those of comparable youths processed in the juvenile justice system. Through a comprehensive review of published studies and government-conducted examinations of policies allowing youth to be transferred to the adult criminal justice system, the US Centers for Disease Control Task Force found that youth were 34% more likely to be rearrested after going through the adult system (USDHHS-CDC, 2007).

Similarly, the US Department of Justice, Office of Juvenile Justice and Delinquency Prevention, reviewed the results from six large studies on the impact of youth in adult court. These studies matched youth who were sent through the adult system with those who remained in the juvenile justice system. The studies matched youth according to geography, gender, age, race, gang involvement, number of previous juvenile arrests, most serious prior offense, current offense, victim injury, property damage, use of weapons, and more. Every study of these comparable youth found higher recidivism rates for youth processed through the adult system, even when youth were given probation instead of incarceration (Redding, 2010). These studies identified a number of significant factors influencing higher youth recidivism rates in the adult system, including socializing with adult criminals; the stigma associated with adult felony convictions; trauma from incarceration; lack of rehabilitation focus in adult facilities; loss of employment opportunities after incarceration; decrease in lifelong earning potential; and lack of emphasis on family support in the adult system (Redding, 2010).

Impact of "Adult Consequences" to Deter Youth Offenders

In a study by the John Jay College of Criminal Justice comparing youth in states where 17-year-olds are subject to juvenile court jurisdiction to states were 17-year-olds are handled in adult court, researchers found that available evidence indicates that adult transfer policies do more harm than good and are counterproductive to reducing juvenile violence and enhancing public safety (Butts, 2012). In other words, the threat of being transferred to the adult system as a deterrent for youth offenders appears unsubstantiated. One reason is the disparity between the intent of these policies and adolescent immaturity is relevant in both assessing culpability but also the efficacy of deterrence (Ward, 2003). Following a decade of recent Supreme Court rulings, youth offenders are fundamentally different developmentally than adults.

It then stands to reason that adult processes and consequences are not designed to be responsive to an adolescent's rehabilitation needs. The threat of transferring or handling youth in the adult system seems to fail as a deterrent. In light of adolescent brain development, this makes logical sense as these youth have developmentally immature impulse control capacities, poor decision-making abilities, and an increased, often negative, impact from peer influence.

Harm of Exposure of Youth to Adult Criminal Justice Systems

Investigations consistently show that youth processed through juvenile courts and juvenile facilities are safer and more likely to experience better outcomes than those sent to adult facilities (Campaign for Youth Justice, 2007; Human Rights Watch, 2012; USDOJ-NIC, 2011).[5] Whether housed with the adult population or kept separate while still in adult facilities, juveniles are exposed to far more dangerous environments in these facilities as compared to juvenile facilities. According to the National Institute of Corrections of the US Department of Justice, "jail administrators can face a difficult choice on this issue: They can house youth in the general population where they are at a differential risk of physical and sexual abuse, or, house youth in a segregated setting where isolation can cause or exacerbate mental health problems" (USDOJ-NIC, 2011; p. 12). Furthermore, whether isolated from adults or not, youth will face challenges in these facilities simply because they are not designed, intended, or equipped, to manage youth (USDOJ-NIC, 2011). To this point, even at a minimal standard of management, staff in most adult facilities often do not have the necessary training or skills essential for working with juvenile offenders (NCSL, 2012).

The US Department of Justice's Bureau of Justice Statistics reports that prison inmates under the age of 18 are 8 times more likely than the adult prison inmate to experience sexual abuse from other inmates while in prison (BJS, 2015).[6] Investigations also indicate that youth are "twice as likely to be beaten by staff and fifty percent more likely to be attacked with a weapon than minors in juvenile facilities" (Human Rights Watch, 2012; p. 19). Isolation of youth in adult facilities also appears to fail to offer greater safety as mental health problems are exacerbated. As a number of studies report, "75 percent of all deaths of youth under 18 in adult jails were due to suicide" (USDOJ-NIC, 2011; p. 11).

5. This disparity in safety between youth and adult facilities pertains to both jails and prisons.

6. National Standards to Prevent, Detect, and Respond to Prison Rape, 77 Fed. Reg. 37,106 (June 20, 2012) (to be codified at 28 C.F.R. pt. 115). Likewise, the Bureau of Justice Statistics found that youth under 18 in adult prisons have the highest sexual victimization rate of any prisoner demographic. US Department of Justice, Bureau of Justice Statistics, Sexual Victimization Reported by Former State Prisoners 16 tbl.8 (2008).

PROMISING PRACTICES FOR YOUTH IN
THE CRIMINAL JUSTICE SYSTEM

There are no known models for keeping youth in adult prisons. This makes sense, as the United States has been moving away from this type of system of justice in sometimes sweeping and, more often, incremental steps for the past century. However, there are emerging practices that show promise of a more developmentally responsive treatment of youth while serving adult sentences. In fact, leading models keep youth in separate juvenile facilities as they begin their sentences before ultimately being transferred, between the ages of 18 and 21, to adult facilities. Other practices focused on more developmentally responsive interventions to limit, or eliminate, holding youth in isolation (a practice commonly done in adult facilities to comply with PREA—see earlier section), having adult correctional facilities exclusively serving adolescents and transitional age young adults, and training correctional staff on the unique developmental considerations for working with adolescent populations.

Separate facilities for youth sentenced as adults or delayed transfer is showing promise in several places. California, Massachusetts, and the District of Columbia have statutes that require those under 18 to be served in juvenile facilities even when convicted in the adult criminal court. Many other states operate adult correctional facilities exclusively for their adolescent and young adult offender populations. In both these scenarios, the critical shift is access to more developmentally responsive services while being surrounded by more similar aged peers. A main focus of many of these facilities is on education and job training. Education alone has been shown as one of the strongest deterrents to future criminal behavior (Lochner, 2004). In conjunction with the US Supreme Court's rulings on eligibility for parole for the vast majority of people convicted in their youth (see section on "Trends and Future Directions"), there has been a paradigm shift in youth gaining access to programming that they were previously deemed ineligible because there was no immediate gain believed when anticipating a life sentence. Beyond education, services that are youth focused also include job training, certifications, and mental health services.

Another promising practice reform has been mounting change in the use of isolation in recent years as rates of suicide and exacerbated mental health issues have been exposed. Isolation has been used throughout correctional facilities in response to behavioral problems associated with acting-out youths who are mentally challenged, chronically violent, or gang involved—a type of behavior management system (CJCA Toolkit, 2015). Regardless of behavioral problems, many facilities also use isolation in an attempt to comply with the requirements to separate youth from adults outlined in PREA. The issue is that studies of youth who serve long periods in isolation, even when done for the sake of their own protection in adult facilities, have demonstrated detrimental repercussions. For instance, over half of all youth suicides in facilities occurred while young people were isolated, and more than 60% of youth that committed suicide, while in custody, had significant histories of being held in isolation (Hayes, 2004). Other issues shown in research are that isolation, particularly solitary confinement (i.e., physical and social isolation in a cell for 22 to 24 hours per day), is psychologically damaging, denies access to education and rehabilitation, and stunts development (ACLU, 2015; Human Rights Watch, 2012). Reform efforts, including those being recently espoused by correctional administrators (CJCA Toolkit, 2015), are guiding facilities to reduce the use of isolation as a measure of absolute last resort, including limiting the time youth spend in isolation when used.

Finally, many proponents of reform suggest looking beyond a system of incarceration, and minimizing the use of incarceration at all for youthful offenders. These reforms rely on evidence-based programs in communities and outside of facilities. For example, Multisystemic Therapy (MST) has been shown to treat even violent offenders in the community with a higher likelihood of improved public safety outcomes and psychosocial functioning as compared to treatment-as-usual controls. This includes serious, antisocial, substance-abusing, and sex-offending youth without incarceration (Blueprints, 2016a; Borduin et al., 1995; Henggeler et al., 1993). Similarly, Functional family Therapy (FFT), a community-based cognitive-behavioral and relational intervention program for high-risk youth and their families, has been shown to be effective in reducing not only recidivism but also the cost of treating youth when compared to other interventions, including incarceration (Alexander et al., 2000; Aos, Barnoski & Lieb, 1998; Blueprints, 2016b). There are these and others in the research, such as Multidemensial Treatment Foster Care, or Treatment Foster Care Oregon, that have been shown to be a cost-effective alternative to incarceration (Blueprints, 2016c).

TRENDS AND FUTURE DIRECTIONS

At the national level, adolescents are more consistently being viewed as a distinct population, with unique and particular needs. Recent research has concluded that adolescents are in the midst of significant neurological and psychosocial development different from adults (NCSL, 2012; Steinberg, 2008; Steinberg et al., 2015). In the legal realm, three US Supreme Court decisions since 2005 recognize the behavior, reasoning, and judgment of adolescents as fundamentally different from adults and warranting developmentally responsive treatment.[7] Furthermore, research has shown that youth sent through the adult criminal justice system are more likely to recidivate compared to similar youth who remain in the juvenile justice system (USDHHS-CDC, 2007).

Beginning in the 1960s, the US Supreme Court began to consider adolescent development as a deciding factor in youth culpability. In 1966, the Supreme Court in *Kent v. U.S.* created standards for determining juvenile maturity and sophistication. In 1967 through the *In re Gault* case, the Supreme Court established due process provisions for individuals within the juvenile system. Most recently, the Supreme Court has specifically recognized the emerging adolescent development

7. *Roper v. Simmons* (2005); *Graham v. Florida* (2010); *Miller v. Alabama* (2012).

research and ruled that youth are fundamentally different from adults and must be treated differently under the law. Citing that adolescence is a mitigating factor in culpability, the Supreme Court abolished the juvenile death penalty for crimes committed when the defendant was younger than 18 (*Roper v. Simmons*, 2005); prohibited life sentences for juveniles convicted of nonhomicide offenses (*Graham v. Florida*, 2010); and prohibited automatic life sentences, without the possibility of parole, for juveniles convicted of any crime (*Miller v. Alabama*, 2012). With a developmentally informed view based on research, the Supreme Court noted that because adolescents are still developing, they "are more capable of change than are adults, and their actions are less likely to be evidence of 'irretrievably depraved character' than are the actions of adults."[8] As supported in the Graham decision, youth are capable of remarkable positive change and growth and can benefit greatly from rehabilitative services and support, and according to the Supreme Court, youth should be given the opportunity and resources to rehabilitate.[9] Further emphasizing this point, the court decisions since 2005 have consistently ruled that a criminal offense does not turn youths into adults.

Mass Incarceration Implications

In reality, releasing every youthful offender from adult facilities is unlikely to happen and would not put a dent in the overwhelming number of people locked up in the United States. That number currently sits at about 2.2 million people (Prison Policy Initiative, 2015). However, to take on the real reform being sought as the United States continues to lock up more people, per capita, than any other nation, every single option for reducing the population needs to be considered. Not sentencing youth offenders to adult prisons in the first place seems like one logical step.

The difference in keeping youth in juvenile justice system versus adult criminal justice systems is apparent when looking at them side by side in terms of incarceration and permanency of criminal records (see Tables 7.1 and 7.2).

Age of Criminal Culpability: The Future of Automatic Transfers of 16- and 17-Year-Olds

As of 2017, nine states continue to automatically transfer all 16- and/or 17-year-olds to the adult criminal justice systems, including adult jails and prisons. New York and North Carolina continue to transfer both 16- and 17-year-olds, while Georgia, Louisiana, Michigan, Missouri, South Carolina, Texas, and

---

8. *Graham v. Florida*, 130 S. Ct. 2011, 2025–2026 (2010) (citing "developments in psychology and brain science" showing "fundamental differences between juvenile and adult minds" and concluding that offenses committed by youth younger than 18 are "not as morally reprehensible as that of an adult").

9. *Graham*, 130 S. Ct. at 2030 ("[T]he State must . . . give defendants . . . some meaningful opportunity to obtain release based on demonstrated maturity and rehabilitation.").

Table 7.1. INCARCERATION

Delinquency Adjudication— Juvenile Justice System	Adult Conviction— Criminal Justice System
Juvenile judge may impose a determinate disposition of commitment to juvenile custody until the juvenile's 18th or 21st birthday (depending on state) provided that period does not exceed the maximum term of imprisonment established in the state statutes for the adjudicated offenses; judge may also commit the juvenile to the custody of a private or public institution or agency.	Judge may sentence defendant to a set term of incarceration up to the maximum term of imprisonment provided in state statutes.
Juvenile judge maintains authority to modify disposition to more or less restrictive conditions or settings based on rehabilitative needs of the juvenile for all but most serious offenses; in some states, considerable discretion is given to the juvenile justice agency to modify placement levels.	
Upon commitment, juvenile justice agencies must assess the child's academic grade level, develop an individualized learning plan, and often report to the juvenile court on the child's academic progress.	Any educational programming is voluntary, subject to availability, and not monitored by the court.
Prior to a juvenile's release from commitment, transitional plans must be developed addressing the juvenile's needs related to education, health, permanent connections, living arrangements, independent living skills, and employment.	Defendants are typically released with little or no support upon the expiration of their term as reentry supports and requirements vary widely in states.

Wisconsin automatically transfer all 17-year-olds. This means that these youth are not protected by juvenile delinquency proceedings and processes and are, instead, subject to adult criminal statutes and practices at all points, including questioning, arrest, detainment, court, incarceration, probation, and parole. Most of these states have active legislation to raise the age of juvenile culpability to at least 18.[10] For example, Louisiana passed legislation in 2016 that will raise the age of juvenile court jurisdiction to include 17-year-old misdemeanor offenses by 2018 and felony offenses by 2020.

10. US Department of Justice, OJJDP Statistical Briefing Book. Data are available at https://www.ojjdp.gov/ojstatbb/structure_process/qa04101.asp.

Table 7.2. RECORDKEEPING AND EXPUNGEMENT

Delinquency Adjudication—Juvenile Justice System	Adult Conviction—Criminal Justice System
Confidentiality rules apply to arrest and court records; court hearings are typically closed to the public except in cases in some states involving violent felonies and second or subsequent felony-grade adjudications.	Arrest and court records are public records; court hearings are open to the public.
Commercial background checks do not reveal juvenile arrests or adjudications, but they are available to law enforcement, courts, and other state agencies.	Commercial background checks by employers, educational institutions, and insurance carriers reveal arrests and convictions.
Juvenile expungement statutes apply to arrests, misdemeanor adjudications, and felony adjudications for offenses other than murder, manslaughter, any sexual crime, kidnapping, or armed robbery in most states.	Expungement is not permitted for felony, convictions for any crime of violence, sexual offenses, and many violations of the Uniform Controlled Dangerous Substances Law in many states.
Expungement order requires the destruction of all records and an absolute bar to the release of any information that cannot be destroyed.	Expungement of adult records means certain convictions may be sealed and closed to the general public, but it does not result in the destruction of records; information may still be released to law enforcement, courts, and licensing boards.

CASE EXAMPLE

Calvin, a 17-year-old African American youth, was arrested for battery. Because he was arrested in Michigan, he was charged as an adult. His parents were not contacted; arresting officers communicated his rights; he was interviewed by police without anyone present; and he was booked into the local jail. The local jail did not have the capacity to immediately separate him from adults, so he was held in a booking cell with 10 other men who ranged in age from 22 to 54 years.

The arrest took place at his high school. This was Calvin's first arrest as "an adult." The arrest stemmed from a fight with a 16-year-old fellow student in the bathroom of the high school. Both Calvin and the other student's behavior had been escalating during the day over a dispute involving Calvin's girlfriend. By the end of the fight, both students had thrown punches, but the fight ended with Calvin tackling the other student as the school resource officer ran into the bathroom to break it up. As Calvin tackled the student, the student's head hit the ceramic sink, and he was knocked unconscious. The other student was transported to the local ER and Calvin was taken to the local jail.

After being booked into the jail, Calvin was told he could make a phone call, but he was unable because officers had taken his cell phone and he did not know any of his relatives' phone numbers by memory. Unless the school had called his parents, he was not certain if anyone even knew he had been arrested. Without the ability to make a call, the jail staff continued his intake to the jail. Calvin was told he had to "voluntarily" submit to a drug screen at the jail or, if he refused, he would automatically be given a date to appear for a hearing at the local drug court after his release. He didn't understand why they were insisting on the drug screen since that wasn't what he was arrested for, but he also knew he didn't want to be sent to drug court. He submitted to the drug screen and it was positive for marijuana.

Calvin was held in the booking cell with no contact with anyone outside of the jail. After 2 days, his name was called and he exited the cell. He was told he was to stand in line with several other adults as they were handcuffed and their legs shackled. Just before moving the line, they were told they were going to their court hearing. Jail staff directed the line out a door and into a sheriff's van marked "inmate transport." Once at a secure prisoner holding space at the court, Calvin met a public defender who had been assigned to his case. He found out that the other student was still hospitalized and in serious condition. The attorney explained that this hearing was to review if he was to remain in jail or be considered for bail. Calvin asked if he could talk to his parents, but the attorney could not tell him if his parents were even present. At the hearing, the judge set his bail at $50,000, and he was to be held in jail until bail had been met or he was ordered differently at his next court date. That date was set in 6 months. Calvin saw his mother present in the court and briefly exchanged words while he walked with his attorney to return to the court holding cell. His mother said she would try to post bail and get him home as soon as she could.

Up until this point in Calvin's life, he was a "C student" and had made it to his junior year of high school. He had participated in football but didn't care much for being at school activities any more than necessary. He was from a low-income family and lived in a rough neighborhood with his mom, stepfather, older sister, and younger brother. He had gotten in trouble once before for shoplifting when he was 13. He was adjudicated as a juvenile delinquent for theft and was placed on probation for 6 months with community service to complete. As a teen, he smoked marijuana fairly consistently and mostly with his older sister, her boyfriend, or other kids in the neighborhood. He didn't get in much trouble at school for behavioral problems but was known to skip school several times a semester.

His mother never made bail due to her lack of resources, and Calvin was moved from the booking cell into the main population of the jail awaiting trial. The jail was not equipped to offer him high school coursework while there, so he failed his junior year. Jail administrators were also worried about his age, so they put him in isolation to "protect him from the other inmates." Calvin's attorney visited him once and recommended he take a plea deal from the District Attorney since the other student had sustained permanent injuries and Calvin's statement to the police and eyewitnesses could testify to his guilt. Calvin pled guilty to felony battery and was sentenced to 5 years in prison with the possibility of parole in 2 years. He spent 3 months in the local jail before being transferred to the adult prison over a hundred miles from his community.

In prison, Calvin was kept alone in a cell 23 hours a day for what prison guards described as "his own protection." He tried to earn his high school equivalency diploma but struggled with depression, anxiety, and suicidal thoughts throughout his imprisonment. He never completed his school and, outside of some antidepressants prescribed by the prison psychiatrist, he never received any treatment. He was released after serving 2 years in prison and returned home on parole.

On parole, he struggled to find a job and attempted to work on his high school equivalency certificate. He felt far behind and isolated from those he had known in high school. Calvin told his family that he felt he could never fit in again. He also described being constantly paranoid that, while on parole, something would go wrong and he would end up back in prison. In many ways he almost re-created the conditions of his isolation and solitary confinement at his own home, shutting himself in his bedroom for long periods. Calvin's depression worsened, and, just before his twentieth birthday, he hanged himself in his bedroom at his mother's home.

WEB-BASED RESOURCES

Accounting from 2014 of the state statues regarding those under 18 housed in adult prisons: http://cfyj.org/images/pdf/Zero_Tolerance_Report.pdf

http://www.jjgps.org/jurisdictional-boundaries#transfer-discretion

National PREA Resource Center: https://www.prearesourcecenter.org/about

The Sentencing Project. How tough on crime became tough on kids; prosecuting teenage drug charges in adult courts: http://www.sentencingproject.org/publications/tough-crime-became-tough-kids-prosecuting-teenage-drug-charges-adult-courts/

Trying juveniles as adults: An analysis of state transfer laws and reporting. US Department of Justice, Office of Juvenile Justice and Delinquency Prevention: https://www.ncjrs.gov/pdffiles1/ojjdp/232434.pdf

REFERENCES

Alexander, J. F., Pugh, C., Parsons, B. V., & Sexton, T. L.(2000). Functional family therapy. In D. C. Elliott, *Blueprints for violence prevention* (2nd ed.). Boulder, CO: Center for the Study and Prevention of Violence, Institute of Behavioral Science, University of Colorado.

American Civil Liberties Union. (2015). Ending the solitary confinement of youth in juvenile detention and correctional facilities. Retrieved from https://www.aclu.org/issues/juvenile-justice/youth-incarceration/youth-solitary-confinement

Aos, S., Barnoski, R., & Lieb, R. (1998). *Watching the bottom line: Cost effective interventions for reducing crime in Washington.* Unpublished report. Olympia, WA: Washington State Institute for Public Policy.

Blueprints for Health Youth Development. (2016a). Multisystemic therapy. Retrieved from http://www.blueprintsprograms.com/factsheet/multisystemic-therapy-mst

Blueprints for Health Youth Development. (2016b). Functional family therapy. Retrieved from http://www.blueprintsprograms.com/factsheet/functional-family-therapy-fft

Blueprints for Health Youth Development. (2016c). Treatment foster care Oregon model. Retrieved from http://www.blueprintsprograms.com/factsheet/treatment-foster-care-oregon

Borduin, C. M., Mann, B. J., Cone, L. T., Henggeler, S. W., Fucci, B. R., Blaske, D. M., & Williams, R. A. (1995). Multisystemic treatment of serious juvenile offenders: Long-term prevention of criminality and violence. *Journal of Consulting Clinical Psychology, 63,* 569–578.

Borum, R. (2003). Managing at-risk juvenile offenders in the community: Putting evidence-based principles into practice. *Journal of Contemporary Criminal Justice, 19,* 114.

Bureau of Justice Statistics (BJS). (2015). Prison Rape Elimination Act. [Data file]. Retrieved from http://www.bjs.gov/index.cfm?ty=tp&tid=20#data_collections

Butts, J. A. (2012). *Transfer of juveniles to criminal court is not correlated with falling youth violence.* New York, NY: John Jay College of Criminal Justice. Retrieved from http://johnjayresearch.org/wp-content/uploads/2012/03/databit2012_05.pdf

Campaign for Youth Justice. (2007). Jailing juveniles: The dangers of incarcerating youth in adult jails in America. Retrieved from http://www.campaign4youthjustice.org/Downloads/NationalReportsArticles/CFYJ-Jailing_Juveniles_Report_2007-11-15.pdf

Carson, A. E. (2015). *Prisoners in 2014.* Washington, DC: US Department of Justice, BJS. Retrieved from https://www.bjs.gov/content/pub/pdf/p14.pdf

Council for Juvenile Correctional Administrators (CJCA) (2015). Council of Juvenile Correctional administrators toolkit: Reducing the use of isolation. Retrieved from http://cjca.net/attachments/article/751/CJCA%20Toolkit%20Reducing%20the%20Use%20of%20Isolation.pdf

Daugherty, C. (2015). *Zero tolerance: How states comply with PREA's youthful inmate standard.* Washington, DC: Campaign for Youth Justice. Available at http://cfyj.org/images/pdf/Zero_Tolerance_Report.pdf

Griffin, P., Addie, S., Adams, B., & Firestine, K. (2011). *Trying juveniles as adults: An analysis of state transfer laws and reporting.* Washington, DC: US Department of Justice, Office of Juvenile Justice and Delinquency Prevention. Retrieved from https://www.ncjrs.gov/pdffiles1/ojjdp/232434.pdf

Hayes, L. (2004). *Juvenile suicide in confinement: A national study.* Washington, DC: US Department of Justice, Office of Justice Program, OJJDP. Retrieved from https://www.ncjrs.gov/pdffiles1/ojjdp/213691.pdf

Henggeler, S. W., Melton, G. B., Smith, L. A., Schoenwald, S. K., & Hanley, J. H. (1993). Family preservation using multisystemic treatment: Long-term follow-up to a clinical trial with serious juvenile offenders. *Journal of Child and Family Studies, 2,* 283–293.

Human Rights Watch. (2012). Growing up locked down: Youth in solitary confinement in jails and prisons across America. Retrieved from https://www.aclu.org/sites/de-fault/files/field_document/us1012webwcover.pdf

Lochner, L. (2004). Education, work, and crime: A human capital approach. *International Economic Review, 45*(3), 811–843.

Lowencamp, C. T., & Latessa, E. J. (2004). Understanding the risk principle: How and why correctional interventions can harm low risk offenders. National Institute of Corrections. Retrieved from http://www.yourhonor.com/dwi/sentencing/RiskPrinciple.pdf

Miller v. Alabama. (2012). Supreme Court of the United States. June 25, 2012. Available at https://origin-www.bloomberglaw.com/public/desktop/document/Miller_v_Alabama_No_Nos_109646_109647_2012_BL_157303_US_June_25_2?1516682884

Mulvey, E. P. (2011). Highlights from pathways to desistance: A longitudinal study of serious adolescent offenders. US Department of Justice. Retrieved from https://ncjrs.gov/pdffiles1/ojjdp/230971.pdf

Mulvey, E. P., Steinberg, L., Piquero, A. R., Besana, M., Fagan, J., Schubert, C., & Cauffman, E. (2010). Trajectories of desistance and continuity in antisocial behavior following court adjudication among serious adolescent offenders. *Development and Psychopathology, 22*, 453–470.

National Conference of State Legislatures (NCSL). (2012). Adolescent development & competency. *Juvenile Justice Guidebook for Legislators.* Retrieved from http://www.ncsl.org/documents/cj/jjguidebook-adolescent.phf.

Phillippi, S., Siegel, G., Scharf, P., Atkinson, R., McCann, E., & Arteaga, P. (2016). A legislated study of raising the age of juvenile jurisdiction in Louisiana: The future of 17-year-olds in the Louisiana justice system. In response to Louisiana House Concurrent Resolution No. 73 of the 2015 Regular Session. New Orleans, LA: Louisiana State University Institute for Public Health & Justice. Retrieved from http://lsuhsc.wpengine.com/wp-content/uploads/2016/07/RAISE_THE_AGE_DRAFT_20160128Final.pdf

Prison Policy Initiative. (2015). Mass incarceration: The whole pie 2015. Retrieved from http://www.prisonpolicy.org/reports/pie2015.html

Redding, R. E. (2010). *Juvenile transfer laws: An effective deterrent to delinquency?* Washington, DC: US Office of Juvenile Justice and Delinquency Prevention. Retrieved from https://www.ncjrs.gov/pdffiles1/ojjdp/220595.pdf

Roper v. Simmons. (2005). Official U.S. Supreme Court opinion March 1, 2005. Available at https://www.supremecourt.gov/opinions/04pdf/03-633.pdf

Steinberg, L. (2008). Adolescent development and juvenile justice. *Annual Review of Clinical Psychology, 16*(3). Retrieved from http://fairsentencingofyouth.org/wp-content/uploads/2010/02/Adolescent-development-and-juvenile-justice.pdf

Steinberg, L., Cauffman, E., & Monahan, K. (2015). *Psychosocial maturity and desistance from crime in a sample of serious juvenile offenders.* Washington, DC: OJJDP Juvenile Justice Bulletin. US Department of Justice. Retrieved from https://www.ojjdp.gov/pubs/248391.pdf

Terrance Jamar Graham, Petitioner v. Florida. (2010). Supreme Court of the United States. May 17, 2010. Available at https://www.supremecourt.gov/opinions/09pdf/08-7412.pdf

US Department of Health and Human Services—Centers for Disease Control (USDHHS-CDC) (2007). Effects on violence of laws and policies facilitating the transfer of youth from the juvenile to the adult justice system: A report on recommendations of the Task Force on Community Preventive Services. *Morbidity and Mortality Weekly Report, 1*(6). Retrieved from http://www.cdc.gov/mmwr/ PDF/rr/rr5609.pdf

US Department of Justice, National Institute of Corrections (USDOJ-NIC) (2011). You're an adult now: Youth in adult criminal justice systems. 9, 15. https://s3.amazonaws. com/static.nicic.gov/Library/025555.pdf

Ward, J. M. (2003). Deterrence's difficulty magnified: The importance of adolescent development in assessing deterrence value of transferring juveniles to adult court. *U.C. Davis Journal of Juvenile Law & Policy, 7*, 253–267.

8

Substance Abuse Treatment in Prison

The Therapeutic Community

MATTHEW HILLER AND CHRISTINE SAUM

The mass incarceration of nonviolent drug offenders, as a sequela of the "War on Drugs," has created a nexus where both public safety and public health issues can be effectively addressed.[1] With respect to public safety, prisons function in multiple roles, including retribution, incapacitation, and deterrence. Correspondingly, prisons punish those who have broken society's laws, separates these individuals from the law-abiding population, and shows other potential offenders they will face similar consequences if they too break the law. Within prisons, safety and security are the primary foci, with the majority of staff devoted to maintaining order through continual surveillance of the inmate population, movement of inmates from one place to another, searches for contraband (including alcohol and illicit drugs), and intervention (possibly with force) when an inmate fails to abide by the rule, and or threatens or assaults another inmate or staff. Indeed, prisons are mandated with providing for the safety and welfare of their inmate population. And, since the Supreme Court rulings in *Estelle v. Ruiz* (1976) and *Bowring v. Goodwin* (1977), prisons are also responsible for ensuring inmates have access to adequate health and behavioral health care (Soderstrom, 2007). However, it is less clear what responsibilities correctional systems have as far as providing rehabilitation to their offenders. Though there is some consensus that recently there has been a paradigm shift occurring in the field where there is more of an emphasis on correctional rehabilitation (Tripodi, 2014), there exist many

---

1. Although both prisons and jails are the primary correctional institutions in the United States, the only focus of this chapter is on prisons. Prisons and jails are different on key dimensions, making them distinct and each deserving their own focus. That is, prisons incarcerate only sentenced offenders who have committed crimes for which they received a sentence of 1 year or more. Jails may include numerous types of offenders, including sentenced, awaiting trial, newly booked, and awaiting transfer. Jail stays, except for sentenced offenders, are typically very brief, and most sentenced offenders have fewer than 1 year to serve.

inconsistencies with regard to the provision and availability of substance abuse treatment to correctional populations. This raises the significance of health issues among prisoners for prison administrators and for policymakers. And a significant amount of research shows the public health problems affecting prisoners are diverse and significantly more common than in community populations. These include infectious diseases like HIV, hepatitis and tuberculosis, physical health problems, violence and trauma-related problems, and substance abuse and its frequent co-occurrence with serious mental health problems (Belenko, Hiller, & Hamilton, 2013; Belenko & Peugh, 2005; Blevins & Soderstrom, 2015; Ditton, 1999; Magaletta, Diamond, Faust, Daggett, & Camp, 2009; Mumola & Karberg, 2006; Soderstrom, 2007). The latter is the focus of this chapter, which will first describe the scope of the problem of substance use (and frequent co-occurring serious mental health) disorders among prisoners; highlight an evidence-based intervention model, the therapeutic community (TC), for addressing substance abuse (and co-occurring disorders); describe specific examples of TCs and corresponding research; and address policy implications and issues. Also presented is a case analysis of in-prison therapeutic communities in the Pennsylvania Department of Corrections.

SCOPE OF PROBLEM

Although 2014 was the first time in 36 years that both state and federal prison populations decreased, there were still more than 1.5 million men and women in prison at the end of 2015 (Carson, 2015; Carson & Anderson, 2016). State prisoners were the majority (about 1.3 million), and federal prisons held about 200,000 inmates. About 15% of state and almost half (49.5%) of federal prisoners were incarcerated for drug offenses (Carson & Anderson, 2016). But defining the scope of the problem of substance abuse problems among prisoners must also incorporate other indicators. In an update to its *Behind Bars* (CASA, 1998) report, the National Center on Addiction and Substance Abuse (CASA, 2010) conducted an in-depth analysis of multiple inmate data sources and estimated that 86% of federal and 85% of state prison inmates were substance involved.[2] Focusing on more direct measures, CASA (2010) estimates that 64.5% met criteria of alcohol or illicit drug use dependence disorders in the year prior to incarceration. Illicit drug use is highly implicated in crime, with "54.3 percent of alcohol law violators, 77.2 percent of those who committed a property crime, 65.4 percent of inmates who committed violent crimes, and 67.6 percent of those who committed other crimes either committed their crime to get money to buy drugs, were under the

2. Substance involved was defined as having any of the following indicators: history of regular illicit drug use, met medical criteria for as substance abuse disorder, were under the influence of alcohol or drugs when committing their crime, history of alcohol treatment, incarcerated for a drug law violation, committed their offense to get money to buy drugs, or were incarcerated for an alcohol law violation (see CASA, 2010, p. 10)

influence of drugs at the time of the crime, had a history of regular drug use or had a drug use disorder" (CASA, 2010, p. 13).

Further complicating matters is the large number of seriously mentally ill prisoners who often have co-occurring substance abuse problems (Diamond, Wang, Holzer, Thomas, & des Agnes, 2001; Lurigio, 2011, Rojas & Peters, 2016). Serious mental illness[3] has been estimated to affect 16% of state and 4.4% of federal prison inmates (Ditton, 1999). Magaletta and colleagues (2009),[4] using data from the Mental Health Prevalence Project, report that 15.2% of federal inmates need some level of psychiatric care. Nearly 7% of prisoners have schizophrenia, compared to 1.4% in the general community population (Peters, Sherman, & Osher, 2008). The conclusion by many is that jails and prisons have become the de facto mental health system for the seriously mentally ill who lack the resources or access to community mental health treatment (Lamb & Weinberger, 2005; Lurigio, 2011).

The focus of this chapter on the in-prison therapeutic community as an evidence-based practice is appropriate because it is one of the best-researched modalities, and it has been adapted to focus on prisoners with co-occurring disorders. In fact, therapeutic communities were originally developed for psychiatric patients, then adapted for substance abuse treatment, modified to operate with in correctional institutions, and then adapted again to address specially populations, like those with co-occurring mental health and substance abuse problems in the correctional system. To provide insight into this treatment modality, we first present a brief summary of the theoretical underpinnings of therapeutic communities.

THERAPEUTIC COMMUNITIES

The scholarship of George De Leon and colleagues has largely defined modern therapeutic community (TC) treatment theory and methods for substance abuse disorders. A comprehensive review of this modality is found in De Leon (1995, 2000; De Leon, Perfas, Joseph, & Bunt, 2015; National Institute on Drug Abuse, 2015), who presents a theoretical framework for TCs focused on perspective, model, and method. This also is often referred to in the literature as the essential elements of the TC (De Leon et al., 2015; Melnick & De Leon, 1999; Melnick, De Leon, Hiller, Knight, & Simpson 2000).

Therapeutic Community Perspective

Perspective explains the theory behind therapeutic community treatment in four areas, including the view of the disorder, view of the person, view of recovery, and view of right living (De Leon, 2000). The first highlights the perspective that the

3. Serious mental illness was defined as a self-reported mental or emotional condition or an overnight stay in a mental hospital or program.

4. A conservative definition of serious mental illness was used, focused on schizophrenia, schizoaffective disorder, major depression, and bipolar disorder.

disorder is not only substance abuse, but it is only one of the multiple problems faced by the individual whose life is in crisis, and who is unable to maintain sobriety or abstinence on his or her own. Etiology of substance abuse lies in biomedical (e.g., genes) and social and psychological factors, with antecedents, including low socioeconomic status, dysfunctional parenting, and negative role models and deviant social modeling. Psychologically, the person may be self-medicating painful, negative affective states, avoiding reality (including everyday stress as well as histories of trauma and abuse), or seeking pleasure and stimulation. Regardless of the etiology, the TC perspective is that the person is responsible for his or her own recovery. Related to this is the view that substance abuse is a disorder of the "whole person." Individuals are steeped in the drug abuse lifestyle and have taken little responsibility for themselves nor have they engaged in socially normative behavior. Unemployment and poor educational achievement are common, and familial duties have been ignored or neglected for a considerable time. Beyond immediate family, other social relationships are strained or nonexistent, with estrangement from parents, siblings, and friends not involved in drug use likely. A variety of negative cognitions are evident, including poor self-awareness of how their actions affect others around them, poor judgement and decision making, poor reality testing, and lack of insight into how they are harming themselves or into the relationship between their drug use and their emotions. Other personal characteristics include low self-esteem, low self-control, unrealistic self-appraisal, low tolerance for discomfort, guilt, anger, and hostility, dysphoria, poor emotional self-regulation, narcissism and entitlement, dishonesty, and a lack of responsibility and accountability. A change in the aforementioned characteristics is essential for stable recovery (De Leon et al., 2015). The drug abuse lifestyle is inherently antisocial, devoted to illegal drug use or procurement and criminal activity, prompting De Leon (2000) to note in regard to the TCs view of recovery, "Many other TC residents have never acquired functional lifestyles . . . . For these residents, their tenure in the TC is usually their first exposure to orderly living. Recovery for them involves habilitation, or learning the behavioral skills, attitudes and values associated with socialized living for the first time" (p. 66). The view of right living inculcates the resident to these values and morals, which include honesty, learning to learn, personal accountability, responsibility, social manners, community involvement, and a work ethic (De Leon, 2000; De Leon et al., 2015).

Therapeutic Community Model

Collectively, the TC model[5] reflects the social structure of the community, staff and peer roles, group and individual counseling, community meetings, and program stages. Each is designed to use the *community as method* (see next section),

---

5. The TC perspective, model, and method sections in this chapter are highly condensed summaries of a much broader treatment of this by De Leon (2000), *The Therapeutic Community: Theory, Model, and Method* (New York, NY: Springer). For those interested in learning about TCs, we strongly encourage them to get a copy of this book because it is an exhaustive description of this treatment modality.

promote affiliation with the community, and lead to prosocial self-change (De Leon et al., 2015). Socially, the community is structured with staff and senior members of the community at the top of the hierarchy and new residents at the bottom. Often a "structure board" is visibly prominent showing the stratification of the program into staff, peer level (junior, intermediate, and senior), treatment phase, and specific job within the community (De Leon, 2010). The purpose of the structure is to promote the sense of an ordered community, carefully specifying the relationships of mutual responsibility of staff and particularly the residents for themselves and for contributing to the self-help of others. Practically, it ensures the day-to-day operation of the TC by specifying the roles and tasks assigned to residents. Staff function as monitors of the TC environment, ensuring the structure is running smoothly and the day-to-day activities are accomplished. Continual monitoring helps ensure a safe and secure environment. Staff and resident serve as peer role models (De Leon et al., 2015). Staff also provide both individual and group counseling to program residents, which at their core are based on 12-step self-help (e.g., Alcoholics Anonymous) (De Leon, 2010). Other TC clinical groups (i.e., encounter, probes, and marathon) are key intervention points. These are led by staff (residents have primary responsibility in encounter groups) and are focused specifically on treatment issues (De Leon, 2000). Daily community meetings (i.e., morning meeting, seminar, and house) are usually led by senior peer residents and are used to initiate a positive outlook for the day, motivate participation in the community, teach TC concepts and perspective, and manage community business (De Leon, 2000, 2015).

TC phases include induction, primary treatment, and reentry (De Leon, 2000). The Induction Phase (the first 30 days following entry) focuses on bringing the new resident into the community, teaching him or her community norms, orienting him or her to how the community operates, setting expectations for self-help and affiliation with the community, and the inception of substance abuse treatment sessions (De Leon, 2000). After meeting specific community and clinical benchmarks, one is promoted to the second, Main Treatment, phase (De Leon, 2000). During the 10-month duration of this phase, which is often segmented into three subphases (Junior, Intermediate, and Senior), individuals are immersed in the community as method (also see next section) and provided individual and group counseling. Within this TC phase, social structure is linked to program phase, with higher status and greater responsibility added at each phase shift (De Leon, 2000). For the first subphase (Junior Peer), intraindividual changes are made, including acceptance of being a community member, acknowledgment of the problems that drug use has caused in their life, and reduced dysphoria (De Leon, 2000). For the second subphase (Intermediate Peer), social status within the community is elevated and greater responsibility is placed on the individual for being a full member engaged in self-change and helping others to change. Internal changes during this subphase include fully accepting personal responsibility for past and current behavior, improved honesty, improved self-esteem, deeper self-awareness, and personal growth reflecting these (De Leon, 2000). In the final subphase, Senior Peer, the resident is an established role model for others in the program, has significant roles in running the community as a coordinator, and also assists staff with treatment groups. Internal changes include insight into, as well as taking responsibility for, their drug problems, higher, more stable self-esteem, and high willingness to disclose information about oneself during group meetings. The Senior Peer subphase helps the resident transition to the next and final program stage, Reentry (De Leon, 2000).

The Reentry phase is typically divided into an early residential subphase and a nonresidential subphase, both lasting about 6 months. During this phase, the resident begins his or her separation from the TC community as he or she transitions back to society, which is done gradually with increasing levels of autonomy and longer lengths of time spent outside of the community. Ultimately, the individual transitions to living in society, has a job or is going to school, is actively self-monitoring for relapse situations, and interacts informally with the community by giving back to others through sharing experiences openly and honestly with the rest of the residents.

Therapeutic Community

"The quintessential element of the TC is community. What distinguishes the TC from other treatment approaches . . . is the purposive use of the community as the primary method for facilitating social and psychological change" (De Leon, 1995, p. 1611). The TC represents a 24-hour immersive treatment experience that requires the individual to assimilate into the community, which is also sometimes referred to as "the family." The idea of being a member of the larger TC community is paramount, with numerous activities (e.g., see earlier) geared specifically to reinforcing this. The community becomes the most important and omnipresent force for change, with peers mutually fostering self-change and habilitation by serving as active role models and engaging in pull-ups (verbal confrontation of a fellow resident's antisocial behavior) and push-ups (verbal praise to a fellow resident for a positive behavior) and actively engaging as intermediate and senior peers in TC groups and meetings. For example, peer encounter groups are used to confront destructive past or present attitudes and behaviors that do not support the values of the community; individuals are confronted for the purpose of assisting them to get rid of this undesirable conduct by bringing awareness of the attitudes and behaviors and how they contribute to a destructive lifestyle. Moreover, the community follows clear, specific rules that set the expectations of "right living," mirroring the social norms of the larger society to which one will return. Privileges are used to promote individual socialization and personal growth (De Leon, 2000, p. 212), and sanctions are used to reinforce the rules of the community, serving as vicarious learning experiences for the other individuals who were not sanctioned. Ultimately, internalization of all of the community expectations, values, norms, knowledge, and structure facilitates self-change, habilitating or rehabilitating the individual into positive, prosocial members of society (De Leon, 2000).

MODIFICATIONS TO THE THERAPEUTIC COMMUNITY
FOR PRISONS

Few community-based TC programs adhere fully to the traditional (as described earlier under perspective, model, and method) model, and from our experience, this also is particularly true for in-prison therapeutic communities (De Leon, 2000; De Leon et al., 2015; Saum et al., 2007; Wexler & Prendergast, 2010). Modifications made to the TC model stem from Department of Corrections' policies and procedures for practical and budgetary reasons (including availability of trained staff and space limitations, and for accommodating special populations like women and the seriously mentally ill). Modifications made for these special populations are addressed later in this chapter.

For example, for traditional TCs, staff typically play background roles, monitoring the residents' activities and the physical aspects of the program because the whole community is the change agent. From our experience, however, in-prison TCs rely much more heavily on professional staff to initiate and conduct most of the therapeutic activities. Ideally, professional staff for traditional TCs are recovering individuals who themselves have completed a TC, and from De Leon's (2000) perspective, these are the individuals who will be viewed as most credible by TC residents. However, most prison systems have policies that expressly preclude the employment of ex-offenders as staff. This dramatically limits the ability of agencies to recruit TC-trained staff because these individuals themselves have extensive criminal histories and prior convictions. To help address this limitation, one agency with whom we have worked developed an extensive, standardized TC curriculum to facilitate the training of new in-prison TC staff (Welsh & Zajac, 2004a,b). Manual-based treatment, in and of itself, also represents a modification to the traditional TC model.

Traditional TCs seek to maintain boundaries separating the community from the setting in which they are located (De Leon, 2000), to limit the influences of anything external to the program. In many prisons, this is addressed by designating a TC housing wing or pod. In this setting, residents are almost completely shielded from the procriminal influences of being a general prison inmate, with external contact limited to assembling in the prison yard for the "count" (correctional staff count prisoners several times a day to ensure security and limit escapes) and meals. However, space is a real concern with many prisons, especially of those with crowded and overcapacity housing conditions, and a separate physical space for the TC is impractical. One of us worked closely with a TC without a designated housing unit that developed a novel solution to this problem. This program provided orange safety vests to all residents to set them "apart" from the general inmate population. Residents were restricted from interacting with the general population, and when one broke this rule, the resident who witnessed it was expected to give a "pull-up" to the individual.

The pull-up, as a method for peers reprimanding each other's' antisocial behavior (e.g., rule breaking; not engaging in the TC process), is difficult to put in practice in in-prison therapeutic communities (McGrain, 2006). Anecdotally, professional staff in multiple in-prison therapeutic communities with whom we have worked, have described the unwillingness of residents to verbally reprimand other TC residents. This is usually attributed to the fact that most residents reside in the general prison population for many years before beginning a TC (usually in the last few months before their parole eligibility or serve-out dates). Longer incarceration tends to increase prisonization, the socialization of the individual into the antisocial culture and norms of inmate life. Prison inmate social norms, like don't "snitch," and retaliation against others who have "wronged" them, are incongruous with pulling up another person. Ironically, the TC goals of habilitating and rehabilitating an inmate into a prosocial individual is greatly complicated by the social learning experience that inmates go through prior to becoming TC residents.

As noted earlier, space has been a major concern for prison systems, though TCs housed separately from the general population often are exempt from agency directives to increase the number of bunks in prison cells to accommodate crowding. However, because parole boards may be influenced by an inmate's programming (see Vilcica, 2015, 2016), in-prison TCs also may serve as a way to get inmates released more quickly, freeing space and possibly reducing crowding problems. A solution that one department of corrections tried was developing TC programs of different duration (i.e., 4, 6, 9, and 12 months). The annual inmate capacity of a 4-month program is 1 ½ times that of a 6-month program and 3 times more than a 12-month program. The idea here was that if the same benefits (e.g., reduced recidivism post-release) were evident for shorter durations as they were for longer durations, then the agency could convert all extant programs to that shorter duration. Despite the willingness of this agency to randomly assign inmates with substance abuse problems to programs with different durations, and despite several attempts by researchers to conduct this study, it ultimately was abandoned because grant applications to federal agencies were not successful in getting funding for this study. This is unfortunate because there are few studies on the ideal program length for a TC to achieve reduced recidivism (see Wexler & Prendergast, 2010).

Separate housing for in-prison TCs also introduces issues related to management of inmate and staff security and safety. Interestingly, there are several scientific studies that show that in-prison TCs improve safety and make the institution easier to manage because TC inmates commit few (compared to the general prison population) infractions (Dietz, O'Connell, & Scarpitti, 2003; Prendergast, Farabee, & Cartier, 2001; Zhang, Roberts, & McCollister, 2009). For example, Dietz, O'Connell, and Scarpitti (2003) found significantly lower rates of violent (7.6 per 100 versus 49 per 100) and nonviolent infractions (21.2 per 100 versus 60.4 per 100) as well as lower rates of inmate grievances (41.5 per 100 versus 129.4 per 100) for in-prison TC compared to nontreatment prison units. This is consistent with one of our experiences where the residents of an in-prison TC alerted the warden to a security staff member who was bringing drugs and other contraband into the prison. Reduced infraction rates have a tangible positive economic impact on prison expenditures. Illustrating this, Zhang, Roberts, and McCollister

(2009) found that in-prison TC s were more cost-efficient relative to nontreatment prison units by generating significantly lower administrative costs for disciplinary actions, grievances, and major incidents like lockdowns. Moreover, one of the authors of this chapter noted, anecdotally, that it is very common for correctional officers to request placement in TCs because of the better overall working environment compared with the general population. However, not all studies have found a significant impact of in-prison TC on prison management (Welsh, McGrain, Salamatin, & Zajac, 2008).

Effectiveness of In-Prison Therapeutic Communities

The evidence base for in-prison therapeutic communities includes reviews and meta-analyses of the empirical literature (Belenko, Hiller, & Hamilton, 2013; Galassi, Mpofu, & Anthansou, 2015; Mitchell, Wilson, & MacKenzie, 2007; Vanderplasschen et al., 2013), as well as evaluations of single programs (e.g., Hiller, Knight, & Simpson, 1999; Inciardi, Martin, & Butzin, 2004; Prendergast, Hall, Wexler, Melnick, & Cao, 2004). General conclusions drawn from this literature are that in-prison therapeutic communities are most effective when continuity of care is maintained during reentry through community-based aftercare and when used with the inmates with the most severe clinical profiles. In addition, general findings are that in-prison TCs have stronger impacts on recidivism than on drug use following community reentry, but these impacts are seen in shorter (e.g., 1-year) rather than longer (e.g., 5-year) follow-up intervals. These points are emphasized in our review of the best-known in-prison TCs provided in the next section. However, additional caveats apply. Many urge caution when drawing interpretations from the empirical literature on the effectiveness of prison-based TCs (Belenko, Hiller, & Hamilton, 2013; De Leon, 2010; Jensen & Kane, 2012) because research designs are typically weak and are based on single programs. Further complicating inferences about TC effectiveness is that there has been very little done with respect to assessing the fidelity to which programs adhere to the TC theory and methods (described earlier); thus, it is unclear to what extent each TC was actually a therapeutic community program. Also, more recent studies have sought to correct this significant problem by using multiple sites (Jensen & Kane, 2010, 2012; Welsh, 2007; Welsh & Zajac, 2013) and randomized designs (Welsh, Zajac, & Bucklen, 2014), and these are summarized in a later section of this chapter.

The research summarized in the next section highlights specific in-prison therapeutic community programs as well as programs that have been specifically modified to address co-occurring disorders and women inmates. Most of these are listed on CrimeSolutions.gov, the national repository for evidence-based programs and practices (EBPPs) for addressing delinquency, crime, and crime prevention. One of these, the Kyle New Vision program, is not listed but is included because of one of the author's extensive experience with it. First, in-prison TCs focused on male prisoners with drug and alcohol disorders (Stay'n Out, Key/

Crest, Amity, and Kyle New Vision), and then adaptations for special populations, including women (Forever Free), and for those with co-occurring disorders (MICA TC) are discussed.

In-Prison Therapeutic Community

STAY 'N OUT

The Stay 'N Out program implemented in New York State prisons is recognized as the primary model for prison-based TCs for substance abusers because it has been replicated throughout the United States and internationally (Wexler, Falkin, & Lipton, 1990; Wexler & Prendergast, 2010; Wexler & Williams, 1986). In this program, participants in both a male and a female institution attended group and individual counseling sessions and special workshops while maintaining jobs within the dedicated residential unit. Participants advanced through three program phases as they successfully moved forward in the program. Graduates were encouraged to continue in aftercare treatment in the community.

The first major evaluation of TCs for substance abusers was completed on the Stay 'N Out program. This large study (n = 1,500+) compared the program participants to a no-treatment control group (volunteers who never participated) and to convenience samples of inmates who participated in other types of substance abuse treatment programs in different prisons. As far as criminal activity, male Stay 'N Out offenders were significantly less likely to be arrested (27%) compared with the control offenders who had no treatment (41%) and the comparison groups who had other forms of treatment (35%–40%). Women study participants also had significantly better arrest outcomes (18%) compared with the control (24%) and one of the other treatment groups (30%). Moreover, strong relationships found between time in program and treatment outcomes established the norm for correctional TCs in the United States to last between 9 and 12 months (Wexler & Prendergrast, 2010).

KEY/CREST

Based in Delaware, the KEY is a prison-based TC for substance abusers and the CREST is a residential work release program where offenders can continue their in-prison treatment in the community. To ensure a better reintegration process, there is also an aftercare component that helps participants with the transition from incarceration back to society. Thus, as a multistage treatment program, KEY/CREST provides a treatment continuum of primary (prison), secondary (work-release), and tertiary (aftercare), which follows the participant from prison through the reentry period. Beginning with the KEY program during the last 12–18 months of their incarceration, participants reside in a total treatment environment with programming each day of the week that is designed to change negative behaviors and thinking patterns. Treatment includes group sessions, program assignments, and individual counseling. As participants move forward in the program, they move up a hierarchy of responsibility but are subject to discipline as required.

Once released, graduates of the KEY move on to the CREST community-based program where they live and continue treatment on a full-time basis. After about 3 months, participants are permitted to begin the work-release program where they work part of the day, still living at the residence and receiving treatment during their nonworking hours. After CREST completion, offenders on probation take part in the aftercare component, where offenders return weekly for group sessions, counseling, and drug testing.

Based on the CrimeSolutions.gov rating scale, the KEY-CREST program has earned a "Promising" score. One study conducted interviews with treatment participants and comparison offenders that were completed several times beginning at 6 months post incarceration. Study groups that were examined at each time period included those who participated in KEY only, CREST only, both KEY and Crest, and those who also participated in the aftercare component. The no-treatment comparison group was comprised of offenders who were assigned to an HIV/AIDS prevention education program only. Results from the 6-month follow-up study indicated that the KEY-CREST and the CREST-only groups did significantly better (more likely to be drug and arrest free) than the KEY-only and comparison groups (Martin, Butzin, & Inciardi, 1995). At 1 and 3 years post prison, crime and drug-free status was significantly better for the treatment groups compared with the no-treatment group (Martin, Butzin, Saum, & Inciardi, 1999). Moreover, 5 years after prison, Inciardi and his colleagues (2004) found that participation in treatment increased the odds of remaining drug- and arrest-free compared with the no-treatment group.

AMITY

The Amity In-Prison Therapeutic Community located in California is an all-male intensive substance abuse treatment program. Participants reside in a dedicated unit during the last 9 to 12 months of their prison term. The program consists of three phases where Amity volunteers receive a variety of treatment services while helping to maintain the TC and also working within the larger prison industry. Treatment includes counseling sessions, encounter groups, and informal teaching sessions but also uses a formal curriculum for some components. As participants make successful progress in the program, they are given positions where they have increasing responsibilities within the TC. A unique part of the program are the "lifer mentors," who under supervision of program staff, provide support and counsel to participants. Finally, to increase the likelihood of a smoother reentry, participants work on postdischarge planning with parole staff prior to release and have the option to participate in a community residential aftercare program (Wexler et al., 1999b).

Crimesolutions.gov lists a "Promising" rating for the Amity TC program. The original study of Amity by Wexler and his colleagues (1999a) using random selection of participants ($n = 715$) in an intent-to-treat design found that 1 year post release, 34% of the participants in the study group were reincarcerated compared with 50% of the no-treatment control group. Moreover, the subgroup of participants who completed both the in-prison and aftercare TCs had a reincarceration rate of only 8% percent. Significantly greater levels of recidivism were also found 3 years post release for the control group (75%) compared with the community treatment group completers (27%). A 5-year postprogram follow-up study by Prendergast and his colleagues (2003), who located and interviewed a large majority (81%) of the original sample of Amity participants, found 76% of the treatment group had at least one reincarceration over the 5 years, compared to 83% percent of the control group. Finally, a cost-effectiveness study found that Amity participants had 81 fewer incarceration days compared to the control group, leading to the conclusion that prison treatment followed by aftercare is a cost-effective criminal justice strategy (McCollister et al., 2004).

KYLE NEW VISION
Located in Texas, the Kyle New Vision program is a prison-based TC that incorporates a three-stage treatment process. Participants begin treatment while in prison, continue with residential corrections-based TC treatment as part of a work-release model in the community, and then take part in the required outpatient aftercare component while they are under parole supervision. Participants move through the stages as they complete required tasks and learning activities as they are gradually reintegrated back into society. New Vision helps participants make positive behavioral changes and stresses personal development and responsibility.

Examinations of the New Vision program have yielded positive results. Hiller and colleagues (1999) compared released TC participants on parole (n = 293) with a matched sample of parolees who were eligible but did not re-ceive treatment (n = 103). The researchers found that during the 13–23-month follow-up period, over 40% of the no-treatment parolees were rearrested compared with 36% of those who participated in the prison TC only and 30% of participants who completed the three-phase model. Three years after prison re-lease, the same sample was analyzed and results indicated that only one quarter of graduates who had completed the full treatment model returned to prison compared to over two fifths of the untreated comparison group (Knight et al., 1999). These studies find that completing all of the treatment phases of the program has a better and longer impact than only completing the prison-based component and that aftercare is integral to correctional treatment (Knight et al., 1999). Moreover, a cost-effectiveness study of New Vision concluded that the program was only economically viable when the three stages are completed and that the biggest cost savings were found for the highest risk participants (Griffith et al., 1999).

Modified In-Prison Therapeutic Communities for Special Populations

FOREVER FREE
Forever Free is credited with being the first comprehensive intensive prison-based substance-abuse treatment program for women. This California-based voluntary

TC program utilized a cognitive-behavioral curriculum and a focus on relapse prevention. Many of the educational topics such as self-esteem, co-dependency, healthy relationships, and posttraumatic stress disorder (PTSD) were designed to be women centered. The 6-month program was provided to women nearing the end of their incarceration period and also included a 6-month voluntary community residential component for graduates once on parole. Program participants resided in a special unit where they received treatment and services for part of the day while also participating in work and education programs throughout the prison. Forever Free was closed in 2010 due to budget cuts; however, a program based on this model was developed for women substance abusers in another California prison (Crimesolutions.gov).

An evaluation of the Forever Free program earned it a "Promising" rating from Crimesolutions.gov. A study by Hall and colleagues (2004) examined 119 women who participated in the Forever Free program and 95 women who participated in a comparison group of women enrolled in an 8-week substance abuse education course. Multivariate results showed that at 6 months after release, about 13% of the study group had been reincarcerated compared with about one third of the comparison group. At 1 year post release, about one third of the Forever Free women were reincarcerated compared with about 44% of the comparison women. Additional analyses highlighted the importance of aftercare; researchers found that as treatment exposure increased from no treatment in prison or on parole to treatment both in prison and during parole, reincarceration significantly decreased (Hall et al., 2004).

MICA

A specialized TC program was created for the growing group of offenders with co-occurring disorders of drug abuse and mental health: Modified Therapeutic Community for Offenders with Mental Illness and Chemical Abuse (MICA) Disorders. This Colorado prison program was based on the first MICA program, which was developed for homeless persons referred to residential substance abuse treatment facilities in the community. MICA programs differed from typical TCs in that they were more individualized while being less intensive and more flexible to better meet the needs of offenders with mental health disorders. Additionally, to adapt the MICA for an offender population, there was an added focus on changing criminal thinking patterns and on participants understanding the relationship between drugs, crime, and mental health.

Crimesolutions.gov lists MICA as a "Promising" program. A randomized study of 185 inmates by Sullivan, McKendrick, Sacks, and Banks (2007) compared MICA inmates in a 1-year prison program to a control group that received the customary treatment for mental health and relapse prevention. The treatment group also had the option to continue the program in aftercare for 6 months after release. Both groups were followed up 1 year post discharge; interviews were conducted with the 75% of participants that could be located. Researchers found that the participants in the specialized MICA program had better outcomes for all variables related to substance use; they were significantly less likely to report using drugs, to be drug-free for a longer period, and for those who did return to drug use, it was less often and less severe.

Similarly, Sacks, Sacks, McKendrick, Banks, and Stommel (2004) examined crime outcomes for this sample and found that inmates in the MICA treatment group and MICA treatment group plus aftercare had statistically significantly lower rates of incarceration (9%, 5%) compared with the control group (33%). These researchers also found MICA + aftercare clients to have significantly lower overall rates of criminal activity, concluding that policy makers should strongly consider implementing integrated TC programs for offenders with mental health issues.

More Recent Research on In-Prison Therapeutic Communities

As noted previously, the two most prominent methodological flaws of the earlier summarized studies is that research designs were weak and the evaluations examined only single programs. More recently published research on in-prison therapeutic communities has sought to address these limitations (e.g., Jensen & Kane, 2010, 2102; Welsh, 2007, 2010; Welsh & Zajac, 2013; Welsh & Zajac, 2004a,b; Welsh, Zajac, & Bucklen, 2014).[6] One example of this is the multisite evaluation of four in-prison TCs in Idaho[7] conducted in 2004 by Jensen and Kane (2010, 2012). Important improvements over the single-site studies noted earlier included using NCIC data (therefore, arrests outside of Idaho were included), multiple programs, and the use of propensity scores to adjust for difference between TC and non-TC parolees (significantly reducing the probability of a selection artifact affecting the study findings), and up to 4 years of postrelease follow-up data.[8] Important characteristics of these TC programs included average TC stays of 9–12 months, nonvoluntary participation (i.e., inmates were referred by case supervisors), use of evidence-based assessments (i.e., the LSI-R), and a mandatory postrelease aftercare lasting 1 year. Two-year follow-up findings reported in Jensen and Kane (2010) noted that completion of an in-prison therapeutic community was associated with a longer interval between release and first rearrest. Updating this

6. The work of Welsh and colleagues is referenced here, but a fuller description of this work is provided in the Case Study section of this chapter.

7. Jensen and Kane (2010, 2012) note that all male inmates from all four of Idaho prisons released in 2004 comprised the sample for their study. However, we were unable to find the exact number of TCs examined in their publications; therefore, assume it was four TCs (three state operated and one operated by a private vendor).

8. Although including several important improvements over previous studies, a number of methodological issues are noted for this evaluation. These include the fact that only a few TC programs were examined, precluding the use of multilevel modeling to assess whether outcomes varied significantly across program and whether variations between programs in the manner in which they were implemented explained this. Also, the sample automatically excludes any individuals who had been reimprisoned for a technical violation because it could not be determined whether these were due to a technical violation of parole conditions or new criminal behavior.

evaluation, Jensen and Kane (2012) found a significantly lower likelihood of re-arrest (but not reconviction) for inmates classified as moderate need and who had completed a TC. Another multisite evaluation of in-prison TCs (Welsh, 2007; Welsh & Zajac, 2013) is discussed in the case study section of this chapter.

Other recent work has focused on evaluating in-prison TC programming across multiple sites. For example, working with the Minnesota Department of Corrections, which follows a TC model for all of its substance abuse programs, Duwe (2010) used a sophisticated propensity score matching procedure to compare treated versus nontreated inmates, controlling for 17 other covariates, on recidivism outcomes that ranged from 36 to 48 months post release. Several treatment variables were examined, enabling comparisons of length of treatment (90, 180, 365 days), treatment completion, and treatment dropout. Findings were that TC inmates had significantly lower recidivism across three measure, including rearrest, reconviction, and reincarceration. Compared to untreated inmates, inmates who received short (90-day) and medium (180-day) programs had significantly lower risk for all three recidivism measures. A comparison of completers, noncompleters, and untreated comparison groups found that completing a program was associated with a significantly lower rate of recidivism, but noncompletion was not significantly related to these outcomes. Duwe (2010) draws an interesting comparison of these findings to the Stay n' Out program. More specifically, like Wexler and colleagues (1990), the findings that short- and medium-length programs had significantly lower recidivism rates (long-term program results were not statistically significant) suggests that longer treatment duration improves outcomes, but that is evident only up until a certain point.

In 2004, the Illinois Department of Corrections opened Sheridan, a prison dedicated to substance abuse treatment following a modified TC model (Olson & Lurigio, 2014; Olson, Rozhon, & Powers, 2009), where all inmates participate in process and encounter groups, cognitive restructuring, TC structures and responsibilities, support groups, didactic groups, and aggression management and domestic violence groups. Following extensive prerelease planning, and under mandatory supervised release, the individuals are required to participate in aftercare, with intensive outpatient, outpatient, and recovery homes the most common placements. Olson and Lurigio (2014) reported recidivism findings for both the in-prison TC and aftercare components relative to a similar group of untreated releasees. Findings showed that, net the effect of multiple covariates, the in-prison TC group had significantly lower recidivism rates. Further analysis that divided the TC group into those who did/not complete aftercare showed a substantially reduced rate of recidivism for the former (did complete) and a significantly greater rate for the latter (did not complete) relative to the nontreatment comparison group.

Policy Implications and Other Issues

Our review of the in-prison TC literature led us to three policy implications focused on aftercare, attention to implementation and fidelity to the TC model, and the need for more rigorous multisite studies. Each of these is described, respectively, in the following paragraphs.

Although a few evaluations (Duwe, 2010; Welsh & Zajac, 2013) have found significantly reduced chances for recidivism following in-prison TC treatment only, the majority of studies (e.g., Hiller, Knight, & Simpson, 1999; Inciardi et al., 2004; Olson & Lurigio, 2014) found aftercare following prison release was essential for realizing significantly reduced recidivism rates. Interestingly, many of these studies were conducted prior to offender reentry becoming a significant issue with policymakers and researchers. Those who conducted these earlier studies puzzled over why in-prison treatment alone did not seem to realize significantly improved outcomes, but with the extensive research on reentry and the specific conditions (e.g., lack of employment, housing, education, and treatment) that predict high recidivism rates, it is clear that the continuum of care these earlier studies first advocated for facilitated offender reentry by addressing two of these conditions, specifically in the areas of housing (Olson & Lurigio, 2014) and additional substance abuse treatment in community-based programs (Hiller, Knight, & Simpson, 1999; Inciardi et al., 2004; Olson & Lurigio, 2014), with some studies indicating that residential and outpatient aftercare are equally effective following release from an in-prison TC (Burdon, Dang, Prendergast, Messina, & Farabee, 2007).

However, surprisingly little is known about what predicts aftercare completion. Exceptions to this include Hiller, Knight, and Simpson (1999), who used demographics and criminal history (e.g., race/ethnicity, age, admitting offense, prior incarceration), psychosocial factors (e.g., self-esteem, depression, anxiety, motivation for treatment), ratings of their experiences in their in-prison community (e.g., rapport with their counselor and with the other TC participants, perceptions of safety), and ratings of their satisfaction (e.g., a nine-item composite composed of items like your counselor was caring and helpful, and quality individual and group therapy) with their aftercare placement. Only two factors emerged as significant predictors, showing that those who had a higher degree of rapport with the other inmates during the in-prison therapeutic community and a lower degree of satisfaction with their aftercare were less likely to complete their aftercare placement. Another study by Olson, Rozhon, and Powers (2009) reported that 56.5% of Sheridan TC graduates completed aftercare, and they also examined predictors of aftercare completion, including sociodemographics and criminal history (e.g., race/ethnicity, age, marital status, education level, gang member, total number of prior arrests, prior prison sentences), length of stay in the prison, release cohorts, region, and type of aftercare referral. Multivariate analysis indicated a number of variables were significantly related to aftercare completion. More specifically, higher rates of aftercare completion were observed among older, non-White, and more highly educated individuals. Criminal history also predicted a greater likelihood of aftercare completion, with individuals who had more prior arrests for drug law violations, convicted of more serious felonies, and longer stays at Sheridan completing their aftercare. Having been previously imprisoned was related to lower rates of aftercare completion. The strongest predictor of aftercare completion was whether one was referred to residential aftercare, which included residential treatment, halfway houses, and recovery homes. Because the literature "appears to have reached the consensus that the benefits of in-prison treatment are magnified and sustained when offenders participate in aftercare services following their release from prison" (Olson, Rozhon, & Powers, 2009, p. 301), it is clear that not only should aftercare follow in-prison TC treatment, but also significantly more research needs to be done on the individual- and program-level predictors of aftercare completion to inform changes and interventions needed to improve retention rates. The expected benefits for focusing more research on this may include improved public safety through reduced recidivism and more efficient and effective use of limited aftercare resources.

One area of implementation science research (also called translational research) (Fixsen, Naoom, Blase, Friedman, & Wallace, 2005; Proctor et al., 2009) that is especially important to consider in relation to in-prison therapeutic communities is assessing the degree to which programs are implemented, with fidelity, to the theory and design with which they were developed. This idea is implicit in the previous section that reviewed common modifications to the TC for implementation in a correctional institution. Seldom has the in-prison TC literature answered the critical question of whether and to what extent the specific program examined adhered to TC theory and methods. Short descriptions of programs often are given with TC argot (e.g., community as method, pull-ups, encounter groups) included; but few have examined this at any great depth. Therefore, perhaps the proverbial Achille's heel of most in-prison TC research is that it isn't conclusively shown that the programs examined had actually adhered to TC model and methods. This, however, is not unique to in-prison TCs; it is also true for most criminal justice interventions.

There are a number of resources aimed at informing, measuring, and ensuring the integrity of TC programs. Professional organizations like the Treatment Communities of America (formerly the Therapeutic Communities of America), The Consortium for Therapeutic Communities, and the European Federation of Therapeutic Communities provide in-depth information on TCs, including consensus statements on TC elements and general guidance related to standards for TC implementation (e.g., Criminal Justice Task Force on Standards of Therapeutic Communities in America, 1997; Criminal Justice Committee on Therapeutic Communities of America, 1999). The *Survey of Essential Elements Questionnaire* (SEEQ; De Leon & Melnick, 1993; Goethals, Soyez, Melnick, De Leon, & Broekaert, 2011; Melnick & De Leon, 1999; Melnick, De Leon, Hiller, & Knight, 2000) was developed to measure the degree to which a program adheres to TC theory, model, and method. Grounded in TC theory (De Leon, 1995, 2000), it includes 139 questions for six global dimensions, "including (a) TC perspective, (b) the agency treatment structure and approach, (c) community as therapeutic agent, (d) educational and work activities, (e) formal therapeutic agents, and (f) process" (Melnick et al., 2000, p. 1824). Melnick and De Leon (1999) report results from a field survey of 59 agency directors affiliated with Therapeutic Communities of America. Differentiation of traditional and modified TCs on SEEQ elements is provided in Melnick et al. (2000), and a comparison of it between American and European TCs is presented by Goethals et al. (2011). In practice, it can identify departures from the traditional TC model, which can then be "corrected" through staff retraining to ensure program integrity.

Adding to the discussion of the fidelity of the implementation of in-prison TC communities, researchers have noted significant departures from good clinical practices as well as situational elements that affect the quality of program implementation (Farabee et al., 1999; Linhorst, Knight, Johnston, & Trickey, 2001; Saum et al., 2007). Following their experience with a quick expansion of TCs within the California Department of Corrections, and their evaluations of some of these programs, Farabee and colleagues (1999) shared six lessons they had learned. It is notable that two of the authors (Knight and Wexler), evaluators of programs like Kyle New Vision and Stay n' Out, respectively, added their experiences to this paper as well. The first lesson was that standard clinical practice for screening, assessment, and referral (see also Hiller, Belenko, Welsh, Zajac, & Peters, 2012) were not always followed. Some correctional systems with large capacities struggle to keep programs full, so there may be a tendency to make quick intake decisions using only limited information instead of basing who goes to the program on the results of evidence-based assessment practices. Also, there may be pressure from within a system, regardless of their treatment need, to send inmates who cause problems to new treatment programs. This may have a deleterious impact on the TC environment, particularly because individuals who don't belong there become a part of the community, unbalancing it and its therapeutic activities. Enforcing good clinical practice around assessment and referral, although difficult due to time pressures and resource limitations, may realize the goal of treating only those who have significant substance abuse problems who are in need of intensive treatment like that provided in the in-prison TC (Farabee et al., 1999).

The second and third insights shared by Farabee and colleagues (1999) were related to staff in the in-prison TCs. Because many prisons (and TCs) are located in rural areas, there are few professional clinicians to hire, and once hired, they often find the prison environment very different from their community-based practices. Being open and honest, sharing emotions, and mutual self-disclosure between client and counselor are difficult to encourage among inmates so steeped in the prison culture that emphasizes strength, being unemotional, and keeping things to oneself. And the overarching mission is to maintain security, setting up potential conflict between correctional staff and counselors, who tend to emphasize rehabilitation as their primary mission. Furthermore, staff retention is very problematic. Correctional institutions and systems see high turnover among both security and treatment staff. When staff leave, especially longer term employees, this can destabilize and reduce the efficiency and efficacy of the program (see Saum et al., 2007). Possible solutions offered include training "lifers" to serve as peer counselors and augment treatment staff; cross-training between correctional and treatment staff to reduce the tensions between staff charged with safety and/or rehabilitation; and specialized staff trainings. Closely related to this, Farabee and colleagues

(1999) provide a fourth insight, which relates directly to those just described, further underscoring the divide between the dual missions of operating a safe prison and the rehabilitation of the individual prisoner. Sanctions in a TC are designed for therapeutic aims, whereas institutional sanctions (e.g., administrative segregation) are geared toward punishing the infraction and promoting a safe and orderly institution. They recommend that treatment and security staff cooperate to find the best possible resolution that represents a compromise between the two missions.

The fifth insight is the need for aftercare (discussed more fully earlier), and the sixth relates to coercion. Highlighting this, Farabee and colleagues (1999) note that prisons by their nature are coercive environments, with many inmates required to participate in the TC program (see also McGrain, 2006; Welsh & McGrain, 2008). The extent to which external motivators (i.e., coercion) and internal motivation are needed for genuine behavioral change is unclear, although research does show internal motivation is important to treatment engagement (Hiller, Knight, Leukefeld, & Simpson, 2002; Rosen, Hiller, Webster, Staton, & Leukefeld, 2004) and to entering aftercare following release (Melnick, De Leon, Thomas, Kressel, & Wexler, 2001), and that external and internal motivation may have independent, additive effects on treatment retention (Knight, Hiller, Broome, & Simpson, 2000).

Linhorst and colleagues (2000) add two more situational influences that can have negative effects on program integrity. They first relate their experience with the imposition of a smoking ban that affected only the inmates in treatment, and not the staff. This example is included because it shows how changes to prison policies can alter the therapeutic environment of a TC. With respect to the ban, staff reported that it distracted inmates from their treatment because a prison economy arose around tobacco, and up to 25% of inmate infractions were violations of this policy. Moreover, inmate morale was low and resentment grew against the staff who continued to smoke, damaging therapeutic rapport. Ultimately the smoking ban was rescinded.

Another institutional change involved a change in treatment providers (Linhorst et al., 2001), an experience echoed in Saum and colleagues (2007). Many in-prison TCs are run by external providers (both nonprofit and for profit agencies) contracted to operate the TC. Because contracts are finite, a different provider with a lower "bid" for operating the program may be selected. This transition to a new provider represents a difficult time for TC residents because the staff with whom they have developed rapport and trusting relationships are suddenly replaced by a new staff member under the new contracted provider. The difficult transition isn't the fault of the contracting agency, but it is advisable that when this does occur, correctional administrators should develop a staff retention plan with the new provider (Saum et al., 2007).

Implicit in the earlier description of implementation issues is the need to understand how variation in program implementation affects outcomes like recidivism and relapse to drug use. Multisite evaluations like those conducted by Welsh (2007) and Duwe (2010) are an important step toward this because they noted between-program differences in implementation, but both lacked enough sites to conduct multilevel analyses to predict outcomes to examine between program, individual, and the interactions between program- and individual-level characteristics. This is an important point because multisite studies of community-based therapeutic communities show that participant outcomes vary significantly across programs. Moreover, individual level (e.g., race/ethnicity, age, marital status, legal pressure for treatment) and program level (i.e., proportion of clients under moderate-to-high legal pressure) significantly predict treatment stays of 90 days or longer (Hiller, Knight, Broome, & Simpson, 1998). Therefore, the final recommendation for policy is that a large multisite study of in-prison therapeutic communities be conducted. Characteristics of both the programs (e.g., degree of fidelity to TC perspective, model, and method) and individuals should be measured. Moreover, this study should collect data for multiple outcome measures (e.g., retention in treatment, relapse to drug use, health and health services use) in addition to recidivism. The culmination of this study would provide significant insight that could be used to improve programs, individual outcomes, and ultimately public safety. Absent this information, it will be very difficult to move research, practice, and policy for in-prison TCs to the next level of clarity regarding what it is about these programs and the interaction between the program and individual characteristics that affect lower recidivism and other outcomes.

CASE STUDY

The case study focuses on in-prison therapeutic communities in the Pennsylvania Department of Corrections (PADOC), which have been extensively examined by Welsh and colleagues. The first set of studies focused on describing the implementation and integrity of PADOC TCs (Welsh & Zajac, 2004a,b); the second was a multisite evaluation of five in-prison therapeutic communities (Welsh, 2007; Welsh & Zajac, 2013); and the third was a study that randomly assigned individuals to either TC treatment or an intensive outpatient model (within the same prison; Welsh, Zajac, & Bucklen, 2014).[9]

The importance of effective collaboration between researchers and departments of correction as an essential component of quality research on prison TCs cannot be understated. Welsh and Zajac (2004a) describe the research partnership between Temple University and the PADOC that was implemented to create strong working relationships so that treatment programs in the state prison could be successfully planned, implemented, and evaluated and the policy-making process could be enhanced. This partnership resulted in the construction of a survey that assessed 118 drug treatment programs, including 6 TC programs in 24 of the PA prisons. An in-depth process evaluation was also completed at two of the

9. CrimeSolutions.gov includes a summary of the findings related to one TC program, but it erroneously concludes that the PADOC TCs do not work. Conclusions were based only on the randomized study (Welsh, Zajac, & Bucklen, 2014), and they did not incorporate the findings from the five-site evaluation study (Welsh, 2007; Welsh & Zajac, 2014).

institutions with the goal of providing insight into survey results. The system-wide survey or census and the evaluations were used to examine and increase discussion in areas such as program differences, implementation problems, and fidelity issues, and to inform outcome evaluation efforts as part of the advancement of a future research agenda (Welsh & Zajac, 2004b). Thus, this census was one of the first steps in identifying TC program needs and in developing the methods and research designs by which the PA TCs could be systematically assessed.

Building on the well-maintained Temple–PADOC partnership and descriptive research discussed earlier, a quasi-experimental study of five of the state's in-prison TCs was completed (Welsh, 2007). Postrelease outcomes for participants in five male TCs ($n = 217$) and a comparison group (inmates assigned to less intensive forms of treatment due to shortage of TC beds, $n = 491$) were examined up to 2 years after program discharge. One notable difference between the TCs in this study and several of the TC models described earlier is that there was no mandatory community aftercare program for program graduates. Results indicated that the comparison inmates were about 1.5 times more likely to be rearrested and reincarcerated, though there were no statistically significant differences between groups for drug relapse (Welsh, 2007). The author concludes that in contrast to previous studies, a major finding from this evaluation was that prison TC treatment reduced recidivism independently of aftercare in the community.

Four-year follow-up results were examined for inmates ($n = 555$) who participated in the same TCs studied earlier along with a comparison group of inmates (n = 998) who were eligible for TC, but due to space issues participated in less intensive programming at the same prisons. A larger sample was utilized in this study because over 1,000 additional inmates had been released from prison since the time of the 2-year follow-up study. Findings indicated that TC inmates had a significantly reduced likelihood of incarceration (again, without having mandatory aftercare), but there were no statistically significant group differences for arrest or drug relapse (Welsh & Zajac, 2013).

We look to outcome studies for evidence of program effectiveness, but just as important are studies that examine what it is about the program that may lead to these outcomes or whether and how change occurs for the participants. A study of 347 PADOC inmates in one TC looked at inmate responsiveness to treatment during their time in the program (Welsh, 2010). Findings revealed that psychological and social functioning improved while in the TC, but these improvements varied according to individual factors such as motivation and risk level as well as the time period examined. Implications of this study pointed to the need for better screening and assessment procedures, improved identification of inmates who may benefit from interventions that facilitate engagement and retention, and a greater understanding of the interaction between individual and programmatic factors and how this may influence inmate response to treatment.

Inmate characteristics and treatment modality were addressed by Welsh, Zajac, and Bucklen (2014) as they examined which inmates benefited from prison TC treatment compared with less intensive prison-based group counseling (outpatient). Upon admission to a specialized drug treatment prison in the PADOC, inmates were randomized into the TC ($n = 286$) or outpatient program ($n = 318$). Contrary to expectations from previous TC research, findings revealed that there was no advantage of TC treatment because participants in both programs had similar rates of reincarceration. Interestingly, inmates with the highest risk levels who had TC treatment had higher incarceration rates than those in the outpatient program. The researchers suggested that ongoing assessment of treatment participants' progress while in the program and a greater emphasis placed on individual responsivity to treatment would improve posttreatment outcomes.

WEB-BASED RESOURCES

https://Crimesolutions.gov

http://www.eftc-europe.com/

https://www.samhsa.gov/nrepp

https://www.samhsa.gov/gains-center

http://www.treatmentcommunitiesofamerica.org/

https://www.therapeuticcommunities.org/

https://www.drugabuse.gov/publications/research-reports/therapeutic-communities/
what-are-therapeutic-communities

REFERENCES

Belenko, S., Hiller, M., & Hamilton, L. (2013).Treating substance use disorders in the criminal justice system. *Current Psychiatry Reports, 15,* 1–17.

Belenko, S., & Peugh, J. (2005). Estimating drug treatment needs among state prison inmates. *Drug and Alcohol Dependence, 77,* 269–281.

Blevins, K. R., & Soderstrom, I. R. (2015). The mental health crisis grows on: A descriptive analysis of DOC systems in America. *Journal of Offender Rehabilitation, 54,* 142–160.

Bowring v. Godwin, 551 F.2d 44 (4th Cir. 1977).

Burdon, W. M., Dang, J., Prendergast, M. L., Messina, N. P., & Farabee, D. (2007). Differential effectiveness of residential versus outpatient aftercare for parolees from prison-based therapeutic community treatment. *Substance Abuse Treatment, Prevention, and Policy, 2,* 1–14.

Carson, E. A. (2015). Prisoners in 2014 (Bureau of Justice Statistics, NCJ 248995). Retrieved from https://www.bjs.gov/content/pub/pdf/p14.pdf

Carson, E. A., & Anderson, E. (2016). *Prisoners in 2015.* US Bureau of Justice Statistics Report, NCJ 250229. Retrieved from https://www.bjs.gov/content/pub/pdf/p15.pdf.

Criminal Justice Committee on Therapeutic Communities of America. (1999) *Therapeutic communities in correctional settings: The prison based TC standards development project final report of phase II.* Washington, DC: The White House Office of National Drug Control Policy.

Criminal Justice Task Force on Standards of Therapeutic Communities of America. (1997). *Therapeutic communities correctional settings: The standards development phase: Phase I report.* Washington, DC: Author.

De Leon, G. (1995). Therapeutic communities for addictions: A theoretical framework. *International Journal of the Addictions, 30,* 1603–1645.

De Leon, G. (2000). *The therapeutic community: Theory, model, and method.* New York, NY: Springer.

De Leon, G. (2010). Is the therapeutic community an evidence-based treatment? What the evidence says. *Therapeutic Communities, 31,* 104–128.

De Leon, G., & Melnick, G. (1993). *Therapeutic community scale of essential elements questionnaire (SEEQ).* New York, NY: Center for Therapeutic Community Research at National and Development and Research, Inc.

De Leon, G., Perfas, F. B., Joseph, A., & Bunt, G. (2015). Therapeutic communities for the addictions: Essential elements, cultural, and current issues. In N. el-Guebaly et al. (eds.), *Textbook on addiction treatment: International perspectives* (pp. 1033–1047). New York, NY: Springer.

Diamond, P. M., Wang, E. W., Holzer, C. E, Thomas, C., & des Agnes, C. (2001). The prevalence of mental illness in prison. *Administration and Policy in Mental Health, 29,* 21–40.

Dietz, E. F., O'Connell, D. J., & Scarpitti, F. R. (2003). Therapeutic communities and prison management: An examination of the effects of operating an in-prison therapeutic community on levels of institutional disorder. *International Journal of Offender Therapy and Comparative Criminology, 47,* 210–223.

Ditton, P. M. (1999). *Mental health treatment of inmates and probationers* (NCJ Publication no. 174483). Washington, DC: Office of Justice Programs.

Duwe, G. (2010). Prison-based chemical dependency treatment in Minnesota: An outcome evaluation. *Journal of Experimental Criminology, 6,* 57–81

Estelle v. Gamble, 426 U.S. 97 (1976).

Farabee, D., Prendergast, M., Cartier, J. E., Wexler, H., Knight, K., & Anglin, M. D. (1999). Barriers to implementing effective correctional drug treatment programs. *The Prison Journal, 79,* 150–162.

Fixsen, D. L., Naoom, S. F., Blase, K. A., Friedman, R. M., & Wallace, F. (2005). *Implementation research: A synthesis of the literature* (FMHI Publication #231). Tampa, FL: University of South Florida, Louis de la Parte Florida Mental Health Institute, The National Implementation Research Network.

Galassi, A., Mpofu, E., & Athanasou, J. (2015). Therapeutic community treatment of an inmate population with substance use disorders: Post-release trends in re-arrest, re-incarceration, and drug misuse relapse. *International Journal of Environmental Research and Public Health, 12,* 7059–772.

Goethals, I., Soyez, V., Melnick, G., De Leon, G., & Broekaert, E. (2011). Essential elements of treatment: A comparative study between European and American therapeutic communities for addiction. *Substance Use and Misuse, 46,* 1023–1031.

Griffith, J. D., Hiller, M. L., Knight, K., & Simpson, D. D. (1999). A cost-effectiveness analysis of in-prison therapeutic community treatment and risk classification. *The Prison Journal, 79,* 352–368.

Hall, E. A., Prendergast M. L., Wellisch, J., Patten, M., & Cao, Y. (2004). Treating drug-abusing women prisoners: An outcome evaluation of the Forever Free program. *The Prison Journal, 84,* 81–105.

Hiller, M. L., Belenko, S., Welsh, W., Zajac, G., & Peters, R. H. (2012). Screening and assessment: An evidence-based process for the management and care of adult drug-involved offenders. In C. G., Leukefeld, J. Gregrich, & T. Gullotta (Eds.), *Handbook on evidence based substance abuse treatment practice in criminal justice settings* (pp 45–62). New York, NY: Springer Verlag.

Hiller, M. L., Knight, K., Broome, K. M., & Simpson, D. D. (1998). Legal pressure and treatment retention in a national sample of long-term residential programs. *Criminal Justice and Behavior, 25,* 463–481.

Hiller, M. L., Knight, K., Leukefeld, C. G., & Simpson, D. D. (2002). Motivation as a predictor of therapeutic engagement in mandated residential substance abuse treatment. *Criminal Justice and Behavior, 29,* 56–75.

Hiller, M. L., Knight, K., & Simpson, D. D. (1999). Prison-based substance abuse treatment, residential aftercare, and recidivism. *Addiction, 94,* 833–842.

Inciardi, J. A., Martin, S. S., & Butzin, C. A. (2004). Five-year outcomes of therapeutic community treatment of drug-involved offenders after release from prison. *Crime & Delinquency, 50,* 88–107.

Jensen, E. L., & Kane, S. L. (2010). The effect of therapeutic community on time to first re-arrest: A survival analysis. *Journal of Offender Rehabilitation, 49,* 200–209.

Jensen, E. L., & Kane, S. L. (2012). The effects of therapeutic community on recidivism up to four years after release from prison: A multisite study. *Criminal Justice and Behavior, 39,* 1075–1087.

Knight, K., Hiller, M. L., Broome, K. M., & Simpson, D. D. (2000). Legal pressure, treatment readiness, and engagement in long-term residential programs. *Journal of Offender Rehabilitation, 31,* 101–115.

Knight, K., Simpson, D. D., & Hiller, M. L. (1999). Three-year reincarceration outcomes for in-prison therapeutic community treatment in Texas. *The Prison Journal, 79*(3), 337–351.

Lamb, H., & Weinberger, L. (2005). The shift of psychiatric inpatient care from hospitals to jails and prisons. *Journal of the American Academy of Psychiatry and the Law, 33,* 529–534.

Linhorst, D. M., Knight, K., Johnston, J. S., & Trickey, M. (2001). Situational influences on the implementation of a prison-based therapeutic community. *The Prison Journal, 81,* 436–453.

Lurigio, A. J. (2011). People with serious mental illness in the criminal justice system: Causes, consequences, and correctives. *Prison Journal, S91,* 66s–86s.

Magaletta, P. R., Diamond, P. M., Faust, E., Daggett, D. M., & Camp, S. D. (2009). Estimating the mental illness component of service need in corrections: Results from the mental health prevalence project. *Criminal Justice and Behavior, 36,* 229–244.

Martin, S, S., Butzin, C. A., & Inciardi, J. A. (1995). Assessment of a multistage therapeutic community for drug-involved offenders. *Journal of Psychoactive Drugs, 27,* 109–116.

Martin, S. S., Butzin, C. A, Saum, C. A., & Inciardi, J. A. (1999). Three-year outcomes of therapeutic community treatment for drug-involved offenders in Delaware: From prison to work release to aftercare. *The Prison Journal, 79,* 294–320.

McCollister, K., French, M., Prendergast, M. L., Hall, E., & Sacks, S. (2004). Long-term cost effectiveness of addiction treatment for criminal offenders. *Justice Quarterly, 21,* 659–679.

McGrain, P. N. (2006). *An examination of therapeutic engagement in a prison-based drug treatment therapeutic community* (Doctoral dissertation). Retrieved from ProQuest Dissertations Publishing, 3211892.

Melnick, G., & De Leon, G. (1999). Clarify the nature of therapeutic community treatment: The Survey of Essential Elements Questionnaire (SEEQ). *Journal of Substance Abuse Treatment, 16*, 307–313.

Melnick, G., De Leon, G., Hiller, M. L., & Knight, K. (2000). Therapeutic communities: Diversity in treatment elements. *Substance Use and Misuse, 35*, 1819–1847.

Melnick, G., De Leon, G., Thomas, G., Kressel, D., & Wexler, H. K. (2001). Treatment process in prison therapeutic communities: Motivation, participation, and outcome. *American Journal of Drug and Alcohol Abuse, 27*, 633–650.

Mitchel, O., Wilson, D. B., & MacKenzie, D. L. (2007). Does incarceration-based drug treatment reduce recidivism? A meta-analytic synthesis of the research. *Journal of Experimental Criminology, 3*, 353–375.

Mumola, C. J., & Karberg, J. C. (2006). Drug use and dependence, state and federal prisoners, 2004 (Bureau of Justice Statistics Report NCJ 213530). Retrieved from https://www.bjs.gov/content/pub/pdf/dudsfp04.pdf.

The National Center on Addiction and Substance Abuse (CASA) at Columbia University. (1998). *Behind bars: Substance abuse and America's prison population*. New York, NY: Author.

The National Center on Addiction and Substance Abuse (CASA) at Columbia University. (2010). *Behind bars II: Substance abuse and America's prison population*. New York, NY: Author.

The National Institute on Drug Abuse (NIDA). (2015). *Therapeutic communities* (NIH Publication 14–4877. Rockville, MD: Author.

Olson, D. E., & Lurigio, A. J. (2014). The long-term effects of prison-based drug treatment and aftercare services on recidivism. *Journal of Offender Rehabilitation, 53*, 600–619.

Olson, D. E., Rozhon, J., & Powers, M. (2009). Enhancing prisoner reentry through access to prison-based and post-incarceration aftercare treatment: Experiences from the Illinois Sheridan Correctional Center therapeutic community. *Journal of Experimental Criminology, 5*, 299–321.

Peters, R. H., Sherman, P. B., & Osher, F. C. (2008). Treatment in jails and prisons. In K. T. Mueser & D. V. Jeste (Eds.), *Clinical handbook of schizophrenia* (pp. 354–364). New York, NY: Guilford.

Prendergast, M., Farabee, D., & Cartier, J. (2001). The impact of in-prison therapeutic community programs on prison management. *Journal of Offender Rehabilitation, 32*, 63–78.

Prendergast, M. L., Hall, E. A., Wexler, H. K., Melnick, G., & Cao, Y. (2004). Amity prison-based therapeutic community: 5-year outcomes. *The Prison Journal, 84*, 36–60.

Proctor, E., Landsverk, J., Aarons, G., Chambers, D., Glisson, C., & Mittman, B. (2009). Implementation research in mental health services: An emerging science with conceptual, methodological, and training challenges. *Administration and Policy in Mental Health, 36*, 24–34.

Rojas, E. C., & Peters, R. H. (2016) Evidence-based practices for co-occurring disorders in offenders. *Addiction Research & Theory, 24*, 223–235.

Rosen, P., Hiller, M. L., Webster, J. M., Staton, M., & Leukefeld, C. G. (2004). Treatment motivation and therapeutic engagement in prison-based substance use treatment, *Journal of Psychoactive Drugs, 36*, 387–396.

Sacks, S., Sacks, J. Y., McKendrick, K., Banks, S., & Stommel, J. (2004). Modified TC for MICA offenders: Crime outcomes. *Behavioral Sciences and the Law, 22*, 477–501.

Saum, C. A., O'Connell, D. J., Martin, S. S., Hiller, M. L., Bacon, G. A., & Simpson, D. D. (2007). Tempest in a TC: Changing treatment providers for in-prison therapeutic communities. *Criminal Justice and Behavior, 34*(9), 1168–1178.

Soderstrom, I. R. (2007). Mental illness in offender populations: Prevalence, duty, and implications. *Journal of Offender Rehabilitation, 45*, 1–17.

Sullivan, C. J., McKendrick, K., Sacks, S., & Banks, S. (2007). Modified therapeutic community treatment for offenders with MICA disorders: Substance use outcomes. *The American Journal of Drug and Alcohol Abuse, 33*, 823–832.

Tripodi, S. J. (2014). Emphasis on rehabilitation: From inmates to employees. *International Journal of Offender Therapy and Comparative Criminology, 58*, 891–893.

Vanderplasschen, W., Colpaert, K., Autrique, M., Rapp, R. C. Pearce, S., Broekaert, E, & Vandevelde, S. (2013). Therapeutic communities for addictions: A review of their effectiveness from a recovery-oriented perspective. *The Scientific World Journal.* Available on-line at https://www.hindawi.com/journals/tswj/

Vilcica, E. R. (2015). The influence of inmate visitation on the decision to grant parole: An exploratory study. *Journal of Criminal Justice, 43*, 498–509.

Vilcica, E. R. (2016). Studying parole in the spotlight: Lessons from a large American jurisdiction. *European Journal on Criminal Policy and Research, 22*, 61–88.

Welsh, W. N. (2007). A multisite evaluation of prison-based therapeutic community drug treatment. *Criminal Justice and Behavior, 34*, 1481–1498.

Welsh, W. N. (2010). Inmate responses to prison-based drug treatment: A repeated measures analysis. *Drug and Alcohol Dependence, 109*, 37–74.

Welsh, W. N., & McGrain, P. N. (2008). Predictors of therapeutic engagement in prison-based drug treatment. *Drug and Alcohol Dependence, 96*, 271–280.

Welsh, W. N., McGrain, P., Salamatin, N., & Zajac, G. (2008). Effects of prison drug treatment on inmate misconduct: A repeated measures analysis. *Criminal Justice and Behavior, 34*, 600–615.

Welsh, W. N., & Zajac, G. (2004a). Building an effective research partnership between a university and a state correctional agency: Assessment of drug treatment in Pennsylvania prisons. *The Prison Journal, 84*, 143–170.

Welsh, W. N., & Zajac, G. (2004b). A census of prison-based drug treatment programs: Implications for programing, policy, and evaluation. *Crime and Delinquency, 50*, 108–133.

Welsh, W. N., & Zajac, G. (2013). A multisite evaluation of prison-based drug treatment: Four-year follow-up results. *The Prison Journal, 93*, 251–271.

Welsh, W. N., Zajac, G., & Bucklen, K. B. (2014). For whom does prison-based drug treatment work? Results from a randomized experiment. *Journal of Experimental Criminology, 10*, 151–177.

Wexler, H. K., De Leon, G., Thomas, G., Kressel, D., & Peters, J. (1999a). The Amity prison TC evaluation: Reincarceration outcomes. *Criminal Justice and Behavior, 26*, 147–67.

Wexler, H. K., Falkin, G. P., & Lipton, D. S. (1990). Outcome evaluation of a prison therapeutic community for substance abuse treatment. *Criminal Justice and Behavior, 17*, 71–92.

Wexler, H. K., Melnick, G., Lowe, L. L., & Peters, J. (1999b). Three-year reincarceration outcomes for Amity In-Prison Therapeutic Community and aftercare in California. *The Prison Journal, 79*, 321–336.

Wexler, H. K., & Prendergast, M. L. (2010). Therapeutic communities in United States' prisons: Effectiveness and challenges. *Therapeutic Communities, 31*, 157–175.

Wexler, H. K., & Williams, R. (1986). The Stay 'n Out therapeutic community: Prison treatment for substance abusers. *Journal of Psychoactive Drugs, 18*, 221–230.

Zhang, S. X., Roberts, R. E. L., & McCollister, K. E. (2009). An economic analysis of the in-prison therapeutic community model on prison management costs. *Journal of Criminal Justice, 37*, 388–395.

9

Sexuality on the Inside

Lesbian, Gay, and Bisexual Inmates

JAMES ROFFEE AND ANDREA WALING

It is well documented that members of the lesbian, gay, and bisexual (LGB) community have long faced discrimination and persecution based on their identity, although the level of acceptance and discrimination toward those who identify as LGB has varied across place and time. Although there is increasing global recognition of LGB rights, such recognition occurs within a dominant heteronormative context and hence within a world that has normalized heterosexual identity and sexual practices. The resulting privilege given to dominant masculinities and femininities has rendered (and, in many settings, continues to render) those who practice and perform anything other than the dominant tropes as deviant (Duggan, 2003).

LESBIAN, GAY, AND BISEXUAL INMATE POPULATIONS

The societal structures that are so heavily reliant on the gender binary of men and women thus act to privilege heterosexual relationships and sexual dynamics (Ingraham, 2005). This impacts all aspects of our criminal justice system, including police, courts, and corrections. Men who "appropriately" perform masculinity and women appropriately who "appropriately" perform femininity operate in a privileged space within society and the institutions of the criminal justice system. With an understanding and awareness of the privilege of heterosexuality, it becomes possible to identify, highlight, and respond to practices that adversely impact those who are not performing in ways aligned with the dominant heterosexual and gender identities. Gay men, lesbian women, and bisexual people are performing sexual orientation in ways that have been viewed as nonnormative (Duggan, 2003). It is therefore imperative to investigate how those engaging with the criminal justice system, including those who are incarcerated, have their lives adversely impacted, constrained, and controlled due to their sexual orientation and performance of "appropriate" gender.

In this chapter, we explore the importance of understanding the differing needs of LGB prisoners. We begin with a brief overview of some of the historical approaches to homosexuality within corrections and the conflation of sexual activity and sexual orientation. We then look at international best practice in the management of vulnerability of particularly gay and bisexual male prisoners to physical and sexual assault. The importance of adequately trained custodial staff and their impact on the detention experiences is explored before we look at several policy issues and implications, such as application and availability of conjugal visitation, and specific health care needs of LGB prisoners. The scope of this chapter will be restricted to the primary impacts of gendering on sexual orientation and the incarceration experience, and we review the use of segregation as a management tool as well as the use of policies preventing pornographic materials being used to target LGB inmates. We conclude with the case study of *X v. Turkey*, detailing the severe impact of inappropriate corrections response to LGB inmates, before presenting some web-based resources.

Sexuality Within an Institutional Environment and Historical Approaches

There has been a long-standing and well-documented fascination with the topics of homosexuality, and sexual activity, in prison. The study of homosexuality has adapted to the differing social and cultural contexts over time. Eigenberg (1992) suggested that literature on homosexuality has employed two basic perspectives to the topic: an essentialist approach and a social constructionist approach. In the former, sexual orientation is viewed as static and permanent, and this approach fails to explain or accommodate bisexuality and/or the changing nature of a person's sexual orientation. The constructionist approach frames sexual orientation as existing on a spectrum or continuum that ranges from "exclusive homosexuality to exclusive heterosexuality" (Eigenberg, 1992, p. 220). As such, from a constructionist perspective, sexual orientation is fluid and it is possible for a persons' sexual orientation to change over time. The reliance on an essentialist perspective has resulted in much literature that approaches inmates' sexuality and sex in prison from a perspective of deviance, and which seeks to place binary categorizations on inmates' identities and activities. Such binary categorizations neglect to capture the complexity of the impacts of incarceration for all inmates, and not simply who choose to be labeled as LGB.

The sexual orientation and identity of an inmate can impact all aspects of their life while incarcerated. It has been recognized for some time that incarcerated LGB persons are at significantly increased levels of risk to their safety and well-being (United Nations High Commissioner for Human Rights [UNHCR], 2011). The United Nations have acknowledged that:

> members of sexual minorities are disproportionately subjected to torture and other forms of ill-treatment because they fail to conform to socially constructed

gender expectations. Indeed, discrimination on grounds of sexual orientation or gender identity may often contribute to the process of the dehumanization of the victim, which is often a necessary condition for torture and ill-treatment to take place. (UNHCR, 2011, p. 12)

The United Nations Special Rapporteur on torture noted that in detention facilities, gay, lesbian, and bisexual people alongside trans persons, are at the bottom of the hierarchy, and often suffer double or triple discrimination (Nowak, 2010). The treatment of sexual minorities as a subcategory of prisoners results in them being detained in worse conditions of detention than the larger prison population (Rodley, 2001). LGB prisoners' identity can therefore be used as a reason to further punish this group of inmates. For example, prison guards are believed to use the threat of transfer to main detention areas, where members of sexual minorities would be at high risk of sexual attack by other inmates, to intimidate LGB inmates (Rodley, 2001).

As knowledge about, and acceptance of, those with LGB identities increases, criminal justice systems have begun to pay more attention to the needs of this population. In the context of corrections, careful consideration should be given to how an inmate's identity impacts intake procedures, classification, placement, and housing within an establishment, the types of medical and health care received, and efforts to prevent suicide and victimization. Staff and offenders should be educated on the policies relating to LGB inmates, which should be robust and enforced. Although this chapter discusses LGB inmates, it should be noted that although LGB inmates are often discussed together, there are gendered differences impacting on experiences of incarceration.

Gendered Institutions, Sexuality, and Inmate Experience and Victimization

Prisons as gendered institutions (see Acker, 1990) operate utilizing (and expecting) the appropriate performance of gender. Sabo (2005) suggests that prisons exhibit earmarks of patriarchal institutions such as sex segregation, hierarchical relationships, and social control through aggression and violence (Sabo, 2005). When discussing prisons and their operations and in thinking about whom they contain, Rafter suggests there is a "monolithic image of the men's prison" adopted by film directors, novelists, policymakers, social historians, and sociologists (Rafter, 1990, p. xii). The fact that prisons are gendered institutions, reflecting and reinforcing beliefs about sexual difference has largely been ignored (Rafter, 1990). One of the reasons for this, it is argued, is that gender roles are so pervasive and taken for granted that it is difficult to recognize them as anything other than natural (Rafter, 1990). Prisons are "melded to the social landscape and to the social relations of men and women" (Sabo, Kupers, & London, 2001, p. 5). That prisons are therefore gendered institutions and operate in a hierarchical way whereby men dominate women and other men is of little surprise. Although the focus of this chapter is on sexual orientation, it should also be noted that intermale dominance hierarchies also exist on the basis of race, ethnicity, and class (Sabo, Kupers, & London, 2001). As such, it is important to understand the structures in place that facilitate this dominance, in order to respond to these forms of social control and their unwanted consequences.

It is within this context of historically male institutions that prisons and jails operate today. Although there is a growing body of literature on the problems of normative male gendering of the operations and practices within prisons and jails generally (Britton, 1997; Davis, 2003; Zaitzow, 2003), the scope of this chapter will be restricted to the primary impacts of normative gendering found in prisons on those who are LGB. Before beginning to look at the evidence-based practices to respond to LGB inmates, the importance of performance of masculinity, femininity, and sexualities in male and female prisons will be discussed. Further, the lack of knowledge of bisexual people and incarceration, and the confusion and conflation surrounding sexual orientation and the act of sex within prison establishments, will be discussed.

SEXUALITY, GENDER, AND MASCULINITY WITHIN MALE PRISONS AND CORRECTIONS

The body of literature on sexual activity and sexuality within prisons and corrections is both significant and continues to grow. The higher rates of incarceration of males and a prurient interest in the fate of men behind bars has resulted in a wealth of academic and popular culture literature on the topic. There has been a particular focus on the traits of incarcerated men, an attempt to understand the socialization of inmates and its impact on their fate behind bars. There has been a growth in interest in the topic of masculinities from the 1980s, and the more recent literature on sexual orientation and experiences of imprisonment draws and takes inspiration from much of the masculinities literatures.

In the prison context, research has identified the importance of understanding masculinity narratives of those imprisoned and their impact on experiences of imprisonment (Sim, 1994). Whereas a full discussion of masculinities is outside the scope of this chapter, it is important to briefly mention hegemonic masculinity. This form of masculinity "stabilizes a structure of dominance and oppression in the gender order as a whole. To be culturally exalted the pattern of masculinity must have exemplars who are celebrated as heroes" (Connell, 1990, p. 94). Donaldson (1993) suggested that "heterosexuality and homophobia are the bedrock of hegemonic masculinity" and that a "fundamental element of hegemonic masculinity . . . is that women exist as potential sexual objects for men while men are negated as sexual objects for men" (p. 645). Male homosexuality is counterhegemonic: Hostility to homosexuality is fundamental to male heterosexuality; homosexuality is associated with effeminacy; homosexual pleasure is considered subversive (Donaldson, 1993; see also Carrigan, Connell, & Lee, 1985; Coston & Kimmel, 2012). Hegemonic masculinity is therefore defined in relation to other subordinated masculinities (Connell, 1987).

Toxic masculinity (Kupers, 2005), sometimes also understood as hypermasculinity in certain contexts, involves the need to aggressively compete and dominate others and encompasses the most problematic proclivities in men. Although there are a number of definitions of hypermasculinity, Mosher and Sirkin (1984) suggest this form of masculinity has three key traits, being a callous sexual attitude toward women, a belief in and acceptance of the use of violence, and viewing excitement in danger. Dolovich (2012) suggests that for those incarcerated there is a hypermasculinity imperative; the need to maintain a reputation that they are "not to be messed with" as well as the requirement to forge self-protective alliances such as gangs. This is not only found in the United States; Bandyopadhyay's (2006) research into Indian prisons suggests that aggressive, violence-prone men are found in the elites of the prison hierarchy, with the softer and feminized inmates being afforded lower status.

Kupers (2001) argues that "hyper-masculinity reinforces the misogyny and toxic masculinity that are central to the male prison culture" (p. 115). As such, the ideal performance of masculinity in prison is the display of being a "manly man"; this man fails to display any weakness and vulnerability, shows only anger as an emotion, does not depend on others, will not inform on others, does not cooperate with the guards, and suffers pain in silence (Kupers, 2010). The lack of development of meaningful relationships in male prisons is in notable contrast to those in female prisons. The performance of appropriate masculinity within prison thus prohibits men from forming relationships of dependence without being labeled as a member of the LGB community. Labeling as gay or bisexual is seen as a marker of weakness and thus opens men to attack from other men who are seeking to assert their masculinity and themselves avoid being the victim of others within the prison environment.

Sexuality, Gender, and Femininity Within Female Prisons and Corrections

The claim by Hensley, Tewksbury, and Koscheski (2002) that little has been said on female prison sexuality has been countered by Severance (2004), who suggested that this aspect of women's imprisonment has received consistent scholarly and public attention and interest. Although compared to the body of literature on male sexuality in prison settings, there is less text on incarcerated female sexualities, there has nonetheless been a long-standing and growing interest in the topic. Literature dates from as early as 1913 on the "unnatural relationships" between women inmates of different races (Otis, 1913).

Freedman (1996) provided a notable and comprehensive discussion of lesbians in prison in the United States. Freedman (1996) suggested that the "prison lesbian" represented the inverse of the ideal White woman of the 1950s and the "prison lesbian" became a symbol of social disorder. Further, she noted that White middle-class women saw value in using their race and class privilege to distance themselves from the "outlaw" identity of the prison lesbian (Freedman, 1996). It is suggested that this historical construction of an aggressive female homosexual outlaw has continued to this day and as such lesbians in prison continue to get treated more harshly than other women (Freedman, 1996).

While in women's prisons, homosexual relationships have historically been tolerated or ignored (Bennett, 2000), the relationships that develop between women can pose a number of significant issues for management. These include health issues, predatory behaviour, jealous, co-dependency, and sexual activities (Bennett, 2000), though Bennett notes that it is not the homosexual nature of the relationships that is the concern, but the behavioral problems arising from them. As will be discussed later, there is often a conflation of the acts of sex and other activities typically found in romantic relationships, and what occurs between inmates, inmate identities, and sexuality. The literature on female prison sexuality is often nuanced in its understanding of the complexities of sexuality. As such, the literature is far more likely to recognize the different forms of prisoner relationship, including prison families, friendships, and romances (Bennett, 2000).

Similar to the research on male sexuality in prison, there is a desire to explain why women who are not " 'homosexually oriented' turn to this way of life while incarcerated" and literature has suggested that women engage in lesbian activity as an imitation of heterosexuality (Forsyth, Evans, & Foster, 2002, p. 69). However, literature on women's identities challenges understandings of prison sexuality as simply a response to women's sexual deprivation and lack of men, and suggests that it is the experience of incarceration, removing women from their networks, that is significant in understanding women's entire incarceration experience. It is thought that it is not the sexual component of these relationships that is the most important (Severance, 2004). Zaitzow's (2003) work suggested that the use of pseudofamilies is an adaptation by female inmates to the loss of their free world networks. The lack of contact with the outside world and loss of close connections give women a reason to create relationships that provide emotional support and assistance in undertaking routine activities of daily life (Heffernan, 1972). The creation of pseudofamilies involves women grouping together and taking on family roles (Blackburn, Fowler, & Mullings, 2014). It has also been suggested that a subculture of new group values and norms which arise from the need to adjust and cope with the impacts of confinement are thus attempts to make doing time easier (Forsyth et al., 2002; Owen, 1998).

Other research has suggested that the interpersonal and supportive relationships between women in prison have been replaced by issues of mistrust, manipulation, and loneliness as found in male prisons (Greer, 2000). Whereas the data informing such studies did not suggest a significant or formal enactment of familial networks (Greer, 2000), they did suggest that the movement toward isolation was one of self-protection and this may well be because of the changing nature of incarceration. This includes women inmates being more closely monitored than they once were, being uniformed rather than able to wear their own clothes, and more heavily policed in their contact with others than they have previously been (Forsyth et al., 2002). The increasing severity with which relatively minor crimes are being treated, and the move toward zero-tolerance policies of law and order, will mean larger numbers of women will enter the criminal justice system. Therefore, there is greater need to investigate the impact of incarceration on women and their identity. Although the calls for corrections departments to be gender responsive is no longer treated with suspicion, there is still much to be learned by corrections concerning how to appropriately support inmates, to prevent maladjustment to the often-alien landscape of carceral spaces (Jiang & Winfree Jr, 2006).

BISEXUAL "ERASURE" IN PRISON AND CORRECTIONS

There is often a failure to mention those holding a bisexual identity within literature on corrections and incarceration. Literature that does mention bisexuality in prisons often relegates it to a space after discussion of prisoners who identify as gay, possibly due to the greater volume of prisoners who identify as gay rather than bisexual and as a result less literature produced on the topic of bisexuality and imprisonment. Noting that discussion in this chapter is after gay and lesbian inmates, it is worth highlighting some observed differences in incarceration experiences of bisexual inmates so as to not further contribute to erasure of the experiences of bisexual inmates.

Alarid (2000) noted that bisexual offenders who preferred women to men more often sought protection from another inmate, reported more pressure from others to have sex, and felt less safe in jail than gay or bisexual men who preferred men over women. Bisexual men also reported lower levels of institutional adjustment and less satisfaction with regard to their sexual identity (Alarid, 2000). There has been recent suggestion by Robinson (2011) that some specific housing units, for example K6G in Los Angeles, discriminate against bisexual people. It was argued that bisexual prisoners are denied access to the K6G Unit (reserved for gay men and trans-women), relegating bisexual men to the general population with a greater risk of victimization. Further research on the impacts of incarceration of bisexual inmates is undoubtedly required. A greater understanding of the needs of bisexual people can come from corrections officials engaging with members of the LGB community in order to undertake needs assessments and impact assessments/audits, as suggested later within the sections on the evidence-based practices and, trends and directions, which will help combat further bisexual erasure.

Corrections and the Conflation of Sexuality and Sexual Activity

As alluded to earlier, there is a need to differentiate the decision by a person to engage in sexual acts and activity, from one's sexual identity and sexual orientation. Within much of the early research on those incarcerated, there was a failure to distinguish between sexual activity occurring in prison and the sexual orientation of those engaging such activity. That is, the research struggled to explain incidents where a person held a heterosexual sexual orientation, yet engaged in sexual activity that is commonly partaken by those who identify as gay and/or bisexual. Eigenberg (1992) has sought to explain the confusion by researchers and corrections officials in their understanding of homosexuality in prison, and acts of sex and rape. She suggested that reliance on an essentialist understanding of sexuality created a paradox whereby researchers were forced to explain why heterosexual men engaged in homosexual behavior and such researchers were simultaneously able to avoid challenging essentialist assumptions by including rape victims and rapists in their classification schemes designed to address homosexuality. Eigenberg (1992) argued that reliance on an essentialist approach to sexuality resulted in a failure of understanding in much of the early discussion of situational-homosexuality which concerned incidents involving nonvoluntary participants and thus victims of rape.

Hensley, Tewksbury, and Wright (2001) found that many inmates who admitted to participating in sexual relationships with other inmates of the same sex did not identify as homosexual. Similarly (Egelund, 2014) found that the majority of men in her Zambian study who had sex with other men did not consider their practices an expression of a homosexual identity. Equally, the creation of pseudofamilies in women's prisons is a response to women's deprivation from nonsexual relationships and the experience of incarceration, rather than the creation of such groupings for sexual purposes. This is a particularly important distinction and must be understood by those working within corrections as well as those seeking to undertake research on those incarcerated.

Societal discrimination and stigma surrounding homosexuality has resulted in inadequate responses to consensual and nonconsensual sexual activity occurring within prisons and jails between members of the same sex. Similarly, the historical lack of understanding and unease with homosexuality has resulted in the production of research that has failed to adequately account for the complexities and navigation of sexual interactions and sexual identities between those incarcerated (Eigenberg, 1992). The lingering impact of discrimination and failure to distinguish between sexual identity of participants and sexual activity continues to impact the safety of those incarcerated. For example, corrections officials in Jamaica refused to provide condoms to prisoners to allow for the practice of safer sexual activity, as this was thought to promote homosexuality (for elaboration, see later discussion on prisoner health and condom distribution; Andrinopoulos, Figueroa, Kerrigan, & Ellen, 2011).

There have been attempts to correct this lack of understanding and knowledge held by prison officials, from the highest levels. In 1978, the Director of the Federal Bureau of Prisons issued a policy statement to clarify confusion surrounding the use of the words "homosexual rape." The director stated that "the use of the terms 'homosexual assault' and 'homosexual rape' to describe assaults or raped committed by one prisoner on another is misleading. Through the use of such terms, the public is led to believe that these assaults are committed by persons who are homosexual . . . the vast majority of rapes and assaults are committed by persons who are not homosexual" as cited by Howarth (1980). Therefore, attention should be paid to all inmates from the risks posed by sexual activity. This should include focus on the risks posed to those with LGB identities. Although there is an increased risk for LGB prisoners of unwanted sexual activity during incarceration, there remain problems with continued conflation of unwanted sexual activity and perpetrators' identities. Other problems for LGB inmates include pressing issues such as nondiscriminatory access to safe housing, conjugal and family visitation rights, health care needs, and civil rights, all of which are discussed later in this chapter.

EVIDENCE-BASED PRACTICES, SEXUAL ORIENTATION, AND DETENTION

If it is recognized that a prison or jail may be inadequately responding to the needs of LGB prisoners housed within it, and there is a desire to change the status quo, then a decision on how to proceed often follows. Although there may be many reasons for the inadequate responses from prisons and jails to the needs of LGB prisoners, the failure to have adequate standards and policies in place and appropriate training of staff are two areas where significant improvements can often be made. The relatively recent rise in visibility and recognition of and response to LGB prisoner issues means there are limited examples of evidence-based practice. However, there has been some progress internationally to improve standards of care for LGB prisoners and in the delivery of training on the needs of such populations.

International Best Practice on Sexual Orientation Management and Prison Standards

Although an example of an attempt to increase the safety of all prisoners from sexual violence, and not simply those who identify LGB, the US Prison Rape Elimination Act (PREA) enacted at federal level, is a practical response to an issue with a disproportionate impact on LGB prisoners (Shay, 2014). In the United States during the 1990s, a significant body of literature and research was growing on the prevalence of sexual coercion within the incarcerated population. The PREA was the culmination of a collaborative effort between human rights, faith-based, and prison rape advocacy groups (Smith, 2008) that were responding to calls for action and the research being generated. Although several factors were at play in bringing the issue of prison rape to the fore, Smith suggests that the Human Rights Watch report on male rape (Mariner, 2001) contributed the most to the passage of the PREA. It was suggested that until the Act's passage, prison rape was America's most ignored crime problem (Lehrer, 2001). The speed with which it passed Congress has been described as "surprising" (Mair, Frattaroli, & Teret, 2003) and since the Act's entry into force, there has been a comprehensive attempt to begin tackling this serious and destructive issue. Although critical of some of the reasons for the swift passage of the Act, after a long period of ignorance toward crimes of rape and sexual assault against those in detention, Smith noted that the PREA "signaled an important shift toward more humane treatment of persons in custody" (Smith, 2008, p. 11).

The Prison Rape Elimination Act has as its purpose the "provision for the analysis of the incidence and effects of prison rape in Federal, State and local institutions and to provide information, resources, recommendations and funding to protect individuals from prison rape." The Act simultaneously created the National Prison Rape Elimination Commission and charged it with developing draft standards for the elimination of prison rape. Those standards were published in June 2009, reviewed by the Department of Justice, and then passed as a final rule becoming effective August 20, 2012. The importance of this Act should be underscored. Many corrections departments created specific units to respond to the requirements of the Act and ensure compliance. Compliance with the Act is linked to accreditations and federal funding, and this has resulted in a number of changes to operating procedures and practices across different establishments after the publication of the standards (National Center for Transgender Equality, 2012). Such standards for adult prisons and jails include the requirements such as:

§ 115.11 Zero tolerance of sexual abuse and sexual harassment; PREA coordinator.

(a) An agency shall have a written policy mandating zero tolerance toward all forms of sexual abuse and sexual harassment and outlining the agency's approach to preventing, detecting, and responding to such conduct.

(b) An agency shall employ or designate an upper-level, agency-wide PREA coordinator with sufficient time and authority to develop, implement, and oversee agency efforts to comply with the PREA standards in all of its facilities.

(c) Where an agency operates more than one facility, each facility shall designate a PREA compliance manager with sufficient time and authority to coordinate the facility's efforts to comply with the PREA standards.

In addition to the important zero-tolerance approach, a key component of the Act relates to the collection and publishing of information on rape and sexual assault occurring against both inmates or staff. This collection and publishing of information includes the requirement of regular auditing in each establishment. The PREA standards require that every confinement facility be audited at least every 3 years and at least one third of each facility type operated by an agency or organization be audited each year. The audit must be conducted using a US Department of Justice designated instrument. Auditors are required to possess mandated qualification and perform audits as independent contractors. The audit comprises interviews with staff, contractors, and volunteers as well as inmates, viewing the operation of the establishment as well as reviewing documentation and records. Importantly the audit must be advertised in each housing unit for at least 6 weeks prior to it taking place, allowing inmates to contact the persons conducting the audit.

Although auditing alone is insufficient, the importance of external oversight and benchmarking of progress undertaken toward increasing prisoner safety and reducing victimization should not be lightly dismissed. The external oversight of prisons is recognized as crucial in ensuring fair and humane standards of detention (Owers, 2006) and can be successfully undertaken by paid professionals as well as volunteers (Roffee, 2017). A crucial component in ensuring compliance is that the assessment of compliance with standards of humane detention is completed by those who are adequately trained and have sufficient knowledge to make an informed assessment (Roffee, 2017).

At a minimum, the creation of the PREA and associated standards have a symbolic function. The Act's mere existence increases attention on issues within the establishment that affect the safety of inmates. Corrections departments across the United States have responded to the PREA and have begun to identify and remedy policies, practices, and places creating a risk to inmates. As a result, there are likely to be fewer incidents of sexual violence within detention establishments, which has multiple benefits for inmates and flow on benefits for corrections departments. As detailed next, there are significant links between sexual orientation and identity, and the safety and health risks posed by inadequate and unsafe housing. Unsafe housing and discriminatory treatment of LGB prisoners leads to exposure to increased risk of mental health issues and sexually transmitted infections. Higher rates of victimization resulting from systematic failures to protect vulnerable LGB inmates from other inmates means that LGB inmates suffer disproportionately. Adopting standards and policies such as the PREA, which recognize the presence of LGB prisoners, can thus have tangible effects on both ending sexual victimization and prison rape of all prisoners. However, for the standard and policies to have an impact they must be complemented with staff training and robust reporting processes, in order to create a situation where inmates are more likely to seek help and assistance and report incidents.

Staff attitudes toward inmates remain important in determining the institutional effectiveness of responses to inmates' needs. Moster and Jeglic (2009) conducted research on prison wardens' attitudes toward prison rape and sexual assault. The results of their research indicate that of the wardens surveyed, 48.3% believed staff training can be completely effective at preventing sexual assault, whereas 29.3% believed institutional policies and procedures can be completely effective at preventing sexual assault (Moster & Jeglic, 2009). Although the confidence displayed by these wardens in these results may be surprising, effectively responding to the needs of LGB prisoners and those suffering from rape and sexual assault remains a complex task. It requires a combination of appropriate policies and procedures, alongside well-trained staff in sufficient numbers to ensure adequate and safe supervision of inmates. The importance of staff training and the impact of their responses to LGB prisoners will be considered next.

Custodial Staff, Training, and the Detention Experience

Although the sexuality of some LGB inmates may have no adverse impact on their experience in detention, for those inmates whose sexual orientation has become known or has made them a target of unwanted attention, there can be significant and severe consequences. Wolfe (2008, para.17) suggests that "gay and lesbian prisoners continue to face manipulation of their housing at the whim of prison officials." One of the most crucial decisions made by corrections staff for all inmates on entering custody is the assignment of housing and with it is the exposure to risk of assault. There are conflicting approaches and commentary on the best practice of placement and housing of LGB (and trans) inmates. Depending on the institution and corrections department in question, inmates that identify as LGB can be housed in specific "gay" prisoner units, mission-specific housing for vulnerable prisoners, or housed within the general population.

On entry into custody and often when transferred between institutions, prisoners are screened for the risk of experiencing or perpetrating abuse, and this is now mandated in PREA Standards discussed earlier. The risk of experiencing or perpetrating abuse is often used by staff to help decide on an appropriate housing unit for an inmate. A significant body of literature has been generated detailing that sexual orientation is a potential risk factor for experiencing abuse (Hensley, Koscheski, & Tewksbury, 2005; Simpson et al., 2016; Struckman-Johnson & Struckman-Johnson, 2006). However, there is little research and information on the knowledge on LGB issues held by custodial staff or the way in which this information is used by them in their daily duties to make decisions such as housing inmates. However, there is research relating to correctional officers' definitions of rape and sexual assault conducted by Eigenberg (2000), which found that issues of homosexuality and consensual activity were blurred by correctional officers. Correctional officers saw homosexual inmates as more likely to be victims and, problematically, were more likely to blame them for the incidents (Eigenberg, 2000). Training of staff should therefore ensure that such stereotypes and assumptions are tackled and challenged in order for staff to appropriately respond to the needs of inmates.

It requires restating that sexual orientation is not a risk factor for perpetrating abuse; most of the perpetrators of sexual assault in prison view themselves as heterosexuals and see the victim as substituting for a woman (Mariner, 2001). Although the myth of the homosexual predator in prison has been shown to fail to withstand scrutiny (Mariner, 2001), and that the majority of victims of sexual assault while in custody are gay and bisexual, it should be noted that those who perpetrate sexual assault can be any sexual orientation (Alarid, 2000). It is therefore important for staff to be trained to understand that individuals belonging to these groups are more at risk of assault and a number of strategies can be used to mitigate such risk. One such best practice strategy found in the PREA standards is the requirement that an individual's own perception of his or her vulnerability must be considered when making housing determinations. In line with research on trans inmates, it is recognized that an individual's own perception of risk is often the most accurate.

Responses to LGB prisoners at risk should be carefully considered and should not rely exclusively on measures that simply single out those at risk (Simpson et al., 2016). The PREA standards similarly require an approach that uses all available information to make appropriate individualized decisions about both the security classification of an inmate and their housing allocation. However, if those making decisions are not trained in how to interpret the information given to them, and they simply rely upon their long-held beliefs, stereotypes, and preconceived notions, then the standards alone will fail to improve the situation for LGB and at-risk inmates. The PREA standards place a number of safeguards around the use of separate housing for LGB (and trans and intersex) people (see PREA § 115.42 Use of Screening Information). Rather than mandate or force inmates who identify as LGB to reside in specific LGB housing, the standards allow for placement in dedicated housing units on a voluntary basis; or where it is mandated, the decision to house the inmate in a dedicated unit follows a case-based assessment. Staff training is thus essential to ensuring that the standards are properly applied in practice to have the desired effect.

A number of compelling arguments have been made for utilizing housing dedicated for LGB prisoners. Such dedicated housing units can be found across the world in countries such as Thailand (Associated Press, 2017), Italy (Civillini, 2016), and Turkey (Hurtas, 2015). However, there have been significant concerns raised about the stigmatizing effect of such prisons and suggestions that such units would lead to more discrimination, including concerns raised by global human rights organizations (Benson, 2014). Discussing the K6G unit in Los Angeles, Dolovich (2012) argues that:

> residents experience K6G as a relatively safe space. They thus feel no need to resort to the self-help of gang membership or hypermasculine posturing and are able to forego the hypervigilance that often defines life in GP [general population]. As a consequence, life in K6G is less dehumanizing than life in GP and is even in some key respects affirmatively humanizing, providing space for residents to retain, express, and develop their personal identity and sense of self in a way that is psychologically healthier than the typical carceral experience. (p. 966)

Nonetheless, this unit has been heavily criticized by others, including Robinson (2011), on the basis that it uses, among other things, biased processes to determine who is allowed to be housed in the unit through the use of stereotypes. Also, it poses risks to those who pass the biased entry requirements in exposing gay and trans inmates to heightened HIV risk and chance of victimization through coercing them to come out. In particular, there was concern that White gay males were privileged due to the lack of knowledge concerning diversity of experience (and stereotypes) held by those in positions of power and who make discretionary decisions on who is permitted to be housed in the unit (Robinson, 2011).

There are cases where LGB inmates have been housed within the general population successfully without incident or cause for concern. Wolfe (2008) details the case of a prisoner from Illinois, where the prisoner was housed in the general population and when transferred to a different establishment, the prisoner was placed under protective custody. The inmate objected to this differential treatment by staff who made the decision to segregate him based solely on his sexual orientation. The inmate brought a case and while the court did not find in the inmate's favor, as he was lacking basis for a legal claim, there was concern with the operation of custodial staff discretion (Wolfe, 2008). Unbridled discretion acts as an open in-vitation to prejudice on the part of the prison officials (Wolfe, 2008), and as such there should be appropriate safeguards in place for review of decisions.

The case of *Johnson v. Johnson* (2004) involved the detention of a prisoner after the revocation of a sentence of probation. Johnson was known to be gay and ef-feminate, and he made it known on arrival to the Texan prison system that he had previously been housed in "safekeeping." Safekeeping is a housing status that separates vulnerable individuals from more aggressive offenders. The Texas Department of Criminal Justice (TDCJ) regulations indicate that safekeeping occurs when an inmate is at risk of victimization, has enemies in the general population, has a history of homosexuality, or possesses other characteristics that mark the offender as vulnerable. The case report suggests that, according to Johnson, one of the members of the classification committee told him: "that '[w]e don't protect punks on this farm'—'punk' being prison slang for a homosexual man. Johnson was put in the general population. He was raped by other inmates almost immediately" (*Johnson v. Johnson*, 2004, p. 10).

The case file indicates that a gang member asserted ownership of Johnson and forced him to become a sexual servant. This gang member then started to rent Johnson to other prisoners to perform sexual acts on them. He was beaten and raped on numerous occasions over 18 months and made repeated requests for assistance to prison officials, including requests to be put on safekeeping status as well as to be placed in protective custody and transferred to a different in-stitution. These were ignored by custodial staff. Thus, the detention experience can be directly impacted by both deliberate acts and omissions on the part of custodial staff. Johnson's requests for appropriate housing and adequate medical treatment went ignored. The failure on the part of custodial officials to respond to the requests for assistance facilitated continued victimization. Ultimately the failure of staff to respond to the inmate's needs opened the state to a claim for damages and compensation for the horrendous acts suffered while Johnson was in state custody and care.

Although the aforementioned case is an example of blatant disregard by custo-dial staff for prisoner safety (and thus suggests inadequate or ineffective training), some prison officials have indicated that they do not report instances of prison rape even when they believe the reporting party, because they have not been properly trained on how to handle the situation (Wyatt, 2005). Staff training thus remains a crucial component to ensure staff hold an appropriate level of knowl-edge, allowing staff to recognize and respond to the presence of LGB prisoners and issues concerning this inmate population. Corrections departments can begin the process of engaging with LGB organizations to help provide training and to get external accreditation for their work interacting with members of LGB communities. Whereas organizations may believe they are LGB friendly, this does not mean that their services are responsive to and meet the needs of LGB persons. Within Australia, a Rainbow Tick accreditation scheme has been devised to assist services from moving from being in a position of being LGBTI-friendly to being LGBTI-inclusive (GLHV@ARCSHS, 2016). External bodies can assist corrections departments in responding to the needs of LGB persons and in helping to assess the impact of measures on LGB persons. It is therefore worthwhile for corrections to begin engaging with their LGB populations and external actors when seeking to train staff on the impact of discretion on the detention experience. As suggested earlier, many seemingly innocuous measures and decisions can have adverse impacts on LGB populations; in the next section, the policy issues surrounding availability of conjugal and family visitation rights and health care needs, including condom availability, will be addressed.

CRIMINAL JUSTICE SYSTEM POLICY ISSUES AND IMPLICATIONS

Availability of Conjugal and Family Visitation Rights

Internationally, there is a significant degree of controversy over the use of conjugal visitation, defined as private meetings in prison between an inmate and their partner, during which time the pair are about to engage in whatever legal activity they desire, which may include but is not limited to sexual activity (Einat & Rabinovitz, 2013). There has been a decline in the use of such visits, which has been attributed to the adoption of cost-saving measures: In the early 1990s the United States had 17 states offering conjugal visitation, although this had dwindled to just four states in 2016: California, Connecticut, New York, and Washington. There has been a focus on the rehabilitative nature of the visits and the ability for inmates to maintain personal ties with the world outside of the prison or jail. Such visits may be known as extended family visits or family reunion visits. In addition to conjugal visits in prison, there are also home visits; for example, in the United Kingdom, where conjugal visits are not available to prisoners, home visits are permitted for the inmate to begin rebuilding links with the life outside of prison that they will be returning to.

Conjugal visits have generally not always been available to those in same-sex relationships as many of the restrictions and requirements concerning the availability of visits were limited to those who were formally married. Wilkinson (2003, p. 1) suggested that while disputable, "the majority of programs tend to place undue emphasis on the sexual aspects of a relationship" and their availability to those in nontraditional families has opened administrators to claims of discrimination. The unavailability of marriage to those in same-sex relationships in many jurisdictions thus acted (and continues to act where it is not available) as a discriminatory barrier. However, despite the reduction in use of conjugal visitation across the country, some states in the United States—notably New York and California, have recently expanded the availability of conjugal visitation to those in same-sex relationships. In New York, the decision to expand availability was formalized by a regulation of 2011. The regulation codified the practice of same-sex visitation for inmates in gay or same-sex marriages or civil unions which had been in place since 2008 when Gov. David Paterson required New York State agencies to end discrimination and recognize same-sex unions (Blain, 2011). In

California, the Department of Corrections began to allow same-sex visitation from June 2007, after being required to comply with antidiscrimination legislation that required equal recognition of rights between partners of heterosexual couples as those found in same-sex relationships. In California the rules allow visitation for partners of inmates who are in a registered marriage or domestic partnership and are not incarcerated (Associated Press, 2007).

There have been several countries who have recently extended the availability of conjugal visits to same-sex couples after repeatedly denying same-sex couples the right to visits. The Israel Prison Service (IPS) indicated in 2013 that it would grant visits to same-sex couples under the same circumstances they are granted to heterosexual couples (Lior, 2013). This was following several cases where gay inmates had petitioned the Tel Aviv and Central District Courts for access to conjugal visits and were denied. These claims had been routinely denied by the IPS and Courts (Lior, 2013). To be eligible for such visits in Israel, inmates must be married or in a common-law relationship confirmed by an affidavit; alternatively, the prisoner should have received continuous visits from the partner for over 2 years in order to be eligible (Ben-Zur, 2012; Lior, 2013). The relaxation of the rules in many jurisdictions thus appears to be prompted by legal challenges or threatened challenges.

A number of legal challenges have been brought globally, and the Colombian Supreme Court issued a verdict in October 2001 in favor of conjugal visitation rights for a lesbian woman, in a case brought by Alba Nelly Montoya, who was denied access to her partner. The court rules that that the Director of Risaralda Women's Prison's decision to deprive lesbian inmates of conjugal visits violates their constitutionally protected rights to privacy (Article 15 of the Colombian Constitution), to freedom from discrimination based on sex, and to equality before the law (Article 13 of the Colombian Constitution) (OutRight, 2002). Importantly the Judge ruled that access to conjugal visitation should be available to all lesbian women under the same conditions of security and privacy as given to those inmates accessing heterosexual visits. Nonetheless, it has been reported that another female inmate in Colombia was refused visits from her same-sex partner (GayLawNet, 2017). Thus, while the legal cases are important, they can have limited impact if corrections officials choose to ignore them.

The key issue for corrections regarding the availability of conjugal visitation is the equal treatment of persons in same-sex and opposite-sex relationships. Where rules are in place to allow conjugal visitation to opposite-sex couples (in both registered and unregistered partnerships), then rules of equal treatment indicate that such visits should also be available to prisoners in same-sex relationships (in both registered and unregistered partnerships). Where national law does not yet permit same-sex couples the right to marry, and the right to conjugal visitation is restricted to those in registered partnerships, this will have an indirectly discriminatory impact on LGB persons. Those who are LGB and are in long-term committed relationships will therefore be unable to access conjugal visitation due to the state's discriminatory failure to provide equal marriage. In such circumstance, it is worth considering whether prisons and jails can extend the availability of conjugal visitation to those who can show they are in de facto relationships. This would help mitigate the problems caused by discriminatory responses to same-sex relationships and help ensure greater parity between inmates who are in genuine relationships, thus giving all inmates the access to rehabilitative programs.

Specific Health Care Needs, Prisoner Safety, and Condom Availability

To detain LGB prisoners in humane conditions, it is necessary for prison administrators and custody officials to recognize the specific health care needs of this group of prisoners. The right to access nondiscriminatory health care has been a significant concern for LGB prisoners and while there have been improvements in many jurisdictions, there is still scope for further advances. Although there may be no anatomical differences between heterosexual prisoners and their LGB counterparts, there are a number of specific health care needs arising from the impacts of holding an LGB identity. Particular attention should be given to the mental health of LGB inmates. Although holding an LGB identity was declassified as a mental/behavioral disorder in 1992 (World Health Organization, 1992), there remain lingering impacts of the discrimination faced by LGB persons in their daily lives, thus impacting their mental and physical health. Being lesbian, gay, or bisexual is not in itself a health problem or concern. It is the exposure to and fear of discrimination and isolation resulting from others' responses to sexual orientation that impact peoples' mental health, causing stress, psychological distress, and suicidality (Hillier et al., 2010; Rosenstreich, Comfort, & Martin, 2011).

The high rate of mental illness found in those incarcerated has been well documented; and mental illness may play a significant part in the reasons for incarceration (Hiday & Moloney, 2014; Lamb & Weinberger, 1998), in addition to being triggered or exacerbated by the experience of incarceration (Haney, 2002; Schnittker & John, 2007). Thus, LGB individuals entering the prison system are starting from a point of greater risk of, and exposure to, mental illness due to the impacts of societal discrimination and marginalization. It is therefore crucial that custodial staff are trained to be culturally competent toward LGB prisoners, and this includes recognizing the heightened risk factors for mental illness. Staff should be trained to understand how exhibiting inclusive behaviors and cultural competency toward LGB populations can aid recovery (Ida, 2007) and thus have positive implications for rehabilitation and prisoner release (Ryan, Russell, Huebner, Diaz, & Sanchez, 2010). Ensuring staff are adequately trained and have sufficient cultural competency in working with diverse populations will help address many of the issues raised; however, it should not be treated as a "cure-all" solution to all the problems faced by members of the LGB community (LaViolette, 2013). Corrections departments should thus begin to implement competency training for staff that contains information on the heighted risk of mental illness, reasons for this, and ways to mitigate risk.

The remainder of this section will address health care responses to increase prisoner safety and reduce risk, and focus on the distribution of condoms and sexual protection to inmates. The Prison Rape Elimination Act (42 U.S.C. § 15601) states that the issue of prison rape undermines public health by contributing to the spread of diseases. Noting that the issue of prison rape is not solely related to LGB prisoners as victims, it should be restated that it disproportionately affects gay and bisexual male prisoners (as well as trans persons discussed elsewhere in this volume) who are singled out as targets of sexual violence and nonconsensual sexual activity. Many correctional administrations have displayed extreme reluctance to acknowledge that sexual activity takes place inside their prisons (Gopal, 2015). The reasons behind the failure to recognize that sexual activity occurs is beyond the scope of this chapter. However, much of the sexual activity that occurs in prisons is contrary to legislation, regulations, and ordinance governing the operation of prisons and jails.

Much thought has been given by corrections officials to reduce both unwanted sexual conduct between prisoners and the harmful effects of sex (both consensual and nonconsensual) in prison. A number of strategies can be undertaken to reduce the harm from and transmission of sexually transmitted infections and bloodborne diseases. The provision of condoms is one potential solution to some of the risks posed by sex in prison, though the provision of condoms to prisoners is uncommon globally and remains contentious (Butler, Richters, Yap, & Donovan, 2013). In some prisons, rather than being considered as potential life-saving devices, condoms are considered as contraband (Leibowitz, Harawa, Sylla, Hallstrom, & Kerndt, 2013). There have also been suggestions that supplying condoms to prisoners encourages prisoners to break the law (Fine-Maron, 2013), that it may increase rates of sexual assaults (Butler et al., 2013), and they may be used as weapons (Butler et al., 2013) or for hiding contraband.

The State of Vermont has allowed the distribution of condoms since 1987 and has been overt in stating that its support for them is grounded in a harm-reduction approach. Then Corrections Commissioner Joseph Patrissi noted that "[corrections] has a responsibility . . . to make sure [HIV] doesn't get spread to the general population" and that he was "sure as heck not going to stand in the way [of condom distribution] if it's the best medical practice even though it may not be the best corrections practice" (Associated Press, 1987). Other US states have been slow to follow Vermont in adopting this public health and harm-reduction-based approaches. There have been several progressive detention establishments on a local level and several counties, particularly within California, that have made condoms available to prisoners, including San Francisco in 1989 and Los Angeles in 2001. The K6G unit, which houses gay men and trans women, is the only carceral complex within Los Angeles County to allow condom distribution and this project was launched in November 2001 (Harawa, Sweat, George, & Sylla, 2010). Outside of the United States, Australia is notable for having jurisdictions that have had long-standing policies of provision of condoms. Condoms have been available in prisons in New South Wales, Australia, since 1996 following a legal challenge by inmates (Butler et al., 2013) and are now available across other Australian jurisdictions.

The distribution and use of condoms is likely to have some affect in reducing risk, though this is likely to improve when education is provided to prisoners.

Peer-led prison-supported education has also been shown to be effective at reducing risky behavior (Sifunda et al., 2008). There are examples of corrections employees and spokespersons who have testified that the introduction of condom distribution and associated safe-sex counseling has resulted in a decrease in disease transmission (Associated Press, 2013). Research undertaken in Australia by Butler et al. (2013) indicates that, if available, condoms were much more likely to be used by prisoners during anal sex. Research also indicates that sexual activity is not likely to increase after condoms become available and condoms do not impede custody operations (Sylla, Harawa, & Grinstead Reznick, 2010). In a study undertaken in K6G in Los Angeles, of the inmates who reported not using condoms when engaging in anal sex, 32% reported that this was because they had run out, 13% stated that they were unavailable, and 8% reported that the lack of lubricant was the reason for not using a condom (Harawa et al., 2010).

Key to any effective change in prison regime is staff participation. Staff in Los Angeles County Jail indicated that it was the result of forward thinking in the upper levels of prison administration along with the identified public health needs that facilitated the development of the program (McCuller & Harawa, 2014). Sylla et al. (2010), when investigating a trial condom program in San Francisco, found that staff acceptance of condom access for prisoners increased after a trial started. Thus, corrections administrators should be aware that while staff may be reluctant to trial condom distribution, in previous trials staff support had grown during program rollout (Sylla et al., 2010).

Responding to the health care needs of incarcerated LGB populations often requires complex solutions. The distribution of condoms alone will not stop prison rape, and an appropriate response requires both staff training and provision of appropriate housing. Yet training and condom provision can help prevent some potential harm from unwanted sexual activity. Improving prisoner safety through housing is crucial to stopping sexual assault and rape, and it can also positively impact prisoner mental health. Establishments need to have LGB-inclusive practice to ensure that prisoners' mental health is adequately considered and not overlooked. Although beyond the scope of this chapter, custodial officers should be aware of the effectiveness of screening for mental illness and bloodborne diseases on entry into the establishment. One concern with screening is that once the institution's awareness of a situation is raised, it then must act and the level of duty of care is raised. Willful blindness within corrections toward incidents and issues arising in their establishments is nothing new, and Wyatt (2005) has argued that for many years, "prison rape has been a problem that has been largely ignored by corrections officers and law enforcement agencies" (Wyatt, 2005, p. 614).

Corrections policies and practices must be better informed to respond to prisoners with diverse needs to ensure they fulfill their obligations and maintain prisoners' rights. Although conjugal visitation remains contentious, in those jurisdictions that have chosen to maintain the practice, access to such visits has been extended to same-sex couples. In many cases, this has been the result of litigation brought against corrections departments. However, like the provision of condoms, there are several progressive penal establishments. The leaders of such departments have seen the value in adopting a harm-minimization approach and associated benefits for those in detention as well as the wider community. Prisoner health, both mental and physical, is impacted by the entire detention experience. As such, the following section on trends and future directions for corrections will address two key issues for LGB prisoners: housing and staff discretion.

TRENDS AND FUTURE DIRECTIONS

The management of all offenders should be in line with the rules and regulations of the institution as decried by those in positions of authority and in line with relevant laws and statutes. The rules and regulations regarding individual detention institutions should be formulated to comply with state, national, and (where applicable) international law. With growing developments in terms of equal rights and antidiscrimination practices, the rules and regulations applied to inmates should be assessed for their compatibility with these equal protection and antidiscrimination requirements. One way of doing this is through an impact audit. An impact audit of the processes and procedures in place within an organization will allow for a snapshot to be taken of how the institution currently responds to LGB prisoners. As with needs assessments, there are a wealth of resources from LGB organizations that custody officers and prison administrators can refer to on how to undertake an impact assessment. When undertaking an impact assessment, it is worthwhile engaging local LGB organizations to ensure the impact assessment is appropriately tailored to the local conditions and responsive to the needs of the population impacted. The following sections will review recent trends concerning staff discretion in housing LGB prisoners and application of policies regarding prisoner mail.

Housing LGB Prisoners: Segregation, Separate Facilities, or General Population?

It has long been recognized that segregation can have adverse impacts on individuals in detention, including impacts on their physical and mental well-being, leading to self-harm and increase the risk of recidivism on release (Kaba et al., 2014; Lovell, 2008; Lovell, Johnson, & Cain, 2007; Metzner & Fellner, 2010). The key task for jail and prison administrators is to safely house inmates, including those at risk of mental, physical, and sexual abuse, without exposing them to further trauma.

There is no shortage of awareness of the risk to LGB inmates from placement within the general population, and some custodial administrators have responded by placing LGB inmates in protective custody. Protective custody involves removing the inmate from the general population of the prison and may encompass segregating the inmate and holding them individually in similar conditions to rule violators. Alternatively, it may comprise placing the inmate within a specialist housing unit with others deemed to be a similar level of risk. Housing LGB inmates in administrative segregation severely limits opportunities for access to programs, exercise, education, face-to-face mental health interventions, and other activities and services available to individuals in the general population (Hastings, Browne, & Kall, 2015). As such, policies and practices that routinely place LGB people in segregated housing for protection "thus penalize these individuals for their vulnerability and significantly worsen their conditions of confinement" (Hastings et al., 2015, p. 16). The concept of segregation, also known as but not limited to, solitary or temporary confinement or administrative segregation, was originally designed to respond to inmates who committed serious rule violations while incarcerated (Browne, Cambier, & Agha, 2011). However, as detailed in the case study that follows, the severe traumas arising from the solitary confinement of inmates based on their sexual orientation can have effects that are of such magnitude as to be considered inhumane punishment and prohibited by international legal instruments against the use of torture (see later). Therefore, inmates should not be in isolation based solely on the reason of their sexual orientation.

There are two primary options remaining for custodial administrators in relation to housing LGB inmates: in specialist housing or within the general population. Mission-specific housing refers to housing designated for subgroups of prisoners who may be allocated to a unit, block, or wing on the basis of particular characteristics. In the United Kingdom, Her Majesty's Prison Service operates what is known as the Vulnerable Prisoner Unit (VPU) (also known as "rule 45"). Mission-specific housing may also refer to housing reserved for those with mental illness or physical disabilities or other prisoners with specific needs such as those housed in drug and alcohol rehabilitation units. Similar to concerns raised with solitary confinement or individual segregation, inmate mission-specific units may restrict prisoner access to education, jobs, and other programs and opportunities (National Center for Transgender Equality, 2012). It has been argued that specific units might pose a risk of further stigmatizing inmates and making them more vulnerable to harassment and abuse by staff (National Center for Transgender Equality, 2012). There is no doubt that such units are controversial and having been conceptualized as the lesser of two evils (Dolovich, 2011), given the high levels of violence and levels of risk faced by LGB inmates when in the general population and can be understood as a double-edged sword (Shay, 2011).

Los Angeles County Men's Jail operates the now famous K6G unit, housing gay men and trans women. This unit is has received significant attention and criticism based on the operational features and admissions process of the unit, with Spade (2012) suggesting its screening process is terrifying and absurd. Sitting behind such criticisms are different normative positions, including those that hold the belief that places of detention should be safer than they currently are, and those that take issue with the unit through its failure to admit all those who wish to be housed within it and thus reject its discretionary approach. There is concern that staff discretion and decision making, including utilization of "cultural questions" posed to inmates to determine eligibility further entrench stereotypes of race, gender, and class (see Robinson, 2011). Data from a study by Blackburn, Fowler, Mullings, and Marquart (2011) found that female inmates disagreed with a statement suggesting that lesbians should be segregated, yet other groups, including male inmates, heterosexual inmates, and young people housed in a juvenile training institution, were significantly more likely to agree that gay inmates should be segregated. The segregation of LGB inmates may further entrench stereotypes and counter advances within detention establishments to provide equal treatment and protection to all inmates.

Further, Robinson (2011) suggests that housing offenders within K6G and similar units labels and stereotypes inmates through clothing; exposes them to a heightened risk of HIV transmission; and disrupts relationships that cut across gender identity and sexual orientation. At issue is the state-sponsored nature of the segregation, which requires government officials to intrude into the most private and intimate details of detainees' lives. Although these arguments are compelling and may be factually correct, such critics do not cast doubt on claims that such units are safer for the gay and bisexual (as well as trans) inmates (than being housed within general population) (Robinson, 2011). Research by Dolovich (2011), who undertook in-depth research into the K6G unit, indicates that the unit is "relatively free from the sexual harassment and forced or coerced sexual conduct that can be the daily lot of sexual minorities in other men's carceral facilities" (Dolovich, 2011, p. 4). However, Dolovich (2011) suggests that should an inmate try to challenge the regime in court, the unit would most likely survive a constitutional challenge. Rather than attempt to challenge and problematize the existence of the unit as others such as Robinson have done, it has been suggested that different questions ought to be asked. These include holistic questions concerned with not "whether the program ought to be allowed, but what would it take to maintain the protection it provides while minimizing the dangers posed whenever the state authorizes differential treatment on the basis of identity" (Dolovich, 2011, p. 7).

Policies on Prisoner Mail—Kentucky and "Homosexual Mail"

Rights-based approaches may be usefully utilized to respond to some of the discriminatory policies and practices adversely impacting LGB prisoners. However, the adoption of policies that allow for a significant degree of unstructured decision making and discretion may simply continue to permit direct and indirect discrimination. Policy makers are therefore advised to limit staff discretion to prevent staff from applying rules in ways contrary to state and national civil rights law and ensure compliance with antidiscrimination statutes. Policy makers must think through the impact of discretionary powers provided to corrections staff and policies that use amorphous phrases and terms, that while not intended to be discriminatory, can be operationalized to have adverse impacts on LGB minority and vulnerable populations.

The American Civil Liberties Union (ACLU) contacted the Warden of Eastern Kentucky Correctional Complex (EKCC) in March 2016, claiming that EKCC used its mail policy dated 2013, on at least occasions during late 2015, to confiscate mail from LGB prisoners. The confiscated mail included magazines such as *Out* and *The Advocate*. The ALCU argued that the state mail policy denied inmates' their First Amendment Rights (Bittenbender, 2016). A similar issue regarding the right to receive information had been litigated in 2005 with the US District Court in Indiana, hearing claims that a prison in Indiana refused to allow copies of the same publications. The prison officials justified their decision to ban the materials on the basis that to allow such material would single out inmates as targets for abuse (Wolfe, 2008). The court in that case agreed with the prison, that banning the publications promoted safety and security, as those who received such materials would be perceived as gay and thus targeted (Wolfe, 2008). The court was silent on the need to provide a safe environment for all inmates, and thus failed to protect LGB inmates' equal rights to access information about communities of which they are part.

Corrections utilized a policy on inmate correspondence dated 2013 that contained direct discrimination against LGB persons. This policy detailed the rules concerning the receipt of incoming mail. Within this policy under a section titled "Pornography and Sexually Explicit Materials," it stated:

> Pornography or sexually explicit material which poses a threat to the security, good order, or discipline of the institution may be disapproved for receipt. Exclusion shall not be based upon sexual content alone.

> a. The Warden shall designate a staff member or members to review incoming publications.
> b. A list shall not be maintained of specific publications that shall be rejected.
> c. Types of materials that may justify rejection include those which depict: homosexuality, sadism, masochism, bestiality, and sexual acts or nudity with children.
> d. Rejection shall not be based upon the grounds set forth above if the material does not pose a threat to any aspect of the institution.

> Sexually explicit and nude photographs or reproductions sent to an inmate from non-publishers or on-line services shall be rejected. (Kentucky Corrections, 2013)

The ACLU legal director responsible for the challenge noted that "safety concerns aren't valid arguments for withholding items that mention homosexuality" (Wire Report, 2016). Concern from the ACLU was that "such policies single out pro-LGBT messages for unfavorable treatment. And that type of viewpoint discrimination by the government is precisely what the First Amendment is designed to prevent" (ACLU Kentucky, 2016). However, another related concern was that the exercise of discretion was inappropriate under the original mail policy. The types of publications that resulted in denial of delivery to prisoners were not pornographic or sexually explicit materials. The materials (publications *Out* and *The Advocate*) were not sexual in content and instead were LGB community magazines; the former describes itself as "A gay and lesbian perspective on style, entertainment, fashion, the arts, politics, culture, and the world at large" (*Out*, 2017) and the latter as "Gay news—commentary, arts and entertainment, health, parenting, and politics. The Advocate is the leading source for up-to-date and extensive LGBT news" (*The Advocate*, 2017).

In addition to listing homosexuality with other illegal conduct, including sex with children and bestiality, the inappropriate exercise of discretion by those applying the mail policy, possibly from discriminatory beliefs and anti-LGB sentiment, resulted in the materials being denied entry. The materials were not sexually explicit, yet they were deemed a threat to the security, good order, or discipline of the institution. The Commissioner of Kentucky Corrections ordered staff to investigate the refusal to allow the materials to the prisoners and issued a revised draft copy of the inmate correspondence policy dated June 2, 2016. Following the Commissioner issuing a state-wide memo prohibiting the use of the 2013 policy, the draft policy became operative with immediate effect:

Prohibited or Sexually Explicit Materials

Sexually explicit as defined by pictorial depictions of nudity in books, pamphlets, magazines, periodicals, and any other graphic images, or any other publication or any personal pictures, drawing, or photocopies of any of these items are prohibited.

1. Nudity for purposes of this policy means a pictorial depiction where male or female genitalia, anus or the nipples or areola of female breasts are exposed.
2. Sexually explicit for purposes of this policy means a pictorial depiction of actual or simulated sexual acts including sexual intercourse, oral sex, or masturbation.
3. Sexually explicit material which poses a threat to the security, good order, or discipline of the institution may be disapproved for receipt. Exclusion shall not be based upon sexual content alone.
4. The Warden shall designate a staff member or members to review incoming publications.
   a. A list shall not be maintained of specific publications that shall be rejected.
   b. Material rejected under this section shall be held by the appropriate staff and notice of the rejection with the reason therefor shall be provided to the inmate and to the sender. The inmate shall have the same appeal process as set forth above. (Kentucky Corrections, 2016a)

This draft policy removed any reference to homosexuality and incorporated an improved set of definitions. These definitions explained in greater detail the types of materials that were prohibited. This clarification to the definition of materials permitted helped to remove some discretion and allowed for a more transparent

protection of the rights of minority populations. This is because the rules are sufficiently clear to allow for manipulation by staff biased against LGB inmates, with
the regulations applying to both male and female sexually explicit materials and
nudity. However, in both policies, entry into the facility was not simply precluded
because the material was of the type listed: It must also pose a threat. Therefore,
it was the discretion exercised by the staff in late 2015 that determined that the
material was a threat. The draft policy of June 2 also prevented staff rejecting the
material based on the sexual content alone and again required there to be a threat
to security, good order, or discipline of the institution. Unfortunately, it does not
prevent staff from using prisoner bias and intolerance toward other prisoners to
qualify as a threat. Staff therefore remain able to argue that banning the materials
would promote good order and prevent biased inmates from creating a threat.
Thus, it remains arguable that a court would find in favor of corrections, even
though corrections would be mounting the argument that they are unable to operate a prison safe enough for LGB prisoners to access community publications.

A new policy, dated January 2017, replaced the interim policy of June 2016,
and although this policy is not openly averse to homosexuality, it may continue to
impact LGB inmates due to the wide level of discretion given to officers. It is unfortunate that the improved definition of sexually explicit materials found in the
draft policy (see earlier) has been removed. The new January 2017 policy states:

Prohibited Sexually Explicit Materials

1. Sexually explicit materials pose a threat to the security, good order, and
   discipline of the institution and may facilitate criminal activity. Sexually
   explicit materials further present a significant risk of sexual harassment
   of employees.
2. Sexually explicit materials shall be prohibited, including pictorial
   depictions in books, pamphlets, magazines, periodicals, and any other
   graphic images, or any other publication or any personal pictures,
   drawing, or photocopies of any of these items.
3. The Warden shall designate a staff member or members to review
   incoming publications to determine if they violate this policy and shall
   be rejected.
   a. A list shall not be maintained of specific publications that shall be
      rejected.
   b. Material rejected under this section shall be held by the appropriate
      staff and notice of the rejection with the reason therefor shall be
      provided to the inmate and to the sender. The inmate shall have the
      same appeal process as set forth above. (Kentucky Corrections, 2016b)

The removal of the definition and clarification of what constituted nudity and
sexually explicit material found in the June 2, 2016, draft policy is a backward
step. ACLU will likely continue to monitor the implementation and impact of new
policy on LGB prisoners. However, best practice would indicate that Kentucky

Corrections ought to conduct an impact audit to investigate how staff apply the new policy and its impact on LGB correspondence. Additionally, it would be useful for Kentucky Corrections to provide guidance to assist staff and inmates in understanding what materials comprise those within the class prohibited, to ensure security, good order, and discipline of the institution. Training staff to be competent and aware of LGB prisoner needs is incredibly important. This training should ensure that staff can recognize the value for minority and vulnerable inmates, including LGB populations, in receiving correspondence that comprises information about a community of which they are part. In addition, training should teach staff to discern publications fitting within a category of lifestyle or community magazines that may include pictures that may be revealing but not overtly sexual in nature and, as such, can be permitted. Training staff on respectful engagement with members of minority communities and on the need for appropriate treatment for LGB prisoners may also help staff to avoid making discriminatory decisions that may then result in legal challenges, as well as adverse impacts on already vulnerable inmates.

CASE EXAMPLE

European Human Rights and *X v. Turkey*: Treatment Amounting to Torture

This case example concerns the detention experience and segregation of a gay inmate after a request for protection. The inmate sought redress before the prison administrators and domestic courts, and after receiving insufficient responses, he decided to exercise his rights under the European Convention on Human Rights (ECHR), bringing a case before the European Court of Human Rights (ECtHR). Although there are many claims concerning inhuman and degrading treatment from incarcerated LGB people that have been made to the ECtHR, this was first case where the court recognized that a failure of the state (through the prison service) was sufficiently serious to violate Article 3 and found the state's treatment of the prisoner amounted to torture.

X was born in 1989, identified as a gay man, and was on remand in Eskişehir Prison in 2008 after being charged with forgery, deception, credit card fraud, and misrepresentation offences. The inmate requested to be removed from the accommodation he shared with heterosexual inmates due to the intimidation and harassment he was facing based on his sexual orientation, and he asked to be placed with other homosexual inmates. The prison removed him to a single cell 7 m² in size and similar to cells intended for those in solitary confinement as a disciplinary measure or accused of pedophilia or rape. The cell had a bed and toilet, was without washbasin or adequate lighting, and was dirty and rat infested. His prison regime did not involve contact with other prisoners nor outdoor exercise, and he had only been outside of his cell to see his lawyer. The inmate sought relief through application to a domestic Judge; however, this was unsuccessful. The Judge noted that the prison authorities did not have specific rules for considering the wishes of remand prisoners, unlike the rules in place for convicted prisoners. The domestic Judge held "it has been established that the applicant is being detained as a preventive measure in an individual cell as the State cannot run the risk of a transvestite being lynched [in a prison]" (*X v. Turkey*, 2013, para. 14). There were indications that the solitary confinement was having irreparable psychological effects on the prisoner. He sought to challenge the conditions of detention through the national courts with no success. However, a domestic court in which he sought relief did send a letter to the prison authorities requesting them to take all necessary measures regarding the applicant's complaints about the conditions of detention (*X v. Turkey*, 2013, para. 17). The domestic court found that in total the inmate was deprived of contact form other inmates and in solitary confinement for 8 months and 18 days.

The European Convention requires the rights of prisoners be respected and the conditions of detention be compatible with human dignity. Article 3 of the ECHR provides that "no one shall be subjected to torture or to inhuman or degrading treatment or punishment." Article 3 compels States to ensure that the conditions of detention are compatible with respect for human dignity and that there is not distress or hardship of an intensity exceeding the unavoidable level of suffering inherent in detention. The ECtHR found that, in addition, and notwithstanding the practical demands of imprisonment, the health and well-being of the inmate should be adequately secured. The ECtHR noted that the prison authorities were concerned that the applicant was at risk of physical abuse—which cannot be deemed unfounded as the applicant complained of intimidation and bullying. Nevertheless, it was found that these fears did not justify a measure totally isolating the inmate. This solitary confinement, although not imposed as a punishment, had the effect of imposing substantial limitations on the applicant's rights. The conditions of detention were capable of causing mental and physical suffering and a feeling of profound violation of his human dignity (*X v. Turkey*, 2013, para. 45). The ECtHR found there was a violation of Article 3 and Article 14 (right to nondiscrimination) and awarded damages to the applicant in the case.

Although much of the criticism was directed at conditions of detention that both heterosexual and gay prisoners face, it was the sexual orientation of the prisoner and not his offending history that caused his exposure to the severe conditions of detention. The Turkish authorities within this case claimed that their decision to remove the prisoner was both at the prisoner's request and to ensure the safety of the prisoner facing threats. However, it is also clear that the prisoner made a recommendation as to his placement, which was ignored by the prison. Implicit within the case are several significant points of learning for prison authorities. The protection of prisoners should remain paramount in decisions being made regarding the housing of LGB inmates. The prisoner was housed with another gay prisoner for a period during which there was no suggestion of any threat to safety or concern about mental health due to isolation. Whereas in the United States the PREA forbids segregation solely on the basis of sexual orientation, the option of housing LGB prisoners with other LGB prisoners may help alleviate some of the safety concerns arising from housing LGB prisoners with non-LGB inmates. In addition, the opportunity to review the case was presented to a domestic Judge who looked at legal compliance without paying attention to the merits of the case. The opportunity for an early intervention and remedy was presented when the case was raised by the inmate. However, the refusal by the State authorities (both the prison and the domestic Judge) to investigate the matter led to a situation that had sufficient duration and severity as to be regarded as torture, inhuman and degrading treatment. Responding appropriately to claims by LGB prisoners concerning risks to safety and security and giving weight to the prisoner's indications of appropriate placement are paramount in ensuring that the conditions of detention are not likely to lead to rights breaches or be regarded as torturous.

Although engaging with persons who are incarcerated, to learn of their needs, may be less palatable in jurisdictions that experience high levels of penal populism, there are a number of benefits to engaging with LGB inmates in order to undertake a needs assessment. A needs assessment is a process for determining the needs and priorities of a particular population cohort (Queensland Government, n.d.). As Gupta, Sleezer, and Russ-Eft (2011) suggest, conducting a needs assessment allows an organization to figure out how to close a learning or performance gap. The learning that may come from this needs assessment will enable corrections staff to make better decisions about inmate safety, security, and care of LGB offenders.

Ideally, a needs assessment that is concerned with improving conditions of detention for LGB prisoners would directly engage with LGB inmates and ensure that they are active participants in the process of undertaking the needs assessment. However, LGB inmates may be unwilling to participate due to the risks of taking part and being identified as a member of a minority community, singling them out for further discrimination. There may be other reasons for an unwillingness; for example, they may approach the institution with mistrust following previous bad experiences during incarceration. In such situations, corrections departments can engage with local LGB organizations and advocacy groups (who may comprise former incarcerated persons) and others with specific cultural knowledge who can help the establishment undertake a needs assessment focused on LGB inmates. Many of these organizations may have ready access to the knowledge and information required for corrections to begin developing standards, policies, and training that are responsive to the needs of LGB prisoners. Although the advocacy work of lobby groups concerned about the lack of safety for LGB (and trans) prisoners in the United States from the 1980s to the early 2000s resulted in an unprecedented national reformist effort in US corrections regulation (Shay, 2014), there is still a great deal of work to be done to improve the conditions of detention for LGB people globally.

WEB-BASED RESOURCES

Bent Bars Project—letter writing for LGBTIQ prisoners in Britain: http://bentbarsproject.org

Black and Pink—open family of LGBTQ prisoners and "free world" allies who support each other: http://blackandpink.org

Just Detention International (JDI)—health and human rights organization that seeks to end sexual abuse in all forms of detention. Free support packet for survivors of sexual abuse in prison/detention: http://justdetention.org

Lambda Legal—committed to achieving full recognition of the civil rights of lesbians, gay men, bisexuals, transgender people and everyone living with HIV through impact litigation, education and public policy work: http://lambdalegal.org

National PREA Resource Centre—website funded through grants from Bureau of Justice Assistance, Office of Justice Programs, US Department of Justice. The aim is to aid those who operate detention establishments, and the inmates and their families in their efforts to eliminate sexual abuse in confinement: http://prearesourcecenter.org

Out Side In (OSI)—a prisoner support group for LGBT prisoners and their families, friends, partners and children. OSI operates a penpal system for LGBT inmates who may feel lonely and isolated: email: osiuk@hotmail.co.uk

Prisoner Correspondence Project—solidarity project for gay, lesbian, transsexual, transgender, gender variant, two-spirit, intersex, bisexual and queer prisoners in Canada and the United States, linking them with people a part of these same communities outside of prison: http://prisonercorrespondenceproject.com

The Prisoners' Advice Service—an independent legal charity providing information and representation to adult prisoners in England and Wales: http://prisonersadvice.org.uk

Prison Reform Trust—an organization working to create a just, humane, and effective penal system: http://prisonreformtrust.org.uk

REFERENCES

Acker, J. (1990). Hierarchies, jobs, bodies: A theory of gendered organizations. *Gender & Society, 4*(2), 139–158.

ACLU Kentucky. (2016). Victory! Prison's anti-LGBT literature ban lifted. Retrieved from http://www.aclu-ky.org/articles/victory-prisons-anti-lgbt-literature-ban-lifted/

The Advocate. (2017). Gay news, LGBT rights, politics, entertainment. Retrieved from http://www.advocate.com

Alarid, L. F. (2000). Sexual orientation perspectives of incarcerated bisexual and gay men: The county jail protective custody experience. *The Prison Journal, 80*(1), 80–95.

Andrinopoulos, K., Figueroa, J. P., Kerrigan, D., & Ellen, J. M. (2011). Homophobia, stigma and HIV in Jamaican prisons. *Culture, Health & Sexuality, 13*(2), 187–200.

Associated Press. (1987, March 8). Vermont prisons give inmates condoms on request. *The New York Times*. Retrieved from http://www.nytimes.com/1987/03/08/us/vermont-prisons-give-immates-condoms-on-request.html

Associated Press. (2007, June 6). Calif. gay, lesbian inmates get conjugal visits. *NBC News*. Retrieved from http://www.nbcnews.com/id/18994457/ns/us_news-life/t/calif-gay-lesbian-inmates-get-conjugal-visits/#.WSObc47LWZY

Associated Press. (2013, July 7). State considers condoms in prison to cut STD rate. *NBC10*. Retrieved from http://www.nbcphiladelphia.com/news/local/State-Considers-Condoms-in-Prison-to-Cut-STD-Rate-214532391.html

Associated Press. (2017, January 29). World first: Thailand considers opening "gay prison," already separating LGBT prisoners. *South China Morning Post*. Retrieved from http://www.scmp.com/news/asia/southeast-asia/article/2066325/world-first-thailand-considers-opening-gay-prison-already

Bandyopadhyay, M. (2006). Competing masculinities in a prison. *Men and Masculinities, 9*(2), 186–203.

Ben-Zur, R. (2012, 11 October). Conjugal visits for gay prisoners? Not in Israel. *Y Net*. Retrieved from http://www.ynetnews.com/articles/0,7340,L-4291171,00.html

Bennett, L. (2000, November). *Managing Sexual Relationships in a Female Prison*. Paper presented at the Women in Corrections: Staff and Clients Conference, convened by the Australian Institute of Criminology in conjunction with the Department for Correctional Services SA, Adelaide, South Australia.

Benson, T. (2014, April 16). Turkey is planning the world's first openly gay prison. *VICE News*. Retrieved from https://news.vice.com/article/turkey-is-planning-the-worlds-first-openly-gay-prison

Bittenbender, S. (2016, March 21). Kentucky prisons mail policy on homosexuality under review—official. *Reuters*. Retrieved from http://www.reuters.com/article/kentucky-prison-homosexuality-idUSL2N16T22Y

Blackburn, A. G., Fowler, S. L., & Mullings, J. L. (2014). Gay, lesbian, bisexual and transgender inmates. In C. D. Marcum & T. L. Castle (Eds.), *Sex in prison* (pp. 87–112). Boulder, CO: Lynne Reiner.

Blackburn, A. G., Fowler, S. K., Mullings, J. L., & Marquart, J. W. (2011). Too close for comfort: Exploring gender differences in inmate attitudes toward homosexuality in prison. *American Journal of Criminal Justice, 36*(1), 58–72.

Blain, G. (2011, April 23). Conjugal visits allowed for inmates and partners in same-sex marriages, civil unions. *Daily News*. Retrieved from http://www.nydailynews.com/new-york/conjugal-visits-allowed-inmates-partners-same-sex-marriages-civil-unions-article-1.114818

Britton, D. M. (1997). Gendered organizational logic. *Gender & Society, 11*(6), 796–818. doi:10.1177/089124397011006005

Browne, A., Cambier, A., & Agha, S. (2011). Prisons within prisons: the use of segregation in the United States. *Federal Sentencing Reporter, 21*(1), 46–49.

Butler, T., Richters, J., Yap, L., & Donovan, B. (2013). Condoms for prisoners: no evidence that they increase sex in prison, but they increase safe sex. *Sexually Transmitted Infections, 89*(5), 377–379. doi:10.1136/sextrans-2012-050856

Carrigan, T., Connell, B., & Lee, J. (1985). Toward a new sociology of masculinity. *Theory and Society, 14*(5), 551–604.

Civillini, M. (2016, 14 April 2016). Le "sezioni gay" nelle carceri italiane esistono davvero—e per una ragione precisa. *VICE News*. Retrieved from https://news.vice.com/it/article/sezioni-gay-carceri-italiane

Connell, R. W. (1987). *Gender and power*. Cambridge, UK: Polity Press.

Connell, R. W. (1990). An iron man: The body and some contradictions of hegemonic masculinity. In M. Messner & D. Sabo (Eds.), *Sociological perspectives in sport: The games outside the games*. Champaign, IL: Human Kinetics Books.

Coston, B. M., & Kimmel, M. (2012). Seeing privilege where it isn't: Marginalized masculinities and the intersectionality of privilege. *Journal of Social Issues, 68*(1), 97–111.

Davis, A. Y. (2003). *Are prisons obsolete?* New York, NY: Seven Stories Press.

Dolovich, S. (2011). Strategic segregation in the modern prison. *American Criminal Law Review, 48*(1), 1–110.

Dolovich, S. (2012). Two models of the prison: Accidental humanity and hypermasculinity in the LA County Jail. *Journal of Criminal Law and Criminology, 102*(4), 965–1118.

Donaldson, M. (1993). What is hegemonic masculinity? *Theory and Society, 22*(5), 643–657. doi:10.1007/bf00993540

Duggan, L. (2003). *The twilight of equality? Neoliberalism, cultural politics, and the attack on democracy.* Boston, MA: Beacon Press.

Egelund, A. (2014). Masculinity, sex and survival in Zambian prisons. *Prison Service Journal, 212,* 16–20.

Eigenberg, H. M. (1992). Homosexuality in male prisons: Demonstrating the need for a social constructionist approach. *Criminal Justice Review, 17*(2), 219–234.

Eigenberg, H. M. (2000). Correctional officers' definitions of rape in male prisons. *Journal of Criminal Justice, 28*(5), 435–449. doi:10.1016/S0047-2352(00)00057-X

Einat, T., & Rabinovitz, S. (2013). A warm touch in a cold cell. *International Journal of Offender Therapy and Comparative Criminology, 57*(12), 1522–1545. doi:10.1177/0306624X12461475

Fine-Maron, D. (2013, 18 September). Condoms behind bars: A modest proposal to cut STIs in Calif. prisons. *Scientific American* [Web log post]. Retrieved from https://blogs.scientificamerican.com

Forsyth, C. J., Evans, R. D., & Foster, D. B. (2002). An analysis of inmate explanations for lesbian relationships in prison. *International Journal of Sociology of the Family, 30*(1/2), 67–77.

Freedman, E. B. (1996). The prison lesbian: Race, class, and the construction of the aggressive female homosexual, 1915–1965. *Feminist Studies, 22*(2), 397–423. doi:10.2307/3178421

GayLawNet. (2017). Laws: Colombia. Retrieved from http://www.gaylawnet.com

GLHV@ARCSHS, La Trobe University. (2016). The Rainbow Tick guide to LGBTI-inclusive practice. P. Kennedy (Ed.). Melbourne, Australia: La Trobe University.

Gopal, N. (2015). Lesbian relationships in correctional settings—"Let our voices be heard." *Agenda, 29*(4), 103–113. doi:10.1080/10130950.2015.1114305

Greer, K. R. (2000). The changing nature of interpersonal relationships in a women's prison. *The Prison Journal, 80*(4), 442–468. doi:10.1177/0032885500080004009

Gupta, K., Sleezer, C. M., & Russ-Eft, D. F. (2011). *A practical guide to needs assessment* (2nd ed.). San Francisco, CA: John Wiley & Sons.

Haney, C. (2002, January). *The psychological impact of incarceration: Implications for post-prison adjustment.* Paper presented at the From Prison to Home Conference of the U.S. Department of Health and Human Services, at National Institutes of Health Natcher Conference Center, MD.

Harawa, N. T., Sweat, J., George, S., & Sylla, M. (2010). Sex and condom use in a large jail unit for men who have sex with men (MSM) and male-to-female transgenders. *Journal of Health Care for the Poor and Underserved, 21*(3), 1071–1087. doi:10.1353/hpu.0.0349

Hastings, A., Browne, A., & Kall, K. (2015). *Keeping vulnerable populations safe under PREA: alternative strategies to the use of segregation in prisons and jails.* New York, NY: Vera Institute of Justice & Bureau of Justice Assistacne, U.S. Department of Justice.

Heffernan, E. (1972). *Making it in prison: The square, the cool, and the life.* New York, NY: Wiley-Interscience.

Hensley, C., Koscheski, M., & Tewksbury, R. (2005). Examining the characteristics of male sexual assault targets in a southern maximum-security prison. *Journal of Interpersonal Violence, 20*(6), 667–679.

Hensley, C., Tewksbury, R., & Koscheski, M. (2002). The characteristics and motivations behind female prison sex. *Women & Criminal Justice, 13*(2–3), 125–139.

Hensley, C., Tewksbury, R., & Wright, J. (2001). Exploring the dynamics of masturbation and consensual same-sex activity within a male maximum security prison. *The Journal of Men's Studies, 10*(1), 59–71. doi:10.3149/jms.1001.59

Hiday, V. A., & Moloney, M. E. (2014). Mental illness and the criminal justice system *The Wiley Blackwell Encyclopedia of Health, Illness, Behavior, and Society*. Hoboken, NJ: John Wiley & Sons, Ltd.

Hillier, L., Jones, T., Monagle, M., Overton, N., Gahan, L., Blackman, J., & Mitchell, A. (2010). *Writing themselves in 3: The third national study on the sexual health and wellbeing of same sex attracted and gender questioning young people*. Melbourne, VIC: La Trobe University, Australian Research Centre in Sex, Health and Society.

Howarth, J. W. (1979–1980). The rights of gay prisoners: A challenge to protective custody. *Southern California Law Review 53*(4), 1225–1276.

Hurtas, S. (2015, January 21). Turkey's "pink prison." *Turkey Pulse Al-Monitor*. Retrieved from http://www.al-monitor.com/pulse/originals/2015/01/turkey-gay-lesbian-lgbt-special-prison.html

Ida, D. (2007). Cultural competency and recovery within diverse populations. *Psychiatric Rehabilitation Journal, 31*(1), 49–53.

Ingraham, C. (2005). Thinking straight: An introduction. In Chrys Ingraham (Ed.), *Thinking straight: The power, the promise and the paradox of heterosexuality*. (pp. 1–14) New York, NY: Routledge.

Jiang, S., & Winfree Jr, L. T. (2006). Social support, gender, and inmate adjustment to prison life: Insights from a national sample. *The Prison Journal, 86*(1), 32–55.

Johnson v. Johnson. (2004). 385 F.3d 503, 512 (5th Cir. 2004) US.

Kaba, F., Lewis, A., Glowa-Kollisch, S., Hadler, J., Lee, D., Alper, H., . . . & Venters, H. (2014). Solitary confinement and risk of self-harm among jail inmates. *American Journal of Public Health, 104*(3), 442–447. doi:10.2105/AJPH.2013.301742

Kentucky Corrections. (2013). *Policies and procedures: Inmate correspondence 16.2.* (August 2013) Kentucky Corrections, Commonwealth of Kentucky. Retrieved from http://corrections.ky.gov/communityinfo/Policies%20and%20Procedures/Documents/CH16/16-2%20Inmate%20Correspondence.pdf

Kentucky Corrections. (2016a). *Policies and procedures: Inmate correspondence 16.2.* (June 2016) Kentucky Corrections, Commonwealth of Kentucky. Retrieved from http://www.aclu-ky.org/wp-content/uploads/2016/06/New-Policy.doc.

Kentucky Corrections. (2016b). *Policies and procedures: Inmate correspondence 16.2.* (November 2016) Kentucky Corrections, Commonwealth of Kentucky. Retrieved from http://corrections.ky.gov/communityinfo/Policies%20and%20Procedures/Documents/CH16/CPP%2016.2%20eff%201-6-17.pdf

Kupers, T. A. (2001). Rape and the prison code. In D. Sabo, T. A. Kupers, & W. London (Eds.), *Prison masculinities* (pp. 111–117). Philadelphia, PA: Temple University Press.

Kupers, T. A. (2005). Toxic masculinity as a barrier to mental health treatment in prison. *Journal of Clinical Psychology, 61*(6), 713–724. doi:10.1002/jclp.20105

Kupers, T. A. (2010). Role of misogyny and homophobia in prison sexual abuse. *UCLA Women's Law Journal, 18*(1), 107–130.

Lamb, H. R., & Weinberger, L. E. (1998). Persons with severe mental illness in jails and prisons: A review. *Psychiatric Services, 49*(4), 483–492.

LaViolette, N. (2013). Overcoming problems with sexual minority refugee claims: Is LGBT cultural competency training the solution? In T. Spijkerboer (Ed.), *Fleeing homophobia. Sexual orientation, gender identity and asylum.* Oxford, UK: Taylor & Francis.

Lehrer, E. (2001). Hell behind bars. *National Review, 53*(2), 24–25.

Leibowitz, A. A., Harawa, N., Sylla, M., Hallstrom, C. C., & Kerndt, P. R. (2013). Condom distribution in jail to prevent HIV infection. *AIDS and Behavior, 17*(8), 2695–2702. doi:10.1007/s10461-012-0190-5

Lior, I. (2013, 3 July). Gay prisoners in Israel granted right to conjugal visits. *Haaretz.*

Lovell, D. (2008). Patterns of disturbed behavior in a supermax population. *Criminal Justice and Behavior, 35*(8), 985–1004. doi:10.1177/0093854808318584

Lovell, D., Johnson, L. C., & Cain, K. C. (2007). Recidivism of supermax prisoners in Washington State. *Crime & Delinquency, 53*(4), 633–656. doi:10.1177/0011128706296466

Mair, J. S., Frattaroli, S., & Teret, S. P. (2003). New hope for victims of prison sexual assault. *The Journal of Law, Medicine & Ethics, 31*(4), 602–606.

Mariner, J. (2001). *No escape: Male rape in U.S. prisons.* Retrieved from Human Rights Watch, https://www.hrw.org/reports/2001/prison/

McCuller, W. J., & Harawa, N. T. (2014). A condom distribution program in the Los Angeles men's central jail. *Journal of Correctional Health Care, 20*(3), 195–202. doi:10.1177/1078345814530870

Metzner, J. L., & Fellner, J. (2010). Solitary confinement and mental illness in U.S. prisons: A challenge for medical ethics. *Journal of the American Academy of Psychiatry and the Law Online, 38*(1), 104–108.

Mosher, D. L., & Sirkin, M. (1984). Measuring a macho personality constellation. *Journal of Research in Personality, 18*(2), 150–163. doi: 10.1016/0092-6566(84)90026-6

Moster, A. N., & Jeglic, E. L. (2009). Prison warden attitudes toward prison rape and sexual assault. *The Prison Journal, 89*(1), 65–78. doi:10.1177/0032885508329981

National Center for Transgender Equality. (2012). LGBT people and the prison rape elimination act. [Fact sheet]. Washington, DC: National Center for Transgender Equality.

Nowak, M. (2010). *Report of the Special Rapporteur on torture and other cruel, inhuman or degrading treatment or punishment.* Retrieved from United Nations General Assembly A/HRC/13/39/Add.5: http://www.un.org/en/documents/index.html

Otis, M. (1913). A perversion not commonly noted. *The Journal of Abnormal Psychology, 8*(2), 113–116.

OUT. (2017) Out Magazine—Gay & lesbian travel, fashion & culture. Retrieved from http://www.out.com

OutRight. (2002, June 10). Colombia: Discrimination in prisons must end. Retrieved from www.outrightinternational.org

Owen, B. A. (1998). *In the mix: Struggle and survival in a women's prison.* Albany, NY: SUNY Press.

Owers, A. (2006). The protection of prisoners' rights in England and Wales. *European Journal on Criminal Policy and Research, 12*(2), 85–91. doi:10.1007/s10610-006-9013-4

Queensland Government. (n.d). *Guide: Undertaking needs assessments*. Brisbane, Queensland: Health and Community Services Workforce Council, Queensland Government.

Rafter, N. H. (1990). *Partial justice: Women, prisons, and social control* (2nd ed.). Brunswick, NJ: Transaction Publishers.

Robinson, R. K. (2011). Masculinity as prison: Sexual identity, race, and incarceration. *California Law Review, 99*(5), 1309–1408.

Rodley, N. (2001). *Question of torture and other cruel, inhuman or degrading treatment or punishment*. Retrieved from United Nations General Assembly A/56/156: http://www.un.org/en/documents/index.html

Roffee, J. A. (2017). Accountability and oversight of state functions. *SAGE Open, 7*(1), 2158244017690792. doi:10.1177/2158244017690792

Rosenstreich, G., Comfort, J., & Martin, P. (2011). Primary health care and equity: the case of lesbian, gay, bisexual, trans and intersex Australians. *Australian Journal of Primary Health, 17*(4), 302–308.

Ryan, C., Russell, S. T., Huebner, D., Diaz, R., & Sanchez, J. (2010). Family acceptance in adolescence and the health of LGBT young adults. *Journal of Child and Adolescent Psychiatric Nursing, 23*(4), 205–213. doi:10.1111/j.1744-6171.2010.00246.x

Sabo, D. (2005). *Handbook of studies on men & masculinities*. Thousand Oaks, CA: Sage.

Sabo, D. F., Kupers, T. A., & London, W. J. (2001). Gender and the politics of punishment. In D. F. Sabo, T. A. Kupers, & W. J. London (Eds.), *Prison masculinities* (pp. 3–18). Philadelphia, PA: Temple University Press.

Schnittker, J., & John, A. (2007). Enduring stigma: The long-term effects of incarceration on health. *Journal of Health and Social Behavior, 48*(2), 115–130. doi: 10.1177/002214650704800202

Severance, T. A. (2004). The prison lesbian revisited. *Journal of Gay & Lesbian Social Services, 17*(3), 39–57. doi:10.1300/J041v17n03_03

Shay, G. (2011). Double-edged paring knives: Human rights dilemmas for special populations. *Human Rights, 38*(3), 17–20.

Shay, G. (2014). PREA's elusive promise: Can DOJ regulations protect LGBT incarcerated people? *Loyola Journal of Public Interest Law, 15*(2), 343–356.

Sifunda, S., Reddy, P. S., Braithwaite, R., Stephens, T., Bhengu, S., Ruiter, R. A. C., & Borne, B. V. D. (2008). The effectiveness of a peer-led HIV/AIDS and STI health education intervention for prison inmates in South Africa. *Health Education & Behavior, 35*(4), 494–508. doi:10.1177/1090198106294894

Sim, J. (1994). Tougher than the rest? In T. Newburn & E. A. Stanko (Eds.), *Just boys doing business?* (pp. 100–117). London, UK: Routledge.

Simpson, P., Reekie, J., Butler, T., Richters, J., Yap, L., & Donovan, B. (2016). Sexual coercion in men's prisons. In A. Dwyer, M. Ball, & T. Crofts (Eds.), *Queering criminology* (pp. 204–228). London, UK: Palgrave Macmillan.

Smith, B. V. (2008). The Prison Rape Elimination Act: Implementation and unresolved issues. *Criminal Law Brief, 3*(10), 10–18.

Spade, D. (2012). The only way to end racialized gender violence in prisons is to end prisons: A response to Russell Robinson's "Masculinity as prison." *California Law Review Circuit, 3*, 184–190.

Struckman-Johnson, C., & Struckman-Johnson, D. (2006). A comparison of sexual coercion experiences reported by men and women in prison. *Journal of Interpersonal Violence, 21*(12), 1591–1615.

Sylla, M., Harawa, N., & Grinstead Reznick, O. (2010). The first condom machine in a US jail: The challenge of harm reduction in a law and order environment. *American Journal of Public Health, 100*(6), 982–985. doi:10.2105/AJPH.2009.172452

United Nations High Commissioner for Human Rights. (2011). *Discriminatory laws and practices and acts of violence against individuals based on their sexual orientation and gender identity.* Retrieved from United Nations General Assembly A/HRC/19/41: http://www.un.org/en/documents/index.html

X v. Turkey. (2013). Application No 24626/09 Judgment Final 27/05/2013 European Court.

Wilkinson, R. A. (2003). The cost of conjugal visitation outweighs the benefits. *Corrections Today* (June 2003). Retrieved from https://www.highbeam.com/doc/1G1-123688030.html

Wire Report. (2016, March 25). *ACLU challenges policy banning gay content in Kentucky prison.* Retrieved from www.watermarkonline.com

Wolfe, Z. (2008). Gay and lesbian prisoners: Recent developments and a call for more research. *Prison Legal News, 19*(10), 1–6.

World Health Organization. (1992). *The ICD-10 classification of mental and behavioural disorders: Clinical descriptions and diagnostic guidelines.* Geneva, Switzerland: World Health Organization.

Wyatt, R. (2005). Male rape in US prisons: Are conjugal visits the answer. *Case Western Reserve Journal of International Law, 37*(2), 579–614.

Zaitzow, B. H. (2003). "Doing gender" in a women's prison. In B. H. Zaitzow & J. Thomas (Eds.), *Women in prison: Gender and social control* (pp. 21–38). Boulder, CO: Lynne Rienner.

10

Trans People and Responding to Need

Improving Carceral Management

JAMES ROFFEE

Rights for lesbian, gay, bisexual, transgender, intersex, and queer (LGBTIQ) people are being rapidly advanced across the globe. As more people feel able to express and disclose their identity, traditional structures of social order face the challenge of how to respond appropriately to the increased diversity of genders, sex, and sexualities. Criminal justice institutions, including correctional facilities and jails, often face particular and difficult challenges when responding to the needs of minority populations and trans prisoners, inmates, and detainees. Globally, trans women housed with men are most at risk of sexual victimization from other inmates, and they are often targeted by male staff members for "random" strip searches and frisking. Many jails and prisons operate without an understanding of trans inmates' needs, and trans people are conspicuously absent in many policies or procedures.

This chapter will detail across several jurisdictions the challenges associated with the increasing number of incarcerated trans people. Recent examples of best practice are contrasted against practice that has proved to be severely harmful to trans inmates. A number of current challenges for trans inmates are reviewed, as are the serious consequences of failing to adequately meet the needs of incarcerated trans offenders.

Drawing from examples in different states in Australia and the United States, and from the United Kingdom, the chapter details several evidence-based practices that seek to ensure improved incarceration outcomes for trans inmates. Examples of housing policy and practice are used to delineate the need for institutional understandings of, and responses to, diverse genders and sexes. The chapter closes with a number of future directions for those seeking to respond to and work with incarcerated trans people. In particular, it challenges those resistant to change to think about both the benefits and how to best meet the needs of trans prisoners, and to think through the implications of failing to respond to this increasing population.

INTRODUCTION TO THE POPULATION AND SCOPE OF THE PROBLEM

The rights and recognition of *transgender* (hereafter "trans") and *intersex* people worldwide remains a contentious issue that shows no sign of reaching resolution soon. The requirement and necessity, even within this chapter, to explain what is meant by trans and intersex persons indicates that significant steps are required to help address some of the pervasive issues profoundly affecting trans and intersex people. Many such issues can be found in their interactions with the criminal justice system. The criminal justice systems that operate within our societies are shaped by the citizens that they serve; such systems reflect those societies and their citizens' views concerning the appropriate treatment of those within them. This chapter therefore begins by explaining what is meant by the terms *trans* and *intersex persons* and by situating their treatment within a broader global context of lack of recognition and invisibility.

The definition and understandings of what is meant by a trans person have seen recent development. No one specific definition enjoys universal acceptance, although all definitions tend to describe an individual who was born with the physical characteristics of one sex but feels aligned with the other (see Glezer, McNiel, & Binder, 2012). For example, *transgender* is defined by the American Psychological Association as a person whose gender identity, gender expression, or behavior does not conform to that typically associated with the sex to which they were assigned at birth (American Psychological Association, 2014). The introduction to the Yogyakarta Principles on the Application of International Human Rights Law in Relation to Sexual Orientation and Gender Identity defines gender identity as:

> Each person's deeply felt internal and individual experience of gender, which may or may not correspond with the sex assigned at birth, including the personal sense of the body (which may involve, if freely chosen, modification of bodily appearance or function by medical, surgical or other means) and other expressions of gender, including dress, speech and mannerisms. (International Commission of Jurists, 2007, p. 8)

Accordingly, it is generally accepted that being a trans person entails issues concerning appropriate gender identity for the individual concerned. The American Psychiatric Association's *Diagnostic and Statistical Manual of Mental Disorders* (*DSM-5*) (American Psychiatric Association, 2013) recognizes gender dysphoria as a mental health condition which replaces the nomenclature of gender identity disorder in the previous edition, *DSM-IV*. A diagnosis of gender dysphoria is not necessary for a person to be considered trans and not all trans people experience signs of gender dysphoria. Significant emphasis has been placed on the diagnosis of gender dysphoria (previously gender identity disorder) and professionals recognize many issues surrounding the continued medicalization of trans experiences (Lev, 2013). Medicalization and reference to experiencing medical conditions and states of being are integral to those who present as intersex. *Intersex* refers to a variety of conditions, known as *intersex conditions*, that can include external genitals that cannot easily be classed as male or female, or internal reproductive organs being incomplete. It may involve having uncommon development; an inconsistency between the genitals and the internal organs; over- or underproduction of sex-related hormones; and or the body's inability to respond as expected to sex-related hormones (APA Task Force on Gender Identity, 2006).

Internationally, there have been unprecedented efforts in attempting to ensure that people of all gender identities can begin to enjoy equal dignity and respect to which all persons are entitled under international law. Many states now have legal instruments guaranteeing the principles of equality and nondiscrimination without distinction based on sex, sexual orientation, or gender identity. Nonetheless, as Simopoulos and Khin (2014) note, there remains a constant struggle on the part of trans persons to combat discrimination and stigma and secure basic human rights.

There is no shortage of literature detailing the higher rates of discrimination and consequent poverty, low employment levels, and homelessness experienced by trans and intersex individuals. The impacts of discrimination and lack of opportunity can result in trans and intersex individuals engaging in criminal activity, such as survival sex and prostitution, as well as petty theft and robbery (Nadal, Davidoff, & Fujii-Doe, 2014; Reisner, Bailey, & Sevelius, 2014). The discrimination against trans and intersex persons exists across all ages and races and can result in high levels of physical victimization (Stotzer, 2009). Trans and intersex people are forced to look to the illegal and informal economies to survive due to the pervasive discrimination they face that leads to high levels of unemployment, homelessness, and marginalization (Spade, 2008b). Research has indicated that trans peoples' inability to receive health care is a contributing factor to the high rates of trans incarceration (Gehi & Arkles, 2007; Spade, 2008b). Gehi and Arkles (2007) note that the lack of access to trans health care increases exposure to violence. Those in need of health care support may engage in and commit survival crimes (for example, prostitution and/or sex work) and are exposed to consequent victimization, including being harassed, attacked, beaten, or raped on the job, as well as the dangers from further violence once incarcerated.

Trans persons who are not incarcerated are at significantly higher risk of reduced life expectancy due to psychosis, depression, and HIV, and they are 9 times more likely to commit suicide than the general population within the United States (Brennan et al., 2012; Coleman et al., 2012; Dhejne et al., 2011; Kessler, Borges, & Walters, 1999). While in the community, trans individuals face inadequate medical care and the burden of paying for medical treatment. Many health insurance plans do not cover the cost of mental health services, cross-sex hormone therapy, or gender affirmation surgery (American College of Obstetricians and Gynecologists, 2011). The Committee on Health Care for Undeserved Women noted that the consequences of inadequate treatment are staggering; 54% of transgender youth have attempted suicide, 21% have self-mutilated, and over half of all people surveyed who identify as trans have injected illegally obtained hormones (American College of Obstetricians and Gynecologists, 2011).

Trans and intersex people occupy a particularly unique and consequently problematic space for the criminal justice system and criminal justice system actors. There are no reliable figures on the number of trans inmates within jurisdictions because such data are not accurately captured; however, it is estimated that there are approximately 100 trans prisoners in the United Kingdom (Women and Equalities Committee, 2016), approximately 400 in California, and 27 in New York City (Jaffer et al., 2016), with Brown and McDuffie (2009) estimating that there are approximately 850 across the United States. Although such numbers are relatively small in comparison to the total prison populations, a large proportion of the trans and intersex population experiences incarceration. As such, trans and intersex prisoners suffer from a disproportionate level of vulnerability as a discrete section of the already vulnerable prison population (Blight, 2000). Rosenblum has suggested that "transgendered prisoners' needs constitute one of many challenges facing correctional authorities who need to balance calls for humane treatment and Constitutional requirements with staffing and budget limitations" (Rosenblum, 1999, p. 519). Situated within a world that adheres rigidly to a gender binary, trans people act as challengers to the current status quo. Their mere presence within society calls into question ways of knowing that have been learned by men and women worldwide. Their presence is thus seen by many as a challenge to current social order and ways of knowing; it is therefore the case that many (including those within the criminal justice system) seek to control and censor those who step outside the learned gender binary. Trans people therefore suffer from higher rates of victimization and dangers to their health, and they are at severe risk of physical and sexual violence.

Trans inmates often experience a prison regime riddled with pervasive discrimination and inappropriate trans-specific practices that treat trans inmates as being an additional problem to be managed while incarcerated. Trans inmates have been conceptualized as presenting problems for corrections facilities and staff; an example of the problems facing staff in correctional facilities was given by Smith (1995), who detailed her concerns with deciding which color jumpsuit to give the prisoner, who should be present during a strip search, and where to house a trans inmate. It would be hoped that significant progress would have been made in the over 20 years since Smith's contribution; sadly, these administrative problems continue to burden correctional managers and contribute to the continued discrimination against trans inmates. The successful management of trans and intersex inmates will not simply come from the ad-hoc imposition of trans-friendly policies, although it is acknowledged that such policies are helping to progress the situation for many of those experiencing incarceration. Instead, a holistic approach is required that values the equal treatment and dignity of all those incarcerated, and recognizes the vulnerable position of some of society's most vulnerable and discriminated citizens.

EVIDENCE-BASED PRACTICES FOR THE TARGET POPULATION

There remains a dearth of evidence-based practices concerning the management of incarcerated trans and intersex populations. Responses to incarcerated trans inmates have been improving, as knowledge on and visibility of trans people have increased worldwide. That the numbers of trans inmates are relatively small in proportion to different countries' and jurisdictions' entire prison populations has resulted in such populations receiving little interest and attention. Instances of egregious treatment, many in the United States (although examples can be found globally), have resulted in extensive litigation that has significantly improved the conditions of detention and treatment received by trans inmates.

Nonetheless, despite the small number of trans inmates, there is a growing body of practice in responding to their needs. In addition to the increasing attention paid to trans and intersex inmates by different corrections departments, there has been an expansion of literature on improving corrections practices by practitioners, activists, and scholars. Before reviewing some examples of corrections best practice, a brief review of some approaches to working with trans and intersex people utilized within education, government departments, and by medical professionals will be reviewed.

Best Practice From Outside Jails and Prisons

The growing recognition of the existence of trans and intersex people within jails and prisons has been the result of increased visibility as part of a diverse (LGBTIQ) community, and acknowledgment of members of such communities is found in all areas of life. Dean Spade's work on the growing visibility of trans and intersex people has led to the identification of "three myths regarding transgender identity [that] have led to conflicting laws and policies that adversely affect transgender people" (Spade, 2008b, p. 35). Spade (2008b) highlights how reliance on structures of knowledge and knowing impact trans and intersex people and suggests that the reliance on official documentation (combined with the refusal of governments and identity document–issuing agencies to recognize change or anything outside of the binary male/female) is a serious impediment to progress. This refusal to accept that trans people exist, Spade argues, is a key factor in the high rates of sexual assault perpetrated against trans people in prisons due to their inappropriate placing within sex-segregated facilities. Further, Spade argues that it is the belief that the birth-assigned gender is the only true gender an individual can have that leads to and results in trans peoples' identities being treated as fraudulent or false and remaining unrecognized and illegitimate (Spade, 2008b).

The second myth refers to trans people only being understood or recognized through medical authority. The medical profession has been key in helping trans people achieve visibility and recognition. However, Spade notes the significant problem with the overreliance on medical intervention or evidence to support a person's claim to a trans identity (Spade, 2008b). Linked to this is the belief that a trans person requires surgery to be complete in their "new" gender. Surgery or medical intervention is not a prerequisite for a person to identify as trans, and many trans and intersex people function without having need to engage with medical professionals. It is therefore essential to remove the fallacy of the necessary association between trans identity and medical intervention into people's lives. The final myth is that trans people's gender-conforming health care is not legitimate medicine. Spade lists examples, such as the refusal of public and private health care to cover the costs of medical intervention, as well written policies and unwritten blanket practices of denying gender-conforming care to those in custody, including those in foster care, juvenile detention, and prisons (Spade, 2008b). As noted earlier, this results in severe consequences for those seeking, but unable to access, appropriate health care.

Only when armed with the knowledge of the precarious position that trans and intersex people occupy within society can we begin to adopt tailored and appropriate practices to respond to the needs of this marginalized population. There are several organizations led by trans and intersex people that are generating and distributing materials on best practice toward trans and intersex people on national and international levels (see websites listed at the end of this chapter). The best practice being generated by these groups routinely draws from individual and collective community experiences and seeks to integrate this knowledge to help improve operations, practices, and procedures impacting trans and intersex people.

EDUCATION AND GOVERNMENT

In the education sphere, there has been a recent focus on improving the support available for trans students to increase student outcomes and well-being. Invariably, best practice concerns training of staff in ally-related information and practice as developing trans-supportive policies. Both training and policies should be easily accessible. Best practice policies and guidelines often concern the adoption and operationalization of empowering practices such as enabling students to use their preferred name rather than legal name, allowing students to change gender markers without legal documentation, and providing gender-neutral bathrooms (Self, 2014). Other suggested best practice policies include reducing routine requests for gender identity often found in enrollment forms, library registrations, and application forms for field trips. It is suggested that before asking for gender identity, the person seeking the information should critically examine if knowledge of a student's gender is needed (Lambda Legal, 2016). Thus, the training of staff is integral to best practice outcomes. Such training should ideally be delivered by or with the assistance of trans and intersex people. In addition, critical attempts to think through the impact and necessity of simple acts such as data gathering, and open-minded approaches such as the willingness to question sex-based distinctions, help organizations to avoid excluding trans and intersex people.

The UK Home Office has provided detailed guidance on the care and management of transsexual detainees (Home Office, 2015). Although the nomenclature used (transsexual, as opposed to trans) has been superseded, the updated guidelines are a positive attempt to treat trans detainees appropriately and with dignity. The Home Office details that detainees should be treated as they present (Home Office, 2015, p. 3). If there is uncertainty, then the detainee should be consulted and treated accordingly. Where there is doubt and the detainee refuses to state the gender they consider themselves to be, they are to be treated consistently with any documentation provided such as birth certificate or passport (Home Office, 2015, p. 3). This policy places the wishes of the trans individual first and does not privilege the legal status of the individual, unless the individual is unwilling to detail how they wish to be treated. In addition, policy dictates that a care plan should be generated, and this plan is to be designed in consultation and agreed with the individual detainee. The care plan is a voluntary written agreement entered between the detention establishment (immigration removal center, short-term holding facility, or predeparture accommodation) and the detainee. The plan is designed to provide information for the detainee and staff concerning the requirements, obligations, and entitlements of the individual detainee. The contents cover matters such as the housing and accommodation, dress code, access to facilities, and matters of searching (Home Office, 2015). The plan is voluntary and is regarded as a living document that can be amended as necessary. It is also possible for detainees to withdraw from the plan at any time; however, the advantages of entering a plan are carefully explained to the detainee (Home Office, 2015, p. 4). The Home Office therefore seeks to balance the wishes of the trans detainee with operational requirements and potential staffing issues that may arise, for example, when having to search a detainee. The Home Office place the detainee's dignity as the primary consideration, and it clearly states that under no circumstances should a physical search or examination of a detainee be conducted for determining a detainee's gender (Home Office, 2015, p. 4). Government organizations often operate within rigid rules and structures and with significant legal burdens, thus the adoption of policies that focus on considering the detainees' wishes stand in stark contrast to such rigid approaches. The disproportionate and unintended harms created by the historical invisibility and lack of recognition of trans people can be eased, and potential suffering alleviated, though proactive engagement and consultation with trans and intersex people.

MEDICAL CARE

The World Professional Association for Transgender Health (WPATH) has generated medically accepted guidelines for the treatment of gender dysphoria (see World Professional Association for Transgender Health, 2011). The conceptualization and recognition that medical treatment and support for trans and intersex inmates is not a choice nor a luxury but a medical necessity had begun to help to challenge some of the long-standing misapprehension with the provision of medical treatment. In the United States, the failure to provide adequate health care to inmates constitutes cruel and unusual punishment prohibited by the Eighth Amendment of the US Constitution (see, among others, *Kosilek v. Maloney*, 2002).

There is a significant body of literature within the medical field on the treatment of trans people. This is beyond the scope of this chapter; however, there are many accounts concerning best practice approaches to working with trans people useful for criminal justice system actors seeking to engage in positive interactions with trans and intersex populations. One best practice guide targeting health workers sets out several "central axes" designed to deliver specific changes to traditional models of operating when working with trans populations (Stop Trans Pathologization, 2012). Of relevance is the need for workers to adopt an approach of "depathologization" whereby positive engagement can flow from a concerted effort to avoid viewing trans people as people with an illness or mental disorder. In addition, the guideline suggests engaging with trans people in an approach that values "de-medicalization": whereby the person's gender identity is no longer simply seen as a problem calling for medical intervention. Best practice within this model indicates that the relationship between trans and intersexuality should not simply be separated, and instead we should no longer ignore the fact that "ignoring the incidence of intersexuality in a trans health care system is a medical strategy aimed at erasure" (Stop Trans Pathologization, 2012, p. 19). Approaches from counseling toward decision making, that seek to promote and respect individuals' autonomy, should also be at the heart of the interaction between the worker and the trans person. The workers should also be able to engage in a process of supporting the subjective self-worth of patients and begin connecting them to local support groups (Stop Trans Pathologization, 2012). Finally, this model requires the appropriate training of professionals working with trans and intersex people and that knowledge and competence in understanding gender and identity is a core part of a professionals' training.

Many simple and small changes can be made to improve the interaction between workers in any organization and trans and intersex clients. The National LGBT Health Education Center notes that "every single interaction counts for a transgender person in a health care setting" (National LGBT Health Education Center, 2013, p. 6). While trite, it is worth noting that every interaction, in every setting, counts—this extends to interactions with all actors within the criminal justice system. Like what is seen within educational best practice, the importance of addressing people in a gender-neutral way, and using people's first and last name as appropriate, is noted. The use of preferred names and pronouns (that may or may not match legal documentation)—and having a system that can capture this information is regarded important in health settings to avoid misgendering trans and intersex people (National LGBT Health Education Center, 2016). When a mismatch occurs between the gender disclosed and the records or data held, it is possible to enquire about alternative names and/or date of birth, thus preventing the client from being outed or embarrassed in front of other people within hearing distance. In addition, the best practice guide recommends a genuine apology for any mistakes that are made (National LGBT

Health Education Center, 2016). The best practice guide notes that maintaining a respectful workplace culture is crucial to fostering and ensuring appropriate interactions with trans and intersex clients, including not gossiping or joking about the person's status. Using the person's preferred names and pronouns even when the person is not present and creating an environment of accountability is important, and where possible politely correcting colleagues for using the wrong names or wrong pronouns, or making insensitive comments, is deemed appropriate (National LGBT Health Education Center, 2016, p. 12). Thus, there are numerous examples of how positive interactions with trans and intersex people can be achieved: Key to this is the acknowledement of the existence of trans and intersex people and their varied needs, and a willingness to afford them with respectful and dignified interactions.

REVIEW OF CURRENT INTERNATIONAL CRIMINAL JUSTICE RESPONSES

Prisons and jails have legal obligations, including a duty of care toward the people detained within them. These obligations extend to the provision of food, shelter, safety, and medical treatment. As warehouses of some of society's most vulnerable people, prisons and jails contain populations with low levels of education and training, including literacy, and complex social needs. As highlighted earlier, many trans prisoners enter the criminal justice system because of their inability to gain and hold stable employment and housing (see Davis & Wertz, 2009). Although outside the scope of this chapter, a holistic response is needed to tackle the causes of discrimination against trans people resulting in their difficulties in accessing basic human needs, which is very often the reason for their engagement with the criminal justice system.

The United Nations Office on Drugs and Crime (UNODC) recognizes that lesbian, gay, bisexual, and transgender prisoners are a group of prisoners with special needs (United Nations Office on Drugs and Crime, 2009). Noting that these groups of persons comprise a particularly vulnerable group in the criminal justice system and in prisons, the UNODC recognizes globally that very little attention has been paid to their special needs, and most jurisdictions have no policy to guide prison management and prison personnel in relation to the special needs of LGBT prisoners (United Nations Office on Drugs and Crime, 2009). Guidance and best practice on the management of trans and intersex inmates is at an early stage in many jurisdictions, including those with larger trans populations.

The following section will explore several corrections practices that have been modified to more effectively engage with inmate populations, within jurisdictions with experience in managing trans and intersex inmates. The aim is to highlight and contrast differing approaches. Many of these approaches have been modified and revised from their initial versions and iterations: All effort has been made to ensure the approaches detailed appropriately reflect current operational practice as of January 1, 2017.

Australia

Australia has a comparatively low relative prison population across all states, although inmate numbers have been rising steadily for the last decade, increasing about 50% over this time. Although the prison total population was 38,845 in June 2016, there are relatively few trans inmates housed within Australian prisons. Australia is a Federal state: in what follows the policies and practice of the states of New South Wales, known for having a long-standing transgender prisoner policy, and Queensland, known for taking a very traditional approach to law and order, are reviewed.

New South Wales

With one of the largest state prison populations, the state of New South Wales is one of the first jurisdictions globally to have devised comprehensive policies and procedures, in May 2002, for the management of transgender and intersex inmates. These were recently revised in December 2015. The policy is broad in its application, and to ensure that staff are able to apply the policy where necessary, it provides useful definitions for staff working with inmates. As part of the update, revised terms including "recognized transgender" and "intersex" were incorporated into the policy (see Table 10.1).

The policy requires that a custodial staff treat "recognized transgender" person in a way to similar people who are members of the sex recorded on the person's identification. The policy dictates that self-identification as a member of the opposite gender is the only criterion for identification as "transgender" and that both "transgender" and "intersex" inmates are to be managed per their identified gender. Inmates who have previously been incarcerated are to be treated according to their gender at the time of incarceration and not in accordance with any previous periods of incarceration. If a person in custody makes an application to be treated as a "transgender" person, then that person is to be treated as a "transgender" person who had just been taken into custody. Security concerns can override the inmate's wishes only after a case management process taking into account issues of offence, safety, previous issues during custody and custodial history, and perceived risk to the inmate and to others. The policy also requires that all three groups of inmates, "recognized transgender," "transgender," and "intersex" inmates, are to be afforded the same classification and placement options as other inmates and that they have the same access to services and programs in the center in which they are housed.

The policy details several specific procedures relating to addressing and escorting prisoners, procedures for reception and screening, searching, clothing, and access to health care. New South Wales Corrections policy now affirms and recognizes the existence of trans and intersex inmates using their preferred names:

Table 10.1. CORRECTIVE SERVICES NEW SOUTH WALES, OPERATIONS PROCEDURES
MANUAL, MANAGEMENT OF TRANSGENDER AND INTERSEX INMATES - DEFINITIONS

Intersex	An intersex person is a person who has physical, hormonal, or genetic features that are: • neither wholly female nor wholly male • a combination of female and male • neither female nor male An intersex person must be treated as a member of the gender with which they identify.
Recognized transgender	A recognized transgender person is a person who has undergone gender reassignment surgery and who has successfully applied for their birth registration and birth certificate to be altered, or for a change to be registered to show their new sex. Recognized transgender persons must be treated as a member of the sex recorded on their new birth certificate or recognized details certificate.
Transgender	A transgender person is a person: • who identifies as a member of the opposite sex by living, or seeking to live, as a member of the opposite sex, or • who, being of indeterminate sex, identifies as a member of a particular sex by living as a member of that sex

SOURCE: NSW Government (2015).

7.23.3.1 Addressing recognized transgender, transgender and intersex inmates

Recognised transgender inmates are to be addressed by name and according to their recognized sex.

Transgender and intersex inmates are to be addressed by their chosen name and according to their identified gender. Male-to-female transgender inmates are not to be called by their male given names (regardless of what is recorded on their warrant file) or referred to as "he"; they are to be called by their female names and referred to as "she." A similar principle applies for female-to-male transgender inmates. Accordingly, all accommodation records are to be amended to reflect the inmate's identified gender.

An inmate who does not identify as either male or female is to be addressed by their chosen name and clarification sought from the inmate as how they are to be addressed. (NSW Government, 2015)

With regard to health care, care plans must be put in place and any existing medication continued. Corrections policy recognizes the need for an approach that considers mental health practitioners, psychologists, and general practitioners. In addition, trans and intersex inmates may have elective gender surgery, hormone therapy, or other therapies of their choice and specific to their needs at their own expense, and guidelines on this are provided. In relation to clothing, all prisoners have the right to dress in clothing that is appropriate to their recognized sex and appropriate to their gender of identification, including inmates housed in centers of their biological sex.

QUEENSLAND

The state of Queensland has been slower in its recognition of the needs of trans and intersex inmates. During the admissions process, Queensland Corrective Services' policy requires a small number of additional considerations to be taken into account on admission and induction of a prisoner. There is no publicly available information on how staff are to address inmates, conduct searches, or provide for medical needs. The QCS Custodial Operations Practice Directive states that on arrival into custody:

When a prisoner who identifies as transgender is admitted to a corrective services facility the General Manager of the corrective services facility must:

- ensure that the prisoner is immediately accommodated in a single cell or separated on a safety order in a way that ensures appropriate management of any risks posed in relation to the prisoner, including risk of harm to the prisoner until an assessment for determining the prisoner's placement can be made
- forward the prisoner's details for purposes of the assessment to the Assistant Director-General or General Manager, Operational Service Delivery. (Queensland Corrective Services, 2014)

Queensland Police in its Operational Procedures Manual (OPM) sets out the standards to be followed when searching a trans person. They define a transgender person as:

A person who has undergone sexual reassignment surgery or treatment, or is in the process of undergoing sexual reassignment, and identifies with being a person of the opposite biological sex, and is accepted as being a transgender person by the community in which that person resides. (Queensland Police, 2016)

The policy on searching requires the responsible officer to ask the person if they "wish to be classed as a male or a female" (Queensland Police, 2016). If the person wishes to be treated as a female, then they will be searched as a female and similarly if they wish to be treated as a male, then they will be searched as a male. However, the OPM requires that transgender persons who have not undergone sexual reassignment surgery are to be searched by a person of the same biological sex (Queensland Police, 2016). The preference for housing trans persons is in an empty cell. However, where an empty cell is not available, they then require the prisoner to be placed with other prisoners who have the same type of genitalia. This approach is therefore in stark contrast to the approach of NSW that places the prisoner's wishes at the forefront of the decision-making process. The approach is Queensland relies on a medical model of recognizing trans status and indicates overriding concern with operational needs with regard to safety, as opposed to a holistic response ensuring dignified treatment of trans and intersex persons.

United Kingdom (England and Wales)

In the United Kingdom, the Women and Equalities Select Committee Into Transgender Equality recently published the Parliamentary Report Into Transgender equality (Women and Equalities Committee, 2016). The report published in January 2016 has resulted in significant action by the British government on trans equality matters. The report noted the progress made within the Her Majesty's Prisons Service (HMPS) in relation to the care of trans people; however, it noted that further improvement was still required. Although there had been a Prison Service Instruction on trans prisoners in place since 2011, it was noted that prison staff often had to be reminded of its existence and many staff may lack awareness and training (Women and Equalities Committee, 2016). The Committee noted:

> While the safety and welfare of all offenders is paramount, caring for and managing trans offenders appropriately is crucial. There is clear risk of harm (including violence, sexual assault, self-harming and suicide) where trans prisoners are not located in a prison or other setting appropriate to their acquired / affirmed gender. Neither is it fair or appropriate for them to end up in solitary confinement solely as a result of their trans status. (Women and Equalities Committee, 2016)

An updated Prison Service Instruction, which entered into practice from January 1, 2017, is an extensive 58-page document with the explicitly stated aim "To treat all transgender offenders in our care and under our supervision fairly, decently and lawfully" (National Offender Management Service, 2016). The document acknowledges continued and recent developments with the managing of trans inmates and now uses the term "transgender" to replace the term "transsexual."

The Instruction reflects and acknowledges the ability of persons to have fluid and neutral approaches to gender identity with the altered policy covering treatment of individuals who identify as nonbinary, gender fluid, and/or transvestite (National Offender Management Service, 2016). Although the latter groups of persons will continue to be managed in accordance with their legal gender assigned at birth, access to the facilities list (containing personal items such as cosmetics and deodorant) will be afforded to enable expression of the gender the offender identifies with. The Prison Service recognizes that known risk, security, and operational factors may impact on the implementation of the policy.

Of all the approaches discussed within this chapter, England and Wales have most recently altered their approach to managing trans inmates. The updated approach is system-wide to ensure consistency in treatment and to ensure that there are no areas where there can be a disproportionate impact on the welfare of the trans inmate. There is a stated goal of maximizing opportunities for early decision-making and contingency planning, which extends to those who express an intention to permanently change their gender. The case management process occurs through the use of Transgender Case Boards.

Transgender Case Boards are convened on the initial detention of an offender and may be reconvened to help guide prison staff of the management of complex cases. The policy recognizes the need for support and guidance to be available to staff across a varied range of issues they may face when managing an inmate in custody. Importantly, there are now provisions for the establishment of a Transgender Advisory Board to help develop policy and guide good practice across the entire detention estate.

Outside of the criminal justice context, the United Kingdom affords significant legal protections provided to trans persons in relation to the use and disclosure of the information that a person has obtained a Gender Recognition Certificate. As such, trans prisoners are asked by HMPS for written consent for the disclosure of this information, and if it is withheld, it can only be disclosed if a legal exemption applies.

Initial decisions in relation to placement and location within the detention estate require the trans offender to be asked their view on which part of the prison estate reflects the gender with which they identify. Any decision to locate an offender in part of the estate that is not consistent with their legal gender is only possible once a Transgender Case Board has been convened. If the prisoner's view of their placement is in accordance with their legally recognized gender, then they must be located accordingly. Where an offender expresses a view that is not consistent with their legally recognized gender, then evidence (of living in the gender with which they identify) must be provided by the offender. Guidance on this evidence is provided (see Figure 10.1). This evidence will then be considered by a Transgender Case Board, convened for this purpose.

The Instruction details the requirement to allow all prisoners covered within the policy to express their gender identity, including dressing in clothes of the gender with which they identify, or to adopt a gender-neutral presentation, in line with relevant dress codes and subject to any requirement to wear prison-issued clothing. It details that dress codes must be based on decency and consider prisoner vulnerability. Trans prisoners can adopt gender-appropriate or gender-neutral names. Those prisoners who identify as nonbinary, gender fluid, or transvestite, or who are intersex are allowed to express themselves according to the gender with which they identify or as gender neutral, subject only to risk, security, and operational assessments (National Offender Management Service, 2016). Importantly, the Instruction requires a fair approach to be taken to all requests, including not being unduly restrictive, requiring that any restrictions must be based on justifications that are properly evidenced and reasoned as well as the restrictions being proportionate. Thus, the implications of the policy are that corrections staff are required to give careful consideration to all requests and

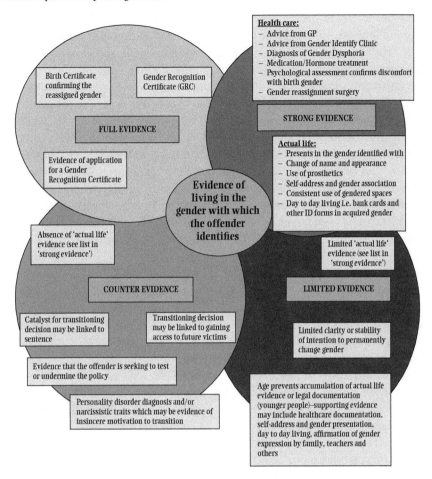

Figure 10.1 Evidence of living in the gender with which the offender identifies. When an offender discloses that they are transgender, this chart may assist in assessing the strength of evidence of living in the gender the offender identifies with in order to inform location decisions and sentence plans.

although the policy does not require staff to accede to every request, it reverses the burden and now requires staff to evidence why any reasonable or unreasonable change should not be accommodated.

United States

Like Australia, the United States is a federal state, and criminal matters that are not federal in nature are generally dealt with at the state level. State laws, rules, and regulations govern the treatment of inmates in state custody within the United States, and where competence is held at federal levels, Congress can pass legislation seeking to improve the conditions of detention. One such example of legislation passed by Congress with a direct impact on the imprisonment of trans and intersex inmates is the Prison Rape Elimination Act (PREA) 2003. (See later discussion for more on the disproportionate impact of sexual violence facing trans and intersex inmates.) The purpose of this act is to provide for the analysis of the incidence and effects of prison rape in federal, state, and local institutions and to provide information, resources, recommendations, and funding to protect individuals from prison rape. In 2004 a commission was convened with the intention of drafting standards for the elimination of prison rape with the intention that the Department of Justice would create rules to support the Act. These rules became effective in 2012, and there have been changes made to ensure compliance at varying levels across the different states. Later in this chapter the policies and practices of two states (California and New York) toward trans prisoners will be reviewed. California is known for its high number of trans prisoners with an estimated incarcerated trans population at 385 in 2015 (Egelko, 2015), and New York (trans population at 27 in 2016) is known for its long-standing and historical approach to the differential treatment of trans inmates.

CALIFORNIA

The state of California is notable for having a high number of trans people in its incarcerated population (Egelko, 2015). Although many activists and scholars have noted significant improvements in the way in which trans inmates have been managed within California, the California Department of Corrections and Rehabilitation has surprisingly little to say on the management of transgender inmates within its Operations Manual (California Department of Corrections and Rehabilitation, 2016). Of relevance to the differential approach to the incarceration of trans and intersex inmates, the Operations Manual details the procedure for an unclothed and clothed body search of an inmate. It provides that where an inmate self-identifies as transgender or self-identifies with a "gender that seems not to match their biological sex," the search will be conducted by staff of the same biological sex as the inmate. Where "an individual's genital status is ambiguous, the search shall be conducted by a staff member that is the same biological sex as indicated in the inmate's records" (California Department of Corrections and Rehabilitation, 2016, p. 390).

In relation to housing of inmates, the Manual states that "If staff are unable to determine the genital status through medical records or an interview with the inmate, the inmate shall be placed on single-cell status or in administrative segregation, for his/her safety, until the standard intake medical evaluation is completed. This standard medical examination will establish the genital status of the inmate. Once the information is collected and documented . . . the Institution Classification Committee should determine appropriate classification and housing placement" (California Department of Corrections and Rehabilitation, 2016, p. 390). Repeated and abusive strip searches conducted by guards to "determine" an inmate's sex, even after an inmate has been assigned a housing unit are widely recognized as damaging. Although the OM states this search and investigation can occur as part of a standard medical examination, it may also cause undue distress for the inmate as it adopts a medicalized approach to trans status and privileges the presence or absence of sexed body parts.

The Operations Manual details that many inmates consider their gender identity to be private information and states that widespread knowledge of this information could impact the safety of trans and intersex inmates. It also details that the information is considered sensitive and thus should be handled sensitively. Importantly, it details that the information should only be communicated to staff where there is a justified need to know, and that such information should never be communicated to other offenders. This is appropriate and although there are no penalties for failing to comply with this requirement, the acknowledgment of the sensitivity of the information and presence of the requirement is a positive step to improving the experience of incarceration for trans and intersex persons.

In relation to the use of management cell regime or placement in a management cell, different personal item allowances apply to trans inmates in male and female institutions. Whereas nontrans males housed in male institutions are issued one t-shirt and one pair of boxer shorts, "male to female" trans inmates housed in the same institution can have one brassier. Whereas in female institutions, inmates can have three brassieres and three pairs of panties, the regulations state that "female to male" trans inmates can retain up to three pairs of boxer shorts (California Department of Corrections and Rehabilitation, 2016, p. 416). The disparity in treatment is based on the gendered nature of the institutions, yet it fails to accord trans males and females equal treatment to nontrans inmates of the same sex.

In late 2015, the state of California reached a legal settlement with the inmate Shiloh Quine (in the case of *Quine v. Beard et al.*, 2016) to allow Quine to undergo sex-reassignment surgery while incarcerated. The State then reviewed its existing guidelines on sex-reassignment surgery (California Corrections Health Care Services, 2015) and California Corrections Health Care Services issued supplementary guidelines (California Corrections Health Care Services, 2016) to clarify the position of Corrections in reviewing requests for sex-reassignment surgery. The new guidelines set out the composition of a committee charged with making any decision on the permissibility of the sex-reassignment surgery: The committee will comprise two physicians from medical services, two physicians from the mental health program, and two psychologists from the mental health program. The guidelines provide that patients who are not approved for the surgery may submit a new request no sooner than 1 year from the date of the letter informing them of the decision to deny their request (California Corrections Health Care Services, 2016).

Thus, although there have been a number of incremental improvements in the treatment of trans and intersex prisoners, there remain significant gaps within the Operations Manual. The Operations Manual is silent on many issues capable of adversely impacting trans and intersex inmates, including the use of appropriate names, and it privileges a medicalized approach to trans and intersex status.

New York

From the late 1970s to 2005, the New York City Department of Corrections (DOC) operated a specialist housing unit for gay and transgender inmates who were in pretrial detention. To be housed in the unit, inmates had to "declare homosexuality, or appear to be transgender, and ask to be kept out of Rikers's main jails" (Zielbauer, 2005). In 2005, then City Corrections Commissioner Martin Horn, suggested the removal of the specialist unit was part of a reorganization to help improve security and suggested that over time the unit had become dangerous due to the presence of inmates seeking to be placed there to take advantage of vulnerable prisoners. The unit had space for 146 prisoners, with 126 housed within it when closure was initiated (Associated Press, 2005). The rules that repealed and replaced the separate housing unit stipulated that inmates who wanted protection from the general population (including but not limited to trans inmates) were required to apply for protective custody and seek a hearing. If protection was granted, they would then be on a protective custody regime, which included lockdown for up to 23 hours per day (Zielbauer, 2005). There was significant controversy over the closure and several organizations, including the Sylvia Rivera Law Project, Lambda Legal Defense and Education Fund, the New York Civil Liberties Union, and the National Gay and Lesbian Task Force, contacted the Commissioner to request a reconsideration of the decision (Associated Press, 2005). The unit was ultimately closed and the situation of protective custody prevailed in New York City until late 2014.

The Department of Corrections issued a press release in November 2014 concerning the opening of a new housing unit for trans women (Campbell, 2014). The unit was unveiled as part of a comprehensive reform aimed at making jails safer and improving inmate outcomes. The new Transgender Housing Unit is a 30-bed unit, although the DOC acknowledges that it usually houses anywhere between 30 and 35 trans inmates across the estate, indicating that demand would outstrip capacity. The DOC Commissioner Joe Ponte noted that "providing [trans inmates] with specialized housing and services is good policy and meaningful reform and is expected to reduce incidents involving these individuals while also leading to better long-term outcomes, including possible reductions in recidivism" (Campbell, 2014, p. 1). However, Department of Corrections data indicate they house an average daily population of 12 transgender prisoners (New York City Department of Corrections, 2017).

Although little is mentioned regarding the needs of trans prisoners within specific rules and practices of the Department of Correction, the New York City Board of Correction recently agreed to adopt final rules to designed to "detect, prevent, and respond to sexual abuse and sexual harassment of persons incarcerated in jails and other facilities operated by the NYC Department of Correction." These new standards are effective from January 2, 2017, and incorporate many of the requirements of the Prison Rape Elimination Act standards and are the first set of new minimum standards issued by the City of New York since 1991 (Stein, 2016). The rules now provide that:

- DOC and Health + Hospitals will implement new training for staff working with inmates who are transgender or intersex, designed to

heighten awareness of their psychosocial and safety needs and ensure communication and custody that is respectful of gender identity.
- DOC will not assign a transgender or intersex inmate to a men's or women's facility based solely on the inmate's external genital anatomy. (Stein, 2016)

The rules also require that the DOC inform the NYC Board of Correction in writing each time a placement of a trans or intersex inmate occurs, including within the document all the information considered in making the decision and the reasons for the determination (New York City Board of Correction, 2016). Consistent with other best practice jurisdictions, the inmates' views on their own safety are to be given serious consideration. Other rules relating to the cross-gender viewing and searches have been put in place, including prohibiting searches or physical examinations solely to determine an inmate's genital status, and trans and intersex inmates will be given the opportunity to shower separately (New York City Board of Correction, 2016). Additional provisions relating to staff training were adopted, including the training of staff on working with inmates who are trans or intersex and includes "psychosocial and safety needs of such persons in custody and instructions on communicating with them in a manner that is respectful of their gender identity" (New York City Board of Correction, 2016, p. 9). The Department is required to complete training on working with trans and intersex inmates (but not on how to conduct searches) by January 2, 2018. Thus, although the New York City DOC took retrograde steps in 2005, there has been recent progress to reverse the serious concerns around trans and intersex prisoners' safety and well-being.

CRIMINAL JUSTICE POLICY ISSUES AND IMPLICATIONS—THE DOUBLE PUNISHMENT

Incarceration exposes trans and intersex people to a situation of double punishment. The first layer of punishment comes from the deliberate act of holding a person within a correctional institution and includes the loss of liberties and freedoms that similarly apply to nontrans people. However, a second layer of punishment comes from the inherent dangers, lack of safety, and treatment received as the result of being a trans or intersex person within a correctional facility. Being highly gendered institutions, male and female prisons and jails categorize and handle trans and intersex people within their current operational boundaries. As such, trans and intersex people are often not treated as trans or intersex; but are treated and expected to act like others housed within the gendered institution to which they are placed—with corrections showing little acknowledgment of, or allowance for, variation or difference. The framing of appropriate criminal justice policies and responses requires both an understanding of the contemporary position of trans and intersex people within society and how to best meet the needs of these target populations without creating additional forms of punishment for trans and intersex people.

Trans People and Higher Rates of Victimization and Physical/Sexual Violence

At the outset, the vulnerability of all persons in prison to physical and sexual violence, both from inmates and staff, should be recognized. There are varying reported rates of physical and sexual violence against inmates across all nations. It is widely accepted that rates of reporting such violence by all persons are below the actual level of incidents due to the stigma attached to reporting physical and sexual violence offences. A robust body of international empirical data suggests that transgender people's subjection to violence commences early in life and continues throughout their lives (Stotzer, 2009). The comprehensive report of the United States' National Transgender Discrimination (USNTD) survey (Grant et al., 2011) illustrates that it is more likely than not for a trans person to experience harassment in their day-to-day lives. Furthermore, of the 6,450 transgender and gender nonconforming participants taking part in the USNTD, 16% of respondents who had been to jail/prison reported being physically assaulted and 15% reported being sexually assaulted (Grant et al., 2011, p. 6). Trans people are also routinely victimized by police: 22% of respondents were harassed by police, 6% were physically assaulted by police, and 2% were sexually assaulted by police (Grant et al., 2011, p. 6).

As within all other social institutions, hierarchies exist within the prison system. The extremely weak positions of power held by trans inmates, particularly those inmates with other intersecting characteristics, such as having a disability or being a person of colour, can result in further victimization and violence. Persons with multiple intersecting characteristics may be targets of victimising behavior directed at these multiple characteristics, either individually or combined. Research indicates that incarcerated trans people suffer higher rates of brutality and sexual assault, which is often precipitated against them due to their heightened visibility and through deliberate targeting by perpetrators (Bassichis, 2007, p. 19). Such violence can be directed at trans and intersex inmates based on homophobic to transphobic beliefs (Bassichis, 2007).

Failures in appropriate management of trans inmates also places them at heightened risk for physical and sexual violence. International examples of poor prison management (see later for further detail on housing decisions) leading to severe trauma to trans inmates can be found with shocking ease; recent examples include a case from Auckland, New Zealand, where a trans woman was repeatedly raped after being placed in a cell with a male inmate. The prison was aware she was taking hormones as part of her transition, yet housed her in a male facility and removed her from protective segregation (Blackstock, 2015). Another recent example from New Orleans includes a 19-year-old trans woman, detained for disturbing the peace who was housed in a cell with a male inmate being held for armed robbery. In a lawsuit for damages, the plaintiff claims she repeatedly screamed for help during a rape she suffered and no deputy ever attended (McGill, 2016). The risk of physical and sexual violence comes not only from other inmates but also from guards and correctional officers. There are examples of failures to adequately investigate incidents and allegations of sexual assault at the hands of other inmates and guards (see McSweeney, 2016). Although research indicates that it is not simply trans inmates, nor only members of the LGBT community that suffer from unwanted sexual activity while incarcerated, research suggests these populations suffer from high levels of unwanted sexual conduct (see Mariner, 2001).

The increased attention over several decades paid to the subject of unwanted sex in prison has brought greater attention to the existence of trans inmates, who are often victims of this unwanted sexual activity. Schuster (2014) noted that some officials in some prisons and jails in the United States presumed from the moment of intake that LGBTI inmates were more likely to sexually abuse other inmates. However, in the extensive testimony before the PREA Commission "it was made clear that LGBTI inmates are far likelier to be the victims of sexual abuse than the perpetrators" (Schuster, 2014, p. 13).

Although starting from a relatively low baseline, there have been great improvements in countries such as the United States when responding to the issue of unwanted sexual activity in carceral spaces. The enactment of legislation, such as the Prison Rape Elimination Act 2003, has been key to this and has been described as an example of "unprecedented national reformist effort in corrections regulation" (Shay, 2014, p. 343). Although the Act itself has been lauded by many, such acts risk remaining merely symbolic without leading to concrete measures and larger structural changes, including altered visions of the use of incarceration as a form of discipline and punishment (Ristroph, 2006). Nonetheless, beyond its symbolic function, the PREA is a huge step towards improving incarceration for trans and intersex (as well as LGB) prisoners, acting to both educate and elicit compassion, and helping to prevent the continued drafting of policies based on misunderstanding or prejudice (Schuster, 2014, p. 10). The misunderstanding and prejudice in the management of trans people results in victimization and physical and sexual violence against this population, which places greater risks on trans and intersex inmates' health.

Trans People, Imprisonment, and Vulnerabilities and Dangers to Health

Violence reported by trans and intersex inmates coming from staff and other inmates ranges from discrimination and bulling to physical assaults of varying degrees, sexual assaults leading to physical and mental health complaints, contracting HIV and other communicable diseases through such assaults and illegal drug use (self-medication and hormones), to examples of self-harm, bodily mutilation, and suicide due to conditions of imprisonment. All such violence, irrespective of the causes, has the capacity to endanger the health of the inmate and others.

Like the sexual violence detailed earlier, physical violence and assaults against trans inmates come from both other inmates and prison personnel. In addition to the damage inflicted by the physical injuries caused by both staff and inmates, there is the mental anguish and trauma caused through the fear of assault and lack of safety. This includes beatings and being cut for refusing to perform sexual acts (Goring & Sweet, 2011). There are reports of prison staff using excessive force against trans inmates who are alleged to have broken prison rules, and there are graphic images of the result of violence being used against trans inmates. In one reported case of excessive force in Brazil, Veronica Bolina was physically restrained and beaten until she was unrecognizable, with her hair shaved off and breasts exposed (Malone, 2015). She is shown photographed with a prison guard standing above her with a gun out of its holster (Malone, 2015).

It is well documented that many transgender persons are on low incomes with lack of access to adequate health care. The lack of resources means they resort to black-market access to hormones and other drugs. On entering the criminal justice system, these individuals thus often lose access to these drugs and hormones from their black-market suppliers. Prison officials' use of policies, for example the "freeze frame policy" whereby medical treatment to trans prisoners is frozen at the level prescribed on entry into incarceration, thus has an adverse impact on trans inmates. Such policies prevent trans people who have previously been accessing health care through alternative (black-market) means from accessing the drugs they are self-administering. These "freeze frame" policies thus deny and fail to recognize the realities of the lived experience of many trans persons. Extensive legal challenges to the "freeze frame" approach, including in the case of *Kosilek v. Maloney* (2002), have resulted in US courts finding that such policies prevent prisoners from receiving adequate treatment (Casazza, 2013).

Although the mental health care needs of prisoners are outside the scope of this chapter, it is important to note that there are significant mental health care needs for trans inmates (see later discussion for denial of appropriate medical care), and the failure to recognize and respond to the needs of such prisoners results in deteriorating levels of mental as well as physical health. The case of *Gammett v. Idaho State Board of Corrections* (2007) set an important precedent in the United States for the health of trans inmates. The case concerned Jenniffer Spencer, a trans woman serving a 10-year sentence who made repeated requests (75 in total) for treatment of her condition (gender identity disorder). Spencer attempted suicide on learning that the prison doctors were unwilling to provide treatment and later performed castration of a testicle, losing a life-threatening volume of blood. Rather than beginning to provide hormone therapy after castration, the Idaho Department of Corrections offered her male hormones. The Judge ruled that when left untreated gender identity disorder is a life-threatening mental health condition. It was also held that the offer of male hormones was medically unacceptable and that the "choice" offered to the plaintiff was no choice at all.

The failure on the part of corrections staff to treat trans and intersex inmates with appropriate levels of dignity and respect can often result in severe consequences. There is no shortage of examples of the extreme measures taken by trans inmates in distress ostensibly to mitigate, not the consequences of their offending, but by the impact of state-sanctioned failures to recognize their gender and identity. The suicide risk to trans people within the community caused by failure to receive appropriate medical assistance is already well documented (Haas et al., 2010).

Inadequate treatment at the hands of the state during periods of detention thus amplifies the number of risk factors for trans inmates. In the United Kingdom, the death of Vicky Thompson, a 21-year-old trans woman, made headline news: It was known that she had indicated she intended to take her own life if she was sent to a male prison (BBC News, 2015). Shortly after the death of Vicky Thompson, another trans prisoner, Joanne Latham, was found unconscious in her cell in the male prison HMP Woodhill (Chidzoy, 2015). Another inmate, Jenny Swift, was found dead in her cell in the all-male HMP Doncaster after she had been refused housing in a female establishment and her hormone medication had been denied. Before her death it was reported that "Jenny said that not having [the medication] was making her legs shake, making her feel sad and ill—she said it was like coming off drugs. It made her miserable" (ITV, 2017). Shortly thereafter, it was reported in the British Houses of Parliament that another woman in an all-male facility was reported as having injected herself with bleach and attempting to remove her own scrotum out of desperation (Lee, 2016). Inappropriate decisions on housing, medical, and safety needs thus contribute to incidents of self-harm and have serious impacts on inmates' health.

Research indicates that the prevalence of AIDS infection is 4 times higher in US state and federal prisons than among the general US population (Krebs, 2006). It is well known globally that prisons are known as sites of transmission for bloodborne viruses (Hellard & Aitken, 2004). Research from countries in the Global North, including Scotland, indicates that during periods of incarceration, there can be outbreaks of bloodborne illnesses, including HIV and Hepatitis B, among those who are intravenous drug users, both prior to prison and while incarcerated (Riley et al., 1993). Transmission can also occur through sexual encounters and through prison tattooing (Hellard & Aitken, 2004). The danger to health posed by bloodborne illnesses and sexually transmitted infections within the incarcerated population (Hammett, 2006) is amplified within the trans and intersex community due to their regular appearance, and status, as victims of nonconsensual and unwanted sex. In addition, it is noted by Stephens, Cozza, and Braithwaite (1999) that it is not uncommon to find transsexual inmates housed in correctional facilities in close quarters with inmates with HIV/AIDS. Although there remains a risk of acquiring a bloodborne infection when incarcerated, dangers of incarceration are amplified for those who are already suffering from bloodborne infections, including from the routine denial of access to health care for trans inmates with AIDS (Potts, 2011). Thus, trans prisoners face significant vulnerabilities to their health while incarcerated, ranging from denial of medically necessary care to new and emerging risks due to poor management and lack of safety afforded to trans and intersex prisoners.

Appropriate Housing and Medical Care for Improving Trans Safety During Incarceration

The perceived failure by trans and intersex persons to adhere to the societally imposed gender binary leaves this group of prisoners particularly vulnerable to administrative decision making. It has been the case that many practitioners

240

SERVING THE STIGMATIZED

often seek to do the best that they can while working within the boundaries of the system as they know it (see Smith, 1995). As has already been established, some groups within the many populations incarcerated face significant risk during the period of incarceration when compared to other groups: Trans and intersex inmates are one such group. The risks to trans and intersex inmates are amplified with incorrect placement and housing decisions and decisions on the appropriate level of medical care received. The safety of such prisoners is directly linked to the administrative and management decisions taken by those running the corrections facilities. The following sections will address the impact of the use of solitary confinement and segregation to manage the problems facing trans and intersex inmates, as well as the denial of appropriate medical care to this vulnerable population.

The Use of Solitary Confinement and Segregation From General Populations

It has been argued cogently by scholars, practitioners, and activists that the use of solitary confinement and segregation is a form of torture to all persons (Hresko, 2006). The negative effects of segregation on mental well-being of prisoners are well documented (Metzner & Fellner, 2010; P. S. Smith, 2006) as are the significant impacts of segregation on those with already-existing mental health issues. The psychological effects of segregation include anxiety, confusion, hypersensitivity, impulsive behavior, and lethargy, leading to eating disorders and communication problems (Hresko, 2006).

Because prison administrators are unsure how to deal with the risks posed to trans prisoners from others in custody, trans prisoners are routinely segregated, either mandatorily or voluntarily. The segregated prisoners are unable to access the educational and recreational activities as well as often unable to engage in prison work (Peek, 2003). The failure to adequately respond to the needs of trans and intersex inmates leading to the decision to segregate is a form of discrimination and denial of equal protection. This decision to place a trans inmate into segregation, often for a long period of time, can lead to other severe mental health conditions. Barnes (1998) argues that "placing transsexual prisoners in protective custody, given their status, compounds the unconstitutionality of such a practice" (p. 644). The decision to segregate trans inmates effectively treats trans people as the problem rather than addressing the underlying issues of transphobia in prison and prevents rethinking of existing policies around sex-segregation (Lamble, 2012).

There is increasing recognition by many corrections departments that although trans women are often housed within male prisons, they remain at risk and severely vulnerable within the general population of the establishment (see earlier on bullying and physical/sexual violence). To respond to these unacceptable levels of violence and risk, and to avoid the problems associated with segregation, prison officials have sought to house trans inmates (and other vulnerable prisoners) separately from the general prison population. Although some prisons and jails use a "pod model" to remove vulnerable prisoners, this is not the norm (Mann, 2006; Mintz, 2013). Prisons have used a multiplicity of modes of segregation to house trans and intersex prisoners, including protective custody, administrative segregation, administrative detention, or administrative confinement (see Mann, 2006). Although the systems vary somewhat, the general result is that trans people end up being confined to a small cell for 21–24 hours a day, with little human contact (Arkles, 2009). The situation is no different when placement is voluntary, with use of voluntary segregation having been documented as resulting in negative effects on the mental well-being of trans prisoners (Cassaidy & Lim, 2016). Although legitimate safety concerns exist, the use of segregation for protective reasons limits a prisoner's privileges and constitutional rights, and ultimately such confinement becomes punitive and results in a disproportionate sentence (see Barnes, 1998). Thus, the use of segregation causes trans prisoners to endure more onerous conditions of detention than other inmates (Edney, 2004).

The use of segregation to protect prisoners from risks posed by other prisoners is therefore inappropriate. Removal of trans inmates from the general population places additional burdens on the prisoner rather than placing the focus on the establishment to reduce the level of risk to all prisoners. Although often politically unpalatable to an electorate, the levels of risk to all prisoners should be reduced to ensure humane conditions of detention. This may include operational decisions such as increasing staffing levels, reducing the density of prisoners sharing cells and dormitory accommodation, and ensuring that all prisoners have access to education, training, exercise, and other recreational activities. The risk to the health of trans and intersex prisoners is exacerbated by poor operational decision making, including the denial of appropriate medical care.

Denial of Appropriate Medical Care

The denial of appropriate medical care is a serious problem for trans and intersex inmates, and it has been suggested that trans prisoners pose special challenges to policy makers in US prison systems (Brown & McDuffie, 2009). Although it is recognized globally that prisoners have access to less than desirable levels of health care, the problem is amplified for specific populations and those with distinct health care needs such as women, younger offenders, and older prisoners (Harris, Hek, & Condon, 2007) as well as those who are trans or intersex. Researchers have suggested that Department of Correction (DOC) health services providers (or contract providers) "usually do not have the training or expertise to manage inmates with severe gender identity disturbances" (Brown & McDuffie, 2009, p. 281).

In addition to standard health care needs found within the general prison population, trans populations have specific health care requirements, including hormone and transition-related treatments and mental health conditions. Although medical experts agree that the gender-related health care requirements of trans people are medically necessary and are safe and effective (Michel et al., 2002), they are still not provided on a systematic and routine basis to those in detention. There are reports of inconsistent levels of treatment, including incorrect dosages of hormones and arbitrary termination of hormone therapy (Bassichis, 2007, p. 27). There have been deliberate and calculated attempts by state legislators to put in place legislation that justifies and permits discriminatory and unconstitutional conduct, for example, Wisconsin's 2005 Inmate Sex Change Prevention Act (Wis. Stat. para 302.386 (5m) (2005)). These have been heavily criticized (see Cox, 2009) and have been found to be unconstitutional under the Eighth Amendment in cases where treatment has been taking place for gender identity disorder and then denied due to such legislation (see *Fields v. Smith*, 653 F.3d 550 (7th Cir. 2011)).

The understanding of what constitutes appropriate medical care has improved since the limited responses to gender identity disorder (as it was then recognized), and there is an extensive and growing literature surrounding high-profile legal cases within the United States, featuring trans plaintiffs who are seeking to either continue, begin, or improve their medical care while incarcerated (see Alexander, 2013; Alexander & Meshelemiah, 2010; Andreopoulos, 2005; Bendlin, 2013; Colopy, 2012; Cooper, 2014; Levine, 2016; Wykoff, 2014). Today, appropriate medical care requires the continuation of treatment that has already started and may require supplementing and beginning new forms of medically necessary care. With the increase in litigation and advancing medical developments and methods of treating trans and intersex people, there has been an increased interest in attempting to identify when, for example, sex reassignment surgery is appropriate for those who are incarcerated (Osborne & Lawrence, 2016). The awareness of the need for providing medically necessary care, which can include sex reassignment surgery, is growing among prisons and jails within the United States. Nonetheless, it should not be for corrections officials to continue to overrule the clinical findings and judgement of medical professionals as to the types of medical treatment that are necessary for trans inmates. Criminal justice actors must therefore recognize the diverse medical needs of trans and intersex inmates and defer to the judgment of medical professional when determining medical care needs. This includes training staff in the types of care that may be necessary and the adverse impacts of not providing the care to inmates.

STAFF KNOWLEDGE, TRAINING, CONDUCT, AND USE OF PROACTIVE MANAGEMENT PRACTICES

Although many corrections staff may feel concerned they are continually attending training and although corrections managers may be concerned with the often significant costs attached to the implementation of any training regime, it is crucial for corrections staff to be adequately trained to ensure humane conditions of detention for those incarcerated. There are multiple and varying needs of the different inmate populations that comprise those incarcerated. The UNODC makes it clear that it is essential to have an adequate number of well-trained staff to ensure the security and protection of LGBT prisoners and to address their special needs in prison (United Nations Office on Drugs and Crime, 2009). The UNODC also suggests that management policies and practices must be unequivocal that staff complicity in sexual or other violence or harassment, or a failure by staff to respond to fears or incidents of violence or harassment, will result in disciplinary action (United Nations Office on Drugs and Crime, 2009). Where there is little recognition of trans and intersex people and their needs within a society, it is understandable though regrettable that staff are more likely to be untrained and engage in inappropriate conduct toward trans and intersex inmates.

Identity, Denial of Self-Definition, and Imposition of External Classification and Housing

Prisons often restrict the rights of transgender and intersex people to define, self-determine, and express their gender identity. The ability to self-determine, to make decisions about one's body and expression, and to present an identity is regarded as central to the sense of self and group belonging, and it is crucial to an individual's ability to maintain dignity, autonomy, and privacy (Arkles, 2012). Staff classification of an inmate's gender is one of the key decisions made on behalf of prisoners and is most acutely seen through the housing determination and placement. The staff may rely upon or make the classification inaccordance with the legal or birth sex or through the presence of sexed genitalia. It is the case that across the United States as well as the United Kingdom that transgender people are usually placed in prison according to the sex with which their genitals accord (see Lamble, 2012). However, this is not always the case, and some countries, such as the Philippines, have housed transgender inmates together for some time (Glezer et al., 2012). The decisions made for prisoners on aspects such as their sex directly correlate with housing determinations and relate to their safety and security.

In the United Kingdom prior to 2009 even in cases where a person obtained a Gender Recognition Certificate, which is the legal means to acquiring a new gender under the Gender Recognition Act 2004, the person was still classified and thus housed according to their birth-assigned gender (Lamble, 2012). This was challenged in the case of *AB v Secretary of State for Justice* (2009), where a trans woman housed in a male facility was refused transfer to a woman's prison even where she had a Gender Recognition Certificate. However, the Ministry of Justice has since indicated that prisoners should be placed according to their gender as recognized in law, and that is the gender stated on the birth certificate, which is reissued after the person obtains a Gender Recognition Certificate.

The recent high-profile British case of Tara Hudson, a transgender woman, involved her being sent to a men's prison for 12 weeks after admitting a charge of assault (Somerset, 2015). Tara had reconstructive surgery and lived as a woman all her adult life; however, she legally remained a man. Supporters rallied around Hudson and claimed that she would suffer from sexual violence if she continued to be detained in a men's prison. Reportedly, over 159,000 signatures (Lee, 2016) were obtained and presented to the British government in support of Tara, and her case was raised in Parliament, which secured her move to a female establishment. The rules in place at the time allowed for the placement of a trans person without a Gender Recognition Certificate (such as Tara) into a prison of their acquired gender even where the law does not yet recognize they are of that gender. However, prison service staff placed her in a male establishment despite being sufficiently advanced in the gender reassignment process and despite having lived as a woman for many years. As such, a key problem with the guidelines is their highly discretionary nature, leaving considerable room for discrimination to persist (Lamble, 2012). The discretion afforded to prison staff afforded them significant latitude to make the decision that created a significant risk to the inmate's well-being.

The problem of where to house trans inmates is not without a solution. It is suggested that a shift from the traditional strict genitalia-based classifications to more flexible identity-based classification would help reduce the risk of violence against trans inmates (Mintz, 2013). Peek (2003) has argued that women's prisons are unable to deal with the requirements of trans women; however, with greater training and resource provision, this is easily overcome. There has been much made of the concern that trans women are going to sexually offend against the other women within prison (see Peek, 2003). Although the safety of all prisoners is of concern, such generalizations should not be the basis for denying trans inmates access to appropriate and safe housing, and Mann (2006) has suggested that this approach is a failure to show concern for safety of trans women housed in male establishments.

It can be seen from the latest policies from the United Kingdom (also detailed earlier) that the wishes of the inmate in relation to housing decisions are not determinative but carry significant weight. In deciding where to place an inmate, it has been suggested that "a better solution is to prevent transgender inmates from being housed in the 'wrong' facility in the first place" (Mann, 2006, p. 109). The attempt to identify a "true" gender and not accord weight to the inmate's feelings toward their identity appears to be a significant hurdle to providing appropriate incarceration regimes. As seen earlier, policy development in different jurisdictions has included strict regulations banning unclothed searches of inmates for determining the inmates' gender. Although the development of guidelines is important to the improvement in the care received by trans inmates, the gap between policy and practice is likely to remain while knowledge and training on trans issues is sparse and attitudinal barriers persist.

Action and Conduct of Corrections Employees

Both within and outside of the criminal justice system, trans and intersex people routinely see their identity and status being used against them. The actions of officials within the criminal justice system, including following long-standing gendered practices or by making discriminatory decisions, for example, making an arbitrary determination on entry into custody that a trans inmate is not trans but is simply "pretending," are a direct failure to adhere to statutes and instruments designed to ensure the rights and equal protection of all citizens.

There are numerous examples of corrections staff abusing the positions of power they hold over those whose lives they are paid to manage. The UN Special

Rapporteur on violence against women has detailed cases of appalling violence at the hands of officials, including in 2011 the case of an El Salvadorian trans woman detained in a male-only prison, in a cell with only gang members, who "was raped more than 100 times, sometimes with the complicity of prison officials" (Manjoo, 2011, p. 9). Although this is a case of sexual and physical assault, it occurred because of discriminatory action and conduct by corrections employees. That corrections officials would knowingly place a vulnerable prisoner with gang members known for their offending against women can only be described as inhumane.

The higher rates of physical and sexual violence experienced by trans and intersex inmates is linked to the censorship and management of the performance of gender and physical bodies within the carceral space. Unnecessary and abusive strip searches have been used to determine their inmates' sex and to harass and humiliate them (Rosenblum, 1999). There are examples of intersex inmates who have been "repeatedly strip searched by custody staff for no other reasons than to see [their] genitalia" (Bassichis, 2007, p. 20). These acts and the discriminatory results, for example, housing trans women who may or may not have male genitalia in male establishments and vice versa, have significant adverse impacts and result in further violations of trans and intersex prisoners' rights.

Staff disinterest in providing safe environments and deliberate indifference from staff towards the harms and abuse suffered by trans and intersex inmates, at the hands of others, constitute an omission and a failure to provide care at an appropriate standard (see Mariner, 2001). This lack of safety results in more vulnerable inmates taking actions to render their time while incarcerated more safe and they may do this by trading sex for protection (B. V. Smith, 2006). Sex can be traded with both prison guards and other inmates, and this can often result in the sex appearing to be consensual, yet it exists within a "protective pairing" whereby inmates submit and trade sex with one inmate for their safety (Davies, 2002; Mariner, 2001; B. V. Smith, 2006).

In addition to the mistreatment through omissions and indifference is the mistreatment resulting from overt and deliberate actions of corrections staff. This is often found in relation to an inmate's presentation and clothing. There are reports that "Guards beat, subdue and forcibly shave the heads of Native men and transgender women" (Arkles, 2012, p. 861). The use of clothing and hair styling by trans and intersex inmates is often integral to their gendered presentation. Spade (2008a) notes that for trans people "who wish to enhance the masculinization or feminization of their appearance, changing external gender expressions such as hairstyle, clothing, and accessories is often an effective, affordable, noninvasive way to alter how they are perceived in day-to-day life" (p. 754). In male prisons in the United States, bras and cosmetics are often considered contraband (Arkles, 2012; Oparah, 2010; Sumner & Jenness, 2014). However, in New York, juvenile facilities stock both bras and panties in young male facilities and boy's underwear in the female juvenile centers to respond to the needs of trans youth (Girshick, 2011). However, there are numerous examples where corrections officers have removed gendered items such as padded bras from trans women, including

Jean-Marie Druley, and made comments that items such as bras are not men's clothing and that "they would treat 'him' like 'everyone else'" (Rosenblum, 1999, p. 549).

The refusal to provide razors and care products to trans women to masculinize them and the requirement for trans men housed in female establishments to shave is reported in firsthand accounts (Bassichis, 2007; Girshick, 2011). Often this is justified based on the items being contraband, though it can also be part of the corrections officers' deliberate attempts to masculinize and feminize the inmates. In an account of masculine-identified people in female prisons, Girshick (2011, pp. 197–198) recalls the case of an inmate, Cookie, who was prevented from wearing boxer shorts and was forced by guards to wear women's underwear, including panties. Girshick reports that Cookie stated, "Boxers don't make me act more aggressive. Boxers don't make me break more rules, they don't make me want to use more drugs, they don't make me want to do anything but feel more comfortable when walking around . . . . Like I said, it's forced feminization, they're going to make us wear those panties. They've determined what women wear and that's it."

During their time while incarcerated some inmates may decide it is appropriate for them to begin to transition or to affirm a gender that may not be in accordance with their sexed body. There can be skepticism and concern that decisions to transition while incarcerated may be for a multiplicity of false reasons, including for trans women, the opportunity and perceived benefit of being housed in female prisons. It was cited in the case of *Gammett v. Idaho* (2007) that the prison staff thought that Gammett's claim of gender dysphoria was to obtain some secondary gain (Rogers, 2015). These so-called secondary gains that prisoners are thought to receive have never been clearly articulated. In addition, the veracity of the claims that prisoners "pretending to be of a different sex" obtain benefits should be questioned with a full consideration of the vulnerability and harassment, including sexual violence, that occur after beginning a transition. Many prison staff fail to regard the act of transitioning or gender affirmation as a positive thing for inmates.

Other seemingly innocuous actions, such as those of the K6G team (in Los Angeles) who attempt to identify gay men and trans inmates in order to segregate them into the special protective unit, have unintended impacts, including the labeling of inmates. There has been criticism that the unit uses outdated, raced, and gendered stereotypes in order to conduct the eligibility determinations (Robinson, 2011). Openly labeling or "outing" prisoners through asking questions about their sexuality, often in front of other prisoners, means that many prisoners may not identify themselves as "homosexual" or trans. Labeling also occurs through the use of powder-blue uniforms which identify that these prisoners are housed in the K6G unit, meaning they become vulnerable to harassment (Arkles, 2012).

Other long-standing practices such as addressing prisoners using the inmates' birth names instead of any adopted names and their desired pronouns act to discriminate against trans and intersex inmates (Simopoulos & Khin, 2014, p. 33). Although the regulations regarding name use by prisoners, particularly found in US jails and prisons, are designed to avoid violence linked to gang-based nicknames, the refusal to use and acknowledge trans prisoners' names does not have the same security concerns. By using the trans inmate's legal name, corrections staff are continuing to deny the experience of trans and intersex inmates, and this continues to perpetuate the discrimination against such populations. Where legitimate reasons for not using inmates' preferred names exist, these should be weighed against the potential harm caused by the continued use of legal or birth names.

TRENDS AND FUTURE DIRECTIONS

Globally there has been increasing acknowledgment of the rights of trans and intersex people, including to rights to equal treatment and freedom from discrimination. The increased visibility of trans and intersex people has resulted in the inclusion of these groups of people into some policies and statutes which has also led to a number of improvements when trans and intersex people are incarcerated. The problems for trans and intersex people created by a binary vision of gender, has led to increased societal recognition of the importance of differential treatment in appropriate circumstances. Within some correctional settings, individualized approaches to case management that are particularly important for these groups of prisoners, have become elements of best practice. However, what is meant by an individualized approach to case management, and the application from policy to practice, vary markedly. In a number of cases, there has been a movement away from the expectation that prisoners to fall into line with a binary understanding of gender. That several correctional facilities have recognized that gender identity exists on a spectrum has resulted in a sometimes radical rethinking of prison and jail operations. Appropriate housing decisions, use of alternative names, and provision of medically necessary care are now standard operating practice for several of these corrections facilities. However, this is still not the norm with many corrections departments continuing to ignore, downplay, and deny the existence of trans and intersex inmates within their facilities.

Although compliance with legal rights and obligations should not be seen as optional, there is an added incentive for corrections departments and for-profit corrections providers in providing secure, safe, and legally compliant facilities. The benefits of recognizing and responding to the needs of trans and intersex inmates, extend far beyond the huge sums that can be spent on litigating claims and can directly impact the effectiveness of efforts to rehabilitate and reform offenders.

Addressing Trans Invisibility Within the Criminal Justice System

Addressing the issue of trans and intersex invisibility is crucial to progressing improvements in the treatment of such populations within the criminal justice system. It is regularly the case that ad-hoc improvements in the treatment of those incarcerated often follow high-profile examples of maltreatment. These often shocking examples have led to the investigation and review of policies and practices of prisons and jails and those working within them. In addition, they have led to reviews by police forces of their practices during arrest and detention. Seminal pieces of corrections legislation such as the US Prison Rape Elimination Act 2003, that have contributed toward increasing safety and strengthening of protections for those housed within jails and prisons, are the result of decades of work by community activists, academics, and interested parties.

To begin making changes, those in corrections can engage with and draw on the knowledge held by trans and intersex people within the wider community. Corrections departments should therefore seek to engage with community actors to improve their policy and practice. This can be done through inviting feedback, engaging stakeholders and working groups, and through the dialogue with staff employed within the criminal justice system and beyond, who hold valuable knowledge. In the short term, prisons, jails, and other custodial institutions can work with knowledge holders to undertake an immediate review to see how their operations impact the trans and intersex people housed within them.

Improved recognition of trans people within the criminal justice system can begin through altering policies and procedures. Corrections facilities should not wait until they are faced with housing a trans inmate before they adopt policies and train staff. Detailed guidelines and policies can be developed immediately and other jurisdictions looked to for examples of best practice. Mandating simple and easy training for staff on the needs of trans and intersex people, in appropriate ways of interacting in a respectful way, can have subtle yet important effects.

Sultan's assertion (2002) that trans prisoners are often in prison for heinous acts and should not be treated with any more sympathy or concern than any other convicted killer or thief is factually erroneous. Most trans and intersex inmates are incarcerated for petty offending and survival crimes; they face a disproportionate impact and significant danger during their time in custody. The evidence concerning the life-threatening consequences of detaining trans and intersex people in inappropriate circumstances is overwhelming. After commuting Chelsea Manning's sentence, then President Barack Obama noted that Manning had already "served a tough sentence" (Obama, 2017). This was in reference to her identity as a trans person within a criminal justice system inadequately designed to handle inmates like her. All trans and intersex prisoners are serving tougher sentences than need be the case, and prisons and jails often fail to consider their needs or provide adequate, safe and nondiscriminatory care. Although their status as a trans or intersex person provides no reason to excuse their offending, the impact of incarceration on different groups of prisoners requires rethinking the ways in which imprisonment occurs.

CASE EXAMPLE

The disproportionate impact of incarceration on trans inmates is illustrated in the case of Ashley Diamond (*Diamond v. Owens et al.*, 2015), a trans woman from Rome, Georgia, who was remanded into custody after a probation violation for a theft offence. She had received an 11-year sentence for nonviolent burglary and theft. The actions of staff from Georgia's Department of Corrections created a situation that saw a vulnerable prisoner housed in the wrong-sex prison, treated like a person of the opposite sex with her hair shaved, denied clothing and amenities, refused medically necessary care, and bullied, harassed, sexually assaulted, and raped on numerous occasions, leading to self-harm and attempted suicide.

Diamond, who was 34 years old, had been on hormone therapy for 17 years; however, she was taken off it when arrested. Despite making numerous requests to continue to receive hormone therapy, Diamond was refused. Her female undergarments were confiscated, and she was not permitted to wear long hair or express herself in other gender-affirming ways (Disposition in *Diamond v. Owens*, 2015). She was housed with men in numerous closed-security facilities (equivalent to maximum-security institutions), including Macon State Prison, Baldwin State Prison, and the medium-security facility Rutledge State Prison, before being returned to a closed-security facility, Valdotsa State Prison. After this, she returned to Baldwin, before being placed in Augusta State Medical Prison (Disposition in *Diamond v. Owens*, 2015). She alleged that she was the victim of numerous and repeated sexual and physical assaults and near-daily verbal abuse throughout her time in the numerous prisons within which she was housed.

Abuse included being called a "he-she thing" as well as being told to "guard your booty" and "act like a man" to avoid being raped (Disposition in *Diamond v. Owens*, 2015). Diamond said, "I am constantly misgendered by GDC personnel who insist on referring to me using male pronouns, calling me demeaning names like 'faggot,' 'he/she' and 'it' " (The Southern Poverty Law Center, 2015). She was put into solitary confinement for "pretending to be a woman" (Disposition in *Diamond v. Owens*, 2015). The state prison doctor recommended access to hormone treatment, but the department of corrections administration continues to fail to provide her access to this medically necessary transition related care. The mental health professionals that evaluated Diamond diagnosed her with posttraumatic stress disorder and found that the sexual assaults were having a "clinically significant effect on her health and well-being" (Disposition in *Diamond v. Owens*, 2015, p. 17).

Diamond filed a federal lawsuit against the Georgia Department of Corrections on February 19, 2015, alleging they breached the Eighth Amendment by not providing access to medically necessary hormone treatments and from failing to protect her from repeated rapes and harassment. She claimed that her treatment (or lack thereof) resulted in anxiety and depression, as well as suicidal feelings. Diamond reported that the lack of female hormones resulted in a reduction in breast tissue and her attempts at self-castration and suicide. The US Department of Justice filed a statement of interest in the lawsuit and issued a statement in support of Diamond's case. The Department of Justice reminded the Georgia Department of Corrections that gender dysphoria is a condition requiring medically necessary treatment, and issued a statement noting that prisoners should continue to receive the same medically necessary health care they received in the community prior to incarceration (US Department of Justice, 2015). The Georgia Department of Corrections claimed that it had been providing hormone therapy to Diamond since March 2015; however, Diamond's legal team argued that the dosage was so low as to have no therapeutic effect (Testa, 2015).

Before the case was heard and after serving 3 years in prison, Diamond was released from the Augusta State Medical Prison on August 31, 2015 (Abeni, 2016). On February 12, 2016, the State reached a settlement with Diamond in her case for an undisclosed amount. Diamond's early release is a rare occurrence, and it may act as a precedent for Corrections Departments on recognizing their inability to guarantee the safety of trans people housed within their establishments. This safety of Diamond during her period incarcerated could easily have been secured at the time of Diamond's entry into the corrections facility. A combination of appropriate training and the presence and utilization of appropriate policies would have provided greater opportunity to house Diamond in safe and humane conditions. Initial failures to acknowledge Diamond's status as a trans woman and refusal to house Diamond in a female facility directly impacted her custodial experience and the abuse she suffered. Although the "freeze frame" health policy utilized by Georgia Corrections (noted as unconstitutional by the Department of Justice) was not applied in Diamond's case, the fact that she was classified by corrections as male resulted in no continuation of the treatment that she received within the community. Further, there were serious shortcomings in staff training: with allegations of staff making jokes about Diamond's status as a trans woman, as well as failing to recognize and respond to her safety needs. The use of solitary confinement in her case was inappropriate as were the incidents of staff disclosing information to other inmates concerning Diamond's allegations of sexual assault. Thus, several changes to policy and practical operations could have resulted in a very different and more positive outcome for Diamond and inmates in similar circumstances. The changes would improve conditions of detention and simultaneously curtail opportunities for inmates to claim damages and reasons for early release.

WEB-BASED RESOURCES

BentBars—A letter-writing project supporting LGBT prisoners: http://bentbarsproject.org

Black and Pink—Advocacy and connections between queer and trans prisoners of all genders within the US prison and jail system through a free newsletter of information, art, and pen pals: http://blackandpink.org

Center of Excellence for Transgender Health—Housed at the University of California, a world-leading center of excellence seeking to increase access to comprehensive, effective, and affirming health care services for trans communities: http://transhealth.ucsf.edu

The Gender Identity Research and Education Society—Giving voice to trans and gender nonconforming individuals, by educating, training, and informing: http://gires.org.uk

National Center for Transgender Equality—An organization making policy change to advance transgender equality: http://TransEquality.org

Power Inside—Works with women, including trans women and trans men, who feel they would benefit from women-centered services. They offer support and advocacy for those who are incarcerated, homeless, addicted, or in the sex trade: http://powerinside.org

Press for Change—Legal advice on discrimination and human rights laws for trans people: pfc.org.uk

SafeT—Advocacy, Buddying, Social Contact, Information, and Training: http://safeTuk.org

Sylvia Rivera Law Project—Free legal services for low income people in New York City: http://srlp.org

TGEU: Transgender Europe—Giving voice to, advocating for, raising awareness on, supporting, and researching to benefit trans people and the trans movement: http://tgeu.org

TGI Justice Project—Challenging and ending the human rights abuses committed against transgender, gender variant/genderqueer, and intersex (TGI) people in California prisons and beyond: http://tgijp.org

Trans prisoners—Grassroots project providing solidarity and supporting incarcerated trans people, supporting those outside to help support trans inmates: http://transprisoners.net

World Professional Association of Transgender Health—Standards of care for transgender people: http://wpath.org

REFERENCES

Abeni, C. (2016). Trans woman Ashley Diamond reaches settlement with Georgia Department of Corrections. *Advocate*. Retrieved from http://www.advocate.com/

AB, R (on the application of) v Secretary of State for Justice. (2009). EWHC 220 (Admin) (September 4, 2009) UK.

Alexander, R. (2013). Transgendered prisoners in the United States: A progression of Laws. *Laws, 2*(4), 428–439.

Alexander, R., & Meshelemiah, J. C. (2010). Gender identity disorders in prisons: What are the legal implications for prison mental health professionals and administrators? *The Prison Journal, 90*(3), 269–287.

American College of Obstetricians and Gynecologists. (2011). Health care for transgender individuals: Committee Opinion No. 512. *Obstetrics and Gynecology, 118*, 1454–1458.

American Psychological Association. (2013). *Diagnostic and statistical manual of mental disorders* (5 ed.). Arlington, VA: American Psychiatric Publishing.

American Psychological Association. (2014). *Answers to your questions about transgender people, gender identity, and gender expression* (3rd ed.). Washington, DC: APA Lesbian, Gay, Bisexual, and Transgender Concerns Office and APA Public and Member Communications.

Andreopoulos, N. (2005). Criminal law–Kosilek v. Maloney: In prison while imprisoned in the body of the opposite sex: Examining the issue of cruel and unusual punishment presented by an incarcerated transsexual. *Western New England Law Review, 27,* 219–260.

APA Task Force on Gender Identity, Gender Variance, and Intersex Conditions. (2006). *Answers to your questions about individuals with intersex conditions.* Washington, DC: American Psychological Association.

Arkles, G. (2009). Safety and solidarity across gender lines: Rethinking segregation of transgender people in detention. *Temple Political & Civil Rights Law Review, 18*(2), 515–560.

Arkles, G. (2012). Correcting race and gender: Prison regulation of social hierarchy through dress. *New York University Law Review, 87,* 12–49.

Associated Press. (2005, December 29). Jail for gay, transgender inmates to close. *USA Today.* Retrieved from http://www.usatoday.com/

Barnes, A. C. (1998). The sexual continuum: Transsexual prisoners. *New England Journal on Criminal & Civil Confinement, 24*(2), 599–646.

Bassichis, D. M. (2007). *"It's war in here": A report on the treatment of transgender and intersex people in New York State men's prisons.* New York, NY: Sylvia Rivera Law Project.

BBC News. (2015, November 19). Transgender woman Vikki Thompson found dead at Armley jail. *BBC News.* Retrieved from http://www.bbcnews.com/

Bendlin, S. (2013). Gender dysphoria in the jailhouse: A constitutional right to hormone therapy? *Cleveland State Law Review, 61*(4), 957–982.

Blackstock, R. (2015, October 3). Jail attack inmate transgender. *The New Zealand Herald.* Retrieved from http://www.nzherald.co.nz/

Blight, J. (2000). *Transgender inmates* (Trends and Issues in Crime and Criminal Justice, No. 168). Canberra: Australian Institute of Criminology.

Brennan, J., Kuhns, L. M., Johnson, A. K., Belzer, M., Wilson, E. C., & Garofalo, R. (2012). Syndemic theory and HIV-related risk among young transgender women: The role of multiple, co-occurring health problems and social marginalization. *American Journal of Public Health, 102*(9), 1751–1757.

Brown, G. R., & McDuffie, E. (2009). Health care policies addressing transgender inmates in prison systems in the United States. *Journal of Correctional Health Care, 15*(4), 280–291.

California Corrections Health Care Services. (2015). *CCHCS/DHCS care guide: Gender dysphoria.* Elk Grove: State of California.

California Corrections Health Care Services. (2016). *Supplement to CCHCS/DHCS care guide: Gender dysphoria: Guidelines for review of requests for sex reassignment surgery (SRS).* Elk Grove: State of California.

California Department of Corrections and Rehabilitation. (2016). *Operations mannual for California Department of Corrections and Rehabilitation Adult Institutions, Programs and Parole.* Sacramento: State of California.

Campbell, R. (2014). DOC opens new housing unit for transgender women on Rikers Island [Press release]. Retrieved from http://www1.nyc.gov/assets/doc/downloads/press-release/DOC_OPENS_NEW_HOUSING_UNIT_n.pdf

Casazza, J. L. (2013). Sex reassignment surgery: Required for transgendered prisoners but forbidden for Medicaid, Medicare, and Champus beneficiaries. *William & Mary Journal of Women & the Law, 20*(3), 625–653.

Cassaidy, M., & Lim, L. (2016). *The rights of transgender people in prisons* [Research paper]. Retrieved from http://equaljusticeproject.co.nz/2016/05/the-rights-of-transgender-people-in-prison-symposium-paper/

Chidzoy, S. (2015, December 1). Transgender inmate found dead in Woodhill prison cell. *BBC News*. Retrieved from http://www.bbcnews.com/

Coleman, E., Bockting, W., Botzer, M., Cohen-Kettenis, P., DeCuypere, G., Feldman, J., . . . & Meyer, W. J. (2012). Standards of care for the health of transsexual, transgender, and gender-nonconforming people, version 7. *International Journal of Transgenderism, 13*(4), 165–232.

Colopy, T. W. (2012). Setting gender identity free: Expanding treatment for transsexual inmates. *Health Matrix, 22(1)*, 227–272.

Cooper, M. (2014). Gender identity behind bars: An analysis of Kosilek v. Spencer. *Buffalo Journal of Gender, Law & Social Policy, 23*, 101–116.

Cox, T. (2009). Medically necessary treatments for transgender prisoners and the misguided law in Wisconsin. *Wisconsin Journal of Law, Gender, & Society, 24*(2), 341–370.

Davies, M. (2002). Male sexual assault victims: a selective review of the literature and implications for support services. *Aggression and Violent Behavior, 7*(3), 203–214. doi:http://dx.doi.org/10.1016/S1359-1789(00)00043-4

Davis, M., & Wertz, K. (2009). When laws are not enough: A study of the economy health of transgender people and the need for a multidisciplinary approach to economic justice. *Seattle Journal of Social Justice, 8*(2), 467–495.

Dhejne, C., Lichtenstein, P., Boman, M., Johansson, A. L., Långström, N., & Landén, M. (2011). Long-term follow-up of transsexual persons undergoing sex reassignment surgery: Cohort study in Sweden. *PloS One, 6*(2), e16885.

Diamond v. Owens et al. (2015). Case 5:15-cv-50-MTT-CHW (2015) US.

Disposition in *Ashley Diamond v. Brian Owens et al.* (2015). Disposition. Retrieved from https://www.splcenter.org/sites/default/files/d6_legacy_files/downloads/case/complaint_2.pdf

Edney, R. (2004). To keep me safe from harm: Transgender prisoners and the experience of imprisonment. *Deakin Law Review, 9*(2), 327–338.

Egelko, B. (2015, October 23). California prisons break ground with sex-reassignment policy. *San Francisco Cronicle*. Retrieved from http://www.sfgate.com/

Fields v. Smith. (2011). 653 F.3d 550 (7th Cir. 2011) US.

Gammett v. Idaho State Board of Corrections. (2007). Case CV05–257–S–MHW Not Reported, F.Supp.2d (D. Idaho 2007) US.

Gehi, P. S., & Arkles, G. (2007). Unraveling injustice: Race and class impact of medicaid exclusions of transition-related health care for transgender people. *Sexuality Research & Social Policy, 4*(4), 7. doi:10.1525/srsp.2007.4.4.7

Girshick, L. (2011). Out of compliance: Masculine-identified people in women's prisons. In E. A. Stanley & N. Smith (Eds.), *Captive genders: Trans embodiment and the prison industrial complex* (pp. 189–208). Oakland, CA: AK Press.

Glezer, A., McNiel, D. E., & Binder, R. L. (2012). Transgendered and incarcerated: a review of the literature, current policies and laws, and ethics. *Journal of the American Academy of Psychiatry and the Law, 41*(4), 551–559.

Goring, C., & Sweet, C. R. (2011). Being an incarcerated transperson: Shouldn't people care? In E. A. Stanley & N. Smith (Eds.), *Captive genders: Trans embodiment and the prison industrial complex* (pp. 185–188). Oakland, CA: AK Press.

Grant, J. M., Mottet, L., Tanis, J. E., Harrison, J., Herman, J., & Keisling, M. (2011). *Injustice at every turn: A report of the national transgender discrimination survey.* Washington, DC: National Center for Transgender Equality and National Gay and Lesbian Task Force.

Haas, A. P., Eliason, M., Mays, V. M., Mathy, R. M., Cochran, S. D., D'Augelli, A. R., . . . & Clayton, P. J. (2010). Suicide and suicide risk in lesbian, gay, bisexual, and transgender populations: Review and recommendations. *Journal of Homosexuality, 58*(1), 10–51. doi:10.1080/00918369.2011.534038

Hammett, T. M. (2006). HIV/AIDS and other infectious diseases among correctional inmates: Transmission, burden, and an appropriate response. *American Journal of Public Health, 96*(6), 974–978. doi:10.2105/AJPH.2005.066993

Harris, F., Hek, G., & Condon, L. (2007). Health needs of prisoners in England and Wales: the implications for prison healthcare of gender, age and ethnicity. *Health & Social Care in the Community, 15*(1), 56–66. doi:10.1111/j.1365-2524.2006.00662.x

Hellard, M. E., & Aitken, C. K. (2004). HIV in prison: What are the risks and what can be done? *Sexual Health, 1*(2), 107–113. doi:10.1071/SH03018

Home Office. (2015). *Detention Services Order 11/2012: Care and management of trans-sexual detainees*, London: Immigration and Border Policy Directorate, Criminality and Enforcement Policy.

Hresko, T. (2006). In the cellars of the hollow men: Use of solitary confinement in US prisons and its implications under international laws against torture. *Pace International Law Review, 18*(1), 1–27.

Inmate Sex Change Prevention Act. (2005). (Wis. Stat. para 302.386) US.

International Commission of Jurists. (2007). *Yogyakarta principles—Principles on the application of international human rights law in relation to sexual orientation and gender identity*, March 2007. Retrieved from http://yogyakartaprinciples.org/

ITV. (2017). Transgender woman remanded in male prison found dead in cell. *ITV Report*. Retrieved from http://www.itv.com/

Jaffer, M., Ayad, J., Tungol, J. G., MacDonald, R., Dickey, N., & Venters, H. (2016). Improving transgender healthcare in the New York City correctional system. *LGBT Health, 3*(2), 116–121. doi:10.1089/lgbt.2015.0050

Kessler, R. C., Borges, G., & Walters, E. E. (1999). Prevalence of and risk factors for lifetime suicide attempts in the National Comorbidity Survey. *Archives of General Psychiatry, 56*(7), 617–626.

Kosilek v. Maloney. (2002). 221 F. Supp. 2d 156, 174 (D. Mass. 2002) US.

Krebs, C. P. (2006). Inmate factors associated with HIV transmission in prison. *Criminology & Public Policy, 5*(1), 113–135. doi:10.1111/j.1745-9133.2006.00101.x

Lambda Legal. (2016). Best practices for supporting transgender students [Fact sheet]. Retrieved from http://www.lambdalegal.org/

Lamble, S. (2012). Rethinking gendered prison policies: impacts on transgender prisoners. *ECAN Bulletin, 16*, 7–12.

Lee, P. (2016, March 11). Placing a transgender woman in a men's prison is a cruel punishment. *Independent*. Retrieved from http://www.independent.co.uk/

Lev, A. I. (2013). Gender dysphoria: Two steps forward, one step back. *Clinical Social Work Journal, 41*(3), 288–296. doi:10.1007/s10615-013-0447-0

Levine, S. B. (2016). Reflections on the legal battles over prisoners with gender dysphoria. *Journal of the American Academy of Psychiatry and the Law Online, 44*(2), 236–245.

Malone, L. (2015, April 20). Beating of transgender prisoner causes outrage in Brazil. *Vocativ*. Retrieved from http://www.vocativ.com/

Manjoo, R. (2011). *Report of the Special Rapporteur on violence against women, its causes and consequences, Addendum—Follow-up mission to El Salvador*. Retrieved from United Nations General Assembly A/HRC/17/26/Add.2

Mann, R. (2006). The treatment of transgender prisoners, not just an American problem—A comparative analysis of American, Australian, and Canadian prison policies concerning the treatment of transgender prisoners and a "universal" recommendation to improve treatment. *Law & Sexuality, 15*, 91–133.

Mariner, J. (2001). *No escape: Male rape in U.S. prisons.* Human Rights Watch [Report]. Retrieved from https://www.hrw.org/reports/2001/prison/

McGill, K. (2016, September 21). Lawsuit: Transgender inmate raped at New Orleans' new jail. *Associated Press: The Big Story.* Retrieved from http://www.bigstory.ap.org/

McSweeney, P. (2016, April 22). Transgender woman alleges rape in men's prison *National.* Retrieved from https://www.stuff.co.nz/

Metzner, J. L., & Fellner, J. (2010). Solitary confinement and mental illness in U.S. prisons: A challenge for medical ethics. *Journal of the American Academy of Psychiatry and the Law Online, 38*(1), 104–108.

Michel, A., Ansseau, M., Legros, J. J., Pitchot, W., & Mormont, C. (2002). The transsexual: what about the future? *European Psychiatry, 17*(6), 353–362. doi:10.1016/S0924-9338(02)00703-4

Mintz, J. E. (2013). Treatment of transgender inmates—The double punishment. *Seton Hall University—Law School Student Scholarship* (Paper 271), 1–31.

Nadal, K. L., Davidoff, K. C., & Fujii-Doe, W. (2014). Transgender women and the sex work industry: Roots in systemic, institutional, and interpersonal discrimination. *Journal of Trauma & Dissociation, 15*(2), 169–183.

National LGBT Health Education Center. (2013). *Affirmative care for transgender and gender non-conforming people: best practices for front-line health care staff* (updated Fall 2016). Boston, MA: National LGBT Health Education.

National LGBT Health Education Center. (2016). *Affirmative care for transgender and gender non-conforming people: Best practices for front-line health care staff.* Boston, MA: National LGBT Health Education.

National Offender Management Service. (2016). *Prison service instruction 17/2016: The care and management of transgender offenders.* London, UK: NOMS Agency Board.

New York City Board of Correction. (2016). *Notice of adoption of rules: Rules relating to the detection, prevention and response to sexual abuse and sexual harassment of persons incarcerated in jails and other facilities operated by the Department of Correction.* New York, NY: New York City Board of Correction.

New York City Department of Corrections. (2017). *Population demographics report FY17 Qtr. 1.* New York, NY: New York City Department of Corrections.

NSW Government. (2015). *Operations procedures manual section 7.23: Management of transgender and intersex inmates.* Sydney, NSW: Author.

Obama, B. (2017). Remarks by the President in final press conference [Press release]. Retrieved from https://obamawhitehouse.archives.gov/the-press-office/2017/01/18/remarks-president-final-press-conference/

Oparah, J. C. (2010). Feminism and the (trans) gender entrapment of gender nonconforming prisoners. *UCLA Women's Law Journal, 18*(2), 239–271.

Osborne, C. S., & Lawrence, A. A. (2016). Male prison inmates with gender dysphoria: when is sex reassignment surgery appropriate? *Archives of Sexual Behavior, 45*(7), 1649–1663.

Peek, C. (2003). Breaking out of the prison hierarchy: Transgender prisoners, rape, and the Eighth Amendment. *Santa Clara Law Review, 44*(4), 1211–1248.

Police, Q. (2016). *Operational procedures manual issue 55: Public edition*. Brisbane, QLD: Queensland Police.

Potts, M. C. (2011). Regulatory sites: Management, confinement and HIV/AIDS. In E. A. Stanley & N. Smith (Eds.), *Captive genders: Trans embodiment and the prison industrial complex*. Oakland CA: AK Press.

Queensland Corrective Services. (2014). *Custodial operations practice directive: Admission and induction*. Queensland, Australia: Queensland Corrective Services.

Quine v. Beard et al. (2016). C 14-02726 JST US.

Reisner, S. L., Bailey, Z., & Sevelius, J. (2014). Racial/ethnic disparities in history of incarceration, experiences of victimization, and associated health indicators among transgender women in the US. *Women & Health, 54*(8), 750–767.

Riley, A., Dunn, J., Emslie, J. A. N., Goldberg, D. J., Gruer, L., Reid, D., . . . & McKeganey, N. (1993). Transmission of HIV in prison. *BMJ: British Medical Journal, 307*(6904), 622–623.

Ristroph, A. (2006). Sexual punishments. *Columbia Journal of Gender and Law, 15(1)*, 139–184.

Robinson, R. K. (2011). Masculinity as prison: Sexual identity, race, and incarceration. *California Law Review, 99*(5), 1309–1408.

Rogers, J. (2015). Being transgender behind bars in the era of Chelsea Manning: How transgender prisoners' rights are changing. *Alabama Civil Rights & Civil Liberties Law Review, 6*(2), 189–203.

Rosenblum, D. (1999). Trapped in Sing Sing: Transgendered prisoners caught in the gender binarism. *Michigan Journal Gender & Law, 6*(2), 499–571.

Schuster, T. (2014). PREA and LGBTI rights. *American Jails, 28*(1), 8–13.

Self, J. (2014). Suggested best practices for supporting trans students [Press release]. Retrieved from http://www.lgbtcampus.org/

Shay, G. (2014). PREA's elusive promise: Can DOJ regulations protect LGBT incarcerated people? *Loyola Journal of Public Interest Law, 15*(2), 343–356.

Simopoulos, E. F., & Khin, E. K. (2014). Fundamental principles inherent in the comprehensive care of transgender inmates. *Journal of the American Academy of Psychiatry and the Law Online, 42*(1), 26–36.

Smith, B. V. (2006). Rethinking prison sex: Self-expression and safety. *Columbia Journal of Gender & Law, 15*(1), 185–234.

Smith, P. S. (2006). The effects of solitary confinement on prison inmates: A brief history and review of the literature. *Crime and Justice, 34*(1), 441–528. doi:10.1086/500626

Smith, R. (1995). Transgendered . . . and taken to jail. *Journal of Psychosocial Nursing and Mental Health Services, 33*(9), 44–46.

Somerset, B. (2015, October 30). Transgender woman Tara Hudson moved to female prison. *BBC News*. Retrieved from http://www.bbcnews.com/

The Southern Poverty Law Center. (2015). Transgender inmate Ashley Diamond released from Georgia prison after pressure from SPLC lawsuit [Press release]. Retrieved from http://www.splcenter.org/

Spade, D. (2008a). Documenting gender. *Hastings Law Journal, 59*(1), 731–842.

Spade, D. (2008b). Trans formation. *Los Angeles Lawyer, October*, 35–41.

Stein, B. (2016). NYC Board of Correction adopts rules to detect, prevent, and respond to sexual abuse and sexual harassment in city's jails [Press release]. Retrieved from http://www1.nyc.gov/site/boc/news/prea-press-release.page/

Stephens, T., Cozza, S., & Braithwaite, R. L. (1999). Transsexual orientation in HIV risk behaviours in an adult male prison. *International Journal of STD & AIDS, 10*(1), 28–31.

Stop Trans Pathologization. (2012). *Best practices guide to trans health care in the National Health System* [Report]. Retrieved from http://www.stp2012.info/

Stotzer, R. L. (2009). Violence against transgender people: A review of United States data. *Aggression and Violent Behavior, 14*(3), 170–179.

Sultan, B. A. (2002). Transsexual prisoners: How much treatment is enough. *New England Law Review, 37*(4), 1195–1230.

Sumner, J., & Jenness, V. (2014). Gender integration in sex-segregated U.S. prisons: The paradox of transgender correctional policy. In D. Peterson & V. R. Panfil (Eds.), *Handbook of LGBT communities, crime, and justice* (pp. 229–259). New York, NY: Springer.

Testa, J. (2015, April 11). Pressured by feds, Georgia changes policy on trans prisoners. *BuzzFeed News*. Retrieved from http://www.buzzfeed.com/

United Nations Office on Drugs and Crime. (2009). *Handbook on prisoners with special needs*. Vienna: United Nations Office on Drugs and Crime. Retrieved from http://www.unodc.org/

US Department of Justice. (2015). *Statement of interest of the United States in the case Ashley Diamond v. Brian Owens et al.* Retrieved from http://www.justice.gov/file/387296/download

Women and Equalities Committee. (2016). *Transgender equality: First report of Session 2015–16*. London, UK: The Stationery Office.

World Professional Association for Transgender Health. (2011). *WPATH Standards of Care Version 7*. Retrieved from https://s3.amazonaws.com/amo_hub_content/Association140/files/Standards%20of%20Care%20V7%20-%202011%20WPATH%20(2)(1).pdf

Wykoff, J. K. (2014). All prisoners are equal, but some prisoners are more equal than others: An inmate's right to sex reassignment surgery after Kosilek v. Spencer, 889 F Supp. 2D 190 (D. Mass. 2012). *Southern Illinois University Law Journal, 39*(1), 143–161.

Zielbauer, P. V. (2005, December 30). New York set to close jail unit for gays. *The New York Times*.

11

The Role of Race/Ethnicity in Criminal and Juvenile Justice

SUSAN MCCARTER

Of the myriad of phenomena studied in the social sciences, few others are as controversial as the intersection of race/ethnicity and criminal and juvenile justice. Disproportionate minority contact (DMC) scholars carefully examine that intersection. And when those scholars are social workers, they are also guided by ethics that charge them to promote social justice and social change, understand and emphasize cultural and ethnic diversity, and strive to end discrimination, oppression, poverty, and other forms of social injustice. DMC scholars have found that despite the fact that minorities (in this case categorized by African American/Black, Hispanic, Asian, American Indian/Alaska Native, Native Hawaiian/Other Pacific Islander, and those identifying as multiracial) comprise approximately 38% of the estimated US population in 2015 (http://quickfacts.census.gov), they comprise more than 66% of adults incarcerated in that same year (Carson & Anderson, 2016) and more than 68% of those juveniles in residential justice placements in 2013 (the latest statistics available; The Office of Juvenile Justice and Delinquency Prevention [OJJDP], 2015). This chapter examines the definitions, scope, and prevalence of disproportionality and disparity in the criminal and juvenile justice systems. It examines current policy, assesses the measurement of racial and ethnic disparities, and explores the contributing factors and analysis trends, including relative rate indices and racial equity impact analyses. Creative youth case examples describe three parallel paths distinguished by race and ethnicity. Finally, readers are also presented with evidence-based interventions and Web-based resources for programs and contacts in jurisdictions successfully addressing racial and ethnic disproportionality and disparity in both justice systems.

DEFINITIONS

Disproportionality

Disproportionality occurs when categories are out of proportion (or are in disproportion) by size or number (Oxford Dictionary, 2017). When the number of individuals present in a specific category is greater than/less than the number of those individuals typically found in the general population, overrepresentation/underrepresentation is said to occur. This discrepancy is also termed "disproportionality" since the occurrence suggests a statistic that is not proportionate to the general population (Vallas, 2009). The term "disproportionality" itself is not pejorative. Judgment regarding over/underrepresentation depends on context, goals, and desired outcomes.

Disparity

Parity means equality (as measured by distribution, pay, status, or privilege) (Oxford Dictionary, 2017). Disparity indicates an unequal status or unequal treatment, and these differences can result in disparate outcomes (e.g., health disparities, income disparities). Unlike disproportionality, if the goal is parity or even equity and the outcomes are disparate, the term and the result are both negative.

Discrimination

The Oxford Dictionary (2017) suggests that discrimination occurs when the disproportionality or disparity can be attributed to differential treatment based on, for example, race/ethnicity, age, sex, and so on.

Race

Race is a historically provisional social construct or characterization (Bobo & Fox, 2003) that most often categorizes people based on physical characteristics such as skin color, bone structure, hair type, or eye color. Biologists can determine the difference between humans and birds or dogs or cats, for example, but other than being able to tell that two humans come from geographically different lineages, there is no scientific mechanism to determine someone's race (Gannon, 2016). In the 2010 US Census, race categories included the following: White or Caucasian, Black or African American, American Indian or Alaska Native, and Native Hawaiian or Other Pacific Islander (Humes, Jones, & Ramirez, 2011). The 2000 US Census was the first to give individuals the option of identifying as more than one race and in the 2010 US Census, 9 million people (3% of the US population) chose "Two or More Races" (Humes et al., 2011).

Ethnicity

Ethnicity refers to individuals with a shared heritage. This heritage can include nationality, culture, language, religion, and so on. The US Census Bureau is guided by the US Office of Management and Budget's (OMB) 1997 *Revisions to the Standards for the Classification of Federal Data on Race and Ethnicity* (Humes et al., 2011). OMB requires that federal agencies include a minimum of two ethnicities: Hispanic or Latino and Not Hispanic or Latino. For the 2010 Census, the ethnicity Hispanic/Latino was defined as "a person of Cuban, Mexican, Puerto Rican, South or Central American, or other Spanish culture or origin regardless of race" (Humes et al., 2011, p. 2). (In this chapter, individuals of Hispanic or Latino heritage will be referred to using the term "Latinx," which does not demonstrate a gender preference nor does it perpetuate a gender binary.)

Consider: What are the goals of US service providers, for example in education, health care, housing, and justice? Are their goals to deliver equal or equitable services? How are their outcomes measured? Are their goals for service delivery achieved? Consider your own system or agency, what are its goals for service delivery? How are your outcomes measured? Are your goals for service delivery achieved?

Prevalence of Disproportionality

Current US Population Demographics

The 2015 US Census estimated the national population to be 321,418,820. Of those 321 million people, approximately 61% identified as White, 17% Hispanic/Latino, 13% Black/African American, 5% Asian, 2.5% multiracial, 1.2% American Indian or Alaskan Native, and 0.2% were classified as Native Hawaiian or other Pacific Islander (http://quickfacts.census.gov; see Figure 11.1).

Current US Criminal and Juvenile Justice Demographics

For those individuals who were held in state and federal adult prisons on December 31, 2015 (1,476,847), 33.8% were classified as White (499,400), 36% were Black (523,000), 21.6% were Hispanic (319,400), and 9.1% (135,100) were included in the category labeled American Indian and Alaska Native; Asian, Native Hawaiian, and Other Pacific Islander; and persons of two or more races (Carson & Anderson, 2016). The Bureau of Justice Statistics estimates that the rate of Black adults in prison in December 2015 was 1,745 inmates per 100,000 Black US residents aged 18 or older. This is compared to a rate of 820 per 100,000 for Hispanic adults and 312 per 100,000 White adults (Carson & Anderson, 2016). That statistic suggests that in the United States, the rate of imprisonment for Hispanics is 2.63 times that of Whites and the rate of imprisonment for Blacks is 5.59 times that of Whites.

The latest data from OJJDP suggest that minority youth comprised 68% of those in residential treatment in 2013 (Hockenberry, 2016). Although the number of

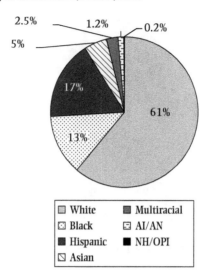

Figure 11.1 The 2015 estimated US Census.
SOURCE: US Census (2015), http://quickfacts.census.gov

youth in national juvenile justice placements continues to decline, youth of color are still significantly overrepresented. In 1997, there were 105,055 youth held in out-of-home justice facilities, and in 2013, that number had decreased 50% to 54,148, its lowest level. Of the 54,148 youth in residential placements in 2013, 1% were 12 or younger, 4% were 13, 9% were 14, 17% were 15, 26% were 16, 28% were 17, and 15% were 18–20 years old; and 32% were classified as White, 40% were Black, 23% were Hispanic, 2% were American Indian/Alaska Native, 1% were Asian, and 2% were classified as "Other." The statistics for that same year indicate that the rate of residential placement for Black youth was 6 times higher than White youth and the rate for commitments for Black youth was 4 times higher than for White youth (Hockenberry, 2016; see Figures 11.2 and 11.3).

Factors Affecting Disproportionality

What accounts for the overrepresentation of individuals of color in the criminal and juvenile justice systems? Criminologists, sociologists, and DMC scholars have two overarching notions about why disproportionality and disparate outcomes in criminal and juvenile justice systems occur. The first is differential involvement, and the second is a combination of differential selection and processing.

DIFFERENTIAL INVOLVEMENT

This notion suggests that minority overrepresentation in the justice systems is as a result of individuals of color committing more crimes, more serious crimes, and more crimes for a longer period of their lives as compared to Whites. In other words, minorities behave differently and that is why arrest, detention, conviction,

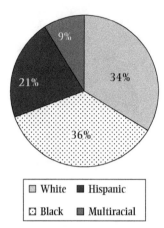

Figure 11.2 Adults in state and federal prisons, 2015.
SOURCE: BJS, https://www.bjs.gov/content/pub/pdf/p15.pdf

and incarceration rates, for example, differ by race/ethnicity. Differential involvement is most accurately measured using self-report since contact points within systems can potentially introduce bias. But very few studies are able to test this hypothesis using reliable self-report data. One of the largest and most reliable measures of self-report data is the Centers for Disease Control's national Youth Risk Behavior Surveillance Survey for students in 9th–12th grade across the United States (https://www.cdc.gov/healthyyouth/data/yrbs/). Figure 11.4 presents self-reported behaviors for four questions from the national survey in 2013. A larger percentage of Latinx youth report having ever used cocaine followed by White youth and then Black youth and the highest percentage of youth who have ever

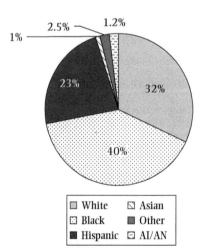

Figure 11.3 Juveniles in residential placement, 2013.
SOURCE: OJJDP - https://www.ojjdp.gov/pubs/249507.pdf

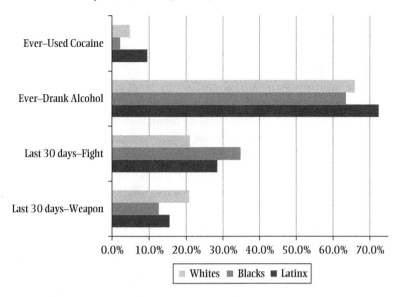

Figure 11.4 Self-reported Youth Risk Behavior Surveillance System data, 2013.
SOURCE: CDC—YRBSS, 2013 https://www.cdc.gov/healthyyouth/data/yrbs/

drank alcohol self-identify as Latinx, followed by White and then Black youth. Black youth, however, are the most likely to have been in a fight in the last 30 days, followed by Latinx, and then White youth. And finally, White youth are the most likely to have carried a weapon in the last 30 days as compared to Latinx, and then Black youth.

Similarly, for adults, the Substance Abuse and Mental Health Services Administration (SAMHSA) reports that in the United States in 2013, 24% of individuals using crack cocaine identified as African American and 72% as White or Latinx American, yet in that same year, more than 80% of adult defendants sentenced for offenses with crack cocaine were African American (SAMHSA, 2014, p. 7). SAMHSA's National Survey on Drug Use and Health (2013) lists the rate of current illicit drug use as 3.1% for Asians, 8.8% for Latinos, 9.5% for Whites, 10.5% for Blacks, 12.3% for American Indians/Alaska Natives, 14.0% for Native Hawaiians/Other Pacific Islanders, and 17.4% for persons self-identifying as multiracial (SAMHSA, 2014). That same year, SAMHSA suggested that although each year past month, past year, and lifetime marijuana usage rates varied slightly, overall Blacks and Whites use marijuana at similar rates. Yet Uniform Crime Reporting Data from the Federal Bureau of Investigation (2013) from all 50 states and the District of Columbia found that between 2001 and 2010 there were over 8 million arrests for marijuana and African Americans were 3.73 times more likely to be arrested for marijuana possession than Caucasians (Black marijuana possession arrest rate is 716 per 100,000; White arrest rate is 192 per 100,000). In 2010 in the United States, an individual was arrested for marijuana possession every 37 seconds (for a total of 889,133 arrests—300,000 more than for all violent crimes combined), for an overall cost of $3.6 billion to enforce marijuana possession laws (ACLU, 2013).

Though there are some trends in self-reported data by race and ethnicity (e.g., proportionately, White youth tend to commit more arson, Black youth tend to commit more petit larceny, Hispanic youth tend to commit more alcohol-related offenses), the majority of scholars suggest that these variations in crime commission rates by race/ethnicity cannot explain the current rates of disproportionality in either the juvenile or criminal justice systems (Huizinga, Thornberry, Knight, & Lovegrove, 2007; Leiber, 2002; Piquero & Brame, 2008).

DIFFERENTIAL SELECTION AND DIFFERENTIAL PROCESSING

A second theory is that minority overrepresentation can be explained by differences in selection and processing for individuals of color such that a combination of differential "selection" (differing police presence, patrolling, and profiling in minority and nonminority neighborhoods) and differential "processing" (discrimination in the courts and correctional systems) lead to the disproportionate arrest, conviction, and incarceration rates of individuals of color. In other words, individuals of color are treated differently (either consciously or not) by law enforcement and the courts based on their race/ethnicity. There is substantial empirical support for this theory. In 1999, North Carolina became the first state to pass a law requiring the collection of race/ethnicity for all motorists stopped by the police (NC General Statutes § 114-10-1). Baumgartner, Epp, Shoub, and Love (2016) analyzed data over 18 million traffic stops in North Carolina between 2002 and 2013 and found that Black and Latinx motorists were consistently, statistically more likely to be stopped, searched, and arrested as compared to Whites for all varieties of stops, including speeding, running a stop light, and so on. The greatest disparities, however, occur when the law enforcement officer's discretion is the highest (e.g., seat belts, vehicle equipment, tag/registration issues). Once stopped, Black and Latinx drivers were much more likely to be searched, but when searched they were less likely to have contraband as compared to White drivers. And this disparity is growing over time—in 2002, officers were almost 125% more likely to use probable cause to search Black drivers as compared to Whites, and in 2013, that figure had risen to 250% more likely to use probable cause as a justification for searching Black drivers' cars, where they were less likely to find contraband (Baumgartner et al., 2016; LaFraniere & Lehren, 2015).

Given the preponderance of evidence supporting differential selection and processing (Cole, 1999; Fabelo et al., 2011; Kann et al., 2014; Kempf-Leonard, 2007; Leiber, 2002; McCarter, 2009), most current scholarship seeks to investigate this theory more fully in order to determine how to use it to inform and address disproportionate minority contact. In addition, several scholars suggest moving beyond the differential involvement/differential selection and processing debate to focus on seeking evidence-based solutions for addressing DMC (Piquero, 2008). But one challenge with establishing a strong evidence base for DMC, however, is that addressing the intersection of race and crime is significantly hampered by the quality of the data collected.

Consider: *What factors do you think affect the overrepresentation of individuals of color in the criminal and juvenile justice systems? Where would you suggest putting the focus on addressing DMC? How would you go about collecting data? How would you test your ideas?*

CURRENT MEASUREMENT AND TRENDS

Data Limitations

Despite the federal classification requirements from OMB, most state law enforcement, juvenile/criminal justice, and courts do not collect accurate racial and ethnic data. Many intake workers visually identify their clients instead of asking their clients to classify themselves and still others do not disaggregate ethnicity but instead consider ethnicity another race category (e.g., "Indicate your race/ethnicity: White, Black, Hispanic, America Indian/Alaska Native") instead of within racial categories (e.g., "Indicate your race: White, Black, American Indian/Alaska Native, etc." and then "Indicate your ethnicity: Hispanic/Latino or non-Hispanic/Latino"). Both of these data collection methods compromise the validity of the data as well as the capacity to compare the data across agencies or institutions.

Moreover, very few empirical sources include self-report and official or agency records on the same individuals measured over time. Most official measures of criminal offenses are collected at the law enforcement level and then reported to the FBI or another federal agency, and these statistics are not consistently disaggregated by race and ethnicity. Alex Piquero (2008) suggests that "data for nonblack minorities, including Hispanics, Native Americans, and Asian Americans, are virtually nonexistent in longitudinal self-report studies of crime and delinquency" (p. 67).

Using a Relative Rate Index

The relative rate index (RRI) is a method used to compare the volume of crime or delinquency for minorities with the volume of those same activities for Whites at the same decision points and then compares that to the percentage of minority/majority individuals in the general population. The RRI is a single statistic calculated by dividing the rate of activity for minorities by the rate of activity for Whites. If the rates are the same, the RRI = 1. If the RRI is < 1, individuals of color are underrepresented and if the RRI is > 1, individuals of color are overrepresented. In other words, if a group has an RRI of 2.0 compared to the standardized RRI of 1.0 for Whites, that group is represented at that decision point at twice the rate of the majority group (see Figure 11.5).

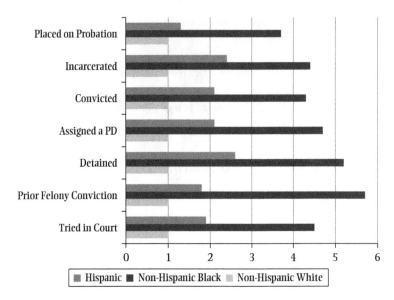

Figure 11.5 Relative rate index of felony defendants in urban counties, 2004.
SOURCE: State Processing Statistics, 2004. http://www.nccdglobal.org/sites/default/files/
publication_pdf/created-equal.pdf

Researchers consider each decision stage within the criminal and juvenile justice system not as distinct—but instead as interrelated contact points. OJJDP uses
the RRI concept with that in mind. For example, using population as the denominator for the juvenile court referral rate yields a rate whose magnitude could
depend on many factors (e.g., the amount of delinquent behavior, the level of
reporting to police, any biases in the contact points), and OJJDP already has a
measure of disparity at the arrest decision. Thus, applying population as the denominator in the court referral rate, the figure is actually a combination of the
disparity at the arrest decision plus any additional disparity added at the court
referral stage. To help isolate the disparity introduced at court referral, a stronger
denominator for the court referral stage would be the number of arrests because
to a large extent, arrests influence juvenile court referral. If arrests increase, then
most likely juvenile court referrals will also increase. Certainly additional paths
to juvenile court exist beyond arrest (e.g., parents may refer the youth, school resource officer may refer, probation violations), but arrest is the most significant
preceding stage. Thus, the magnitude of racial disparity at any contact point is a
combination of the disparities introduced at prior decision points plus that added
by the decision point of interest. Examining the RRIs for specific decision points
helps us to see the contributions made by each decision point to the overall disparity in the system (see Table 11.1).
    Thus, the RRI attempts to show data in context of proportionality (relative to
the expected percentage represented in the overall population) and taking into
consideration the decision points prior and following the current point being

Table 11.1. 2013 CASE PROCESSING SUMMARY: RATES BY DECISION POINTS RELATIVE
RATE INDICES FOR DELINQUENCY OFFENSES

Relative Rates	Minority	Black	AIAN	AHPI
Arrest rate	1.8	2.4	1.0	0.2
Referral rate	1.1	1.1	1.1	1.1
Diversion rate	0.7	0.7	0.8	0.9
Detention rate	1.3	1.3	1.3	1.1
Petitioned rate	1.2	1.2	1.1	1.1
Adjudicated rate	0.9	0.9	1.1	1.0
Probation rate	1.0	0.9	0.9	1.1
Placement rate	1.2	1.2	1.1	0.8
Waiver rate	1.3	1.3	1.4	*0.6

NOTE: All RRIs are relative to Whites. Interpret data with caution; rates and RRIs are
based on a small number of cases.

AHPI: Asian, Hawaiian, or Pacific Islander; AIAN: American Indian or Alaskan
Native.

SOURCE: Puzzanchera, C., & Hockenberry, S. (2016). National disproportionate minority contact databook. Developed by the National Center for Juvenile Justice for the
Office of Juvenile Justice and Delinquency Prevention. Retrieved from http://www.
ojjdp.gov/ojstatbb/dmcdb/

assessed. Moreover, scholars also suggest that there is a "cumulative effect" or
"amplification phenomenon" for individuals who become court involved (DMC
TA Manual, 2009; Piquero, 2008).

Unfortunately, the RRI has five profound limitations: (1) it is not a standardized
measure in that RRIs can vary considerably based on the percentage of individuals
of color in any given jurisdiction (counties with a low minority percentage could
have a higher RRI, whereas a higher minority percentage can have an artificially
low RRI), (2) an RRI cannot measure statistical significance, (3) it cannot suggest
causality or explain why a group is over- or underrepresented, (4) it in no way can
tease out the influence of individual versus system-level variables nor can they
differentiate legal variables from extralegal variables, and finally, (5) it cannot explain why any disproportionality or disparities exist.

Explicit and Implicit Bias

The National Center of State Courts defines explicit bias as the attitudes or beliefs
that one endorses at a conscious level. Because explicit biases are accessible
through introspection, individuals can choose to conceal or hide explicit biases
in order to appear more socially or politically correct (Casey, Warren, Cheesman,

& Elek, 2012). Implicit bias, on the other hand, operates outside of our aware-ness and is the judgment or behavior that results from subtle cognitive processes that operate at a level below conscious awareness and without intentional control (Casey et al., 2012).

Considering differential selection and processing as central to explaining the role of race and ethnicity in juvenile and criminal justice systems, could explicit and, more important, implicit biases affect outcomes for individuals of color? In February of 2015, FBI Director James Comey spoke about law enforcement at Georgetown University and said, "Much research points to the widespread exist-ence of unconscious bias" and how these unconscious racial biases can affect how people respond to individuals of different racial groups (Comey, 2015). Implicit bias was also mentioned in both the 2016 Vice Presidential as well as Presidential debates, with candidates arguing whether everyone has implicit bias [they do] and suggesting that African American police officers could not be biased against members of their own race [they can].

Dr. Jennifer Eberhardt, Stanford University social psychologist, has conducted several studies to explore the role of race and ethnicity and implicit bias in criminal and juvenile justice (Hetey & Eberhardt, 2014). One specific study uses line drawings that begin as blurry images in Frame 1, and as the frames advance to Frame 41, they become much clearer. Study participants seated at computers are asked to identify the images as quickly as possible. The images are classified in two categories: crime-irrelevant objects (e.g., sta-pler, cup and saucer, bugle) and crime-relevant images (e.g., knife, gun, hand-cuffs). Participants are randomly assigned to three groups. Group 1 receives no priming. Group 2 is "primed" with photographs of White university fac-ulty, staff, and students at the rate of 30 milliseconds, which is undetectable to the conscious mind, in between the frames depicting the line drawings. And Group 3 is "primed" with photographs of Black university faculty, staff, and students, also at the undetectable speed of 30 milliseconds. All three groups are able to identify crime-irrelevant objects in approximately 22–24 frames. Group 1 participants who are shown no photographs, then identify crime-relevant objects in a similar response time, average about 23 frames. However, for those primed with White photographs, participants averaged 27 frames to identify crime-relevant images—a statistically significantly longer response time. And for those primed with Black photographs, participants averaged 18 frames to identify crime-relevant images—a statistically significantly shorter response time (Hetey & Eberhardt, 2014). (See the Kirwan Institute's State of the Science: Implicit Bias Review 2016 for more on implicit bias, http:// kirwaninstitute.osu.edu/.)

Consider: *Could implicit bias be a factor that affects the overrepresentation of individuals of color in the criminal and juvenile justice systems? Can RRIs cap-ture this? If so, how? If not, why? And what other type of measurement would you suggest? Would you include policy or practice to complement your efforts?*

CURRENT POLICIES TO ADDRESS DISPROPORTIONATE MINORITY CONTACT

Disproportionate Minority Contact in Juvenile Justice— The Juvenile Justice and Delinquency Prevention Act of 1974

The Juvenile Justice and Delinquency Prevention Act (JJDPA) was enacted in 1974 and mandates that in order for states to receive federal juvenile justice funding, they have to meet three requirements: (a) discontinue holding juvenile status offenders in secure detention or confinement; (b) create separate confinement facilities for youth, in order to protect juveniles and guard them from further corruption by adult offenders; and (c) in situations where children must be placed in an adult facility, state placements must maintain sight and sound separation such that the youthful offenders could not be held next to adult cells, share dining rooms, or any other common spaces (P.L. 93-415).

When the Act was first legislated, though demographic data were collected, there was no focus on minority overrepresentation. The Office of Juvenile Justice and Delinquency Prevention (OJJDP) defined minorities as African Americans, American Indians, Asians, Pacific Islanders, and Hispanics (OJJDP Regulations 28 CFR Part 31). Congress addressed minority overrepresentation by amending the JJDP Act of 1974 to reduce racial disproportionality in the juvenile justice system. In 1988, a fourth requirement was added to the JJDPA requiring states to assess and address the disproportionate number of minorities in juvenile secure confinement:

> In accordance with regulations which the Administrator shall prescribe, [the state plan] shall ... address efforts to reduce the proportion of juveniles detained or confined in secure detention facilities, secure correctional facilities, jails, and lock ups who are members of minority groups if such proportion exceeds the proportion such groups represent in the general population. (Juvenile Justice and Delinquency Prevention Act of 1974, as amended [P.L. 93-415, Section 223 [a] [23])

Congress amended the JJDPA in 1992, for the second time. This amendment elevated DMC to a core requirement of the Act, such that 25% of each state's Formula Grant allocation could be withheld from states found to be out of compliance (P.L. 102-586). Yet youth of color continued to be overrepresented at every decision point in all states reporting data (Leiber, 2002). So, in 2002, for the third time the JJDPA was amended to address DMC. The 2002 amendment includes a specific language change from "disproportionate minority confinement" to "disproportionate minority contact," and this amendment noted racial disproportionality at contact points prior to incarceration and recognized that macro factors in addition to micro- and mezzo-level factors also required examination. In order for states to comply with the third amendment to address DMC, OJJDP stipulates that they must participate in five sustained efforts: (1) identify the extent to which

DMC exists, (2) assess the reasons for DMC if it exists, (3) develop an intervention plan to address these identified reasons, (4) evaluate the effectiveness of strategies to address DMC, and (5) monitor DMC trends over time (Pope, Lovell, & Hsia, 2002).

That was the last time that the JJDPA was reauthorized (2002), and although parts of the Act expired in 2007 and in 2008, many programs continue to receive appropriations. Various legislators have introduced reauthorization and related bills most recently in 2015 and 2016, but neither of them was passed by their respective Congress (see S. 1169 Juvenile Justice and Delinquency Prevention Reauthorization Act of 2015—introduced on April 30, 2015, and sponsored by Charles Grassley [R-Iowa] and Sheldon Whitehouse [D-RI] but held up in the Senate by Tom Cotton [R-AR]; and H.R. 5963—Supporting Youth Opportunity and Preventing Delinquency Act of 2016—introduced on September 8, 2016, and sponsored by Carlos Curbelo [R-FL]; passed by the House, but not by the Senate in the 114th Congress).

Disproportionate Minority Contact in Criminal Justice— No Comparable Legislation

In 2009, Christopher Hartney and Linh Vuong of the National Council on Crime and Delinquency (NCCD) composed a national report titled "Created Equal: Racial and Ethnic Disparities in the US Criminal Justice System." NCCD's report was created because "increased focus on DMC in the juvenile system has no similar federal counterpart concerning adults" (Hartney & Vuong, 2009, p. 7).

Consider: *What are the implications of not reauthorizing the JJDPA? What are the implications of having no federal mandate to identify, assess, intervene, evaluate, and monitor DMC in the adult criminal justice system?*

EVIDENCE-BASED PRACTICES AND NEXT STEPS

Nine Jurisdictions Reducing Disproportionate Minority Contact

The evidence base is not new. With the 2002 amendment to the JJDPA, states were required to begin collecting and analyzing DMC data in the juvenile justice system, and in 2005, states began inputting their juvenile justice DMC data into a national database. But it is novel to have those data analyzed and disseminated and to be able to identify the few jurisdictions across the United States that have demonstrated a reduction in disproportionate minority contact. The DMC Reduction Cycle includes five phases: identification, assessment, intervention, evaluation, and monitoring (see Figure 11.6). The Office of Juvenile Justice and Delinquency Prevention contracted with the Development Services Group to, for the first time, analyze all the states' reports and data submitted to OJJDP as part of the federal JJDPA—DMC requirement (Spinney et al., 2014). Spinney and her

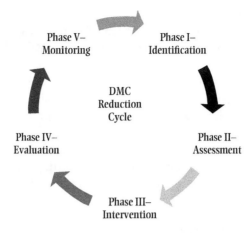

Figure 11.6 Office of Juvenile Justice and Delinquency Prevention's (OJJDP's) Disproportionate Minority Contact (DMC) reduction cycle.

colleagues (2014) identified nine jurisdictions that systematically demonstrated a reduction in DMC; they are Bernalillo County, NM; Clark County, NV; the state of Connecticut; Essex County, NJ; Hillsborough County, NH; Montgomery County, AL; Philadelphia, PA; Tulsa County, OK; and Utah County, UT. Following are the highlights of their accomplishments.

Bernalillo County, New Mexico
Bernalillo County is the largest county in New Mexico, and their youth population has increased 11% over the last decade. In the 1990s, Bernalillo was selected as an Annie E. Casey Foundation JDAI (Juvenile Detention Alternatives Initiative) site and spent years strengthening their data collection and reforming the juvenile system. From 2004 to 2010, the county demonstrated a reduction in disparities for African American, Hispanic, and Native American youth for cases referred from law enforcement to probation and for cases diverted from court. And to improve reentry and wrap-around services, Bernalillo has developed working relationships with multiple youth-serving partners, increased access to diversion through a Prevention Unit, and created a mental health clinic adjacent to the detention facility to serve court-involved youth.

Clark County, Nevada
Clark County has been working since 2007 to employ improved technology and data-analyses techniques, strengthen community relationships, use a new risk-assessment instrument to inform detention decisions, increase access to detention and confinement alternatives, and transform the culture in juvenile justice from primarily enforcing the law to addressing children's needs. Using Relative Rate Indices, from 2007 to 2011 they were able to document a reduction in secure detention for African American youth from 1.7 to 1.4 and in confinement from 2.4 to 1.7, while the rates for Hispanic youth remained at a consistent 1.0 for both contact points.

THE STATE OF CONNECTICUT

Since the 1990s, Connecticut has published three comprehensive DMC assessment studies to assist lawmakers in resource allocation for DMC-reduction strategies. From 2006 to 2012, the state focused on workforce development, training, and public awareness of disproportionality and disparities in juvenile justice across the state, including JUST.Start, Right.ResponseCT, and the Effective Police Interactions with Youth training curriculum used to train more than 1,500 law enforcement officers across Connecticut and from other states. For those same years, their RRIs at referral decreased from 2.9 to 1.6 for Hispanic youth and from 6.3 to 4.7 for African American youth. They have also developed a memorandum of understanding between law enforcement, the schools, and the courts to reduce school-based arrests and referrals to court.

ESSEX COUNTY, NEW JERSEY

Almost 71% of youth aged 10–17 who live in Essex County (the third most populated county in NJ) identify as youth of color with most as African-American/Black. Just as Bernalillo County, Essex County benefitted from its participation in the AECF—JDAI. Essex County used JDAI technical assistance (TA) to improve its workforce and use of data in decision making, and this helped create alternatives to detention and increase diversion options. From 2004 to 2011, their RRI at referral dropped from 4.9 to 3.5 for African American youth and from 2.2 to 1.1 for Hispanic youth, and their diversion RRIs improved from .59 to .87 for African American youth and from .71 to .93 for Hispanic youth.

HILLSBOROUGH COUNTY, NEW HAMPSHIRE

Despite the small minority population in Hillsborough, the DMC Coordinator, several chiefs of police, and other community stakeholders were determined to improve their DMC results. They worked to engage law enforcement leadership in addressing DMC, to train police officers in diversity and youth interactions, and to improve data collection, accuracy, and analyses. From 2007 to 2011, Hillsborough's arrest rates have declined for White and Hispanic youth and their RRI for arrests for Hispanic youth decreased from 1.8 to 1.3.

MONTGOMERY COUNTY, ALABAMA

Montgomery County is the smallest county in the report, and their goals were on reducing racial disparities at the detention and confinement contact points with government partners from the judicial and executive branches—as well as from JDAI. They have developed a risk assessment instrument to reduce detention rates and from 2009 to 2011 were also able to decrease their RRI from 1.6 to 1.3 at detention and from 1.3 to 1.1 for confinement for African American juveniles.

PHILADELPHIA, PENNSYLVANIA

Philadelphia leveraged several city-wide initiatives as well as an active DMC working group to build relationships between law enforcement and youth, create a Graduated Response Court, and launch a Global Positioning Satellite (GPS) program as an alternative to detention. Between 2006 and 2010, their detention RRI decreased from 1.6 to 1.3 for African American youth and from 2.3 to 1.3 for Hispanic youth.

Tulsa County, Oklahoma

Tulsa County started by hiring a local DMC Coordinator, forming a DMC Steering Committee, and then conducting strategic planning with community stakeholders. From there, they have trained law enforcement and have established a crisis intervention center as an alternative to detention for police to take youth who commit low-level offenses. From 2005 to 2011, Tulsa's detention RRI improved from 1.4 to 1.1 for African Americans, and for those same years, their detention RRI for Hispanic and Native American youth has remained at 1.0.

Utah County, Utah

Between 2007 and 2011, Utah County's RRIs improved across four different contact points: arrest, referral, diversion, and detention. From 2007 to 2010, arrests went from 5.7 to 3.6 for African Americans and 2.8 to 2.2 for Latinx. They attribute these changes to obtaining technical assistance, hiring a DMC Coordinator, improving data collection, delivering training to police cadets, and building DMC awareness across the state (Spinney et al., 2014). OJJDP identified eight themes of strategies across the jurisdictions reducing DMC: Data, Collaboration, Culture, Affiliation, Alternatives, DMC focus, Leadership, and Priorities (see Figure 11.7).

Interestingly, Spinney et al. (2014, p. 84) note at the end of their report that more research is needed because many of the strategies used by these nine jurisdictions have not been successful in other jurisdictions, and in some jurisdictions these strategies have exacerbated RRIs statistics instead of improving them. Moreover, as the limitations of using the RRI were noted, if this is the sole determinant of a jurisdiction's ability to reduce DMC, it is also limited. Race Matters for Juvenile Justice (RMJJ) (http://www.rmjj.org) asserts that attempting to reduce DMC without a race analysis will, in fact, result in a variety of intended and unintended outcomes (McCarter et al., 2017). RMJJ suggests that the DMC Reduction Model should be informed and shaped with an understanding of and focus on race and ethnicity (consistent with the work of others include The Kirwan Institute and Race Forward). This would include an exploration of implicit bias at the individual level (see http://implicit.harvard.edu) as well as an examination of institutionalized racism at the system level (see http://raceforward.org and http://rmjj.org).

Consider: *Many of the nine "successful" jurisdictions include workforce development and "training law enforcement." Most of these include studying race and racism. Why is it important for service providers, including law enforcement, to be knowledgeable about the effects of race and racism, implicit bias, and differential selection and processing? Might adding knowledge, values, and skills improve the effects and sustainability of DMC reduction (King, Gulick, & Avery, 2010)?*

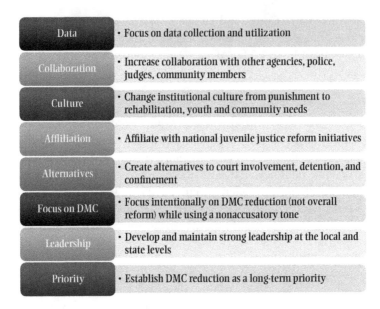

Figure 11.7 Strategies most noted from nine Disproportionate Minority Contact-reducing jurisdictions.
SOURCE: Spinney et al., 2014, p. 2. https://www.ncjrs.gov/pdffiles1/ojjdp/grants/250301.pdf

Using a Racial Equity Impact Analysis

Racial equity impact analyses (REIAs), also known as racial equity impact assessments, are systematic examinations of outcomes or impacts upon various racial and/or ethnic groups. REIAs help decision makers anticipate negative outcomes of potential policies, programs, resource allocations, and institutional practices, and they can help identify and eliminate existing disproportionality and disparities. According to Race Forward: The Center for Racial Justice Innovation,

> REIAs are used to reduce, eliminate and prevent racial discrimination and inequities.
> The persistence of deep racial disparities and divisions across society is evidence of institutional racism––the routine, often invisible and unintentional, production of inequitable social opportunities and outcomes. When racial equity is not consciously addressed, racial inequality is often unconsciously replicated.
> (http://www.raceforward.org/practice/tools/racial-equity-impact-assessment-toolkit)

Using an REIA, the city of Seattle was able to identify and assess racial and ethnic disparities across systems. They discovered disproportionality in income and poverty, noting that despite the fact that people of color comprise a relatively small percentage of the population, they represent a disproportionate number of those living in poverty in Seattle. They also found disparities in education as evidenced by varying school discipline and graduation rates by race and ethnicity. Health disparities were also evident in diabetes, asthma, and HIV/AIDS rates. And finally, the REIA also revealed DMC in criminal justice, as minorities were overrepresented in incarceration rates across Washington State (Nelson & Harris, 2008; https://www.seattle.gov/rsji).

The Race and Social Justice Initiative began in 2007 with the hopes of eliminating racial disparities and achieving racial equity for their community, and since then, Seattle, Washington, has implemented an REIA and developed an evidence-based practice with solid initial results. Through the Race and Social Justice Initiative, over 7,000 employees (more than 75% of the total city's workforce) have been trained in a race analysis and in addressing institutional racism. The city has purposefully and thoughtfully expanded its engagement with historically un-derrepresented communities, doubled its contracts with women and minority-owned businesses, awarded over $1 million in grants to community efforts that address race and social justice at the neighborhood level, and mandated that all city departments provide essential translation and interpretation services for any non-English-speaking customers (Nelson & Harris, 2008; https://www.seattle.gov/rsji).

CONCLUSION AND NEXT STEPS

How can we explain the fact that minorities comprise approximately 38% of the estimated US population in 2015 (http://quickfacts.census.gov), but more than 66% of adults incarcerated (Carson & Anderson, 2016) and more than 69% of the juveniles in residential justice placements in that same year (Puzzanchera & Hockenberry, 2017? (Included at the end of this chapter are several web-based resources—see Table 11.2). Is this a function of differential involvement or dif-ferential selection and processing—or a combination of both? Many systems use the RRI to assess racial and ethnic disproportionality and disparities, but per-haps the REIA is a better measure. Regardless, several successful jurisdictions point to the importance of data, community collaboration, workforce de-velopment/race analysis, and the examination of outcomes across systems. Reauthorization of the JJDPA and developing a federal mandate for the criminal justice system that is similar to the DMC mandate in juvenile justice would help address racial and ethnic disproportionality in an era of mass incarceration. Finally, as social work considers practice within the categories of its 12 Grand Challenges, consider how reducing DMC will need to effectively straddle three of the challenges: Ensure healthy development for all youth, Promote smart decarceration, and Achieve equal opportunity and justice. As was evident in JDAI and as we are beginning to see with smart decarceration efforts, you can reduce jail and prison populations without affecting racial and ethnic dispro-portionality. At the root of the issue of DMC is the intersection of what it means to be White, Black, or Brown and court involved. (To that end, please see the powerful case examples presented next.)

Table 11.2. Web-Based Resources

The Annie E. Casey Foundation—Juvenile Detention Alternatives Institute (JDAI)	http://www.aecf.org/work/juvenile-justice/jdai/	One of two AECF Juvenile Justice Initiatives. JDAI is a site-based effort to reduce the use of detention—the holding of youth before adjudication—and increase more effective interventions.
W. Haywood Burns Institute	http://www.burnsinstitute.org/	W. Haywood Burns Institute's website contains information on community action approaches to reducing DMC and an interactive data map of juvenile justice disparities across the United States.
Center for Children's Law and Policy	http://www.cclp.org/ http://www.cclp.org/wp-content/uploads/2016/06/RED-Practice-Manual-Chapters-1-7.pdf	The Center for Children's Law and Policy helps jurisdictions across the country create youth justice systems that are developmentally appropriate, free of racial and ethnic bias, and focused on building strengths that help youth avoid further involvement with the justice system.
John D. and Catherine T. MacArthur Foundation—Models for Change DMC Action Network Goals and Structure	http://www.modelsforchange.net/about/Action-networks/Disproportionate-minority-contact.html	Models for Change Initiative for Juvenile Justice Reform of the MacArthur Foundation also houses research, reports, and resources and information from the 16 states involved in comprehensive juvenile justice reform, as well as updates from its DMC Action Network.
Kirwan Institute for the Study of Race and Ethnicity	http://kirwaninstitute.osu.edu/	The Kirwan Institute uses research, engagement, and communication to connect individuals and communities with opportunities needed for thriving by educating the public, building the capacity of allied social justice organizations, and investing in efforts that support equity and inclusion.

Table 11.2. CONTINUED

National Conference of State Legislatures	http://www.ncsl.org/research/civil-and-criminal-justice/racial-and-ethnic-disparities-in-the-juvenile-justice-system.aspx http://www.ncsl.org/documents/cj/jjguidebook-dmc.pdf	NCSL (National Conference of State Legislature) is a bipartisan organization that conducts policy research in a variety of areas ranging from agriculture and budget and tax issues and education to health care and immigration and transportation.
National Juvenile Justice Network	http://www.njjn.org/our-work/reducing-racial-and-ethnic-disparities-in-juvenile-justice-systems-promising-practices	The NJJN (National Juvenile Justice Network) leads state-based juvenile justice reform and advocacy. The NJJN employs education, technical assistance, community building, and leadership development to improve juvenile justice.
Race Matters for Juvenile Justice	http://www.rmjj.org	Race Matters for Juvenile Justice (RMJJ) is a collaborative leadership group working within their community to reduce disproportionality and disparate outcomes for children and families of color through institutional organizing, education, and workforce development.
Seattle's Race and Justice Initiative	https://www.seattle.gov/rsji	The Seattle Race and Social Justice Initiative (RSJI) is a citywide effort to end institutionalized racism and race-based disparities in city government. RSJI builds on the work of the civil rights movement and the ongoing efforts of individuals and groups in Seattle to confront racism. The Initiative's long-term goal is to change the underlying system that creates race-based disparities in our community and to achieve racial equity.
US Dept. of Justice: Office of Justice Programs— Office of Juvenile Justice & Delinquency Prevention	https://www.ojjdp.gov/dmc/	The DMC (Disproportionate Minority Contact) Virtual Resource Center is a forum for state and local DMC Coordinators, State Advisory Group members, JJ Specialists, Compliance Monitors, practitioners, and other system stakeholders to access a variety of tools and resources to help support their state and local DMC efforts.

Consider: *Since race is a nonbiological/nonscientific, social construct and individuals often have the ability to select multiracial as a classification, should service providers in juvenile and criminal justice systems continue to collect this less-than-perfect demographic data? DMC scholars suggest that as long as outcomes vary by race and ethnicity, we should continue to collect, disaggregate, and analyze racial and ethnic disproportionality.*

CASE EXAMPLES

(The following are as demonstrated through young people's own words in slam poetry.)

The Evidence
By Camisha L. Jones

There was a gun
There was a cop
There was a Black boy

The Black boy had no gun
The Black boy had
   His skin
   His breath
   His hands
The Black boy had enough

For the cop to be afraid

The Black boy ran
The Black boy ran
The Black boy ran

The cop chased
The cop was not chased

The cop had
   a gun
   a badge
   a car
The cop had fear
It leaned into his car
Ugly words all in its mouth
Strong arms bruising his thinking

About the boy

The cop said
The kid's hands were thieves
The kid's hands were violent

The kid's hands forgot how history stutters new names
At the trigger of white men's fear

They say that evidence
Doesn't change
That evidence is fact

They say the boy is dead
And that is a fact
They say the cop had a right to deadly force
And that is another kind of fact

They never say
The boy was afraid
That fear put running in his legs

They say the child with no gun
Rushed toward the cop
And the cop saw the darkest brutality
Growing in the guilt of his skin

They say the kid forgot
What his momma taught him 'bout
Black boys and police officers
They say the cop had a right to his fear

No one is sure where the boy's hands were
Some say the boy
Had his hands up
Had his hands over his head
Had his hands in front of him,
Palms up, ready to receive

What we know is
His hands were his hands
His hands had nothing in them
His hands couldn't hold him to this life
Or innocence

What we know is
The cop was afraid
And the kid was
Breathing
And Black

The cop held his fear
Like the weapon it is
In this land of liberty and amnesia
And the gun
It knew the boy
Like any precious prey
Would run

The Ten Commandments of Being Mexican

By José Martinez

Number one:
Thou shall eat tortillas and frijoles with every meal
even on Thanksgiving
because you know your damn turkey
could always use a little bit of salsa.

Number two:
Always respect your nana, abuela, abuelita
because you know she'll beat your a**, cabrón,
even if she's under five feet tall.

Number three:
Never let anyone make fun of your shoes
just because you got them at the swap meet.
They don't understand that churros, kettle corn, bargains, and good deals
a random guy selling his chickens is
a cool place to spend your Friday and Saturday nights.

Number four:
Follow the path of no white man
because we are our own race
And we are our own people
And this is our revolution
And the day that the minority becomes the majority
is closer than we think
and no ignorant, unfair, inhumane law will get in our way.

Number five:
Look in your mother's eyes and swear to her
that you will make it in this world
and you will make something of yourself
And every damn burrito she rolled
Every damn taco she served
Every damn restaurant she worked in
Every damn insult spit in her face by bosses
who abused the fact that she had no papers
Every damn trailer park,
every damn sleepless night
counting numbers that will never make ends meet
making sure we had the damn tortilla on our stomachs,
would not go to waste.
Because that one tortilla in my stomach has become a fire
and I will redeem myself, Mom,
I will redeem myself,
and every sacrifice you made for us will not go to waste

Number six:
Don't forget where you came from
Whether you're a Dominguez, García, Lopez, Montaño, Terrazas
Vásquez, Moreno, Cruz, Martínez, or any other name
Don't forget where you came from

Number seven:
French is not the language of love.
lo siento por los que nunca van a saber lo caliente que es el lenguaje
español, el amor y hermoso que son las palabras que corren por mis venas
hispanas

Numero ocho:
Can you hear the sweat dripping,
Dripping puddles of generations into the dirt
Evaporating in the hot desert sun
like we never existed
the eighth commandment is the sound of his knees
dropping to the ground
jagged pebbles of the American Dream stabbing into his knees
lost somewhere between Rio Rico
and a family praying to the Virgen De Guadalupe
to protect him from the green monsters
that guard the land of opportunity
not knowing that God is no longer the only one that can judge us once
you are in the land of America

Number nine:
Don't let them take away years of blood, sweat, and tears
Books, classrooms, racial discrimination, what's next?
Will history repeat itself?
I dare you to try to burn through this calloused skin
The harder it gets, the harder we work,
you say we're working so we can take your jobs?
Do you know what hard-working Mexican hands taste like?
Try not to choke on your tomatoes.

Number ten:
Always remember that no matter how much soap you use
you'll always be brown.

White Boy Privilege
By Royce Mann

Dear women, I'm sorry.
Dear black people, I'm sorry.
Dear Asian-Americans, dear Native Americans, dear immigrants who come here
    seeking a better life, I'm sorry.

Dear everyone who isn't a middle or upper-class white boy, I'm sorry.

I have started life in the top of the ladder while you were born on the first rung.

I say now that I would change places with you in an instant, but if given the opportunity, would I?

Probably not.

Because to be honest, being privileged is awesome. I'm not saying that you and me on different rungs of the ladder is how I want it to stay.

I'm not saying that any part of me has for a moment even liked it that way.

I'm just saying that I f------ love being privileged and I'm not ready to give that away. I love it because I can say 'f------' and not one of you is attributing that to the fact that everyone with my skin color has a dirty mouth.

I love it because I don't have to spend an hour every morning putting on makeup to meet other people's standards.

I love it because I can worry about what kind of food is on my plate instead of whether or not there will be food on my plate.

I love it because when I see a police officer I see someone who's on my side.

To be honest I'm scared of what it would be like if i wasn't on the top rung if the tables were turned and I didn't have my white boy privilege safety blankie to protect me.

If I lived a life lit by what I lack, not what I have, if I lived a life in which when I failed, the world would say, 'Told you so.'

If I lived the life that you live.

When I was born I had a success story already written for me.

You—you were given a pen and no paper.

I've always felt that that's unfair but I've never dared to speak up because I've been too scared.

Well now I realize that there's enough blankie to be shared. Everyone should have the privileges I have.

In fact they should be rights instead.

Everyone's story should be written, so all they have to do is get it read.

Enough said.

No, not enough said.

It is embarrassing that we still live in a world in which we judge another person's character by of the size of their paycheck, the color of their skin, or the type of chromosomes they have.

It is embarrassing that we tell our kids that it is not their personality, but instead those same chromosomes that get to dictate what color clothes they wear and how short they must cut their hair.

But most of all, it is embarrassing that we deny this. That we claim to live in an equal country and an equal world.

We say that women can vote. Well guess what: They can run a country, own a company, and throw a nasty curve ball as well. We just don't give them the chance to.

I know it wasn't us 8th-grade white boys who created this system, but we profit from it every day.

We don't notice these privileges though, because they don't come in the form of
   things we gain, but rather the lack of injustices that we endure.
Because of my gender, I can watch any sport on TV, and feel like that could be me
   one day.
Because of my race I can eat at a fancy restaurant without the wait staff expecting
   me to steal the silverware.
Thanks to my parents' salary I go to a school that brings my dreams closer instead
   of pushing them away.
Dear white boys: I'm not sorry.
I don't care if you think the feminists are taking over the world, that the Black
   Lives Matter movement has gotten a little too strong, because that's bulls---.
I get that change can be scary, but equality shouldn't be.
Hey white boys: It's time to act like a woman. To be strong and make a difference.
   It's time to let go of that fear.
It's time to take that ladder and turn it into a bridge.

REFERENCES

American Civil Liberties Union. (June 2013). The War on Marijuana in Black and White.
   https://www.aclu.org/sites/default/files/field_document/1114413-mj-report-rfs-rel1.
   pdf
Baumgartner, F. R., Epp, D. A., Shoub, K., & Love, B. (2016). Targeting young
   men of color for search and arrest during traffic stops: Evidence from North
   Carolina, 2002–2013, politics, groups, and identities. http://dx.doi.org/10.1080/
   21565503.2016.1160413
Bobo, L. D., & Fox, C. (2003). Race, racism, and discrimination: Bridging problems,
   methods, and theory in social psychological research. *Social Psychology Quarterly,*
   66, 4. Retrieved from http://uncc.worldcat.org/oclc/4583634469&referer=brief_
   results
Bonczar, T. P., & United States. (2003). *Prevalence of imprisonment in the U.S. population,*
   1974–2001. Washington, DC: US Department of Justice, Office of Justice Programs.
   Retrieved from https://www.bjs.gov/content/pub/pdf/piusp01.pdf
Carson, E. A., & Anderson, E. (December 2016). *Prisoners in 2015*. Washington,
   DC: Bureau of Justice Statistics, NCJ 250229.
Casey, P. M., Warren, R. K., Cheesman, F. L., & Elek, J. K. (2012). *Helping courts address*
   implicit bias: Resources for education. Williamsburg, VA: National Center for State
   Courts. http://www.ncsc.org/ibreport
Cole, D. (1999). *No equal justice: Race and class in the American criminal justice system*.
   New York, NY: The New Press.
Comey, J. B. (2015). *Hard truths: Law enforcement and race*. Speech delivered at
   Georgetown University on February 12, 2015.
DMC TA Manual. (2009, July). *Disproportionate minority contact: Technical assistance*
   manual (4th ed.). Washington, DC: US Department of Justice, Office of Justice
   Programs, Office of Juvenile Justice and Delinquency Prevention. http://www.ncjrs.
   gov/html/ojjdp/dmc_ta_manual/

Fabelo, T., Thompson, M. D., Plotkin, M., Carmichael, D., Marchbanks, M. P., & Booth, E. A. (2011). *Breaking schools' rules: A statewide study of how school discipline relates to students' success and juvenile justice involvement.* New York, NY: Council of State Governments Justice Center. http://csgjusticecenter.org/wp-content/uploads/2012/08/ Breaking_Schools_Rules_ Report_Final.pdf

Eitle, T. M. N., & Eitle, D. J. (2004). Inequality, segregation, and the overrepresentation of African Americans in school suspensions. *Sociological Perspectives, 47,* 269–287.

Federal Bureau of Investigation. (2013). Uniform crime reporting program data: Arrests by age, sex, and race, summarized yearly, 2011. ICPSR34581-v1. Ann Arbor, MI: Inter-university Consortium for Political and Social Research, 2013-07-17. http://doi.org/ 10.3886/ICPSR34581.v1

Gannon, M. (2016, February 5). Race is a social construct, scientists argue. *Scientific American.* Retrieved from https://www.scientificamerican.com/article/ race-is-a-social-construct-scientists-argue/

Hartney, C., & Vuong, L. (2009, March). *Created equal: Racial and ethnic disparities in the U.S. criminal justice system.* Washington, DC: The National Council on Crime and Delinquency. http://www.nccdglobal.org/sites/default/files/publication_pdf/created-equal.pdf

Hetey, R. C., & Eberhardt, J. L. (2014). Racial disparities in incarceration increase acceptance of punitive policies, *Psychological Science, 25,* 1949–1950. doi:10.1177/ 0956797614540307

Hockenberry, S. (2016, May). *Juveniles in residential placement, 2013.* The Office of Juvenile Justice and Delinquency Prevention, National Report Series Bulletin NCJ 249507. https://www.ojjdp.gov/pubs/249507.pdf

Hockenberry, S., Puzzanchera, C., & National Center for Juvenile Justice. (2015). *Juvenile court statistics, 2013.* Pittsburgh, PA: National Center for Juvenile Justice.

Huizinga, D., Thornberry, T., Knight, K., & Lovegrove, P. (2007). *Disproportionate minority contact in the juvenile justice system: A study of differential minority arrest/referral to court in three cities.* Washington, DC: US Department of Justice, Document No. 219743.

Humes, K. R., Jones, N. A., & Ramirez, R. R. (March, 2011). *Overview of race and Hispanic origin: 2010. 2010 Census Briefs.* US Department of Commerce. Economics and Statistics Administration. Washington, DC: US Census Bureau. C2010BR-02

Juvenile Justice and Delinquency Prevention Act of 1974, Public Law No. 93-415, 88 Stat. 1109, as amended P. L. 114-22.

Kann, L., Kinchen, S., Shanklin, S. L., Flint, K.H., Kawkins, J., Harris, W. A., . . . Zaza, S. (2014). Youth risk behavior surveillance—United States, 2013. MMWR, 63(4), 1–172.

Kempf-Leonard, K. (2007). Minority youths and juvenile justice: Disproportionate minority contact after nearly 20 years of reform efforts. *Youth Violence and Juvenile Justice, 5*(1), 71–87.

King, E., Gulick, L. M. V., & Avery, D. (2010). The divide between diversity training and diversity education: Integrating best practices. *Journal of Management Education, 34*(6), 891–906. doi:10.1177/1052562909348767

LaFraniere, S., & Lehren, A. W. (2015, October 24). The disproportionate risks of driving while Black. *The New York Times.* https://www.nytimes.com/2015/10/25/us/racial-disparity-traffic-stops-driving-black.html

Leiber, M. J. (2002). Disproportionate minority confinement (DMC) of youth: An analysis of state and federal efforts to address the issue. *Crime & Delinquency, 48*(1), 3–45.

McCarter, S. A. (2009). Legal and extralegal factors affecting minority overrepresentation in Virginia's juvenile justice system: A mixed method study. *Child and Adolescent Social Work Journal, 26*(6), 533–534. doi:10.1007/s10560-009-0185-x

McCarter, S. A. (2011). Disproportionate minority contact in the American juvenile justice system: Where are we after 20 years, a philosophy shift, and three amendments? *Journal of Forensic Social Work, 1*(1), 96–107. doi:10/1080/1936928X.2011.541217

McCarter, S. A., Chinn-Gary, E., Trosch, L. A., Toure, A., Alsaeedi, A., & Harrington, J. (2017). Bringing racial justice to courtroom and community: Race matters for juvenile justice and the Charlotte model. *Washington and Lee Law Review, 73*(2), 641–686.

Nelson, J., & Harris, G. (December, 2008). Report 2008: Looking back, moving forward. *The Race and Social Justice Initiative,* 9–11. https://www.seattle.gov/Documents/Departments/RSJI/Jan20FINALRSJIrept.pdf

Oxford Dictionary. (2017). Definitions of "discrimination." Retrieved from https://en.oxforddictionaries.com/definition/discrimination; "disproportionality/disproportion." Retrieved from https://en.oxforddictionaries.com/definition/disproportion; "parity/disparity." Retrieved from https://en.oxforddictionaries.com/definition/parity; https://en.oxforddictionaries.com/definition/disparity;

Peguero, A. A., & Shekarkhar, Z. (2011). Latino/a student misbehavior and school punishment. *Hispanic Journal of Behavioral Sciences, 33*(1), 54–70.

Piquero, A. (2008). Disproportionate minority contact. *The Future of Children, 18*(2), 59–80.

Piquero, A. R., & Brame, R. W. (2008). Assessing the race-crime and ethnicity-crime relationship in a sample of serious adolescent delinquents. *Crime and Delinquency, 54*(3), 390–422. doi:10.1177/ 0011128707307219.

Pope, C. E., Lovell, R. D., & Hsia, H. M. (2002). *Disproportionate minority confinement: A review of the research literature from 1989 through 2001.* Washington, DC: US Department of Justice, Office of Justice Programs, Office of Juvenile Justice and Delinquency Prevention. Retrieved from https://www.ncjrs.gov/App/Publications/abstract.aspx?ID=198428

Puzzanchera, C. & Hockenberry, S. (2016). National disproportionate minority contact databook. Developed by the National Center for Juvenile Justice for the Office of Juvenile Justice and Delinquency Prevention. Retrieved from http://www.ojjdp.gov/ojstatbb/dmcdb/quickfacts.census.gov

Puzzanchera, C. & Hockenberry, S. (July 2017). Census of Juveniles in Residential Placement. National Center for Juvenile Justice, Office of Juvenile Justice and Delinquency Prevention. Washington, DC: U.S. Census Bureau. https://www.ojjdp.gov/ojstatbb/snapshots/DataSnapshot_CJRP2015.pdf

Spinney, E., Cohen, M., Feyerherm, W., Stephenson, R., Yeide, M., & Hopps, M. (2014). Case studies of nine jurisdictions that reduced disproportionate minority contact in their juvenile justice systems. Development Services Group for the Office of Juvenile Justice and Delinquency Prevention. No. 2009-JF-FX-0103. https://www.ncjrs.gov/pdffiles1/ojjdp/grants/250301.pdf

Substance Abuse and Mental Health Service Administration (SAMHSA). (2014). Results from the 2010 National Survey on Drug Use and Health: Summary of National Findings, NSDUH Series H-41, HHS Publication No. (SMA) 11-4658: 2011. http://www.samhsa.gov/data/nsduh/2k10NSDUH/tabs/Sect1peTabs1to46.htm

Uniform Crime Reporting Data [United States]: Arrests by Age, Sex, and Race [Alternative Title: ASR], 2001–2010.

Uniform Crime Reporting Data [United States]: County-Level Detailed Arrest and Offense Data, 1995–2010.

United States Census Bureau. (2015). *Quickfacts: United States* [Data file]. Retrieved from http://www.census.gov/quickfacts/table/PST045216/00

Vallas, R. (2009). The disproportionality problem: The overrepresentation of Black students in special education and recommendations for reform. *Virginia Journal of Social Policy & the Law, 17*(1), 181–208.

Youth Violence: A Report of the Surgeon General. (2001). Rockville, MD: Office of the Surgeon General. http://www.surgeongeneral.gov/library/ youthviolence/chapter2 / sec12.html#differences.

12

Coming Home

Challenges and Opportunities to Enhance Reentry Success

KATIE ROPES BERRY, MATTHEW GILMOUR,
STEPHANIE C. KENNEDY, AND STEPHEN J. TRIPODI

This chapter explores evidence-based reentry practices for people returning home from jails and prisons.

CASE EXAMPLES

Thomas

Thomas was sent to prison just a few months after his 15th birthday. He had just gotten his learner's permit, and he and his friends were out joyriding in his grandmother's car on a warm summer evening. His friends joked about going to a convenience store so that could "score some cash." Thomas was pretty sure that they were joking, until they stopped for sodas and he watched through the window as they held the cashier at gunpoint, screaming at her to empty the register, before turning and running back toward the car. He stared at them, mouth gaping, speechless, heart pounding in his chest when they jumped back into to the car and began to scream at him to drive. The police came to his house 2 days later and Thomas broke down and told them everything. Thomas had wanted so badly to fit in and seem tough with these friends, but at the trial he couldn't stop sobbing. One of the other boys' lawyers used his tears to paint him as the mastermind of the event—the "bad kid" who stole a car and orchestrated a complex and violent heist.

Thomas spent the next 21 years in a few different prisons. He had a 30-year sentence and hadn't really thought about what would happen when he "got out." Instead, he channeled his energy into prison programs, trying to take advantage of whatever opportunities were available to him. He finished his GED just before his 20th birthday, took several college correspondence courses in psychology and law, and completed a number of vocational programs. He had little contact with his mother, his father had died in prison when he was just a boy, his siblings rarely visited, and he had no real friends on the outside. Thomas did his best to work hard and to help other inmates struggling to cope with life on the inside; he was, by all accounts, a model prisoner. He was diagnosed with a major depressive disorder shortly after his 30th birthday; since that time he accessed mental health services whenever they were available to him. Before his diagnosis, he spent several months battling a deep depression which left him both physically and emotionally drained as well as consumed with thoughts of suicide.

When Thomas received the news from a lawyer that he would be released in just a few months, he felt a strange mixture of happiness, dread, and nothing at all. Where would he go? How would he get by? If he couldn't live life on the outside, what would that say about him as a person?

Sharon

Sharon was 25 years old in 1992 when she was convicted of conspiracy to commit felony possession with intent to distribute a Schedule I substance. It was her third drug charge, and she was subject to a wave of new mandatory minimum sentencing structures which had just been implemented in her state. She was sentenced to 35 years, despite the fact that she had just given birth to her second child weeks before her arrest, her husband was her "co-conspirator," and in the past year alone, he had beaten her so badly she'd been hospitalized four times.

Over the next 26 years, Sharon worked to create a life for herself in prison while maintaining a strong connection to her family on the outside. She was fortunate enough to be serving time in a prison just 20 miles from her hometown and her children, who now had children of their own. Her parents, sisters, children, grandchildren, and friends came to visit as often as possible. Sharon made helping other survivors of domestic violence inside her passion, and she ran an informal weekly support group with the help of a staff social worker. She petitioned the Warden to bring domestic violence classes to the prison and volunteered for every class, program, and research project which came to her facility. She completed the Certified Nursing Assistant program at the prison and hoped to work with women and their children experiencing domestic violence in the community after her release.

Unfortunately, Sharon's physical health had been waning. She was diagnosed with hypertension, hyperlipidemia, and Type II diabetes. She was also diagnosed with hypothyroid several years ago, was referred for surgery, and suffered several long-term adverse effects from both the surgery and her inconsistent access to medication. Although she had planned to be released in 4 years, her caseworker had contacted her just this morning to tell her that her release date had been changed and she would now be going home in 10 short months. Sharon bounced out of her caseworker's office—she couldn't wait to tell her family the good news. She was finally coming home.

SCOPE OF THE PROBLEM

There are over 2.1 million people behind bars in the United States, held in local jails as well as in state and federal prisons (Carson & Anderson, 2016). Men comprise the overwhelming majority of those incarcerated (approximately 93% of the total correctional population is male), although the rate of incarceration for women has increased sharply over the last four decades (Glaze & Herberman, 2013). More than 95% of incarcerated men and women will eventually be released from jail or prison back into their communities, which translates into approximately 630,000 people released each year (Kaeble & Glaze, 2016). The process during which a person transitions from incarceration back to the community is called "reentry," and it includes people released from jail or prison to probation, parole, or community supervision, as well as those released without any continued criminal justice supervision (James, 2015; Jonson & Cullen, 2015).

A successful reentry is almost always defined in terms of recidivism (whether or not a person returns to jail or prison after release), although some scholars suggest that a focus on recidivism obscures important nuances about the reentry process (e.g., Miller, 2014; O'Hear, 2007; Richie, 2001). In this chapter, recidivism is defined as rearrest or reincarceration after release. Unfortunately, recidivism rates for this population are very high based on a number of factors which will be discussed later; the Bureau of Justice Statistics estimates that nearly 77% of people released from jail and prison will recidivate within the first 5 years after release (Durose, Cooper, & Snyder, 2014). Nearly a third of those who recidivate will do so within the first 6 months, and more than half will recidivate within the first year after release. Although these rates are alarmingly high, recidivism is largely driven by high rates of technical violations (e.g., noncriminal violations of the terms of the conditions of release or parole, including missing an appointment or curfew or failing a drug screen) in tandem with the commission of new crimes (Travis, 2007). Estimates suggest that nearly two thirds of recidivism is propelled by technical violations, a practice known "back-end sentencing," which has increased exponentially in the past three decades (Travis & Christiansen, 2006). Regardless, the majority of people released from jail and prison who fail to meet the terms of the conditions of their release or parole or who are rearrested for a new crime will be reincarcerated (Markman, Durose, Rantala, & Tiedt, 2016).

The hundreds of thousands of men and women who are released from jail or prison each year encounter a litany of barriers to success. Both individual-level and structural factors influence the reentry process. Individual-level predictors of recidivism include being male, less than 30 years old, and a member of racial or ethnic minority group (Visher, Debus-Sherrill, & Yahner, 2011; Walters, 2014). Further, much research has evaluated the relationship between individual-level cognitive characteristics, such as criminal thinking, or the thoughts and beliefs associated with antisocial and criminal offending behaviors, and recidivism (e.g., Skeem & Lowenkamp, 2016; Vaske, Gehring, & Lovins, 2017; Walters, 2014). In general, an increased level of criminal thinking translates into increased rates of recidivism, although education may have an unexpected moderating effect on the relationship (with higher levels of education predicting recidivism for people with high levels of criminal thinking). Individual-level protective factors generally include education, vocational skills, employment, marriage, and the quality of family and social support (Kim & Clark, 2013; Seiter & Kadela, 2003). These factors are associated with decreased rates of recidivism in most samples (e.g., Pettus-Davis, Howard, Roberts-Lewis, & Scheyett, 2011; Tripodi, 2010; van der Knapp, Alberda, Oosterveld, & Born, 2012).

Both substance use and mental health status are also significant predictors of reentry success for men and women leaving jail or prison (Duwe & Clark, 2015). Substance use is prevalent among justice-involved men and women, with estimates suggesting that nearly 60% of the men and women in jail or prison were using drugs, alcohol, or both at the time of their arrest or report committing a crime to support their drug or alcohol use (Mumola & Karburg, 2007). Although substance use is, in and of itself, a crime, substance use also contributes to criminal offending behavior and creates a variety of barriers to reentry (Mallik-Kane & Visher, 2008). Substance use issues intersect with housing, employment, and quality of family and social support, and often result in poor outcomes. Although there is strong evidence that providing residential substance use treatment in prison and after release (especially when services are provided in intensive therapeutic communities) decreases recidivism and improves a variety of subjective well-being outcomes (James, 2015; Seiter & Kadela, 2003), few eligible men and women receive these services at any point after making contact with the criminal justice system (Malik-Kane & Visher, 2008; SAMHSA, 2016).

In addition to high rates of substance use, more than half of men (55%–63%) and three quarters of women (73%–75%) in jails and prisons have been officially diagnosed with a mental disorder or meet criteria for a mental disorder using standardized psychiatric measures (James & Glaze, 2006). Of the men and women identified with mental health issues, nearly three quarters also met psychiatric criteria for a substance use disorder (James & Glaze, 2006; Kennedy, Tripodi, Pettus-Davis, & Ayers, 2015; Mumola & Karberg, 2007). The presence of mental health issues is associated with higher rates of homelessness, both in the year prior to incarceration and after release (Roman & Travis, 2006), a history of prior physical and/or sexual abuse, and in-prison behavior infractions (James & Glaze, 2006). These factors muddle the reentry process as mental health issues may also be associated with housing and employment instability and reduced quality of family and social support.

Results are mixed, however, on the exact nature of the relationship between mental health and recidivism. In some samples, people leaving jail or prison who are diagnosed with schizophrenia (or other psychotic disorders), dissociative identity disorder, or a major depressive disorder are more likely to recidivate than people with no such mental health diagnoses (Baillargeon, Binswanger, Penn, Williams, & Murray, 2009; Cloyes, Wong, Latimer, & Abarca, 2010). In other samples, mental health status in general and specific psychiatric diagnoses have not been statistically associated with recidivism (Begun, Early, & Hodge, 2016; Bonta, Law, & Hanson, 1998; Ostermann et al., 2014; Wilson & Wood, 2014).

Regardless of the predictive relationship between mental health status and recidivism, mental health care is a profound need for the majority of people leaving jail or prison and reentering the community.

Structural factors also complicate the reentry process and restrict opportunity and choice for many people leaving jail or prison. These factors include deficiencies in the housing market, issues with employment, and the collateral consequences of criminal justice sentencing. In sum, many people leaving jail or prison come home to disadvantaged neighborhoods with higher than average rates of poverty, unemployment, and single-parent households, and lower than average rates of homeownership and educational achievement (Petersilia, 2001; Roman & Travis, 2006; Seiter & Kadela, 2003; Wang, Mears, & Bales, 2010; Wehrman, 2010). These structural factors have been associated with increased rates of technical violations and lower rates of employment when outcomes are compared to people released to more affluent neighborhoods (Morenhoff & Harding, 2011).

Finding, securing, and maintaining stable housing is one of the most important aspects of and challenges to a successful reentry. Unfortunately, securing stable housing is fraught with obstacles, including the overall scarcity of affordable, accessible, and appropriate housing and individual difficulty obtaining deposits and clearing a credit check (Chin, 2017). The range of estimates from housing data suggest that approximately half of the men and women who leave jail or prison will live with family, friends, or significant others, around 10% end up homeless, and the remaining population will end up in a halfway house or other transitional housing program (Roman & Travis, 2006). There are many factors which prevent people leaving jail or prison from living with family members, including the conditions of release or parole, as well as space availability and interpersonal dynamics. For many people, this begins a complex search for approved housing with private landlords or companies, halfway houses, transitional housing services, or emergency sheltering systems while they apply for (and are placed on long waiting lists) federal public housing benefits (Roman & Travis, 2006). Although public housing is a good resource for some people who leave jail or prison, the local and state interpretation of many federal housing policies often excludes many low-income people with criminal records, regardless of the category of charge (felony versus misdemeanor) or crime type and disposition (Miller, 2014). These often faulty, narrow interpretations of (in)eligibility contribute to housing instability and, ultimately, to homelessness (Carey, 2004).

Employment is another critical factor for reentry success, due to the strong, protective effect of employment on recidivism (meaning that stable employment is associated with decreased recidivism; Tripodi, 2010; Tripodi et al., 2010; Visher et al., 2011). Although two thirds of people are employed when they are arrested and incarcerated, those jobs are rarely waiting for them upon release (Visher et al., 2011). This reality is complicated by the fact that people leaving jail or prison, on average, have less education, experience, and job skills when compared to people who have never been incarcerated, making them less attractive candidates on the job market (Tripodi et al., 2010). Additionally, it is more difficult to secure employment with a potentially long gap in work history and without valid identification (Tripodi, 2010).

Further, many people leaving jail or prison also face employment discrimination or are prohibited from working in a variety of industries with a criminal record (Petersilia, 2001; Pinard, 2010; Visher et al., 2011). To reduce stigma and promote employment, some states have recently begun to enact "Ban the Box" policies to prevent applicants from being forced to disclose a criminal record prior to interview (Agan & Starr, 2016). However, as a criminal background check is often required during the final hiring process, the future impact of such policy changes is still unclear. Unemployment rates among this population are exceedingly high, with estimates suggesting that approximately 60% of people leaving jail or prison will be unemployed 1 year after release (Petersilia, 2000). Of those who are working 1 year post release, they will earn less on average than workers with comparable work histories who have never been incarcerated (Visher et al., 2011).

As noted earlier, the quality of family and social support is a powerful predictor of recidivism for people leaving jail or prison (Pettus-Davis et al., 2011; Tripodi, 2010; van der Knapp et al., 2012). Social support also appears to have a strong cyclical relationship with employment stability. That is, increased quality of family and social support helps people leaving jail or prison to find and maintain employment, and workers succeed in their jobs based on the social support they receive from family, friends, neighbors, religious contacts, and coworkers (Pettus-Davis et al., 2017; Visher et al., 2011). In addition, these positive family and social supports are also associated with decreased substance use after release, increased ability to meet the terms of probation or parole, and lower rates of recidivism (Naser & La Vigne, 2006; Skeem, Louden, Manchak, Vidal, & Haddad, 2009).

Finally, in addition to housing and employment barriers, many people leaving jail or prison suffer a variety of collateral consequences to their incarceration, including being stripped of their civil and political rights (e.g., voting in political elections, serving on a jury, and holding political office) as well as their socioeconomic rights to retain or reclaim child custody and receive many public benefits, including federal welfare or federal student loans and education grants (Petersilia, 2001; Pinard, 2010). Finally, although not all incarcerated men and women come from and release back to impoverished communities, many of them will (Roman & Travis, 2006). Scarce resources, lack of public transportation, and decentralized services problematize reentry as people seek to find housing and employment and reconnect with their families (Petersilia, 2001; Taxman, 2005; Visher, Debus-Sherrill, & Yahner, 2011; Wehrman, 2010). This "concentrated disadvantage" (Wehrman, 2010, p. 538) tends to be disproportionately present in poor Black neighborhoods and other poor communities of color, which suffer from oversurveillance and hostile relationships between community members and law enforcement, in addition to reduced housing and employment opportunities. All of these factors result in lower rates of successful reentry for the men and women who return to these communities (Miller, 2014).

RISK–NEED–RESPONSIVITY MODEL

The Risk–Need–Responsivity (RNR) model provides the foundation for comprehensive risk/needs assessment and referral to appropriate intervention for justice-involved people, including people leaving jail or prison (Andrews, Bonta, & Hoge, 1990; Austin, 2003; Lowenkamp, Latessa, & Holsinger, 2006). The risk principle suggests that program intensity should match the risk level of a prisoner; that is, high-risk individuals should receive the most intensive programs and low-risk individuals the least intensive programs (or no program at all). The needs principle examines the individual-level factors related to criminal offending behavior, including criminal thinking, substance use and mental health, education, housing, and employment (Andrews, Bonta, & Wormith, 2011). Finally, the responsivity principle considers an individual's skills and abilities when appropriate interventions are identified to ensure a good fit (Bonta & Andrews, 2007).

Although lawmakers and policymakers, and individuals working within the criminal justice system understand the powerful influence of both individual-level and structural factors on reentry success, few cohesive reentry programs exist. A barrier to widely implementing effective reentry practices and programs is that the scientific literature is inconclusive about what definitively "works" to reduce recidivism for people leaving jail or prison (James, 2015; Jonson & Cullen, 2015). Evidence-based reentry practices take place both during incarceration and after an individual has been released to his or her community, although the vast majority of current evidence-based programming occurs during incarceration (e.g., substance use and mental health treatment and education programs; James, 2015). As people leaving jail or prison transition back into their communities, housing and employment programs may be available to them. In a review of the effectiveness of specific interventions, James (2015) identified few rigorous studies proving evidence of effectiveness of existing programs. Taken together, however, it appears that intensive programs provided to high-risk offenders within the first year after release were generally effective. In another review, Ndrecka (2014) noted that reentry programs which occurred in multiple phases (e.g., beginning in prison and continuing in the community), offered multiple services tailored to the needs of each individual, and were at least 13 weeks in length were more successful than programs without these characteristics.

This chapter presents four categories of reentry practices (and associated empirically supported programs) in detail, all of which meet the aforementioned criteria and have some level of empirical evidence to suggest their effectiveness for men and women leaving jail or prison. These include coordinated case management, coordinated mental health treatment services, transitional housing plus supportive services, and in-prison substance use treatment. The chapter then shifts to highlight challenges to evidence-based reentry and highlights directions for future research and practice to improve outcomes for the hundreds of thousands of men and women leaving jails and prisons every year. The case examples are revisited at the end of the chapter to guide application.

Coordinated Case Management

The creation of a continuum of care to provide targeted in-prison services in tandem with in-prison and community-based case management and service referrals represents the most holistic and comprehensive reentry programs. Many such programs exist in jails and prisons across the country, although very few have been rigorously evaluated. In general, coordinated case management programs have two phases. Phase one typically involves a risk/needs assessment and referral to a variety of existing in-prison services (e.g., cognitive-behavioral programs, in-prison substance use treatment, and in-prison mental health services). During phase one, inmates are connected to a Reentry Coordinator who helps to identify and link the inmate to community services and serves as a liaison with a probation or parole office, or a community-based reentry team. In phase two, supportive services and targeted referrals are typically provided to the offender, helping connect the person with community supports to enhance success and reduce or eliminate recidivism. Although a few coordinated case management programs have a limited evidence base suggesting modest effectiveness (e.g., San Diego SB 618 program; Mulmat, Burke, Doroski, Howard, & Correia, 2009; Mulmat et al., 2010, 2012), the Allegheny County, PA Jail-Based Reentry Specialist Program (Willison, Bieler, & Kim, 2014) is highlighted next because of the comprehensiveness of the program and the rigor of the existing evidence.

Phase one of the Allegheny County, PA Jail-Based Reentry Specialist Program begins with the identification of eligible jail inmates via a comprehensive risk/needs assessment. Eligible inmates are then provided with at least 5 months of in-jail programming and services. A team of five (including a community-based probation officer) coordinate services and liaise with the inmate in a "Reentry Pod"—a dedicated space to increase access reentry services and program staff and improve communication and planning. In-jail services include a variety of services that span individual-level and structural factors: criminal thinking, substance use and mental health, family and social support, housing, and employment. Specifically, program participants receive an empirically supported cognitive-behavioral intervention called "Thinking for a Change" to decrease criminal thinking attitudes and promote critical thinking. Wrap-around substance use services are provided, including abuse prevention, gender-responsive treatment, and relapse prevention. Healthy family functioning and positive relationships are promoted through parenting and relationship classes, as well as increased visitation with participants' children.

A family support specialist liaises between the inmate and his or her family to prepare everyone for release. Housing opportunities are enhanced though community-based supportive housing services when necessary. And finally, participants receive educational and apprenticeship services, which began in jail and continue in the community after release, and intensive employment services, including job readiness and preparation for a job search and improving occupational balance (or helping connect inmates to satisfying and sustaining work rather than encouraging them to "just find a job"). Once the inmate is released, he or she remains connected with the program probation officer. Risk/needs assessments are continuously implemented and modified to ensure success, and the program probation officer coordinates with the offender's probation or parole officer and helps ensure compliance with the terms of release (Willison et al., 2014).

A rigorous evaluation supported the program's feasibility and suggested that program participants had significantly lower rates of rearrest in the follow-up period (10% rearrest rate) when compared to members of a matched, weighted comparison group (34% rearrest rate; Willison et al., 2014). Further, for those members of the sample who were arrested, program participation was associated with spending more days in the community prior to rearrest. The program is currently rated as effective, with more evaluations necessary to demonstrate efficacy.

Coordinated Mental Health Treatment Services

Although evidence suggests that mental health treatment has a protective effect on recidivism for people leaving jail or prison who have been diagnosed with a mental disorder (Duwe & Clark, 2015), few empirically supported programs exist (James, 2015). The Mental Health Services Continuum Program (MHSCP) is one such program with limited evidence suggesting short-term decreases in recidivism for people leaving custody who require ongoing mental health treatment. The MHSCP is a two-phase program that begins in prison and continues in the community after release. The program works collaboratively between in-prison social work or case management services, parole officers, and outpatient clinics (Farabee, Bennett, Garcia, Warda, & Yang, 2006). The first phase of the program occurs in prison. During this phase, offenders are enrolled in the Transitional Case Management Program and they receive a face-to-face risk/needs assessment within 90 days of their parole. Information is shared with the person's parole officer, and an appointment is made for the offender to receive treatment at a Parole Outpatient Clinic within a week of release. During phase two of the program, the offender receives ongoing no-cost mental health services at the clinic on a schedule determined by both the in-prison risk/needs assessment and the initial clinical interview.

The primary goal of MHSCP is to reduce recidivism for people with mental health diagnoses released from jail or prison to parole with a secondary goal of protecting public safety. An evaluation of outcomes for people who participated in the program, received a prerelease risk/needs assessment and referrals, or who had one or more contacts with the Parole Outpatient Clinic suggested significant decreases in recidivism when compared to matched controls. Farabee et al. (2006) note that although completion of the program increased both mental health treatment access and the number of days before recidivism, at 1 year postrelease rates of recidivism were no different when compared to members of a control group. Farabee et al. (2006) also highlight challenges to program implementation in their evaluation. Namely, communications breakdowns between in-prison and outpatient staff members and a surplus of eligible inmates who, due to time and caseload constraints, could not be assessed prior to their release. Both of these factors hampered implementation and limited the reach of the program. The program is currently rated as promising.

Transitional Housing Plus Supportive Services

Halfway houses are the most prevalent form of reentry housing support; they provide transitional living to people leaving jail or prison as they search for employment and secure permanent living arrangements. Evidence suggests that halfway houses are a good fit for high-risk men and women leaving jail or prison and contribute to significantly decreased rates of recidivism when compared to other high-risk offenders in alternative living situations (James, 2015; Latessa & Lowenkamp, 2005; Lowenkamp & Latessa, 2002). In nearly every case, halfway house services had a negative effect on low-risk offenders and have been associated with increased recidivism for this group.

Ohio's halfway house programs provide a comprehensive model of supportive housing and have a strong, emerging evidence base to suggest reduced recidivism for moderate- and high-risk offenders (Lowenkamp, 2004; Lowenkamp & Latessa, 2002, 2005). Although service provision varies by specific facility location, all halfway house programs in the state offer some measure of additional services beyond housing and curfew-keeping. Ninety-five percent offer substance use treatment, more than 80% offer employment services, and nearly two thirds offer some form of educational support and services.

An analysis of data from 22 halfway house facilities across the state found that participation in the halfway house programs was associated with significant decreases in recidivism for moderate- and high-risk offenders (Lowenkamp & Latessa, 2002, 2005). When women were analyzed as a stand-alone group, the trend held: Moderate- and high-risk female offenders in halfway house programs had lower rates of recidivism when compared to low-risk female offenders, for whom rates of recidivism actually increased (Lovins, Loewenkamp, Latessa, & Smith, 2007). Further, fidelity to the model strongly affected outcomes, with those halfway houses who consistently provided the additional supportive substance use, employment, and educational services as intended demonstrating the lowest pooled rates of recidivism for participants (Lowenkamp & Latessa, 2005). The initial evaluations were used to improve model fidelity (e.g., Andrew & Janes, 2006), highlighting the iterative and complementary cycle of program implementation and evaluation to improve outcomes overall. This program is currently rated as effective.

In-Prison Substance Use Treatment

As noted earlier, substance use is a prevalent issue for people who make contact with the criminal justice system, and substance use is strongly associated with recidivism after release (Mallik-Kane & Visher, 2008). The evidence suggests a strong association between high intensity, residential substance use treatment (during custody and/or after release) and improved outcomes for people with substance use issues leaving jail or prison (James, 2015; Seiter & Kadela, 2003). Seeking Safety (Najavits, 2002) is a gender-responsive and trauma-informed in-prison substance use treatment program designed especially for women. Seeking safety is a manualized intervention that contains 25 sessions covering four domains: interpersonal, cognitive, behavioral, and case management (Najavits, 2002). The program is adaptable to both group and individual settings, and the sessions are designed to stand alone, allowing group or individual counselors to tailor the topics to the immediate needs of the client(s).

Seeking Safety is grounded in cognitive-behavioral techniques, present-focused, and specifically addresses the link between posttraumatic stress and substance misuse. When implemented within the prison milieu, program participants reported significant pre- to postintervention decreases in mental health symptoms and behavioral infractions, as well as statistically significant increases in coping and self-reported wellness (Messina, Grella, Cartier, & Torres, 2010; Wolff, Frueh, Shi, & Schumann, 2012; Zlotnick, Johnson, & Najavits, 2009). Long-term recidivism analyses also indicate clinically meaningful, although not statistically significant decreases in recidivism after release for intervention completers (Saxena, Messina, & Grella, 2014; Zlotnick et al., 2009). This program is currently rated as promising.

CRIMINAL JUSTICE POLICY: ISSUES AND IMPLICATIONS

The financial costs associated with mass incarceration have profoundly damaged state budgets, in most cases diverting resources away from education and health care (Leachman, Chettiar, & Geare, 2012). Consequently, criminal justice reform currently has strong bipartisan support, and many states have begun to enact new laws and policies to release people from jail or prison and provide services to help them succeed in the community. To this end, in 2007, the Second Chance Act Demonstration Project (SCA), a federal funding opportunity, was passed to enhance reentry program development, implementation, and evaluation (Henry, 2009).

A decade later, more than 600 programs have been funded and are in some phase of delivery and evaluation (James, 2015).

The challenges to sustaining political support for the SCA in specific and reentry program development in general are multifaceted (O'Hear, 2007). In general, a political demand for results is incongruent with the nascent stages of development of most existing reentry interventions (James, 2015). As described earlier, the lack of additional resources to support the implementation and evaluation of new interventions hampers results and confounds outcomes (Leachman et al., 2012). Further, few empirically supported reentry programs exist, and many are tailored specifically to just one subset of the highly heterogeneous population of men and women leaving jails or prisons across the county (James, 2015; Jonson & Cullen, 2015). When effective or promising programs are implemented in the field, the resources and technical skills needed to conduct a rigorous evaluation are often lacking, which creates a translational gap in our understanding of whether these programs are truly effective (Mears & Cochran, 2014).

Although many jails and prisons attempt to provide transitional services to the men and women they release every day, there is no standard application of services and no "best practices" have been formulated (Roman & Travis, 2006). State and municipal policies, as well as the depth of resources in the local community, create the context within which reentry is managed. Finally, the thousands of men and women who are released from jails or prisons every day face tremendous barriers to success. Although empirically supported interventions are a step in the right direction to helping these individuals succeed in the community, it is unlikely that one practice or program will be able to create sustainable change. A call for the creation of comprehensive, wrap-around services tailored to individual needs has been made in the literature, and the evidence-based practices and programs highlighted in this chapter support this movement (Ndrecka, 2014; O'Hear, 2007).

TRENDS AND FUTURE DIRECTIONS

Although a variety of challenges to improving the reentry process exist, there is evidence of exciting changes on the horizon. The movement for criminal justice reform is gaining traction, and stakeholders at all levels of the criminal justice system are beginning to prioritize building evidence for effective reentry practices. One promising development is the 5 Key Reentry model, an overarching flexible model for practice, which provides a blueprint for jails, prisons, and community-based organizations to begin the process of tailoring comprehensive reentry programs to both the local community context and the needs of the individual (Veeh, Renn, & Pettus-Davis, 2017). The 5 Key Reentry model represents a synthesis of the aspects of the most promising empirically supported reentry programs into one manual. This model is not intended to be a "one-size-fits-all" program, but rather a platform by which a program can be tailored to the needs of individuals, starting with the five most essential and common elements of reentry success: (1) healthy thinking patterns, (2) occupational balance, (3) positive coping strategies, (4) positive social activities, and (5) positive social relationships. In this model, practitioners and offenders work together collaboratively and actively, creating a plan for success that resonates with the needs and goals of each individual. It is our hope that evidence-based reentry practices will continue to be implemented and evaluated in a variety of correctional settings and that new programs will be developed to more effectively meet the needs of the hundreds of thousands of men and women who leave jails and prisons every year and return home.

Thomas

A few days after the lawyer visited with news of Thomas's early release from prison, the reality of the message was still sinking in for Thomas. Thomas hadn't even known that someone was working on his case, but apparently a team of lawyers had been working for years to change the sentencing guidelines for people like him who had been sentenced as minors to extremely long sentences. Charles, the prison's new Reentry Coordinator, met with Thomas to explain the change in the law and calculate his new time sheet. They had 5 months and 8 days to help create a solid reentry plan to ensure success after release. Charles said they had a lot of work to do together, but that some exciting new practices and programs were being implemented in the prison based on this change in the law. Twenty-four men, all convicted as juveniles and serving long sentences, would be released within the next year. Therefore, the prison was experimenting with a comprehensive new reentry practice to see if they could improve outcomes. Charles told Thomas that all 24 men would move into one cellblock, called a "Reentry Pod," based on a promising reentry program run out of a large county jail in Pennsylvania. In the Pod, a team of support staff would provide individualized services, including individual sessions with the social worker, support groups to help problem-solve common issues after release, and even a weekly meeting with the parole officer assigned to work with all of them after release. Charles assures Thomas that they will do everything they can to help him feel capable and competent and that Thomas will leave prison with a solid plan for success. Thomas feels hopeful for the first time in years.

Charles and Thomas immediately begin their work by completing a series of standardized instruments together to assess Thomas's risks and needs, and identify key areas for intervention. Thomas is categorized as high-risk because he has no family or social support in the community, a history of serious mental health issues, and he has neither lived independently nor held a job in the community. Based on these factors, Charles suggests that they identify a halfway house that offers supportive employment services and connect him with a local outpatient mental health clinic.

The following day, Thomas and the others move into the Reentry Pod, meet the team, and begin the process of familiarizing themselves with the depth and breadth of what they will need to do before going home. Over the next few months, Charles helps Thomas and the others apply for Medicaid and gathers the forms to request Social Security cards and birth certificates so that everyone can apply for state identification cards or driver's licenses after release. Charles and Thomas meet weekly to connect Thomas to community-based mental health services, housing, employment, and transportation. Charles also facilitates a weekly support group for the men in the Pod to help them connect to each other and talk through their fears about release. Thomas develops a strong friendship with two of the men in the Pod, and they bond over their shared experiences.

Charles finds a halfway house with an innovative job readiness and training program that includes a weekly support group for residents with mental health issues. The halfway house is on a bus line and is just a few miles from the clinic and his parole officer's office. Thomas is thrilled to learn that one of his friends in the Pod will also be going to the same halfway house program. His confidence is bolstered knowing that he will have support and connection on the outside. Charles also connects Thomas and a few other men to a community-based agency that provides culinary training and employment for formerly incarcerated men and women. For the first time, Thomas begins to imagine what his life will feel like and he is excited about building a community and a life for himself.

Six months after his release, Thomas is still in touch with Charles and has become an informal point of community contact for many men released through the program. He tells Charles that he has found a surprising amount of pleasure in baking and is now the manager of the "cupcakes and confections" food truck at work. He also tells Charles that he and a friend from the Pod have a plan to rent an apartment together, once they save enough for the deposits. Charles contacts the halfway house with a new resource he learned about at a professional development conference that provides deposit and utilities assistance for eligible parolees securing an independent lease. Charles feels sure Thomas will qualify.

Sharon

Sharon met with her caseworker, Liz, several times in the week following the news of her release. Although the prison didn't have a formal reentry program, Liz was committed to helping women succeed after release and, over the years, had developed a wealth of strong community connections. Liz had been reading about evidence-based reentry practices and suggested that she and Sharon begin by completing a comprehensive risk/needs assessment together. Using the assessment results, Sharon was classified as low-risk; her physical health concerns, history of substance use, and the length of her time served were her primary risk factors. Her strengths included vocational training, family and social support, and the availability stable housing with her oldest daughter. Liz connected Sharon with a new community-based wraparound reentry program modeled on the empirically supported Mental Health Services Continuum Program. The local program, however, had recently received a grant to extend services to men and women leaving prison with both chronic mental health and physical health issues. The program provided all participants with Medicare and Medicaid benefits applications, appointment services, and transportation. After their meeting, Liz sent Sharon's application, and she was approved for entrance into the program beginning at her release date. By the time Liz notified Sharon of her approval, the program emailed to notify that they had already scheduled Sharon for a comprehensive physical exam 4 days after her release.

Liz then began to work with the judge on Sharon's case and the district social worker to remove the provision for Sharon to release to a halfway house. Liz cited several empirical articles which demonstrated that halfway house programs had a harmful effect on low-risk offenders like Sharon. She further detailed the commitment of Sharon's family, the deep bond the family has created and sustained over the past two-plus decades, and highlighted Sharon's family as having both the practical and emotional capacity to help her succeed.

After reviewing the results of the assessment, Liz was surprised to see that Sharon met criteria for posttraumatic stress disorder (PTSD) in addition to reporting problematic substance use prior to her incarceration. In all of their meetings, Sharon had never mentioned experiencing any of the characteristic symptoms of PTSD, although Liz knew her history. Liz met with Sharon to discuss the assessment and asked Sharon why she never mentioned the flashbacks, intrusive memories, and physical re-experiencing of her abuse. Sharon smiled and said that she assumed "those issues" were simply life. Liz then told her about Seeking Safety, a new empirically supported, gender-responsive, and trauma-informed program, which was scheduled to come to the prison in the upcoming months. Sharon was excited to be eligible for participation, and she hoped that the group might help her heal.

In the months leading up to her release, Sharon completed the Seeking Safety group curriculum and reported feeling calmer and having fewer PTSD symptoms. Her participation in the group also ignited her passion for helping other women move forward from abuse and trauma. Liz connected Sharon to a community-based family violence advocacy group looking to hire someone with lived experience of the consequences of family violence to manage community education and advocacy campaigns. Although they were hesitant at first to even consider hiring someone with a felony record, Liz persuaded the Executive Director and Community Outreach coordinator to come to the prison and interview Sharon. After the interview, Sharon felt like the position was tailor-made for her, and she and her family were hopeful that the context of her incarceration would be considered an asset, rather than a liability. A few days after the interview the Executive Director called to offer Sharon the job. They would write in a 6-month probationary period to the offer letter, but salary and benefits would begin immediately. Sharon was overjoyed and she hugged Liz tightly, thanking her for always believing that good things could and would happen.

A year after her release, Liz received a letter from Sharon filled with smiling family pictures and drawings made by her grandkids. Sharon wrote that she was still working with the family violence agency and had recently developed a 12-week group curriculum for use with middle and high school girls at risk for domestic violence. She said that she felt like she was finally making a difference for her family and for the women and girls in her community.

WEB-BASED RESOURCES

Crimesolutions.gov: A complete registry of programs and practices pertaining to adult and juvenile justice populations that have been evaluated by the number and rigor of studies on specific and categories of interventions: https://www.crimesolutions.gov/Programs.aspx

The National Inventory of the Collateral Consequences of Conviction Exit Notice (Berson, 2012) is an interactive database that allows users to search sanctions and restrictions by state: http://www.nij.gov/journals/272/pages/collateral-consequences-database.aspx

The National Reentry Resource Center (NRRC) is an online clearinghouse of information regarding reentry, including summaries of existing research, available reentry resources and programs, and evaluation summaries of existing reentry programs: https://csgjusticecenter.org/nrrc

Smart Decarceration Initiative (SDI): The Smart Decarceration Initiative (SDI) is a collaboration of social work scholars and other professionals that aim to improve practices and policies associated with the adult criminal justice system: https://csd.wustl.edu/ourwork/socialjustice/decarceration/pages/default.aspx

The What Works in Reentry Clearinghouse provides information about programs and practices and the empirical evidence substantiating their efficacy: https://whatworks.csgjusticecenter.org

REFERENCES

Agan, A. Y., & Starr, S. B. (2016). Ban the box, criminal records, and statistical discrimination: A field experiment. *University of Michigan Law & Economics Research Paper, 16-012.*

Andrews, D. A., Bonta, J., & Hoge, R. D. (1990). Classification for effective rehabilitation: Rediscovering psychology. *Criminal Justice and Behavior, 17,* 19–52.

Andrews, D. A., Bonta, J., & Wormith, J. S. (2011). The risk-need-responsivity (RNR) model: Does adding the good lives model contribute to effective crime prevention? *Criminal Justice and Behavior, 38,* 735–755.

Andrews, S., & Janes, L. (2006). Ohio's evidence-based approach to community sanctions and supervision. *Topics in Community Corrections: Effectively Managing Violations and Revocations, Annual Issue.* Washington, DC: US Department of Justice, National Institute of Corrections.

Austin, J. (2003). Findings in prison classification and risk assessment. *National Institute of Corrections. US Department of Justice, Federal Bureau of Prisons, 25,* 2–3.

Baillargeon, J., Binswanger, I. A., Penn, J. V., Williams, B. A., & Murray, O. J. (2009). Psychiatric disorders and repeat incarcerations: The revolving prison door. *American Journal of Psychiatry, 166,* 103–109.

Begun, A. L., Early, T. J., & Hodge, A. (2016). Mental health and substance abuse service engagement by men and women during community reentry following incarceration. *Administration and Policy in Mental Health and Mental Health Services Research, 43,* 207.

Berson, S. B. (2013). Beyond the sentence-understanding collateral consequences. *National Institute of Justice Journal, 272,* 25–28.

Bonta, J., & Andrews, D. A. (2007). Risk-need-responsivity model for offender assessment and rehabilitation. *Rehabilitation, 6,* 1–22.

Bonta, J., Law, M., & Hanson, K. (1998). The prediction of criminal and violent recidivism among mentally disordered offenders: A meta-analysis. *Psychological Bulletin, 123*(2), 123.

Carey, C. A. (2004). No second chance: People with criminal records denied access to public housing. *University of Toledo Law Review, 36,* 545–594.

Carson, E. A., & Anderson, E. (2016). *Prisoners in 2015* (NCJ 250229). Washington, DC: Bureau of Justice Statistics.

Chin, G. (2017). Collateral consequences of criminal conviction. In E. Luna (Ed.), *Academy for Justice: A Report on Scholarship and Criminal Justice Reform*. https://papers.ssrn.com/sol3/papers.cfm?abstract_id=2948025

Cloyes, K. G., Wong, B., Latimer, S., & Abarca, J. (2010). Time to prison return for offenders with serious mental illness released from prison: A survival analysis. *Criminal Justice and Behavior, 37*, 175–187.

Durose, M., Cooper, A., & Snyder, H. (2014). Recidivism of prisoners released in 30 states in 2005: Patterns from 2005 to 2010 (NCJ 244205). Washington DC: Bureau of Justice Statistics.

Duwe, G., & Clark, V. (2015). *Moving on: An outcome evaluation of a gender-responsive, cognitive-behavioral program for female offenders*. St. Paul, MN: Minnesota Department of Corrections.

Farabee, D., Bennett, D., Garcia, D., Warda, U., & Yang, J. (2006). Final report on the Mental Health Services Continuum Program of the California Department of Corrections and Rehabilitation—Parole Division. *UCLA Integrated Substance Abuse Program, Neuropsychiatric Institute, 30*, 202.

Glaze, L. E., & Herberman, E. J. (2013). *Correctional populations in the United States, 2012* (NCJ 243936). Washington, DC: Bureau of Justice Statistics.

Henry, J. S. (2009). The Second Chance Act of 2007. *Criminal Law Bulletin, 45*, 3–19.

James, N. (2015). *Offender reentry: Correctional statistics, reintegration into the community, and recidivism*. Congressional Research Service, Library of Congress. Retrieved from https://fas.org/sgp/crs/misc/RL34287.pdf

James, D. J., & Glaze, L. E. (2006). *Mental health problems of prison and jail inmates* (NCJ 213600). Washington, DC: Bureau of Justice Statistics.

Jonson, C. L., & Cullen, F. T. (2015). Prisoner reentry programs. *Crime and Justice, 44*, 517–575.

Kaeble, D., & Glaze, L. (2016). *Correctional populations in the United States, 2015* (NCJ 250374) Washington, DC: Bureau of Justice Statistics.

Kennedy, S. C., Tripodi, S. J., Pettus-Davis, C., & Ayers, J. (2015). Examining dose-response relationships between childhood victimization, depression, symptoms of psychosis, and substance misuse for incarcerated women. *Women & Criminal Justice*. Advance online publication. doi:10.1080/08974454.2015.1023486

Kim, R. H. & Clark, D. (2013). The effect of prison-based college education programs on recidivism: Propensity score matching approach. *Journal of Criminal Justice, 41*, 196–204.

Latessa, E. J., & Lowenkamp, C. (2005). What works in reducing recidivism. *University of St. Thomas Law Journal, 3*, 521.

Leachman, M., Chettiar, I. M., & Geare, B. (2012). Improving budget analysis of state criminal justice reforms: A strategy for better outcomes and saving money. Retrieved from https://www.aclu.org/other/improving-budget-analysis-state-criminal-justice-reforms-strategy-better-outcomes-and-saving

Lowenkamp, C. T. (2004). Correctional program integrity and treatment effectiveness: A multi-site, program-level analysis. *Dissertation Abstracts International: Section A: Humanities and Social Sciences, 65*(2), 706–A.

Lowenkamp, C., & Latessa, E. (2002). *Evaluation of Ohio's community-based correctional facilities and halfway house programs*. Cincinnati, OH: University of Cincinnati, Center for Criminal Justice Research.

Lowenkamp, C. T., & Latessa, E. J. (2005). Increasing the effectiveness of correctional programming through the risk principle: Identifying offenders for residential placement. *Criminology & Public Policy, 4,* 263–290.

Lowenkamp, C. T., Latessa, E. J., & Holsinger, A. M. (2006). The risk principle in action: What have we learned from 13,676 offenders and 97 correctional programs?" *Crime & Delinquency, 52*(1), 77–93.

Lovins, L., Lowenkamp, C., Latessa, E., & Smith, P. (2007). Application of the risk principle to female offenders. *Journal of Contemporary Criminal Justice, 23,* 383–398.

Mallik-Kane, K., & Visher, C. A. (2008). *Health and prisoner reentry: How physical, mental, and substance abuse conditions shape the process of reintegration* (p. 82). Washington, DC: Urban Institute Justice Policy Center.

Markman, J. A., Durose, M. R., Rantala, R. R., & Tiedt, A. D. (2016). *Recidivism of offenders placed on federal community supervision in 2005: Patterns from 2005 to 2010* (NCJ249734). Washington, DC: Bureau of Justice Statistics.

Mears, D. P., & Cochran, J. C. (2014). *Prisoner reentry in the era of mass incarceration.* Thousand Oaks, CA: Sage.

Messina, N., Grella, C. E., Cartier, J., & Torres, S. (2010). A randomized experimental study of gender-responsive substance abuse treatment for women in prison. *Journal of Substance Abuse Treatment, 38,* 97–107. doi: http://dx.doi.org/10.1016/j.jsat.2009.09.004

Miller, R. J. (2014). Devolving the carceral state: Race, prisoner reentry, and the micropolitics of urban poverty management. *Punishment & Society, 16,* 305–335.

Morenoff, J. D., & Harding, D. J. (2011). *Final technical report: Neighborhoods, recidivism, and employment among returning prisoners.* Ann Arbor, MI: Institute for Social Research, University of Michigan.

Mulmat, D. H., Burke, C., Doroski, E., Howard, L., & Correia, D. (2009). *Improving reentry for ex-offenders in San Diego County: SB 618 second annual evaluation report.* San Diego, CA: San Diego Association of Governments.

Mulmat, D. H., Doroski, E., Howard, L., Correia, D., Keaton, S., Rohanna, K., & Burke, C. (2010). *Improving reentry for ex-offenders in San Diego County: SB 618 third annual evaluation report.* San Diego, CA: San Diego Association of Governments.

Mulmat, D. H., Doroski, E., Howard, L., Rohanna, K., & Burke, C. (2012). *Improving reentry for ex-offenders in San Diego County: SB 618 final evaluation report.* San Diego, CA: San Diego Association of Governments.

Mumola, C. J., & Karberg, J. C. (2007). *Drug use and dependence, state and federal prisoners, 2004* (NCJ 213530). Washington, DC: Bureau of Justice Statistics.

Najavits, L. M. (2002). *Seeking safety, a treatment manual for PTSD and substance abuse.* New York, NY: Guilford.

Naser, R. L., & La Vigne, N. G. (2006). Family support in the prisoner reentry process: Expectations and realities. *Journal of Offender Rehabilitation, 43,* 93–206.

National Institute of Corrections. (2014). Gender-responsive policy and practice (Library ID 028130). Retrieved from http://nicic.gov/library/028130

Ndrecka, M. (2014). The impact of reentry programs on recidivism: A meta-analysis (Doctoral dissertation, University of Cincinnati), no. 3639194.

O'Hear, M. M. (2007). The Second Chance Act and the future of reentry reform. *Federal Sentencing Reporter, 20,* 75–83.

Ostermann, M., & Matejkowski, J. (2014). Exploring the intersection of mental health and release status with recidivism. *Justice Quarterly, 31,* 746–766.

Petersilia, J. (2000). When prisoners return to communities: Political, economic, and social consequences. *Federal Probation, 65*, 3–8.

Petersilia, J. (2001). Prisoner reentry: Public safety and reintegration challenges. *The Prison Journal, 81*, 360–375.

Pettus-Davis, C., Dunnigan, A., Veeh, C. A., Howard, M. O., Scheyett, A. M., & Roberts-Lewis, A. (2017). Enhancing social support postincarceration: Results from a pilot randomized controlled trial. *Journal of Clinical Psychology, 73*, 1–21.

Pettus-Davis, C., Howard, M. O., Roberts-Lewis, A., & Scheyett, A. M. (2011). Naturally occurring social support in interventions for former prisoners with substance use disorders: Conceptual framework and program model. *Journal of Criminal Justice, 39*, 479–488.

Pinard, M. (2010). Collateral consequences of criminal convictions: Confronting issues of race and dignity. *NYU Law Review, 85*, 457.

Richie, B. (2001). Challenges incarcerated women face as they return to their communities: Findings from life history interviews. *Crime and Delinquency, 47*, 368–389.

Roman, C. G., & Travis, J. (2006). Where will I sleep tomorrow? Housing, homelessness, and the returning prisoner. *Housing Policy Debate, 17* 389–418.

Saxena, P., Messina, N., & Grella, C. E. (2014). Who benefits from gender responsive treatment? Accounting for abuse history on longitudinal outcomes for women in prison. *Criminal Justice Behavior, 41*, 417–432. doi:10.1177/0093854813514405

Seiter, R. P., & Kadela, K. R. (2003). Prisoner reentry: What works, what does not, and what is promising. *Crime and Delinquency, 49*, 360–388.

Skeem, J., Louden, J. E., Manchak, S., Vidal, S., & Haddad, E. (2009). Social networks and social control of probationers with co-occurring mental and substance abuse problems. *Law and Human Behavior, 33*, 122.

Skeem, J. L., & Lowenkamp, C. T. (2016). Risk, race, and recidivism: Predictive bias and disparate impact. *Criminology, 54*, 680–712.

Substance Abuse and Mental Health Services Administration (SAMHSA). (2016). Criminal and juvenile justice. Retrieved from https://www.samhsa.gov/criminal-juvenile-justice.

Taxman, F. S. (2005). Brick walls facing reentering offenders. *International Journal of Comparative and Applied Criminal Justice, 29*, 5–18.

Travis, J. (2007). Back-end sentencing: A practice in search of a rationale. *Social Research, 74*, 631–644.

Travis, J., & Christiansen, K. (2006). Failed reentry: The challenges of back-end sentencing. *Georgetown Journal on Poverty, Law & Policy, 13*, 249–260.

Tripodi, S. J. (2010). The influence of social bonds on recidivism: A study of Texas male prisoners. *Victims & Offenders, 5*, 354–370.

Tripodi, S. J., Kim, J. S., & Bender, K. (2010). Is employment associated with reduced recidivism? The complex relationship between employment and crime. *International Journal of Offender Therapy and Comparative Criminology, 54*, 706–720.

van der Knaap, L. M., Alberda, D. L., Oosterveld, P., & Born, M. P. (2012). The predictive validity of criminogenic needs for male and female offenders: Comparing the relative impact of needs in predicting recidivism. *Law and Human Behavior, 36*, 413–422.

Vaske, J. C., Gehring, K. S., & Lovins, B. (2017). Gender differences in the measurement of criminal thinking. *Criminal Justice and Behavior, 44*, 395–415.

Veeh, C., Renn, T., & Pettus-Davis, C. (2017). Promoting reentry well-being: A novel assessment tool for individualized service assignment in prisoner reentry programs. *Social Work, 63,* 91–96.

Visher, C. A., Debus-Sherrill, S. A., & Yahner, J. (2011). Employment after prison: A longitudinal study of former prisoners. *Justice Quarterly, 28,* 698–718.

Walters, G. D. (2014). Relationships among race, education, criminal thinking, and recidivism: Moderator and mediator effects. *Assessment, 21,* 82–91.

Wehrman, M. M. (2010). Race, concentrated disadvantage, and recidivism: A test of interaction effects. *Journal of Criminal Justice, 38,* 538–544.

Wang, X., Mears, D. P., & Bales, W. D. (2010). Race-specific employment contexts and recidivism. *Criminology, 48,* 201–241.

Willison, J. B., Bieler, S. G., & Kim, K. (2014). *Evaluation of the Allegheny County Jail Collaborative Reentry Programs.* Washington, DC: Urban Institute.

Wilson, J. A., & Wood, P. B. (2014). Dissecting the relationship between mental illness and return to incarceration. *Journal of Criminal Justice, 42,* 527–537.

Wolff, N., Frueh, B. C., Shi, J., & Schumann, B. E. (2012). Effectiveness of cognitive-behavioral trauma treatment for incarcerated women with mental illnesses and substance abuse disorders. *Journal of Anxiety Disorders, 26,* 703–710. doi:http://dx.doi.org/10.1016/j.janxdis.2012.06.001

Zlotnick, C., Johnson, J., & Najavits, L. M. (2009). Randomized controlled pilot study of cognitive-behavioral therapy in a sample of incarcerated women with substance use disorder and PTSD. *Behavior Therapy, 40,* 325–336. doi:http://dx.doi.org/10.1016/j.beth.2008.09.004

13

Incarcerated Veterans

EVAN R. SEAMONE, KATE H. THOMAS, AND
DAVID L. ALBRIGHT

The first national survey of incarcerated veterans occurred in the 1920s following World War I with the startling statistic that, by 1922, more than 20,000 veterans were incarcerated throughout the nation (Casey, 1923). Even then, almost a century ago, medical professionals hypothesized that wartime trauma contributed in some significant way to their incarceration (Seamone, 2013a). Point-in-time surveys occurred haphazardly over time. By 2015, the Bureau of Justice Statistics released a periodic study of veterans in prisons and jails focusing on data collected in 2011 and 2012. The study concluded that 181,500 veterans accounted for roughly 8% of the population in prisons and jails in the United States, which represented a slight decrease since the last study using data from 2004 (Bronson, Carson, Noonan, & Berzofsky, 2015).

Regardless of their precise number within correctional settings, inmates with prior military experience are a special population, based on unique needs and characteristics (Gideon, 2013).Unlike other special populations, such as gay, lesbian, bisexual, or transgender inmates, or individuals convicted of terrorism offenses, inmates with military experience are characterized by a shared set of cultural experiences, complete with their own set of common values, codes of conduct, and even a separate language of acronyms (Malmin, 2013). Although branches of service, military occupational specialties, combat experience, and other factors distinguish *subcultures* within the overarching military culture (Seal et al., 2009), common staples of *all* military service include at the very least: (1) basic combat training; (2) supplication to authority; (3) lethal use of force; (4) serving a purpose larger than one's self; and (5) teamwork in the face of adversity (Tanielan & Jaycox, 2008; Thomas & Plummer Taylor, 2015). Much like society at large, the corrections community has learned that these indelible influences offer both *challenges* and *attributes*.

With an eye toward attributes of military service, wardens and sheriffs—like in many businesses—have learned that veterans are generally more responsible and adaptable to change than inmates without military experience (e.g., Bennett, 1954, p. 42; MacPherson, 1993, p. 579; Roth, 1986, p. 3C). Sheriff John Dart at Chicago's Cook County Jail, for example, capitalized on this sense of responsibility by using veteran inmates to replace the prison industry laundry service, saving hundreds of thousands of dollars in the process (Beggs, 2010). In contrast, an enduring challenge presented by veterans is a largely ad hoc approach to postservice community reintegration. Although the military has gone to great lengths to transform citizens into warriors who are ideally ready to follow orders without question and obliterate any force within their path (Grossman, 2009), the transition back to civilian life following military service is much more of an enigma with societal responsibility falling largely on a civilian society that is not prepared to tailor special responses (Schaller, 2012).

Many military members are so influenced by their service that they find great difficulty abandoning routines they depended upon for their very survival (Sigafoos, 1994). Service-related trauma greatly amplifies already significant challenges in readjustment (Spelman, Hunt, Seal, & Burgo-Black, 2012). Indubitably, these challenges translate to confined settings where, for example, it is not uncommon for combat veterans, particularly, to adopt their past survival mode while incarcerated because of the striking similarities in settings, which causes veterans to lack insight into the future consequences of their day-to-day behaviors (Sigafoos, 1994).

True to the moniker of "special population," the criminal justice system has begun to address veterans in a special manner that recognizes that the violation of civilian laws is often a predictable byproduct of difficulties in community reintegration or is symptomatic of untreated or poorly treated mental health conditions sustained during military service (Seamone & Albright, 2017). Poor mental health is a major health problem in the military veteran community, with estimated rates of stress injury and depression varying from 15% to 50% (Acosta, Adamson, Farmer, Farris, & Feeney, 2014; Coughlin, 2012).

The response to criminogenic influences on veterans places an emphasis on providing treatment for mental conditions incurred during military service over punishment with a premium on "decarceration"—the objective to avoid confinement in the first place (McCloed, 2012). With more than 461 specialized veterans treatment court (VTC) dockets devoted to decarcerating veterans by 2016 (Flatley, Clark, Blue-Howells, & Rosenthal, 2016), it is easy for the public to forget that many—in fact, most—veterans in the criminal justice system are ultimately incarcerated for their offenses. As this chapter explains, a number of factors contribute to undue emphasis on pretrial diversion of veterans, including the inability of prisons and jails to meet the mental health needs of their general populations (Sieleni, 2011), let alone combat veterans who may need specialized interventions for combat trauma and laws that prohibit the federal Department of Veterans Affairs from offering any tangible health care treatment to veterans during their term of incarceration in a state or federal correctional facility (38 C.F.R. § 17.38(c)(5)).

Today, in the midst of widespread recognition that justice-involved veterans have special needs, and while the focus remains mostly upon programs and approaches that can be implemented outside of institutional settings, the time is ripe to explore solutions that can be attained during the veteran's period of incarceration. From various interventions implemented in times of war and peace, there are lessons to be learned about what works best for this population. This chapter explores both contemporary and historic approaches to the management of incarcerated veterans with special attention to program attributes that leverage their attributes to overcome the challenges.

The second section emphasizes the lack of an evidence base for current interventions that is largely attributable to the initial development of most approaches in the mid-to-late 2000s and the dissimilar structures of programs, even within the same states. The dilemma here is whether the nature of veterans' needs should allow for more flexibility in interventions within systems, whether the current perception of widespread success in these programs is accurate, and especially whether programs for incarcerated veterans should be adopting the same evaluative criteria as programs based on a diversion model. Certain characteristics of incarceration in jails versus prisons will dictate widely divergent objectives with jails offering less time to address deep-seated mental health concerns and placing a premium instead on stabilization of one's acute symptomology.

The third section of this chapter explores the policy issues and implications of a specialized approach to veterans often viewed by other inmates and correctional officers as *preferential treatment*. Skeptics rightfully question whether jails and prisons can ever justify treating veteran inmates differently from individuals who did not have the opportunity to serve in the military, but who may have nevertheless suffered trauma in civilian life and who have just as pronounced needs for empathic treatment, support, and consideration. The reasoned response to these concerns straddles the justifications of shared cultural experience that often makes veterans inaccessible to persons who cannot understand the realities of their lived experiences and, separately, the integral value of earned entitlements based upon their military service that can be used to enhance reentry in a manner not possible for nonveteran inmates. Although these responses are not ideal, especially when a given inmate is not eligible for VA benefits, they provide a solid foundation on which to justify most veteran-specific interventions within correctional settings, strictly from a perspective of optimal allocation of resources.

When considering trends and future directions for veterans in correctional settings, the fourth section focuses on the recent phenomenon of specializing housing units for veterans in prisons and jails. Sometimes called "pods," "dorms," or veterans service units (VSUs), already more than a dozen states have instituted some sort of similar approach, with a federal correctional institution in Florida confirming its far reach (Seamone, 2016). Similar to VTCs, while no two specialized housing units are identical in operation or objectives, segregated housing—in both theory and practice—offers a method to streamline resource allocation, capitalize on the value of peer support, and increase perceptions of officer and inmate safety. In discussing this growing trend, which attempts to identify and respond to veterans' needs, the chapter also addresses a long-neglected population of veteran sex offenders who have largely escaped a specialized approach that integrates their military experience. We consider veteran sex offenders as a population deserving of institutional intervention mainly because veterans are consistently incarcerated for violent sex offenses at rates far greater than civilians, sometimes at more than double the rate.

The fifth section of this chapter uses the example of the Incarcerated Veterans of Roxbury (I.V.O.R.) in Hagerstown, Maryland, to demonstrate how a group of veterans and correctional officers who served in the US Marine Corps capitalized on the inmates' shared military culture to transform incarceration into an opportunity to continue serving the community and embody the values that defined their proudest moments of service to the nation. The final section concludes with various web-based resources to assist readers in identifying organizations, benefits related to military service, legal considerations, and other resources to help prisons and jails support incarcerated veterans.

EVIDENCE-BASED PRACTICES

Current institutional and organizational outreach to incarcerated veterans focuses on both diversion and reentry programming along phases of the sequential intercept model (Munetz & Griffin, 2006). The model for impact includes the following four intercept points, along which specific programs are deployed to support veterans in contact with the justice system: first-response services, initial detention and court hearings, jails and court systems, and reentry from correctional sites (Blue-Howells, Clark, van Berk-Clark, & McGuire, 2013). The US Department of Veterans Affairs (VA) Veterans Justice Programs (VJP) attempts to reach justice-involved veterans at these critical junctures through two nationwide programs, Veterans Justice Outreach (VJO) and Healthcare for Reentry Veterans (HCRV).

At intercept point one, programming focuses on diversion and involves the cooperation of law enforcement personnel and VA Emergency Care Centers to offer rapid assessment and care for veterans in trouble, rather than confinement. Although such communication and cooperation sound simplistic, it is a complex interagency process requiring procedures, training, and agreement that differ wildly between localities (Clark, McGuire, & Blue-Howells, 2010). Because the focus of this chapter centers on veterans already incarcerated, best practices along intercept points two, three, and four are salient.

Critical to reaching incarcerated veterans is the simple issue of identification. No national process exists for identifying former-military inmates, but in areas where at intake (intercept point 2), corrections personnel identify veterans and cooperate with VJP to issue reports, the VA becomes a partner. As such, the VJP can use information about the incarcerated veterans' location and projected release date to plan outreach. Identification and initial partnership with VJP are crucial first steps toward more impactful measures for the veteran subpopulation. Without national guidelines and because agencies are diverse and geographically disparate, this basic interorganizational communication at intake is not yet status quo (Blue-Howells et al., 2013).

Once the veteran moves to interaction with the courts system, an important opportunity for coordination presents (sequential intercept point 3). VJO and court partnerships allow medical care (typically mental health and substance abuse treatment) to craft treatment plans desperately needed and not typically available to nonmilitary inmates (Greenberg & Rosenheck, 2009). A step beyond such cooperation is the VTC, which uses the same medical information release and cooperation processes in a dedicated, veteran-only court setting. In approximately 461 court systems nationwide, the VJO and local court partner with dedicated VA treatment clinicians in VTCs. Because approximately 10% of inmates are veterans and large proportions of them suffer from medical and social problems, the numbers indicate need and utility of such dedicated courts (Mumola, 2000; Noonan & Mumola, 2007).

At reentry (intercept four), the VA's HCRV program offers opportunity for the prison's case manager to work with a health care case manager and potentially the VA residential program to reduce recidivism by ensuring that a treatment, housing, and support plan is in place for a veteran leaving an incarcerated environment (Greenberg & Rosenheck, 2008). Enabling this care planning is the creation of all-veteran housing units in prisons and jails (Mumola, 2000). None of these programs are standardized nationwide, and a vital area of future research and practice is to establish best practices that include the mentioned partnerships and outreach options, plus the important, needed programs beyond.

There is a notable dearth of strong evaluation results that would validate these models for intervention development aiming to improve the well-being of veterans in correctional settings. A key reason for this is that underlying issues of veteran mental health are not easily categorized, labeled, and treated (Hendricks Thomas, 2015). Gaining a better understanding of stress injury and depression in the incarcerated veteran population is vital (Hoge, 2010). A number of studies have attempted to explore the issue of depression and posttraumatic stress (PTS) in veterans, but ranges and rates vary widely, and predictive models that could guide programming are lacking (Gironda, Clark, Massengale, & Walker, 2006; Seal et al., 2009; Tanielian & Jaycox, 2008). As outlined in the first part of this chapter, long-term and short-term, targeted programming is needed for veterans in correctional institutions to improve *de*carceration outcomes, reduce recidivism, decrease violence, and improve mental health outcomes that contribute to incarceration issues generally.

Current VJO initiatives are a vital starting point for linking justice-involved veterans to resources along intercept points, and national application and program expansion are indicated by preliminary feedback (Blue-Howells et al., 2013). Progressing beyond veteran identification and connection to Veterans Health Administration (VHA) and Veterans Benefits Administration (VBA) resources in prisons and courtrooms would greatly benefit incarcerated veterans.

Interestingly, a review of successful practices indicates a cultural truism that transcends settings and applies in institutions of incarceration as much as it does in local civilian community settings. More than service provision, jailed veterans may benefit from community-cultivation and interactive efforts to help them build a high level of support. Such support can offer mental health protective effects that will positively impact this inmate subgroup (Hoge, 2010). Warrior culture is characterized by team emphasis and community; perhaps more than other incarcerated subpopulations, social cohesion issues are uniquely salient to questions of mental health, behavioral improvement, and reentry enabling; programs that intend to offer opportunities for purposeful group effort are uniquely successful in reaching veterans (Malmin, 2013).

The research literature shows that for both the general population and for military veterans, a high level of social support offers s protective effect against poor mental health outcomes and the symptoms associated with them, which include self-medication and violence that can land an individual in contact with some level of the justice system (Cohen, Underwood, & Gottlieb, 2000; Egolf, Lasker, Wolf, & Potvin, 1992). Whether social support programs are delivered through government agencies, communities, social networks, families, interpersonal relations, or agents of the criminal justice system, they reduce criminal involvement (Cullen, 1994).

Studying social support development efforts to improve quality of life and reduce mental health symptomology for National Guard soldiers in the pos-deployment period translates well to the general veteran population struggling to connect to the civilian community after service. This liminal period of reconnection is a time of significant social and psychological risk for military veterans (Friedman, 2015; Junger, 2015). National Guard soldiers, like all reservists, often face stresses additional to those faced by active-duty troops. Reservists do not come from as insular of a military community as active-duty service members and may lack support services in civilian community settings. Particularly because PTS symptoms are very likely to be misread as behavioral deviance, stigma is even more difficult to overcome in community settings removed from the active-duty military component (Friedman, 2015; Greden et al., 2010).

A 2010 case study highlights one Michigan pilot program's experience with buddy-to buddy peer support programs. A team from the University of Michigan and Michigan State worked with the Army National Guard (ANG) to address the constellation of issues facing soldiers returning from a deployment to Iraq. The University of Michigan researchers also understood the need for audience-centered communication and partnered with unit leadership to institute a program that was completely peer led. This decision came out of the qualitative research they conducted in the unit prior to developing a program. Interviewees said things such as "If you haven't been there, you don't get it" and "Other veterans can be trusted" (Greden et al., 2010, p. 93). The research team considered concepts of warrior culture and sought to design a program that spoke the correct language, using an understanding of social norms to change the culture of treatment avoidance (Greden et al., 2010). The researchers trained 350 peer leaders, called "Buddy Ones" by the program.

Evaluation results were encouraging. Ninety percent of participants understood program intent, received regular calls and contact from their buddies, and felt comfortable with their trained peer. More than 20% were referred to formal treatment by their buddy, and that percentage affirmed using the recommended services. In settings where soldiers and veterans are struggling with social support, a program that brings them together in purposeful, service-driven fashion, informed by warrior culture and using unit-specific language, peer leadership, and insider message delivery can aid in suicide prevention and lower behavioral issues (Greden et al., 2010).

To this end, programs that reach veterans at intercept point four in veteran-housing settings have real potential for lasting impact. Inmates with purposeful work opportunities and team support are less likely to create behavioral issues while incarcerated (Vergakis, 2012). Partnerships with nonprofit organizations that offer social connectivity, communities of faith that minister to inmates, and relationship cultivation with other veteran inmates who have walked similar paths are indicated by what we have seen work successfully with military veterans in non-justice settings and with inmates in general (Rose & Clear, 2003).

It is important to remember that the service member and veteran population is made up of many subpopulations with unique needs. For example, lesbian, gay, and questioning service members and veteran students are more likely to report feelings of depression and other mental health challenges than heterosexual veterans (Pelts & Albright, 2015).

Women suffer significantly higher rates of stress injury than male veterans and are more likely to have experienced sexual trauma (Duhart, 2012; Kelly, Skelton, Patel, & Bradley, 2011; Thomas et al., 2016). Research has shown that women are more likely to screen positively for depression both before and after deployments (Koo & Maguen, 2014). Female service members and veterans also have health care needs that are often unmet and misunderstood by Department of Defense and Veterans Administration providers (Carlson, Stromwall, & Lietz, 2013; Elnitsky et al., 2013).

In reality, the nature of warfare today has added to mental health issues for all veterans. High operational tempos and short garrison time between deployments means that service members frequently do not have the time to get the help they need. Additionally, a smaller percentage of the American public volunteers for service and deployment, leading to minority stress for military personnel as they reintegrate into a civilian society that may struggle to understand their experiences (Hendricks Thomas, 2015; Malmin, 2013). These factors have led to much higher levels of undiagnosed PTS than in prior generations, and the problems are particularly significant for veterans who fall into a minority category (Held & Owens, 2013; Thomas et al., 2015).

The answers lie beyond programming along key intercepts, and cultural competence is important (Hoge & Castro, 2012). Correctional institutions should provide officers and staff deeper knowledge about these inmates' needs by educating them on military culture and the inherent diversity in how service members and veterans experience and contextualize their military experiences. Cultural competence with the service member and veteran inmate subpopulation is a challenge, and peer leadership can help (Greden et al., 2010). Implementing institutional programs that promote socially supportive environments is indicated. Successful programs with post 9-11 veterans have reported tremendous impact using both peer mentors and clinically trained outreach personnel who have served (Thomas et al., 2015). Ultimately, correctional institutions must assess their specific veteran populations at a given time and invest in these inmates by tailoring current programs that are in place to ensure that needs are being met.

Comprehensive evaluation of existing programs aiming to serve the needs of incarcerated veterans is indicated; establishing best practices in short-term jail settings and long-term prison settings would assist correctional professionals as they work to reach out to their veteran population and prevent recidivism, inmate violence, and mental health symptomology. Rendering targeted programs culturally palatable in order to resonate with incarcerated veterans and rigorously evaluating them will go a long way toward serving the needs of a population struggling with the impact of civilian reintegration after 15 years of war.

CRIMINAL JUSTICE POLICY ISSUES AND IMPLICATIONS

Two major policy concerns involving incarcerated veterans are (1) lack of evidence-based studies on in-prison programs and interventions and (2) the concern that any program developed specifically for veterans improperly singles out inmates based solely on their status. Both questions have far-reaching implications because they offer no fixed or easy answers and sometimes require corrections professionals to respond to critics of veteran-based initiatives.

Lack of Evidence-Based Studies

For the most part, VTCs emerged after 2008 in the midst of a two-front war in Iraq and Afghanistan; the existing specialized housing units for veterans in prisons and jails emerged after that with the majority coming into existence after 2010 (Seamone & Albright, 2016). Any effort to collectively explain all of these programs' operation and, more specifically, successes will necessarily fail based on the variety of approaches adopted. The variables are simply too great, and some critics point out that current reviews of VTCs have tended to focus on "safe" definitions of effectiveness in an effort to promote future grant funding for specific programs (Brooke & Baldwin, 2016). For example, when program evaluators do not track a participant's time penalties for infractions in a VTC, program completion reporting has the potential to paint a misleading picture (Brooke & Baldwin, 2016). Nevertheless, VTC programs have expanded at unprecedented rates, even outpacing the explosive growth of drug courts by three times (Justice for Vets, 2010).

From the standpoint of program evaluation, specialized housing units for veterans in prisons and jails pose even greater dilemmas than VTCs, considering their smaller number and the overlay of each institution's correctional culture, which alone can significantly transform any jail- or prison-based program for any category of inmate. Respecting VSUs, perhaps the oldest program that has continuously operated is the New York Department of Corrections Veterans Residential Treatment Program (VRTP), which initially rolled out a dormitory at Arthur Kill Confinement Facility in 1987 (Marks, 2001). As only one example, the VRTP's objectives and methods to achieve them, as well as the program's development, would not be generalizable to other VSUs because of VRTP's genesis from specialized Vietnam veterans' rap groups (Marks, 2001) and substantial changes in the program's structure that occurred as the Department of Veterans Affairs removed counselors in accordance with VA's stricter policies (S.M. Verbeke, personal communication, September 16, 2013). In contrast with VRTP, nearly all VSUs operating today grew at a time when VA employees are barred from providing any type of group or individual therapy during the period of incarceration. Further, current programs lack the experience of a core group of incarcerated veteran advocates who demonstrated the value of the program through sustained advocacy efforts. Although it is tempting to pose the general question of whether housing veterans together in the same unit increases desirable outcomes within prison and jail populations, such broad questions would, in fact, obscure the unique aspects of these programs that truly account for success, such as the quality of programming for veterans while in the program, the involvement of correctional officers who have prior military experience, and specific initiatives to reinvigorate the pride and esprit de corps once enjoyed by these inmates during their most productive years as citizens and soldiers. (See the fourth section of this chapter for further discussion of these VSU attributes.)

The ultimate policy question is whether veterans present such substantial needs and offer such substantial opportunities to remedy the needs through targeted interventions that the corrections and criminal justice systems can justify these interventions without the benefit of traditional longitudinal studies. The short answer to this question is yes, mainly because this group, unlike other groups of inmates and offenders, shares three important attributes: (1) specialized training in the use of lethal force that can increase risk of suicide and harm to others when combined with symptoms of PTS and other "invisible wounds of war"; (2) unique cultural experiences that make interventions more effective in a group setting among similarly situated inmates who can relate to one another; and (3) more often than not, eligibility for VA benefits that derive exclusively from time spent in military service. When considered in combination, a maxim becomes quite clear: Efforts to minimize stressors on members of this population while incarcerated, to capitalize on unique cultural experiences that are conducive to mission accomplishment, and to generate hope by confirming and exploiting benefit eligibility contributes to order within the correctional institution, reducing opportunities for disciplinary infractions and maximizing the constructive use of inmate time prior to release. The ultimate effect of instituting veteran-focused programming also has the indirect second- and third-order effects of promoting public safety following the veteran's release into the community (Seamone, 2013b; Seamone et al., 2014).

Although correctional administrators currently lack the studies that would normally indicate the success of veteran-specific interventions, they do have other statistics that emphasize the pressing needs of this group specifically. Current statistics regarding veterans' severe challenges with readjustment to and reintegration into society following their separation from service—including the increased risk of substance abuse, unemployment, and especially suicide—underscore the need for aggressive, specially targeted, veteran-based programs in any setting to promote veteran well-being. For example, respecting corrections, a number of mental health professionals highlighted some of these factors in support of the position that veterans were a population at greater risk of suicide while incarcerated (Wortzel, Binswanger, Anderson, & Lawrence, 2009) and noted the responsibility to take immediate action to minimize this risk, even with a lack of traditional studies to confirm the exact contours of the risk (Frisman & Griffin-Fennell, 2009). In sum, the institution of segregated housing units and other specially tailored approaches to veterans in prisons and jails is supported by the policy of the precautionary principle to risk mitigation, which justifies allocation of resources to reduce significant risks, even though they do not occur regularly (Seamone 2013b; Seamone et al., 2014).

Preferential Treatment for Veterans

Despite advocates for veteran-specific programming, some departments of correction have adopted polices limiting programming for veterans, specifically, on the basis that expansive programs would show preferential treatment based on an inmate's status with the potential to cause friction among the inmate population. For example, although California may now be revisiting its policy, at one time, the Department of Corrections firmly disavowed the creation of VSUs on these grounds, indicating that the Department would, instead, allow veterans to join prison "veterans-only discussion groups" to address common concerns like other inmates with similar experience (Perry, 2013). Others share this sentiment. Notably, in addressing VTCs, retired Connecticut Supreme Court Justice Barry Schaller has suggested that programs that divert veterans from incarceration based upon veteran status raise constitutional concerns of equal protection under the law (2012). A key policy consideration is whether these veteran-specific interventions represent preferential treatment for veterans that excludes other inmates simply because they were never in a position to serve in the United States Armed Forces (Schaller, 2012, p. 208).

Correctional administrators and others in the criminal justice system have pondered this question. Most offer the explanation that specialized programs do not amount to preferential treatment but rather represent *different* treatment that is tailored to the unique needs of this group (McCormick-Goodhart, 2013; Pentland, 1979, p. 526). Given that the VA Office of Justice Programs estimates that the majority of justice-involved veterans (roughly 80%) are eligible for VA benefits because they meet statutory requirements: (1) minimum time in service; (2) service-connected disabilities; and (3) a discharge that is other than Dishonorable for VA purposes (McGuire, 2007), efforts to connect those veterans with counseling regarding such federal entitlements is not preferential, but rather necessary as part of planning for reintegration. In fact, to the extent that special programming exists in direct relation to VA benefit eligibility, this entitlement is the reason for separate and different treatment. Concerns over preferential treatment are justified when there is no difference between veterans and other inmates but veterans are singled out for certain privileges. For those veterans who do not have eligibility for VA benefits, the concern has greater applicability.

Even for those without benefit eligibility, segregated housing units for veterans represent only one of a number of existing approaches that recognize the significance of inmates' cultural experiences. Currently, using the Muscogee County Jail in Columbus, Georgia, as an example, the Sheriff has developed segregated housing pods for inmates affiliated with a faith tradition, inmates pursuing their GEDs, and incarcerated fathers. In the "fatherhood dorm," incarcerated fathers are housed together and agree to commit their time to better assume responsibility for being good parents to their children (Gierer, 2013). To accomplish this goal, the living area is decorated with positive attestations about being parents. Inmates attend regular lectures from guest speakers on what it means to be a responsible father. Fatherhood Dorm members have the opportunity to take parenting classes. And, most important, participants enjoy streamlined visitation with their children during program participation (Gierer, 2013). One might question whether the existence of the Fatherhood Dorm prejudices the rights of other inmates who have children but do not want to participate in the program or who would be ineligible for a host of reasons. Despite such concerns, the Fatherhood Dorm flourishes because of its ability to accomplish goals of reentry, contribute to family stability, and promote officer and inmate safety at the jail (N. Richardson, personal communication, November 4, 2013).

The unifying justification for specialized housing units, including VSUs, is the ability of these programs to tap into a shared cultural experience that creates strong bonds between inmates who are more willing to work with one another to succeed in correctional settings. Rather than spending time confined, incarceration has a purpose. For veterans, incarceration while participating in a VSU gives them a "mission" similar to the one they had when they served on active duty or in the reserve component. This phenomenon answers one of the greatest problems veterans face in community and workforce reintegration, which is the sense that they have lost a meaningful mission for their lives after leaving the Armed Forces.

For veterans, many adopt the position that it is impossible for nonveterans to understand their problems since they have not experienced the realities of war and having to depend on others for sheer survival. This byproduct of military culture, which begins from the time that recruits are reconditioned, forced to abandon their "civilian identity" and adopt a warrior identity, creates impediments for veterans embedded in the general population, where the majority of inmates lack military experience and do not subscribe to the core set of military values. To house inmate veterans together provides a sense of belonging and the ability for veterans to rely upon their past instinct to work as a team to accomplish common goals.

As a consequence, the impact of military culture alone, even without VA benefit eligibility, is a strong enough reason to justify treating veteran inmates differently by offering specific services at times when the group can benefit. When considering the manner in which certain gangs are housed together to avoid conflict and promote the safety of inmates and correctional officers, it is possible to recognize the aim of different treatment without adopting a view that inmates who receive such different treatment are automatically favored above others. Accordingly, the policy justification of responding to military culture and using its themes to maximize resource allocation, order, and discipline within institutions should allay concerns of equal protection violations.

TRENDS AND FUTURE DIRECTIONS

One of the biggest developments that has placed incarcerated veterans' needs on the radar is a computerized program called the Veterans Reentry Research Service (VRRS). This program, developed through pilot programs in 2009, finally answered earlier calls for a system to match inmate Social Security Numbers with Department of Defense (DoD) personnel data. To use this system, corrections personnel need only submit inmate information to VA Justice Programs personnel, who will run the identifying information against DoD's comprehensive list of all veterans who have served for several of the last decades (McCabe, 2013). The VRSS program finally provided the justice system with a method for identifying veterans that is not dependent upon self-identification. The impact of this development is quite significant because of veterans' widespread, traditional reluctance to self-identify due to a host of reasons, including shame for violating the law they once were required to uphold as service members.

In the first implementation of VRSS at pilot sites around the country, the program proved indispensable because it confirmed that state departments of correction had largely underestimated their population of incarcerated veterans. As one prominent example, in California, VRSS established that there were more than two times as many incarcerated veterans (7.9%), compared with prevailing inaccurate estimates (2.7%) (J. McGuire, personal communication, December 30, 2013). The effect of VRSS has been to eliminate the notion that veterans' needs while confined are merely hypothetical because the actual number of veterans can now be ascertained, at least for those corrections systems that subscribe to VRSS. A major and recent trend within corrections regarding veterans has thus become how to meet their needs once the population is identified, especially where the population is much larger than estimated prior to confirmation through VRSS. Within the backdrop of this recent capacity to identify incarcerated veterans, this section explores two other trends that fall on contrasting ends of the spectrum: (1) the emergence of VSUs in prisons and jails and (2) the continuing recognition that veterans make up a substantial population of incarcerated sex offenders, whose needs seem to be perpetually unmet as a result of the criminal justice system's great animosity for this group.

The Veterans Dorm Phenomenon

At present, there are at least 24 states operating VSUs across the country; 14 state prisons operate them, 16 jails operate them, and two federal correctional institutes, in West Virginia and Florida, operate one (Seamone 2016).[1] The sparks that ignited to bring these programs to fruition are varied. In 2012, the Large Jail Network meetings began tracking issues related to VSUs as part of a special update on developments in corrections related to veterans (National Institute of Corrections, 2012, pp. 40–41). Word of mouth regarding Florida's model inspired Virginia to launch a similar program that includes special uniforms for inmates, daily formations in accordance with drill, ceremonies like military training, and other hallmarks of service in the Armed Forces. At the same time, unlike the boot camp model that strives to bring inmates together as teams through a forma-tive experience overcoming hardship, other VSUs focus instead on minimizing stress and creating a therapeutic environment, especially for inmates who suffer symptoms of untreated PTS or other service-related conditions. In this respect, when he was Sheriff of Kennebec County Jail in Maine, Randal Liberty realized that aspects of incarceration aggravated symptoms of his PTSD from combat in Operation Iraqi Freedom, motivating him to take measures for similarly situated inmates. Not only did Liberty, who is now Warden of the Maine State Prison, house veterans together under the supervision of sheriffs' deputies with prior mil-itary service, but he instituted programming to help veteran inmates with PTSD focus on tasks that helped them maintain concentration, and he disabled the au-tomatically locking doors in the dorm because they sounded too much like auto-matic machinegun fire (*A Matter of Duty*, 2013).

As addressed earlier, one could not simply compare Warden Liberty's Veterans' Dorm with the Florida Department of Corrections' Veterans Dorm because the programs have such different objectives. But it is fair to say that from the ex-isting programs, some standard formats are beginning to emerge. At least three include (1) programs instituted to help veterans meet objectives for reintegration; (2) programs instituted to limit triggers for mental health conditions that com-monly exist in prison settings; and (3) programs that celebrate and honor the veterans' prior service. A given VSU program could theoretically combine more than one objective, but salient features of one track often negate features of the others. As just one example, a program wishing to celebrate and honor one's prior military service would not likely seek to enroll inmates with less-than-honorable discharge characterizations because this might undermine the idea that members performed valuable service to the nation.

Commonly, the first category of programs tailored specifically for community reintegration normally limit participation to those inmates who have served most of their sentences and are nearing the time of their release, which can be anywhere from no more than 24 months prior to release, as in the case of Virginia's VSU

---

1. The author's published research does not reflect the identification of another Veterans Dorm operated by the Central Mississippi Correctional Facility.

program (Hixenbaugh, 2012, p. A1), to no less than 6 months prior to release, as in the case of the Florida Department of Corrections (Kamal, 2013). Within the construct of these short-term programs, the emphasis is mainly on linking the veteran with benefits that he or she will be able to use upon release, which coincides with the VA's limited role of offering counseling on benefits. These programs do not normally offer programming for inmates serving sentences of many years, raising a slew of questions regarding problems that could arise within the short window of release, such as time to appeal the denial of benefits, which might exceed even a 24-month period, or methods to address symptoms of un-treated mental health conditions during the course of confinement.

In contrast to the first short-termer category of reintegration VSUs, the second type of program is concerned mainly with the very real consequences of incarcer-ation on a group of inmates that is more susceptible to triggers for stress reactions. Although these programs face severe limitations as a result of VA prohibitions on treatment during confinement, they prepare for the mitigation of acute stressors through peer counseling, support, and integration of stress-reduction strategies. Whereas the program in Kennebec County Jail, addressed earlier, incorporated fly-fishing instruction to help veterans improve their concentration as they approach complex tasks (*A Matter of Duty*, 2013), other programs, such as the VRTP in New York, use a system of specially trained "cadre"—inmates who have risen through the leadership ranks within the program—to look out for symptoms in other inmates and render psychological first aid in the form of peer-based crisis intervention and de-escalation techniques (Groveland Correctional Facility, n.d., p. 7). Recognizing that some veterans may have experienced conflicts with the military institution and may be distrustful of it, the program is less focused on regimens that resemble military service and adhere to a cadre concept more for the purpose of identifying shared responsibilities within the program.

The third type of VSU that celebrates military service is the most representa-tive of a boot camp approach to incarceration, which attempts to revive a sense of pride and esprit de corps by emulating some of the key characteristics of military service. Normally, enrollment is limited to individuals who exited the military with an honorable characterization of service. Inmates in these programs must also normally agree to conduct themselves in a manner that reflects their military training, which is explicitly recognized by the program participants as more de-manding than the social standards to which the general population is held. These programs, for example, carry severe consequences for the use of profanity, or the failure to keep grooming or living quarters in strict accordance with program guidelines. In some cases, these programs will require a physical fitness regimen. In the most representative example in the Belmont Correctional Institute in Ohio, their VSU offers exceptional inmate graduates the possibility of an appointment to a position where they could work for the state's emergency reserve in a quasi-military capacity (DeFrank, 2012).

Although these programs have been instituted too recently to reach any clear conclusions on the most effective format, it is important to recognize that programs with specific objectives will normally be limited to a range of program attributes to meet those objectives, and it is very difficult to mix and match between programs. To this end, it behooves correctional administrators to identify the aims of their programs and consider methods to achieve them before implementation.

From the experience of the VRTP, another important lesson to emerge regarding VSUs is the importance of permitting participants to stay in the program after they have been admitted to it. Oftentimes, inmates may require modules of training and residential participation in substance abuse or other issues related to their offense(s). Because VSUs build on the veteran's identity as the member of a team with loyalties to other members of the program, it can be particularly devastating to remove the veteran from the VSU or intermittently rotate him in and out of the program while the veteran undergoes correctional treatment.

A final lesson from the growing trend of VSUs is the importance of alternatives and supplements to the federal VA in order to meet program objectives. For example, while the VA may not provide any type of therapy to the inmates during incarceration, this is not true of university graduate students, mental health providers affiliated with nonprofit groups, or other volunteers from the community. Increasingly, these programs are adopting a multifaceted approach to VSUs, which includes the initial involvement of VA and non-VA entities in planning stages and beyond.

The impact of VSUs is being felt throughout criminal justice systems, even without hard data on recidivism rates or other traditional measures of success. The foremost example of this system-wide effect is inclusion of VSUs in the approach of VTCs. In an increasing number of scenarios, VTC judges have incorporated VSUs in their planning, such as housing potential participants in VSUs prior to arraignment, or other measures to recognize the benefit of a veteran-focused experience even when a defendant is not eligible for diversion or *de*carceration. Often, the existence of a VSU will motivate agreements in which counties without VSUs will agree to transfer veterans to the county with the VSU for ease of processing, with VSUs acting as an "outgrowth" of VTCs (Lionti, 2013). In some cases, in fact, VSUs have motivated counties to establish VTC dockets, such as the program that grew from Sheriff Glenn Boyer's VSU in Jefferson County, Missouri (Carbery, 2013, p. 11B). As these programs continue to grow across the nation, it is hoped that they will be studied in concert with VTCs as part of a comprehensive societal approach to address the unique needs of veterans in the criminal justice system at large.

Inertia in Responding to the Significant Population of Veteran Sex Offenders

Sex offenders have been compared to "terrorists and perpetrators of genocide" in the criminal justice system (Zilney & Zilney, 2009, p. xiii) with many jurisdictions openly pursuing political agendas to make living conditions so onerous on sex offenders that they will be forced to leave the state in order to survive (Saxer,

2009). These goals have materialized in the form of severe restrictions on places where sex offenders are able to live and work. In an effort to protect the community and vulnerable populations of children, some living restrictions are so harsh that sex offenders have been forced to reside under freeway overpasses and uninhabitable areas located away from schools and other public places (DeGregory, 2009). This despised status is relevant to veterans for an important reason. Namely, in repeated evaluations of veterans in the civilian criminal justice system, veterans are represented among violent sex offenders at significant rates, often many times greater than civilians incarcerated for the same offenses (Mumola, 2000, pp. 1, 5): 18% of veterans incarcerated in prisons as opposed to 7% of civilians incarcerated in prisons and 6% of veterans incarcerated in jails as opposed to 3% of civilians incarcerated in jails (Noonan & Mumola, 2007, p. 1); 23% of veterans incarcerated in prison as opposed to 9% of civilians incarcerated in prisons (Bronson, Carson, Noonan, & Berzofsky, 2015, pp. 5, 6); 35% of veterans incarcerated in prisons as opposed to 23% of civilians incarcerated in prisons; and 11.8% of veterans incarcerated in jails as opposed to a standardized rate of 6.5% of civilians incarcerated in jails. These statistics are consistent in both prison and jail populations, raising an important question of whether there are any aspects of military or combat service that may relate to sex offending by veterans. The question is noteworthy because violent sex offenses represent *the only* type of offense for which veterans are represented more than civilian offenders, with veterans committing comparatively fewer offenses of all other types.

One of the reasons why the nation's prisons and jails are influenced by these phenomena is simply the fact that nearly all VTCs refuse to enroll veteran sex offenders for diversion from incarceration. In 2015, Judge Robert Russell Jr., the innovator of the contemporary model, acknowledged that, akin to premeditated murderers, no sex offenders should have the opportunity to participate in a VTC docket (Russell, 2015, p. 395). In fact, while noting the standard of complete disinterest, only one VTC judge to date, Judge Stephen Manley, admitted that he has permitted sex offenders to participate in his program (Manley, 2016).

The dilemma presented is two-fold. First, for those veterans who have committed sexual offenses as a result of mental health conditions related to their military service, the inability to connect with programs that can address those symptoms ironically increases the chances of recidivism. Second, because civilian criminal offending—even sex offending—does not divest one of VA benefits for which they are eligible, sex-offending veterans who face the ultimate handicaps for community readjustment could be greatly assisted by VA programs to prevent homelessness and assist with employment.

With more than 460 VTC dockets devoted to diversion from confinement, only two federal courts currently operate VTC dockets that manage offender reentry into the community (Seamone, Brooks-Holliday, & Sreenivasan, 2018 forthcoming). In Utah, one of these programs has managed a sex offender through the process of reentry into the community (Seamone, Brooks-Holliday, & Sreenivasan, forthcoming). In recognition of the growing number of veterans incarcerated for violent sex offenses, with consistent data from 1983 to 2015, another trend in programming for incarcerated veterans is the establishment of reentry courts using the same apparatus as pretrial diversion courts for veterans.

Although it would be counterproductive to pair diverted veteran participants with incarcerated sex-offender veterans, the data suggest that there exists a large enough population of sex-offender veterans to use as the basis for a reentry docket. Surely, the attributes that have led to successes within existing VTCs—including veteran mentors from the community, regular appearances before the treatment court judge, and intensive involvement of the interdisciplinary treatment team—can assist in addressing the special needs of this severely at-risk population of veteran sex offenders.

CASE EXAMPLE

The Incarcerated Veterans of Roxbury (I.V.O.R.) is a prison-based veterans' organization that has operated at Maryland's Roxbury Correctional Institute for decades. In a noteworthy development in 1988, the inmate members used more than 4,200 bricks donated by community organizations to construct one of the few veterans' memorials on prison grounds (Inmates Building Memorial to Vets, 1988, p. A3). Dedicated to the veterans who risked their lives in service of the nation, as depicted in Figure 13.1, the memorial exists as a place where I.V.O.R. color guard members have raised and retired the colors since its development.

Beyond this, on Memorial and Veterans Days, the prison hosts elaborate ceremonies at the foot of the memorial. The landscaped walkway features dedications to the veterans of specific campaigns from the War of 1812 to the Persian Gulf War. As noteworthy as the memorial and the place of honor in which it is held at Roxbury, the inmate members of I.V.O.R. have also developed into a distinctive presence at the institution.

In 2012, a former Marine Sergeant named Corporal John J. Worgul, Jr., became the prison staff sponsor for I.V.O.R. Corporal Worgul assessed the organization and, with the participation and support of its members, developed I.V.O.R. into an organization capable of making sustained contributions not only to the institution but beyond its walls in service to the local community (J. J. Worgul, personal communication, September 20, 2013). Corporal Worgul's initiatives provide an important example of the possibilities for correctional institutions that seek to capitalize on the strengths and experiences of veteran inmates.

One of Corporal Worgul's first transformations of the I.V.O.R. program was to recognize the personal accomplishments of the veteran members during their service to the nation. To accomplish this goal, Corporal Worgul instituted a new arrangement in which he would use the prison industry for clothing development and create individualized polo shirts that program participants could wear during I.V.O.R. activities and visitations with family members. The shirts not only depicted the member's years of service with bars on the shoulder but also permitted the veteran to display his name and branch of service. As depicted in Figures 13.2 through 13.4, participants were also able to memorialize individual contributions to the institution and the community in the form of illustrated decorations akin to military medals.

Figure 13.1 (A and B) Views of the Memorial to Veterans and Their Families, which was built entirely by incarcerated veterans at Roxbury Correctional Institute in Hagerstown, Maryland.
Copyright 2013 Evan R. Seamone.

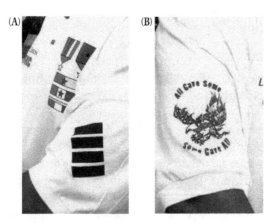

Figure 13.2 (A and B) Depicted here are the left and right sleeves of the I.V.O.R. polo shirt worn by members of the organization. Whereas the right sleeve is generic, the left sleeve uses black bars to signify the number of years the veteran served in the US military.
Copyright 2013 Evan R. Seamone.

Figure 13.3 Depicted here is the back of the I.V.O.R. polo shirt for all members of the organization.
Copyright 2013 Evan R. Seamone.

Figure 13.4 Depicted here is the I.V.O.R. polo shirt of a more decorated veteran officer within the organization, who had prior service in the United States Army.
Copyright 2013 Evan R. Seamone.

To Corporal Worgul, it was vital that the decorations represented present contributions rather than medals awarded during military service, since current recognition would incentivize further contributions to the program rather than reminiscence for an era that had passed (J. J. Worgul, personal communication, September 20, 2013).

The memorialization of inmates' identities as program participants and veterans in the form of polo shirts cemented the functions played by the inmates, including writing for the newsletter, participating on the color guard, and participating in other community service, such as facilitating other inmates' graduations from educational programs or fundraising for community organizations beyond the facility. In reflecting on I.V.O.R.'s activities, Warden Gregg Hershberger commented, "Like I always say, you're the group I wish I had more of. If I did, I wouldn't be here" (Hershberger, 2013).

Through participation in I.V.O.R., some veterans gain the opportunity to train service dogs from the time they are puppies to serve wounded warriors (Demetrick, 2013; Maryland Department of Public Safety and Correctional Services, 2012). Veterans in the Maryland Department of Corrections also have the opportunity to work in landscaping and care for veterans' cemeteries in Maryland under an innovative partnership with the VA, which has in some cases led to the placement of program participants in VA jobs following their release (Maryland Department of Public Safety and Correctional Services, n.d.). Although such opportunities could very well exist without the existence of I.V.O.R. or the leadership of Corporal Worgul, the I.V.O.R. program has done a tremendous job of harnessing and operationalizing the attributes of the veterans at Roxbury, ensuring that their skills are put to maximum use for the benefit of the entire institution. This model is but one example of the benefits of developing a well-thought-out approach to veterans incarcerated in prisons and jails across the nation. As reflected in the I.V.O.R. example, perhaps the greatest attribute for developing any prison- or jail-based program is the veterans who can act as peer support to other veterans and the correctional officers and sheriff's deputies who themselves have prior military experience. In the most basic sense, the only other necessary ingredients are space to house the veterans and "two or three gallons of paint" to adorn their living/work space (Lionti, 2013).

WEB-BASED RESOURCES

The entries that follow briefly describe organizations, laws, government benefits, and other resources to assist prisons and jails in developing programs to support incarcerated veterans. Within each category, we include a brief synopsis and a web address.

Organizations That Assist Incarcerated Veterans

Justice for Vets is a special organization that falls under the National Association of Drug Court Professionals (NADCP). Although the program largely focuses on establishing VTCs, it researches issues related to veterans in the criminal justice system and methods to address their unique needs (http://www.justiceforvets. org).

Vietnam Veterans of America (VVA) is a nonprofit veterans service organization developed with the specific aim of supporting veterans of the Vietnam War. Since its inception, VVA has concerned itself with incarcerated veterans and the development of VVA chapters in prisons throughout the nation. The address below links to the VVA's Incarcerated Veterans section (https://vva.org).

The National Institute on Corrections (NIC) is a professional organization that studies issues related to incarcerated populations and promulgates guidelines to help prisons and jails. A recent program developed by the NIC is crisis intervention training, part of which has a veteran focus. The materials (National Institute of Corrections, 2010: Facilitator's Guide § 5) are available at http://nicic.gov/.

Legal Provisions Applicable to Incarcerated Veterans

BAR TO VA HEALTH CARE DURING INCARCERATION
The Code of Federal Regulations provision governing the bar for VA health care during periods of incarceration can be found at https://www.law.cornell.edu/cfr/text/38/17.38

APPORTIONMENT OF BENEFITS TO FAMILY MEMBERS DURING INCARCERATION
A flyer produced by the Department of Veterans Affairs describes the process of apportioning VA disability and pension benefits to family members during the course of one's incarceration under certain circumstances. See http://www.benefits.va.gov/BENEFITS/factsheets/misc/incarcerated.pdf

Government Benefits Applicable to Incarcerated Veterans

Healthcare Reentry for Veterans (HCRV) is a program operated by the VA's Office of Justice Programs. The purpose of HCRV is to provide counseling to incarcerated veterans to better prepare them for reentry into the community following their period of incarceration. See https://www.va.gov/homeless/reentry.asp.

Other Resources Applicable to Incarcerated Veterans

The Veterans Survival Guide is a comprehensive handbook originally developed by Veterans for America. It is now made available free of charge by the National Veterans Legal Services Program on their website at http://www.nvlsp.org/images/products/survivalguide.pdf. The guide is intended to address specific issues related to veterans in a single location. Chapter 14 describes issues related to incarcerated veterans.

REFERENCES

Acosta, J., Adamson, D., Farmer, C., Farris, C., & Feeney, K. C. (2014). *Improving programs that address psychological health and traumatic brain injury: The RAND toolkit.* Santa Monica, CA: RAND.

Beggs, B. (2010, November 29). Veterans gain job skills, get "clean start" in jail program. *American Laundry News.*

Bennett, J. V. (1954). The criminality of veterans. *Federal Probation, 18*(2), 40–43.

Blue-Howells, J. H., Clark, S. C., van den Berk-Clark, C., & McGuire, J. F. (2013). The U.S. Department of Veterans Affairs veterans justice programs and the Sequential Intercept Model: Case examples in national dissemination of intervention for justice-involved veterans. *Psychological Services, 10*(1), 48.

Bronson, J., Carson, A., Noonan, M., & Berzofsky, M. (2015). *Veterans in prison and jail, 2011–12.* Washington, DC: US Department of Justice, Office of Justice Programs, Bureau of Justice Statistics.

Brooke, E. J., & Baldwin, J. M. (2016, November 17). Ethical issues in veterans treatment courts. Presentation at the American Society of Criminology Annual Conference, New Orleans, LA.

Carbery, K. (2013, November 7). Helping troubled veterans: Sheriff implements veterans program at county jail. *Jefferson County Leader* (St. Louis, Mo.).

Carlson, B. E., Stromwall, L. K., & Lietz, C. A. (2013). Mental health issues in recently returning women veterans: Implications for practice. *Social Work, 58*(2), 105–114.

Casey, R. J. (1923, September 28). The lost legion: 20,000 veterans are in prison—How many of them ought to be in hospital. *The American Legion Weekly, 7*, 24–27.

Clark, S., McGuire, J., & Blue-Howells, J. (2010). Development of veterans treatment courts: Local and legislative initiatives. *Drug Court Review, 7*(1), 171–208.

Cohen, S., Underwood, L., & Gottlieb, B. H. (2000). *Social support measurement and intervention: A guide for health and social scientists.* New York, NY: Oxford University Press.

Coughlin, S. S. (Ed.). (2012). *Posttraumatic stress disorder and chronic health conditions* (1st ed.). Washington, DC: American Public Health Association.

Cullen, F. T. (1994). Social support as an organizing concept for criminology: Presidential address to the Academy of Criminal Justice Sciences. *Justice Quarterly, 11*(4), 527–559.

DeFrank, R. (2012, December 11). Military unit opens at BCI. *The Times Leader* (Ohio).

DeGregory, L. (2009, August 14). Miami sex offenders limited to life under a bridge. *Tampa Bay Times.*

Demetrick, A. (2013, October 24). Three pups complete Md. prison vet dog training. *CBS Baltimore.*

Duhart, O. (2012). PTSD and women warriors: Causes, controls and a congressional cure. *Cardozo Journal of Law & Gender, 18*, 327–331.

Egolf, B., Lasker, J., Wolf, S., & Potvin, L. (1992). The Roseto effect: A 50-year comparison of mortality rates. *American Journal of Public Health, 82*(8), 1089–1098.

Elnitsky, C. A., Andersen, E. M., Clark, M. E., McGarity, S., Hall, C. G., & Kerns, R. D. (2013). Access to the U.S. Department of Veterans Affairs health system: Self-reported barriers to care among returnees of Operations Enduring Freedom and Iraqi Freedom. *BMC Health Services Research, 13*(1), 1–20.

Flatley, B., Clark, S., Blue-Howells, J., & Rosenthal, J. (2016). *Veterans Treatment Court Inventory Update*. Unpublished raw data. US Department of Veterans Affairs, Veterans Justice Programs, Philadelphia, PA.

Friedman, J. (2015). Risk factors for suicide among army personnel. *Journal of the American Medical Association, 11*, 1154–1155.

Frisman, L. K., & Griffin-Fennell, F. (2009). Commentary: Suicide and incarcerated veterans: Don't wait for the numbers. *Journal of the American Academy of Psychiatry and the Law, 37*, 92–94.

Gideon, L. (Ed.) (2013). Introduction: Special needs offenders. In *Special needs offenders in correctional institutions* (pp. 1–20). Thousand Oaks, CA: Sage.

Gierer, L. (2013, September 21). Church recovery program helps those in need. *Columbus Ledger-Enquirer* (Georgia), p. 1.

Gironda, R. J., Clark, M. E., Massengale, J. P., & Walker, R. L. (2006). Pain among veterans of Operations Enduring Freedom and Iraqi Freedom. *Pain Medicine, 7(4)*, 339–343.

Greden, J. F., Valenstein, M., Spinner, J., Blow, A., Gorman, L. A., Dalack, G. W., & Kees, M. (2010). Buddy-to-buddy, a citizen soldier peer support program to counteract stigma, PTSD, depression, and suicide. *Annals of the New York Academy of Sciences, 1208*, 90–97.

Greenberg, G. A., & Rosenheck, R. A. (2008). Jail incarceration, homelessness, and mental health: A national study. *Psychiatric Services, 59(2)*, 170–177.

Greenberg, G. A., & Rosenheck, R. A. (2009). Mental health and other risk factors for jail incarceration among male veterans. *Psychiatric Quarterly, 80(1)*, 41–53.

Grossman, D. (2009). *On killing: The psychological cost of learning to kill in war and society* (2nd ed.). New York, NY: Back Bay Books.

Groveland Correctional Facility. (n.d.). *Veterans residential therapeutic program: Groveland correctional facility vets dorm overview*. Groveland, NY: New York State Department of Correctional Services.

Held, P., & Owens, G. P. (2013). Stigmas and attitudes toward seeking mental health treatment in a sample of veterans and active-duty service members. *Traumatology, 19(2)*, 136–145.

Hendricks Thomas, K. (2015). *Brave, strong, and true: The modern warrior's battle for balance*. Clarksville, TN: Innovo.

Hershberger, G. (2013, September 20). Comments at POW/MIA Remembrance Day memorial service, Roxbury Correctional Institution, Hagerstown, MD.

Hixenbaugh, M. (2012, December 27). Veterans say uniform treatment in own prison wing helps healing. *The Virginian-Pilot* (Norfolk, VA).

Hoge, C. W. (2010). *Once a warrior, always a warrior* (1st ed.). Guilford, CT: Lyons.

Hoge, C. W., & Castro, C. A. (2012). Preventing suicides in U.S. service members and veterans. *Journal of American Medical Association, 308(7)*, 671–672.

Inmates building memorial to vets. (1988, October, 25). *Altoona Mirror*, p. A3.

Junger, S. (2015, June). How PTSD became a problem far beyond the battlefield. *Vanity Fair*. Retrieved from http://www.vanityfair.com/news/2015/05/ptsd-war-home-sebastian-junger

Justice for Vets. (2010, November 11). SITREP 005-10. Retrieved from http://www.nadcp.org/sites/default/files/nadcp/SITREP%20005-10%20FINAL_2.pdf.

Kamal, S. (2013, May 1). Veteran prisons pave path to re-rntry. *Columbia News Service*.

Kelly, U. A., Skelton, K., Patel, M., & Bradley, B. (2011). More than military sexual trauma: Interpersonal violence, PTSD, and mental health in women veterans. *Research in Nursing & Health, 34*(6), 457–467.

Koo, K. H., & Maguen, S. (2014). Military sexual trauma and mental health diagnoses in female veterans returning from Afghanistan and Iraq: Barriers and facilitators to Veterans Affairs care. *Hastings Women's Law Journal, 25*(1), 27–38.

Lionti, K. (2013, October 24). Holding center to help rehabilitate incarcerated veterans. YNN Buffalo.

MacPherson, M. (1993). *Long time passing: Vietnam and the haunted generation.* New York, NY: Doubleday.

Malmin, M. M. (2013). Warrior culture, spirituality, and prayer. *Journal of Religion and Health, 52*(3), 740–758.

Manley, S. (2016, May 7). Determining scope and eligibility of veterans treatment courts. Panel at Stanford Law School, Stanford University, CA.

Marks, A. (2001). Giving extra help to imprisoned vets. *Christian Science Monitor*, 3.

Maryland Department of Public Safety and Correctional Services. (2012, September 24). Western Correctional Institution inmates are training service dogs for wounded U.S. veterans. Townson, MD: Maryland Department of Public Safety and Correctional Services.

Maryland Department of Public Safety and Correctional Services. (n.d.). Community revitalization. Retrieved from http://msa.maryland.gov/megafile/msa/speccol/sc5300/sc5339/000113/014000/014589/unrestricted/20120425e.pdf

A Matter of Duty: The Continuing War Against PTSD. (2013, November 10). Bangor, ME: Maine Public Broadcasting Network.

McCabe, K. (2013, November 10). A helping hand for veterans: Many behind bars are finding there's a network of services to help them rebuild their lives. *The BostonGlobe.*

McCormick-Goodhart, M. (2013). Leaving no veteran behind: Policies and perspectives on combat trauma, veterans courts, and the rehabilitative approach to criminal behavior. *Pennsylvania State Law Review, 117*, 895–926.

McGuire, J. (2007). Closing a front door to homelessness among veterans. *Journal of Primary Prevention, 28*, 389–400.

McLoed, A. M. (2012). Decarceration courts: Possibilities and perils of a shifting criminal law. *Georgetown Law Journal, 100*, 1587–1674.

Mumola, C. J. (2000). Veterans in prison or jail. *Alcohol, 23*, 30–36.

Munetz, M. R., & Griffin, P. A. (2006). Use of the sequential intercept model as an approach to decriminalization of people with serious mental illness. *Psychiatric Services, 57*(4), 544–549.

National Institute of Corrections. (2010). *Crisis intervention teams: A frontline response to mental illness in corrections [Lesson Plans and Participant's Manual].* Washington, DC: National Institute of Corrections. Retrieved from http://nicic.gov/Library/024797.

National Institute of Corrections. (2012, March 18–20). *Proceedings of the large jail network.* Washington, DC: NIC Jails Division.

Noonan, M. E., & Mumola, C. J. (2007). *Veterans in state and federal prison, 2004.* Washington, DC: US Department of Justice, Office of Justice Programs, Bureau of Justice Statistics.

Pelts, M. D., & Albright, D. L. (2015). An exploratory study of student service members/ veterans' mental health characteristics by sexual orientation. *Journal of American College Health, 63*(7), 508–512.

Pentland, B. (1979, July 11). Prepared statement as coordinator, Veterans in Prison Project, Veterans Administration Medical Center (Brentwood), Los Angeles, CA, pp. 523–528. *Oversight on issues related to incarcerated veterans. Hearing before the Committee on Veterans' Affairs, United States Senate.* 96th Cong. 1st Session. Washington, DC: USGPO.

Perry, T. (2013, November 18). Separate jail facilities seek to cut recidivism rates among veterans. *Los Angeles Times.*

Rose, D. R., & Clear, T. R. (2003). Incarceration, reentry, and social capital. In *Prisoners once removed: The impact of incarceration and reentry on children, families, and communities* (pp. 189–232). Urban Institute and Washington, D.C.

Roth, J. B. (1986, November 8, 9). Guilty conscience. *The Gettysburg Times* (Pennsylvania), p. 3C.

Russell, R. T. (2015). Problem-solving court: Veterans treatment court. *Touro Law Review, 31*, 385–401.

Saxer, S. R. (2009). Banishment of sex offenders: Liberty, protectionism, and alternatives. *Washington University Law Review, 86*, 1397–1453.

Schaller, B. R. (2012). *Veterans on trial: The coming battles over PTSD.* Washington, DC: Potomac Books.

Seal, K. H., Metzler, T. J., Gima, K. S., Bertenthal, D., Maguen, S., & Marmar, C. R. (2009). Trends and risk factors for mental health diagnoses among Iraq and Afghanistan veterans using Department of Veterans Affairs health care, 2002–2008. *American Journal of Public Health, 99*(9), 1651–1658.

Seamone, E. R. (2013a, November/December). A historical touchstone for Nebraska in the mission to divert criminally-involved veterans from confinement. *Nebraska Lawyer, 16*(6), 7–15.

Seamone, E. R. (2013b). Dismantling America's largest sleeper cell: The imperative to treat, rather than merely punish, active-duty offenders with PTSD prior to discharge from the Armed Forces. *Nova Law Review, 38*, 73–117.

Seamone, E. R., McGuire, J., Sreenivasan, S., Clark, S., Smee, D., & Dow, D. (2014). Moving upstream: Why rehabilitative justice in military discharge proceedings serves a public health interest. *American Journal of Public Health, 104*(10), 1805–1811. doi:10.2105/AJPH.2014.302117

Seamone, E. R. (2016). Specialized housing units for veterans in prisons and jails: Solution-based incarceration as the counterpart to problem-solving veterans' courts. Washington, DC: Bureau of Justice Assistance and American University School of Public Affairs.

Seamone, E. R., & Albright, D. L. (2017). Veterans in the criminal justice system. In L. Hicks, E. L. Weiss, and J. E. Coll., *Civilian lives of U.S. veterans: Issues and identities* (vol. 2, pp. 481–506). New York, NY: Prager/ABC-CLIO.

Seamone, E. R., Brooks-Holliday, S., & Sreenivasan, S. (forthcoming 2018). Veteran *non grata*: Veteran sex offenders with service-related mental health conditions and the need to mitigate risk. *Virginia Journal of Criminal Law,*

Sieleni, B. (2011). Addressing the mental health crisis in corrections. *Corrections Today, 73*(5), 10.

Sigafoos, C. E. (1994). Post-traumatic stress disorder program for combat (Vietnam) veterans in prison. *International Journal of Offender Therapy and Comparative Criminology, 38*, 117–130.

Spelman, J. F., Hunt, S. C., Seal, K. H., & Burgo-Black, A. L. (2012). Post-deployment care for returning combat veterans. *Journal of General Internal Medicine, 27*(9), 1200–1209.

Tanielan, T., & Jaycox, L. H. (2008). *Invisible wounds of war: Psychological and cognitive injuries, their consequences, and services to assist recovery.* Santa Monica, CA: RAND.

Thomas, K. H., Albright, D., Shields, M., Kaufman, E., Michaud, C., Plummer Taylor, S., & Hamner, K. (2016). Predictors of depression diagnoses and symptoms in United States female veterans: Results from a national survey and implications for programming. *Journal of Military and Veterans' Health, 24*(3), 6–17.

Thomas, K. H., & Plummer Taylor, S. (2015). Bulletproofing the psyche: Mindfulness interventions in the training environment to improve resilience in the military and veteran communities. *Advances in Social Work, 16*(2), 312–322.

Thomas, K. H., Plummer Taylor, S., Hamner, K., Glazer, J., & Kaufman, E. (2015). Multisite programming offered to promote resilience in military veterans: A process evaluation of the just roll with it bootcamps. *Californian Journal of Health Promotion, 13*(2), 15–24.

Thomas, K. H., Turner, L. W., & Kaufman, E., Paschal, A., Knowlden, A. P., Birch, D. A., & Leeper, J. (2015). Predictors of depression diagnoses and symptoms in veterans: Results from a national survey. *Military Behavioral Health, 3*(4), 255–265.

Vergakis, B. (2012, November 25). Va. prison groups veterans together for support. Associated Press.

Wortzel, H. S., Binswanger, I. A., Anderson, C. A., & Lawrence, E. A. (2009). Suicide among incarcerated veterans. *Journal of the American Academy of Psychiatry and the Law, 37*(1), 82–94.

Zilney, L. J., & Zilney, L. A. (2009). *Reconsidering sex crimes and offenders: Prosecution or persecution.* New York, NY: Prager/ABC-CLIO.

14

Immigrant Inmates in the Correctional System

KHADIJA KHAJA AND JEREMIAH W. JAGGERS

In the last 20 years, the immigrant population has increased by "70 percent to about 43 million," making up about "13 percent of the population" with "one in every four Americans" being "either an immigrant or the child of one" with estimates that "one million immigrants have come legally to the United States each year" since 2000 (Preston, 2016, p. 1). The Pew Research Center (2008) illustrated that by 2050 one in five Americans (19%) will be foreign born; non-Hispanic Whites who comprised 67% of the population in 2005 will now be 47%; Hispanics will rise from 14% of the population in 2005 to 29%; Blacks will represent around 13%; and Asians, who were 5% of the population in 2005, will be at 9%. By 2050, 54% of the American population will be minorities. With this changing cultural landscape has come some contentious political divides. For example, recently the United States presidential election of 2016 brought to the forefront a growing public perception that immigrants take jobs away from Americans by lowering wages because they work for less, and if they are undocumented or from certain geographic regions, they are more prone to violence. In 2016, during the presidential election, one candidate when speaking about illegal immigrants said they "compete directly against vulnerable American workers" and that he would "boost wages and ensure jobs were offered to American workers first" (Preston, 2016, p. 1). However, a 2016 report by the National Academies of Sciences, Engineering and Medicine that conducted research from 14 leading economists, demographers, and various other scholars did not support the stereotype that illegal immigrants are taking away jobs (Blau & Mackie, 2016). Numerous researchers have found that the "most commonly invoked explanation for why native populations express negative views towards newcomers" is they fear that "immigrants threaten the social position and control over valued resources of the native born" (Timberlake & Williams, 2012, p. 870). Negative societal perceptions of immigrants have generally occurred in areas with "high visibility due to dense settlement in major cities, distinctly different patterns of dress or religious-cultural customs, or darker skin" (Timberlake & Williams, 2012, p. 868). Anti-immigrant public opinion has also been affected by whether immigrants are unauthorized to work, also referred to generally as undocumented or illegal workers (Timberlake & Williams, 2012). All these factors have led to increasing antagonism directed toward immigrants living in the United States. In addition, the global widespread terrorist acts committed by ISIS followers who have often videotaped their gruesome and horrific acts have led to growing fear and anxiety about immigrants coming especially from Islamic geographical regions. The reality is that many studies have shown that immigrants have "lower crime rates than natives" living in the United States and that "immigrants are only one-fifth as likely to be incarcerated for crimes" (Somin, 2015, p. 1). The growing public perception, which has been fueled by some political leaders, that we can reduce violent crime rates by "reducing immigration or deporting more illegals" is not accurate or realistic (Somin, 2015, p. 1). Research shows that "within the native-born population, there are a number of demographic groups that have much higher than average crime rates. For example, a hugely disproportionate percentage of violent crimes are committed by young males, particularly homicides" (Somin, 2015, p. 1). Adult men born in the United States are incarcerated 2.5 times more than men born in other countries (Butcher & Piehl, 2008). There is growing concern today that immigration detention and incarceration has an uncanny resemblance to the "policies of criminal sanctions and mass incarceration used to fight the war on drugs" during the 1980s that led to the "overincarceration of African American males" also known as the "browning of our American prison" system (*USA Today*, 2006, p. 7). Others argue that that "deportation of so-called 'criminal aliens' has become the driving force in U.S. immigration enforcement" (Chazaro, 2016, p. 594).

MIGRATION

During the 20th century, the geographical origin of immigrants went through a major shift. In the 1900s, approximately 80% of immigrants came from Europe, with much smaller populations from Latin American, Asia, and other areas. However, by 2000 about 16% of people living in the United States who were born in foreign lands came from Europe with "half of all immigrants from Latin America, over a quarter from Asia, and another 6% from other regions" (Timberlake & Williams, 2012, p. 869). Undocumented migration to the United States started back in 1965 because of changes to the US immigration policy. Before this time, Mexicans had been given opportunities to access temporary worker programs easily with no numerical legal permanent residency restrictions. However, around the "end of 1964, the US Congress abruptly terminated the Bracero program, and in 1965, it imposed the first ever numerical limitations on legal immigration from the Western Hemisphere" (Massey, Durand, & Pren, 2014, p. 1029). However, due to the organized migrant networks and monetary needs in Mexico, "migrants simply drew on network ties to continue migrating without authorization to jobs waiting for them north of the border" because there were many employers willing to hire them in the undergrown economy (Massey, Durand, & Pren, 2014, p. 1030). By 2010 there were at least 47 million Latinos living in the United States, with undocumented immigrants making up one fifth (19%) of this population (Arbona et al., 2010). The population today for undocumented residents is about 11 million; 60% are from Mexico and about 15% are from Central America with 5% having Latin American or Caribbean origins (Massey, Durand, & Pren, 2014).

The latest figures from 2014 illustrate that there are approximately 42.4 million immigrants who live in the United States, 13.3% of the total population of 318.9 million (Zong & Batalova, 2016). However, immigrants and their US-born children number about 81 million people, about 26% of the total population. Currently, the Census Bureau describes immigrants as being foreign-born individuals, which includes "lawful permanent residents, temporary nonimmigrants, and unauthorized immigrants" (Zong & Batalova, 2016, p. 1). The largest immigrant group that makes up 28% of the 42.4 million foreign-born population are Mexicans. Immigrants to the United States from India, China (including Taiwan), and the Philippines make up about 5% each; El Salvador, Vietnam, Cuba, and Korea represent 3% each; and the Dominican Republic and Guatemala make up 2% each. The immigrants from these 10 countries represent 60% of the US immigrant population (Zong & Batalova, 2016). In 2014, 48% of the foreign-born population described their race as White, 26% as Asian, 9% as Black, and 15% as a different race, with 2% having two or more racial backgrounds (Zong & Batlova, 2016). "In 2014, the top five U.S. states by number of immigrants were California (10.5 million), Texas and New York (4.5 million each), Florida (4 million), and New Jersey (2 million)" (Zong & Batalova, 2016, p. 1).

IMMIGRANT DETENTION AND DEPORTATION

A lot of the debate and controversy by policy makers and activists on detention of undocumented immigrants has focused on "whether the well-being of individuals should supersede economic and security concerns" (Rocha, Hawes, Fryar, & Wrinkle, 2014, p. 79). At the same time the enactment in 1986 of the Immigration Reform and Control Act (IRCA) and the Immigration Act of 1990 led to a dramatic increase in resources for Border Patrol and the Immigration and Naturalization Service (INS). The budget of Border Patrol increased substantially from $151 million in 1986 to surpassing 1 billion in 2000 (Rocha, Hawes, Fryar, & Wrinkle, 2014). The US government can now detain and deport "immigrants whom they find undesirable either because they are in the United States without authorization or because they have past criminal convictions" (Sladkova, Garcia-Mangado, & Quinteros, 2012, p. 78). This was made possible by laws that included the 1996 Illegal Immigration Reform and Responsibility Act (IIRIRA) and the Antiterrorism and Effective Death Penalty Act (AEDPA), which further broadened the definition of which types of people could be detained or removed from the United States. The IIRIRA law is also retroactive, which makes it possible for immigrants to be deported "for offenses they committed before 1996 and for which they have already served their sentences" (Sladkova, Garcia-Mangado, & Quinteros, 2012, p. 79). Studies have found that legal permanent residents have been incarcerated and deported for "shoplifting, jumping turnstiles, drunken driving, urinating in public, forgery, receipt of stolen property, petty drug crimes, or non-violent offenses" with poor access to judicial due process (Sladkova, Garcia-Mangado, & Quinteros, 2012, p. 79).

> There were 679,996 apprehensions in 2014 by U.S. Customs and Border Protection (CBP) and U.S. Immigration and Customs Enforcement (ICE), the two agencies within DHS responsible for the identification and removal of inadmissible noncitizens. The Border Patrol reported 486,651 apprehensions (72 percent of all apprehensions) in 2014, a 16 percent increase from 420,789 in 2013. About 99 percent of Border Patrol apprehensions (479,371) occurred along the Southwest border. Additionally, ICE Enforcement and Removal Operations made 181,719 administrative arrests (27 percent of total apprehensions in 2014) and ICE Homeland Security Investigations made 11,626 administrative arrests (2 percent). (Zong & Batalova, 2016, p. 1)

The majority of people apprehended in 2014 came from Mexico, Honduras, Guatemala, and El Salvador, making up 93% of all apprehensions (Zong & Batalova, 2016). Shankar (2010) reported that approximately half of the people removed from the United States had a criminal record with most of it related to drunk driving or drug-related offenses. A study done by Sladkova, Garcia-Mangado, and Quinteros (2012) and other studies have illustrated concerns about the serious impact of detention and deportation of a parent(s) on their children. Such children are at greater risk of living in poverty; experiencing trauma related to emotional distress; having feelings of abandonment due to a parent(s) who disappeared suddenly; facing educational challenges; having more chances of their health being impacted; having more vulnerability to joining gangs; and so on. The study recommended "lawyers, community leaders, immigrant-serving and faith-based organizations, and other trusted community members should educate parents about the best ways to respond when they are detained" and found that more education was needed to ensure that eligible immigrants apply for US citizenship (Sladkova et al., 2012, p. 92).

HISTORY OF IMMIGRATION POLICY

The "United States was founded by immigrants, colonists who came to the shores of the New World for economic gain and religious freedom" (Jaggers,Gabbard, & Jaggers, 2014, p. 3). Yet historically there have always been attempts to control immigration by citizenship processes and implementation of border control for certain populations (Jaggers et al., 2014). From the early beginnings, the US vision had not initially been about restricting immigration as the country needed more population. However, "late in the nineteenth century, nativism would take hold and incrementally, laws would slowly be implemented to regulate immigration" (Jaggers et al., 2014, p. 4) with five eras of immigration policy that framed the New World. During the *Open Door Era: 1776–1881*, the Naturalization Act of 1790 granted citizenship "to all white men of good moral character" with women getting citizenship via their husband or father (Jaggers et al., 2014, p. 4). The Alien and Sedition Acts of 1798 permitted "the president to deport any alien that was considered harmful to the safety of the United States" or "any alien from a country at war with the U.S." (Jaggers et al., 2014, p. 4). Slaves initially were not seen as citizens, but that decision was reversed with "the passing of the 13th and 14th amendments to the Constitution in 1865 and 1868" (Jaggers et al., 2014, p. 4). The *Era of Regulation: 1882–1916* occurred as increasingly more immigrants started to come from China and Europe. This led to formulation of the Chinese Exclusion Act of 1882, which stopped immigration of both skilled and unskilled labor from China for a decade, and was later extended. Although Chinese already living in the United States could stay, they still experienced a great deal of discrimination and resentment and were essentially viewed as a threat to nativists getting higher wage increases and jobs. The Scott Act of 1888 did not permit Chinese from returning to the United States if they left, further isolating them from their cultural roots. Ellis Island reviewed immigrant applicants from Europe, and Angel Island became the entry point for Asian immigrants who wanted to live in the United States. In 1906 the Naturalization Act was enacted, which "required" all immigrants to learn English to get citizenship (Jaggers et al., 2014). In 1907, the Dillingham Report, which examined the effects of migration for Congress, recommended that immigration had to be less and could pose a risk to "American culture and society" (Jaggers et al., 2014, p. 6). Subsequently, the Era of Restriction: 1917–1964 led to more groups being denied entry into the United States with the passage of the Immigration Act of 1917. A literacy test was now required to enter the United States with people from areas in Asia and the Pacific Islands barred from entry into the United States. The Emergency Quota Act of 1921 provided specific "formula on how many could enter from a given country" (Jaggers et al., 2014, p. 7). Then in 1952 Congress enacted the McCarran-Walter Act that got rid of racial and ethnic descriptors of who could enter the United States and created "three classes of immigrants-the skilled immigrant or related to a U.S. citizen, the average immigrant and the refugee" (Jaggers et al., 2014, p. 7). The Era of Liberalization: 1965–2000 was symbolic of "equalizing immigration policy, migration into the United States began to shift from predominantly European nations to Asian and other American countries" (Jaggers et al., 2014, p. 8) based on a "first come, first-served basis instead of using race or other sociocultural markers for distribution" (Jaggers et al., 2014, p. 8). The Era of Devolution: 2001–present was symbolized by the terrorist attacks on September 11, 2001, against the World Trade Centers in New York City. Implementation of the Patriot Act of 2001 gave the "government the ability to deny admission or to deport any immigrant who is politically or socially affiliated with a group that undermines U.S. anti-terrorist activities, has been in a position to endorse such activity or intends to participate in terrorist activity against the U.S." (Jaggers et al., 2014, p. 9). Immigration security concerns led to a number of propositions being passed in different states. In Arizona this included restricting undocumented individuals from getting state benefits, being allowed to have a bail if they were involved in particular crimes, restrictions to in-state tuition or financial aid if they were attending public universities or colleges, and so on.

DELINQUENCY AND IMMIGRANT YOUTH

Defining who is an immigrant isn't nearly as easy as many consider. The oft-cited definition is any individual who resides and was born in the country and comes into the United States. However, the spectrum of immigration types is far more complicated. Unfortunately, foreign-born families are often treated similarly, with some variation based on country of origin and ethnicity (Bui & Thongniramol, 2005; Fridrich & Flannery, 1995). Further complicating the immigrant definition are first- and 1.5-generation youth. First-generation immigrants are those born abroad who later migrate to the United States (Portes & Rumbaut, 2005; Sharpton, 2012). Between 1990 and 2015, the number of children with immigrant parents in the United States doubled to over 17 million (Migration Policy Institute, 2015). Although not explicitly outlined, there is an underlying assumption that first-generation immigrants are older youth or adults capable of *deciding* to migrate to a new country. On the other hand, 1.5-generation youth are born abroad but *accompany* parents, family, or other adults into another country. In contrast to 1.5-generation youth, children born in the United States to immigrant parents are referred to as second-generation "immigrants."

Migrating to the United States presents specific challenges to immigrant youth—namely acculturation. There is much variation in the conceptualization of acculturation, yet most definitions include aspects of psychological and social adaptation to new and different norms and values. This is cited as a major concern for those immigrating to a new country. Although there is great variation in the impact of acculturation, it is widely accepted that the acculturation process can be difficult, and it may result in adverse social, emotional, and familial problems (Berry, 1997, 2003).

One problem often encountered is *dissonant acculturation*, also known as the acculturation gap-distress hypothesis (Tezler, 2010). Immigrant adults arriving in the United States bring the norms, values, and cultural aspects from their home country with them. That is, they do not automatically adopt the values and norms of their host country. Instead, acculturation is a process of learning and of behavioral change. However, this can present some unique problems for children born in the United States (or those that migrated with their parents at a very young age). Parents encourage the uptake of values and norms that they themselves were taught, and this seems to be the basis of dissonant accultura-tion. As youth mature and have greater involvement with nonimmigrant youth and families, their belief system is influenced by that of their parents and by the larger society, which has its own set of norms and values. The difference in values and norms expected by the parents, and those that are actually learned means that parent and child, have different social and cultural perspectives. These differences are at least partially responsible for family conflict and maladjust-ment (Costigan & Dokis, 2006).

Preference given to American cultural values by Hispanic youth is associated with high-risk behaviors such as school conduct problems and psychosocial impairment, impacting the youth's ability to successfully function in society (Lau et al., 2005). Aggression, isolation, and poor academic performance are all associated with juvenile delinquency leading to incarceration. These concerns are hardly addressed by current migration policy. At the time this chapter was written, the President of the United States was advocating for a $20 billion border wall between the United States and Mexico, while also restricting entry to Muslims from the Middle East, a move not seen since the late 19th century.

CRIME AND ADULT IMMIGRANTS

Popular perception is that recent immigrants to the United States are more likely to commit crime, especially violent crime, than those native to the United States. However, recent immigrants are far less likely to commit crime or to engage in antisocial behavior, even when accounting for education, income, and residence in urban communities (Ewig, Martinez, & Rumbaut, 2015; Sampson, 2008; Vaughn, Salas-Wright, DeLisi, & Maynard, 2014), a fact established in the early part of the 20th century (Speranza, 1911–1912). The question remains as to why do people *believe* that immigrants frequently engage in criminal acts? Martinez and Lee (2000) proffer a number of theories, such as limited opportunity structures (Bankston, 1998), the culture of poverty hypothesis (Lewis, 1965), and social disorganization (Bursik, 1988; Tjomas & Znaniecki, 1920) that may account for these factual discrepancies. Stumpf (2006) suggests group membership may also play a major role in the treatment of immigrants. The criminal justice system engages in discrimination (even if unintended) against immigrants who are then denied the same rights as US citizens. Still, these suggestions are all undergirded by negative public opinions about immigrants, opinions that have existed and developed since the early 19th century (Roper Reports, 1995; Simon, 1993).

Popular perception has led to moral panic, a condition resulting in discriminatory legislation and intensified police enforcement in immigrant communities (Sabina, Cuevas, & Schally, 2013; Zatz & Smith, 2012). However, *victimization* of immigrants is a substantial problem, and it is especially bad for immigrants from Latin America, and specifically Mexico, who are more socially disadvantaged (Tonry, 1997). Consequently, immigrants are less likely to report crimes against them or their community (Davis & Henderson, 2003). The popular fearmongering perception that immigrants engage in more criminal behaviors than US citizens, combined with serious victimization, may exacerbate already existing legal and political problems. The reluctance to engage with law enforcement, even though prudent given known prejudices, may actually worsen perceptions.

CHILD WELFARE INVOLVEMENT AND IMMIGRANT FAMILIES

Immigrant families often have difficulty with child welfare agencies. Besides limitations imposed by poverty, immigrants face a unique set of problems. Among the most common are caseworkers' inadequate knowledge of immigration, cultural differences and acculturation, and challenges arising from language differences (Earner, 2007; Johnson, 2007). Despite opinions otherwise, child maltreatment is more common among native families than in immigrant families (Dettlaff, Earner, & Phillips, 2009). Unfortunately, child welfare practitioners' limited understanding of immigrant experiences, combined with negative perceptions about immigrants, involvement with the child welfare system results in unique problems that may yield serious family trauma (Pine & Drachman, 2005).

Often times, families involved with the child welfare system are provided services directed toward family unification, including health and mental health services. Those families who are undocumented and/or have limited English proficiency have a more difficult time *accessing* services, even when court mandated (Ayon, 2009). Moreover, non-White families often experience longer out-of-home placement and limited *availability* of services to reunify families (Chow, Jaffee, & Snowden, 2003; Lu et al., 2004). This is especially problematic since immigrant caregivers involved with the child welfare system demonstrate serious mental illness, greater cognitive impairment, and more involvement with the justice and the incarceration system (Rajendran & Chemtob, 2009). There is also some evidence that children in Latino families receive fewer mental health services (Dettlaff & Cardoso, 2010).

Immigrant families have serious difficulties accessing and using services designed to facilitate family reunification. There is a strong association between histories of child maltreatment and delinquency (Landsford et al., 2009), adult criminality (Elklit, Karstoft, Armour, & Feddern, 2013), and future abuse of one's own children (Heyman & Slep, 2002). Limited access to services that help to reunify families most certainly has a significant negative effect on the long-term well-being of immigrant youth and families. Increasing access to high-quality services for families involved in the child welfare system is an essential component for ensuring well-being into adulthood.

SERVICES TO IMMIGRANTS

Immigrants are already one of the most underserved populations. Similarly, individuals with previous criminal justice system involvement have difficulty accessing and using health and mental health services (Berk, Schur, Chavez, & Frankel, 2000; Kim et al., 2011). Moreover, there is limited access to legal representation for poor immigrants (Katzman, 2007). The resulting "storm" of limited access has been blamed for making the plight of immigrants in the United States worse, potentially restricting any opportunity for upward mobility.

The health care system imposes a number of barriers, such as cost of care, which limits access and use of health care. Prevention of medical disease is a public health concern. In addition, prevention efforts serve an economic function, limiting individual expenditures on health care by maintaining health rather than fixing existing problems. Unfortunately, there are barriers specifically targeting immigrants that limit their use of health care. Inconsistent involvement with public health agencies places a significant burden on the health care system. Immigrants with chronic conditions such as HIV, and who need prenatal care or vaccination, further exacerbate community health problems that could otherwise be addressed through increased access to health care (Kullgren, 2003).

A number of political determinants are associated with use of health care. Despite policy mechanisms like the Affordable Care Act, immigrants' often do not have health insurance. Undocumented immigrants are explicitly prevented from receiving the benefits provided by the Affordable Care Act (National Immigration Law Center, 2014), and undocumented immigrants are only allowed Medicaid services in exceptional cases (Center for Medicare & Medicaid Services, 2014).

While married, older females are far more likely to have insurance and to access health care than other demographics (Nandi et al., 2011), many are left uninsured or underinsured. Many times immigrants from Mexico and Central America are forced back across the border into Mexico to receive treatment. Although mostly self-initiated (Wallace, Mendez-Luck, & Castaneda, 2009), some formal mechanisms have been established for Mexican immigrants to receive treatment in Mexico (Warner, 2012). Still, children from immigrant families are far more likely to be unhealthy (Huang, Yu, & Ledsky, 2006). Because adult well-being is largely influenced by health status, immigrant children do not have the best start. Poor health then likely perpetuates difficulties in accessing and using health care services.

Mental illness is often a major concern among immigrant groups. The source and severity of mental illness are affected by a number of unique circumstances not necessarily problematic in the native-born population. For example, Latino immigrants must often acculturate to the social norms and expectations of individuals and groups in the United States. This entails, to a certain degree, rejection (or at least suppression) of one's own beliefs in order to adapt to a new set of attitudes and beliefs (Pumariega, Rothe, & Pumariega, 2005).

There is also a significant difference in access to and use of mental health services when compared to native-born populations (Nandi et al., 2011). This may be due in part to socioeconomic circumstance; those in poverty are less likely to receive treatment for mental illness (Chow, Jaffee, & Snowden, 2003). However, a number of barriers specifically applicable to non-European immigrants have been identified. Whitley and colleagues (2006) found that immigrants were reluctant to use services because of the overuse of medications, dismissive attitudes by practitioners, and beliefs in "nontraditional" techniques not employed by Western practitioners.

Surprisingly, many immigrants are unwilling to access community-based mental health services but are more enthusiastic about seeking mental health treatment from physicians (Kiramyer et al., 2011; Vega et al., 1999). Among other approaches, school-based treatment has shown some success in providing accessible treatment for Latino children (Kataoka et al., 2003). This reluctance to seek out and receive mental health treatment by immigrants, especially Latino immigrants, is most certainly related to cultural, familial, and legal concerns. Providing access to treatment in "sheltered" conditions, conditions where these concerns are adequately addressed should be implemented to ensure the well-being of families and to ensure fewer chances of getting involved with the judicial system.

CONCLUSION

With the growth of the immigration detention population, more private immigration facilities have been created in the United States. The Department of Homeland Security is relying more on "private companies to detain an immigrant detainee population that's reaching historic highs" (Speri, 2016a, para.1). In 2014 the immigration detention population was reported to have increased by 47% during the last decade (Speri, 2016). A 2016 report commissioned by the Department of Homeland Security that involved law enforcement, national security, and military experts was critical of private immigration detention centers, finding that correctional services, programs, resources, safety, and security measures were not at the standards of general correctional services and did not result in significant cost-saving measures.

Immigration and Customs Enforcement (ICE) reports that "70 percent of its detainees are held in privately run facilities" (Speri, 2016b, para 11). Currently there are approximately 41,000 immigrants in detention, with this number expected to rise to 45,000 soon. Detention Watch Network's (2016) report states that the "U.S. immigration detention system is the largest in the world" with "over 200 detention facilities" and American tax payers paying "more than 2 billion each year to main the detention system" (Detention Watch Network, 2017, p. 2). In August 2016, the Department of Justice announced that it would begin phasing out private prisons with some reasons related to "investigative reporting on deaths as a result of medical neglect and other serious deficiencies" and also "years of careful research and advocacy by non-profit organizations, and organizing and resistance by people incarcerated in the facilities" (Detention Watch Network, 2016, p. 2).

The federal government of the United States has pledged to deport millions of immigrants who did not come here legally, causing a serious crises for the emotional well-being of these families, many of whom are reporting severe anxiety, fear, and stress. Research by the Sentencing Project, which is a criminal justice research and advocacy group, found that residents not born in the United States will engage in crime less often than citizens born in the United States. Another study by the Cato Institute reported that immigrants are "less likely to be incarcerated" relative to native "shares of the population" (Bernal, 2017, para. 3). One presidential candidate during the 2016 campaign tstated that he felt illegal immigrants further posed an economic threat and were one of the reasons for crime increases. The 2018 federal budget of the Department of Homeland Security (the DHS budget) will increase by 3 billion to fund a "proposed border wall and executive orders on immigration" (Bernal, 2017, para. 4). Further, during the 2016 presidential election on various occasions one candidate stated that he felt that immigrants "bring crime" often specifically mentioning individuals who had been murdered by immigrants who were not here legally (Bernal, 2017, para.

5). Many have been deeply troubled by such statements, feeling it is creating societal hysteria, and increasing discriminatory views about immigrants that they are more prone to crime, factors that could explain increases in hate crimes toward immigrant populations living in the United States. The Cato Institute and the Sentencing Project do not support findings that immigrants commit more crimes than people born in the United States. Further, the Cato Study found that "there are about 2 million U.S. born citizens, 123,000 undocumented immigrants and 64, 000 documented foreign citizens in jails" (Bernal, 2017, para. 9). Many families who may have had children born here but who did not come here legally and who have lived here for years now face threat of incarceration and ultimately deportation. This has heightened anxiety levels for many communities. Further, Attorney General Sessions has "threatened to strip Justice Department funding from what are known as sanctuary city jurisdictions that don't comply with a particular federal law about sharing information with Immigration and Customs Enforcement" (Zapotosky, 2017, para. 8). There is now an increase in lawsuits against the federal government because of this. Others are concerned that "crime victims, victims of sexual abuse and domestic violence, witnesses to crimes who are aiding law enforcement, limited English speakers" and others who come to the courts for help who did not come here legally face a double jeopardy as they could be incarcerated and eventually deported if it is learned they are here illegally, making them more vulnerable to be repeated crime victims (Zapotosky, 2017, para. 13). The federal government's persistent attempts to ban people coming from seven Muslim majority countries have also led to increasing fears within this community as well. The Southern Poverty Law Center reported that "at least 700 hateful incidents of harassment around the country against immigrants were reported during the week after the presidential election" (Davis, 2017, closing paragraph).

All of these potential changes also increase the risk that immigrant youth will not receive the services they need to address the psychosocial correlates of delinquent behavior. With a strong emphasis on deportation, youth who would have previously been provided services (i.e., probation, family therapy, etc.) may find themselves incarcerated for otherwise minor offenses. This approach serves to support political ideals about the supposed economic problems arising from immigration. Moreover, the belief that immigrants are criminals, despite evidence to the contrary, has previously enforced populist ideas (c.f. Arizona SB 1070) about the treatment of immigrants in the criminal justice system.

TRENDS AND FUTURE DIRECTIONS

In May 2017, immigration and customs enforcement conducted the biggest antigang operation to date, which led to 1,300 arrests in the United States. Contrary to stereotypes "of the arrests, 933 were US citizens and 445 were foreign nationals, with 384 in the country illegally" (Kopan, 2017, para. 2). Further, "of the 1,378 total arrests, 1,095 were confirmed to be gang members or affiliates of a gang, ICE said, including mostly Bloods, followed by Surenos, MS-13 and the Krips" (Kopan, 2017, para. 5–6). Some have argued that the aggressive commitment by ICE to target gangs whose membership includes people of color, or diverse ethnicities, is leading to higher incarceration rates of this population. However, various studies have shown that "immigrants are less likely to commit serious crimes or be behind bars than the native-born" and that "high rates of immigration are associated with lower rates of violent crime and property crime," which "holds true for both legal immigrants and the unauthorized, regardless of their country of origin or level of education" (Ewing, Martinez, & Rumbaut, 2015, para. 1). Thus, contrary to myths and stereotypes, strict immigration laws and policies do not appear to be an appropriate strategy to address crime. The growing stigma of immigrants being associated with "criminality" had led to common misconceptions that immigrants are threats to the national security, which is contrary to empirical evidence. What is deeply troubling is that "whole new classes of felonies have been created which apply only to immigrants, deportation has become a punishment for even minor offenses, and policies aimed at trying to end authorized immigration have been made more punitive rather than rational or practical. In short, immigrants themselves are being criminalized" with more immigrant communities fearing their incarceration rates will increase (Ewing, Martinez, & Rumbaut, 2015, para. 1).

> The United States is in the midst of a "great expulsion" of immigrants, both lawfully present and unauthorized, who tend to be non-violent and non-threatening and who often have deep roots in this country. This relentless campaign of deportation is frequently justified as a war against "illegality"—which is to say, against unauthorized immigrants. But that justification does not come close to explaining the banishment from the United States of lawful permanent residents who committed traffic offenses and who have U.S.-based families. Nor does it explain the lack of due-process rights accorded to so many of the immigrants ensnared in deportation proceedings. Likewise, the wave of deportations we are currently witnessing is often portrayed as a crime-fighting tool. But, as the findings of this report make clear, the majority of deportations carried out in the United States each year do not actually target "criminals" in any meaningful sense of the word. (Ewing, Martinez, & Rumbaut, 2015, para. 8)

Today more immigrant families are being separated with billions being spent on border enforcement. Many immigrants come to the United States to pursue better lives for their families. As Ewing, Martinez, and Rumbaut (2015) state, "public policies must be based on facts, not anecdotes or emotions" and the continued increases in the "detention-and-deportation machine is designed to primarily track down and expel non-violent individuals, including legal residents of the United States who have worked and raised families here for many years" (Ewing, Martinez, & Rumbaut, 2015, para. 11). It is critical that as we move into the future that "US immigration policies accurately reflect the diversity and complexity of immigration to this country, based not on a reflexive politics of fear and myth, but on sound analysis and empirical evidence with due process rights accorded to so many of the immigrants ensnared in deportation proceedings" (Ewing,

Martinez, & Rumbaut, 2015, pp. 12–13). Undocumented workers who work in the "underground economy" are not protected by labor laws and have justifiable fears of being incarcerated and deported, leading to more opportunities for unethical employers to intimidate, abuse, and exploit them for profit. More advocacy agencies, volunteer lawyers, and mental health supports systems must be put into place to support such workers who face increasing anxiety and stress about what the future holds for them and their children in the United States.

CASE EXAMPLE

Juan is a 16-year-old Hispanic adolescent with no known criminal record who was arrested for suspicion of trafficking marijuana. Juan's primary language is Spanish. At the time of his arrest, his citizenship status was unknown. Juan is an American citizen who was born in Puerto Rico. He and his father moved to a rural county in the Southeastern United States when he was 12 to find stable employment. Initially, Juan was referred to Immigration and Customs Enforcement for processing. After determining his citizenship status, he was remanded to the jail in his hometown without bail pending trial. Juan met with the prosecutor. He was not afforded a translator. Subsequent to his meeting, Juan pled to possession of a controlled substance and was sentenced to 6 months in jail and 2 years of probation. Even though he was a first-time offender, Juan's conviction for possession of a controlled substance meant he did not qualify for the county's diversion program. Diversion programs, such as Juvenile Detention Alternatives Initiative (JDAI), are designed to reduce the number of juveniles detained in prisons and jails. However, the county's diversion program excludes youth convicted of drug or violent offenses.

Three days after arriving in jail, Juan was assigned a Spanish-speaking mental health provider—Amanda. Amanda told Juan that she would be assessing him to identify any areas of concern. Amanda used the MAYSI-2 (Massachusetts Youth Screening Instrument) to identify potential mental health concerns. The MAYSI-2 identifies concerns with alcohol/drug use, angry-irritable behavior, somatic complaints, suicidal ideation, thought disturbances, and traumatic experiences. The MAYSI-2 provides three levels of concern: no concern, caution, and warning. Warning is the most urgent outcome for each of the subscales, and it indicates a need for immediate intervention by a mental health professional. Based upon discussions with Juan and an evaluation using the MAYSI-2, Amanda determined Juan had two areas of concern; the MAYSI-2 indicated "caution" for somatic complaints and "warning" for alcohol/drug use. To address the somatic complaints, Amanda referred Juan to the jail's nurse practitioner to evaluate his physical health. At admission to the jail, Juan tested positive for marijuana and admitted to drinking vodka prior to his arrest. Further assessment of Juan's substance use revealed that he drinks alcohol three or more times per day. Consequently, Amanda referred Juan to a substance abuse treatment program within the jail that included an abstinence-based peer support group and weekly meetings with a substance abuse counselor to address his needs and progress toward sobriety.

Juan's time in jail was difficult. The county where he resided was a poor, rural area of the state. The population was largely English-speaking, White individuals. Besides Amanda, no one in the jail spoke Spanish. Juan's limited ability to communicate using English made things even more difficult. He was unable to connect with any of the other inmates and most regarded him as just another immigrant. Moreover, neither his substance use therapist nor members of his peer support group spoke Spanish. Near the end of his jail time the substance use therapist expressed concerns that Juan had not taken his treatment seriously. After reporting her concerns to Juan's probation officer, he required Juan to continue his treatment after leaving jail.

Prior to his arrest, Juan and his father had summer jobs working for a landscaping company. However, Juan was released during the winter and had no prospects for employment. Similarly, his father had not secured employment since the fall. A condition of Juan's release is that he become employed within 30 days, and that he begin substance use treatment immediately, something he must pay for himself. In addition, he was required to stay in the county for 6 months. Since Juan wasn't able to secure employment in his home county, he moved to a large city 100 miles away and secured a job at a fast food restaurant. He also began treatment with a Spanish-speaking therapist at a community mental health center. Despite his success in meeting most of the requirements, he was rearrested.

WEB-BASED RESOURCES

Juvenile Detention Alternative Initiative (JDAI): http://www.aecf.org/work/juvenile-justice/jdai/

Massachusetts Youth Screening Inventory: http://www.nysap.us/MAYSI2.html

The Sentencing Project: http://www.sentencingproject.org/

REFERENCES

Arbona, C., Olvera, N., Rodriquez, N., Hagan, J., Linares, A., & Wiesner, M. (2010). Acculturative stress among documented and undocumented Latino immigrants in the United States. *Hispanic Journal of Behavioral Sciences, 32*(3), 362–384.

Ayon, C. (2009). Shorter time-lines, yet higher hurdles: Mexican families' access to child welfare mandated services. *Children and Youth Services Use, 31*(6), 609–616.

Bankston, C. L. (1998). Youth gangs and the new second generation: A review essay. *Aggression and Violent Behavior, 3*(1), 35–45.

Berk, M. L., Schur, C. L., Chavez, L. R., & Frankel, M. (2000). Health care use among undocumented Latino immigrants. *Health Affairs, 19*(4), 51–64.

Bernal, R. (2017). Reports find that immigrants commit less crimes than US-born citizens. Retrieved from http://thehill.com/latino/324607-reports-find-that-immigrants-commit-less-crime-than-us-born-citizens

Berry, J. W. (1997). Immigration, acculturation, and adaptation. *Applied Psychology, 46*(1), 5–34.

Berry, J. W. (2003). Conceptual approaches to acculturation. In K. M. Chen, P. B. Organista, and G. Marin (Eds.), *Acculturation: Advances in theory, measurement, and applied research* (pp. 17–38). Washington, DC: American Psychological Association.

Blau, F. D., & Mackie, C. (2016*). The economic and fiscal consequences of immigration report.* Report of the National Academies of Sciences, Engineering, and Medicine. Washington, DC: National Academies Press.

Bui, H. N., & Thongniramol, O. (2005). Immigration and self-reported delinquency: The interplay of immigration generations, gender, race, and ethnicity. *Journal of Crime and Justice, 28*(2), 71–99.

Bursil, R. J. (1988). Social disorganization and theories of crime and delinquency: Problems and prospects. *Criminology, 23*, 519–551.

Butcher, K. F., & Piehl, A. M. (2008). Crime corrections and California. *Public Policy Institute of California, 9*(3), 1–23. Retrieved from http://www.ppic.org/content/pubs/cacounts/CC_208KBCC.pdf2008

Center for Medicare & Medicaid Services. (2014). Eligibility for non-citizens in Medicaid and CHIP. Retrieved from https://www.medicaid.gov/medicaid/outreach-and-enrollment/downloads/overview-of-eligibility-for-non-citizens-in-medicaid-and-chip.pdf

Chazaro, A. (2016). Challenging the criminal alien paradigm. *UCLA Law Review, 63*(3), 594–664.

Chow, L. C. C., Jaffee, K., & Snowden, L. (2003). Racial/ethnic disparities in the use of mental health services in poverty areas. *American Journal of Public Health, 93*(6), 792–797.

Costigan, C. L., & Dokis, D. P. (2006). Relations between parent-child acculturation differences and adjustment within immigrant Chinese families. *Child Development, 77*(5), 1252-1267.

Davis, M. (2017). Rise in hate crimes, divisive rhetoric prompts bar group to act. Retrieved from http://www.abajournal.com/magazine/article/bar_resists_hate_crime_rhetoric/

Davis, R. C., & Henderson, N. J. (2003). Willingness to report crimes: The role of ethnic group membership and community efficacy. *Crime & Delinquency, 49*(4), 564–580.

Detention Watch Network. (2017). A toxic relationship: Private prisons and U.S. immigration detention. Retrieved from http://www.detentionwatchnetwork.org/sites/default/files/reports/A%20Toxic%20Relationship_DWN.pdf

Dettlaff, A. J., & Cardoso, J. B. (2010). Mental health need and service use among Latino children of immigrants in the child welfare system. *Children and Youth Services Review, 32*(10), 1373–1379.

Dettlaff, A. J., Earner, I., & Phillips, S. D. (2009). Latino children of immigrants in the child welfare system: Prevalence, characteristics, and risk. *Children and Youth Services Review, 31*(7), 775–783.

Earner, I. (2007). Immigrant families and public child welfare: Barriers to services and approaches for change. *Child Welfare, 86*(4), 63–91.

Elklit, A., Karstotf, K, Armour, C., Feddern, D., & Christoffersen, M. (2013). Predicting criminality from child maltreatment typologies and posttraumatic stress symptoms. *European Journal of Psychotraumatology, 4*(1), 19825. doi:10.3402/ejpt.v4i0.19825

Ewig, W., Martinez, D. E., & Rumbaut, R. G. (2015). *Special Report: The criminalization of immigration in the United States.* Washington, DC: American Immigration Council.

Fridrich, A. H., & Flannery, D. J. (1995). The effects of ethnicity and acculturation on early adolescent delinquency. *Journal of Child and Family Studies, 4*(1), 69–87.

Heyman, R. E., & Slep, A. M. S. (2002). Do child abuse and interparental violence lead to adulthood family violence? *Journal of Marriage and Family, 64*(4), 864–870.

Huang, Z. J., Yu, S. M., & Ledsky, R. (2006). Health status and health service access and use among children in U.S. immigrant families. *American Journal of Public Health, 96*(4), 1–7.

Jaggers, J., Gabbard, W. J., & Jaggers, S. J. (2014). The devolution of U.S. immigration policy: An examination of the history and future of immigration policy. *Journal of Policy Practice, 13*(3), 3–15. Retrieved from http://dx.doi.org/10.1080/15588742.2013.855695

Johnson, M. A. (2007). The social ecology of acculturation: Implications for child welfare services to children of immigrants. *Children and Youth Services Review, 29*(11), 1426–1438.

Kakota, S., Stein, B. D., Jaycox, L. H., Wong, M., Escudero, P., Tu, W., Zaragoza, C., & Fink, A. (2003). A school-based mental health program for traumatized Latino immigrant children. *Journal of the American Academy of Child & Adolescent Psychiatry, 42*(3), 311–318.

Katzmann, R. (2007). The legal profession and the unmet needs of the immigrant poor. *The Report, 62*(2), 287–311.

Kim, G., Loi, C. X. A., Chirboga, D. A., Jang, Y., Parmelee, P., & Allen, R. S. (2011). Limited English proficiency as a barrier to mental health service use: A study of Latino and Asian immigrants with psychiatric disorders. *Journal of Psychiatric Research, 45*(1), 104–110.

Kiramyer, L. J., Narasiah, L., Munoz, M., Rashid, M., Ryder, A. G., Guzder, J., Hassan, G., Rousseau, C., & Pottie, K. (2011). Common mental health problems in immigrants and refugees: General approach to primary care. *Canadian Medical Association Journal, 183*(12), 1–7.

Kopan, T. (2017). Ice announces major anti-gang operation, mostly US citizens arrested. Retrieved from http://www.cnn.com/2017/05/11/politics/ice-gang-arrests-operation/index.html

Kullgren, J. T. (2003). Restrictions on undocumented immigrants' access to health services: The public health implications of welfare reform. *American Journal of Public Health, 93*(10), 1630–1633.

Lansford, J. E., Miller-Johnson, S., Berlin, L. J., Dodgen, K. A., Bates, J. E., & Pettit, G. S. (2009). Early physical abuse and later violent delinquency: A prospective longitudinal study. *Child Maltreatment, 12*(3), 233–245.

Lau, A. S., Yeh, M., Wood, P. A., McCabe, K. M., Garland, A. F., & Hough, R. L. (2005). The acculturation gap-distress hypothesis among high-risk Mexican American families. *Journal of Family Psychology, 19*(3), 367–375.

Lewis, O. (1965). *La vida: A Puerto Rican family in the culture of poverty.* New York, NY: Random House.

Lu, Y. E., Landsverk, J., Ellis-Macleod, E., Newton, R., Ganger, W., & Johnson, I. (2004). Race, ethnicity, and case outcomes in child protective services. *Children and Youth Services Review, 26*(5), 447–461.

Martinez, R., & Lee, M. T. (2000). On immigration and crime. *The Nature of Crime: Continuity and Change, 1*, 485–524.

Massey, D. S., Durand, J., & Pren, K. A. (2014). Explaining undocumented migration to the U.S. *International Migration Review, 48*(4), 1028–1061. doi: 0.1111/imre.12151

Migration Policy Institute. (2015). Children in U.S. immigrant families by age group and state, 1990 versus 2015. Retrieved from http://www.migrationpolicy.org/programs/data-hub/charts/children-immigrant-families

Nandi, A., Galea, S., Lopez, G., Nandi, V., Strogarone, S., & Ompad, D. C. (2011). Assess to and use of health services among undocumented Mexican immigrants in a US urban area. *American Journal of Public Health, 98*(11), 2011–2020.

National Immigration Law Center. (2014). Immigrants and the Affordable Care Act. Retrieved from https://www.nilc.org/issues/health-care/immigrantshcr/

Pine, B. A., & Drachman, D. (2005). Effective child welfare practice with immigrant and refugee children and their families. *Child Welfare, 84*(5), 537–562.

Portes, A., & Rumbaut, R. G. (2005). Introduction: The second generation and the children of immigrants longitudinal study. *Ethnic and Racial Studies, 28*(6), 983–999.

Preston, J. (2016, September 21). Immigrants aren't taking American jobs, new study finds. *New York Times.* Retrieved from http://www.nytimes.com/2016/09/22/us/immigrants-arent-taking-americans-jobs-new-study-finds.html?_r=0

Pumariega, A. J., Rothe, E., & Pumariega, J. B. (2005). Mental health of immigrants and refugees. *Community Mental Health Journal, 41*(5), 581–597.

Rajendran, K., & Chemtob, C. M. (2009). Factors associated with service use among immigrants in the child welfare system. *Evaluation and Program Planning, 33*(3), 317–323.

Rocha, R. R., Hawed, D. P., Fryar, A. H., & Wrinkle, R. D. (2014). Policy climates, enforcement rates and migrant behavior: Is self-deportation a viable immigration policy? *The Policy Studies Journal, 2*(1), 79–100.

Roper Reports (1995). *Roper Reports 95–4.* New York, NY: Roper Starch Worldwide.

Sabina, C., Cuevas, C. A., & Schally, J. (2013). The effect of immigration and acculturation on victimization among a national sample of Latino women. *Cultural Diversity and Ethnic Minority Psychology, 19*(1), 13–26.

Sampson, R. J. (2008). Rethinking crime and immigration. *Contexts, 7*(1), 28–33.

Shankar, V. (2010, October 7). U.S. deportations reach record high. *The Washington Post.* Retrieved from http://www.washingtonpost.com.

Sharpton, A. N. (2012). First generation immigrants. In *Encyclopedia of Immigrant Health* (pp. 702–703). New York, NY: Springer.

Simon, R. J. (1993). Old minorities, new immigrants: Aspirations, hopes, and fears. *Annals of the American Academy of Political and Social Science, 30*, 61–73.

Sladkova, J., Garcia-Mangado, S. M., & Quinteros, J. R. (2012). Lowell immigrant communities in the climate of deportations. *Analyses of Social Issues and Public Policy, 12*(1), 78–95.

Somin, L. (2015, July 14). Immigration and crime. *Washington Post.* Retrieved from https://owl.english.purdue.edu/owl/resource/560/10/2915

Speranza, G. C. (1911–1912). Crime and immigration. *Journal of Criminal Law and Criminology, 2*(4), 546–553.

Speri, A. (2016a). The Justice Department is done with private prisons: Will ice drop them too? Retrieved from https://theintercept.com/2016/08/18/justice-department-done-with-private-prisons-will-ice-drop-them-too/

Speri, A. (2016b). Private prisons are really bad, but good enough for immigrants, concludes homeland security report. Retrieved from https://theintercept.com/2016/12/05/private-prisons-are-really-bad-but-good-enough-for-immigrants-concludes-homeland-security-report/

Stumpf, J. (2006). The crimmigration crisis: Immigrants, crime, and sovereign power. *American University Law Review, 56*(2), 367–419.

Telzer, E. H. (2010). Expanding the acculturation gap-distress hypothesis model: An integrative review of the research. *Human Development, 53*, 313–340.

Thomas, W. I., & Znaniecki, F. (1920). *The Polish peasant in Europe & America*. Chicago, IL: Chicago University Press.

Timberlake, J., & Williams, R. H. (2012). Stereotypes of U.S. immigrants from four global regions. *Social Science Quarterly, 93*(4), 867–890.

Thomas, W. I., & Znaniecki, F. (1920). *The Polish peasant in Europe and America*. Chicago, IL: University of Chicago Press.

Tonry, M. (1997). Ethnicity, crime, and immigration. *Crime & Justice, 1*, 1–29.

USA Today Magazine. (2006, September). Is immigrant detention mimicking drug policies? *USA Today Magazine, 135* (2736), 7–7.

Vaughn, M. G., Salas-Wright, C. P., DeLisi, M., & Maynard, B. R. (2014). The immigrant paradox: Immigrants are less antisocial than native-born Americans. *Social Psychiatry and Social Epidemiology, 49*(7), 1129–1137.

Vega, W. A., Kolody, B., Aguilar-Gaxola, S., & Catalano, R. (1999). Gaps in service utilization by Mexican Americans with mental health problems. *American Journal of Psychiatry, 156*(6), 928–934.

Wallace, S. P., Mendez-Luck, C., & Castaneda, X. (2009). Heading south: Why Mexican immigrants in California seek health services in Mexico. *Medical Care, 47*(6), 662–669.

Warner, D. C. (2012). Access to health services for immigrants in the USA: From the Great Society to the 2010 Health Reform Act and after. *Ethnic and Racial Studies, 35*(1), 40–55.

Whitely, R., Kirmayer, L. J., & Groleau, D. (2006). Understanding immigrants' reluctance to use mental health services: A qualitative study from Montreal. *The Canadian Journal of Psychiatry, 51*, 205–209.

Zapotosky, M. (2017). Top U.S. officials defend courthouse arrests of undocumented immigrants in escalating feud with California Justice. Retrieved from https://www.washingtonpost.com/world/national-security/top-us-officials-defend-courthouse-arrests-of-undocumented-immigrants-in-escalating-feud-with-california-justice/2017/03/31/d92dddfe-1627-11e7-ada0-1489b735b3a3_story.html?hpid=hp_hp-more-top-stories_sessions-705pm%3Ahomepage%2Fstory&utm_term=.3e6866e619a7

Zatz, M. S., & Smith, H. (2012). Immigration, crime, and victimization: Rhetoric and reality. *Annual Review of Law and Social Science, 8*(1), 498.

Zong, J., & Batalova, J. (2016, April 14). Frequently requested statistics on immigrants and immigration in the United States. Migration Policy Institute. Retrieved from http://www.migrationpolicy.org/article/frequently-requested-statistics-immigrants-and-immigration-united-states

15

Terminal Illness in Correctional Settings

STEPHANIE GRACE PROST

Terminal illness, including many cancers, liver disease, and Alzheimer's disease, describes conditions that are unlikely to respond to curative care and, therefore, are likely to result in premature death. Persons may enter correctional facilities with terminal illnesses or may develop such conditions over time. This chapter describes the prevalence, scope, and costs associated with terminal illness in incarcerated populations. Furthermore, this chapter provides an overview of current policies designed to ameliorate the often negative experiences faced by those with terminal illness while incarcerated. Such policies include compassionate release, as well as on-site programming, including hospice care. The chapter concludes with the presentation of early evidence-informed practices, recommendations for next steps, and a case example regarding common correlates faced by prisoners with terminal illness.

TERMINAL ILLNESS BEHIND BARS

Though terminal illness is often associated with older adults, not all older adults develop terminal conditions, nor are all persons with terminal illness older adults—this is also true for incarcerated populations. However, incarcerated persons age 55 and over account for more than half of all deaths in state prisons, the vast majority of which are illness related (Noonan, Rohloff, & Ginder, 2014).

Some scholars indicate older adults are the fastest growing subpopulation of prisoners (Potter, Cashin, Chenoweth, & Jeon, 2007). Some estimates have indicated that the population of prisoners over the age of 55 increased as much as 282% between 1995 and 2010, representing a growth rate 7 times greater than that of the total US prison population during the same period (42.1%; Human Rights Watch [HRW], 2012). More recent estimates indicate the population of older adult prisoners increased 204% between 1999 and 2012 (Pew, 2014). The number of prisoners age 64 and up increased 62.7% in just 3 years between 2007 and 2010—a dramatic contrast to the mere 0.67% increase of the total prisoner population during the same period (HRW, 2012). By 2013, prisoners age 55 and up sentenced to 1 year or more under state or federal jurisdiction accounted for 17.9% of all prisoners, over twice the percentage reported in 2010 and 2011 (8% and 8.2%, respectively; Carson, 2014; HRW, 2012; Pew, 2014). The population of older adult prisoners age 55 and up is expected to balloon to over 400,000 by 2030 (Chari, Simon, DeFrances, & Maruschak, 2016).

The increasing population of older adult prisoners is due to many factors, including the mandatory-minimum, truth-in-sentencing, and three-strikes laws at the root of the nation's greatest mass incarceration (Chiu, 2010; HRW, 2012; Kinsella, 2004; Linder & Meyers, 2007; Snyder, van Wormer, Chadha, & Jaggers, 2009). Thus, some older adults have aged behind bars as a result of having received long sentences at an early age (HRW, 2012; Potter et al., 2007). The revocation of parole, often based on technical violations, alongside increasing use of life-without-parole (LWOP) sentencing further enhances the likelihood of aging behind bars (Chiu, 2010; HRW, 2012). In six states, all life sentences lack the prospect of parole (Nellis & King, 2009). Increasing age of first offense is also an important consideration. In 2002, nearly 534,000 arrests were reported for persons age 50 and older, nearly 6% of all arrests for that year (Aday & Krabill, 2006). As many as 15% of these older adults were arrested for felony offenses. Felony offenses (i.e., murder, heinous sexual offenses, violent crime), generally, result in prison commitment lengths greater than 1 year (Aday & Krabill, 2006). In fact, new commitments for those aged 55 and older have also grown. New commitments reflect first-time incarcerations. Such incarcerations for all persons increased 9.7% between 1995 and 2009. In stark contrast, new commitments of older adult persons age 55 and older increased approximately 109% during this same period (HRW, 2012) with some scholars pointing toward the housing market crash and subsequent economic depression of the mid-2000s as contributors to risks of poverty-related crime commission for older adults.

In addition to these criminogenic characteristics, the larger society is undergoing a demographic shift. The general population has faced a so-called graying as baby boomers enter older adulthood. In addition, technological and medical advances have given way to longer life expectancies (Prost, 2014). Though not all older adult persons face terminal illness and not all persons with terminal illness are older adults, these individuals age 55 and older account for more than half of all deaths behind bars. Thus, older adults entering prison with long sentences give way to the increased potential for the development of terminal illness as nearly 90% of all deaths behind bars are illness related.

It is important to note that some debate exists regarding the age best representing "older" in correctional environments (HRW, 2012). All incarcerated persons endure what is known as "accelerated aging" (Chiu, 2010; Linder & Meyers, 2009; Potter et al., 2007; Yampolskaya & Winston, 2003). Accelerated aging reflects the unique phenomenon of an individual's lived experience as that of someone markedly older (Chiu, 2010; HRW, 2012; Lemieux, Dyeson, & Castiglione, 2002; Linder & Meyers, 2009; Snyder et al., 2009). Incarcerated persons, therefore, are more likely to share the physical and psychosocial attributes of persons that are

10 years older who have never been incarcerated. Accelerated aging results from a variety of factors both prior to prison (e.g., poverty, substance use, violence) and during incarceration (e.g., acute conditions such as pneumonia; Kinsella, 2004; Linder & Meyers, 2009; Pew, 2014). This phenomenon breeds contention regarding appropriate age cut-offs for what constitutes an older adult within correctional settings, though most publications continue to reference prisoners over the age of 50 as older (Chiu, 2010; HRW, 2012; Kinsella, 2004; Potter et al., 2007; Snyder et al., 2009).

CAUSES OF TERMINAL ILLNESS IN PRISONERS

It is a commonly held notion that prisoners' preprison physical and mental health are considered poorer than those who have never been incarcerated. This is a result of two broad factors generally classified as related to either preincarceration experiences or experiences that take place during incarceration. Preincarceration considerations such as poverty and homelessness and limited access to preventative health care must be mentioned (Linder & Meyers, 2009). Such limited access is often linked to low health literacy and the subsequent inability to navigate health care systems. Many incarcerated men and women also deal with undiagnosed and untreated mental illness concerns or have long-standing issues with substance use and dependence as well (Falter, 1999). Exposure to violence prior to incarceration may also affect physical and mental health negatively.

Second, correctional environments exacerbate physical and mental health concerns due to the very nature of incarceration. Mental health issues may predate incarceration, as previously mentioned, but may also develop as a result of the many key components of incarcerated life, including material deprivation, lack of privacy, and increased or sustained levels of fear of violence or victimization (Potter et al., 2007). The threat of violence or victimization may also increase cortisol production—known to have deleterious effects on numerous organ systems (Björntorp & Rosmond, 2000; Burke, Davis, Otte, & Mohr, 2005; Whitworth, Williamson, Mangos, & Kelly, 2005).

All prisoners face varying acute and contagious conditions common in overcrowded settings and, in turn, a high burden of disease (Pew, 2014). The correctional environment is ripe with pneumonia, tuberculosis, and Methicillin-resistant Staphylococcus aureus (MRSA; HRW, 2012; Pew, 2014). These and other infections can complicate preexisting conditions or, with delayed or poorly targeted intervention, lead to increasingly complex, medical problems due to the higher rate of chronic conditions among the incarcerated when compared to the nonincarcerated population (e.g., AIDS, hepatitis C; Pew, 2014). Chronic disease progression, furthermore, may require skilled nursing care or other intensive medical services for the older adult offender with terminal illness (Snyder et al., 2009).

Older adult prisoners, however, must contend with additional hardships. As previously noted, incarcerated men and women face the mental and physical health conditions of persons at least 10 years older in part due to accelerated aging. Simple tasks such as eating, bathing, and ambulation may be impeded entirely or take longer to complete than is anticipated for younger persons (HRW, 2012). Furthermore, structural concerns exist for older adult prisoners and those with terminal illness. If housed within the general population, bunk beds or shared cells may prove problematic for movement and transferring. Ambulation may be arduous as paths can be in disrepair or lack guardrails. Some individuals may also require durable medical equipment such as wheelchairs, walkers, or quad-style canes causing concerns with narrow cells or doorways. The distance between main buildings (e.g., infirmary, dining hall) can increase fall risks and subsequent hospitalizations. These men and women may also endure loss of hearing or vision without adequate intervention (Pew, 2014). This becomes further problematic as prisons constructed prior to the enactment of the Americans with Disabilities Act are not automatically required to retrofit facilities (Aday & Krabill, 2006), leaving many correctional settings unfit for persons facing these and other impairments. Perhaps more troublesome, approximately 20% of prisoners age 50 or older reported having been physically or emotionally victimized due to incontinence, physical disability, or cognitive impairments (HRW, 2012).

CONSEQUENCES OF TERMINAL ILLNESS IN PRISONERS

Terminal illness in prisoners is associated with numerous consequences for the prisoner, health care providers, and larger administration. Death behind bars is often cited as the greatest fear among prisoners, one especially salient for incarcerated older adults (Linder & Meyers, 2007). Researchers have stated this fear is further compounded by experiencing a serious or terminal illness (Linder & Enders, 2011; Linder & Meyers, 2009; Snyder et al., 2009; Waselchuk, 2010). In 2012, 78% of all deaths within correctional settings took place in state prisons (Noonan et al., 2014). This reflects a 2% increase in the prison mortality rate from 2011, with 3,351 deaths occurring in US state prisons. The median mortality rate for the country was 242 deaths per 100,000 prisoners.

In 2012, 88% of state prison deaths ($n = 2,953$) were illness related. Cancer remained the most common cause of death (30.5%; $n = 1,021$) followed closely by heart disease (23.9%; $n = 800$; Noonan et al., 2014). Persons aged 18–24 accounted for approximately 2.1% of all deaths in state prisons in 2012. As previously noted, persons age 55 and over accounted for 55% of all reported deaths in state prisons. That figure balloons to 81.6% if adults over 45 are included, an important consideration given the previous discussion of accelerated aging (Noonan et al., 2014).

Upon acknowledging the growing numbers, proportion, and the health problems faced by these men and women, the population of older adult prisoners has changed the demography of US prisons. Older adults, in general, and older adult prisoners, particularly, require enhanced health care services due to their increased rates of physical and mental health morbidities. These health concerns are both complex and costly—placing health care providers within US prisons in a challenging position as attempts are made to meet the many and costly needs of this vulnerable population (Potter et al., 2007).

Corrections administrators and policy makers are legally bound by case precedent to meet the mental and physical health needs of persons with care equivalent to that of the public sector while simultaneously assuring public safety. The US Supreme Court has previously ruled that substandard health care within correctional settings is not part of legal punishment and that persons must receive health care services parallel to the free world (see *Estelle v. Gamble*, 1976; Linder & Enders, 2011; Linder & Meyers, 2007; Pew, 2014). However, working to meet this obligation comes at a steep price, mostly as a result of elevated health care expenses. Median growth of per-inmate health care spending between 2007 and 2011 was 6%. Health care costs accounted for approximately $6.5 billion of total prison costs in 2008 and $7.7 billion in 2011—averaging about one fifth of overall prison expenditures (Pew, 2014).

Funds directed toward correctional health care are much greater for older adults when compared to their younger counterparts (Pew, 2014). The average cost of incarceration for an older adult inmate (over 55) in the United States during 2011 was approximately $70,000 (HRW, 2012; Kinsella, 2004). These high costs are often due to physical therapy, medical testing, pharmacological and surgical treatments, special dietary requirements, durable medical equipment, and acute hospitalization (Linder & Enders, 2011; Snyder et al., 2009). Further, transportation to and from specialty appointments or overnight stays for emergency care should be considered as states must transport persons with supervision—translating to overtime or temporary-worker costs (Pew, 2014). This creates a significant demand on those states with high and increasing rates of older adult prisoners. Results from a Pew Charitable Trust examination (2014) indicated that 40 of the 42 states surveyed (95% of respondents) experienced a rise in the raw number and proportion of older adult prisoners.

In conclusion, correctional administrators and state leadership face great challenges while assuring the highest quality, individualized care, while managing costs, and guaranteeing public and prison safety. This challenge is perhaps most pressing as related to the care of older adult prisoners, whose rates of acute, chronic, and terminal illness are far greater than their younger counterparts. Efforts to respond to these concerns are discussed next.

STATUS OF CURRENT POLICY

In response to the aforementioned realities of growing populations of prisoners with complex and terminal illness, legal mandates to assure care equivalent to that of the community and growing costs associated with health care service provision, states have adopted and use various solutions. Such solutions extend from initial assessment, through incarceration, and later post release to meet the needs of men and women incarcerated with terminal illness.

Admission and Assessment Phases

Very little is known about health care practices in US prisons (Chari et al., 2016) and less still of end-of-life care for prisoners with terminal illness. Recently, the United

States Department of Health and Human Services released selected findings drawn from the National Survey of Prison Health Care, which provides an initial framework regarding these services throughout varying phases of the criminal justice system (Chari et al., 2016). First, those admitted to prison undergo routine screenings for many infectious conditions. In fact, large proportions of facilities screen for Hepatitis A (77%), Hepatitis B (82%), Hepatitis C (87%), and tuberculosis (100%). Due to the high risk of communicable disease transmission within correctional facilities, screening for these conditions is critical. Such infectious conditions are not necessarily terminal in nature, but acute conditions can complicate other chronic conditions and magnify already complex medical conditions for individuals with compromised immunity. Other common screenings include cardiovascular diseases (83% of responding facilities, per ECG) and high blood pressure (99.8%; Chari et al., 2016). Importantly, no mention of terminal illness screenings at admission were made in the report.

Incarceration Phase

As previously noted, nearly 90% of all deaths in state prisons are illness related. Despite the regularity of illness and death behind bars, great variability exists regarding how facilities manage care for persons with such conditions. In addition to the great inconsistency regarding the type of care employed, the quality of such care is also variable (Aday, 2006; Linder & Meyers, 2009). Two broad treatment options are available to those individuals who are incarcerated with terminal illness. Those include on-site health care programs, such as skilled nursing, and palliative- and end-of-life care, and off-site alternatives, including compassionate release and geriatric parole.

ON-SITE PROGRAMMING

As previously noted, the 1976 Supreme Court ruling of *Estelle v. Gamble* provides precedent regarding the assurance that persons in the United States should receive health care services similar to that of their free counterparts. Use of innovative practices has increased, including the use of telemedicine, and are described as cost-effective alternatives to outpatient hospitalizations and prison transfers. However, the National Survey of Prison Health Care reveals that approximately 45% of responding states (*n* = 31) provided on-site care for chronic diseases, 78% provided long-term or nursing care (*n* = 35), and 78% provided hospice services (*n* = 35). For chronic disease, many facilities provide services within the infirmary, though chronic-condition and disease-dedicated clinics were also used (e.g., cancer centers). Each of the 35 states that indicated use of long-term and nursing care provided such care these services on site. Although these proportions indicate that supportive services available to some men and women serving time in our nation's prisons, these percentages highlight the nearly one quarter of responding states that are not providing such services. Furthermore, these percentages do not reflect service provision for the approximately 728,200 persons housed in local jails at the end of 2015 (Kaeble & Glaze, 2016).

Older adult prisoners, even those facing chronic and terminal illness, often receive standard health care in acute settings rather than more specialized end-of-life care services (Snyder et al., 2009). However, some prisons have adopted more specialized on-site programming to support the needs of this vulnerable group. More often, however, support for such persons is closely parallel to long-term or skilled nursing care (Potter et al., 2007). Such programs may include specialized care dormitories or wings that are within or supported by correctional facilities (Potter et al., 2007). For instance, the Louisiana Correctional Institute for Women (LCIW) maintains an assisted living unit for prisoners with acute physical illness that require "personalized supportive services and healthcare" for activities of daily living (LCIW #4-05-034, ¶5).

Though great variation exists between on-site health care programs, the use of peer caregivers remain core to many services (Chow, 2002; Potter et al., 2007). Peer caregivers are described as fellow incarcerated persons who provide supportive services to an incarcerated peer facing acute, chronic, or terminal illness. Peer caregivers come into their role in various ways. Some are classified to the job, others have been requested to serve by prison administration (e.g., Assistant Warden), whereas others have volunteered for the role (Cloyes et al., 2014; Hoffmann & Dickinson, 2011; LCIW, #4-05-034, ¶7). No research exists regarding paid caregivers (viz. orderlies), though a growing body of knowledge exists related to volunteer caregivers in palliative and end-of-life care programs in correctional facilities.

Caregivers' training often includes issues related to hazardous waste, isolation procedures, universal precaution, confidentiality and privacy, and activities of daily living—further specialized topics may include physical and spiritual dynamics of dying, stress management and self-care, and grief and bereavement (Hoffmann & Dickinson, 2011). Peer caregivers provide a wide range of supportive services, including assistance with housekeeping, feeding, bathing, toileting, transferring, and medication management (Hoffmann & Dickinson, 2011; LCIW #4-05-034, ¶5). In addition, caregivers support their fellow prisoners via companionship, letter writing, and lay counseling (Cloyes et al., 2014; Hoffmann & Dickinson, 2011). On-site programming including prison hospice—especially those using peer caregivers for patient care—have been found to be associated with several benefits, including the provision of quality, comprehensive and compassionate care, the reduction of violent infractions and shifts from a punitive prison climate, support for the transformative experience of caregivers, and the potential for reducing agency costs (Bronstein & Wright, 2007; Cloyes et al., 2014; Wright & Bronstein, 2007).

Initial evidence indicates on-site programming, most notably those hospice services using peer caregivers, is associated with numerous positive outcomes. However, several ethical considerations must be mentioned in light of prisoners with terminal illness. Less than half of responding programs required prisoners with terminal illness to forgo curative care and just over one third of programs required patients to sign do-not-resuscitate orders (Hoffmann & Dickinson, 2011).

Such requirements call into question the role of coercion in correctional health care settings because it is unclear how information regarding such decisions is disseminated, reviewed, and understood by prisoners with terminal illness. However, these criteria were requirements for the minority of programs. Similarly, compulsory curative care for prisoners with terminal illness may foster ethical concerns. The Standard Minimum Rules for the Treatment of Prisoners approved in 1977 dictates that medical teams "shall treat any physical or mental illnesses or defects" (United Nations, 2017, #62). The National Commission on Correctional Health Care (NCCHC) dictates that prisoners can refuse care (Standard I-09; NCCHC, 2016). However, it is possible that curative care may continue against a prisoner's wishes due to the naturally coercive nature of correctional settings and the potential for mistrust between prisoners and service providers. These issues create unique ethical dilemmas for health care providers in prison settings requiring further investigation to assure patient-centered care and quality of life for prisoners with terminal illness.

OFF-SITE ALTERNATIVES: COMPASSIONATE RELEASE

Compassionate release refers to the reduction, termination, or alteration of inmate sentencing that allows eligible persons with chronic or terminal illness to be released into the community (Chiu, 2010; Linder & Enders, 2011; Snyder et al., 2009). By 2003, approximately 36 states had been recognized as providing compassionate or geriatric release options for prisoners (Aday, 2003). More recent estimates indicate an increasing lean toward such off-site practices with nearly all states, the federal government, and Washington, DC, using some form of compassionate or geriatric release policy for older adult persons ($n = 45$; Maschi et al., 2015). Many states have adopted compassionate release policies based on a federal model policy within the Comprehensive Crime Control Act of 1984. Associated procedures for 18 USC §§ 3582(c)(1)(A) and 4205(g), modified in 2013, require that requests for geriatric release for elderly persons be restricted to either (a) persons who are sentenced after 1987, are at least 70 years of age, and have served at least 30 years of their sentence; or (b) are 65 years of age of older, who suffer from chronic or serious medical conditions, where conventional treatment has provided no improvement, and have served at least 50% of their sentence.

Proponents of compassionate release suggest it is an innovative solution to reducing correctional costs associated with health care services (Linder & Enders, 2011) and supports the reduction of the incarcerated population while providing persons the option for death with dignity among friends and family (Russell, 1993). Many policies work to assure appropriate vetting of medical facilities for persons prior to release, and some even include provisions that require holistic or family support systems (Maschi et al., 2015). These protections and potential opportunities for cost savings, though, do not account for the many concerns directly related to compassionate release such as reducing inmate access to long-standing peer social support, community apprehension, and limited access to health care post release (Berry, 2009; Linder & Enders, 2011; Russell, 1993).

Many prisoners have been deserted by family members and have limited support outside prison walls (Linder & Meyers, 2007). Compassionate release may cause prisoners with chronic and terminal illnesses to forgo contact with their prison family, oftentimes the persons' longest-standing and largest source of social support (Linder & Meyers, 2007; Waselchuk, 2010; Yampolskaya & Winston, 2003). Desertion by friends and family often means that compassionate release results in residential placement (Aday, 2006; Linder & Enders, 2011; Snyder et al., 2009).

However, community service providers such as long-term care and skilled nursing facilities are often reticent to admit former prisoners due to stigma or safety concerns—concerns even larger with special subpopulations (e.g., sexual offenders). In fact, many have policies in place where persons with felony convictions are ineligible for admittance (Hoffmann & Dickinson, 2011). Similarly, victim advocacy groups and the public often remain opposed to prisoner release. Public disinterest often hinges upon the desire to assure retribution, to forgo community costs associated with caring for persons with terminal illness, and to preserve public safety (Chihowlas & Chen, 2010; O'Meara, 2010).

Furthermore, many persons will face limited access to health care if released (Linder & Enders, 2011). In fact, prison is often the first time these men and women have had consistent access to health care (Linder & Meyers, 2007). Assuming public or family support is in place, eligibility for compassionate release often requires that persons are bedridden or permanently incapacitated to assure no risk to society (Linder & Enders, 2011; Maschi, Kalmanofsky, Westcott, & Pappacena, 2015; 18 USC §§ 3582(c)(1)(A) and 4205(g)). Those persons who are eligible for compassionate release still face long, complicated proceedings resulting in recurrent continuances and court appearances—most will die before granted release (Berry, 2009; Linder & Enders, 2011; Russell, 1993). This is a much needed area for policy reformation.

A recent analysis of such policies reveals other limitations (Maschi et al., 2015). Critically, five states did not have formal compassionate release policies in place (Illinois, Massachusetts, South Carolina, South Dakota, Utah). Two additional states did not have policies, but instead use case precedent as a framework for release (Iowa, Maine). Only 17 states had distinct, clearly defined compassionate release processes in place. For more than half of the states ($n = 28$), limited transparency existed related to the process by which release determination is made. For the vast majority of policies, little consideration is made regarding the offender's well-being, and only one policy (Oregon) reflects language in accordance with a human-rights perspective, stating that failure to release an offender with such infirmity or advanced age confirms the incarceration as cruel or inhumane.

As a result of these considerations, many persons with chronic or terminal illness may reap greater benefits such as access to their prison family support systems, continuity of care, and a better quality of life behind bars served by on-site programming when compared to a compassionate release into the community, though such decisions are best evaluated on a case-by-case basis using a patient-centered model.

EVIDENCE-BASED PRACTICES AND NEXT STEPS

Little evaluation of practices for prisoners with terminal illness has been completed. As a result, it is inappropriate to identify specific practices as "evidence based." However, national guidelines and promising practices for several on-site and off-site options have been constructed.

On-Site Programming

Hospice services are considered the model of quality, compassionate care (National Hospice and Palliative Care Organization [NHPCO, 2016]). Thus, increasing the use of hospice or similar models is likely to support the needs of men and women facing terminal illness behind bars. The limited use of such models is rooted in multiple factors and one such consideration is the barriers to hospice certification for correctional facilities. Recent research has indicated that many hospice programs in operation are not, in fact, accredited or licensed by any health care organization or agency (Prost, Holland, Hoffman, & Dickinson, 2018). It is possible that the timelines associated with accreditation are burdensome and that correctional facilities are not priorities for granting bodies. Furthermore, efforts must be undertaken to examine components of effective hospice and other palliative care programs, as well as associated outcomes, including the role of caregivers in service provision.

In addition to increasing use of hospice models of care and reducing barriers to accreditation, facility administration is encouraged to make efforts to increase the use of geriatric-specific or end-of-life training to staff and facility personnel (Maschi et al., 2015). Maschi and colleagues (2015) also note that additional efforts should be made to harness the strengths of multidisciplinary teams both within the prison and in the community to refine on-site programs. It is also important to solicit feedback from prisoners receiving care. Patient-centered care models are known to increase positive outcomes for persons receiving care, their caregivers, and the larger health care system (Bergeson & Dean, 2006).

Off-Site Alternatives

Broadly speaking, compassionate release policies should be refined to enhance transparency of decision-making processes and to ease access and utilization of such strategies when desired by prisoners with terminal illness. It is understandable that not all facilities have comprehensive care models available to persons, and that release into the community is likely essential to receive optimum care. When this is the case, prisoner consultation is encouraged (Maschi et al., 2015). Self-determination related to social support networks and prisoner families is critical: a growing body of literature speaks to the limited or absent support systems available to older adult prisoners. This means it is possible that though compassionate release is touted as an ethical and humane alternative to incarceration, some men and women may prefer to remain with their incarcerated families (Linder & Meyers, 2007; Waselchuk, 2010; Yampolskaya & Winston, 2003). Institutionalization is also an important consideration because long-term incarceration may result in deteriorated skills essential to successful re-entry (Atabay, 2009).

Access to services and health care coverage upon release are important considerations that must be made when using off-site alternatives to incarceration for prisoners with terminal illness. Results of the content analysis completed by Maschi and colleagues (2015) reveal that only 11 states include financial coverage as a component of postrelease support; therefore, 75% of the included policies did not speak to supports for re-entry as related to ability to pay for services. Assurance of health care coverage is standard practice in inpatient discharge planning in community settings and, thus, should be provided to previously incarcerated men and women with terminal illness returning to the community. Compassionate release preparation should therefore include application or reinstatement of Medicare and Medicare because many individuals facing re-entry will have limited health care opportunities (Linder & Enders, 2011).

Another important opportunity to support men and women facing terminal illness exists prior to correctional facility admission. Before entering prisons and jails, scholars point to the role of courts in reviewing and revising sentencing structures for persons with terminal illness who do not pose threat to community safety (Maschi et al., 2015). This would also relate to diversion opportunities and alternatives to incarceration.

CASE EXAMPLE

Louis, a 57-year-old, Black male was incarcerated for his most recent charge in his late 30s. He had several previous incarcerations, some were related to violent crimes (e.g., armed robbery), whereas the majority of his criminal history was nonviolent. He is currently serving life without the possibility of parole. Shortly after his 45th birthday, Louis noted discomfort in his jaw beneath his right eye and through his right cheek and neck. He visited the prison infirmary and the staff believed his discomfort was connected to temporomandibular joint (TMJ) concerns as a result of the symptoms he described. He was provided naproxen and other anti-inflammatory medications to reduce his discomfort over the course of several months. He was also encouraged to take small bites when eating and apply hot compresses as needed. This helped to alleviate much of Louis's discomfort for several weeks.

It was only when he noted difficulty reporting to work in the laundry room due to tiredness that his cellmate sought attention. Louis spoke to the infirmary staff and due to increased swelling of his right neck and face, he was referred to a nearby hospital for an X-ray and MRI. After a short delay due to transportation concerns, Louis's diagnostics were completed alongside exploratory bloodwork. Louis learned that he had stage 3 osteogenic sarcoma (OGS), an aggressive form of bone cancer that has metastasized throughout his collarbone and right shoulder.

Louis was encouraged by a peer to request to be transferred to another prison, one with a more comprehensive care model and a geriatric, skilled nursing unit. He agreed that this would be a good move and was excited that the facility was also closer to his oldest sister, his only remaining relative. After 6 months and much paperwork, Louis was granted a transfer. However, the small capacity of the skilled nursing unit has proven problematic, and he must remain in the general population until a bed becomes available. Louis stated that he was "racing towards a red light" and that his voice remains unheard.

After approximately 3 months at the facility, Louis was transferred to the skilled nursing unit. Here he has opted to receive curative cancer care (i.e., chemotherapy and radiation) and has weekly visits to a nearby hospital. He noted, however, that he doesn't like going to the hospital because he has to be handcuffed to the chair while receiving his medication and the staff "give him dirty looks" during his treatment. He further states that the chemotherapy techs are rough during his treatment and are making the bruises on his body worse, though he feels his complaints fall on deaf ears. Currently he is hopeful that after this round of treatment he will be able to return to the general population and secure a job to "keep him busy" and help pass the time. He also mentions that he misses his "brothers" and that his family here (i.e., in the prison) are what really keep him going.

WEB-BASED RESOURCES

Louisiana-Mississippi Hospice and Palliative Care Organization: http://www.lmhpco.org/

National Hospice and Palliative Care Organization Quality Guidelines for Hospice and End-of-Life Care in Correctional Settings: http://www.nhpco.org/sites/default/files/public/Access/Corrections/CorrectionsQualityGuidelines.pdf

Prison Terminal [Documentary film]: https://www.prisonterminal.com/

US Department of Justice National Institute of Corrections: Hospice and Palliative Care in Prisons: http://static.nicic.gov/Library/014785.pdf

REFERENCES

Aday, R. (2003). *Aging prisoners: Crisis in American corrections*. Westport, CT: Praeger.

Aday, R. (2006). Aging prisoners. In B. Berkman (Ed.), *Handbook of social work in health and aging* (pp. 231–241). New York, NY: Oxford University Press.

Aday, R., & Krabill, J. J. (2006). Aging persons in the criminal justice system. *Marquette Elder's Advisor, 7*(2), 237–258. Retrieved from http://scholarship.law.marquette.edu/elders/vol7/iss2/4

Atabay, T. (2009). *Handbook on prisoners with special needs*. United Nations Publication E.09.IV.4.

Bergeson, S. C., & Dean, J. D. (2006). A systems approach to patient-centered care. *JAMA, 296*, 2848–2851. doi:10.1001/jama.296.23.2848

Berry, W. W. (2009). Extraordinary and compelling: A re-examination of the justifications of compassionate release. *Maryland Law Review, 68*(4), 850–888. Retrieved from http://digitalcommons.law.umaryland.edu/mlr/vol68/iss4/6

Björntorp, P., & Rosmond, R. (2000). Obesity and cortisol. *Nutrition, 16*, 924–936.

Bronstein, L. R., & Wright, K. (2007). The impact of prison hospice: Collaboration among social workers and other professionals in a criminal justice setting that promotes care for the dying. *Journal of Social Work in End-of-Life & Palliative Care, 2*, 85–102. doi:10.1300/J457v02n04_05

Burke, H. M., Davis, M. C., Otte, C., & Mohr, D. C. (2005). Depression and cortisol responses to psychological stress: A meta-analysis. *Psychoneuroendocrinology, 30*, 846–856.

Carson, E. A. (2014). *Prisoners in 2013* (NCJ 247282). Washington, D.C.: Bureau of Justice Statistics.

Chari, K. A., Simon, A. E., DeFrances, C. J., & Maruschak, L. (2016). National survey of prison health care: Selected findings. Retrieved from https://www.cdc.gov/nchs/data/nhsr/nhsr096.pdf

Chihowlas, J. A., & Chen, Y. J. (2010). Volunteer prisoners provide hospice to dying inmates. *Annals of Health Law, 19*, 127–132. Retrieved from http://lawecommons.luc.edu/annals/vol19/iss1/26

Chiu, T. (2010). *It's about time: Aging prisoners, increasing costs, and geriatric release. United States.* The VERA Institute of Justice. NCJ 232550.

Chow, R. (2002). Initiating a long-term care nursing service for aging inmates. *Geriatric Nursing, 23*, 24–27. doi:http://dx.doi.org/10.1067/mgn.2002.122562

Cloyes, K. G., Rosenkranz, S. J., Wold, D., Berry, P. H., & Supiano, K. P. (2014). To be truly alive: Motivation among prison inmate hospice volunteers and the transformative process of end-of-life peer care service. *American Journal of Hospice and Palliative Medicine, 31*, 735–748. doi:10.1177/1049909113506035

Estelle v. Gamble, 429 U.S. 97 (1976).

Falter, R. G. (1999). Selected predictors of health services needs of inmates over age 50. *Journal of Correctional Health Care, 6*(2), 149–175.

Hoffmann, H. C., & Dickinson, G. E. (2011). Characteristics of prison hospice programs in the United States. *American Journal of Hospice and Palliative Medicine, 28*, 245–252. doi:10.1177/1049909110381884

Human Rights Watch. (2012). Old behind bars: The aging prison population in the United States. Retrieved from http://www.hrw.org/sites/default/files/reports/usprisons0112webwcover_0_0.pdf

Kaeble, D., & Glaze, L. (2016). *Correctional populations in the United States, 2015* (NCJ 250374). Washington, DC: Bureau of Justice Statistics.

Kinsella, C. (2004). Council of state governments: Corrections healthcare costs. Retrieved from http://www.csg.org/knowledgecenter/docs/TA0401CorrHealth.pdf

Lemieux, C. M., Dyeson, T. B., & Castiglione, B. (2002). Revisiting the literature on prisoners who are older: Are we wiser? *The Prison Journal, 82*, 440–458. Retrieved from http://citeseerx.ist.psu.edu/viewdoc/download?doi=10.1.1.1003.1124&rep=rep1&type=pdf

Linder, J. F., & Enders, S. R. (2011). Key roles for palliative social work in correctional settings. In T. Altilio & S. Otis-Green (Eds.), *Oxford textbook for palliative social work* (pp. 153–166). New York, NY: Oxford University Press.

Linder, J. F., & Meyers, F. J. (2007). Palliative care for prison inmates: "Don't let me die in prison." *JAMA, 298*, 894–901.

Linder, J. F., & Meyers, F. J. (2009). Palliative and end-of-life care in correctional settings. *Journal of Social Work in End-of-life & Palliative Care, 5*, 7–33. doi:10.1080/15524250903173579

Maschi, T., Kalmanofsky, A.,Westcott, K., & Pappacena, L. (2015). *An analysis of United States compassionate and geriatric release laws: Towards a rights-based response for diverse elders and their families and communities.* New York, NY. Be the Evidence Press, Fordham University. Retrieved from http://www.beetheevidence.org

National Commission on Correctional Health Care. (2016). *Right to refuse care.* Retrieved from http://www.ncchc.org/right-to-refuse-treatment

Nellis, A., & King, R. S. (2009). *No exit: The expanding use of life sentences in America.* Sentencing Project. (NCJ: 229164)

Noonan, M. E., Rahloff, H., & Ginder, S. (2014). *Mortality in local jails and state prisons, 2000-2012.* (NCJ 247448). Washington, DC: Bureau of Justice Statistics.

O'Meara, G. J. (2010). Compassion and the public interest: Wisconsin's new compassionate release legislation. *Federal Sentencing Reporter, 23*, 33–38. doi: 10.1525/fsr.2010.23.1.33

Pew Charitable Trusts. (2014). State prison health care spending: An examination. Retrieved from http://www.pewtrusts.org/en/projects/state-health-care-spending

Potter, E., Cashin, A., Chenoweth, L., & Jeon, Y. H. (2007). The healthcare of older inmates in the correctional setting. *International Journal of Prisoner Health, 3*(3), 204–213. doi:http://dx.doi.org/10.1080/17449200701520115

Prost, S. G. (2014). Hospice and self-assessed quality of life in the dying: A review. Journal of *Human Behavior in the Social Environment, 24*, 281–295. doi:10.1080/10911359.2013.820159

Prost, S. G., Holland, M., & Hoffman, G., & Dickinson, G. (2018). Characteristics of prison hospice programs in the United States: An update and five year reflection

Russell, M. P. (1993). Too little, too late, too slow: Compassionate release of terminally ill prisoners—is the cure worse than the disease? *Wiedner Journal of Public Law*, 799–856. Retrieved from http://heinonline.org/HOL/LandingPage?handle=hein.journals/wjpl3&div=24&id=&page=

Snyder, C., van Wormer, K., Chadha, J., & Jaggers, J. W. (2009). Older adult inmates: The challenge for social work. *Social Work, 54*, 117–124. Retrieved from http://sw.oxfordjournals.org/content/54/2/117.full.pdf

United Nations. (2017). *Standard minimum rules for the treatment of prisoners.* Adopted by the First United Nations Congress on the Prevention of Crime and the Treatment of Offenders, held at Geneva in 1955, and approved by the Economic and Social Council by its resolutions 663 C (XXIV) of 31 July 1957 and 2076 (LXII) of 13 May 1977. Retrieved from http://www.ohchr.org/EN/ProfessionalInterest/Pages/TreatmentOfPrisoners.aspx

Waselchuk, L. (2010). *Grace before dying.* Brooklyn, NY: Umbrage Editions.

Whitworth, J. A., Williamson, P. M., Mangos, G., & Kelly, J. J. (2005). Cardiovascular consequences of cortisol excess. *Vascular Health and Risk Management, 1*(4), 291–299.

Wright, K. N., & Bronstein, L. (2007). Creating decent prisons: A serendipitous finding about prison hospice. *Journal of Offender Rehabilitation, 44*, 1–16. doi:http://dx.doi.org/10.1300/J076v44n04_01

Yampolskaya, S., & Winston, N. (2003). Hospice care in prison: General principles and outcomes. *American Journal of Hospice and Palliative Medicine, 20*, 290–296. doi:10.1177/104990910302000411

INDEX

Note: Tables, figures, and boxes are indicated by an italic *t*, *f*, and *b* following the page number.

Housing (*cont.*)
  for parents after prison, 122–123
  on reentry success, 291
  safekeeping, 195
  transgender and intersex, 239–240, 244
  transitional, after imprisonment, 296
Housing, LGB inmates
  manipulation, 192–193
  segregation, adverse effects, 201–202
  trends and future directions, 201–203
  unsafe, 192
Howarth, J. W., 189
Hug, A., 5
Human immunodeficiency virus (HIV). *See*
  HIV/AIDS
Husain, J., 23
Hypermasculinity, 185–186

Ideation, on adolescent help seeking
  attitudes, 20–21
Illegal Immigration Reform and
  Responsibility Act (IIRIRA), 335–336
Immigrant inmates, 333–346
  antagonism *vs.* lower crime rates, 334
  case example, 345–346
  child welfare and immigrant families,
    339–340
  crime and adult immigrants, 339
  delinquency and immigrant youth,
    338–339
  detention and deportation, 335–336,
    344–345
  on family well-being, 342
  immigration policy, history, 336–338
  migration, 334–335
  population, recent increase, 333
  Presidential election (2016), 342–343
  privately run facilities, 342
  public perception and visibility, 333–334
  services, 340–342
  trends and future directions, 343–345
  web-based resources, 346
Immigrants
  countries of origin, 334–335
  criminality myth *vs.* criminalization, 339,
    343–344
  expulsion, current, 344

mental illness, 341
Mexican, 334–335
victimization, 339
Immigration Act of 1917, 337
Immigration policy, history, 336–338
Immigration Reform and Control Act
  (IRCA), 335
Implicit bias, 268
Incarcerated Veterans of Roxbury (I.V.O.R.,
  Hagerstown, MD), 310, 323–326,
  324*f*–325*f*
Incarceration, as trauma, 105
Inciardi, J. A., 165
Individual community-based
  treatment, 8–9
In re Gault, 146–147
Integrated risk-need-responsivity model
  (RNR-I), 9
Intersex people, 217–251. *See also*
  Transgender and intersex people
  definition, 219
  rights and recognition, 218
Intimate partner relationships skills
  training, 121–122

Jails
  function, 155
  vs. prisons, 155, 155n1
James, D. J., 2–5, 6, 293
Jeglic, E. L., 192
Jensen, E. L., 168–169, 168n7
Job training
  on future criminal behavior, 145
  on HIV risk factors for incarcerated, 66
  Ready4Work Reentry Initiative, 124
  youth in criminal justice, 145
Johnson v. Johnson, 195
Jones, K. T., 74
Judicial waivers for youth, local level, 140
Jürgens, R., 78
Justice for Vets, 326–327
Justice Reinvestment Act, Oregon,
  125–126
Juvenile Detention Alternatives Initiative
  (JDAI), 345
Juvenile justice, 21–27
  arrests, prevalence, 21, 22